Frommer's®

S0-BAY-217

Maryland & Delaware

9th Edition

by Mary K. Tilghman

WILEY

Wiley Publishing, Inc.

ABOUT THE AUTHOR

Maryland native **Mary K. Tilghman** is a journalist and editor and has lived and worked all over the state, from small towns to a farm on the Eastern Shore. She and her family have seen just about every corner of their home state and Delaware, by land and on their sailboat on the Magothy River. She currently resides in Baltimore.

Published by:

WILEY PUBLISHING, INC.

111 River St.
Hoboken, NJ 07030-5774

ISBN 978-0-470-58248-0
Editor: William Travis
with Naomi Kraus
Production Editor: Lindsay Conner
Cartographer: Andrew Dolan
Photo Editor: Richard Fox
Production by Wiley Indianapolis Composition Services

Front cover photo: Aerial view of the Eastern Shore of Maryland with sailboats at anchor
© Cameron Davidson / Alamy Images
Back cover photo: Baseball game at Oriole Park at Camden Yards in Baltimore
© Visions LLC / PhotoLibrary

For information on our other products and services or to obtain technical support, please contact our Customer Care Department within the U.S. at 877/762-2974, outside the U.S. at 317/572-3993 or fax 317/572-4002.

Wiley also publishes its books in a variety of electronic formats. Some content that appears in print may not be available in electronic formats.

Manufactured in the United States of America

5 4 3 2 1

CONTENTS

LIST OF MAPS

ACKNOWLEDGMENTS

So many people helped make it a pleasure to write this guide. Special thanks to Lyn Lewis of the Greater Wilmington Convention and Visitor Center, Connie Yingling of the Maryland Office of Tourism Development, Monee Cottman of Visit Baltimore, Jill Jasuta of the Dorchester County Tourism Office, Sarah Duck from the Garrett County Chamber of Commerce, Carl Whitehill of the Gettysburg Convention and Visitors Bureau and Susan Steckman of the Annapolis and Anne Arundel County Conference and Visitors Bureau. My thanks, too, to Frances and Bill Young for their enthusiasm and support as I researched Hagerstown for this new guide.

As always, my thanks to the many innkeepers and restaurateurs who welcomed me warmly. And thanks to the staff and volunteers at museums and historic sites who showed me around with pride and delight. For two such tiny states, Maryland and Delaware have so much to offer and plenty of warm, friendly people thrilled to show visitors a good time.

Finally, I want to thank my husband, Ray; my children, Gina, Sean, and Brigid; and my parents, Pat and Bill, for all their help and encouragement.

—Mary K. Tilghman

HOW TO CONTACT US

In researching this book, we discovered many wonderful places—hotels, restaurants, shops, and more. We're sure you'll find others. Please tell us about them, so we can share the information with your fellow travelers in upcoming editions. If you were disappointed with a recommendation, we'd love to know that, too. Please write to:

Frommer's Maryland & Delaware, 9th Edition
Wiley Publishing, Inc. • 111 River St. • Hoboken, NJ 07030-5774

AN ADDITIONAL NOTE

Please be advised that travel information is subject to change at any time—and this is especially true of prices. We therefore suggest that you write or call ahead for confirmation when making your travel plans. The authors, editors, and publisher cannot be held responsible for the experiences of readers while traveling. Your safety is important to us, however, so we encourage you to stay alert and be aware of your surroundings. Keep a close eye on cameras, purses, and wallets, all favorite targets of thieves and pickpockets.

FROMMER'S STAR RATINGS, ICONS & ABBREVIATIONS

Every hotel, restaurant, and attraction listing in this guide has been ranked for quality, value, service, amenities, and special features using a **star-rating system.** In country, state, and regional guides, we also rate towns and regions to help you narrow down your choices and budget your time accordingly. Hotels and restaurants are rated on a scale of zero (recommended) to three stars (exceptional). Attractions, shopping, nightlife, towns, and regions are rated according to the following scale: zero stars (recommended), one star (highly recommended), two stars (very highly recommended), and three stars (must-see).

In addition to the star-rating system, we also use **seven feature icons** that point you to the great deals, in-the-know advice, and unique experiences that separate travelers from tourists. Throughout the book, look for:

(Finds)	Special finds—those places only insiders know about
(Fun Facts)	Fun facts—details that make travelers more informed and their trips more fun
(Kids)	Best bets for kids, and advice for the whole family
(Moments)	Special moments—those experiences that memories are made of
(Overrated)	Places or experiences not worth your time or money
(Tips)	Insider tips—great ways to save time and money
(Value)	Great values—where to get the best deals

The following **abbreviations** are used for credit cards:

AE	American Express	DISC	Discover	V	Visa
DC	Diners Club	MC	MasterCard		

TRAVEL RESOURCES AT FROMMERS.COM

Frommer's travel resources don't end with this guide. Frommer's website, **www.frommers.com**, has travel information on more than 4,000 destinations. We update features regularly, giving you access to the most current trip-planning information and the best airfare, lodging, and car-rental bargains. You can also listen to podcasts, connect with other Frommers.com members through our active-reader forums, share your travel photos, read blogs from guidebook editors and fellow travelers, and much more.

The Best of Maryland & Delaware

Maryland and Delaware are often overshadowed by their neighbors, including the nation's capital. But thanks to the always-dazzling Chesapeake Bay, ocean beaches, and gently rolling mountains, these two states offer plenty of outdoor charms. The cities of Baltimore, Maryland, and Wilmington, Delaware, are filled with intriguing museums, sophisticated restaurants, and delightful waterfronts that make for a romantic summer evening stroll. Add charming small towns—including Maryland's capital, Annapolis, and Delaware's capital, Dover—friendly people, and a wealth of historic sites, and you've got two states worth a visit whether you have a day, a weekend, or a whole week.

These two states have been shaped by history, from the Colonial days to the Revolutionary and Civil wars; by industry, from the commercial fisheries of ocean and bay to high-tech banking and information technology; and even by sports—what would NASCAR do without Dover twice a year? And what Baltimoreans don't keep up-to-date with their beloved Orioles or stop whatever they're doing for the Preakness?

Every corner of Maryland offers something for those who look. Get off I-95 and you'll find scenic Havre de Grace. Wander through the Eastern Shore for a tableful of hot steamed crabs. Park the car outside Frederick, and you'll find the leafy glens that surround Cunningham Falls.

And don't be fooled by Delaware's small size. Sure, it's got beaches and NASCAR, but it also has mansions tucked in the Brandywine Valley, good food and wine on quiet Wilmington nights, and the town of Lewes—which is so charming, you might forget the ocean is just a short walk across a bridge.

Marylanders and Delawareans look toward the future but remember where they've been, too. They remember their fallen friends with monuments, battlefields, and aging forts that recall battles in 1776, 1812, 1917, and 1945. You can see places where George Washington stood, where brothers died, and where slaves ran for freedom. You can get a glimpse of how people lived when these states were just small colonies, or when the Golden Age made industrialists millionaires.

Whether you visit Maryland and Delaware while on your way to someplace else or because you're drawn to their charm and friendliness, you won't be disappointed.

1 FROMMER'S FAVORITE MARYLAND & DELAWARE EXPERIENCES

- **Raising the Star-Spangled Banner at Fort McHenry** (Baltimore, Md.): The park rangers ask visitors to help with the raising and lowering of the huge flag each day. The nooks and crannies and views keep young ones interested. Outside the fort, the sprawling waterfront park is perfect for families and picnics. See p. 78.

- **Attending the Preakness** (Baltimore, Md.): If you're young and want some serious partying, check out the infield. If you actually want to see the second jewel in the Triple Crown, head for the grandstand. The race is held the third Saturday in May at **Pimlico Race Course** (✆ 410/542-9400). Order grandstand tickets up to a year in advance. Infield tickets are available up to the week before and are sold at area gas stations. See p. 91.

- **Rafting the Yough:** The Youghiogheny (generally just called the "Yock") is Maryland's great white-water river. Its churning waters race through class III/IV rapids, with such names as Gap Falls, Bastard, Triple Drop, Meatcleaver, Lost and Found, and Backbender. The water levels are controlled by dam release, so the river can be ridden almost year-round. See chapter 10.

- **Kayaking among the Cypress Trees** (southern Delaware): A paddle on an early fall day in the cypress swamp of Trap Pond is a peaceful, exhilarating way to get some exercise. The changing leaves are gorgeous, the water is still warm, and most bugs are gone. Coastal Kayak offers tours. See chapter 11.

- **Going to a Baseball Game:** Maryland has baseball's most beautiful stadium—Oriole Park at Camden Yards—and the best team in the world (the Orioles, of course!). The many minor league teams are also fun, and more affordable. See "The Best Baseball in Maryland," p. 8.

- **Walking through 4 Centuries** (Annapolis, Md.): Sailors, statesmen, housewives, and slaves have trod the brick sidewalks of Maryland's capital city since Colonial days. Visit today to see how the city has preserved its memories at the State House and Paca House, while advancing into the modern age at the U.S. Naval Academy and on the water. See chapter 6.

- **Going "Downy Ocean":** Head for the crowded beaches of Ocean City, Maryland (with all those restaurants, shops, and golf courses), or to the quiet public beaches of Rehoboth or Bethany, Delaware. Both have their charms. The sand is white and clean; the waves can be gentle or furious (watch for the red warning flags). The sand crabs are used to being dug up, and the sea gulls will keep an eye on your snacks. (Don't give in and feed them—it can be pretty scary.) See chapter 11.

- **Bicycling at the Delaware Shore:** Grab a helmet and head onto Route 1 for a ride along flat road by the sea. Or, better yet, ride between Rehoboth and Lewes on the Junction and Breakwater Trail. See p. 257.

2 THE BEST LODGING BETS

- **Hyatt Regency Baltimore** (Baltimore, Md.; ✆ 410/528-1234): If you're planning a trip to Baltimore, the Hyatt's location and its spiffy new decor make it a must. Staff here, as well as the incomparable view and the Inner Harbor location, make this more than "just a Hyatt." See p. 58.

- **The Annapolis Inn** (Annapolis, Md.; ✆ 410/295-5200): This sumptuous Georgian-style house was originally the home of Thomas Jefferson's physician in the 1770s. A three-course breakfast is served on fine china in the cranberry-red dining room. Selling points include Jacuzzis, a room with its own deck, and experienced, welcoming hosts. See p. 110.

- **The Tilghman Island Inn** (Tilghman, Md.; ✆ 800/866-2141): Waterfront

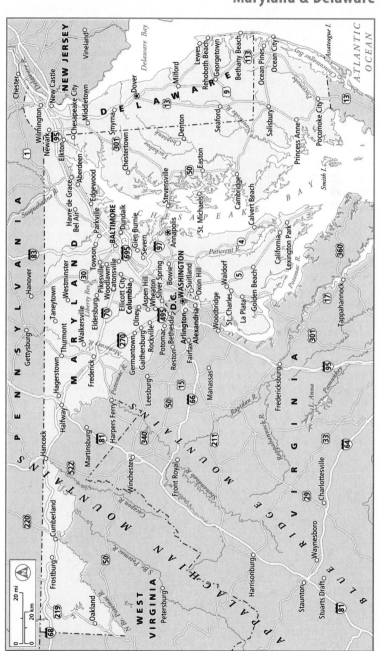

rooms take full advantage of the inn's setting on Knapps Narrows on the Eastern Shore. The bedrooms are spacious and comfy, and the welcome is warm. See p. 164.

- **The Westin Annapolis** (Annapolis, Md.; ℂ 410/972-4300): A bit of 21st-century styling has hit this 18th-century town, and we are so glad. No views to speak of (go to the Annapolis Marriott Waterfront for that), but amenities here are a delight. See p. 114.

- **Rock Hall inns:** The **Osprey Point Inn** (ℂ 410/639-2194) and **Inn at Huntingfield Creek** (ℂ 410/639-7779), two of the Eastern Shore's most gracious getaway locations, are in tiny Rock Hall. Osprey Point offers rooms with a view. Huntingfield Creek is surrounded by fields with water access. Both are serene and beautifully appointed. See p. 185 and p. 184, respectively.

- **The Stonebow Inn** (Grantsville, near Deep Creek Lake, Md.; ℂ 800/272-4090): Location makes the Stonebow, a restored 1877 Victorian, a good bet. It's right on the Casselman River, beside the Spruce Forest Artisan Village, a few minutes from Deep Creek Lake, and as far from the hustle and bustle as you want to be. See p. 234.

- **The Addy Sea Bed & Breakfast** (Bethany Beach, Del.; ℂ 800/418-6764): In a resort filled with condos and rental houses, this B&B offers cozy charm surrounded by beach and surf. It's quiet enough for romance but close enough to beach fun. See p. 260.

- **Lighthouse Club Hotel** (Ocean City, Md.; ℂ 800/371-5400): This hotel was designed for romantic beach getaways. Leave the kids at home and come here for secluded luxury with a view of the bay. Some rooms have fireplaces and Jacuzzis, too. See p. 273.

- **Hotel du Pont** (Wilmington, Del.; ℂ 800/441-9019): Not only is this a showcase of marble, carved paneling, and DuPont's latest fibers, but it also offers its lucky guests palatial surroundings, terrific amenities, and some of the best dining in town. See p. 297.

- **The Inn at Montchanin Village** (Montchanin, Del.; ℂ 800/269-2473): This cluster of buildings was once home for workers of the DuPont powder mills. Now they're charming guest rooms and suites, set in beautiful gardens, located just a few miles from the du Pont homes and gardens. See p. 298.

3 THE BEST DINING BETS

- **Charleston** (Baltimore, Md.; ℂ 410/332-7373): Southern cuisine takes center stage at this restaurant in the trendy Harbor East neighborhood. Expect to be treated like royalty as the waitstaff serves your grilled yellowfin tuna with andouille sausage, and a perfect crème brûlée. See p. 66.

- **The Prime Rib** (Baltimore, Md.; ℂ 410/539-1804): Where Baltimore has gone to celebrate mergers and engagements for decades. It's swank,

romantic, and serves perfect classic steakhouse fare. See p. 72.

- **Carrol's Creek** (Annapolis, Md.; ℂ 410/263-8102): The best views of the waterfront and Annapolis's skyline are paired with imaginative food here. Dine indoors or on the porch, from a seasonally changing menu. The cream of crab soup is always a winner. See p. 117.

- **Green Room** (Wilmington, Del.; ℂ 302/594-3154): Delaware's top restaurant wows diners the minute they see the impressive decor. But the real star here is the food: classic sauces, perfectly cooked entrees, and desserts prepared as art. See p. 299.

- **Krazy Kat's** (Wilmington, Del.; ✆ **302/888-4200**): The Brandywine Valley's finest inn also has the finest classic dining. Enjoy a leisurely meal of exceptionally prepared food in the cozy candlelit dining rooms. See p. 301.
- **The Hobbit** (Ocean City, Md.; ✆ **410/524-8100**): How we missed the charming Hobbit during its reconstruction.

And how much we love the sleek, modern Hobbit, with its water views, cold martinis, and rich seafood dishes. See p. 276.

- **The Buttery** (Lewes, Del.; ✆ **302/645-7755**): For sheer romance and excellent French-inspired food and wine, stop at this bistro set inside a Victorian mansion. The porch is lovely when the weather's warm; the softly lit dining rooms are warm when the weather's cold. See p. 241.

4 THE BEST AFFORDABLE DINING

- **Sabatino's Italian Restaurant** (Baltimore, Md.; ✆ **410/727-9414**): Good food at reasonable prices is the norm at most of Little Italy's restaurants. But Sabatino's also offers cozy dining rooms, an attentive waitstaff, and dinner served late into the night. See p. 69.
- **Gertrude's** (Baltimore, Md.; ✆ **410/889-3399**): This restaurant in the Baltimore Museum of Art goes perfectly with a trip to view the exhibits or as a destination in itself. Gertrude's (as in Gertrude Stein) boasts artfully prepared food and outdoor dining (in season) with beautiful views. See p. 73.
- **Celsius** (Rehoboth, Md.; ✆ **302/227-5767**): Fill your pockets with cash and come early for Mediterranean-inspired seafood and Asian dishes. Prix-fixe

menus and early bird specials make this lovely spot at the beach a good value. See p. 253.

- **Harpoon Hanna's** (Fenwick Island, Del.; ✆ **800/227-0525**): The food is good; the fresh breads and muffins are outstanding. For a beach restaurant, this one is worth the trip. Set on a canal, its big windows let the sunset in. The fish is fresh, the staff hardworking, and children are always welcome. Come early or be prepared for a substantial wait. See p. 263.
- **Mountain State Brewing Company** (McHenry, Md.; ✆ **301/387-3360**): Pizza from a wood-fire oven and locally produced brews, all in a relaxed atmosphere with mountain views. See p. 229.

5 THE BEST SHOPPING BETS

- **Antique Row** (Baltimore, Md.): In a single block of Howard Street, a few blocks north of downtown, serious antiques fans can find old silver, chandeliers, assorted porcelain, and chairs of all sizes and shapes. See p. 142.
- **Downtown Annapolis, Md.:** Main Street and Maryland Avenue offer all

kinds of choices in little shops. Tuscan kitchenware, Christmas ornaments, antique mirrors, and Navy sweat shirts are only a few of the items on these charming streets. There are a few chain stores, but the best shops are locally owned. See p. 127.

- **Tanger Outlets** (Rehoboth Beach, Del.): Wear comfortable shoes for this colossal (tax-free) shopping extravaganza. The three centers have every-

thing from Waterford crystal to OshKosh B'Gosh overalls. There's lots of clothing and home decor, as well as books, food, and other stuff. See p. 255.

6 THE BEST VIEWS & VISTAS

- **From the Severn River Scenic Overlook** (near Annapolis, Md.): On Route 450 outside Annapolis, a beautiful stone porch offers stunning views of the Severn River and the U.S. Naval Academy. It's also the site of a World War II memorial, with summaries of the major battles and obelisks bearing the names of Marylanders who gave their lives in World War II. See p. 125.

- **At Great Falls of the Potomac** (near Potomac, Md.): Just outside of Potomac, on the C&O Canal, a series of walkways will take you over the Great Falls of the Potomac. Stand above the piles of jagged rocks as the Potomac River rushes over them and down to the sea, the steepest and most spectacular fall-line rapids of any Eastern river. On a sunny Sunday, the walkways will be crowded, but the falls are worth the trouble. See p. 142.

- **On the Bay Bridge** (Md.): When you get to the middle of this bridge, you'll have a wonderful view of the Chesapeake. Maryland's Eastern Shore stretches down one terminus, while the view of the Western Shore includes Annapolis south of the bridge, and two lighthouses north of the bridge. The closest is the Sandy Point Light, and the farther one is the Baltimore Light.

- **Atop the Mountain at Wisp Resort** (McHenry, Md.): Ride the ski lift to the top, and before you go schussing down, take in the snow-covered slopes, the vast white expanse of Deep Creek Lake lined with the tracks of the occasional snowmobile, and a sky as blue as it can be. See p. 231.

- **From the Brandywine River Museum** (Chadds Ford, Pa., in the Brandywine Valley): While the art at this museum is dazzling, don't forget to look out the windows. The view of the river meandering under the canopy of trees is peaceful, though a riot of color in fall. See p. 316.

7 THE BEST HIKING

- **Swallow Falls State Park** (Garrett County, Md.): A great place for families to hike in Western Maryland, this park's short trails wind through dark, peaty forest and offer relatively easy access to some stunning scenery. There are overlooks to three waterfalls—Swallow Falls, Tolliver Falls, and the 63-foot-high cascading Muddy Creek Falls. See p. 215.

- **Big Savage Trail in Savage River State Forest** (Garrett County, Md.): This rugged trail extends 17 miles along the ridge of Big Savage Mountain, passing impressive vistas along the way. A tough hike through almost total wilderness, it's the best choice for serious backpacking in Western Maryland. See p. 215.

8 THE BEST FISHING & CRABBING

- **Calvert County Charter Fleets** (Solomons and Chesapeake Beach, Md.): For charter fishing on the Chesapeake, Calvert County, south of Annapolis, is the place to go. The small harbor of Chesapeake Beach is home to the largest charter fleet on the bay. Solomons, south of Chesapeake Beach, has a good fleet, too—with over 30 charter boats and a few headboats (charters for individual fisherman, charged by the "head") of its own. From either one, the captains are glad to take you trolling or chumming along the Western and Eastern shores of the Chesapeake. See p. 133.

- **Point Lookout State Park** (St. Mary's County, Md.): Location is everything at this peninsular park, with the Chesapeake Bay on one side and the Potomac River on the other. Fish from the pier on the bay, or rent a boat at the camp marina. If they aren't biting in the bay, simply stroll over to the Potomac and try again. See p. 137.

- **Casselman River** (near Grantsville, Md.): Cleanup efforts in this area of Western Maryland have paid off. The beautiful and wild Casselman River, once empty of fish because of acid draining from local mines, is now teeming with trout. Fish tales include catches of up to 40 fish a day—and fly-fishing with the bears. One thing is for certain, though: The Casselman is a great place to fish. See chapter 10.

9 THE BEST BIRDING & WILDLIFE-WATCHING

- **Blackwater National Wildlife Refuge** (Eastern Shore, Md.): The Delmarva Peninsula is dotted with wildlife refuges and protected lands, havens for migrating waterfowl and other wildlife. Blackwater is the largest of these. During peak migration season, you'll see ducks, tundra and mute swan, and snow geese, as well as the ever-present herons, Canada geese, and osprey, plus the occasional bald eagle. If you explore the wooded areas, you may even catch sight of the endangered Delmarva fox squirrel. See p. 173.

- **Butterfly-Watching at Eastern Neck National Wildlife Refuge** (Eastern Shore, Md.): The trees here fill up with colorful little travelers as they make their way to South America every fall. Fans of the tundra swan also await the waterfowls' arrival to this resting place. The refuge's website keeps nature lovers up-to-date on the migrating creatures' arrival. See p. 183.

- **Whale- & Dolphin-Watching on the Mid-Atlantic:** The Atlantic coast of Maryland and Delaware, particularly near Cape Henlopen State Park (Del.), is a good place to spot whales and dolphins. The Great Dune at Cape Henlopen is a perfect vantage point (bring binoculars). There are also whale- and dolphin-watching cruises available—even sea kayaking with the dolphins. See p. 243 and chapter 11.

- **Bombay Hook National Wildlife Refuge** (Central Del.): The largest of Delaware's wildlife refuges, Bombay Hook, northeast of Dover, has nearly 16,000 acres of tidal marsh, freshwater pools, and timbered swamps. You'll see a lot of migratory waterfowl in fall and spring; then the migrant shorebirds and songbirds appear in April, May, and June. See p. 329.

The Best Baseball in Maryland

Marylanders love baseball. The Orioles are the big-league team, of course, but the state is also home to seven minor-league teams, three baseball museums, and a monument to a storied slugger.

The **Baltimore Orioles** (☏ **888/848-2473;** http://baltimore.orioles.mlb.com) play at Oriole Park at Camden Yards. The stadium is easy to get to, right off I-95 to I-395 at the bottom of the ramp into town. Parking in lots around the stadium usually costs about $10. The Light Rail also stops here for every game. The ballpark was designed to bring spectators closer to the action, and it does. Watch out for foul balls! There's also a promenade that follows the warehouse building along the outfield wall; stop at the deck overlooking the bullpen to watch the pitchers warm up. Food here is pretty good, ranging from hot dogs to Italian sausage to crab cakes. Former Oriole Boog Powell's barbecue stand sends a cloud of smoke up over the scoreboard wall—the pit-beef sandwiches are worth the wait in line. The park also offers tours that give visitors a chance to sit in the dugout, and in the press box from April to September.

An Orioles game might be a great place to bring a client (the stands are full of them), but a minor-league game is the place for families. In addition to lower ticket prices (less than $10) and more intimate stadiums, many minor-league games offer playgrounds, fireworks, and special family events.

The **Aberdeen IronBirds** (☏ **410/297-9292;** www.ironbirdsbaseball.com), a Class A affiliate of the Orioles, are owned by Aberdeen native and Baseball Hall of Famer Cal Ripken and his brother Billy Ripken. The stadium has remained a popular place to catch a game since it opened in 2002. Nearby youth-size fields copy the dimensions of famous parks; Cal Sr.'s Yard, for instance, is a miniature replica of Oriole Park at Camden Yards. The "warehouse," like the one at the real Camden Yards, houses a 120-unit Courtyard by Marriott (☏ **410/272-0440**). The Ripken Academy here operates a series of baseball clinics, tournaments, and the Cal Ripken World Series.

The **Bowie Baysox** (☏ **301/464-4865;** www.baysox.com), a Class AA Orioles affiliate, usually have a fireworks display after Saturday home games. The team

10 THE BEST CAMPING

- **Janes Island State Park** (Eastern Shore, Md.): For sunset vistas over the Chesapeake Bay, the campsites at this park north of Crisfield can't be beat. Many sites sit on the water's edge, offering unobstructed views and access to the canoe trail. If you prefer less-primitive accommodations, there are a few waterside cabins as well. See p. 178.

- **New Germany State Park** (Garrett County, Md.): It's small, with only 37 well-spaced sites, but they are clean, well kept, and offer easy access to hiking trails, fishing spots in the park's lake, and the facilities of several other Western Maryland state parks and forests. The 11 cabins are great options for winter cross-country skiing trips. See p. 216.

plays in Prince George's Stadium, in Prince George's County, northeast of Washington, D.C.

The **Delmarva Shorebirds** (℃ **888/BIRDS96** [247-3796] or 410/219-3112; www.theshorebirds.com), an Orioles affiliate in the Class A South Atlantic League, play near Ocean City, at Arthur W. Perdue Stadium in Salisbury, Maryland. An Eastern Shore Hall of Fame here celebrates Delmarva baseball from amateur to pro.

The **Frederick Keys** (℃ **877/846-5397;** www.frederickkeys.com), a Class A Orioles affiliate, play at Harry Grove Stadium in Frederick, off I-70 and Route 355 (Market St.). The Keys draw fans from Baltimore and Washington, D.C.

The **Hagerstown Suns** (℃ **800/538-9967** or 301/791-6266; www.hagerstownsuns.com), a Class A affiliate of the Washington, D.C., Nationals, play at Municipal Stadium, on Route 40, in Hagerstown, Maryland.

Hall of Famer and former Oriole Brooks Robinson is part owner of the newest team, the **Southern Maryland Blue Crabs** (℃ **301/638-9788;** www.somdbluecrabs.com). An independent in the Atlantic League, the team plays in Regency Furniture Stadium in Waldorf.

Baltimore City has two sports museums celebrating baseball. Yes, the Babe *was* a Yankee, but he was born in Baltimore in the narrow rowhouse that is now the **Babe Ruth Birthplace and Museum,** 216 Emory St. (℃ **410/727-1539;** www.baberuthmuseum.com). Next door to Oriole Park at Camden Yards is **Sports Legends Museum at Camden Yards,** 301 W. Camden St. (℃ **410/727-1539;** www.baberuthmuseum.com), filled with mementos of Orioles history as well as other local sporting memories. For details on these two museums, see p. 82 and 84.

If you visit **Chestertown,** on the Eastern Shore, look for the life-size statue of **Bill Nicholson** next to the town hall on Cross Street. In the 1940s, the Chestertown native was a home-run king with the Chicago Cubs. He led the majors in home runs and RBIs in 1943 and 1944. During the 1944 season, the New York Giants intentionally walked him with the bases loaded, rather than risk a grand slam. He died in his hometown, Chestertown, in 1996.

- **Potomac–Garrett State Forest** (Garrett County, Md.): For primitive camping in the mountains, head to this state forest in Western Maryland. Nearly all the campsites are within walking distance of one of the forest's mountain streams, and they're so spread out, you'll never know if you have neighbors. See p. 217.
- **Cape Henlopen State Park** (near Lewes, Del.): Summer beach camping is always a tenuous venture, with the heat, the bugs, and the sand. But the facilities at Cape Henlopen make for the best beach experience: There are 159 wooded sites, several with full hookups and all with access to bathhouses and running water. Within the park, you'll find several miles of hiking and biking trails, guarded beaches, and great fishing. See p. 243.

- **Flowermart** (Baltimore, Md.; **410/323-0022**; www.flowermart.org): This 2-day festival is held the first weekend in May, around the Washington Monument on Charles Street. You'll see ladies wearing flower-bedecked hats; traditional Baltimore foods, such as crab cakes and the lemon stick (halve a lemon, stab it with a peppermint stick, and suck the juice through the candy); and, of course, flowers.

- **United States Sailboat Show** (Annapolis, Md.; *©* **410/268-8828;** www.usboat.com): Boat dealers fill the city dock with an array of sailboats, Spartan racing boats, and luxurious floating living rooms. Wear sneakers or boat shoes, and you can climb aboard them all and dream. It takes place the first weekend in October. The **Powerboat Show** is held the following weekend.

- **Waterfowl Festival** (Easton, Md.; *©* **410/822-4567;** www.waterfowl festival.org): This festival, held the second week in November, features paintings of canvasbacks, herons, and Canada geese, decoys both practical and fanciful, and sculptures so lifelike you'll want to smooth their feathers. There are sometimes even tiny sculptures worked in gold. For fun, stop by the duck-calling contest.

- **Christmas at Longwood Gardens** (Kennett Square, Pa., in the Brandywine Valley; *©* **610/388-1000**): Everyone forgets that it's cold as they slow down to gaze at the thousands of lights—maybe millions—that turn the gardens into pure magic. Then they go into the conservatories to see the poinsettias and Christmas decorations. "Winter wonderland" is such a cliché, but it's really true in this case.

12 THE BEST FAMILY ACTIVITIES

- **B&O Railroad Museum** (Baltimore, Md.): Kids of every age are entranced by the gigantic iron horses that fill the roundhouse where American railroading got its start. See p. 83.

- **Art and Industry** (Baltimore, Md.): Baltimore's museums have a few attractions the kids are sure to like. The **Walters Art Museum** (p. 87) has a great armor collection, while the sculpture garden at the **Baltimore Museum of Art** (p. 88) delights even the youngest children. And the guides at the **Baltimore Museum of Industry** (p. 78) offer insights on kids' levels and even let them try out some of the machines.

- *Harbor Queen* **Boat Ride** (Annapolis, Md.): The kids love leaning over the rail as waves hit the boat, and it's a great way to see the bay. There's a little history lesson, but mostly this is a wind-in-your-face, sun-in-your-eyes ride. See p. 126.

- **Delaware History Museum** (Wilmington, Del.): Toddlers can run up and down the ramps, school-age children can try out the interactive displays, and everybody will get a kick out of the "Distinctly Delaware" exhibit. Grandma's Attic adds hands-on activities to the fun. See p. 303.

Maryland & Delaware in Depth

Tucked in the Philadelphia–Washington, D.C., megalopolis are two of America's smallest states. But don't be fooled. Maryland and Delaware aren't places you want to pass by as you speed over the interstate. Nor should you make the mistake of assuming they are two parts of the same geographic location. Far from it.

Marylanders consider their state "America in miniature." In the space of 300 miles, a visitor can travel over mountains, past rolling farmlands, and across a mighty body of water to the flat coastal plains that end at the Atlantic Ocean. For every season, there's a pretty-as-a-postcard view: spring tulips in north Baltimore, summer skies over ocean and bay, autumn leaves along the Gunpowder and the Potomac, and snow-topped mountains filled with skiers.

Delaware has its own delights. "The First State" revels in its history: Dutch whalers created an outpost along the Delaware Bay; Caesar Rodney raced on horseback to ensure passage of the Declaration of Independence; the state was the first to ratify the U.S. Constitution. And it makes the most of its natural beauty: White sands line its Atlantic Ocean shores; cypress trees wade in the tranquil waters of inland ponds; rolling hills traverse the Brandywine Valley.

As you travel through these two states, you'll have the opportunity to peer into the age of dinosaurs, see where Native Americans made their marks, trace the route of European settlers and runaway slaves, and marvel at the advances of the Industrial Revolution, the Space Age, and the Digital Age.

What's your pleasure? **Food:** You can't beat the seafood restaurants along the Chesapeake Bay or in the ocean resorts. **Wine:** Believe it or not, Maryland wineries have produced some pretty decent vintages. **Architecture:** Colonial gems in New Castle, Delaware, and Annapolis, Maryland, are the real deal, protected for more than 200 years; and mansions, castles really, dot the Brandywine. **Music:** Wilmington has both a symphony and an opera company, while Charm City's Baltimore Symphony Orchestra and its musical director Marin Alsop are wowing audiences at home and at Carnegie Hall.

Outdoor adventures: These states have got it all, from kayaking and white-water rafting to sailing, fishing, surfing, mountain biking, and camping. Whatever you like, if you can't find it in either Delaware or Maryland, you're not looking hard enough.

1 LOOKING BACK AT MARYLAND & DELAWARE

MARYLAND
Early Days

When Lord Baltimore and 140 fellow English men and women landed on the shores of the St. Mary's River in 1634, the area was already settled by Native American tribes, including the Yaocomaco people, an Eastern Woodland group, with whom the first colonists traded. Also living in the state were the Algonquin, Leni-Lenape, and Nanticoke. These people are responsible for naming the places still so valued here today: the Chesapeake Bay, Potomac River, and Assateague.

Maryland's first capital, St. Mary's City, was founded by a Catholic nobleman who enacted the first Freedom of Conscience law in the world. Settlers were free to worship as they saw fit, and to hold office no matter what their religion. There were other precedents set here, too. The first man of color held office in Maryland, and the first Catholic church to be built in the English colonies was built here. A woman sought the opportunity to vote here, but, as progressive as the settlers were, they turned her down. The first print shop south of Boston was established here (and run by a woman) in the 1600s.

Meanwhile, 75 miles to the north, another Englishman, William Claiborne, had established in 1631 a trading post in the Chesapeake Bay for the colony of Virginia. Now known as Kent Island (the eastern terminus of the Chesapeake Bay Bridge), the settlement became a source of conflict even after it was absorbed into Lord Baltimore's colony.

The colony, centered in St. Mary's City, grew in strength and number. Demand for Maryland tobacco grew in Europe, making the noxious plant the currency of the day. The economy boomed and the town grew with the construction of inns, a statehouse, and a chapel. By the late 1600s, some 20,000 people lived there.

But the days of St. Mary's City were coming to an end. Tensions from an English revolution spilled into the Catholic colony, and disgruntled Protestants led a revolution against Lord Baltimore in 1689. The crown appointed royal governors who moved the capital from St. Mary's City to Annapolis in 1695.

The first capital all but disappeared under cornfields and woodlands. Hidden below ground were all sorts of treasures—shards of glass, rosary beads, lead coffins, and shadows of hearths and posts—valuable markings that would enable archaeologists and historians to piece together the design and history of the first capital and rebuild parts of it, now known as Historic St. Mary's City.

Revolution & Statehood

The colony continued to grow. Annapolis became the hub of government and the center for exports, most notably tobacco but, to its shame, for the slave trade, as well. As the home of the state legislature, it attracted the wealthy and the powerful, the trader and the barrister, and the waterman and the farmer.

Farther north, in a deep harbor of the Patapsco River, another city was taking shape. Formed from the shipbuilding center of Fell's Point and the industrial center of Jonestown, the new city, named after the colony's founder, was founded in 1729. Baltimore grew quickly as a center of trade and industry. It became the home port of a fleet of speedy trading vessels, the Baltimore clippers.

As the colony grew, the desire for independence from England grew as it did in the other 12 English colonies. Annapolis became a center for revolutionary thought. The tax on tea prompted protest. The *Peggy Stewart,* a ship laden with a ton of tea, was burned when its owner paid the tax. Protesters tossed shipments of tea overboard in the Eastern Shore city of Chestertown, in response to the closing of the Boston harbor.

Marylanders, including three Carrolls—Charles Carroll the barrister, his son Charles Carroll of Carrollton, and Daniel Carroll, the barrister's nephew—and two Chases—Jeremiah and Samuel—took part in the Continental Congresses in Philadelphia. When the time came to sign the Declaration of Independence, Maryland's four delegates stepped up: Charles

Carroll of Carrollton, Samuel Chase, William Paca, and Thomas Stone.

As the conflict with England escalated, Annapolis became the United States's first peacetime capital. From November 26, 1783, to August 13, 1784, the legislature met in the State House, where the Maryland General Assembly continues to gather every January through April. This was the site of the ratification of the Treaty of Paris, the document in which Great Britain recognized American independence. It was also here that George Washington resigned his commission as commander in chief of the army.

When the Constitution came before the General Assembly in April 1788, Maryland became the seventh of the original 13 colonies to ratify it. Peace and prosperity continued as the new state grew. Maryland had been virtually untouched during the American Revolution, but this would not be the case when the British Navy returned to reclaim its colonies in 1812. This time, a single flag flying over Baltimore's harbor would become a symbol of America's independence.

The War of 1812 began with a British blockade of the Chesapeake and Delaware bays. Many small towns along the Chesapeake found themselves facing British warships. The Battle of Baltimore, on the night of September 13, 1814, is remembered every time we sing the national anthem. American forces were ready for the British. Ships were deliberately sunk near Fort McHenry to keep the British and their powerful cannons away from Baltimore and its harbor. Instead, the British aimed their guns at the fort through the night. The siege was witnessed by Francis Scott Key, a young attorney who had met with the British while seeking the release of a doctor captured during the British march toward Washington. Though the doctor was freed, he and Key were forced to stay aboard the British ship until the battle was over. Seeing the giant

flag sewn by Mary Young Pickersgill flying over the fort the following morning inspired Key to write "The Star Spangled Banner." Set to the tune of a drinking song, it became the national anthem in 1931.

A Time of Growth

The 19th century was a time of immense growth for Maryland, especially for its most industrialized city, Baltimore. The first sugar refinery was built here, and saccharine and Bromo Seltzer antacid were developed here. The first American umbrella factory opened here, as did the first commercial ice-cream factory. Samuel Morse created the first American telegraph line here.

But it was in transportation that Baltimore—and the state—made its mark. The first national road from Baltimore to the frontier began construction in 1806. (Much of it is intact, from Baltimore to Western Maryland, as part of the National Historic Road.)

George Washington envisioned a watery highway between Washington, D.C., and the fertile Ohio Valley. The C&O Canal, which stretches through the Potomac Valley from Georgetown to Cumberland in Western Maryland, includes a towpath for mules to haul the barges along the canal. A newfangled invention, the railroad, made the canal obsolete even before it was begun. But the towpath has been preserved as a national park and offers visitors 184 miles of trails for biking and hiking from Georgetown to Cumberland.

America's first commercial railroad, the Baltimore and Ohio, got its start in Baltimore in 1828. "Tom Thumb," the first steam-burning locomotive, even proved in a race between Baltimore and Ellicott City that it was faster than a horse. (Alas, a technical malfunction enabled the horse to win the race but the point had been made.) Though the Tom Thumb was not preserved, a replica built in 1926 is on display at the B&O Railroad Museum in Baltimore, site of the original B&O headquarters.

Civil War & the Underground Railroad

Baltimore earned its most detested moniker in the opening days of the Civil War. When the Sixth Massachusetts Union Army troops and the Pennsylvania Volunteer Washington brigade passed through Baltimore's President Street Station on their way to Washington, D.C., they had to march through the city's streets to reach the Camden Station, a few blocks away. But an angry mob gathered and blocked their passage. The skirmish resulted in the "First Blood of the Civil War." Four soldiers and 12 civilians were killed that day, April 19, 1861. And the city became known as "Mobtown."

Maryland was deeply divided during the War Between the States, with many loyal to the South. These divided loyalties caused federal troops to be deployed to Baltimore and martial law enacted. Guns set up on Federal Hill in the Inner Harbor were trained on the city to ensure loyalty to the Union—and guarantee that Washington, D.C., would not become surrounded by Confederate States.

Soldiers crisscrossed Maryland several times in the course of the war, including the July 1863 battle that came to be known as the "high-water mark of the Confederacy" and General Robert E. Lee's final great campaign, Gettysburg. The tiny town of Sharpsburg witnessed the bloodiest day of the Civil War. The battle at Antietam, in September 1862, marked the bloodiest day of the war—and of any war since, even D-day. Some 23,000 Americans were killed or wounded that day.

The war touched other Maryland towns, as well. Ransoms were demanded of the citizens of Frederick and Hagerstown to save them from torching. In southern Maryland, John Wilkes Booth made his way through Waldorf and Clinton both before he assassinated Abraham Lincoln and then as he attempted to escape.

Though the Civil War never came to the Eastern Shore, the Underground Railroad had many routes through the flat farmlands here, where slaves escaped north to freedom. Harriet Tubman was the most famous of the Underground Railroad conductors. A slave in Dorchester County, she escaped to lead several hundred people to freedom. Frederick Douglass, who was enslaved in Talbot County, escaped the bonds of slavery while working in Baltimore and became a renowned abolitionist. Tubman and Douglass are remembered in both counties, as well as other places where they led enslaved people to freedom.

Modern Maryland

Industrial Baltimore continued to grow through the 20th century. It became a major manufacturing city, home to General Motors and Bethlehem Steel plants, Domino Sugar and McCormick Spice, Noxell, and Westinghouse.

During the world wars, Maryland turned its talents to the creation of military material, planes, and ships. Defense contractors built up around Fort Meade, the Patuxent Naval Air Station, and Aberdeen Proving Ground—places that will continue to see growth as defense workers relocate here from closed military bases over the next decade.

Modern medicine has made its mark in Baltimore as well, thanks largely to the efforts of health professionals at the Johns Hopkins Hospital and University of Maryland Medical System. These two centers of healthcare attract patients from around the world. The shock trauma center at the University of Maryland, pioneered by Dr. R. Adams Cowley, is a model for emergency rooms around the world.

"The land of pleasant living" was once an advertising slogan, but Marylanders have taken it to heart. Playgrounds have developed around the state to take advantage of its natural wonders. Ocean City was established as the state's first beach resort in 1875. A year later, a summer resort opened near the B&O railroad line in Garrett County.

The advent of the automobile and new roads, bridges, and other engineering marvels made these attractions popular with the average Joe and Jo. The Chesapeake Bay bridges, built in 1952 and 1973, brought the Eastern Shore's delights and the beaches of Ocean City closer to Baltimore and Washington residents. Construction of Deep Creek Lake in Western Maryland in 1925 turned the Appalachian Mountains into a family resort. A Pittsburgh resident named Helmuth Heise turned a little hill above the lake into a ski resort he named Wisp. Once I-68 was complete, the trip to Western Maryland got a lot easier and Western Maryland resorts became year-round attractions.

Baltimore, which had seen the rise of industry, a devastating fire in 1905, and civil strife in the 1960s, began to turn around in the 1970s—and continues to do so today. James Rouse's vision of Harborplace became a model re-created as far as Sydney, Australia. The immense popularity of Harborplace in 1980 led to further development of the Inner Harbor, including new stadiums for the Baltimore Orioles and the Baltimore Ravens. Harbor East is Baltimore's newest gathering spot, with other neighborhoods around the waterfront showing signs of rebirth.

Even St. Mary's City, the state's first city, has experienced a renaissance. Now a living history museum, its State House, print house, taverns and ordinaries, even its Brick Chapel, have been re-created as a testimony of those early days of trial, bravery, and freedom.

DELAWARE
In the Beginning

Henry Hudson first saw the Delaware Bay in 1609, but he was discouraged by the dangerous shoals and turned north to discover the Hudson River. Another Englishman, Samuel Argall, came the next year, but determined that he'd made a mistake, named the bay the Delaware—after the governor of Virginia, Thomas West, Lord de La Warr—and headed south to his original destination of Virginia.

Dutch fishermen arrived in 1631 to settle on a tiny cape of land lying between the Delaware Bay and the Atlantic Ocean—they called it Zwaanendael, the Valley of the Swans. It didn't last. A dispute arose between the settlers and the Leni-Lenape tribes, and the Dutch were massacred.

Swedish settlers came next. In 1637, the *Kalmar Nyckel* and *Vogel Grip* sailed into the Delaware Bay and headed north to a narrow river the settlers called the Christina, after their queen. They built a fortress and log cabins—the first built in the New World—and called their settlement New Sweden. The Swedes adapted well to their new home. They raised livestock and grew corn, a staple introduced to them by their Native American neighbors.

The settlement prospered, but it wasn't long before the Dutch returned to claim the land. In 1655, a group of settlers under the leadership of Peter Stuyvesant, established Fort Casimir, 7 miles south of New Sweden. Hungry for more land, the Dutch sent troops to the Swedish settlement and forced their surrender. The Swedish settlers were allowed to remain in the newly renamed New Amstel, under Dutch governance.

Change would come again in 1664 when King Charles II of England granted this land to the duke of York, thus giving England control of most of the Atlantic seaboard. The settlement became known as New Castle and soon became Delaware's first capital and a major Colonial seaport. During this first English rule, a Colonial court was established and the streets were resurveyed. The town developed into a seat of government and Delaware's first capital.

The Dutch returned to power briefly in 1673 but in 1684, William Penn arrived with his Quaker followers to take possession of the Pennsylvania colony granted to him. He arrived first in New Castle before sailing up the Delaware River to establish Philadelphia. Penn, who had been given Delaware as part of Pennsylvania, divided the lands south of Philadelphia into the counties of New Castle, Kent, and Sussex. By 1704, residents of the counties of Delaware became dissatisfied with Pennsylvania, and Penn granted them the right to form their own assembly.

The colony of Delaware flourished. New colonists arrived to develop Wilmington on the site of Fort Christina, and Dover was plotted in 1717 according to a street plan of Penn's devising. Sixty years later, the capital was moved to this city in the center of the state.

The First State

Although Delaware is tiny in size, its people played important roles in the establishment of a free United States. Look at a Delaware quarter, and you'll see an image of a man on horseback. This commemorates the ride of Caesar Rodney of Kent County, who broke a deadlock on the vote for independence in 1776 in Philadelphia. Though he was suffering from cancer, he rode 80 miles on horseback through the night to Philadelphia so he could cast his crucial vote in favor of the Declaration of Independence.

To meet the English redcoats in battle, Delaware raised an army of 4,000 soldiers clad in blue coats who became known for the blue hens they carried with them.

The Revolution bypassed Delaware except for a skirmish at Cooch's Bridge near Newark. From here, the British

would meet George Washington's army at the Battle of Brandywine, just north of Delaware, in one of the largest battles of the Revolutionary War.

Delaware had one more crucial role to play in the formation of the new nation. When the Constitution was brought before the state legislature December 7, 1787, Delaware voted aye and became "The First State," the first to ratify the document.

Of Transportation & Chemicals

Delaware's location along the Delaware Bay and Atlantic Ocean, downstream from powerful Philadelphia, made it ideal for industrial development, especially with the coming of the railroad and the steamboat to ship these new products as well as crops from Delaware's fertile farmlands. The 1829 construction of the Chesapeake and Delaware Canal offered shippers a shortcut from the Chesapeake Bay (and Baltimore, Washington, and points south) to the Atlantic Ocean. With that, Wilmington grew in size and stature.

The arrival of a French aristocrat, E.I. du Pont, would bring great change to Delaware. He established his black powder mill on the banks of the Brandywine River in 1802. This endeavor grew as the du Pont family extended their research into a wide variety of chemical products used by the military, aerospace industry, and homeowner alike as du Pont became the largest chemical manufacturer in America.

The chemical industries of DuPont continue to pump millions of dollars into the Delaware economy. DuPont money is also responsible for the famous "châteaux" of the Brandywine Valley that visitors flock to each year: Winterthur, Nemours, and Longwood Gardens, as well as Hagley, home of the original powder mill.

With an eye on Baltimore's Inner Harbor, the city planners of Wilmington have developed the Riverfront in the past decade in an effort to revive the downtown district. Museums, restaurants, a new stadium, and tall residential buildings have changed the waterfront significantly.

Tourists come to Delaware for many other reasons, as well. Slots at Delaware Park, Harrington, and Dover Downs have made the state a gambling mecca. Twice a year, NASCAR fans descend on Dover by the tens of thousands. Sales-tax-free shopping makes the Rehoboth outlets even better. And then there are the beaches: The quiet resorts of Fenwick and Bethany, the party known as Dewey, and the towns of Rehoboth and Lewes not only have lovely beaches but attractive small-town charm as well. Add the outdoor delights of a network of great state parks—though not even one national park—and you've got lots of fun things to choose from.

2 THE LAY OF THE LAND

MARYLAND
Western Maryland

Lovers of the outdoors adore this part of Maryland. It has biking and hiking trails, lakes, and white water. It has the Catoctin Mountains and Deep Creek Lake, charming towns, and historic sites.

Everything west of Frederick County is considered Western Maryland. Although development has begun here, particularly around Hagerstown and Cumberland, the atmosphere is peaceful. You can expect a smile and a welcome from the people you meet.

It used to take hours driving over small winding roads to get to the far reaches of Western Maryland. That's no longer true since the construction of Route 68, which continues westward when Route 70 heads north near Hancock. Route 68 bypasses the small towns and slices right through a mountain at Sideling Hill.

Now skiing at Wisp Resort is just a few hours away from the more populous eastern part of the state. Hiking a trail at Swallow Falls can take longer than driving to it. And many visitors frequent Deep Creek Lake and Rocky Gap State Park and Resort.

Summer and winter are the best times to visit. Summer offers hot sunshine and cool shade for outdoor activities. State parks beckon in winter with cross-country skiing, snowshoeing, tobogganing, and rides in horse-drawn sleighs. Spring and fall are the seasons for hiking, biking, horseback riding, fishing, and sometimes boating. Colorful foliage also makes this a popular spot in fall, but sometimes spring can be a little cold and wet for activities other than shopping and limited sightseeing. The Wisp Resort keeps visitors coming year-round, with golf, a white-water course, hiking, and biking, as well as downhill skiing.

The Washington, D.C., Suburbs

A lot of territory is dumped into this region. All roads—or at least highways—lead to Washington, D.C., and so do many of the people who live in these Maryland counties. But the counties of Frederick, Montgomery, Prince George's, Howard, and Carroll are distinctly different. Frederick's history is tied more to that of Western Maryland, though you'd never know it if you were driving the highways around rush hour. It's part of the Civil War crossroads, so you can't go far without finding another reminder of the War Between the States. The area is also home to Camp David, the presidential retreat, and rolling hills covered with orchards and dairy farms. A drive up Route 15 toward Gettysburg offers one of Maryland's best day trips.

The other four counties have mostly given themselves over to urban sprawl. There are still some gems, such as the

Charm City Architecture

ROWHOUSES

Part of what makes Baltimore "Charm City" is its rowhouses: long rows of flat fronted houses. Three marble steps lead to the front door. A pink Baltimore brick probably faces the exterior—but you just might see the pink-and-gray fake-stone veneer known as Formstone. Baltimore's rowhouses have been undergoing a renaissance since the 1970s, when the city sold vacant houses for a buck apiece. You'll find these beauties in Otterbein, near Oriole Park, in Federal Hill, Canton, and Fell's Point. The longest row of rowhouses, at 1,800 feet, is in the 2600 block of Wilkens Avenue in west Baltimore.

MANSIONS

If you want to see really spectacular houses, castles really, you'll want to go to the Brandywine Valley near Wilmington. Sure, there are great houses in Maryland (the Carroll and Garret mansions in Baltimore, p. 81 and 88, and the Paca House in Annapolis, p. 124, for example) but the du Pont family has built the most striking examples open to the public. Not only houses, but gardens, too, make Nemours, Winterthur, Longwood Gardens, and Hagley spectacular.

COLONIAL STYLE

Williamsburg's Colonial streets may be famous, but Annapolis's and New Castle's buildings were actually built in the 1700s, and some even in the 1600s. Carefully preserved Georgian and Federal beauties line these streets.

BEAUX ARTS STYLE

Tired of those symmetrical brick buildings? For a taste of architecture with a European flair, you've got to take a walk up Charles Street in Baltimore. You'll find palatial homes facing the parks around the Washington Monument.

Great Falls of the Potomac and the home of Clara Barton, the founder of the American Red Cross. Theme-park fans can head for Six Flags America in Prince George's County.

Baltimore Metropolitan Area

The heavily populated region around Baltimore and Annapolis is home to most Marylanders. Baltimore keeps attracting more businesses and residents as it continues to transform from aging industrial town to up-to-the-minute cosmopolitan city. Annapolis, 25 miles away, works hard at staying just the way it has always been.

That Colonial style, with the U.S. Naval Academy and Chesapeake Bay as charming backdrops, still attracts plenty of visitors.

Southern Maryland

Tobacco once was king in Southern Maryland, and reminders are still evident. As you drive through Charles, Calvert, and St. Mary's counties, you can see tobacco-curing barns with the long narrow slits that open up to the air.

St. Clement's Island, where Maryland's first settlers stepped upon the New World in 1634, is still a very remote place. St. Mary's City disappeared after Annapolis became the capital, but archaeologists are rediscovering and restoring the 374-year-old buildings in a fascinating work in progress.

Surrounded by the mouth of the Potomac River and the Atlantic Ocean, this is fishing territory. At Point Lookout State Park, anglers can try their luck in both. In Calvert County, both Chesapeake Beach and Solomons offer many a fishing-boat charter.

The Eastern Shore

This is the home of corn, oysters, and geese. On a flat spit of land that stretches up the eastern side of the Chesapeake Bay, the Eastern Shore is different from the rest of Maryland. Natives have their own accent and are sun- and wind-burned from long hours on a tractor or a workboat. Towns are small, and though many are more busi-nesslike than pretty, some have deserved reputations for charm and history. There are rivers for fishing, boating, and swim-ming. The wide-open spaces attract water-fowl from fall to spring, a delight if you're a hunter or a birder. And the Eastern Shore's flatness makes biking easy.

The Mid-Shore—Talbot, Kent, and Dorchester counties—is the most devel-oped part of the Eastern Shore and the most tourist-friendly. Though fishing and crabbing are important, the main industry here has historically been shipbuilding.

Don't care about any of that? You'll love Route 50 because it will get you "downy ocean" in a hurry, hon.

Down the Ocean

The Atlantic rules here—sun, beach, and miniature golf as far as the eye can see. Here, too, are the lifesaving stations and concrete watchtowers that once housed those on the lookout for sailors in distress and World War II enemy ships.

Ocean City's condos, shops, and high-ways dominate the state's coastline; in summer, it's Maryland's second-largest city. South of the inlet is Assateague

Island, a seashore park renowned for its wild ponies and its pristine landscape.

DELAWARE
Down the Ocean, Continued

In Delaware, much smaller resorts, such as Bethany Beach and Dewey Beach, are located between long stretches of public beach and national seashore. Rehoboth, Delaware's premier beach, retains its small-town charm in spite of the crowds that can make Route 1 impassable on holidays or summer weekends. (An ever-popular dis-trict of outlet stores on Rte. 1 makes the traffic worse—and the bargains more plentiful.) Just north of Rehoboth Beach is Lewes, a quaint Victorian town known as the terminus of the Cape May-Lewes Ferry. It's a nice diversion thanks to its shops, its Delaware Bay beaches, and its many charter fishing boats.

Central Delaware

Kent County, which is primarily farm-land, is Delaware's central county and home of Dover, the state capital. In strik-ing contrast to Annapolis, Dover is a quiet capital town with charming museums and historic sites—but twice a year on race weekends, it fills up with fans of the big NASCAR auto races. Bombay Hook National Wildlife Refuge on the Delaware Bay is a stop along the East Coast for migrating waterfowl and is less developed than Blackwater on Maryland's Eastern Shore.

The Brandywine Valley

This is du Pont country. The American branch of the du Pont family has been in this region since E. I. du Pont opened his black-powder mill on the banks of the Brandywine River in 1802. Their legacy is everywhere, from Longwood Gardens to Winterthur. You could easily spend a week here and not see all the sights. It's not hard to see why the du Ponts, or anyone, would settle here: The rolling hills, the fertile land, and the river itself have served as inspiration for the region's other famous family, the Wyeths.

Wilmington lies at the edge of Brandywine Valley. It's a convenient spot for visiting the valley sites, but it's also got interesting restaurants and museums of its own. The city's Riverfront, now lined with office buildings, restaurants, museums, and tall condos, is worth a visit.

3 MARYLAND & DELAWARE IN POP CULTURE

FILMED IN MARYLAND

Charm City has had a starring, or at least supporting role, in movies since the early 20th century. Alfred Hitchcock re-created a waterfront street for *Marnie,* and James Bond landed at Friendship Airport (now BWI) with Pussy Galore in *Goldfinger.*

Two Baltimoreans have put their hometown in a variety of movies. John Waters filmed lots of movies in Baltimore from the early *Pink Flamingoes* to the more mainstream *Cry-Baby,* with Johnny Depp, and *Serial Mom,* with Kathleen Turner. *Serial Mom* was a homecoming for Turner, who studied drama at the University of Maryland Baltimore County.

The musical version of *Hairspray* wasn't really filmed in Baltimore—that was Toronto, hon. And that's John Travolta trying to sound like he's really from "Muriland." He'd been to B-more before to film *Ladder 49* in 2004, and we loved him then, too.

Local boy Barry Levinson paid homage to our town in a number of his early movies: *Tin Men, Avalon,* and *Liberty Heights,* and the most famous of them all, *Diner.*

We've had our fair share of silver screen beauties here, too. Nicole Kidman was in town to shoot the *Invasion,* released in 2007. Renee Zellweger starred in *He's Just Not That Into You,* with Baltimore stepping into the role of Boston. Diana Ross never actually came to Baltimore when she starred in the 1972 biopic *Lady Sings the Blues,* about Baltimore's Billie Holiday. But that was Whoopie Goldberg in the two-hankie *Clara's Heart.* Elizabeth McGovern came to

town twice for *Bedroom Window,* a 1987 murder mystery, and 1991's *He said, She Said,* which also starred Kevin Bacon, one of the original *Diner* stars.

Thrillers by Marylander Tom Clancy were filmed locally as well. That's the Ravens' stadium being blown up in *The Sum of All Fears.* Annapolis was the setting for Harrison Ford in 1992's *Patriot Games.* Ford had previously been in Baltimore to film the forgettable *Mosquito Coast* in 1986.

Oriole Park at Camden Yards got its star turn, too, in *Major League,* with Charlie Sheen and Tom Berenson; and in *The Babe,* with John Goodman playing Baltimore's Babe Ruth. Kevin Kline came to an Orioles game to throw out the first pitch in *Dave.*

And what better place for a romance than Baltimore, setting for *Sleepless in Seattle* and *The Accidental Tourist* (based on a novel by Baltimorean Anne Tyler). *Step Up* (and *Step Up 2*) showed the grittier side of Baltimore—as well as the refined Baltimore School for the Arts.

The Maryland countryside was the backdrop of a few movies as well. *Wedding Crashers* and *Failure to Launch* are set on the Eastern Shore. Oprah Winfrey starred in *Beloved,* shot in the countryside north of Baltimore in 1988. Sissie Spacek spent time in Ocean City for *Violets Are Blue* in 1986, and then returned to nearby Berlin to film *Tuck Everlasting* in 2002. Little Berlin was turned upside down earlier by Julia Roberts and Richard Gere, when they came to film *Runaway Bride.*

Oh, and one more. The people of suburban Baltimore County and Frederick County would like it if everyone forgot that the *Blair Witch Project* was shot there in 1999.

FILMED IN DELAWARE

In Delaware, Centerville was the spooky setting of M. Night Shyamalan's *The Village* and the not spooky at all backdrop for the Meg Ryan vehicle *Addicted to Love* in 1997.

TV & BOOKS, TOO

Baltimoreans remain proud of their town's starring role in *Homicide: Life on the Streets.* HBO's *The Wire,* also by David Simon, was filmed here, as well.

The good-natured folks of Delaware haven't gotten their own television show (and thank goodness, not even one about urban violence), but the Delaware-based *Punkin' Chunkin'* has given the state its 15 minutes of fame. It's been featured on ESPN and the Smithsonian Channel among other outlets.

A wide variety of books have local settings. James Michener wrote his historical *Chesapeake* (Random House, 1978) while living on the Eastern Shore. Though it's fiction, the book offers a good history of the area and the watermen who make their living on the Bay.

Several other books celebrate the Chesapeake: William H. Warner's *Beautiful Swimmers* (Little, Brown, 1976), a Pulitzer Prize–winning study of the blue crab; *An Island Out of Time* (Norton, 1996), by Tom Horton, chronicles his 3 years living on remote Smith Island. Cambridge native John Barth set his epic *The Sotweed Factor* (Atlantic Books, 1960) on the Eastern Shore. Children have been reading Katherine Paterson's *Jacob I Have Loved,* a Newbery Medal winner, since Crowell published it in 1980.

Roots (Doubleday, 1976) opens in Annapolis. Author Alex Haley and his main character Kunta Kinte are remembered at the City Dock there.

Anne Tyler sets her books in and around the Baltimore neighborhood where she has lived. Several have been made into movies, most notably *The Accidental Tourist* (Knopf, 1985). *Ladder of Years* (Knopf, 1995) takes place at the beach.

Nora Roberts, a prolific romance writer, has set several of her books in her adopted state of Maryland. The four-book Chesapeake Bay collection is set in St. Michaels and Baltimore.

Baltimore native and sportswriter Frank DeFord based his novel *An American Summer* (Sourcebooks, 2002) in 1954 Baltimore County.

The newest Maryland-based book is James McBride's *Song Yet Sung,* published in 2008, which chronicles a runaway slave's experiences on the Eastern Shore.

ONLY IN BALTIMORE, HON

Walk down one of Baltimore's rowhouse-lined streets and you'll probably see a **painted screen.** Idyllic scenes were usually on the window, but some screen doors have been decorated, too. William Oktavec started the art form in 1913 to soften the hard lines of the city streets and provide a little more privacy to the homeowners. The idea caught on with homeowners and artists alike. Screens are part of the collections at the American Visionary Art Museum. (There's a screen painting kit for sale there, too.)

ONLY IN DELAWARE

People all over the world count on DuPont products every day, from cooks and race-car drivers to astronauts.

But in Delaware—where there are DuPont plants, offices, and mansions all over the Wilmington area—the Hagley Museum celebrates the chemical breakthroughs DuPont has made for the past 200 years. It started with gunpowder but has continued with all kinds of products we all use, including nylon and Teflon.

Hagley, of course, was the first DuPont plant.

4 EATING IN MARYLAND & DELAWARE

SEAFOOD

If you visit either Maryland or Delaware, you'll want to order seafood. With the Chesapeake Bay and Atlantic Ocean so close, seafood is taken very seriously here. Crabs used to be available only in the summer, but now you can get crab served any which way year-round. Alas, the crabmeat is often imported from southern waters or, even more shocking, from Asia. It's all blue crab, but it isn't all the same.

The good news is that local cooks have come up with the most creative ways to prepare it: soups (white cream of crab or red Maryland crab soups), crab dip, chicken and steak topped with crabmeat, and crab Imperial, a rich crab dish topped with a mayo mixture and broiled.

By far, though, the most popular ways to enjoy crab is steamed or as a crab cake.

Steamed crabs come piled high under a spicy dose of Old Bay Seasoning. Go ahead, grab a mallet and a knife and get your hands dirty. (Someone will show you how to open the crab.) You'll be delighted by the sweet white meat hidden underneath that bright red shell.

If that's too messy, crab cakes, prepared broiled or fried, are the area's most perfect food.

If the month ends in an *r*, it's oyster season. Fried, swimming in a milky stew, or raw on the half shell, oysters are a seasonal delight that were the cause of "Oyster Wars" a century ago.

Fish lovers await the short seasons for roe shad and rockfish (striped bass) every year. They appear as specials on restaurant menus.

OTHER REGIONAL FAVORITES

Fried chicken fans, though, never have to wait for their favorite dish. Farmers on Delaware and Maryland's Eastern Shore raise thousands of chickens year-round.

Local Flavors

Beer tastes better after an afternoon of paddling, so **Quest Fitness & Kayak** (② **302/644-7020;** www.questfitnesskayak.com) in Lewes has combined a tour of the lazy Broadkill River with a pint and tour of Dogfish Head Brewery in nearby Milton. Don't worry, you won't be pulling up a kayak to the brewery door. After paddling, your guide will drive you to the brewery—no drinking and paddling to worry about. Reservations are required.

Chicken tastes better when it's been barbecued by the Kiwanis. Or the Knights of Columbus. Or the Lions Club. Don't believe it? Drive down Route 404 or Route 50 toward the Atlantic beaches on a summer weekend and stop at one of the roadside stands. For less than $10, you'll get some of the best grilled chicken—most likely from birds raised in one of the numerous chicken coops nearby. The stands sit silent most of the year, but 1 day a week through the summer, fragrant smoke fills the air enticing passersby to stop.

(Tips) The Ice-Cream State

Visitors to Maryland may think the state is defined by the blue crab. And, yes, that's true. But at $25 a pound for a jumbo lump, we really don't eat crab cakes that much. What we line up for on a regular basis is ice cream. Locally made ice cream. And it seems like every town has its own.

You have a Baltimorean to thank for commercial ice cream. Jacob Fussell, the first to built a commercial ice-cream plant, made ice cream from the leftover cream from milk bought from dairy farmers in York County, Pennsylvania, for his Baltimore customers. His first plant was in Pennsylvania but he wised up and moved it to Baltimore.

Taharka Brothers, 1405 Forge Ave., Mount Washington (📞 **410/433-6800**), makes great ice cream (Key Lime is both tart and creamy); look for their carts at Baltimore festivals, too.

Annapolis has **Annapolis Ice Cream,** 196 Main St. (📞 **443/482-3895**). Ice cream is made daily right in their downtown store. They even make the apple pies for the apple pie ice cream.

Western Maryland is home to two creameries. In Deep Creek Lake, order locally made ice cream from the **Lakeside Creamery,** 20282 Garrett Hwy., Oakland (📞 **301/387-2580**). The girls behind the counter also bake vanilla-scented waffle cones. In Cumberland, the choices of frozen custard are limited to three at the **Queen City Creamery,** 108 Harrison St. (📞 **301/777-0011**): chocolate, vanilla, and the flavor of the day. But what flavors—everything from white Russian to pumpkin pie.

In Ocean City, everybody lines up at **Dumser's,** on Coastal Highway at 49th and 124th streets and along the Boardwalk (📞 **410/524-1588**). Made daily, the ice-cream flavors are traditional, except for the fruity Hawaiian Delight. They must be doing something right; Dumser's has been churning ice cream since 1939.

In southern Maryland, the **Ice Cream Factory,** 13700 Old Brandywine Rd., Brandywine (📞 **301/782-3444**), mixes in 1 of 24 flavors when you order their soft frozen custard.

Oxford is home to the **Scottish Highland Creamery,** 314 Tilghman St. (📞 **410/924-6398**), with perfect ice cream made on-site. Fudge, too.

And lucky for the rest of the world: Columbia, west of Baltimore, is home to the headquarters of **Maggie Moo's.** This ice-cream parlor at the Mall in Columbia (📞 **410/730-3313**) mixes various treats into the ice cream on a frozen granite slab. Other "treateries" are scattered across the United States and even Asia.

You'll see Maryland fried chicken on menus, but no one agrees on what that actually is. Often it comes with cream gravy and is deep-fried with a crispy bread coating.

With an international mix of cultures in both states, you'll likely to find any kind of ethnic food you want. Sure, you'll find plenty of Italian and German and Irish dishes from restaurateurs whose ancestors came from the old country. But now, Latino food is growing in popularity with the increase in immigrants from Latin America, especially on the Eastern Shore, in Delaware, and in Baltimore's Fell's Point neighborhood.

Thai, Ethiopian, and Indian foods are appearing on more menus, as well. Tapas and "small plates" may be so yesterday in other parts of the United States, but here, diners are holding on to the concept, thrilled to be able to try so many things without wearing their slacks with the elastic waist.

Diners have become adventurous eaters here, willing to try everything. So restaurants have expanded, improved, and challenged their palates. Nevertheless, show up in a Baltimore diner and you're bound to hear, "What'll you have, hon?" The waitress is asking in the friendliest of ways.

DINING OUT

Dining around here is casual—especially at the seafood houses. In fact, there you can expect to find paper on the table and maybe even a roll of paper towels nearby instead of napkins.

So, unless you're celebrating at Wilmington's Green Room or Baltimore's Prime Rib, you can leave your jacket or cocktail dress at home. "Smart casual" is fine. A pair of clean slacks and polo shirt or sweater is fine for both men and women almost everywhere.

People tend to dine early here. In fact, the most popular time for a reservation in Baltimore is 7pm. At the beach, the lines get really long at no-reservation restaurants at about that time, too. By 9pm, most people have gone home, and the kitchen staff is cleaning up. To skip the crowds, stop on a weeknight or plan on an early or later dinner. You'll get a better table and probably a special deal, too; restaurants are getting creative at finding ways to fill tables during those quiet times.

Lunchtime starts promptly at noon around here, too. By 12:30pm, the crush is on. But lunch is usually served until 2pm or later.

3

Planning Your Trip to Maryland & Delaware

Maryland and Delaware, two of the smaller states in the Union, contain a wide variety of terrain, weather, topography, and urban and rural areas. So a little advance planning can make your trip run smoother. This chapter will answer many questions you may have while preparing for your trip.

For additional help in planning your trip and for more on-the-ground resources in Maryland and Delaware, please see "Fast Facts: Maryland & Delaware," on p. 331.

1 WHEN TO GO

The resort towns on the Atlantic, especially Fourth of July through Labor Day, are most popular in summer and usually quite crowded. The fringe season, May and especially September, is a great time to find cheaper rates, comfortable temperatures, and quieter beaches. Peak season for the Eastern Shore, Annapolis, and Southern Maryland is April through October, when the weather is clear for boating and the fish are biting. Most everything is open in Baltimore year-round, though because of its boating culture and baseball season,

summer is the most popular and crowded time to visit. May and fall bring the convention crowds to Baltimore, but the sunny, less humid weather makes a visit more comfortable. Western Maryland attracts visitors year-round, though spring can be too cool and soggy. Fall is magnificent, especially around mid-October; when it snows, winter is beautiful; summers are cooler here than in the rest of the state. Wilmington and the Brandywine Valley are year-round destinations.

Baltimore's Average Monthly Temperatures & Precipitation

	Jan	Feb	Mar	Apr	May	June	July	Aug	Sept	Oct	Nov	Dec
Temp. (°F)	32	35	44	53	63	73	77	76	69	57	47	37
Temp. (°C)	0	1	6	11	17	22	25	24	20	13	8	2
Precip. (in.)	3.1	3.1	3.4	3.1	3.7	3.7	3.7	3.9	3.4	3	3.3	3.4

Cumberland's Average Monthly Temperatures & Precipitation

	Jan	Feb	Mar	Apr	May	June	July	Aug	Sept	Oct	Nov	Dec
Temp. (°F)	30	33	43	54	63	71	75	74	67	55	45	35
Temp. (°C)	0	0	6	12	17	21	23	23	19	12	7	1
Precip. (in.)	2.38	2.3	3.1	3.2	3.7	3.3	3.4	3.3	3.1	2.8	2.8	2.6

For Baltimore and Annapolis, check on the day's weather forecast by calling ℂ 410/936-1212. In Wilmington, dial ℂ 302/429-9000 for weather, time, and a few ads.

Most attractions offer festivals and events year-round. In the temperature chart above, Baltimore information applies generally to Wilmington and the Brandywine Valley as well; expect summer temperatures to be slightly higher on the southern Eastern Shore and on the coast. Remember that monthly averages can be deceiving: Even though the average temperature in Baltimore during July is 77°F (25°C), days in the 90s (32°C and up) are common.

CALENDAR OF EVENTS

For an exhaustive list of events beyond those listed here, check **http://events. frommers.com**, where you'll find a searchable, up-to-the-minute roster of what's happening in cities all over the world.

JANUARY

Historic Annapolis Antiques Show (Medford National Guard Armory, Annapolis, Md.; ℂ **410/267-8146;** www.annapolis.org): Fine country and period furniture and decorative arts are displayed and sold to benefit London Town Foundation. Second weekend in January.

Chesapeake Bay Boat Show (Baltimore Convention Center, Baltimore, Md.; ℂ **212/984-7000;** www.discover boating.com): Dream of summer while climbing aboard the boats. Nine days in mid-January.

FEBRUARY

Hunt Valley Antiques Show (Timonium, Md.; ℂ **410/366-1980;** www. huntvalleyantiquesshow.org): As good as Annapolis's show (see above). Call for tickets. Last weekend in February.

MARCH

St. Patrick's Day Parade and Festival (Coastal Hwy., Ocean City, Md.; ℂ **800/OC-OCEAN** [626-2326]): The second-largest parade in Maryland features floats and live Irish dancing and entertainment. Saturday nearest the actual day.

Maryland Day (Historic St. Mary's City and Annapolis, Md.; ℂ **800/762-1634** for St. Mary's, or **410/267-8146** for Annapolis): Special tours and ceremonies at historic sites. On or near March 25.

APRIL

My Lady's Manor Steeplechase Races (Ladew Topiary Gardens, Rte. 146 and Pocock Rd., Monkton, Md.; ℂ **410/557-9466**): Annual running of the steeplechase. Saturday in mid-April.

MAY

The Maryland Film Festival (ℂ **410/752-8083;** www.mdfilmfest.com): Venues around Maryland showcase original as well as restored films. First week in May.

Decoy and Wildlife Art Festival (Havre de Grace Decoy Museum, Havre de Grace, Md.; ℂ **410/939-3739;** www. decoymuseum.com): Auctions, retriever demonstrations, and carving competitions. First weekend in May.

Preakness Week (Baltimore area, Md.; ℂ **410/542-9400;** www.preakness.com): The Preakness Stakes, the second jewel of horse racing's Triple Crown, is held at Pimlico Race Course. Gates open at 8:30am. The celebration begins the previous week with a parade and other events. Third Saturday in May.

Wine in the Woods (Symphony Woods, Columbia, Md.; ℂ **410/313-7275;** www.wineinthewoods.com): Maryland wines and gourmet foods, entertainment, arts, and crafts. Preakness Weekend (just by coincidence) from noon to 6pm.

Flowermart (Mount Vernon, Baltimore, Md.; ℂ **410/323-0022;** www.flower mart.org): A charming tradition known for its flowers, lemon sticks, and crab cakes. First weekend in May.

Chestertown Tea Party Festival (Chestertown, Md.; ℂ **410/778-0416;** www. chestertownteaparty.com): Bostonians weren't the only ones throwing tea overboard in the 1770s. This festival has a reenactment of the 1774 Tea Party, a parade, a crafts show, entertainment, and food. Last weekend in May.

U.S. Naval Academy Commissioning Week (Annapolis, Md.; ✆ **410/263-6937**): Activities include an air show by the Blue Angels, several dress parades, and graduation. The air show stops traffic near the Severn River and attracts lots of spectators. Other events are closed to the public. Mid-May.

JUNE

"Monster Mile" NASCAR Weekend (Dover, Del.; ✆ **800/441-RACE** [7223]; www.doverspeedway.com): This 2-day stock-car race draws top drivers from the circuit to Dover International Speedway. Early June.

Arts Alive (Northside Park, Ocean City, Md.; ✆ **800/OC-OCEAN** [626-2326]): Juried art contest and exhibition. First weekend in June.

Columbia Festival of the Arts (Lake Kittamaqundi, Columbia, Md.; ✆ **410/715-3044**; www.columbiafestival.com): Celebration of the arts with local and national stars of theater, music, dance, and visual arts. Ten days in mid-June.

JULY

Salute to Independence (Antietam National Battlefield, Sharpsburg, Md.; ✆ **301/432-5124**; www.nps.gov/anti/salute.htm): The Maryland Symphony Orchestra's annual concert, with cannon fire and fireworks. Saturday after July 4th.

Artscape (Baltimore, Md.; ✆ **410/837-4636**; www.artscape.org): A weekend festival celebrating the visual and performing arts. Nationally known performers join local artists; children's activities are also offered. Mid-July.

Delaware State Fair (State Fairgrounds, Harrington, Del.; ✆ **302/398-3269**; www.delawarestatefair.com): Annual

agricultural showcase, as well as stock-car races, a demolition derby, harness racing, rides, games, and live concerts. Third week in July.

J. Millard Tawes Crab and Clam Bake (Crisfield, Md.; ✆ **410/968-2500**): An all-you-can-eat celebration of crabs, clams, and corn. Wednesday in mid-July.

AUGUST

Kunta Kinte Celebration (Annapolis, Md.; ✆ **410/349-0338**): African-American cultural heritage festival with music, dance, arts, and crafts. Mid-August.

Maryland State Fair (Timonium Fairgrounds, Md.; ✆ **410/252-0200**; www.marylandstatefair.com): Eleven days of farm animals, crafts, produce, rides, entertainment, and thoroughbred racing. From the week before Labor Day through the holiday weekend, daily from 10am to 10pm.

SEPTEMBER

Duck Fair (Havre de Grace Decoy Museum, Havre de Grace, Md.; ✆ **410/939-3739**; www.decoymuseum.com): A celebration of wildlife art, along with food, entertainment, and children's activities. Weekend after Labor Day.

The Star-Spangled Banner Weekend (Fort McHenry, Baltimore, Md.; ✆ **410/962-4290**; www.nps.gov/fomc): Reenactments of the War of 1812, with musket firing and children's activities. Fall weekend near Defender's Day, September 12 (a Baltimore City holiday).

Maryland Wine Festival (Carroll County Farm Museum, Westminster, Md.; ✆ **800/654-4645**): Maryland wines, food, entertainment, and tours of the farm museum. Mid-September.

Baltimore Book Festival (Baltimore, Md.; ✆ **888/BALTIMORE** [225-8466] or 410/837-4636): Features local bookstores and publishers, authors and storytellers, art, entertainment, and food. Weekend in mid-September.

Bethany Beach Boardwalk Arts Festival (Bethany Beach, Del.; ✆ 800/962-7873): Juried show attracts craftspeople and spectators, and takes up the length of the boardwalk. First Saturday in September.

Maryland Million (Laurel Park, Laurel, Md.; ✆ 410/252-2100; www.mdhorse breeders.com): Maryland's own are celebrated in this race of Maryland-bred thoroughbreds. Late September or early October.

"Monster Mile" NASCAR Weekend (Dover, Del.; ✆ 800/441-RACE [7223]; www.doverspeedway.com): This 2-day stock-car race, like June's event, draws dozens of top drivers from around the world. Second or third weekend in September.

OCTOBER

Fells Point Fun Festival (Baltimore, Md.; ✆ 410/675-6756): Largest urban festival on the East Coast. First weekend in October.

United States Sailboat Show (City Dock, Annapolis, Md.; ✆ 410/268-8828; www.usboat.com): Nation's oldest and largest in-water sailboat show. Columbus Day weekend.

United States Powerboat Show (City Dock, Annapolis, Md.; ✆ 410/268-8828; www.usboat.com): Nation's oldest and largest in-water powerboat show. Weekend after sailboat show.

Autumn Glory Festival (Oakland, Md.; ✆ 301/387-4386; www.autumn gloryfestival.com): State banjo and fiddle championship, crafts, and antiques. Second week in October.

Catoctin Colorfest (Thurmont, Md.; ✆ 301/271-4432): Arts and crafts and the beauty of the mountains. Second weekend in October.

Tilghman Island Day (Tilghman Island, Md.; ✆ 410/886-2677): Local seafood, music, watermen contests, and rides on skipjacks and workboats. Saturday in October.

NOVEMBER

Waterfowl Festival (Easton, Md.; ✆ 410/822-4567; www.waterfowl festival.org): An Eastern Shore celebration of decoys, artwork of waterfowl, duck-calling contests, kids' activities, and food. Second weekend in November.

Punkin Chunkin (Bridgeville, Del.; ✆ 302/684-8196; www.punkinchunkin. com): Giant pumpkin hurling contest that draws crowds of competitors and spectators. First weekend in November.

DECEMBER

New Year's Eve Spectacular (Inner Harbor, Baltimore, Md.; ✆ 888/ BALTIMORE [225-8466]): Party suitable for families, featuring entertainment, food, and fireworks. December 31.

Yuletide at Winterthur (Winterthur, Del.; ✆ 800/448-3883 or 302/888-4600; www.winterthur.org): Celebrate the holidays in 19th-century style, with a festive program at the Brandywine Valley museum, featuring entertainment and guided tours. Mid-November through early January.

2 ENTRY REQUIREMENTS

PASSPORTS

Virtually every air traveler entering the U.S. is required to show a passport. All persons, including U.S. citizens, traveling by air between the United States and Canada, Mexico, Central and South America, the Caribbean, and Bermuda are required to present a valid passport. U.S.

and Canadian citizens entering the U.S. at land and sea ports of entry from within the Western Hemisphere will need to present government-issued proof of citizenship, such as a birth certificate, along with a government-issued photo ID, such as a driver's license. A passport is not required for U.S. or Canadian citizens entering by land or sea, but you are highly encouraged to carry one.

VISAS

For information on obtaining a visa, see chapter 15, "Fast Facts."

The U.S. Department of State has a **Visa Waiver Program (VWP)** allowing citizens of the following countries to enter the United States without a visa for stays of up to 90 days: Andorra, Australia, Austria, Belgium, Brunei, Denmark, Finland, France, Germany, Iceland, Ireland, Italy, Japan, Liechtenstein, Luxembourg, Monaco, the Netherlands, New Zealand, Norway, Portugal, San Marino, Singapore, Slovenia, Spain, Sweden, Switzerland, and the United Kingdom. Citizens of the Czech Republic, Estonia, Hungary, Latvia, Lithuania, Malta, the Republic of Korea, and Slovakia are soon to be admitted to the VWP. (*Note:* This list was accurate at press time; for the most up-to-date list of countries in the VWP, consult http://travel.state.gov.) Even though a visa isn't necessary, in an effort to help U.S. officials check travelers against terror watch lists before they arrive at U.S. borders, visitors from VWP countries must register online through the Electronic System for Travel Authorization (ESTA) before boarding a plane or a boat to the U.S. Travelers will complete an electronic application providing basic personal and travel eligibility information. The Department of Homeland Security recommends filling out the form at least 3 days before traveling. Authorizations will be valid for up to 2 years or until the traveler's passport expires, whichever comes first. Currently, there is

no fee for the online application. *Note:* Any passport issued on or after October 26, 2006, by a VWP country must be an **e-Passport** for VWP travelers to be eligible to enter the U.S. without a visa. Citizens of these nations also need to present a round-trip air or cruise ticket upon arrival. E-Passports contain computer chips capable of storing biometric information, such as the required digital photograph of the holder. If your passport doesn't have this feature, you can still travel without a visa, if it is a valid passport issued before October 26, 2005, and includes a machine-readable zone, or between October 26, 2005, and October 25, 2006, and includes a digital photograph. For more information, go to **http://travel.state.gov**. Canadian citizens may enter the United States without visas; they will need to show passports (if traveling by air) and proof of residence, however.

Citizens of all other countries must have (1) a valid passport that expires at least 6 months later than the scheduled end of their visit to the U.S., and (2) a tourist visa.

CUSTOMS
What You Can Bring Into the U.S.

Every visitor more than 21 years of age may bring in, free of duty, the following: (1) 1 liter of wine or hard liquor; (2) 200 cigarettes, 100 cigars (but not from Cuba), or 3 pounds of smoking tobacco; and (3) $100 worth of gifts. These exemptions are offered to travelers who spend at least 72 hours in the United States and who have not claimed them within the preceding 6 months. It is forbidden to bring into the country almost any meat products (including canned, fresh, and dried meat products such as bouillon, soup mixes, and the like). Generally, condiments including vinegars, oils, spices, coffee, tea, and some cheeses and baked goods are permitted. Avoid rice products, as rice can often harbor insects. Bringing fruit and vegetables is not advised, though not prohibited. Customs will allow produce, depending on where you got it and where you're going after you arrive in the U.S. International visitors may carry in or out up to $10,000 in U.S. or foreign currency with no formalities; larger sums must be declared to U.S. Customs on entering or leaving, which includes filing form CM 4790. For details regarding U.S. Customs and Border Protection, consult your nearest U.S. embassy or consulate, or **U.S. Customs** (www.customs.gov).

What You Can Take Home from Maryland & Delaware

For information on what you're allowed to bring home, contact one of the following agencies.

U.S. Citizens: U.S. Customs & Border Protection (CBP), 1300 Pennsylvania Ave., NW, Washington, DC 20229 (© 877/ 287-8667; www.cbp.gov).

Canadian Citizens: Canada Border Services Agency (© 800/461-9999 in Canada, or 204/983-3500; www.cbsa-asfc.gc.ca).

U.K. Citizens: HM Revenue & Customs at © 0845/010-9000 (from outside the U.K., 020/8929-0152), or consult their website at **www.hmce.gov.uk**.

Australian Citizens: Australian Customs and Border Protection Service at © 1300/363-263, or log on to **www. customs.gov.au**.

New Zealand Citizens: New Zealand Customs Service, The Customhouse, 17–21 Whitmore St., Box 2218, Wellington (© 04/473-6099 or 0800/428-786; www.customs.govt.nz).

MEDICAL REQUIREMENTS

Unless you're arriving from an area known to be suffering from an epidemic (particularly cholera or yellow fever), inoculations or vaccinations are not required for entry into the United States.

---

3 GETTING THERE & GETTING AROUND

GETTING TO MARYLAND & DELAWARE
By Plane

The gateway to Maryland is **Baltimore/ Washington International Thurgood Marshall Airport (BWI),** 10 miles south of Baltimore and 20 miles north of Annapolis. Hundreds of domestic and international flights arrive daily, and it's a hub for several airlines. Most cities and towns are also convenient to **Washington Dulles International Airport** and **Ronald Reagan Washington National Airport,** both major international airports but deep in the heart of many D.C. traffic jams.

Most major airlines fly into BWI, including **Air Tran** (© 800/247-8726), **American** (© 800/433-7300), **British Airways** (© 800/247-9297), **Continental**

(© 800/525-0280), **Delta** (© 800/221-1212), **Northwest** (© 800/225-2525), **Southwest** (© 800/435-9792), **United** (© 800/241-6522), and **US Airways** (© 800/428-4322).

Commuter flights fly into **Salisbury– Ocean City–Wicomico Regional Airport,** near Ocean City, Maryland.

Delaware does not have its own major airport. Located within easy reach are **Philadelphia International Airport,** 30 minutes from downtown Wilmington and 1½ hours from Dover; **BWI,** approximately 1½ to 2½ hours to most points in Delaware; and **Washington Dulles International Airport** and **Ronald Reagan Washington National Airport,** approximately 2½ to 3 hours to most points in Delaware. In addition, **New Castle County Airport,** about 5 miles south of Wilmington, serves private craft.

By Car

International visitors should note that insurance and taxes are almost never included in quoted rental car rates in the U.S. Be sure to ask your rental agency about additional fees for these. They can add a significant cost to your car rental.

The Eastern Seaboard's major north-south link from Maine to Florida, **I-95,** passes through Wilmington and Newark in Delaware as well as Baltimore and central Maryland. Other interstate highways that traverse Maryland are **I-83,** which connects Baltimore with Harrisburg and points north, and **I-70** and **I-68,** which connect Western Maryland to the rest of the state and to Pennsylvania, West Virginia, and Ohio. There are no other interstates in Delaware, but to access the state from Maryland and points south, use U.S. **Route 13** or **Route 113.**

Maps and brochures are available at visitor information centers on I-95 and I-70. Most are open only from 9am to 5pm. Some locations even offer hotel reservations services.

By Train

Amtrak (© **800/USA-RAIL** [872-7245]; www.amtrak.com) offers frequent daily service to Baltimore, at both Pennsylvania Station (downtown) and BWI Airport Rail Station, and to the Wilmington station at 100 S. French St. (at Martin Luther King, Jr., Blvd.). There's also daily service to Newark, Delaware; and Aberdeen and New Carrollton, Maryland. Amtrak has limited service to and from the west at Cumberland and Rockville, Maryland. The high-speed Acela train runs along the Northeast Corridor.

MARC (© **800/325-RAIL** [7245]) commuter service runs between Washington, D.C., and Baltimore during the week. MARC also serves Western Maryland in Brunswick and Frederick.

By Bus

Greyhound (© **800/231-2222;** www.greyhound.com) serves major points in Maryland and Delaware, including Wilmington and Dover, Annapolis, Baltimore, Ocean City, Easton, and Frederick, with express service from New York City to Baltimore (at South Baltimore and East Baltimore's Travel Plaza).

By Ferry

The **Cape May-Lewes Ferry** travels daily between southern New Jersey and the lower Delaware coast. This 70-minute crossing is operated on a drive-on, drive-off basis and can accommodate up to 800 passengers and 100 cars. Full details on the ferry are given on p. 238.

By Boat

All cruise vessels depart from the Port of Baltimore's **South Locust Point Marine Terminal,** 2001 E. McComas St., about 5 miles from the Inner Harbor, where many of the best attractions and hotels are located. To get to Baltimore, follow I-195 west to Route 295 north, which will take you into downtown. **Taxis** to downtown attractions run about $22.

GETTING AROUND

By Plane

Commuter flights within Maryland fly from Baltimore and Philadelphia airports to **Salisbury–Ocean City–Wicomico Regional Airport** (© **410/548-4827**), 40 minutes west of Ocean City, on the outskirts of Salisbury.

Some large airlines offer transatlantic or transpacific passengers special discount tickets under the name **Visit USA,** which allows mostly one-way travel from one U.S. destination to another at very low prices. Unavailable in the U.S., these discount tickets must be purchased abroad in conjunction with your international fare.

This system is the easiest, fastest, cheapest way to see the country.

By Car

The most practical way to see both Maryland and Delaware is by car. Depending on traffic, it takes approximately 2 hours to get from Wilmington to Lewes; from 75 minutes to 2 hours, also depending on traffic, from Wilmington to Baltimore; 1 hour from Baltimore to Annapolis; 90 minutes from Baltimore to Washington, D.C.; 90 minutes from Baltimore to Frederick; 2½ hours from Frederick to Cumberland; and 2½ hours from Annapolis to Ocean City.

If you're planning to drive on the **Baltimore Beltway** (I-695), try to avoid rush hour. Congestion, particularly at the junctions north and south of I-95, is terrible. Road widening is underway in some areas, but traffic is at its heaviest from 7 to 10am and 3 to 6pm.

The **I-95 Corridor Coalition** puts out a seasonal "Lane Closings, Bottlenecks, and Upcoming Events" brochure that lists interstate trouble spots for both states with a few alternate routes listed. You'll find the brochure at welcome centers, visitor centers, and online and in real time at **www.i95coalition.org**.

The tourism agencies in Maryland and Delaware both produce good free maps. However, if you plan to do any extensive driving on Maryland's Eastern Shore, you'll need more detail than the state maps provide. Contact the county tourism agencies (especially Somerset, Dorchester, and Talbot) for free county maps. There are a couple of special-interest maps, too. The best is the **Maryland Scenic Byways** map and guide, which offers some off-the-beaten-path routes with scenic stops. (Get them just so you can see what the black-eyed Susan signs along the road are referring to.) The state also puts out an excellent bicycle map.

If you're visiting from abroad and plan to rent a car in the United States, keep in mind that foreign driver's licenses are usually recognized in the U.S., but you should get an international one if your home license is not in English. Check out **Breezenet.com** (www.bnm.com), which offers domestic car-rental discounts with some of the most competitive rates around.

By Train

International visitors can buy a **USA Rail Pass,** good for 15, 30, or 45 days of unlimited travel on **Amtrak** (© 800/USA-RAIL [872-7245]; www.amtrak.com). The pass is available online or through many overseas travel agents. See Amtrak's website for the cost of travel within the western, eastern, or northwestern United States. Reservations are generally required and should be made as early as possible. Regional rail passes are also available.

By Bus

Bus travel is often the most economical form of public transit for short hops between U.S. cities, but it's certainly not an option for everyone. **Greyhound** (© 800/231-2222;** www.greyhound.com) is the sole nationwide bus line. International visitors can obtain the **Greyhound North American Discovery Pass** from foreign travel agents or through **www.discoverypass.com** for unlimited travel and stopovers in the U.S. and Canada. Passes can be activated at the downtown Baltimore bus terminal, 2110 Haines St. (© 410/752-7682), or the Baltimore Travel Plaza, off I-95 (© 410/633-6389). Both are open 24 hours.

You can travel in Baltimore on the Metro, Light Rail, or bus, all operated by the **Maryland Transit Administration** (**MTA;** © 410/539-5000; www.mtamaryland.com). In Wilmington and the Brandywine Valley, **DART First State** (© 302/577-3278; www.dartfirststate.com) runs buses between the downtown business section and suburbs and tourist attractions.

4 MONEY & COSTS

The Value of the U.S. Dollar vs. Other Popular Currencies

US$	Can$	UK£	Euro (€)	Aus$	NZ$
1.00	1.05	0.65	0.70	1.15	1.40

Frommer's lists exact prices in the local currency. The currency conversions quoted above were correct at press time. However, rates fluctuate, so before departing, consult a currency exchange website such as **www.oanda.com/convert/classic** to check up-to-the-minute rates.

It's always advisable to bring money in a variety of forms on a vacation: a mix of cash, credit cards, and traveler's checks—although lots of businesses no longer know how to handle traveler's checks and so won't accept them.

You should also exchange enough petty cash to cover airport incidentals, tipping, and transportation to your hotel before you leave home, or withdraw money upon arrival at an airport ATM.

ATMs are everywhere, even in convenience stores on street corners. Credit and debit cards are accepted almost everywhere. Checks are frowned upon, especially when they aren't local.

What Things Cost in Maryland & Delaware

Shuttle from BWI to Inner Harbor	$22.00
Economy class rental car from Avis for a week (unlimited mileage)	$390.00
Double room at the Intercontinental Harbor Court Hotel (very expensive)	$239.00–$369.00
Double room at the Holiday Inn Inner Harbor (moderate)	$150.00
Double room at Georgian House, a B&B in Annapolis	$189.00–$225.00
Lunch for one at Chick and Ruth's Delly, Annapolis (inexpensive)	$8.00
Dinner for one, without wine, at the Prime Rib, Baltimore (expensive)	$48.00
Dinner for one, without wine, at Domaine Hudson, Wilmington (moderate)	$37.00
Dinner for one, without wine, at Sabatino's, Baltimore (inexpensive)	$20.00
Espresso and dessert at Vaccaro's, Little Italy	$12.00
Full day's parking at the Inner Harbor	$24.00
Orioles' game-day parking	$15.00
Upper reserve ticket to an Orioles' game	$15.00
Adult admission to the National Aquarium in Baltimore	$25.00–$30.00
Adult admission to Winterthur, Wilmington	$22.00
Inner Harbor water taxi fare, all day	$9.00

5 HEALTH

COMMON AILMENTS

LYME DISEASE Maryland and Delaware don't pose any unusual health risks to the average visitor. If you're hiking or camping, be aware that this is deer-tick country, and deer ticks can carry **Lyme disease.** Wear long sleeves and pants tucked into your socks, cover your head, and inspect yourself for ticks later. Insect repellent containing DEET also helps repel ticks. After your trip, watch for a bull's-eye-shaped rash that can appear 3 days to a month following infection (but be aware that not everyone who is infected will get the rash). There is now a vaccine available for Lyme disease; consult your doctor if you're planning to take an extensive trip to deer tick–infested areas.

RESPIRATORY ILLNESSES Baltimore's air quality can be hard on a person suffering from asthma or other lung ailments, especially in the hot, humid summer. Weather reports provide alerts whenever the air quality index is so poor that people are advised to stay inside.

SUN EXPOSURE Visitors should keep applying sunscreen and wear a hat whenever outside as they would at home. This is especially important near the water, where cool breezes or cloudy skies can lull visitors into believing the sun isn't strong.

WHAT TO DO IF YOU GET SICK AWAY FROM HOME

If you face a life-threatening illness, call ✆ 911 anywhere in Maryland or Delaware for an ambulance. Every hospital has an emergency room whose staff won't turn anyone away. Bring your health insurance card, if you have one.

If you suffer from a chronic illness, consult your doctor before your departure. Pack **prescription medications** in your carry-on luggage, and carry them in their original containers, with pharmacy labels—otherwise they won't make it through airport security. Visitors from outside the U.S. should carry generic names of prescription drugs. For U.S. travelers, most reliable healthcare plans provide coverage if you get sick away from home. Foreign visitors may have to pay medical costs upfront and be reimbursed later. See "Medical Insurance," under "Travel Insurance," in chapter 15.

6 SAFETY

While most of Maryland and Delaware enjoy relatively low crime rates, Baltimore has a nagging problem with property and violent crime, and Wilmington also has neighborhoods where visitors are advised not to go. The major tourist areas of both cities are fairly well policed, but be alert and follow common-sense precautions.

If you're using public transport, it's best to travel during the day and to keep valuables out of sight. It is safer and smarter to drive or take a cab between neighborhoods (unless otherwise noted) than to walk, even when the distance is not too great. Keep a good city map at hand to help you out if you're lost. Neighborhoods can go from safe to scary in a matter of a few blocks. It's best to keep on the main routes and turn around if anything looks worrisome.

In addition to the destination-specific resources listed below, please visit Frommers.com for additional specialized travel resources.

GAY & LESBIAN TRAVELERS

In Baltimore, the main resource for gay men and lesbians is the **Gay and Lesbian Community Center of Baltimore,** 241 W. Chase St. (© **410/837-7748**). The center also produces the *Baltimore Gay Paper* (www.glccb.org), available free at area restaurants, nightclubs, bars, and bookstores.

TRAVELERS WITH DISABILITIES

Visitors with disabilities can count on finding accessible hotels, restaurants and attractions throughout Maryland and Delaware. A few B&Bs have found ways to outfit their buildings for the needs of disabled guests, though most would pose a challenge.

Curbs in almost every town have been cut to assist visitors, but brick sidewalks can be difficult in the historic areas of Annapolis.

That having been said, efforts have been made at a majority of attractions to be accessible for travelers with disabilities. Baltimore's buses have "kneeling" buses for wheelchair users and Light Rail stops have ramps.

FAMILY TRAVEL

To locate accommodations, restaurants, and attractions that are particularly kid-friendly, refer to the "Kids" icon throughout this guide.

WOMEN TRAVELERS

For general travel resources for women, go to www.frommers.com/planning.

SENIOR TRAVEL

Most attractions offer senior discounts on admission. You'll find them listed throughout this guide.

SINGLE TRAVELERS

For more information on traveling solo, go to www.frommers.com/planning.

8 SUSTAINABLE TOURISM

Marylanders and Delawareans are recycling their bottles and paper. They're choosing locally produced foods and choosing "green" products.

But if you visit either state, you are going to have a difficult time recycling your own waste, as there are few recycling containers at local attractions and hotels.

There are a few steps visitors can take to protect the fragile Chesapeake Bay, ocean, beach, or mountain environments you've come to enjoy.

Most hotels now ask if you want your linens changed every day. Politely decline.

(Now, you don't change your own sheets every day, do you?) Use them twice, and save gallons of hot water and energy.

Take the bus, the Light Rail, or the train. Public transportation is the way to go, especially in downtown Baltimore and at the beach. Baltimore's public buses are one option. Another is the new Charm City Circulator, which offers free transportation all around the business district. In fact, it's the cool way to go at the beach, both in Maryland and Delaware. All-day passes are available and inexpensive.

General Resources for Green Travel

In addition to the resources for Maryland and Delaware listed above, the following websites provide valuable wide-ranging information on sustainable travel. For a list of even more sustainable resources, as well as tips and explanations on how to travel greener, visit www.frommers.com/planning.

- **Responsible Travel** (www.responsibletravel.com) is a great source of sustainable travel ideas; the site is run by a spokesperson for ethical tourism in the travel industry. **Sustainable Travel International** (www.sustainabletravel international.org) promotes ethical tourism practices, and manages an extensive directory of sustainable properties and tour operators around the world.

- In the U.K., **Tourism Concern** (www.tourismconcern.org.uk) works to reduce social and environmental problems connected to tourism. The **Association of Independent Tour Operators (AITO;** www.aito.co.uk) is a group of specialist operators leading the field in making holidays sustainable.

- In Canada, **Green Living** (www.greenlivingonline.com) offers extensive content on how to travel sustainably, including a travel and transport section and profiles of the best green shops and services in Toronto, Vancouver, and Calgary.

- In Australia, the national body that sets guidelines and standards for ecotourism is **Ecotourism Australia** (www.ecotourism.org.au). The **Green Directory** (www.thegreendirectory.com.au), **Green Pages** (www.thegreen pages.com.au), and **EcoDirectory** (www.ecodirectory.com.au) offer sustainable travel tips and directories of green businesses.

- **Carbonfund** (www.carbonfund.org), **TerraPass** (www.terrapass.org), and **CoolClimate** (http://coolclimate.berkeley.edu) provide info on carbon-offsetting, or offsetting the levels of greenhouse gas emitted during flights.

- **"Green" Hotels Association** (www.greenhotels.com) recommends green-rated member hotels around the world that fulfill the company's stringent environmental requirements. **Environmentally Friendly Hotels** (www. environmentallyfriendlyhotels.com) offers more green accommodations ratings. The Hotel Association of Canada has a **Green Key Eco-Rating Program** (www.greenkeyglobal.com), which audits the environmental performance of Canadian hotels, motels, and resorts.

- **Sustain Lane** (www.sustainlane.com) lists sustainable eating and drinking choices around the U.S.; also visit **www.eatwellguide.org** for tips on eating sustainably in the U.S. and Canada.

- For information on animal-friendly issues throughout the world, visit **Tread Lightly** (www.treadlightly.org). For information about the ethics of swimming with dolphins, visit the **Whale and Dolphin Conservation Society** (www.wdcs.org).

- **International Volunteer Programs Association (IVPA;** www.volunteer international.org) has a list of questions to help you determine the intentions and the nature of a volunteer program. For general info on volunteer travel, visit **www.volunteerabroad.org** and **www.idealist.org**.

Bike paths are everywhere. If you want to leave your car alone for a day or two, you can take a bike ride from Cumberland to Washington. Or along the Allegheny Passage into Pennsylvania. Or at the beach between Lewes and Rehoboth. Or along the Underground Railroad Trail on the Eastern Shore. Even Baltimore has a bike path from north Baltimore into downtown.

The farm-to-table movement has made it into local restaurants. Look for local produce and seafood where you dine. Some shout it out loud in their menus. Others not so much.

For more ideas, go to www.ecodelaware.com. You'll find a list of earth-friendly ideas for where to travel, and when and how to tread lightly when you get there.

9 STAYING CONNECTED

Many convenience stores and packaging services sell **prepaid calling cards** in denominations up to $50; for international visitors, these can be the least expensive way to call home. Many public pay phones at airports now accept American Express, MasterCard, and Visa credit cards. **Local calls** made from pay phones in most locales usually cost 50¢. Most long-distance and international calls can be dialed directly from any phone. **For calls within the United States and to Canada,** dial 1 followed by the area code and the seven-digit number. **For other international calls,** dial 011 followed by the country code, city code, and the number you are calling.

Calls to area codes **800, 888, 877,** and **866** are toll-free. However, calls to area codes **700** and **900** (chat lines, bulletin boards, "dating" services, and so on) can be very expensive—usually a charge of 95¢ to $3 or more per minute, and they sometimes have minimum charges that can run as high as $15 or more.

For **reversed-charge or collect calls,** and for person-to-person calls, dial the number 0 then the area code and number; an operator will come on the line, and you should specify whether you are calling collect, person-to-person, or both. If your operator-assisted call is international, ask for the overseas operator.

For **local directory assistance** ("information"), dial 411; for long-distance information, dial 1, then the appropriate area code and 555-1212.

CELLPHONES

Just because your cellphone works at home doesn't mean it'll work everywhere in the U.S. (thanks to our nation's fragmented cellphone system). It's a good bet that your phone will work in major cities, but take a look at your wireless company's coverage map on its website before heading out.

You can rent a cellphone from **Roberts Rent-A-Phone** (© 800/964-2468; www.roberts-rent-a-phone.com).

INTERNET & E-MAIL
With Your Own Computer

Checking e-mail and getting online is easy just about everyplace in Maryland and Delaware. Wireless connectivity is available throughout both states—a little more difficult to find at the beach and a few B&Bs, but only just a little. Free Wi-Fi is most often available in the less expensive chain hotels, B&Bs, and small business hotels. Even in the pricier places, free Wi-Fi is usually available in the lobby or other public spaces. Most larger hotels also have business centers with printers and computers, so visitors can check their e-mail and print out their boarding passes to go home. Internet connectivity is listed with each hotel throughout this guide, if it is available.

Most laptops sold today have built-in wireless capability. To find public Wi-Fi hot spots at your destination, go to **www. jiwire.com**; its Wi-Fi Finder holds the world's largest directory of public wireless hot spots. Many hotels in the U.S. now also offer free high-speed Internet access.

Wherever you go, bring a **connection kit** of the right power and phone adapters, a spare phone cord, and a spare Ethernet network cable—or find out whether your hotel supplies them to guests.

Without Your Own Computer

Most major airports have **Internet kiosks** that provide basic Internet access for a per-minute fee that's usually higher than cybercafe prices. Also check out such copy shops as **FedEx Office,** which offers computer stations with fully loaded software (as well as Wi-Fi). Public libraries are also good places to get online.

For help locating cybercafes and other establishments where you can go for Internet access, visit **www.cybercaptive.com** and **www.cybercafe.com**.

10 TIPS ON ACCOMMODATIONS

Accommodations in both Maryland and Delaware can be found for everyone from the rock star to the budget traveler.

In Baltimore or Wilmington, your best bet is one of the big hotels in the tourist and business sections of town on a weekend or special package. These are pricier than the motels outside of town, but you'll be closer to major attractions.

Baltimore has three Marriotts, a Hyatt, a Sheraton, and a few independent hotels offering comfortable accommodations near the Inner Harbor.

If you prefer the suburbs, you can find chain hotels and motels near BWI, along Route 40 and I-95, and around the Beltway that circles Baltimore City. Two hotels near the airport are within walking distance of the Light Rail—with stops in downtown Baltimore. That's a good way to avoid the hassles of renting a car, driving in an unfamiliar city, and finding an expensive parking space. The suburbs are home to several Sheratons, a Hilton, and an Embassy Suites. You can usually count on a clean, comfortable room at a Holiday Inn or Best Western, often with a simple continental breakfast included. In most cases, children stay in their parent's room at no extra charge.

Wilmington also has a number of chain hotels in its business district; these usually have plenty of room on the weekends, often with free or reduced price parking. There are also some comfortable hotels on the outskirts of town, convenient to both Wilmington and the Brandywine Valley. Chains include Holiday Inn, Embassy Suites, Quality Inn, and the Hilton.

For bed-and-breakfasts, head for Annapolis, Frederick, or Western Maryland. These areas are rich in B&Bs. Because they are old and often have delicate furnishings, innkeepers require children to be well behaved, if they are welcome at all. There may be no TV or hair dryer—but the bread will be fresh from the oven, and the furnishings usually reflect the locale. Lots of these places now have their own websites, which are accurate, if a bit flowery.

In addition, many B&Bs have made their accommodations as accessible as possible. Call ahead and check to see what can be done for you. Some innkeepers admit they haven't figured out how to accommodate a wheelchair while preserving a fine old house, but they're clearly working on it.

Smokers should be aware that their cigarettes are usually not welcome in the house, not even on the porches.

If you're going to a beach resort in Delaware or Maryland, you've got lots of choices: chains, local hotels, or home and condo rentals. The chains offer predictable accommodations, while the local hotels range from clean and comfy to dazzling. What makes resort destinations really comfortable and economical for families are house and condo rentals. Real-estate agents in each resort (listed in specific chapters) can help you find a place big enough for a family reunion or cozy enough for newlyweds. At the beach, you'll have to pack linens, towels, and paper products, as these aren't provided. But you can count on a pretty well-equipped kitchen, living areas with TVs—and often VCRs—sleeping space, and bathrooms. House rentals have become more popular in Deep Creek Lake as well. Firms in both Annapolis and on the Eastern Shore have lined up an impressive array of homes available to the tourist, as well. In every place, there are lots of choices, many with hot tubs, boat piers, or beach access. Here linens are provided, so just bring paper products.

Suggested Itineraries

Two little states. A prospective visitor might think it would be easy to see either one in just a few days. But a leisurely pace is best for this "Land of Pleasant Living." How much time do you have? How much driving do you want to do? You could come by boat, but most visitors do best with a car when exploring Maryland and Delaware. It's the only way to see the Brandywine Valley or Western Maryland.

So, what are your interests? In a week, you could see the highlights of Maryland or the attractions of the state's Eastern Shore, along with a glimpse of Delaware. But you'll have to make some choices about what to see.

Civil War buffs will want to include a visit to Baltimore with trips to the battlefields around Frederick. Wine lovers might like to plan a weekend to see local wineries, enjoy the seafood, and experience a little culture. History fans should consider taking a walk on the path to freedom trod by slaves on the Underground Railroad. And outdoorsy types, you're in for a treat: Hiking, skiing, fly-fishing, and kayaking await.

1 THE BEST OF MARYLAND & DELAWARE IN 2 WEEKS

Annapolis is a fairly central place to start this trip—especially for those flying into Baltimore/Washington International Thurgood Marshall Airport (BWI). Or, if you're coming from the west, start in Western Maryland and just keep heading east. Coming from the south? Take the Chesapeake Bay Bridge Tunnel and visit Delaware and the Eastern Shore before heading across the other Bay Bridge to see the rest of Maryland.

Maryland requires a lot of driving in order to see everything, from the mountains of Western Maryland to the Eastern Shore to the Atlantic Ocean. Delaware's attractions begin at the beach and end in Wilmington. There's a lot to see in both states: Civil War battlefields, museums of all sorts, the Chesapeake Bay, waterfalls and mountain trails, historic homes and districts, and veritable castles.

I've designed this itinerary for visiting at breakneck speed. Feel free to slow down and savor any place you like.

Day ❶: Annapolis

You could start in Baltimore, but Annapolis offers a slower pace—so you'll feel like you're on vacation right away. **History-Quest** at the **St. Clair Wright Center** makes a good first stop for walking tours and an orientation exhibit on Maryland's capital. Stop for lunch along the **City Dock,** then visit the **State House,** and afterward spend a leisurely afternoon shopping along Maryland Avenue. Have dinner on Main Street or West Street and finish with a carriage ride through the historic district. Get a good night's sleep at a local B&B or one of the **Historic Inns.** Because you want an early start in the morning, it's best to stay downtown.

SUGGESTED ITINERARIES

4

THE BEST OF MARYLAND & DELAWARE IN 2 WEEKS

The Best of Maryland and Delaware in 2 Weeks
The Best of Maryland in 1 Week

NEW JERSEY

Delaware Bay

ATLANTIC OCEAN

Assateague I.

DELAWARE

CHESAPEAKE BAY

PENNSYLVANIA

MARYLAND

WEST VIRGINIA

VIRGINIA

WASHINGTON D.C.

BALTIMORE

Annapolis

St. Michaels

New Castle

Wilmington

Dover

Ocean City

Georgetown

Rehoboth Beach

Bethany Beach

Frederick

Smith I.

Chincoteague Bay

20 mi

20 km

Day ❷: United States Naval Academy & Historic Homes

Head to the **Naval Academy** and sign up for a tour at the visitor center—the best one includes a stop at **Bancroft Hall** about the time the midshipmen line up for noon formation. After they march in for lunch, head into the historic district for your own. Near Maryland Avenue are three houses worth a visit: the **Chase–Lloyd House,** the **Paca House and Gardens,** and the **Hammond–Harwood House.** You can probably see all three in an afternoon, or just go to the Hammond–Harwood, and then spend a leisurely time in the Paca Gardens. (Hours at the Chase–Lloyd are quite limited.) Make reservations at an **Eastport** restaurant and take the water taxi across the harbor for a good seafood meal.

Day ❸: Boat Trip to St. Michaels

You can't be this close to the Chesapeake Bay and not get on it. **Watermark Cruises** offers a boat trip to **St. Michaels,** an Eastern Shore village with a number of shops, restaurants, and the **Chesapeake Bay Maritime Museum.** Not a big boat fan? Try one of the shorter cruises, such as a trip on the *Woodwind,* a schooner with several 2-hour cruises each day, or **Annapolis by Boat,** which offers a variety of short excursions.

Days ❹–❺: Ocean City

Head across the Bay Bridge and down Route 50 to **Ocean City.** The visit to St. Michaels was your only stop along the Eastern Shore; but, if it caught your fancy and you want to see more, stop for lunch in **Easton** or **Cambridge.** Bird lovers may want to make a detour to the **Blackwater National Wildlife Refuge,** which is southwest of Cambridge.

In Ocean City, take a break: Rent an umbrella and a chair and relax by the surf. Plan an early dinner at one of the local restaurants before heading to the **boardwalk** for a little amusement. Or spend the evening playing **miniature golf;** this town is full of courses. Marylanders (and plenty of out-of-state visitors) could do this for a whole week or more. Another way to spend your second day is beachcombing and seeing the ponies on **Assateague Island.**

Day ❻: The Delaware Shore

Delaware's beaches are just like Ocean City's, but **Bethany,** for example, is small and quiet. **Rehoboth** has lots of good restaurants, plus spas, live jazz, and a plethora of tax-free outlet stores. **Lewes** is the First State's First Town and has museums and historic sites. Choose one and go exploring.

Day ❼: Dover

Delaware's capital city has a cluster of unusual museums along with the well-regarded **Biggs Museum of American Art.** The downtown sights, along with the Legislative Hall and state archives, are known as the **First State Heritage Park at Dover,** and could easily be seen in a day. Or chuck all that culture and head to the slots or horse races at **Dover Downs.** Wildlife fans may prefer to wander **Bombay Hook National Wildlife Refuge** for a little bird-watching. Plan to be there for about 2 hours or more—depending on how much walking you want to do.

Day ❽: Historic New Castle

The original capital of Delaware was the waterfront village of **New Castle.** Its historic sites are still lovingly maintained, including the Federal-style **Read House,** home of the son of a signer of the Declaration of Independence. A number of other Colonial-era homes are open most days (except Mon). Have lunch at the Colonial-era **Jessop's Tavern.** Or go modern and stop at the chic **Prince on the Delaware.**

Day 9: Wilmington

Make this a base for your visit to the **Brandywine Valley.** You'll want to see one of the du Pont properties: **Winterthur,** if you love home furnishings; **Nemours,** if you love lavish style; **Longwood Gardens,** if flowers are your passion; or **Hagley,** if you like to learn how things work in a bucolic setting. Or stay in town and visit the 12,000 works of art at the **Delaware Art Museum** or the changing exhibits of the **Delaware Center for the Contemporary Arts.** History buffs should see the **Delaware History Museum** or visit the *Kalmar Nyckel* if it's moored here. Get some rest; it's off to Baltimore tomorrow, a 2-hour drive.

Day 10: Baltimore

If you have only a day to see Baltimore, your first stop has to be **Fort McHenry,** home of the Star-Spangled Banner. Lunch at **Harborplace** while you decide where to go next. Should it be the **National Aquarium** to see the new Australia exhibit? Or the **Reginald F. Lewis Museum of Maryland African American History & Culture?** Art lovers can choose from the **Baltimore Museum of Art,** the **Walters Art Museum,** or the **American Visionary Art Museum.** History buffs may choose from the **Maryland Historical Society,** the **Baltimore Museum of Industry,** or sign up for a **Heritage Walk** (at the visitor center in the Inner Harbor) to get a closer look at Charm City. Prefer a view from the top? Go to the **Top of the World** observation level in the World Trade Center. End the day with dinner in **Little Italy,** tony **Harbor East,** or historic **Fell's Point.**

Day 11: Frederick

The drive to **Frederick** takes about an hour along I-70. After checking into your hotel or B&B, spend the afternoon at **Antietam Battlefield.** Head to Frederick's historic district for dinner.

Days 12–14: Outdoors Maryland

You have a choice: The **Deep Creek Lake** area off I-70 and I-68 has lots to draw an outdoors enthusiast—skiing, dog-sledding, white-water rafting, hiking, and fly-fishing. If you have the time, make sure you include this area on your itinerary; if you're running out of time, head north on Route 15 to **Cunningham Falls State Park.** Here you can hike to a waterfall and swim or canoe in a nearby lake. Stop for local produce along the way, and have a meal at one of the roadside restaurants.

2 THE BEST OF MARYLAND IN 1 WEEK

If you have only a week, put four places on your itinerary: Baltimore, Annapolis, any place on the Eastern Shore (or Ocean City, on the Atlantic), and Western Maryland. You can slow down long enough to see a Civil War battlefield, too. But hurry: There's lots to do in 7 little days.

Day 1: Baltimore Essentials

Baltimore means three things to first-time visitors: Fort McHenry, the Inner Harbor, and the National Aquarium. You can see all three in a day, so put on some comfortable shoes. Get your all-day ticket on the **water taxi** so you can travel to the fort and Fell's Point by water. Start off at the **National Aquarium** (get your tickets online, so you don't have to wait in line). You'll want to see the new Australia exhibit as well as the dolphin demonstration.

Have lunch and shop a bit at **Harbor-place.** Then hop that water taxi for **Fort McHenry.** You'll need most of the afternoon for this visit. In fact, if you can be here at sunset, you may be able to help take down the large flag—it takes about 20 people to fold it. Get on another water taxi for an evening in **Fell's Point,** with dinner and live entertainment at one of the local watering holes.

Day ❷: Baltimore History & Culture

Spend a second day in Baltimore soaking up either the history or the culture. Stop by the visitor center at the Inner Harbor to sign up for a **Heritage Walk,** which will give you a closer look at Charm City. After lunch in **Little Italy,** take in a museum. Baltimore has plenty to choose from: the **Reginald F. Lewis Museum of Maryland African American History & Culture,** the **Baltimore Museum of Art,** the **Walters Art Museum,** the **American Visionary Art Museum,** or the **Baltimore & Ohio Railroad Museum.** End the day at **Power Plant Live** with dinner and music.

Day ❸: Annapolis

If you have only a day, you must go to the **Naval Academy** and sign up for a tour at the visitor center. The best one includes a stop at **Bancroft Hall,** about the time the midshipmen line up for noon formation. The **State House,** where George Washington resigned as commander in chief, and the **Paca House and Gardens** are also good places to visit. Or skip the history for an afternoon on a boat: **Watermark Cruises,** the *Woodwind,* or **Annapolis by Boat** can get you on the Chesapeake Bay and Severn River. Have dinner on Main Street or West Street, and finish with a

carriage ride through the historic district. If you haven't clambered aboard a boat yet, make reservations at an **Eastport** restaurant and take the water taxi across the harbor for a good seafood meal.

Day ❹: Boat Trip to St. Michaels or Day Trip to Ocean City

Get out on the water with a day on Chesapeake Bay. **Watermark Cruises** offers a boat trip to **St. Michaels,** an Eastern Shore village with shops, restaurants, and the **Chesapeake Bay Maritime Museum.** If you need to see the ocean, take the day and drive to **Ocean City.** It's only 2½ hours from here.

Day ❺: Driving to Western Maryland

This is the way settlers headed from the rolling valleys around Baltimore to the hills of Appalachia. The drive to Western Maryland will take up to 4 hours. If you want, stop along I-70. **Ellicott City** has a charming historic district with antiques shops and the oldest railroad station in the world. **New Market** has a street lined with antiques shops. Civil War buffs should plan to stop at **Antietam,** near Frederick. **Frederick** has its own small-town historic district, as does **Cumberland,** a stop along the **C&O Canal.**

Days ❻–❼: Western Maryland's Great Outdoors

Ski at **Wisp** if it's wintertime, or head to **Deep Creek Lake** for a swim if it's warm. Don't miss a chance to hike to Muddy Falls at **Swallow Falls State Park** or enjoy the pristine **Savage River State Forest.** Sign up at one of the outfitters for a white-water rafting trip, fly-fishing, or boat or snowshoe rental. You can even sign up for dog-sledding. Take 2 days. Take 3 if you've got 'em.

These two 1-week itineraries both focus on the outdoors. Start in Baltimore with either one so the kids can see Fort McHenry, the National Aquarium, and the Baltimore & Ohio Railroad Museum. Then head east to the Eastern Shore and Ocean City (or a Delaware beach, if you prefer), or head west to the mountains. End in Annapolis with a visit to the Naval Academy and a boat ride.

Days ❶–❷: Baltimore for Kids

All kids like **Fort McHenry.** The rangers talk on their level, there are lots of cannons to see and nooks and crannies to climb into, and the waterfront lawn outside the fort wall is great for running around or enjoying a picnic. Or have lunch at **Harborplace,** where there's plenty of kid-friendly food. The **National Aquarium** has dolphins and a rainforest, a bit of Australia, and a 4-D movie. You'll probably spend the whole afternoon here. Then head to **Little Italy** for some pasta. Finish with cannoli and gelato at **Vaccaro's.**

On your second day, pick a couple of museums according to your interests—kid-oriented museums are everywhere in Baltimore. **Port Discovery** is a children's museum. The **Baltimore Museum of Industry** has guides who tell great stories and let kids handle some of the artifacts. Everyone likes the massive locomotives and diminutive model trains at the **Baltimore & Ohio Railroad Museum.** Give your children some inspiration at the **Reginald F. Lewis Museum of Maryland African American History & Culture,** where many of the displays tell very personal stories. Sneak a little art education into the day with a visit to the **Walters Art Museum,** home of some impressive armor, or the **Baltimore Museum of Art,** where kids can simultaneously enjoy the outdoors and the arts in the sculpture garden. Baseball fans can spend the afternoon in the presence of greatness at **Sports Legends at Camden Yards** or the **Babe Ruth Museum.**

Days ❸–❺, Option A: Ocean City

Enough city life. Throw the bathing suits into the car and head to **Ocean City** for a couple of days of surf and sun. Spend all 3 days building sand castles and bodysurfing during the day and playing miniature golf in the evening. Or book a fishing trip, rent a kayak, or visit **Assateague Island** or **Frontier Town** amusement park. In the evening, take the kids to **Ocean Downs** to watch the harness races. Admission is free, and the lead horse comes up to the fence so children can pet his nose. Or head to Salisbury for a **Delmarva Shorebirds** minor league baseball game.

Days ❸–❺, Option B: Western Maryland

Get out your hiking boots, your bathing suit, or your skis—whatever the weather, there's something to do here. Base your family at **Deep Creek Lake** so you can ski at **Wisp Resort,** hike to Muddy Falls at **Swallow Falls State Park,** or enjoy **Savage River State Forest.** Sign up at one of the outfitters for a white-water rafting trip, fly-fishing, dog-sledding or a kennel visit, or boat or snowshoe rental.

Days ❻–❼: Annapolis

Two days in Annapolis are plenty for children. Just make sure you visit the **Naval Academy** (sign up for a tour that takes visitors by Bancroft Hall in time for noon formation), and then take a ride on the *Harbor Queen.* Children give both of these high marks. You can easily do this all in a day, with lunch at the **City Dock** in between. Take a carriage ride in the historic district in the evening.

Spend your second day hiking or kayaking at **Quiet Waters Park,** or head down Route 2 to **Six Flags America** for some big-time thrills. Children also like the **State House** and the **Annapolis Maritime Museum** in Eastport.

4 THE BEST OF DELAWARE FOR FAMILIES

Tiny Delaware packs in a lot of fun, history, and culture. This is a 5-day itinerary, but it's easy to pick and choose a couple of days' worth of activity for a long weekend, or stretch out the fun for a whole week's vacation—without getting bored.

Day ❶: A Day at the Beach

Start slow. Unpack your bathing suit or fishing rod and head to **Bethany Beach** or **Fenwick State Park** for a quiet day. Doing nothing will make you hungry, so decide whether you want pizza at **Grotto's** or a heartier dinner at **Frog House** or **Mango Mike's.** Or send the kids to one of those and head to **Sedona** or **Kingston Grille** for fine dining.

Day ❷: Let's Go Shopping

Sales-tax-free Delaware makes shopping even more fun. Head to **Tanger Outlets** in Rehoboth. Or visit the little shops in downtown **Rehoboth Beach** or **Lewes.**

Day ❸: Dover

Delaware's capital city has a cluster of unusual museums, and the well-regarded **Biggs Museum of American Art.** The downtown sights, along with the Legislative Hall and state archives, are now known as the **First State Heritage Park at Dover.** You could easily see them all in a day. Or head to the slots or horse races at **Dover Downs** instead. Wildlife fans may prefer **Bombay Hook National Wildlife Refuge** for a little bird-watching. Plan to be there for about 2 hours or more, depending on how much hiking you can handle.

Day ❹: Historic New Castle

The original capital of Delaware was the waterfront village of **New Castle.** Its historic sites are still lovingly maintained, including the Federal-style **Read House,** home of the son of a signer of the Declaration of Independence. A number of other Colonial-era homes are also open most days. Have lunch at the Colonial **Jessop's Tavern.**

Day ❺: Wilmington & the Brandywine Valley

The castles of the **Brandywine Valley** beckon, but the exhibits at the **Delaware Art Museum** and the **Delaware History Museum** are hard to pass by, too. If you've got only a day, you're going to want to see one of the du Pont properties: **Winterthur,** with its Enchanted Gardens; **Nemours,** if you love lavish style; **Longwood Gardens,** with three great treehouses and children's garden; or **Hagley,** for its bucolic setting and displays made for kids. Wilmington's **Delaware History Museum** makes history fun for kids. We haven't seen it yet, but a new **Delaware Children's Museum** is opening on the Riverfront in mid-2010. Climb aboard the *Kalmar Nyckel* or walk down to the newly opened **Russell W. Peterson Urban Wildlife Refuge** to work up an appetite for dinner. Dinner at the Riverfront is a great way to end the day.

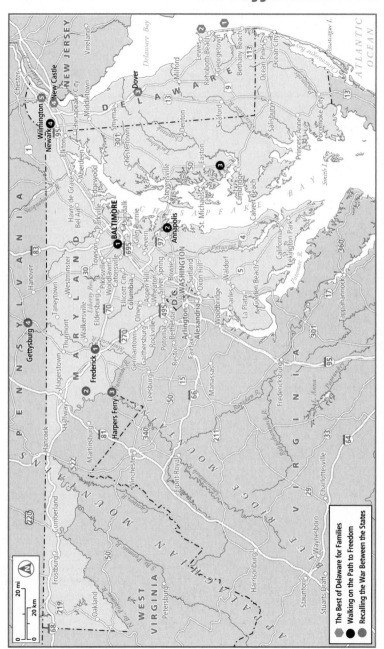

5 WALKING ON THE PATH TO FREEDOM

African-American history has gotten some well-deserved attention throughout the region. From Baltimore to the Eastern Shore, look for the places where people struggled for freedom and the museums that highlight their courage and faith.

Day ❶: Baltimore Museums

Learn about the individuals who found freedom on the Underground Railroad or who made the civil-rights movement their own in three museums here. All eyes are on the **Reginald F. Lewis Museum of Maryland African American History & Culture,** the newest jewel in the city's collection of museums, on the east side of the Inner Harbor. The **National Great Blacks in Wax Museum** is a bit out of the way for downtown visitors, but the figures recall the triumphs and the horrors of slavery in a unique way. The **Eubie Blake Cultural Center** focuses on local musicians, most notably this composer, jazzman Cab Calloway, and others.

Day ❷: Annapolis

Alex Haley, author of *Roots,* has a permanent seat at **City Dock,** a place where people were once auctioned off as slaves. The sculpture is only one such tribute. U.S. Supreme Court Justice Thurgood Marshall and North Pole explorer Matthew Henson are honored with statues on the lawn of the **State House.** Stop in the newly expanded **Banneker–Douglass Museum** for a look at the lives of other prominent African-American Marylanders. A tour focusing on African-American history is available at the **Historic Annapolis** museum store.

Day ❸: Following the Underground Railroad

These roads in Dorchester and Caroline counties on the Eastern Shore, which were traveled by Underground Railroad "conductor" Harriett Tubman, are detailed in the **"Finding a Way to Freedom"** driving-tour brochure and map, available at visitor centers on I-95 and in Cambridge. The roads remain, though most of the buildings, such as Tubman's home, are gone. If you're visiting after 2011, stop by **Harriet Tubman Underground Railroad State Park.** The **Harriet Tubman Museum,** in Cambridge, offers tours to help interpret the places as you go by. The route is about 100 miles long and takes about 4 hours. Most of it goes through farmland, but there are a few places to stop for food and restrooms.

Day ❹: Delaware

If you have only a day, be sure to stop in Newark, Delaware, to see the nationally recognized **Paul R. Jones Collection of African American Art**—the largest and most comprehensive collection of 20th-century African-American art in the world. Mr. Jones's collection, which includes Jacob Lawrence, Carrie Mae Weems, and Elizabeth Catlett, is on display at the University of Delaware's Mechanical Hall. Stop in nearby **New Castle** and visit the old **Court House** to see the stirring exhibit on the Underground Railroad. If you have time, visit **Wilmington** and walk along the **Riverfront** to see the markers recalling Harriet Tubman's efforts here. The riverside Tubman–Garrett Park is named for her and abolitionist Thomas Garrett.

6 RECALLING THE WAR BETWEEN THE STATES

Frederick is your base for a 3- or 4-day visit to three major battlefields: Gettysburg, Antietam, and Harpers Ferry. Or you could spend a week and add Baltimore's Civil War Museum (site of the first bloodshed in the Civil War) and Federal Hill (where U.S. cannons were trained on the city), plus Delaware's Fort Delaware, which served as a prisoner-of-war camp for 33,000 Confederate soldiers.

Day ❶: Frederick
Begin your day in Frederick at the **National Museum of Civil War Medicine** for a different perspective of the war. Frederick was not only a crossroads for soldiers as they headed off to battle but also where many came to recuperate afterward. Take a walk through the historic district, looking for signs that feature photos of the troops as they marched through town. The confrontation between **Barbara Fritchie** and Stonewall Jackson in 1862 was immortalized in poetry; a reconstruction of her house sits along Carroll Creek.

Day ❷: Antietam
More U.S. soldiers were killed, wounded, or missing after the 1-day battle here than at any other time in American history. Stop in the visitor center at **Antietam National Battlefield** to see a film about the battle and get a tour map. There are maps for biking and hiking along these gently rolling hills, too. Battlefield guides are another option. Take a few minutes to stop by the **Pry House Field Hospital,** which was also Gen. George McClellan's headquarters prior to the battle and a field hospital afterward. A visit here takes only a few hours and could be combined with Frederick sightseeing if time is short.

Day ❸: Harpers Ferry
Abolitionist John Brown's plan to start a rebellion was thwarted here by Lt. Col. Robert E. Lee in 1859. The riverfront town was to see Union and Confederate troops several more times before witnessing the war's largest surrender of Federal troops. It's worth a day trip to visit the **Harpers Ferry National Historical Park,** which still appears much as it did during the war. It's a place of natural beauty, too, so bring your hiking shoes or plan a rafting trip on the Shenandoah–Potomac here.

Day ❹: Gettysburg
The 34-mile drive to Gettysburg from Frederick takes you through gently rolling hills, woodlands, orchards, and farms. Take it slowly if you have the time; but, if you have just a day, you'll need to start early so you can fit in the **Gettysburg National Military Park,** including the Gettysburg Cemetery, where President Lincoln delivered his famous address. Driving the battlefield takes a good 2 hours. You'll also want to see the Cyclorama and museum at the new visitor center. A number of companies, including the well-regarded **Association of Licensed Battlefield Guides,** offer guided tours that give good historical perspective on the sites here. The town itself, with a charming historic district, has lots of privately owned museums. If you have time, don't miss the **Shriver House Museum** for a view of how citizens fared during the battle here. One day is enough here, but 2 days gives you time to savor your visit, shop, and dine at a historic inn.

Baltimore

"Hi, hon!" If you're lucky, you just might hear the old Baltimorean greeting. But so many visitors have made "Charm City" their home, the old phrase is disappearing. No matter. The "charm" remains every time Baltimore reinvents itself.

Baltimore has welcomed visitors since 1729. Founded as a port and shipbuilding town, its citizens have adapted to constant change. Baltimore clippers were once cutting-edge technology here. Then it was cars and steel. Now the city is on the rise once again with top-notch healthcare, high-tech industries, and nonprofits.

That doesn't mean Baltimore is all business. Far from it. Arrive on a sunny May weekend for an old-fashioned Flowermart. Come to Harborplace in midsummer and you'll wonder what the party's for. (It's just Baltimore having a good time.) On a wintry night when it looks like the city has gone to bed, head east to Power Plant Live, Fell's Point, or trendy Canton, and you'll find hot crowds and cool music. Baltimore also revels in its historic sites, museums, and neighborhoods, including Federal Hill, Mount Vernon, Fell's Point, and Canton.

As always, Baltimoreans are happy to see new faces. If you hear a "Hi, Hon!" you can be sure you're welcome.

1 ORIENTATION

ARRIVING

BY PLANE **Baltimore/Washington International Thurgood Marshall Airport** (**BWI;** ℂ 800/I-FLY-BWI [435-9294] or 410/859-7111; www.bwiairport.com) is 10 miles south of downtown Baltimore, off I-295 (the Baltimore–Washington Pkwy.). Domestic airlines serving Baltimore include **AirTran** (ℂ 800/247-8726), **American** (ℂ 800/433-7300), **Continental** (ℂ 800/525-0280), **Delta** (ℂ 800/221-1212), **Northwest** (ℂ 800/225-2525), **Southwest** (ℂ 800/435-9792), **United** (ℂ 800/241-6522), and **US Airways** (ℂ 800/428-4322).

To get to Baltimore from the airport, take I-195 west to Route 295 north, which will take you into downtown. **SuperShuttle** (ℂ **800/258-3826;** www.supershuttle.com) operates vans between the airport and all major downtown hotels. The cost is $22 per person one-way. The **Light Rail** also connects the airport and Amtrak station at BWI, with downtown Baltimore stops at Camden Station and Penn Station.

BY CAR **I-95** provides the easiest routes to Baltimore from the north and south. From the north, follow I-95 south through the **Fort McHenry Tunnel** ($2 toll) to exit 53, I-395 north to downtown. Bear left off the exit, and follow signs to the Inner Harbor. From the south, follow I-95 north to exit 53, I-395 north to downtown. Bear left off the exit, and follow signs to the Inner Harbor.

From the west, take **I-70** east to exit 91, I-695 south (the **Baltimore Beltway**) heading toward Glen Burnie. Take exit 11A, I-95, to I-395 north to downtown.

From **I-83** (Pennsylvania to the north), follow I-83 south to where it merges with I-695 (the Baltimore Beltway). Continue on I-83 south for 1 mile to exit 23A (I-83 south, downtown). The Jones Falls Expressway ends at President Street downtown.

Once you arrive, you'll find parking garages and metered on-street parking downtown. Garages charge about $20 a day, or $8 to $12 for special events or evening visits. Parking meters must be fed $1.25 an hour (in quarters only), though most streets now have meters that take both credit cards and cash to pay parking fees.

BY TRAIN   Baltimore is served by **Amtrak** (© 800/872-7245; www.amtrak.com). Trains on the Northeast Corridor route arrive at and depart from **Pennsylvania Station,** 1500 N. Charles St. (© 410/291-4165), north of the Inner Harbor, and **BWI Airport Rail Station** (© 410/672-6169), off Route 170 about 1½ miles from the airport.

In addition, **MARC** (Maryland Area Rail Commuter) trains provide rail service on two routes from Washington, D.C., stopping at BWI en route. One route ends at Camden Station, closest to the Inner Harbor, and the other ends at Penn Station, about 20 blocks north. From here, you can take a taxi or the Light Rail, which runs Monday through Saturday from 6am to 11pm and Sunday and holidays from 11am to 7pm. The MARC fare to the airport is $4 one-way. For more information, call © **800/325-RAIL** (7245) or go to **www.mtamaryland.com**.

BY BUS   Regular bus service is provided to and from Baltimore via **Greyhound** (© **800/231-2222;** www.greyhound.com) and **Peter Pan Bus Lines** (© **800/343-9999;** www.peterpanbus.com). Buses serve two stations in the area: in South Baltimore at 2110 Haines St. (© **410/752-7682**), and in East Baltimore at the **Baltimore Travel Plaza,** 5625 O'Donnell St. (© **410/633-6389**).

VISITOR INFORMATION

Contact **Visit Baltimore,** 100 Light St., Baltimore, MD 21202 (© **877/BALTIMORE** [225-8466]; http://baltimore.org). It has all sorts of information to help you plan your trip, including maps, brochures, and water taxi schedules. The visitor center is open daily at the Inner Harbor, adjacent to Harborplace, at 401 Light St. Stop by for brochures or advice from one of the knowledgeable staffers. A short film shown several times an hour will introduce you to Baltimore. You can even get tickets for attractions, tours, and boat trips. The **Downtown Partnership Baltimore,** 217 N. Charles St. (www.godowntown baltimore.com), also has directions, maps, and other information. **Downtown Baltimore Guides** in the yellow shirts can give directions or provide an escort (© **410/244-8778** daytime, 802-9631 nighttime).

BALTIMORE'S NEIGHBORHOODS IN BRIEF

Baltimore has always been a hardworking town, home to fiercely loyal Orioles fans, with close-knit neighborhoods and families. Below are some neighborhoods you may wish to visit, along with a few of the characteristics that make them unique.

Baltimore's **Inner Harbor** is the obvious starting point for visitors, the focal point of the town's turnaround in the late 1970s. Visitors can get a feel for the city's seafaring days through attractions on the Inner Harbor, harbor cruises, and even water taxis.

The National Aquarium is filled with fish, sharks, and dolphins, and topped with a rainforest. The Maryland Science Center offers an IMAX theater and planetarium. Harborplace Mall and the Gallery are shopping and dining extravaganzas that draw thousands every weekend.

Baltimore has become a destination for pleasure boaters, tall ships, and even high-tech racing sailboats. The Volvo Ocean Race sailors stopped here in 2002 and 2006.

Just past the Inner Harbor are some of Baltimore's oldest neighborhoods.

Little Italy has been home to Italian immigrants and their descendants since the mid-1800s, when they first opened the restaurants that continue to anchor the neighborhood. Some of the city's oldest buildings line the charming, narrow streets—these survived the 1905 fire that destroyed downtown. Before or after dinner, take a walk to see the rowhouses and their famous marble steps, which dominate the Baltimore streetscape—and notice the shrines with flowers and statues that grace windows here and there.

Harbor East, formerly an industrial area, now boasts the city's newest hotels and condos, and some fine restaurants and shops. Young adults moving to Baltimore want to live in this area, which is quite convenient to the other harborside neighborhoods.

Fell's Point was Baltimore's original seaport and home to the first shipyards. Baltimore clippers, swift and elegant topsail schooners, were made here. For years, immigrants to the U.S. arrived in Fell's Point and settled this area, as well as the surrounding neighborhoods of Highlandtown and Canton.

Fell's Point has long been known as a rowdy part of town. Restaurants and entertainment venues keep this neighborhood hopping all night. But don't miss the history. Walking tours bring the past (and a few ghosts) to life as you pass elegant brick rowhouses.

The Recreation Pier will be familiar to TV viewers as the site of police headquarters in the series *Homicide.*

Canton was once home to families whose breadwinners worked at nearby factories, canneries, and breweries. Today, technology firms rent office space here, while families are moving in to rehab the old brick and Formstone rowhouses. O'Donnell Square is surrounded by bars and eateries, and the Can Company has transformed an abandoned can-making operation into a mixed-use space, with offices, a few shops, and restaurants with outdoor patios.

All of the above neighborhoods are connected by a waterfront promenade as well as water taxis.

Mount Vernon, surrounding the Washington Monument (which, as Baltimoreans will remind you, predates the one in D.C.), offers a collection of beautiful buildings from the city's heyday. This tony area is home to the Walters Art Museum and a half-mile walk up Charles Street.

Northern Baltimore City is mostly residential, though **Hampden** and **Mount Washington Village** offer interesting shopping and some good restaurants. If you happen to be in town in December, visit Hampden's **34th Street** ★★ to see how the neighbors dress up their rowhouses for the holidays; people come from all over the city to view the thousands of lights, model trains, and Santas. Mount Washington Village is a short Light Rail trip from downtown, a good side trip if the glitz of the Inner Harbor is too much for you. It's small but offers a handful of fun eateries, as well as some unique shops, plenty of hair salons, and a pottery studio.

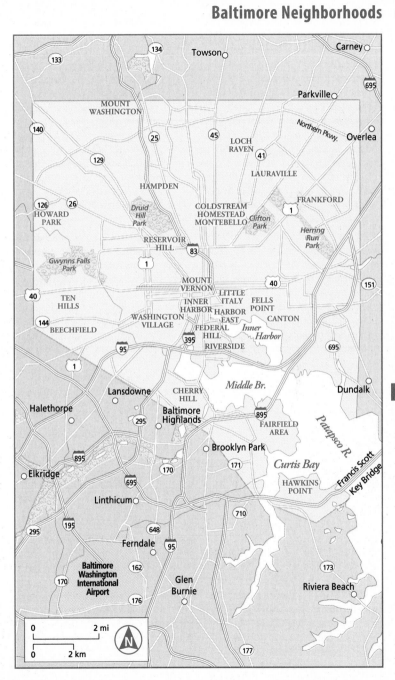

2 GETTING AROUND

BY CAR   If you plan to stay near the harbor, it is easier to walk or take a water taxi than to drive and park. That having been said, driving in downtown Baltimore is fairly easy. The streets are on a straight grid; many are one-way. The major northbound streets are Howard, Charles, and Calvert. Cathedral and St. Paul are southbound. Lombard and Pratt are the major east and west streets. On the west side, Martin Luther King Boulevard connects the harbor with the cultural district; it runs both north and south.

Need to find an address? Buildings are numbered east and west from Charles Street; 100 East Lombard is in the first block to the east of Charles. Baltimore Street is the dividing line for north-south addresses; 100 South Charles is a block below Baltimore.

Car-rental agencies at Baltimore/Washington International Thurgood Marshall Airport include **Alamo** (© 410/859-8092), **Avis** (© 410/859-1680), **Budget** (© 410/859-0850), **Dollar** (© 800/800-4000), **Enterprise** (© 800/325-8007), **Hertz** (© 410/850-7400), **National** (© 410/859-8860), and **Thrifty** (© 410/850-7139).

BY LIGHT RAIL, SUBWAY & BUS   The Maryland Transit Administration (MTA) operates the **Light Rail,** a 27-mile system of aboveground rail lines reminiscent of the city's old streetcars. It travels on one north-south line, from the northern suburb of Timonium to Glen Burnie in the south, with a spur to Penn Station. The key stop within the city is Camden Station, next to the Orioles' ballpark. The Light Rail is the ideal way to get to a game or to travel between Camden Yards and the Inner Harbor, and the train station, the performing-arts district, or Mount Washington. Trains run every 15 to 30 minutes daily between 6am and midnight and Sunday between 11am and 7pm. Tickets, which cost $1.60 one-way, are dispensed from machines at each stop. Better yet, get a day pass for $3.50—it's good on all MTA transportation.

The MTA also operates the **Metro,** a subway system that connects downtown with the northwestern suburbs. Trains run from Johns Hopkins Hospital in East Baltimore through Charles Center and north to the suburb of Owings Mills. Service is available Monday through Friday from 5am to midnight, Saturday and Sunday from 6am to midnight. The fare is $1.60; you can also purchase the aforementioned day pass, which allows unlimited trips on the Light Rail, the Metro, and city buses for $3.50.

A network of **buses,** also operated by the MTA, connects all sections of the city. Service is daily, but hours vary. The base fare is $1.60; exact change is necessary.

The **Charm City Circulator** (www.charmcitycirculator.com), a free shuttle with three routes, was due to begin operations in early 2010.

To get information and schedules for all MTA services, call © **410/539-5000** or visit **www.mtamaryland.com**.

BY TAXI   All taxis in the city are metered; two reputable companies are **Yellow Cab** (© 410/685-1212) and **Arrow Cab** (© 410/358-9697). For airport trips, call **SuperShuttle** (© 800/258-3826; www.supershuttle.com).

BY WATER TAXI   The water taxi makes for a pleasant way to visit Baltimore's attractions. **Baltimore Water Taxis** (© 800/658-8947 or 410/563-3901; www.thewatertaxi. com) runs between about a dozen Inner Harbor locations, including Harborplace, Fell's Point, Little Italy, Canton, and Fort McHenry; the main stop at Harborplace is on the corner between the two pavilions. Just tell the mate where you want to go. The cost is $9 for adults and $4 for children 10 and under for a full day's unlimited use of the water coupons for area restaurants, museums, and shops.

From May through Labor Day weekend, the 13 water taxis generally run about every 15 to 18 minutes, from 10am to 11pm Sunday through Thursday and until midnight Friday and Saturday. From November through March, taxis run from 11am to 6pm, sometimes later. In April, May, and October, Friday and Saturday service runs until 11pm. Service to Fort McHenry runs only April through September. Service is always weather permitting; you can pick up a schedule at the main stop at Harborplace.

Note: A free **Water Taxi Harbor Connector** runs between Tide Point, about a mile from Fort McHenry, and Maritime Park in Fell's Point. Water taxis run every 12 minutes 7am to 7pm daily, except in inclement weather.

ON FOOT   You'll need to know only a few streets to get around. The easiest is the **promenade** around the Inner Harbor, which runs along the water from Federal Hill to Harbor East to Fell's Point and Canton. You can take it to the American Visionary Art Museum, Maryland Science Center, Harborplace, National Aquarium, USS *Constellation,* and Maritime Museum, as well as to shops and restaurants. Biking is permitted from 6 to 10am every day on the promenade.

Pratt and **Lombard** streets are the two major east-west arteries just above the Inner Harbor. Pratt heads east to Little Italy, while Lombard extends west to the stadiums. **Charles Street** is Baltimore's main route north and home to some good restaurants, Baltimore's Washington Monument, and the Walters Art Museum, all within walking distance of the Inner Harbor. **St. Paul Street** is the major route south.

Fast Facts   Baltimore

American Express The office is at 100 E. Pratt St. (© **410/837-3100**).

Area Code The area codes in Baltimore are **410** and **443.**

Car Rentals See "Getting Around: By Car" (p. 54) for car-rental agencies at BWI. Two companies have locations at the Inner Harbor: **Avis,** at the Sheraton, 101 W. Fayette St. (© **410/685-6405**), and **Enterprise,** at the Sheraton, 300 S. Charles St. (© **410/547-1855**).

Emergencies Dial © **911** for fire, police, or ambulance.

Eyeglass Repair Try **For Eyes,** 330 N. Charles St. (© **410/727-2027**).

Hospitals Downtown options include **Johns Hopkins Hospital,** 600 S. Wolfe St. (© **410/955-5000**); **University of Maryland Medical Center,** 22 S. Greene St. (© **410/328-8667**); and **Mercy Medical Center,** 301 St. Paul Place (© **410/332-9000**).

Liquor Laws Restaurants, bars, hotels, and other places serving alcohol may stay open from 6am to 2am. Some opt to close on Sundays and election days. The legal age to buy or consume alcohol is 21.

Newspapers & Magazines The *Baltimore Sun* (www.baltimoresun.com) is the city's daily. *City Paper,* Baltimore's free weekly, is published Wednesdays and has excellent listings. *Baltimore* magazine is published monthly.

Pharmacies Two downtown options are **Rite Aid,** 125 E. Baltimore St. (📞 **410/685-4340**), and **Walgreens,** 19 E. Fayette St. (📞 **410/625-1179**).

Police Dial 📞 **911** for emergencies, or 📞 **311** for nonemergencies requiring police attention.

Post Office The main post office is at 900 E. Fayette St. (📞 **410/347-4202**). It's open Monday through Friday from 8:30am to 7pm. Other area post offices are at 111 N. Calvert (📞 **410/539-2335**), and 130 N. Greene St. (📞 **410/244-1981**). Both are open Monday through Friday from 9am to 5pm.

Safety Baltimore has a nagging problem with both property and violent crime. The Inner Harbor and Mount Vernon areas are fairly safe, thanks to a greater number of police officers, along with the Downtown Partnership's safety guides. Still, be alert and follow some common-sense precautions.

Taxes The state sales tax is 6%. The hotel tax is an additional 7.5%.

Transit Information For bus, Light Rail, and Metro info, call the **Maryland Transit Administration (MTA)** at 📞 **866/RIDE-MTA** (743-3682) or 410/539-5000; or go to **www.mtamaryland.com**.

Weather Call 📞 **410/936-1212.**

3 WHERE TO STAY

Baltimore caters to the business traveler but loves families—there are about 9,000 hotel rooms downtown, with all the expected amenities—with more hotels due to open in 2010. In 2011, the Four Seasons will open a new hotel on Harbor East's waterfront. Bed-and-breakfasts around town offer unique style and comfort.

Every hotel listed is accessible to travelers with disabilities, although specific amenities vary from place to place.

INNER HARBOR

Very Expensive

InterContinental Harbor Court Baltimore ★★ It's a treat just to walk in the front door of Baltimore's finest hotel, part of the InterContinental chain. When you spend the night, prepare to be pampered. Accommodations are exquisitely furnished, from the large standard rooms to the suites, which boast hand-painted decor, marble bathrooms, kitchenettes, and canopy beds. The hotel overlooks the harbor, but only a few rooms have a clear harbor view. Breakfast, lunch, afternoon tea on weekends, and dinner are served at the cheery **Brighton's,** which offers waterfront views; and the **Explorers Lounge** serves lunch, dinner, and late-night fare, as well as live entertainment every night but Monday.

550 Light St., Baltimore, MD 21202. 📞 **800/824-0076** or 410/234-0550. Fax 410/659-5925. www.harborcourt.com. 195 units, 22 suites. $275–$305 double; $450–$3,800 suite. AE, DC, DISC, MC, V. Valet parking $32; self-parking $21. **Amenities:** Restaurant; coffee shop; lounge; health club; Jacuzzi; massage; indoor pool; room service; tanning; tennis courts. *In room:* A/C, TV, CD player, hair dryer, minibar, MP3 player, Wi-Fi (fee).

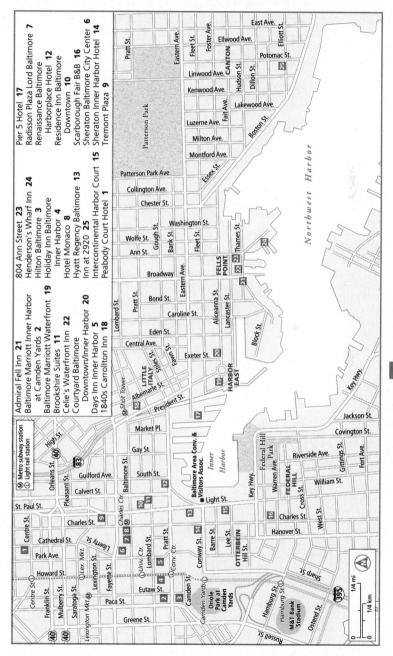

Admiral Fell Inn **21**
Baltimore Marriott Inner Harbor
  at Camden Yards **2**
Baltimore Marriott Waterfront **19**
Brookshire Suites **11**
Celie's Waterfront Inn **22**
Courtyard Baltimore
  Downtown/Inner Harbor **20**
Days Inn Inner Harbor **5**
1840s Carrollton Inn **18**

804 Ann Street **23**
Henderson's Wharf Inn **24**
Hilton Baltimore **3**
Holiday Inn Baltimore
  Inner Harbor **4**
Hotel Monaco **8**
Hyatt Regency Baltimore **13**
Inn at 2920 **25**
Intercontinental Harbor Court **15**
Peabody Court Hotel **1**

Pier 5 Hotel **17**
Radisson Plaza Lord Baltimore **7**
Renaissance Baltimore
  Harborplace Hotel **12**
Residence Inn Baltimore
  Downtown **10**
Scarborough Fair B&B **16**
Sheraton Baltimore City Center **6**
Sheraton Inner Harbor Hotel **14**
Tremont Plaza **9**

Ⓜ Metro subway station
Ⓛ Light rail station

BALTIMORE

5

WHERE TO STAY

Baltimore Marriott Waterfront ★ Kids

This Marriott dominates a prime piece of waterfront—even though it's more than a few steps from the city's best-known attractions and the convention center. Luckily, the water taxi stops nearby. The hotel rises 31 floors above the Harbor East neighborhood. Rooms here, updated in 2008, are standard, with the added pleasures of down duvets and that skyline vista. The suites offer more room. The best views are from the top two floors, which come at a premium.

700 Aliceanna St., Baltimore, MD 21202. © **800/228-9290** or 410/385-3000. Fax 410/895-1900. www. marriott.com/hotels/travel/bwiwf-baltimore-marriott-waterfront. 732 rooms, 21 suites. $299–$425 double. AE, DC, DISC, MC, V. Valet parking $36; self-parking $25. Water taxi stop nearby. **Amenities:** Restaurant; lounge; concierge-level rooms; fitness center; indoor pool. *In room:* A/C, TV, hair dryer, minibar, MP3 player, Wi-Fi (fee).

Hilton Baltimore

It's supposed to be a convention center hotel but for baseball fans, the Hilton is all about the stadium-view rooms. The city's newest and largest hotel has rooms looking right over the outfield wall. Built adjacent to the Baltimore Convention Center, the rooms are standard Hilton comfort. About those ballpark rooms, 10 are suites with balconies in the parlor. Ask for a south-side room to overlook the stadium. Ask about baseball packages and special programs for the kids. The terrace off the lounge faces the stadium, too. It's open to the public.

401 W. Pratt St., Baltimore, MD 21201. © **800/HILTONS** (445-8667) or 443/573-8700. www.baltimore. hilton.com. 747 rooms, 10 suites. $129–$399 double. AE, DC, DISC, MC, V. Valet parking $34; self-parking $26. On Light Rail stop. Pets accepted for fee. **Amenities:** Restaurant; lounge; concierge-level rooms; fitness center; indoor pool; whirlpool; sauna. *In room:* A/C, TV, hair dryer, MP3 dock-radio, Wi-Fi (fee).

Hyatt Regency Baltimore ★★★

Location and smart furnishings make this convenient hotel the city's most stylish. Not only is the all-glass facade eye-catching, you won't want to miss the distinctive blue-and-yellow modern decor inside. The most pleasing feature is the bank of chaise longues tucked under the picture windows. And the location is still the best. It's a short walk across a skywalk to the Inner Harbor, another skywalk to the convention center, and a few blocks to the stadiums.

300 Light St., Baltimore, MD 21202. © **800/233-1234** or 410/528-1234. Fax 410/685-3362. www. baltimore.hyatt.com. 488 units. $199–$399 double. Ask about packages and discounts. Children 17 and under stay free in parent's room. AE, DC, DISC, MC, V. Valet parking $37; self-parking $26. **Amenities:** Restaurant; bar; basketball court; executive-level rooms; health club; outdoor pool; putting green; recreation deck w/jogging track; 2 tennis courts. *In room:* A/C, TV, hair dryer, minibar, Wi-Fi (fee).

Pier 5 Hotel ★ Finds

Be prepared for something wild when you walk into the lobby of the Pier 5. It's bright and airy, with fun, offbeat sofas and a purple, red, and yellow color scheme. The rooms continue the theme, though they're much a quieter and more refined urban chic. Standard units are comfortable, with lots of conveniences for both business and leisure travelers. Suites are luxurious, with one, two, or even three tiny balconies overlooking the harbor or the National Aquarium. Just about every room has a water view—and a much closer one than at any of the other hotels, as this place is only two stories high and right on the harbor. Ask about their packages for family fun or romance. **Pizzazz Tuscan Grille** is open for breakfast, lunch, and dinner; **McCormick & Schmick's** offers lunch and dinner; and **Ruth's Chris Steak House** serves dinner.

711 Eastern Ave. (at the end of Pier 5), Baltimore, MD 21202. © **866/583-4162** or 410/539-2000. Fax 410/783-1787. www.harbormagic.com. 65 units. $179–$399 double; $250–$850 suite. AE, DC, DISC, MC, V. Valet parking $32; self-parking $22. Located at a water taxi stop. Pets welcome. **Amenities:** 3 restaurants; access to exercise room at Brookshire Suites; day pass to Maryland Athletic Club; complimentary shuttle to Brookshire Suites, Admiral Fell Inn, and Johns Hopkins Hospital. *In room:* A/C, fridge, Wi-Fi (fee).

Renaissance Baltimore Harborplace Hotel ★★   The Renaissance is in the middle of everything: Business travelers find it convenient to local firms, the convention center, and restaurants, while tourists like its location across the street from Harborplace and the Inner Harbor. It's part of the Gallery shopping arcade at Harborplace. Guest rooms are the biggest in Baltimore, with comfortable furniture and wide windows (which really open) overlooking the Inner Harbor. The huge rooms on the upper level have the best views. Need extra luxury? Suites have bedrooms connected to a parlor with living room, dining room, and kitchenette; some even have Murphy beds for extra guests. Public spaces, renovated in 2007, include the contemporary-styled **Watertable** restaurant and lounge.

202 E. Pratt St., Baltimore, MD 21202. © **800/HOTELS-1** (468-3571) or 410/547-1200. Fax 410/783-9676. www.renaissanceharborplace.com. 622 units. $199–$349 double; $500–$449 suite. Children 17 and under stay free in parent's room. AE, DC, DISC, MC, V. Valet parking $30; self-parking $27. **Amenities:** Restaurant overlooking harbor; lounge; concierge-level rooms; health club w/harbor view; indoor pool; sauna; whirlpool. In room: A/C, TV, hair dryer, minibar, Wi-Fi (fee).

Moderate

Baltimore Marriott Inner Harbor at Camden Yards ★   This hotel, with a 10-story crescent-shaped facade, is across from Camden Yards and a couple of blocks from the Inner Harbor and the convention center. (Don't confuse it with the Baltimore Marriott Waterfront in Harbor East.). Brightly colored rooms are appointed with white linens and local art. King and two-queen rooms are the same size; king rooms have a single sleeper chair. Executive kings offer a separate sitting area with sofa bed. A panel on the flatscreen TV allows guests to hook up their laptop, game system, or MP3 to the TV.

110 S. Eutaw St., Baltimore, MD 21202. © **800/228-9290** or 410/962-0202. Fax 410/625-7892. www. marriott.com/baltimore. 524 units. $189–$324 double. Weekend discounts available. AE, DC, DISC, MC, V. Self-parking $24. **Amenities:** Restaurant; lounge; coffee shop; concierge; concierge-level rooms; fitness center; room service. In room: A/C, TV, hair dryer, Wi-Fi (fee).

Brookshire Suites ★ **Kids**   This building was once a parking garage, but only the tallest guests might notice its slightly lower ceilings. Accommodations are comfortable, with room to spread out. Separate sitting rooms have wet bars with fridges. Bedding was updated in 2008. The **Cloud Club** has a terrific view, comfortable seating, and TVs. Visiting families will like the breakfast buffet served every morning. On Saturdays, breakfast is hosted by "Bite" the shark. Afternoon receptions feature local foods and brews. The hotel is easy to find, located a block from the Inner Harbor on one of the city's main arteries—convenient for seeing the sights.

120 E. Lombard St., Baltimore, MD 21202. © **866/583-4162** or 410/625-1300. www.harbormagic.com. 97 units. $129–$229 double. Ask about packages. Rates include full breakfast in Cloud Club. AE, DC, DISC, MC, V. Valet parking $33. Pets welcome. **Amenities:** Lounge; fitness room; pass to Maryland Athletic Club; complimentary shuttle to Pier 5 Hotel, Admiral Fell Inn, and Johns Hopkins Hospital; Wi-Fi in public areas. In room: A/C, TV, CD player, fridge, hair dryer, high-speed Internet. .

Courtyard Baltimore Downtown/Inner Harbor ★   Set in the middle of trendy Harbor East, the Courtyard offers comfortable accommodations, which were renovated in 2007. Eight units have Jacuzzis and the 10 corner suites feature kitchenettes, pullout sofas and a curved bank of windows in the bedroom. This hotel is serious enough for business travelers, but casual enough for families on vacation. Though not exactly right at the Inner Harbor, it's near the waterfront promenade, making it an easy 15-minute walk to the Inner Harbor or Fell's Point. The exercise room is small but the complimentary access to the nearby Maryland Athletic Club should please serious fitness buffs.

1000 Aliceanna St., Baltimore, MD 21202. ☏ **443/923-4000.** Fax 443/923-9970. www.marriott.com/bwidt. 195 rooms, 10 suites. $129–$209 double. AE, DC, DISC, MC, V. Self-parking $22. Water taxi stop nearby. **Amenities:** Breakfast cafe; bar; exercise room; indoor pool; whirlpool. *In room:* A/C, TV w/HBO, fridge and microwave on request, hair dryer, free Wi-Fi.

Days Inn Inner Harbor (Value)   If you're willing to give up proximity to the harbor (by 2 or 3 blocks), you can get a great deal at this modern nine-story hotel, located between the 1st Mariner Arena and the convention center, 3 blocks from Camden Yards. It's got a good setup for business travelers, including rooms with large desks, microwaves, and fridges, and a well-equipped business center. All units have the comfort you expect from this chain but, after a 2007 update, a surprisingly high level of style. In fact, this hotel was chosen as the chain's No. 1 hotel in 2008. Most rooms have two double beds, though a few have space for a rollaway cot or just stretching room. Remember to ask for these. Spacious king rooms have a sleeper sofa.

100 Hopkins Place (btw. Lombard and Pratt sts.), Baltimore, MD 21202. ☏ **800/DAYS-INN** (329-7466) or 410/576-1000. Fax 410/576-9437. www.daysinnerharbor.com. 250 units. $109–$229 double. Children 17 and under stay free in parent's room. AE, DC, DISC, MC, V. Valet parking $20. **Amenities:** Restaurant; lounge; fitness center; outdoor pool. *In room:* A/C, TV w/pay movies and Nintendo 64, hair dryer, free Wi-Fi.

Holiday Inn Baltimore Inner Harbor (Kids)   For value and location, it's hard to beat this old-timer, the first major chain property in Baltimore. It's between the 1st Mariner Arena and the convention center, a block from Camden Yards, and 3 blocks from Harborplace. Guest rooms are a good size with traditional furniture and wide windows with skyline views. Some suites have whirlpool tubs.

301 W. Lombard St., Baltimore, MD 21201. ☏ **800/465-4329** or 410/685-3500. www.holiday-inn.com/bal-downtown. 375 units. $129–$189 double; $285 suite. Children 18 and under stay free in parent's room. AE, DC, DISC, MC, V. Self-parking $21. **Amenities:** Restaurant; coffee shop; health club; indoor pool; sauna. *In room:* A/C, TV w/PlayStation, hair dryer, free Wi-Fi.

Hotel Monaco Baltimore   The marble staircase leading to the lobby may fool you that you've entered a grand old hotel. The building *is* historic—a 1906 Beaux Arts glamorpuss—but the Monaco is sleek and modern. Big windows let the light stream into these rooms that hint that this was once Baltimore & Ohio Railroad headquarters. Standard rooms are a nice 385 square feet. Majestic suites are the size of Baltimore rowhouses, at 1,400 square feet. With 12-foot ceilings, tall people should be quite comfortable, but "tall rooms" with special amenities are available.

2 N. Charles St., Baltimore, MD 21202. ☏ **866/973-1904** or 443/692-6170. www.monaco-baltimore.com. 202 units. $129–$449 double. AE, DC, DISC, MC, V. Valet parking $36. Pets accepted. **Amenities:** Restaurant; lounge; concierge-level rooms; fitness center; Kimpton Kids (arranges babysitting, stroller rental); room service. *In room:* A/C, TV, fridge on request, minibar, MP3 dock, Wi-Fi (fee).

Radisson Plaza Lord Baltimore (Moments)   If you love grand old hotels with modern conveniences, this one's for you. The 23-story French Renaissance–style hotel, which opened in 1928, still retains its old-fashioned charm. The grand lobby boasts soaring columns and a glittering chandelier. Those who need extra space should consider a one-bedroom parlor suite or a corner room, which comes with king-size bed and sleeper sofa. Set in the heart of the financial district, the hotel is convenient to Mount Vernon attractions; the Inner Harbor is only 5 blocks away.

20 W. Baltimore St. (btw. Charles and Hanover sts.), Baltimore, MD 21202. ☏ **888/201-1781** or 410/539-8400. Fax 410/625-1060. www.radisson.com/lordbaltimore. 439 units. $99–$279 double. AE, DC, DISC, MC, V. Valet parking $31. **Amenities:** Restaurant; bar; coffee shop; concierge-level rooms; fitness center; Jacuzzi; sauna. *In room:* A/C, TV, hair dryer, free Wi-Fi.

Residence Inn Baltimore Downtown/Inner Harbor   Just a block from the Inner Harbor and tucked into the financial district is a branch of this family- and business traveler–friendly chain. The studio kings, comfortable and reasonably priced, fill up quickly. But families may prefer the other, larger units: One-bedrooms have kitchenettes and pullout sofas, while two-bedroom suites are reserved for extended-stay guests. A hot breakfast is served every morning, with evening receptions Tuesday through Thursday, all complimentary.

17 Light St., Baltimore, MD 21202. ✆ **800/331-3131** or 410/962-1220. Fax 410/962-1221. www.marriott. com/BWIHB. 188 units. $179–$299 double (daily rates decrease for longer stays). Rates include breakfast and evening refreshments. AE, DC, DISC, MC, V. Valet parking $29. Pets okay for fee. **Amenities:** Restaurant; lounge; snack shop; children's playroom; fitness center; laundry room; access to pool at nearby Marriott hotels; Wi-Fi in public areas. *In room:* A/C, TV, hair dryer, high-speed Internet, kitchenette.

Sheraton Baltimore City Center Hotel ★   Renovations in 2007 gave the rooms some new polish. The decor features dark wood, taupe, and navy blue, and the rooms, though not large, are comfortable with flatscreen TVs and wide desks. The hotel is one of Baltimore's largest, with two towers; the south tower is said to have slightly bigger rooms, but the amenities are the same everywhere except on the more upscale concierge level. Because this is a big conference hotel, rooms are set up with the business traveler in mind. Visitors will like the outdoor pool and location 5 blocks from the Inner Harbor and next door to the 1st Mariner Arena (and lower weekend rates).

101 W. Fayette St., Baltimore, MD 21202. ✆ **800/325-3535** or 410/752-1100. Fax 410/385-6865. www. sheraton.com/baltimorecitycenter. 706 units. $149–$189 double. Weekend packages available. Children 18 and under stay free in parent's room. AE, DC, MC, V. Valet parking $34; self-parking $24. Small pets welcome for fee. **Amenities:** 2 restaurants; lounge; concierge level; fitness center; outdoor pool. *In room:* A/C, TV w/movies, fridge on request, hair dryer, Wi-Fi (fee).

Sheraton Inner Harbor Hotel   The Sheraton has a perfect location for convention-eers and Orioles fans (and Red Sox and Yankees fans); the latter will like the location and the packages with tickets to Camden Yards. Furniture and linen upgrades in 2009 have made the sleeping rooms brighter and much more welcome. The suites are a good idea, set up with Murphy beds so they can be turned into mini conference rooms. The fitness center is due to be enlarged in 2010. The **Orioles Grille** has interesting sports memorabilia. **Morton's, The Steakhouse** has a restaurant here.

300 S. Charles St., Baltimore, MD 21202. ✆ **410/962-8300**. Fax 410/962-8211. www.sheraton.com/ innerharbor. 337 units. $179–$429 double; $550–$1,900 suite. Children 18 and under stay free in parent's room. AE, DC, DISC, MC, V. Valet and self-parking. **Amenities:** Restaurant; grill and lounge; club-level rooms; fitness center; indoor pool; sauna; terrace. *In room:* A/C, TV, fridge and microwave on request, hair dryer, Wi-Fi (fee).

Tremont Plaza Hotel ★   You may be surprised by the amount of room in the Tremont's "studio" suites. Really L-shaped rooms, they feature sleeping and sitting areas, as well as kitchenettes. If these aren't not big enough for you, there are one- and two-bedroom suites; these have impressive finishes and fabrics. Upper-floor rooms offer sweeping views of the city. At first glance, the location may seem out of the way—but Charles Street, Baltimore's main drag, is only a block away and the Inner Harbor is 7 blocks away. A free shuttle will take guests anywhere within a 2-mile radius.

222 St. Paul Place, Baltimore, MD 21202. ✆ **800/TREMONT** (873-6668) or 410/727-2222. www. 1800tremont.com. 303 units. $139–$329 studio; $129–$359 1 bedroom, in season. AE, DC, DISC, MC, V. Valet parking $25. **Amenities:** Restaurant; lounge; deli; fitness room; pool; sauna; yoga room; free Wi-Fi in public areas. *In room:* A/C, TV w/pay movies, hair dryer, high-speed Internet, fridge, microwave.

Admiral Fell Inn   Updated and expanded over the years, this charming inn sits just across Thames Street from the harbor in the heart of the Fell's Point Historic District. It spans eight buildings, built between 1790 and 1996, and blends Victorian and Federal-style architecture. Originally a boardinghouse for sailors, later a YMCA, and then a vinegar bottling plant, the inn now features an antiques-filled lobby and library, along with individually decorated guest rooms with Federal-period furnishings. Some units have four-poster beds with lacy canopies and Jacuzzis, two rooms have balconies, and one suite has a fireplace and Jacuzzi. The loft room is more rustic, with sloping ceilings. But from its three dormer windows, the views are among the best in the inn. Evening activities such as ghost tours or wine tastings are offered in the lobby.

888 S. Broadway, Baltimore, MD 21231. ℂ **866/583-4162** or 410/522-7377. Fax 410/522-0707. www.harbormagic.com. 80 units. $149–$229 double. Rates higher during Yankee and Red Sox games. AE, DC, DISC, MC, V. Valet parking $29; self-parking $17. Located across the street from a water taxi stop. Pets welcome. **Amenities:** 2 restaurants; access to Maryland Athletic Club; complimentary shuttle to Pier 5 Hotel, Brookshire Suites, and Johns Hopkins Hospital. *In room:* A/C, TV, fridge and microwave in double rooms, hair dryer, Wi-Fi (fee).

The Inn at Henderson's Wharf ★   From the warm lobby to the courtyard garden, every detail has been chosen for comfort and style. All rooms are on the ground floor (shutters at the windows ensure privacy), with views of the courtyard, the adjacent marina, or the cobblestone streets of Fell's Point. Each is outfitted in soothing neutrals, with dark mahogany furniture and luxurious marble bathrooms.

1000 Fell St., Baltimore, MD 21231. ℂ **800/522-2088** or 410/522-7777. Fax 410/522-7087. www.hendersons wharf.com. 38 units. $189–$259 double. Rates include continental breakfast. AE, DC, MC, V. Free parking. **Amenities:** 256-slip marina. *In room:* A/C, TV w/DVD player available, fridge, hair dryer, minibar, free Wi-Fi.

NORTH OF DOWNTOWN

Inn & Spa at the Colonnade Baltimore ★   If your visit will take you to northern Baltimore, Johns Hopkins University, the Baltimore Museum of Art, or Homeland or Roland Park, this is a stylish choice freshly updated in 2007. Sleek and elegant, the inn offers comfortable rooms, Biedermeier-style furnishings, and lots of amenities, including a spa and free transportation to Baltimore hospitals. Every room has a separate sitting room and sleeping room. Some units have fridges and microwaves. The indoor pool set in a glass-domed solarium is only open in summer. The parking is a bit tricky—you'd do best to pull up and let the valet park your car.

4 W. University Pkwy., Baltimore, MD 21218. ℂ **800/222-8737** or 410/235-5400. Fax 410/235-5572. www.colonnadebaltimore.com. 125 units. $139–$299 double. Weekend discounts available. AE, DC, DISC, MC, V. Valet parking $24; self-parking $20. **Amenities:** Restaurant; coffee shop and bakery; fitness center; 2 Jacuzzis; indoor pool; room service; access to nearby jogging track and tennis courts. *In room:* A/C, TV, hair dryer, free Wi-Fi.

Peabody Court ★   This Mount Vernon boutique hotel, a Clarion property, continues to offer the first-class service that has kept it in business since 1930. The small lobby's luxurious, European-style ambience gives way to polished guest rooms that are some of the most spacious in the city—the light-bathed corner units have upward of 600 square feet. Ask for a room that overlooks Baltimore's most beautiful and historic square. Rooms were refreshed with new duvets and bedding in 2008. The hotel is close to the Peabody Institute, Walters Art Museum, and Mount Vernon restaurants and shops. The walk to

the Inner Harbor takes about 20 minutes—and it's all downhill. The low-key but elegant
George's serves lunch and dinner.

612 Cathedral St., Baltimore, MD 21201. © **800/292-5500** or 410/727-7101. Fax 410/789-3312. www.
peabodycourthotel.com. 104 units. $200–$300 double. Weekend rates available. AE, DC, DISC, MC, V.
Valet parking $29; free self-parking. **Amenities:** Restaurant; lounge; fitness center. *In room:* A/C, TV,
fridge, hair dryer, towel warmers, wet bar in some rooms, free Wi-Fi.

BED & BREAKFASTS

If you prefer accommodations with a bit more individual attention, stop in one of these
city bed-and-breakfasts. Located all over town, each has its own style.

Abacrombie Fine Food and Accommodations (Finds) Guest performers with the
Baltimore Symphony Orchestra often choose this inviting B&B across from the Meyerhoff Symphony Hall. Guest rooms, decorated with vintage furnishings, are cheery and
bright. Rooms can be small, but they have luxe touches such as robes and fine toiletries.
Ask for a room at the end of the hall, if you'd like more space—these have the most
square footage and the biggest windows. Single rooms ($88 a night) are tiny, with charm-
ing beds. Two connect to doubles, making them perfect for families. A restaurant and bar
are located on the ground floor.

58 W. Biddle St., Baltimore, MD 21201. © **410/244-7227.** Fax 410/244-8413. www.abacrombie.net. 12
units. $115–$155 double. Rates include continental breakfast. AE, DC, DISC, MC, V. Free parking. **Amenities:** Restaurant; bar; book/video library. *In room:* A/C, TV/VCR, hair dryer.

Ann Street These two town houses are just around the corner from all of Fell's Point's
hustle and bustle. The suite here has an 18th-century poster bed and a fireplace in the
sitting room. The second bedroom has a poster bed and overlooks the garden instead of
the street (which can be noisy on the weekend).

804 S. Ann St., Fell's Point, Baltimore, MD 21231. © **410/342-5883.** 2 units. $115 double; $125 suite.
Rates include full breakfast. No credit cards. Parking pass for on-street parking. *In room:* A/C.

Celie's Waterfront Inn ★ (Finds) Walk down the sally port of this 18th-century town
house and enter a quiet refuge in bustling Fell's Point. Two units have fireplaces, whirlpool tubs, and harbor views, while two others—with just as nice city views—have private
balconies and whirlpools. Two interior rooms overlooking the flower-filled courtyard are
particularly quiet. Two suites (with full kitchens) can accommodate four or six comfortably. Enjoy breakfast in your room, on the deck, or in the garden.

1714 Thames St., Baltimore, MD 21231. © **800/432-0184.** www.celieswaterfront.com. 9 units. $159–$299
double; $229–$259 suites. Rates include hearty continental breakfast. 2- or 3-night minimum stay may be
required on weekends or holidays. AE, DISC, MC, V. Off-street parking $9. Located across the street from a
water taxi stop. **Amenities:** Roof deck w/harbor views. *In room:* A/C, TV, fridge on request, free Wi-Fi.

1840s Carrollton Inn ★★ Sharing a courtyard with the Carroll Mansion Museum
is this 13-room inn with electric fireplaces, richly carved furniture, whirlpool baths,
sumptuous bedding, Oriental carpets, and silk drapes in every room. Every room has its
own style: The largest is the Carroll Suite, with a separate sitting room and double Jacuzzi
in the bathroom. The Scholars Room has a double Jacuzzi and king-size bed. Light floods
the corner Independence Suite. It's convenient to the Reginald Lewis Museum, the Carroll Mansion, and Little Italy with the Inner Harbor only a short walk away.

50 Albemarle St., Baltimore, MD 21202. © **410/324-5883.** www.1840scarrolltoninn.com. 13 units.
$175–$395 suites. Rates include full breakfast. AE, DISC, MC, V. Discount parking passes for nearby
garages. *In room:* A/C, TV, hair dryer, microwave, free Wi-Fi.

64 **Inn at 2920** ★   This B&B was made for the youthful guests of Canton. A mix of old Baltimore rowhouse and contemporary style, it features five upscale rooms with Jacuzzi tubs, big beds, and modern decor, 15-foot ceilings, and windows that open. The Bordello Room features the only king-size bed (others have queens) and a double whirlpool. A second-level sitting room has videos, books, and games.

2920 Elliott St., Baltimore, MD 21224. ⓒ **877/774-2920** or 410/324-4450. www.theinnat2920.com. 5 units. $170–$220 double. Rates include full breakfast. 2-night minimum required many weekends. AE, DISC, MC, V. On-street parking only. Near water taxi stop. **Amenities:** Concierge services; discount passes to nearby gym. *In room:* A/C, ceiling fan, TV/DVD, hair dryer, whirlpool tub, free Wi-Fi.

Scarborough Fair Bed & Breakfast ★★   New owners are turning this cozy Federal-style town house on a pretty Federal Hill corner into something special. It already offered two rooms with whirlpool tubs and five with fireplaces. Rooms are getting makeovers one at a time and soon they should all have literary themes. The first one finished was the Edgar Allan Poe Suite, a spacious room with fireplace in shades of graphite and lavender with Victorian touches. High ceilings in first-floor rooms make them even airier. Sunnyslope (soon the Brothers Grimm Room) is filled with light. The Hickory Vale Room (soon the Agatha Christi) has a canopy bed, fireplace, and en-suite bathroom with double Jacuzzi.

1 E. Montgomery St., Baltimore, MD 21230. ⓒ **410/837-0010.** www.scarboroughfairbandb.com. 6 units. $169–$259 double. Rates include breakfast. 2-night minimum required many weekends. AE, DISC, MC, V. Off-street parking included. Children welcome. *In room:* A/C, TV/DVD, hair dryer, free Wi-Fi.

NEAR THE AIRPORT

An alternative to staying downtown and worrying about parking—especially if you plan to see only the Inner Harbor attractions—is a hotel near Baltimore/Washington International Thurgood Marshall Airport that offers free shuttle service to the North Linthicum Light Rail station. About 15 airport hotels have such shuttles. From North Linthicum, it's a 15-minute ride to the Camden Yards station, which is just 6 blocks from the Inner Harbor. For a train schedule, see **www.mtamaryland.com**.

Closest to the airport are the **BWI Airport Marriott,** 1743 W. Nursery Rd. (ⓒ **800/596-2376** or 410/859-8300; www.marriott.com), which has an indoor pool; **Country Inn & Suites BWI Airport,** 1717 W. Nursery Rd. (ⓒ **800/456-4000** or 443/577-1036; www.countryinns.com/bwiairport), with an indoor pool; and **Four Points by Sheraton BWI Airport,** 7032 Elm Rd. (ⓒ **800/368-7764** or 410/859-3300; www.bestbwihotel.com), with an outdoor pool. Situated on the same property at 1110 Old Elkridge Landing Rd., the **Sheraton Baltimore Washington Airport Hotel** (ⓒ **443/577-2100;** www.sheraton.com/baltimore) and the **Westin Baltimore Washington Airport** (ⓒ **443/577-2300;** www.westin.com/baltimore) both have indoor pools.

---

4 WHERE TO DINE

Baltimore is known for its seafood, but the city is also home to a variety of ethnic and regional cuisines. There are plenty of good restaurants in the main tourist areas, with excellent choices in Little Italy, Fell's Point, Harbor East, and Mount Vernon.

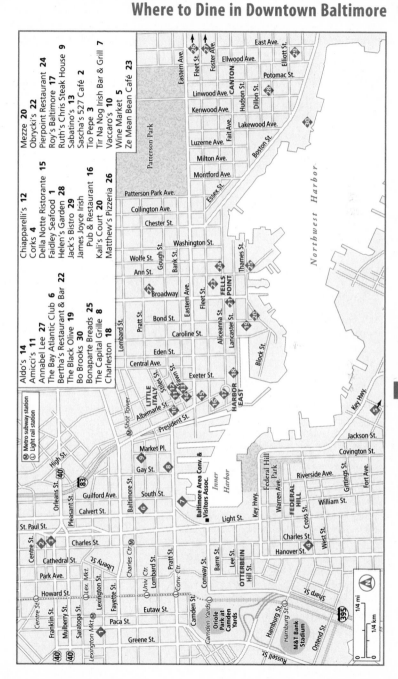

Mezze **20**
Obrycki's **22**
Pierpoint Restaurant **24**
Roy's Baltimore **17**
Ruth's Chris Steak House **9**
Sabatino's **13**
Sascha's 527 Café **2**
Tio Pepe **3**
Tir Na Nog Irish Bar & Grill **7**
Vaccaro's **10**
Wine Market **5**
Ze Mean Bean Café **23**

Chiapparelli's **12**
Corks **4**
Della Notte Ristorante **15**
Faidley Seafood **1**
Helen's Garden **28**
Jack's Bistro **29**
James Joyce Irish
  Pub & Restaurant **16**
Kali's Court **20**
Matthew's Pizzeria **26**

Aldo's **14**
Amicci's **11**
Annabel Lee **27**
The Bay Atlantic Club **6**
Bertha's Restaurant & Bar **22**
The Black Olive **19**
Bo Brooks **30**
Bonaparte Breads **25**
The Capital Grille **8**
Charleston **18**

Ⓜ Metro subway station
Ⓛ Light rail station

BALTIMORE

5

WHERE TO DINE

In recent years, the Inner Harbor has become overrun with chain restaurants serving mediocre fare, but such places as the Hard Rock Cafe and ESPN Zone continue to draw crowds. Power Plant Live, with its mix of restaurants and clubs, is also packed for dinner. You'll find it a block north of Pratt Street, a short walk from the Inner Harbor.

INNER HARBOR & HARBOR EAST
Very Expensive

Charleston ★★★ SOUTHERN   The Charleston is Baltimore's special-night-out place. The food here is the undisputed best in Baltimore. Chef Cindy Wolf has turned Southern cooking into an art form. And the menu, with its tasting sizes so you can choose three to six courses (and count on dessert), is oh-so-imaginative. Whether you choose local seafood or beef, you know the food will be fresh, perfectly cooked, with delightful sauces and accompaniments. Service, though, is so smooth, it may be too cool for Baltimore. As waiters glide by, you might get the feeling of being part of a culinary factory. A tiny quibble, perhaps, but with the elegantly appointed dining room and Southern-style dishes, you hope for Southern hospitality, too. (No grouchiness, of course, just "cool.") Charleston offers a choice of three to six courses: A three-course dinner is $74; a six-course meal will run $109 (wine is extra). The chef's husband and co-owner, Tony Foreman, has selected 600 bottles for the restaurant's wine list, which wins accolades. The couple run a virtual chain in Baltimore nowadays—if you like Charleston, try **Pazo,** 1425 Aliceanna St. (✆ **410/534-7296**), for tapas, or **Cinghiale,** 822 Lancaster St. (✆ **410/547-8282**), for its wine bar and Italian food.

1000 Lancaster St. ✆ **410/332-7373.** www.charlestonrestaurant.com. Reservations recommended. Fixed-price dinners $74–$109. AE, DC, DISC, MC, V. Mon–Sat 5:30–10pm. Free valet parking.

Ruth's Chris Steak House ★★ STEAK   Located on the first floor of the Brokerage, the Baltimore branch of this steakhouse chain is a favorite with the suit-and-tie crowd. The dark-wood furnishings and globe lanterns contribute to its clubby atmosphere. This is a place to come for beef—there are six choices of steak on the menu, all butter-bathed and prepared to order, plus prime rib and filet mignon. Alternatively, you can opt for lobster, salmon, swordfish, or blackened tuna. A second downtown Ruth's Chris is at the Pier 5 Hotel, 711 Eastern Ave. (✆ **410/230-0033**).

600 Water St., btw. S. Frederick and Market sts. ✆ **410/783-0033.** www.ruthschris.com. Reservations recommended Fri–Sat. Main courses $27–$73. AE, DC, DISC, MC, V. Mon–Thurs 5–10pm; Fri–Sat 5–11pm; Sun 4–9pm. Valet parking available.

Expensive

The Capital Grille STEAK   Baltimore is a town big enough for two Ruth's Chris steakhouses, plus the ever-popular Prime Rib. Then there's the new Capital Grille, creating quite a buzz for its clubby atmosphere and sizzling steaks. The food is expertly prepared and the service professional. Lunchtime choices range from sandwiches to salads to steak; at dinner, steak reigns, but there's plenty of seafood, too.

500 E. Pratt St. ✆ **443/703-4064.** www.thecapitalgrille.com. Reservations recommended. Main courses $11–$23 lunch, $23–$39 dinner. AE, DC, DISC, MC, V. Mon–Fri 11:30am–3pm; Sun–Thurs 5–10pm; Fri–Sat 5–11pm.

Roy's ★ HAWAIIAN   This well-regarded chain restaurant next door to the Marriott Waterfront features modern furnishings and a menu quite exotic for Baltimore. Known for its incredible blackened ahi tuna and other tropical delights, the restaurant also does

Baltimore's Best Crab Cakes

A visit to Baltimore means crab cakes—but what makes a good crab cake is for a topic of heated debate. You can expect jumbo lump mixed with a bit of mayo; fried or broiled is often the diner's choice. But each recipe is different. Is Old Bay seasoning required? How much filler is too much? Should you see a fleck of any plant material besides parsley?

Keep in mind a few things: Crabs run from May to September (more or less), so you have a better chance of getting local crab—not Louisiana or Asia imports—then. You don't have to go to a crab house for a decent crab cake. In fact, the number of crab houses has dwindled in recent years, but you can find good seafood at just about every restaurant around. Expect to pay $12 to $18 for a crab-cake sandwich (served on crackers or a bun). A crab-cake platter will be at least $25 and usually comes with fries, coleslaw, and sliced tomato.

Below is my list of where I think you'll find a good crab cake. Are these the best? Have a marvelous time deciding!

The Crab Shanty Restaurant, 3410 Plum Tree Dr. (Rte. 40 W.), Ellicott City (© **410/465-9660;** www.crabshanty.com). Good-size cake, not too much filler. Open Sunday through Friday for lunch, daily for dinner. Carryout is available.

Faidley Seafood, Lexington Market, 400 W. Lexington St. (© **410/727-4898;** www.faidleyscrabcakes.com). The Faidley family has been selling seafood from this stall for 120 years, including a great traditional crab cake. Open Monday through Saturday from 9am to 5pm. Carryout only; shipping is available, too.

Gertrude's, at the Baltimore Museum of Art, 10 Art Museum Dr. (© **410/889-3399;** www.gertrudesbaltimore.com). Noted chef John Shields offers traditional Baltimore-style cakes as well as a creative chef's special. Open Tuesday through Sunday for lunch and dinner.

Kali's Court, 1606 Thames St., Fell's Point (© **410/276-4700;** www.kaliscourt.net). Crab, crab, and not much else. Open daily for dinner.

Nick's Fish House, 2600 Insulator Dr., South Baltimore (© **410/347-4123;** www.nicksfishhouse.com). Maybe the old South Baltimore feel of this casual place swayed me, but this is a great traditional crab cake in a traditional (but new) crab house. Open every day for lunch and dinner.

Obrycki's Crab House and Seafood Restaurant, 1727 E. Pratt St., Upper Fell's Point (© **410/732-6399;** www.obryckis.com). Traditional crab house, traditional crab cake. Open daily for lunch and dinner from mid-March to November.

Pierpoint Restaurant, 1822 Aliceanna St., Fell's Point (© **410/675-2080;** www.pierpointrestaurant.com). Crab cakes here are smoked—different, but well worth a try. Open Tuesday through Sunday for dinner.

local seasonal favorites, including crab cakes, oysters, and softshell crabs. Its prix-fixe menu offers an appetizer sampler, entree, and dessert for $35. The sleek bar is a great place to try one of Roy's Hawaiian martinis.

720B Aliceanna St. ☏ **410/659-0099.** www.roysrestaurant.com. Reservations recommended. Entrees $21–$29. AE, DC, DISC, MC, V. Mon–Thurs 5:30–10pm; Fri 5:30–10:30pm; Sat 5–10:30pm; Sun 5–9pm.

Moderate

Tir Na Nog Irish Pub & Restaurant IRISH   This is not your Grandmother O'Malley's Irish pub. Yes, you'll find Guinness stout and fish and chips. But you'll also find crab cakes, salmon with truffle essence, and fresh fettuccine. The restaurant is a knockout, with two beautifully carved bars and, for diners lucky enough to have window seats, a close-up view of the Inner Harbor. Brunch is served Saturday and Sunday.

Harborplace, Pratt St. Pavilion, Level 2. ☏ **410/483-8968.** www.tnnirishpub.com. Reservations recommended. Main courses $11–$16 lunch, $14–$24 dinner. AE, DC, DISC, MC, V. Mon–Fri 11am–2am; Sat–Sun 10am–2am.

Inexpensive

The Bay Atlantic Club ★ (**Value**) AMERICAN   The students at the Baltimore International College's culinary school work with the head chef to produce wonderful meals at their lunchtime restaurant. The dining room is elegant, with chandeliers and high ceilings painted sky-blue with clouds. And you have to love the young staff, who are obviously proud of their delicious work. Bowing to demand, the menu has gotten more casual with salads, soups, panini, and pizzas—fast food created by culinary students! If you're downtown, this is a pleasant way to break for lunch.

206 E. Redwood St. ☏ **410/752-1448,** ext. 24. www.bic.edu. Reservations recommended. Main courses $6–$11. AE, DC, MC, V. Mon–Fri 11:30am–2pm. Call ahead in summer; students may be on break.

James Joyce Irish Pub & Restaurant IRISH   This handsome, wood-paneled pub in Harbor East attracts conventioneers for hearty fare—from Irish stew to potato soup, crab cakes to steak—and beer. It has a musician crooning Thursday to Saturday nights. There's a children's menu and brunch on weekends.

616 President St. ☏ **410/727-5107.** www.thejamesjoycepub.com. Reservations recommended. Main courses $9–$23. AE, DISC, MC, V. Daily 11am–2am. Valet parking available at Roy's next door.

LITTLE ITALY

In just a few packed blocks, you'll find all the pasta, cannoli, and chianti you could want. Make a reservation if you know where you want to eat beforehand. But if you prefer to wander, plan to eat early or late and choose a place as you stroll through the basil-scented streets. If you don't have room for dessert, remember, there's always Vaccaro's to go. *Tip:* Parking is fairly easy. Choose the garage at Pratt and President streets, opt for the valet parking many restaurants offer, or look for a spot on the street.

Expensive

Aldo's Ristorante Italiano ★★★ NORTHERN ITALIAN   Expect to be treated like royalty here. An elegant setting with small, candlelit rooms and an oh-so-grand atrium dining room, there's also a hefty wine list here. Plates full of perfectly prepared northern Italian cuisine, such as risotto and heavenly lobster-studded mashed potatoes, are stellar. A bit of seafood, as well as veal saltimbocca and *osso buco* make the grade, too. It's a perfect spot for romance or celebration. They'll even arrange a limo.

306 S. High St. ☏ **410/727-0700.** www.aldositaly.com. Reservations recommended on Fri–Sat. Main courses $19–$45. AE, DC, DISC, MC, V. Daily 5–10pm. Valet parking available.

Chiapparelli's SOUTHERN ITALIAN   Southern Italian dishes in red sauce are the trademark at this longtime favorite, but do try Grandma's ravioli stuffed with spinach and ricotta. Pizzas and panini are on the lunch menu, but dinner is the main event, when veal is the star. You'll also find tasty chicken dishes and many classics such as *pescatore Christopher* and shrimp parmigiana. The children's menu includes chicken tenders and pizza bread.

237 S. High St. ℂ **410/837-0309.** www.chiapparellis.com. Reservations recommended. Main courses $7–$16 lunch, $17–$30 dinner. AE, DC, DISC, MC, V. Sun–Thurs 11:30am–9pm; Fri–Sat 11:30am–11pm.

Della Notte Ristorante ★★ ITALIAN   Della Notte is noted for its circular main dining room, lined with banquettes and a huge tree rising in the center. Lunch can be panini, pizza for one, or pasta. At dinner, choose chicken Marsala, a traditional pasta, or something inventive from the night's specials. Jazz brunch is served on Sunday. The impressive wine list includes 46 sparkling wines. The piano lounge is open from 6 to 10pm nightly and until midnight on Saturday. On-site parking is available.

801 Eastern Ave. ℂ **410/837-5500.** www.dellanotte.com. Reservations recommended. Main courses $10–$14 lunch, $20–$39 dinner. AE, MC, V. Sun–Thurs 11am–10pm; Fri–Sat 11am–midnight.

Sabatino's Italian Restaurant ★★ SOUTHERN ITALIAN   For more than 50 years, Sabatino's has been known for its exceptional cuisine. Everyone will tell you to get the house salad with the house dressing, which is thick and garlicky. Simple pasta dishes come in very large portions. The menu also has seafood and meat dishes—*brasciola,* a roll of beef, prosciutto, cheeses, and marinara, is heavenly. Dining rooms fill three floors of this narrow building. It's worth the wait to be seated upstairs, where it's quieter. This is a good spot for late-night dining and people-watching after the bars have closed.

901 Fawn St. (at High St.). ℂ **410/727-9414.** www.sabatinos.com. Reservations recommended. Main courses $12–$27. AE, DC, DISC, MC, V. Sun–Thurs noon–midnight; Fri–Sat noon–3am.

Inexpensive

Amicci's (Kids) (Value) ITALIAN   You'll usually find casual Amicci's crowded with local families and young couples who don't want to spend a lot on good Italian food. Don't be fooled by the small storefront—the restaurant is a maze of dining rooms. If you have to wait, it won't be too long. Start with Amicci's signature *pane rotundo.* Seafood lovers will enjoy that or one of their seafood and pasta dishes—but the pasta should satisfy everyone, even vegetarians. Desserts here come from Vaccaro's. A $5 children's menu is offered all day.

231 S. High St. ℂ **410/528-1096.** www.amiccis.com. Reservations recommended. Main courses $7–$10 lunch, $14–$20 dinner. AE, DISC, MC, V. Daily 11:30am–midnight.

Vaccaro's Italian Pastry Shop ★ ITALIAN DESSERTS   To top off a perfect day, stop at the always-busy Vaccaro's for dessert and coffee. The modern Italian design is new but the old recipes for cannoli, pastries, and tiramisu are still here. If you love gelato, you'll be thrilled by the huge servings—just one scoop is plenty (really!). Vaccaro's also has an outlet in Harborplace's Light Street Pavilion (ℂ **410/547-7169**) and in Canton at 2919 O'Donnell St. (ℂ **410/276-4744**).

222 Albemarle St. ℂ **410/685-4905.** www.vaccarospastry.com. Reservations not accepted. Desserts $4–$10. AE, MC, V. Mon 9am–10pm; Tues–Thurs and Sun 9am–11pm; Fri–Sat 9am–1am.

Expensive

The Black Olive ★★★ GREEK/SEAFOOD   Slip down a quiet residential street and find this taverna, which specializes in fresh, organic Greek treats and an enormous fish selection. The whole-fish preparations are well known among area foodies. Diners can also choose from a variety of small plates and Greek dishes, including chicken souvlaki and village pie. The wine list is hefty, with a lot of options by the glass. Service is smooth but friendly, and the four dining rooms are intimate and comfortable.

814 S. Bond St. ℂ **410/276-7141.** www.theblackolive.com. Reservations required for dinner. Main courses $12–$22 lunch, $27–$40 dinner. AE, MC, V. Daily noon–2pm and 5–10pm. Valet parking for dinner.

Bo Brooks Restaurant ★ SEAFOOD   This is where Baltimoreans take their friends for steamed crabs. It's one of the few places in the city where you can get both a view and a pile of hot steaming crustaceans. And the crabs are fat and spicy. They've got lots of other seafood entrees, as well as sandwiches, salads, and pasta.

2701 Boston St. ℂ **410/558-0202.** www.bobrooks.com. Reservations recommended. Main courses $10–$22; crabs $50–$75 a dozen. AE, MC, V. Mon–Thurs 11:30am–9pm; Fri 11:30am–10pm; Sat 12:30–10pm; Sun 12:30–8pm. Parking available on-site.

Kali's Court ★★ GREEK/SEAFOOD   This two-story cathedral to good food and good times has the most wonderful crab cakes—giant lump crab held together with little more than a prayer and not even a hint of Old Bay Seasoning. The place is known for its grilled whole fish; its bouillabaisse comes highly recommended, too. Make a reservation and plan to wait. The bar in the front can be raucous, but upstairs, the mood is more intimate. Once seated, you'll be treated well and your palate will be delighted. An extravagant brunch of three to five courses is available on Sunday.

Mezze (ℂ **410/563-7600**), right next door, serves Mediterranean-style tapas at affordable prices. It's open Monday to Saturday 4 to 10pm and Sunday 11:30am to 4pm.

A few doors down, **Meli,** 1636 Thames St. (ℂ **410/534-6354**), means honey in Greek so honey-sweetened pastries are featured here. Lunch is served Monday through Friday 11:30am to 2:30pm, with dinner daily 5 to 11pm and dessert served until 1am.

1606 Thames St. ℂ **410/276-4700.** www.kaliscourt.net. Reservations recommended. Main courses $21–$35. AE, DC, MC, V. Daily 5–10pm; brunch Sun 11am–3pm. Free valet parking.

Obrycki's Crab House and Seafood Restaurant ★★ SEAFOOD   Food connoisseurs Craig Claiborne and George Lang have raved about this place in Upper Fell's Point. The decor is charming, with stained-glass windows, wainscoting, and brick archways. It's the quintessential crab house, where you can crack open steamed crabs or choose crab soup, crab cocktail, crab balls, crab cakes, crab imperial, or softshell crabs. The rest of the menu is just as tempting, with options such as lobster, haddock, flounder, and steaks. Service is extremely attentive. Note that Obrycki's is open only during the local crab season.

1727 E. Pratt St. ℂ **410/732-6399.** www.obryckis.com. Reservations recommended, but accepted only until 7pm Mon–Fri, 6pm Sat–Sun. Main courses $17–$37; lunch and light fare $8–$16. AE, DC, DISC, MC, V. Mon–Fri 11:30am–10pm; Sat 11:30am–11pm; Sun 11:30am–9:30pm. Closed Dec to mid-Mar.

Moderate

Annabel Lee Tavern ★ PUB FARE   Baltimore street corners all over the city have these tiny neighborhood taverns. This one is worth going out of the way for—and you'll have to search for it. Phrases from Edgar Allan Poe's famous poem are painted on the walls and the master of horror's portrait is everywhere. But the menu is sheer comfort: crisp salads, upscale appetizers including a yummy flatbread pizza topped with crab dip, burgers, and sandwiches along with the microbrew beers and fancy cocktails.

7601 S. Clinton St. ℂ **410/522-2929.** www.annabelleetavern.com. No reservations but call ahead to get on the seating list. Main courses and appetizers $8–$15. AE, MC, V. Mon–Sat 4pm–1am.

Bertha's Restaurant & Bar ★ INTERNATIONAL/SEAFOOD

This Fell's Point landmark is known for its mussels and music. The decor is shabby chic, with dark walls and plenty of accessories proud of their age. It's a perfect place for a traditional afternoon tea, a dinner featuring Bertha's mussels, or a night of jazz or blues. Mussels are famous here, prepared in a dozen different ways—they're delicious swimming in garlic butter. The entire menu is available all day with a few lunch specials offered daily. It's heavy on seafood. Afternoon tea is served Monday through Saturday from 3 to 4:30pm; reservations are required. Brunch is served on Sundays. The music starts playing most evenings after 9pm.

734 S. Broadway. ℂ **410/327-5795.** www.berthas.com. Reservations accepted only for parties of 6 or more for lunch and dinner; reservations required 24 hr. in advance for afternoon tea. Main courses $7–$19 lunch, $12–$22 dinner; afternoon tea $10. MC, V. Sun–Thurs 11:30am–11pm; Fri–Sat 11:30am–midnight. Bar open until 2pm.

Pierpoint Restaurant ★ REGIONAL

Chef Nancy Longo has won accolades for her creative American cuisine with its Maryland and Italian roots. Smoked crab cakes are a specialty, but you'll also be delighted with the stylish preparations of tenderloin, duck breast, or oysters. Each season brings new dishes. The 44-seat restaurant is a quirky little place with a big bar up front.

1822 Aliceanna St. ℂ **410/675-2080.** www.pierpointrestaurant.com. Reservations required for lunch, recommended for dinner. Main courses $6–$14 lunch, $19–$26 dinner. AE, DC, DISC, MC, V. Tues–Fri 11:30am–2pm; Tues–Thurs 5–9:30pm; Fri–Sat 5:30–10:30pm; Sun 10:30am–1:30pm and 4–9pm.

Ze Mean Bean Café EASTERN EUROPEAN

At this cozy European-style cafe, you can count on an attentive waitstaff, a menu that maintains its ties to Eastern Europe (this area is rich in Polish and Ukrainian heritage) while trying new things, and food that lives up to its promise. Sample the pierogi or borscht, or try the signature chicken Kiev. Thursday is Slavic night with $9.95 dinners. The lunch menu includes salads and sandwiches. Brunch is served Saturday and Sunday, with jazz on Sunday. Acoustic music is offered weekends.

1739 Fleet St. ℂ **410/675-5999.** www.zemeanbean.com. Reservations recommended. Main courses $12–$20 lunch, $12–$23 dinner. AE, DC, DISC, MC, V. Mon–Thurs 11am–11pm; Fri 11am–1am; Sat 9:30am–1am; Sun 9am–11pm.

Inexpensive

Bonaparte Breads BAKERY/FRENCH

This wonderful little spot is part bakery, part cafe, all French. You can take out fresh pastries or bread studded with olives and herbs. Or you can stop in for the breakfast or lunch special. At lunchtime, walk up to the counter and choose from the numerous sandwiches and quiches (the seafood quiche is rich and creamy). Then pull up a leather chair at one of the tables; if you're lucky, you'll sit by the windows looking out at the harbor. After lunch, check out the fresh tarts filled with fruit and sugar, which are all good.

903 S. Ann St. ℂ **410/342-4000.** Reservations not accepted. Breakfast special $7.95; lunch special $15. AE, MC, V. Daily 8am–6pm. Lunch served only until 4pm, but breads and pastries available until 6pm.

Helen's Garden AMERICAN   There's no pretension here, just honest comfort food with a few spicy twists. The dining rooms are set on two floors of two rowhouses with a bar on the lower level. Prix-fixe dinners on Tuesday, a special Wednesday menu, and discounted wines on Thursday keep tables filled. Pork chops are meaty, and burgers come with mango chutney or au poivre. Chicken, catfish, pasta carbonara, and pecan-crusted trout are on the menu, too, along with 50 wines by the glass.

2908 O'Donnell St. ☎ **410/276-2233.** www.helensgarden.com. Reservations accepted Thurs–Tues. Main courses $7–$12 lunch, $17–$25 dinner. DISC, MC, V. Tues–Thurs 11:30am–9pm; Fri–Sat 11:30am–10pm; Sun 11am–2pm and 5–9pm. Valet parking available Thurs–Sun.

Jack's Bistro INTERNATIONAL   The menu offers a variety of meat and seafood dishes—but not what you'd expect in Baltimore. Termed "coastal" cuisine, dishes are prepared with a unique blend of seasonings from Asia to South America, as well as a shot of Guinness stout here and there. A neighborhood gathering spot, Jack's is casual. If you were wondering, the restaurant's name comes from Jack Tripper's place on *Three's Company.*

3123 Elliott St. ☎ **410/878-6542.** www.jacksbistro.net. Reservations accepted only for parties of 6 or more. Main courses $18–$25. AE, MC, V. Wed–Sun 5–10pm.

Matthew's Pizza PIZZA   At this little hole in the wall, they know how to make a perfect pizza: soft chewy crust, tomatoey sauce, and the right amount of gooey cheese. They've had some practice—they've been here since 1943. There is also a location at 2908 O'Donnell St.

3131 Eastern Ave. ☎ **410/276-8755.** www.matthewspizza.com. Reservations not accepted. Main courses $5–$13. AE, DISC, MC, V. Mon–Thurs 11am–10pm; Fri–Sat 11am–11pm; Sun noon–9pm.

MOUNT VERNON

Expensive

The Prime Rib ★★★ STEAK   In the heart of Mount Vernon, this restaurant has been dishing out the beef since 1965. The prime rib is the best in town; the Caesar salad is dressed to perfection; and the lobster bisque is rich and creamy. If you want seafood, there are crab cakes and fish. Everything is a la carte. The classic setting—lots of brass, black leather, and flowers—can get noisy when there's a crowd but mostly is a romantic spot for enjoying classic food. Music almost every night adds to the ambience.

1101 N. Calvert St. (btw. Biddle and Chase sts.). ☎ **410/539-1804.** www.theprimerib.com. Reservations required. Jackets are requested for men on Sat. Main courses $21–$45. AE, DC, MC, V. Mon–Thurs 5–10pm; Fri–Sat 5pm–midnight; Sun 4–10pm. Bar fare until 1am. Free valet parking.

Moderate

Sammy's Trattoria ITALIAN   Casual enough for a quick bite but pretty enough for a romantic dinner, Sammy's has a location that makes it a great choice for pre-symphony dining. The menu is split between pasta dishes and Italian favorites such as chicken Marsala and shrimp scampi. Panini, salads, and smaller versions of dinner entrees are offered at lunch.

1200 N. Charles St. ☎ **410/837-9999.** www.sammystrattoria.com. Reservations recommended. Main courses $15–$29 dinner, $10–$17 lunch. AE, DISC, MC, V. Mon 5–9pm; Tues–Fri 11:30am–10pm; Sat 5–11pm; Sun 5–9pm. Valet parking Thurs–Sun.

Sascha's 527 Café ★ AMERICAN   Sascha's has put together an eclectic menu and a colorful but sophisticated dining room, with high ceilings and velvet banquettes. Dinner choices range from burgers to seafood entrees, but the "taste plates" are where Sascha's shines. These range from a cone of fries to mini bison burgers to Sascha's decadent BLT with lobster. At lunch, the restaurant goes buffet style, with salads, panini, and soup.

527 N. Charles St. (© 410/539-8880. www.saschas.com/restaurant.html. Reservations accepted only for parties of 5 or more. Main courses $6–$9 lunch, $15–$24 dinner; taste plates $5–$13. AE, DC, MC, V. Mon–Fri 11am–3pm; Mon–Wed 5:30–10pm; Thurs 5:30–11pm; Fri–Sat 5:30pm–midnight.

Tapas Teatro ★★ TAPAS   Tapas are big in Baltimore—and as pretty as Sascha's is, the food here is even better. The restaurant, adjacent to the Charles Theatre, is an ode to industrial chic, with exposed-brick walls and metal accents. The refinement is in the food, which changes seasonally: colorful salads, rockfish, country bread rubbed with Maryland tomatoes and Asiago cheese. Need something hearty? Try the paella. Sangria makes a nice accompaniment, or taste one of the 37 wines or 15 beers. The desserts are a delight to the eye and a pleasure to the palate.

1711 N. Charles St. (© 410/332-0110. www.tapasteatro.net. Reservations not accepted. Tapas and main courses $5–$15. AE, DISC, MC, V. Tues–Fri 5pm–2am (tapas served until 11pm); Sat–Sun 4pm–2am (tapas menu served until midnight).

Tío Pepe ★★ SPANISH   Walk down the stairs into whitewashed rooms that resemble a wine cellar. Spanish artwork, wrought iron, and pottery decorate the tiny dining rooms that seem to go on and on. Start with the fruity sangria. The menu's highlights include shrimp in garlic sauce, sole with bananas and hollandaise sauce, and dramatic paella. Dessert is a standout: Try the flan, chocolate soufflé, or the roll cakes. Tío Pepe is a special-occasion restaurant for Baltimoreans, so reservations are a must.

10 E. Franklin St. (off Charles St.). (© 410/539-4675. Reservations recommended (as far as 3 weeks in advance for Sat night). Jackets suggested. Main courses $11–$25 lunch, $18–$35 dinner. AE, DC, DISC, MC, V. Mon–Fri 11:30am–3pm; Mon–Thurs 5–10pm; Fri 5–11pm; Sat 5–11:30pm; Sun 4–10pm.

NORTH OF DOWNTOWN
Moderate
Gertrude's ★★ (Finds) SEAFOOD   Pause at Gertrude's during a visit to the Baltimore Museum of Art. Chef and cookbook author John Shields has created a restaurant filled with local delights—making this place a destination in itself. The sleek space has tall windows overlooking the sculpture garden, with outdoor seating in warm weather. The menu includes soups (such as rich cream of crab) and sandwiches (with plenty of Old Bay Seasoning on the shrimp)—and entrees where Chesapeake seafood has a starring role. If you're feeling adventurous, you might like the small plates, such as citrus barbecue shrimp or portobello crab imperial. Tuesday dinner specials feature $10 entrees. Brunch is served Saturday and Sunday.

At the Baltimore Museum of Art, 10 Art Museum Dr. (© 410/889-3399. www.gertrudesbaltimore.com. Reservations recommended. Main courses $9–$15 lunch, $17–$26 dinner. AE, DC, MC, V. Tues–Fri 11:30am–9pm; Sat 10am–3pm and 5–9pm; Sun 10am–3pm and 5–8pm.

Inexpensive
Cafe Hon (Kids) AMERICAN/DINER   Elvis greets guests, but the real star at this Hampden institution is homey comfort food. The specialty is "Much Better than Mom's" meatloaf with mashed potatoes. At dinner, you'll find spaghetti, pork chops, and roast beef. The lunch menu includes chicken salad, grilled cheese, burgers, and blue-plate specials. Come for breakfast and get killer coffee and "Hon Buns," cinnamon rolls as big as your hand. The menu always lists something any kid will eat.

1002 W. 36th St. (at Roland Ave.). ℂ **410/243-1230.** www.cafehon.com. Reservations not accepted. Main courses $6–$13 lunch, $12–$27 dinner. AE, DC, DISC, MC, V. Mon–Thurs 7am–9pm; Fri 7am–10pm; Sat 9am–10pm; Sun 9am–8pm.

Chocolatea CAFE   It's worth a stop, if only for a couple of truffles and a chai latte, or maybe a salad or sandwich after a visit to the nearby Baltimore Museum of Art. The shop's atmosphere is more Starbucks than Jane Austen. They have good tea, from oolong to pearl jasmine. American-style breakfast every morning gives way to dumplings, rice bowls, and other Asian-style lunch fare. There's free Wi-Fi, too.

39th St. and Canterbury Rd. ℂ **410/366-0095.** www.chocolateacafe.com. Reservations not accepted. Main courses $4–$8 breakfast, $6–$9 lunch. AE, DISC, MC, V. Mon–Fri 8am–9pm; Sat 9am–7pm; Sun 9am–5pm.

The Dogwood ★★★ ORGANIC AMERICAN   Though not yet the Chez Panisse of the East, Dogwood may be on its way. The menu by one of Baltimore's celebrity chefs Galen Sampson features organic meats and produce from Maryland and Pennsylvania outlets in an eclectic combination of creative dinner entrees that celebrate the best of each season. Look for mushroom risotto, rabbit salad, an autumn-root-vegetable cobbler, as well as local beef, chicken, and duck, napped in rich sauces. The basement dining room is sleek and dark with a cool vibe.

911 W. 36th St. ℂ **410/889-0952.** www.dogwoodbaltimore.com. Reservations recommended for dinner. Main courses $16–$31. AE, DISC, MC, V. Mon–Thurs 5–10pm; Fri–Sat 5–11pm.

PaperMoon Diner AMERICAN/DINER   This funky restaurant is a college student favorite, but anyone with a sense of fun will like all the toys and knickknacks lurking about. Though no longer open 24 hours, it's still open very late. The burgers, sandwiches, breakfast items, and vegetarian options served all day are good. So is the cake, lots of cake.

227 W. 29th St. (btw. Remington Ave. and Howard St.). ℂ **410/889-4444.** www.papermoondiner24.com. Reservations not accepted. Main courses $6–$14. MC, V. Sun–Thurs 7am–midnight; Fri–Sat 7am–2am.

MOUNT WASHINGTON VILLAGE

Crêpe du Jour FRENCH   The bright yellow-and-blue porch may attract your eye, but the huge savory and sweet crepes will thrill your taste buds. Crepes come with all kinds of fillings: ratatouille; walnuts, blue cheese, and mesclun; sugar and lemon. At dinner, the menu expands to include French-flavored steak, chicken, and seafood entrees. Sidewalk tables and a deck increase the dining space in warm months.

1609 Sulgrave Ave. ℂ **410/542-9000.** www.crepedujour.com. Reservations suggested for dinner and Sat–Sun brunch. Crepes and sandwiches $4–$16; dinner main courses $14–$26. AE, DISC, MC, V. Mon 11am–3pm and 5–9pm; Tues–Thurs 11am–10pm; Fri 10am–11pm; Sat 10am–11pm; Sun 10am–9pm. Valet parking available.

Ethel and Ramone's ★ CAJUN   On a little street in Mount Washington, you'll be confronted with four intriguing restaurants on the same short block. Ethel and Ramone's is the place for Cajun-style food. The folks who run this offbeat eatery know good food. Get the gumbo—it's spicy, filling, and rich with andouille sausage and chicken. Other Louisiana favorites include red beans and rice, jambalaya, and blackened fish. Lunch is mostly overstuffed sandwiches, including po'boys. Breakfast is offered from 7 to 11am. There's seating outdoors in warm weather.

1615 Sulgrave Ave. ℂ **410/664-2971.** www.ethelandramones.com. Reservations recommended for dinner. Main courses $9–$13 lunch, $13–$25 dinner. AE, DISC, MC, V. Tues–Thurs 7am–3pm and 5:30–9pm; Fri–Sat 11am–3pm and 5:30–10pm; Sun 5:30–10pm.

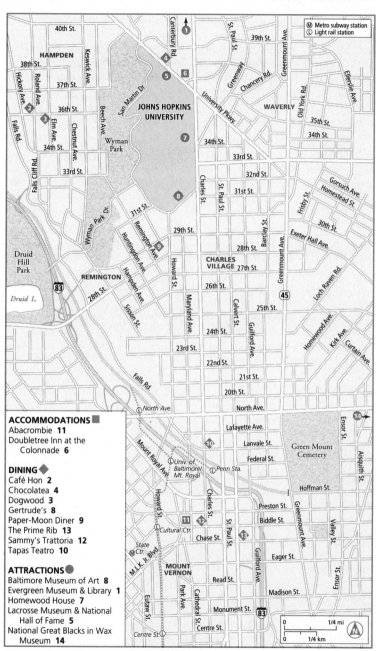

Metro subway station
Light rail station

40th St.

HAMPDEN

38th St.

Keswick Ave.

Hickory Ave.

Roland Ave.

37th St.

36th St.

Elm Ave.

Beech Ave.

Chestnut Ave.

35th St.

34th St.

Falls Rd.

Falls Cliff Rd.

33rd St.

San Martin Dr.

Wyman Park Dr.

JOHNS HOPKINS UNIVERSITY

Wyman Park

Druid Hill Park

Druid L.

REMINGTON

28th St.

Sisson St.

Huntingdon Ave.

Remington Ave.

Hampden Ave.

31st St.

29th St.

Howard St.

Maryland Ave.

Canterbury Rd.

University Pkwy.

Greenway

Chancery Rd.

St. Paul St.

39th St.

Greenmount Ave.

Ellerslie Ave.

WAVERLY

35th St.

34th St.

34th St.

33rd St.

32nd St.

31st St.

Charles St.

St. Paul St.

28th St.

CHARLES VILLAGE 27th St.

26th St.

25th St.

24th St.

23rd St.

22nd St.

21st St.

20th St.

Barclay St.

Guilford Ave.

Calvert St.

Gorsuch Ave.

Homestead St.

Frisby St.

30th St.

Exeter Hall Ave.

Loch Raven Rd.

Homewood Ave.

Kirk Ave.

Curtain Ave.

Old York Rd.

North Ave.

North Ave.

Lafayette Ave.

Lanvale St.

Federal St.

Mount Royal Ave.

Univ. of Baltimore/ Mt. Royal

Penn Sta.

Howard St.

Charles St.

St. Paul St.

Green Mount Cemetery

Hoffman St.

Preston St.

Biddle St.

Ensor St.

Aisquith St.

Valley St.

Ensor St.

Hoffman St.

Cultural Ctr.

Chase St.

State Ctr.

M.L.K. Jr. Blvd.

Eutaw St.

MOUNT VERNON

Park Ave.

Cathedral St.

Charles St.

Read St.

Madison St.

Monument St.

Centre St.

Centre St.

Guilford Ave.

Greenmount Ave.

Eager St.

ACCOMMODATIONS
Abacrombie **11**
Doubletree Inn at the
  Colonnade **6**

DINING
Café Hon **2**
Chocolatea **4**
Dogwood **3**
Gertrude's **8**
Paper-Moon Diner **9**
The Prime Rib **13**
Sammy's Trattoria **12**
Tapas Teatro **10**

ATTRACTIONS
Baltimore Museum of Art **8**
Evergreen Museum & Library **1**
Homewood House **7**
Lacrosse Museum & National
  Hall of Fame **5**
National Great Blacks in Wax
  Museum **14**

0   1/4 mi
0   1/4 km

The Mount Washington Tavern AMERICAN   This sprawling restaurant, beloved by locals, has bars where you can watch the ballgame, wood-paneled nooks for intimate dining, and a garden room elegant enough for special occasions. It's big enough that if the Ravens score, those in the dining room never know it. The menu offers seafood, steaks, and a raw bar. Light fare, crab cakes, sandwiches, and burgers are available at lunch. Try the individual pizzas or come for Sunday brunch from noon to 3pm.

5700 Newbury St. ✆ **410/367-6903.** www.mtwashingtontavern.com. Reservations recommended on weekends. Main courses $7–$13 lunch, $8–$27 dinner. AE, DC, DISC, MC, V. Mon–Sat 11:30am–11pm; Sun 10:30am–10pm. Bar open until 2am daily.

FEDERAL HILL/SOUTH BALTIMORE

Corks ★ WINE BAR   Watch the cooks in action in the front room or head to the back for a cozier, quieter place to savor wine by the glass or the bottle and enjoy a wide variety of choices—everything from cheesy fondue to a burger to a rich vegetable pasta or porterhouse pork chop. Something's going to make you happy here.

1026 S. Charles St. ✆ **410/752-3810.** www.corksrestaurant.com. Reservations recommended for dinner on Sat–Sun. Main courses $7–$11 lunch, $14–$22 dinner. AE, DISC, MC, V. Mon 11:30am–10pm; Tues–Sat 11:30am–10pm; Sun 10am–10pm.

Nick's Fish House Finds SEAFOOD   You're going to have to look for this place. But once you raise a cold beer or savory crab cake to your lips and look out at the old, non-glitzy Patapsco River, you'll be glad you did. Two dining rooms with water views, a bar reminiscent of a beach shack, and waterside dining in summer take full advantage of the location. The menu is seafood all the way, though you can get a pretty good burger (topped with crab if you like). There is live music on Friday nights. Brunch is served Sunday. Plus you can come by boat; there are slips available.

2600 Insulator Dr. (off Hanover St.). ✆ **410/FISH-123** (347-4123). www.nicksfishhouse.com. Reservations recommended on Sat–Sun. Main courses $8–$12 lunch, $18–$27 dinner. AE, DISC, MC, V. Daily 11am–9pm.

The Wine Market ★ WINE BAR   Tucked behind a huge wine shop is this casual food-and-wine fan's paradise. The industrial chic dining room in an old foundry is delightful but in warm weather the patio makes an even better place to sample one of the many wines by the glass and the menu filled with everything from small plates (oysters, flatbread pizza, and cheese) to light fare (sandwiches and salads) to serious entrees such as rib-eye, fish, and braised-meat dishes. Order your wine from the wine list or stop in the shop and pick out your own bottle.

921 E. Fort Ave. ✆ **410/244-6166.** www.the-wine-market.com. Reservations recommended on Fri–Sat. Main courses $10–$14 lunch, $15–$26 dinner. AE, DISC, MC, V. Lunch Tues–Fri 11:30am–4pm; dinner nightly 5–9pm; Sun brunch 11am–4pm.

5 ATTRACTIONS

INNER HARBOR ★★★

Although much of Baltimore's business takes place along Charles Street, the city's focal point for tourism is the Inner Harbor, home of the Baltimore Convention Center, Harborplace shopping pavilions, Oriole Park at Camden Yards, M&T Bank Stadium, National Aquarium, Pier Six Concert Pavilion, and Reginald F. Lewis Museum of Maryland African

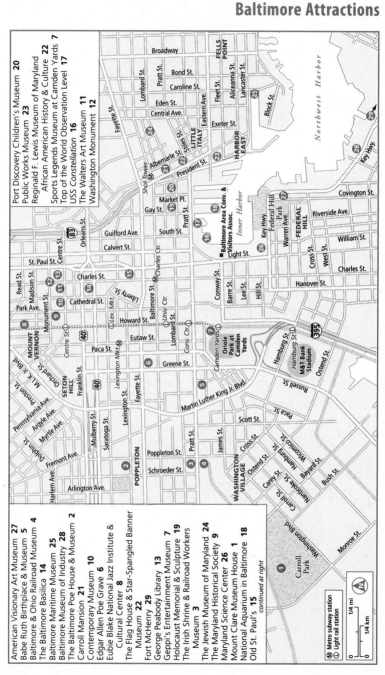

Port Discovery Children's Museum 20
Public Works Museum 23
Reginald F. Lewis Museum of Maryland
African American History & Culture 22
Sports Legends Museum at Camden Yards 7
Top of the World Observation Level 17
USS Constellation 16
The Walters Art Museum 11
Washington Monument 12

American Visionary Art Museum 27
Babe Ruth Birthplace & Museum 5
Baltimore & Ohio Railroad Museum 4
The Baltimore Basilica 14
Baltimore Maritime Museum 25
Baltimore Museum of Industry 28
The Baltimore Poe House & Museum 2
Carroll Mansion 21
Contemporary Museum 10
Edgar Allen Poe Grave 6
Eubie Blake National Jazz Institute &
Cultural Center 8
The Flag House & Star-Spangled Banner
Museum 22
Fort McHenry 29
George Peabody Library 13
Geppi's Entertainment Museum 7
Holocaust Memorial & Sculpture 19
The Irish Shrine & Railroad Workers
Museum 3
The Jewish Museum of Maryland 24
The Maryland Historical Society 9
Maryland Science Center 26
Mount Clare Museum House 1
National Aquarium in Baltimore 18
Old St. Paul's 15
continued at right

BALTIMORE

5

ATTRACTIONS

Value **Money-Saving Harbor Pass**

Baltimore's top tourism spots have teamed up with **Harbor Pass.** For $57 for adults and $38 for kids, visit the National Aquarium, Maryland Science Center, Port Discovery or American Visionary Art Museum, Sports Legends at Camden Yards, and Top of the World Observation Level. The passes are valid for 4 consecutive days, but only one visit per location. Order in advance for a 20% discount at ℂ **877/BALTIMORE** (225-8466) or **www.baltimore.org**. Or pick them up at the Inner Harbor visitor center.

American History & Culture. That having been said, Baltimore is also still a working deepwater port. Boats from all over dock just beyond the Domino Sugar sign. At the Inner Harbor sea wall, it's not unusual to see naval vessels and tall ships and their crews from around the world.

American Visionary Art Museum ★   This curvaceous building is marked by the "Whirligig," a 55-foot wind-powered sculpture at the front. "Visionary" art is created by people who lack artistic training but feel compelled to draw, paint, or build a ship with matchsticks. Everything here is fascinating; some of it can be quite troubling. And the artists' stories are as interesting as their art. You'll be entranced from the moment you set your eyes on Emery Blagdon's "Healing Machines" mobile hanging down three stories. Some work is too strong for children (the museum will alert you to that); other exhibits are a joy for any age. On Thursdays during June through August, a free movie is screened on the side of the museum's building. The museum stays open until 9pm on those days. Check the website for film listings.

800 Key Hwy. (take Light St. south, turn left onto Key Hwy. at the Maryland Science Center; museum is about 3 blocks farther on the right). ℂ **410/244-1900.** www.avam.org. Admission $12 adults; $8 seniors, students, and children. Tues–Sun 10am–6pm. Closed Thanksgiving and Dec 25.

Baltimore Museum of Industry (Finds) (Kids)   Housed in a former oyster-packing house on the harbor's southern bank, this museum gives visitors a look at the industries that made Baltimore a manufacturing capital in the 1880s—canning, printing, and garment-making. It's geared toward children, with exhibits set up so kids can get their hands on the oyster-shucking stations, antique irons, and movable type. Tour guides are sensitive to kids' attention spans and adjust their talks for the younger visitors. You can wander around on your own, but the exhibits aren't as interesting without the guides' stories. Wall-size pictures recall the days before child labor laws, and other displays include a collection of antique delivery trucks and one of only two working steam tugboats in the country. The museum is a few blocks from Fort McHenry; a visit to both—with a picnic on the fort's lawn—could make a great day.

1415 Key Hwy. ℂ **410/727-4808.** www.thebmi.org. Admission $10 adults, $6 students and seniors. Tues–Sat 10am–4pm; Sun 11am–4pm. Closed Memorial Day, Thanksgiving, and Dec 24–25. Bus: 1 to Fort Ave., 1 block south of the museum. Water taxis stop nearby.

Fort McHenry ★★★ (Moments) (Kids)   The flag that flies at Fort McHenry is 30×42 feet, big enough to see "by the dawn's early light." Its 15 stars and stripes still fly as boldly as they did at the Battle of Baltimore, when U.S. soldiers reclaimed American independence from the British in the War of 1812. The star-shaped fort looks much as it did then, and its buildings, repaired in the days following the attack, still stand. The star-spangled banner is central to this fort, a national monument. A talk about the flag is offered every day at noon; Fort McHenry Guardsmen (living-history volunteers) are on duty noon to 4pm on summer weekends. Visitors are invited to take part in the daily changing of the flag (9:30am or 4:30pm, 7:30pm June–Aug)—in fact, because the flag is so big, around 20 people are needed to keep it off the ground. The large flag flies only during daylight hours (weather permitting); a smaller flag flies at night.

Exhibits recall Baltimore under siege during the War of 1812 and the fort's service during the Civil War and as a World War I army hospital. Allow at least 90 minutes for a visit. The 15-minute film shown every 20 minutes is a good introduction to the fort. A new visitor center, with updated exhibits and high-tech displays, will open by early 2011. Fort McHenry sits on a point in the harbor from which visitors can see the Inner Harbor, the Patapsco River, and down to the Chesapeake Bay. Visits to the park outside the fort are free, and picnicking is allowed.

The **Star-Spangled Banner Weekend,** held in mid-September, recalls the British attack on the fort. Flags are everywhere here on **Flag Day,** June 14. On select Sundays from 6 to 8pm, military bands perform with a color guard, drill teams, and the Fort McHenry Guard dressed in 19th-century uniforms, a ceremony that began in 1803. Admission to this ceremony is free; call or visit the website for a schedule.

Fort McHenry National Monument, E. Fort Ave. ℂ **410/962-4290.** www.nps.gov/fomc. Admission $7 adults, free for children 16 and under. Sept–May fort and grounds daily 8am–5pm; June to Labor Day grounds remain open daily until 8pm. Closed Thanksgiving, Dec 25, and Jan 1. Bus: 1. Water taxi stop.

Historic Ships in Baltimore ★★ (Kids)   With the USS *Constellation* as its center-piece, this collection of ships and a lighthouse offers a glimpse at American maritime history. The **Coast Guard Cutter** *Taney* survived the bombing of Pearl Harbor. The submarine USS *Torsk* sank the last two Japanese merchant ships of World War II and still holds the record for the most dives and resurfacings of any sub. The lightship *Chesapeake* spent 40 years anchored near the mouth of the Chesapeake Bay. The **Seven Foot Knoll Lighthouse** once welcomed immigrants to Baltimore—admission here is always free. Each provides an interesting glimpse into the lives of 20th-century sailors. Certainly the star is the *Constellation,* docked in front of Harborplace. A triple-masted sloop-of-war launched in 1854, the *Constellation* is the last Civil War–era vessel afloat. It's most notable for its efforts fighting the transatlantic slave trade. Tour her gun decks, visit the wardrooms, see a cannon fired, and learn about the sailor's life. Demonstrations begin with the raising of the colors at 10:30am and continue on the hour. The Fourth of July picnics and New Year's Eve receptions end with fireworks (tickets are required). Downtown visitors should note that the ship's cannon is fired daily at noon. "Powder Monkey" tours are directed at children 6 and over.

Piers 1, 3, and 5, Inner Harbor. ℂ **410/396-3453.** www.historicships.org. Admission for 1 ship: $10 adults, $8 seniors, $5 children 6–14; for 2 ships: $13 adults, $11 seniors, $6 children; for 4 ships: $16 adults, $13 seniors, $7 children. Buy tickets at the booth near the National Aquarium or beside the *Constellation*. *Constellation, Torsk, Chesapeake* hours: Mar–May and Sept–Oct daily 10am–5:30pm; June–Aug Mon–Fri 10am–5:30pm, Sat–Sun 10am–7pm; Nov–Feb daily 10am–4:30pm. *Taney, Lighthouse* hours: Mar–May and Sept–Oct daily 10am–4:30pm; June–Aug daily 10am–4:30pm; Nov–Dec 10am–3:30pm. Closed Jan–Feb. All ships closed Thanksgiving, Dec 25, and Jan 1.

Maryland Science Center ★ (Kids)   Three floors of exhibits include the popular Our Place in Space—with a huge weather globe display, dazzling Hubble Space Telescope pictures, links to NASA, and spacesuits kids can try on—and the towering dinosaurs of

DinoQuest. Children get a kick out of the hands-on exhibits of Newton's Alley and the Body Link, and everybody likes the IMAX theater and planetarium. The IMAX movies, which range from *Beauty and the Beast* to *Space Station 3D,* are so popular that extra screenings are held Friday and Saturday evenings, for $8 to $12 per ticket. The stars are on display at the Davis Planetarium and the Crosby Ramsey Observatory; the observatory is free to the public on Friday nights, weather permitting (call for hours). On Friday nights, admission to exhibits, the planetarium, and IMAX is $8 from 5 to 8pm, and on autumn Saturday mornings, visitors get a $5 discount and an egg to drop off the roof after designing a protective covering for it.

601 Light St. (south side of the Inner Harbor). ☎ 410/685-5225. www.mdsci.org. Admission varies according to exhibits: core experience with planetarium $15 adults, $11 children 3–12; core experience with planetarium and IMAX film $19 adults, $15 children 3–12; special exhibits additional charge. Oct–Apr Tues–Thurs 10am–5pm, Fri 10am–8pm, Sat 10am–6pm, Sun 11am–5pm; Nov–Mar Thurs–Sat 10am–8pm, Sun–Wed 10am–6pm. Call ahead, as hours change with some exhibits. Water taxi stop.

National Aquarium Baltimore ★★★ (**Kids**) Walk into a room surrounded by patrolling sharks, stroll among coral reefs, and visit a rainforest on the roof of one of the best aquariums in the country. **Animal Planet Australia: Wild Extremes,** set in a 120-foot-tall glass cube at the front of the aquarium, takes visitors to the floor of an Australian river gorge. In this immersion exhibit, wander past tanks filled with death adders, pythons, archer fish, and barramundi, while kookaburras, parrots, and lorikeets fly overhead—1,800 animals, as well as plants native to Australia. On a cold day, skip right to the top of the aquarium and bask in the tropical heat that envelops the brightly colored birds, the shy iguana, and the sloth who reside on this level. (It's best any day to come straight here when the aquarium opens and the animals are most active.) Although you simply walk in front of most exhibits, you walk inside the doughnut-shaped coral reef and shark tanks, getting up close to these exotic creatures. At feeding time in the coral reef, the divers always draw a crowd. The **Marine Mammal Pavilion,** connected by covered bridge to the main hall, is home to the dolphins. Don't miss the presentations—reserve a seat when you pay your admission. Presentations are canceled if a baby dolphin was born recently, but you can stop in and watch the dolphins and stay as long as you want. **4-D Immersion Theatre** shows 3-D movies, with added sensory effect, throughout the day. *Tip:* Crowds are huge in summer. Beat the crush by purchasing timed tickets in advance, either in person or through the aquarium's website. Nonpeak visiting hours are weekday mornings, Fridays when the aquarium stays open until 8pm, and any day after 3pm.

501 E. Pratt St. (on the harbor). ☎ 410/576-3800. www.aqua.org. Admission to aquarium only $25 adults, $24 seniors, $15 children 3–11. Aquarium and dolphin presentation $28 adults, $25 seniors, $18 children. All programs $30 adults, $29 seniors, $20 children. Mar–June and Sept–Oct Sat–Thurs 9am–5pm, Fri 9am–8pm; Nov–Feb Mon–Thurs 10am–4pm, Fri 10am–8pm, Sat–Sun 10am–5pm; July–Aug Mon–Thurs 9am–5pm, Fri–Sat 9am–6pm, Sun 9am–6pm. Hours subject to change; call ahead. Exhibits are open 2 hr. after last ticket is sold.

Port Discovery Children's Museum ★★ (**Kids**) At this kid-powered museum with three floors of exhibits, children of all ages—though mostly ages 2 to 10—can cross the Nile to explore ancient Egypt, crawl through a kitchen drain to solve a mystery in Miss Perception's Mystery House, and climb the three-story-high Kidworks. Walt Disney Company Imagineers designed many of the exhibits. Buy groceries and fill up your car's tank at the convenience store and stop at the diner. Wonders of Water is wet but it sure is fun. Story times for toddlers are offered Tuesday through Friday at 11:30am; Saturday at 11am, noon, and 1pm; and Sunday at 3:30pm. There are also changing exhibits every quarter.

35 Market Place. ☎ **410/727-8120.** www.portdiscovery.org. Admission $13 ages 2 and older. Oct–May Tues–Fri 9:30am–4:30pm, Sat 10am–5pm, Sun noon–5pm; Memorial Day to Labor Day Mon–Sat 10am–5pm, Sun noon–5pm; Sept Fri 9:30am–4:30pm, Sat 10am–5pm, Sun noon–5pm. Bus: 7, 10, 19, or 20. Metro: Shot Tower. Closed Thanksgiving and Dec 25.

Top of the World Observation Level   For a 360-degree view of the city, head to the 27th floor of the World Trade Center, the world's tallest pentagonal building, next to Harborplace. In addition to the view, you can acquire a bit of background about Baltimore from the exhibits, hands-on displays, and multimedia presentations. The area is accessible to visitors with disabilities.

401 E. Pratt St. (on the harbor). ☎ **410/837-8439.** Admission $5 adults, $4 seniors, $3 children 3–16. Sept–May Wed–Sun 10am–6pm; June–Aug Sun–Fri 10am–6pm, Sat 10am–8pm. Tickets sold in the lobby up to a half-hour before closing.

NEAR LITTLE ITALY & FELL'S POINT

Carroll Mansion & Phoenix Shot Tower   When Charles Carroll of Carrollton lived in the mansion here, people knocked on his door to meet the last living signer of the Declaration of Independence. After he died in 1832, in a room on the second floor, this stately home became the German Working Man's Club, and then a tenement filled with Russian-born tailors, and finally a recreation center with a basketball court. Slowly, the home is being restored but Carroll's bedroom and his library are open for visitors. The **Phoenix Shot Tower** nearby is open only by appointment for a 10:30am tour on Saturday or Sunday. Call 2 weeks in advance. Inside the 1828 tower, shot was made by dropping lead down the shaft.

800 E. Lombard St. ☎ **410/605-2964.** www.carrollmuseums.org. Admission $5 adults; $4 students, seniors, and military. Sat–Sun noon–4pm; last tour at 3pm.

Creative Alliance at The Patterson (Finds)   This Highlandtown venue's gallery and performance space celebrate local arts. Contemporary artwork in all mediums is on display, and the auditorium is the site of classic-film series and special events. Though much of the work is edgy, more mainstream works also have their place. It's worth going out of your way for a taste of the Baltimore arts scene. Events are listed on the website.

3134 Eastern Ave. (from downtown, take Pratt St. east, head south around Patterson Park to Eastern Ave., and continue on Eastern Ave. to Highlandtown). ☎ **410/276-1651.** www.creativealliance.org. Free admission to gallery. Tickets for films and performances $5–$20. Gallery Tues–Fri 11am–5pm, Sat 9:30am–5pm; film and performance times vary.

Fell's Point Visitor Center (Finds)   Home to the Fell's Point Preservation Society, the visitor center has maritime and historical exhibits of the people and places that have made Fell's Point unique. Plenty of walking tours depart from here (p. 90). Tours of the 1765 Robert Long House around the corner on Ann Street, the oldest residence in Baltimore Town, are offered Tuesday through Saturday at 1:30pm. There is a gift shop and performance space, too.

1724 Thames St., Fell's Point. ☎ **410/276-1651.** www.preservationsociety.org. Free admission to gallery. Admission to Long House $5. Dec–Mar Sun and Tues–Fri noon–5pm, Sat 11am–7pm; Apr–Nov Sun and Tues–Thurs noon–5pm, Fri 11am–8pm, Sat 11am–7pm.

The Jewish Museum of Maryland   A visit to this compound offers insight into local Jewish history, a glimpse of Jewish traditions, and a look at the immigration experience. The 1845 Lloyd Street Synagogue is Maryland's oldest (and one of the oldest in the U.S.). It's plainer than the nearby B'nai Israel Synagogue, but it has a matzo oven, a mikvah (ritual bath), and a classroom where the first Hebrew school got its start. The building was restored in 2009 in time for the JMM's 50th anniversary in 2010. The Greek Revival–style B'nai Israel Synagogue, built in 1876, contains what may be the oldest Jewish star in one of its stained-glass windows. Its ark is a hand-carved masterpiece. Take a tour of the synagogues at 1 or 2:30pm for the best experience; the guides are full of stories. Between the two synagogues are exhibit space and library. The exhibits change often, but always focus on Jewish religion and culture.

15 Lloyd St. © 410/732-6400. www.jewishmuseummd.org. Admission $8 adults, $4 students, $3 children 12 and under. Sun and Tues–Thurs noon–4pm. Travel east on Pratt St.; turn left on Central St., left on Lombard St., and then right onto Lloyd St. Closed Jewish holidays, Jan 1, Memorial Day, July 4, Labor Day, Thanksgiving Day, and the day after Thanksgiving.

Reginald F. Lewis Museum of Maryland African American History & Culture ★ (Finds)   The building alone makes the Lewis a memorable place. It's striking in its bold use of black, yellow, and red in a distinctly modern design. Inside, the museum is much more personal, detailing individual stories of African-American Marylanders such as Supreme Court justice Thurgood Marshall, gymnast Dominique Dawes, musician Cab Calloway, and religious leader Mother Mary Elizabeth Lange—exhibits designed to give children examples of African Americans who were successful in spite of poverty, discrimination, and poor schooling. On-site are a gift shop and cafe.

830 E. Pratt St. © 443/263-1800. www.africanamericanculture.org. Admission $8 adults; $6 children, students, and seniors. Wed–Sat 10am–5pm; Sun noon–5pm. Closed Thanksgiving, Dec 25, Jan 1, and Easter. Bus: 10. Metro: Shot Tower. Discounted parking available across Pratt Street from museum.

The Star Spangled Banner Flag House & Hofmeister Museum Building (Kids)   Everyone remembers Betsy Ross and the first American flag. Baltimoreans, however, recall Mary Young Pickersgill who stitched the 15-star flag that flew over Fort McHenry during the War of 1812, the flag that inspired Francis Scott Key to write "The Star-Spangled Banner." The flag is now part of the Smithsonian, but Pickersgill's 1793 house, open during guided tours 7 times a day, has period furniture and artifacts of the war. A modern museum addition, whose glass front is dominated by a giant glass flag (the size of the fort's flag), offers additional exhibits, including period uniforms, sheet music for the anthem printed in 1822, and memorabilia of the 1914 centennial celebration. The museum, which is handicapped-accessible, also has an orientation theater and a children's hands-on room.

844 E. Pratt St., at Albemarle St. © 410/837-1793. www.flaghouse.org. Admission including house tour $7 adults, $6 seniors, $5 children. Museum and film only $4. Tues–Sat 10am–4pm. Closed major holidays.

WEST OF DOWNTOWN

Babe Ruth Birthplace and Museum ★   George Herman "Babe" Ruth was born in this rowhouse, where two rooms have been re-created to look as they would have when the Sultan of Swat was a boy. Other exhibits include a wall enumerating his home runs, plus memorabilia from his major league career and his days at St. Mary's Industrial School in Baltimore, where he learned to play the game.

216 Emory St. (from Camden Yards, follow the sidewalk baseballs from the Babe Ruth statue at the north end of the warehouse to the house on this tiny street, 3 blocks away). © 410/727-1539. www.baberuth museum.com. Admission $6 adults, $4 seniors, $3 children 5–16. Combination tickets with Sports Legends available. Tues–Sun 10am–5pm, until 7pm on Orioles home game days. Closed Thanksgiving, Dec 25, and Jan 1.

Baltimore & Ohio (B&O) Railroad Museum ★★ (Kids)   American railroading got its start here when the B&O was chartered in 1827, and the first locomotive, the *Tom Thumb,* was built here. The remarkable roundhouse was restored after the roof collapsed in a 2003 snowstorm and is now more accessible for visitors with disabilities and parents with strollers. As damaged pieces are repaired, they are returned to the roundhouse, but it's still filled with an awe-inspiring collection of engines and rolling stock. A car barn has the largest locomotive ever built. Platforms enable visitors to tour trains outside, including a World War II troop sleeper, a caboose, and a refrigerated car where a train movie runs continuously. A short train ride ($2 adults, $1 kids) takes passengers along some of the oldest train tracks in the world. Trains depart at 11:30am Wednesday through Friday, three times on Saturday and twice on Sunday from April through December; weekends only in January.

901 W. Pratt St. ℂ **410/752-2490.** www.borail.org. Admission $14 adults, $12 seniors, $8 children 2–12. Mon–Fri 10am–4pm; Sat 10am–5pm; Sun noon–5pm. Closed Jan 1, Easter, Memorial Day, July 4, Labor Day, Thanksgiving, Dec 24–25, and Dec 31. Bus: 31.

The Baltimore Poe House and Museum (Moments)   Edgar Allan Poe composed some of his first works in this tiny West Baltimore rowhouse, which contains five rooms (including the garret where Poe slept and wrote). He lived here from 1833 to 1835 with his grandmother, aunt, and cousin, Virginia, whom he later married. You can see portraits, memorabilia, period furniture, changing exhibits, and a video. The house is located on a small one-way street heading south; there is no number, but you will see a black antique streetlamp out front and two markers on the house. Don't try to walk here from downtown—take a car or cab—and call ahead to verify hours.

203 N. Amity St. ℂ **410/396-7932.** www.eapoe.org. Admission $4 adults, free for children 12 and under and military families. Wed–Sat noon–3:30pm. Closed Jan–Mar. Take Charles St. north to Fayette St.; turn left on Fayette and go past Martin Luther King Blvd. to Schroeder St. Turn right on Schroeder; in 2 blocks, turn right on Saratoga St. and continue about 1/4-block to Amity St., the first street on the right. Turn right on Amity and look for the Poe House on the left side, near the end of the block.

Edgar Allan Poe's Grave (Moments)   Three modest memorials in this old graveyard recall the poet who wrote "The Tell-Tale Heart" and "The Raven" (the only poem to inspire an NFL team's name). After his mysterious death in 1849 at age 40, Poe's relatives erected a small gravestone. Before the stone could be installed, however, a train crashed through the monument yard and destroyed it. In the century since, the site has been adorned with three newer monuments: the main memorial, which features a bas-relief bust of Poe; a small gravestone adorned with a raven at Poe's original burial lot; and a plaque placed by the French, who, thanks to the poet Baudelaire, enjoy some of the best translations of Poe's works. The poet is remembered on his birthday every January 19, when a mysterious "Poe Toaster" leaves half a bottle of cognac and three roses at the grave. On the weekend closest to Poe's birthday, a party is held in his honor. Call ahead for tours offered 1st and 3rd Fridays April to November.

Westminster Hall and Burying Grounds, southeast corner of Fayette and Greene sts. ℂ **410/706-2072** (answered by a University of Maryland Law School staffer). Daily 8am–dusk. Closed major holidays.

Geppi's Entertainment Museum ★   This stylishly designed museum on the second floor of the Camden train station (beside Camden Yards stadium) celebrates the comic book. Its founder, Steve Geppi, made his fortune finding, collecting, and selling this amusing slice of Americana, and some of his favorite pieces are located here along with toys and collectibles associated with *Amazing Stories, Superman,* or *Yellow Kid.* Displays offer a historical look at how comics have developed since the 1800s. Other pop culture artifacts, from animation cels and movie posters to TV memorabilia, flesh out the collection. High-tech kiosks allow visitors to thumb through digital comic books. Toys and collectibles—banks, decoder rings, and lunchboxes—are among the most interesting artifacts. Combo tickets with the Sports Legends Museum on the first floor of Camden Station are available. There's lots of cool stuff in the gift shop.

301 W. Camden St. (*C*) **410/625-7060.** www.geppismuseum.com. Admission $10 adults, $9 seniors, $7 children 5–18. Tues–Sun 10am–6pm. Closed Thanksgiving, Dec 25, and Jan 1. Light Rail: Camden Yards.

The Irish Shrine and Railroad Workers Museum   Two 10-foot-wide 1848 brick rowhouses, a block from the B&O Museum, have been restored as a monument to the thousands of Irish workers who lived here and worked for the railroad. One house, with its original plaster walls and floors, is sparsely furnished for a family of eight and a boarder. Next door is a museum devoted to Irish Baltimoreans, with photo displays and a heartfelt video presentation. Volunteer guides are well acquainted with—and may be related to—past residents; their stories are personal and folksy. Even if you're not interested in the Irish, it's worth a visit to see a typical pre–Civil War Baltimore home. Because the back wall has been replaced with glass, it is possible to see inside the house any time; volunteers offer house tours most Saturdays. Always call ahead.

918–920 Lemmon St. (from the Inner Harbor, go west on Lombard St., turn left on Poppleton St., and turn right on Lemmon St.). (*C*) **410/669-8154.** www.irishshrine.org. Free admission. Sat 10am–2pm. Call ahead to confirm opening times.

Mount Clare Museum House   This 1760 summer home of barrister Charles Carroll and Margaret Tilghman Carroll is set on a hill with a sweeping view of the Baltimore skyline. Most of the furnishings belonged to the Carroll family, including a Charles Wilson Peale portrait and a fine collection of Chinese and English porcelain. Washington didn't sleep here, but Martha did—and so did the Marquis de Lafayette.

1500 Washington Blvd. (in Carroll Park). (*C*) **410/837-3262.** www.mountclare.org. Admission $6 adults, $5 seniors, $4 students. Tues–Sat 10am–4pm (tours on the hour until 3pm). Bus: 11.

Sports Legends Museum at Camden Yards (**Kids**)   Two floors of the historic 1856 Camden Station have been lovingly developed as a tribute to local sports. The Orioles have their own Hall of Fame here, as do the Baltimore Colts, with special attention given to star quarterback Johnny Unitas. The Ravens, the Blast soccer team, and the Negro Leagues, particularly the Baltimore Elite Giants, also have their own exhibits. But where else can you find high-school and college sports teams represented, along with a history of stadiums in Baltimore? Bring your camera if you bring your kids: The locker room has uniforms to try on, and you're going to want a photo in that way-too-big Ravens jersey. The museum is at the baseball stadium, 3 blocks west of the Babe Ruth Museum.

301 W. Camden St. (*C*) **410/727-1539.** www.baberuthmuseum.com. Admission $10 adults, $8 seniors, $7 children 2–12. Combination tickets with Babe Ruth Museum available. Apr–Oct Tues–Sun 10am–5pm (until 7pm Orioles home game days); Nov–Mar Tues–Sun 10am–5pm. Light Rail: Camden Yards.

MOUNT VERNON

The Baltimore Basilica ★★   Designed by Benjamin Latrobe—who was working on the U.S. Capitol at the same time—this neoclassical basilica is considered one of America's most beautiful. A national shrine and historic landmark, it was the first cathedral

(Moments) **Only in Baltimore, Hon!**

- **Cannoli at Vaccaro's.** All the desserts are divine, but the cannoli is a tradition. Skip dessert wherever you're having dinner and head straight to Little Italy afterward, or stop by the annex at the Light Street Pavilion.
- **Seventh-Inning Stretch at Camden Yards.** The crowd of 45,000 unites for a rousing rendition of John Denver's "Thank God I'm a Country Boy."
- **Spring in Sherwood Gardens.** This community garden at Highfield Road and Greenway Street, in the Guilford neighborhood of northern Baltimore, is out of the way and hard to find—but it's an oasis in May, when the tulips are in bloom. You'll also go through lovely neighborhoods that tourists seldom see.
- **View from the Glass Elevators at the Hyatt.** Short of a harbor-view room, this is the best view in the city, especially at night—and it's free.
- **Water Taxi Ride to Fell's Point and Little Italy.** It's an inexpensive way to see the harbor—and a great way to avoid the hassle of parking.

built in the United States and has been a monument to religious freedom since 1806. Notable visitors have included Mother Teresa and Pope John Paul II, both of whom now have memorials to their visits. A controversial restoration, including the removal of stained glass and uncovering of 24 skylights in the dome, has resulted in a light-drenched sanctuary filled with glittering details. For natives who remember the dark, solemn space, this was a startling revelation and a welcome one. The project also uncovered balconies once reserved for African-American Catholics and cloistered nuns. The undercroft has reopened with a chapel, museum, and crypt. Tours are available Monday through Friday at 9am, 11am, and 1pm, and Sunday at noon. A prayer garden dedicated to Pope John Paul II is around the corner on Charles Street.

400 block of Cathedral St. (*(C)* **410/727-3565.** www.baltimorebasilica.org. Free admission. Daily 8:30am–4:30pm. Mass Sun 7:30, 9, 10:45am, and 4 and 5:30pm; Mon–Fri 7:15am and 12:10pm; Sat 7:30am and 5:30pm. Take Charles St. north; turn left on Franklin St., and left again on Cathedral St.

Contemporary Museum (Finds) The Contemporary Museum holds shows in its Mount Vernon home but will sometimes exhibit art on the sides of buildings, on buses, or in other community settings as well. Its small storefront galleries are devoted to distinctly contemporary art, ranging from photography and video to paintings and performance art. It's a nice counterpoint to its neighbors, the elegant Walters Art Museum and the traditional Maryland Historical Society, which are a block or so away.

100 W. Centre St. (*(C)* **410/783-5720.** www.contemporary.org. Admission $5 adults, $3 children. Wed–Sun noon–5pm. Hours may vary; calling ahead is a must. Closed btw. exhibits.

Eubie Blake National Jazz Institute and Cultural Center Baltimorean Eubie Blake, the ragtime pianist and Broadway composer, is remembered in this small museum on Howard Street's Antique Row. Exhibits feature local musicians Billie Holiday and Cab Calloway. Eubie Live!, a new performance space, has expanded the number of poetry

Coming Soon—A Star-Spangled Bicentennial

The bicentennial of the War of 1812, and especially the Battle of Baltimore and the writing of the "Star-Spangled Banner," will be celebrated here with 2 years of exhibitions, fireworks, and Tall Ships visits. Mary Young Pickersgill is expected to make appearances throughout the state during those 2 years. Marylanders faced the British in 1813 and 1814 in skirmishes and battles from Havre de Grace to St. Michaels and finally at Fort McHenry. Official commemoration will begin with a 2-week celebration, starting on Defender's Day, September 12, 2012. Other signature events will be held throughout the next 2 years, when a final celebration will conclude the weekend around September 12, 2014. A few of the Baltimore locations sure to be must-sees during the bicentennial are:

Fort McHenry, end of East Fort Avenue (℃ **410/963-4290;** www.nps.gov/fomc), is the site of the Battle of Baltimore, where Francis Scott Key was inspired to write "The Star-Spangled Banner." A new visitor center and revamped exhibits are planned.

The Star Spangled Banner Flag House and Hofmeister Museum Building, 844 E Pratt St. (℃ **410/837-1793;** www.flaghouse.org), was the home of Mary Young Pickersgill, the flag maker, whose flag inspired the writing of "The Star-Spangled Banner." Exhibitions planned will include "Family of Flag Makers," due to open in 2012.

The Maryland Historical Society, 201 W. Monument St. (℃ **410/685-3750;** www.mdhs.org), houses Maryland artifacts including Key's original composition, and plans special exhibits.

Fell's Point Visitor Center, 1724 Thames St. (℃ **410/276-1561;** www.preservationsociety.org) will commemorate the waterfront neighborhood's role during war.

A website has been set up for those interested in keeping up with the star-spangled bicentennial: **www.starspangled200.org**.

readings and musical performances. Check the website for the events calendar. *Tip:* Even when there usually isn't a lot to see here, talk to the docents—many of them knew Blake or Calloway.

847 N. Howard St. ℃ **410/225-3130.** www.eubieblake.org. Admission $5 adults. Wed–Fri noon–6pm; Sat 11am–3pm.

George Peabody Library ★★★   One of Baltimore's hidden treasures, the 1866 Peabody is an architectural gem with the cast-iron balconies soaring five levels to a shining glass ceiling. It's an academic gem as well—the resting place of 300,000 volumes, mostly rare books, with some dating to when the printing press was new. Philanthropist George Peabody provided the funds to build this magnificent "cathedral of books" and ordered that it be filled with the best works on every subject. Literary exhibits change regularly in an adjacent gallery.

Maryland Historical Society ★★ (**Kids**) Three floors of historical artifacts offer interesting glimpses of life in Maryland. The main exhibit "Looking for Liberty" has Francis Scott Key's manuscript of "The Star-Spangled Banner" as its centerpiece. A maritime history display has great ship models. There's art by the famous Peale family of painters, Broadway composer Eubie Blake's glasses and baton, Stieff silver and Baltimore furniture, Baltimore album quilts, and quite a collection of antique toys. Historians and genealogy fans revel in the documents, books, and records in the 7-million item library. It's easy to spend a couple of hours on a visit here, and the society is not far from the Walters Art Museum and the antiques shops of Howard Street.

201 W. Monument St. (*C*) **410/685-3750.** www.mdhs.org. Admission $4 adults, $3 seniors and children 13–17, free for children 12 and under. Free admission 1st Thurs of month. Wed–Sun 10am–5pm. Free parking on-site. Light Rail: Centre St.

Old St. Paul's Episcopal Church Originally founded in 1692 as one of Maryland's first Anglican parishes, this Italian-Romanesque building dates to 1856 and features Tiffany stained-glass windows and mosaics, notably the Tiffany rose window. In addition, two friezes salvaged from the previous church, which burned in 1817, have been incorporated into the portico. The church is no longer open to the public, though services are, of course.

Charles and Saratoga sts. (*C*) **410/685-3404.** www.osp1692.org. Sun services at 8 and 10:30am, and 5:30pm; Wed services 12:15pm.

The Walters Art Museum ★★★ The Walters has always been one of Baltimore's great attractions. Begun with the 22,000-object collection of William and Henry Walters, this gem's ancient and medieval galleries practically sparkle. Walk through the galleries of sculpture, jewelry, mummies, and 19th-century French paintings to see the progress of fine art through 50 centuries. The Knight's Hall displays tapestries, furnishings, and suits of armor from the Middle Ages. The Egyptian collection is one of the best in the U.S. The original Palazzo building features 1,500 works from mostly the Renaissance and baroque periods. Hackerman House, open Saturday and Sunday, features Asian art. The Palace of Wonders is the imaginary gallery of a 17th-century Flemish nobleman with art, collections from nature, and artifacts from around the world. Docents offer free tours Sunday at 2pm. The cafe serves light fare.

600 N. Charles St. (*C*) **410/547-9000.** www.thewalters.org. Free admission; admission is charged for special exhibitions. Wed–Sun 11am–5pm. Closed July 4, Thanksgiving, and Dec 24–25. Bus: 3, 11, 31, 61, or 64. Light Rail: Centre St. Take Charles St. north to the Washington Monument.

Washington Monument This 178-foot-tall column, the country's first major architectural memorial to George Washington, was designed in 1815 by Robert Mills, who also designed the Washington Monument (begun in 1848) in Washington, D.C. To learn the whole story, see the exhibit inside the building. The physically fit can also climb the 228 steps to the top of the tower and see why this spot has what's often called the best view in Baltimore. The monument takes center stage on the city's seal.

Mount Vernon Place and Charles St. (*C*) **410/396-0929.** Suggested donation $1. Wed–Fri 10am–4pm; Sat–Sun 10am–5pm. Take Charles St. north to the monument.

Baltimore Museum of Art ★★★   The largest museum in Maryland, the BMA offers galleries dedicated to modern and contemporary art; European sculpture and painting; American painting and decorative arts; prints and photographs; the arts of Africa, Asia, the Americas, and Oceania; and a 2¾-acre sculpture garden with 35 major works by Alexander Calder, Henry Moore, and others. The BMA is famous for its Matisse collection, assembled by Baltimore sisters Claribel and Etta Cone, who went to Paris in the 1920s and came back with Impressionist and modern art. The $4-million Cone Wing showcases their collection of paintings by Matisse, Cézanne, Gauguin, van Gogh, and Renoir. Visit the special room set up to remember these women, featuring drawers filled with their personal things, pieces of furniture, and a virtual tour of their Baltimore apartments. Other highlights include the 35,000-square-foot West Wing for Contemporary Art, with work by Andy Warhol, Jasper Johns, and Baltimorean Grace Hartigan; Early American decorative arts and a gallery of miniature rooms; European art that includes Impressionist paintings by Monet and Degas; and the Jacobs Wing, a collection of 15th- to 19th-century European art displayed in jewel-toned rooms. Younger visitors can borrow the ART + FUN packs, which will show them museum pieces on their own level as they listen to music or draw. A summer jazz series in the sculpture garden is a delight. Look for two brochures outlining the **Sculpture Garden Cell Phone Tour** and the **Historic Homewood Artwalk.**

10 Art Museum Dr. (at N. Charles St. and 31st St.; take Howard St. north and bear right onto Art Museum Dr., about 3 miles north of the harbor). ⓒ **443/573-1700.** www.artbma.org. Free except for special exhibits. Wed–Fri 10am–5pm; Sat–Sun 11am–6pm. Bus: 3 or 11.

Evergreen Museum & Library (Finds)   What started as a relatively modest Italianate mansion in the mid-1800s became a 48-room marvel of the Gilded Age, with a 23-karat gold-plated bathroom, a theater painted by noted Ballet Russe designer Leon Bakst, and room after room of art, books, and *objets*. Bought in 1878 by the president of the B&O railroad, John W. Garrett, the home grew over the years and became ever more lavish and more famous. Its last owners, John and Alice Garrett, turned it into a glittering salon, where they entertained statesmen, authors, artists, and musicians.

From the moment visitors arrive at the entrance, a *porte-cochere* topped by a Tiffany glass awning, they are treated to a multitude of beautiful rooms, fine arts, and decorative items that reflect the Garretts' travels and interests: a red Asian room displaying Japanese and Chinese items; paintings by Picasso, Modigliani, and Degas; glass by Tiffany; a 30,000-book library; and Dutch marquetry furniture. Tours, offered on the hour, last about an hour. The beautiful formal gardens should be visited as well.

4545 N. Charles St. (btw. Loyola College and the College of Notre Dame). ⓒ **410/516-0341.** www.museums.jhu.edu. Admission $6 adults, $5 seniors, $3 students. Tues–Fri 11am–4pm; Sat–Sun noon–4pm (last tour at 3pm).

Homewood Museum   If you have time, visit both Evergreen (see above) and Homewood (they're a mile apart) to see how differently the rich lived in different centuries. Homewood was designed and built by the son of Charles Carroll of Carrollton, a signer of the Declaration of Independence. Built in 1801, the five-part classic Palladian home is a dazzling example of Federal architecture with superb woodcarving and plaster ornamentation. It's painted in a rainbow of soothing colors and decorated in pieces of the time, some from the Carroll family. Highlights are the main hall, the family sitting room with toys and doll furniture, the music room, the long lemon-yellow hall, and the master bedroom with its high cove ceiling and bookcases tucked into the sides of the fireplace. Tours, offered on the half-hour, last 45 minutes. Changing exhibits in the main hall focus on the decorative arts or architecture.

3400 N. Charles St. ✆ 410/516-5589. www.museums.jhu.edu. Admission $6 adults, $5 seniors, $3 students. Tues–Fri 11am–4pm; Sat–Sun noon–4pm (last tour at 3:30pm). It's on the campus of Johns Hopkins University; drive to the university's north entrance, on University Pkwy., and follow signs to the parking lot. Press the button at the gate to park. The house is on the other side of a building by the lot.

Lacrosse Museum & National Hall of Fame   This museum offers a look at 350 years in the history of lacrosse, America's oldest sport and a passion in Maryland. Displays include photographs and murals of athletes at play, sculptures and paintings, vintage equipment and uniforms, a documentary, and a Hall of Fame.

113 W. University Pkwy. ✆ 410/235-6882. www.uslacrosse.org. Admission $3 adults, $2 children 5–15. Feb–May Tues–Sat 10am–3pm; June–Jan Mon–Fri 10am–3pm; 1st Wed of every month noon–3pm. Hours occasionally change, so call ahead.

The Maryland Zoo in Baltimore (Kids)   The third-oldest zoo in the U.S. is home to some 2,000 animals, including polar bears, penguins, and chimpanzees. The Polar Bear Watch allows visitors a view of Magnet and Alaska. The Chimpanzee Forest, Leopard Lair, and African Watering Hole are fun, but the best part is the children's zoo, with its lily pads, tree slide, farm animals, and Maryland wilderness exhibit. Feeding time for the African penguins, North America's largest collection, at 11am and 3pm, is a highlight. Plan to spend a few hours here. Tram rides are included with admission.

Druid Hill Park (take exit 7, Druid Hill Lake Dr., off I-83 and follow signs for the zoo). ✆ 410/366-LION (5466). www.marylandzoo.org. Admission $15 adults, $12 seniors, $10 children 2–11. $1 discount online. Daily 10am–4pm. Closed Jan–Feb, 2nd Fri in June, Thanksgiving, and Dec 25.

National Great Blacks In Wax Museum (Finds)   The first thing you hear when you enter is the sound of moaning, coming from the Slave Ship exhibit. This wax museum doesn't shy away from the tough topics—a lynching exhibit is in the basement—but it revels in the African Americans, and all people of color, who made a difference. Some are expected: Martin Luther King, Jr., Frederick Douglass, and famous athletes, artists, and entertainers. Some may be people you weren't aware of: rodeo star Bill Pickett, Matthew Henson at the North Pole, and African Americans who made advances in medicine, science, law, and politics.

1601–1603 E. North Ave. ✆ 410/563-3404. www.ngbiwm.com. Admission $12 adults, $11 seniors and students, $10 children 2–11. Feb and July–Aug Mon–Sat 9am–6pm, Sun noon–6pm; Mar 1–June 30 and Sept 1 Tues–Sat 9am–6pm, Sun noon–6pm; Oct 15–Jan 31 Tues–Sat 9am–5pm, Sun noon–5pm.

6 ORGANIZED TOURS & CRUISES

SPECIAL-INTEREST TOURS

A series of guided tours takes tourists around and away from the Inner Harbor, offering a bit of history and culture. The **Heritage Walk** guides tourists through Baltimore's oldest waterfront neighborhoods, including Little Italy and Jonestown. It's offered free May through October weekdays at 10am and weekends at 10am and 1pm. Tours start from the Inner Harbor Visitor Center.

The **Mount Vernon Cultural Walk** goes up Charles Street for a glimpse of Baltimore's financial district and some of its best-known cultural institutions. The tour ends at the iconic Washington Monument in picturesque Mount Vernon. The tour begins at the visitor center daily at 1pm May through October. For a look at Baltimore's African-American Heritage, join the tour on the **Pennsylvania Avenue Heritage Trail.** It's given Sunday mornings May through October to take advantage of a visit to the Arabbers' Market, held only on Sundays. The tour includes a ride on the Metro.

For information on any of the tours, call © **443/984-2369** or visit **www.star spangledtrails.org**.

The **Fell's Point Visitor Center,** 1724 Thames St. (© **410/675-6750;** www.preservation society.com), offers tours of some of Baltimore's oldest streets April through November. Walking tours, including the Immigration Tour at noon and Secrets of a Seaport, depart from here on Saturdays. Authentic Fell's Point Ghostwalks are offered Friday and Saturday at 7pm. African American History Tours get underway at 3pm on Sunday. Tickets are $12 for adults, $8 for children 11 and under; reservations are a must. Tours of the 1765 Robert Long House on Ann Street, the oldest residence in Baltimore Town, are offered Tuesday through Saturday at 1:30pm. Tickets are $5.

African American Cultural Tours focus on contributions of local African Americans, such as Harriet Tubman and Thurgood Marshall, as well as important landmarks, including locations where the TV series *The Wire* was shot. Tours on area movie locations are also available. Call © **410/727-0755;** reservations are essential.

Baseball fans will enjoy the 90-minute tour of **Oriole Park at Camden Yards** (© **410/547-6234;** http://baltimore.orioles.mlb.com). Well-informed guides fill you in on where Hall of Famer Eddie Murray hit his 500th home run, why there are no bat racks in the dugout, and how many miles of beer lines run under the seats. The tour visits places the average fan can't see: the dugouts, scoreboard control room, and the press box. Buy tickets at least 30 minutes beforehand at the box office at the north end of the stadium; prices are $9 for adults and $7 for seniors and children. During the baseball season, tours are conducted on away-game days, four times a day. Call ahead to confirm times.

CRUISES & BOAT TOURS

There's no shortage of options for seeing Baltimore from the water. Several touring boats will inevitably be docked at the Inner Harbor during your visit, but the cheapest way to get on the water is to take **Baltimore Water Taxis** (© **800/658-8947** or 410/563-3901; www.thewatertaxi.com). It provides transportation to various destinations, including Harborplace, Little Italy, Fell's Point, Canton, and Fort McHenry, but you're welcome to stay on for the entire route. See "Getting Around," earlier in this chapter, for details.

Baltimore Spirit Cruises gives 2-hour lunch, 3-hour dinner, and 1-hour sightseeing cruises as well as themed and midnight cruises on two 450-passenger ships, which dock by the Light Street Pavilion (© **866/312-2469;** www.spiritcruisesbaltimore.com). The food is passable, but the cruise is worthwhile. Tickets are $20 for sightseeing tours, $35 for lunch and $70 for dinner cruises. Children's ticket prices begin at $12.

Annapolis-based **Watermark Tours** (© **410/268-7601**) offers 45 minute tours of the Inner Harbor six times a day on weekdays and nine times on weekends May through October. Tickets are $15 for adults and $6 for ages 3 to 11.

The Black-Eyed Susan, a 150-passenger paddle-wheeler, offers Sunday brunch, jazz, sunset, and murder mystery cruises departing from the Broadway Pier in Fell's Point. Cruises cost $30 to $120. Call © **410/342-6960** or visit **www.theblack-eyedsusan. com**.

Bring your Boat

On a summer weekend, the Inner Harbor looks like a boat parking lot. So, c'mon, forget the car and sail into town. Inner Harbor docking fees range from $15 for 5 hours or $1.25 a foot for overnight docking. Contact the dockmaster at VHF68.

Tired of serious cruises? **Urban Pirates** (℃ 410/327-8378; www.urbanpirates.com) leaves Fell's Point five times a day in summer and in spring and fall on weekends only on an adventure involving treasure, enemy ships, and swashbuckling. Daytime tours are kid-friendly; evening tours are best left to the adults. Tickets are $20 for ages 3 and up, $10 for little pirates.

For a tall-ship adventure, plan an autumn trip on a New England schooner that docks in Baltimore for several cruises on the Chesapeake. The 103-foot *Mystic Whaler* (℃ 800/697-8420; www.mysticwhaler.com) offers 3- and 5-day Chesapeake Bay cruises from Baltimore. Prices for 3 days range from $450 to $590.

7 SPECTATOR SPORTS & OUTDOOR ACTIVITIES

BASEBALL   From April to October, you can see the American League's **Baltimore Orioles** play ball. If there's a home game during your visit, try to attend—it's a real Baltimore experience. The team plays at Oriole Park at Camden Yards, 333 W. Camden St. (℃ 888/848-2473 or 410/685-9800; http://baltimore.orioles.mlb.com). Afternoon games are usually at 1:35pm; evening games start at 7:35pm. Ticket prices range from $9 to $55, with bargain night on Tuesday and college-student discounts on Friday, both for the upper deck. Tickets for Yankees or Red Sox games cost more. Tours of the stadium (℃ 410/547-6234) are available every day.

FOOTBALL   The **Baltimore Ravens** play at M&T Bank Stadium, next to Camden Yards at 1101 Russell St. (℃ 410/261-7283; www.baltimoreravens.com). About 5,000 tickets are sold per game (the rest are held by season-ticket holders) and cost $50 to $345.

HORSE RACING   Maryland's oldest thoroughbred track and the site of the annual Preakness Stakes is **Pimlico Race Course,** 5241 Park Heights (℃ 410/542-9400; www. pimlico.com), on the city's northwest side. (Seabiscuit made history at this track, beating Triple Crown winner War Admiral.) The **Preakness** ★ (www.preakness.com), the middle jewel in racing's Triple Crown, is held the third Saturday in May. Clubhouse and grandstand tickets go on sale in October—and go fast. Infield tickets, at $50, are for sale at the box office and online. Post time for regular racing days is 1:10pm; admission is $3 for the grandstand. Self-parking is free; valet parking is $3. Call ahead for opening days.

INDOOR SOCCER   The **Baltimore Blast** (℃ 410/732-5278; www.baltimoreblast.com) have had a loyal following for 30 years. A number of players are local boys. The season lasts October through April; games are played at the 1st Mariner Arena. Tickets cost $16 to $30.

PADDLEBOATS & ELECTRIC BOATS   Paddleboats and little electric boats are available for rent at the Inner Harbor, adjacent to the World Trade Center. Hours vary according to season. Paddleboats, some built like dragons, cost $10 to $16 per half-hour per boat, depending on the number of people riding. Not that energetic? A half-hour ride on an electric boat will run $12 for two passengers or $18 for three.

PUBLIC PARKS

Baltimore has many green spaces, including a couple that deserve special mention.

Cylburn Arboretum Moments   Just off Northern Parkway, a quick run up the Jones Falls Expressway (I-83), Cylburn is a peaceful collection of gardens and mansion. The 100-plus acres include a formal Victorian garden, children's garden, and gardens devoted to butterflies, shade, roses, and vegetables. Woodland trails wind 2.5 miles through the forests of Cylburn. Among the 161 bird species spotted here have been the Baltimore oriole and bald eagle. The ornate stone house with mansard roof and cupola has an equally ornate interior, with inlaid floors, mosaics, and plasterwork. The Maryland Ornithological Society's bird museum and a nature museum for children are in a carriage house behind the mansion.

4915 Greenspring Ave., Mount Washington. © **410/367-2217.** www.cylburnassociation.org. Free admission. Mansion museums Mon–Fri 7:30am–3:30pm. Grounds open daily dawn–dusk.

Federal Hill ★★★   Get a great view of the city from that big hill overlooking the Inner Harbor. Take the 100 steps on the Battery Avenue side, or enter from Warren Avenue, where you won't have any steps to contend with at all, except maybe a curbstone. The hill has been valued for its scenic views since the first Baltimoreans came here to watch construction around the harbor. A single cannon recalls the Civil War, when federal guns were trained on the city. Take your dog (on a leash) or your children. Once the kids get tired of the view, they can play in the fenced-in playground.

Federal Hill Park, Battery and Warren aves. Free admission. Best to visit during daylight hours.

8 SHOPPING

The Inner Harbor is an obvious choice for shoppers. But those who like an adventure will find Fell's Point, Hampden, Mount Washington, Antique Row on Howard Street, and a lot of fun. If your wallet needs emptying, head over to Cross Keys, near Mount Washington, for designer threads. Harbor East is the newest go-to shopping district.

INNER HARBOR

You can find anything from onion rings to diamond rings at the 160 shops that make up **Harborplace Mall** (© **410/332-4191;** www.harborplace.com), which is actually three separate venues: two stand-alone pavilions on Light and Pratt streets, and the Gallery, a vertical mall in the Renaissance Harborplace Hotel. The **Light Street Pavilion** has the most food stalls and restaurants, plus some souvenir shops. The **Pratt Street Pavilion** offers specialty stores, clothing and jewelry shops, and more restaurants. The **Gallery** has three floors of shops, plus a fourth-floor food court. Most of the stores are franchises of national chains, and are open Monday through Saturday from 10am to 9pm and Sunday from noon to 6pm.

The 75 shops in the Gallery (connected via skywalk to the Pratt St. Pavilion) include Banana Republic, Brooks Brothers, Ann Taylor, and Coach. Santa's magical house is located between the Harborplace pavilions from Thanksgiving to Christmas Eve.

Sweet Things in Charm City

Sometimes you just need a sweet—and there are a couple sweet spots around town that shouldn't be missed if you're in the neighborhood. The most famous baker in town, Food Network's *Ace of Cakes* chef, Duff Goldman, has his Charm City Cakes shop in Remington, but it isn't open to the public.

The Baltimore Cupcake Company, 1433 E. Fort Ave. (© **410/783-1600;** www.baltimorecupcakecompany.com). This little pink-and-white shop on the way to Fort McHenry sells cupcakes, other sweets, and Cafe du Monde coffee. Open Tuesday through Friday from 10am to 6pm, Saturday from 9am to 5pm.

Charm City Cupcakes, 326 N. Charles St. (© **410/244-8790;** www.charmcitycupcakes.com). This downtown spot sells tasty cupcakes. Open Tuesday through Saturday, 10am to 5:30pm.

Dangerously Delicious Pies, 1036 Light St., Federal Hill (© **410/522-7437;** www.dangerouspies.com). No fancy stuff here—just honest, homemade, fresh-out-of-the-oven pies. The rock-'n'-roll guys here make all kinds: fruit, Key (Bridge) lime, derby, and a towering lemon meringue. Open Tuesday through Sunday from 7am to 6pm.

Patisserie Poupon, 820 E. Baltimore St. (© **410/332-0390**). You'll find this delightful French pastry shop in the shadow of the Shot Tower and near Port Discovery and Little Italy. (It's safer to drive here, due to traffic.) Stop for coffee and a croissant or a fabulously decorated pastry. Open Monday through Saturday from 7am to 6pm.

FELL'S POINT

Art Gallery of Fells Point   This cooperative gallery features works by regional artists, including paintings, photography, fibers, and jewelry. Open Tuesday through Sunday. 1716 Thames St. © **410/327-1272.** www.fellspointgallery.org.

Brassworks Company   Brass glistens from every shelf here. Fine-quality items include lamps, candlesticks, doorknockers, and more. Open daily. 1641 Thames St. © **410/327-7280.** www.baltimorebrassworks.com.

Robert McClintock Baltimore Seen   Prints and original works of Baltimore scenes in McClintock's unusual style. Open Tuesday through Sunday. 1809 Thames St. © **410/814-2800.**

Sheep's Clothing   Irish woolens and ceramics and Provençal soaps and fragrances. Open Wednesday through Sunday. 1620 Shakespeare St. © **410/327-2222.**

The Sound Garden   One of the best CD stores around. Also has used CDs and new and used DVDs. It's a good place to check for live music around town. Open daily. 1616 Thames St. © **410/563-9011.** www.cdjoint.com.

Ten Thousand Villages   Using the Body Shop model of commissioning handmade products by indigenous peoples, this shop is filled with textiles, pottery, baskets, and coffee, all fairly traded and affordably priced. Open daily. 1621 Thames St. © **410/342-5568.** www.tenthousandvillages.com.

For a neighborhood that didn't even exist a few years ago, this one's thriving, and the shopping is *très* chic. Most shops are on Exeter or Fleet Street. Look for something hot to carry your stuff in at **Handbags and the City,** 612 S. Exeter St. (✆ 410/528-1443), or something cool to sit on at **Arhaus Furniture,** 660 S. Exeter St. (✆ 410/244-6376; www.arhaus.com).

You'll also find plenty of restaurants, including **Mustang Alley's Bar, Bowling & Bistro** 10- and duck-pin bowling and sleek eatery, 1300 Bank St. (✆ 410/522-BOWL [2695]; www.mustangalleys.com). Or stop for a snack or supplies at **Whole Foods,** 1001 Fleet St. (✆ 410/528-1640), or for wine at **Bin 604 Wine Sellers,** 604 S. Exeter St. (✆ 410/576-0444; www.bin604.com), which has wine classes on Saturdays and tastings on Thursdays.

MOUNT VERNON

A People United   This nonprofit shop features goods made by women who are part of development cooperatives in India, Guatemala, Kenya, and other lands. You'll find clothing, jewelry, and accessories; sweaters here are not your average pullovers. Open daily. 516 N. Charles St. ✆ 410/727-4471. www.apeopleunited.com.

Beadazzled   Be dazzled by the array of beads, which come from everywhere and in every color. Jewelry-making classes are available. Open daily. 501 N. Charles St. ✆ 410/837-2323. www.beadazzled.net.

Antique Row ★

On a single block in Mount Vernon—the 800 block of Howard Street—lies an amazing string of antiques shops. The first antiques stores opened here in the 1840s—they were furniture resellers, really—making this the oldest antiques district in the U.S. Most of the shops are open from 11am or noon to 5pm. Street parking is metered—bring quarters or take the Light Rail, which runs up Howard.

Amos Judd and Sons, Inc. (✆ 410/462-2000) is a dark little store filled with cases of English, French, and Italian accessories. The 20 dealers at **Antique Row Stalls** (✆ 410/728-6363), an 8,000-square-foot co-op, sell just about everything. They're closed Tuesdays.

The eclectic **Connoisseur's Connection** (✆ 410/383-2624) has a little of everything and often provides set pieces for locally produced movies. **Dubey's Art and Antiques** (✆ 410/383-2881) boasts a wealth of Chinese export porcelain and other American, English, and Asian treasures. For antiquities from Europe and Asia, see **Richard Sindler** (✆ 410/225-2727).

Check out the old silver at **Imperial Half Bushel** (✆ 410/462-1192)—the shop fairly glitters with flatware and holloware. The **20th Century Gallery** (✆ 410/728-3800) stocks American and European art pottery, as well as prints and paintings. **Crosskeys** (✆ 410/728-0101), which specializes in English, Continental, and American furnishings, is open only Saturday and Sunday.

C. Grimaldis Gallery   Contemporary art is the focus here, with new exhibitions 11
times a year. Open Tuesday through Saturday. 523 N. Charles St. ✆ **410/539-1092.** www.
cgrimaldisgallery.com.

The Woman's Industrial Exchange   Founded in 1880, this shop's mission has
always been to help women by selling their handiwork, originally as part of a national
movement after the Civil War. The work here is finely done: smocked dresses and handmade afghans, quilts, and other wares. Open Monday through Saturday. 333 N. Charles
St. ✆ **410/685-4388.** www.womansindustrialexchange.org.

HAMPDEN

The Antreasian Gallery   Antreasian Gallery features the work of 50 regional artists,
from painting to jewelry to ceramics. Open Wednesday through Sunday. 1111 W. 36th St.
✆ **410/235-4420.** www.antreasiangallery.com.

Charlotte Elliott   Three levels of antiques, vintage clothing, Thai silks, and the like.
Open daily. 837 W. 36th St. ✆ **410/243-0990.**

Form   Designer clothes, including Vera Wang, Anna Sui, and Denim of Virtue, for
"creative women." Open Tuesday through Sunday. 1115 W. 36th St. ✆ **410/889-3116.**

Gotta Have . . . Bags   A basement shop stocked with handbags and things to put
inside them. Open Wednesday through Sunday. 846 W. 36th St. ✆ **410/243-5999.**

Hometown Girl (Finds)   This is the spot for a real Baltimore souvenir, hon. The shop's
soda fountain opens at noon. Open daily. 1001 W. 36th St. ✆ **410/662-4438.**

Ma Petite Shoe   Splurge on two indulgences—eye-catching footwear and gourmet
chocolates—in one shop. Local chocolatiers Cacao Lorenzo and Mouth Party are featured. Open daily. 832 W. 36th St. ✆ **410/235-3442.** www.mapetiteshoe.com.

Mud and Metal   This shop specializes in functional art—lamps, tables, business-card
holders, jewelry—often created from recycled materials by local artists. Open daily. 1121
W. 36th St. ✆ **410/467-8698.** www.mudandmetal.com.

Wild Yam Pottery   The pottery (think lamps, baking dishes, vases) made on these
premises is mostly practical, in soothing earth tones. Special orders and handcrafted
jewelry are available. Open daily. 863 W. 36th St. ✆ **410/662-1123.** www.wildyampottery.com.

The Wine Source   The friendliest wine people staff this big store a block from "the
Avenue." Besides a wealth of wine, they stock beer, spirits, and cheeses. Open daily. 3601
Elm St. ✆ **410/467-7777.** www.the-wine-source.com.

MOUNT WASHINGTON VILLAGE

Baltimore Clayworks   This nonprofit center holds classes, rents studio space, and
runs a gallery and shop. The main building at no. 5707 has a warren of little gallery rooms
where exhibits of art pieces change frequently. The shop has functional pottery, made by
local potters. Open daily. 5706–5707 Smith Ave. ✆ **410/578-1919.** www.baltimoreclayworks.org.

Jurus   I go out of my way to shop at this elegant little store filled with the owner's
handcrafted jewelry and tableware, scarves, and crafts. Open Tuesday through Saturday.
5618 Newbury St. ✆ **410/542-5227.** www.jurusjewelry.com.

Something Else   You won't find the clothing here in a department store. Flowing
dresses, exotic jewelry, and South American sweaters are made of flax, wool, and cotton.
Open Monday through Saturday. 1611 Sulgrave Ave. ✆ **410/542-0444.**

Sunnyfields   Traditional girls will like this shop's Williamsburg reproduction furniture and accessories, porcelain, crystal, and party furnishings. Open Monday through Saturday. 6305 Falls Rd. ℭ **410/823-6666.**

VILLAGE OF CROSS KEYS

This upscale shopping center, at 5100 Falls Rd. in north Baltimore, has local stores, plus a few chains such as Talbots and Williams-Sonoma. Hours are from 10am to 6pm or later. From downtown, take the Jones Falls Expressway north to the Northern Parkway East exit. Turn right at the light at Falls Road; the center is on the right.

The Pied Piper   Spoil your children with these luxurious clothes, everything from christening dresses to bibs. Open Monday through Saturday. ℭ **410/435-2676.**

Ruth Shaw   You need designer clothes, you come here. Where else are you going to get your Jimmy Choo shoes? Open Monday through Saturday. ℭ **410/532-7886.**

The Store Ltd.   Pared down to their simplest form, these home furnishings and personal accessories are contemporary and always fresh. Jewelry here is designed by the store's owner. Open Monday through Saturday. ℭ **410/323-2350.**

MARKETS & MALLS

Baltimore still has several old-fashioned covered markets with vendors selling seafood, baked goods, produce, and sweets. The outdoor farmers' market, held under the Jones Falls viaduct, is a Sunday tradition for many people.

Arundel Mills   Located south of Baltimore, this theme-park-like mall is worth the trek for shopaholics. It's *huge,* with some 200 shops. Larger retailers, such as Off 5th Saks Fifth Avenue Outlet, Neiman Marcus Last Call, and Bass Pro Shops Outdoor World, are joined by smaller shops, a 24-screen movie theater, and lots of restaurants. The combination of games and food at Dave & Buster's is an afternoon's diversion all by itself, and Medieval Times offers dinner and a show. ℭ **410/540-5110.** www.arundelmills.com. Off Rte. 295, 10 miles south of Baltimore. Take Rte. 295 south; pass BWI exit to exit 10 for Arundel Mills.

Baltimore Farmers' Market   For a look at Old Baltimore, stop at this weekly outdoor gathering—a great source for crafts, herbs, jams, jellies, baked goods, smoked meats, cheeses, local produce, and flowers. Saratoga St., btw. Holliday and Gay sts. (under JFX). ℭ **410/752-8632** (for office at 200 W. Lombard St.).

Belvedere Square   If you're in northern Baltimore, near Hopkins or Loyola universities, this market is a great place to stop. A cluster of takeout counters and retail shops offer mouthwatering choices: sushi, fresh fruit and vegetables, baked goods, and organic items. Atwater's soups, breads, and desserts should never be passed up. 540 E. Belvedere Ave. (just south of Northern Pkwy.), Roland Park. ℭ **410/464-9773.** www.belvederesquare.com.

Broadway Market   This 200-year-old market, with two large covered buildings, is staffed by local vendors selling produce and ethnic and raw-bar foods (ideal for a quick lunch). S. Broadway, btw. Fleet and Lancaster sts., Fell's Point. No phone. www.bpmarkets.com.

Cross Street Market   First opened in 1846, Cross Street Market is one of Baltimore's public markets. Local vendors offer produce, seafood, meats, candy, baked goods, and much more. 1065 S. Charles St., at Cross St., Federal Hill. No phone. www.bpmarkets.com.

Lexington Market   Established in 1782, this Baltimore landmark claims to be the oldest continuously operating market in the U.S. Some 140 merchants sell prepared foods (for eat-in or take-away), seafood, produce, meats, baked goods, and sweets. It's worth a visit. 400 W. Lexington St. ℭ **410/685-6169.** www.lexingtonmarket.com.

9 BALTIMORE AFTER DARK

Baltimore is jumping when the sun sets: The Inner Harbor, Federal Hill, Canton, and Mount Vernon have all developed lives after dark.

For major events, check the arts and entertainment sections of the Baltimore *Sun* and the *Washington Post*. The free weekly *City Paper* has very complete listings, down to the smallest bars and clubs. On the Web, try **www.baltimorefunguide.com**.

Tickets for most major venues are available at the individual box offices or through **Ticketmaster** (© **410/547-SEAT** [7328]; www.ticketmaster.com).

THE PERFORMING ARTS

Baltimore has a solid range of resident performing-arts companies, including a nationally recognized symphony, an opera company, a major regional theater, and several local professional theater companies.

Classical Music

The world-class **Baltimore Symphony Orchestra** ★★★ (© **410/783-8000;** www. bsomusic.org) is led by renowned conductor Marin Alsop. The BSO performs classical and pops concerts at the Meyerhoff Symphony Hall, 1212 Cathedral St. In summer, you'll also find the BSO outside at Oregon Ridge Park, north of the city off I-83. Its Fourth of July concerts are terrific fun. Tickets are $25 to $75.

The **Peabody Symphony Orchestra** (© **410/659-8100;** www.peabody.jhu.edu/pso) is one of several performing units of the Peabody Institute of Music; concerts are held in Friedberg Hall, at 1 E. Mount Vernon Place.

Theater

For entertainment by local professional actors at affordable prices, the **Vagabond Players,** in Fell's Point at 806 S. Broadway (© **410/563-9135;** www.vagabondplayers.org), stage a variety of classics, contemporary comedies, and dramas. The **Fell's Point Corner Theatre,** 251 S. Ann St. (© **410/276-7837;** www.fpct.org), presents seven productions a year and is a venue for the annual Baltimore Playwrights Festival.

The city's prominent African-American theater company, **Arena Players,** 801 McCulloh St., off Martin Luther King Boulevard (© **410/728-6500**), presents contemporary plays and romantic comedies.

Everyman Theatre, 1727 N. Charles St. (© **410/752-2208;** www.everymantheatre. org), earns rave reviews for its local Equity productions of classics and new works. It plans to move to the renovated Town Theatre, 315 W. Fayette St., for the 2011 season. The **Theatre Project** ★, 45 W. Preston St. (© **410/752-8558;** www.theatreproject.org), presents experimental and avant-garde work.

Center Stage ★★★ Many major American plays—including works by August Wilson and Eric Overmyer—have been developed at Maryland's state theater, which has presented new and classic work since 1963. Center Stage offers child care at several matinees and "Nights Out" for its gay and lesbian fans. Two theaters offer both traditional seating and a more flexible black-box experience. 700 N. Calvert St. © **410/332-0033.** www.centerstage.org.

The Hippodrome Theatre ★ Located at the France-Merrick Performing Arts Center, this restored former vaudeville venue, built in 1914, now stages national Broadway shows. Orchestra seats and front balcony seats are good, but pass up the back rows of the balcony, unless it's a show you absolutely have to see. A cafe serves light fare, but it's usually crowded; arrive early or eat somewhere else downtown before heading to the theater. 10 N. Eutaw St. ℂ **410/837-7400,** or 547-SEAT (7328) for tickets. www.france-merrickpac.com.

THE CLUB & MUSIC SCENE

Baltimore has a nice variety of small live-performance venues. Major national acts come to the **1st Mariner Arena Baltimore** near the Inner Harbor, 201 W. Baltimore St. (ℂ **410/347-2020;** www.baltimorearena.com), **Pier Six Concert Pavilion** at the Inner Harbor, 731 Eastern Ave. (ℂ **410/783-4189;** www.piersixpavilion.com), and **Rams Head Live** at Power Plant Live, 20 Market Place (ℂ **410/244-1131;** www.ramsheadlive. com). Get tickets at **www.ticketmaster.com** for 1st Mariner Arena and at Rams Head Live for Pier Six and Rams Head.

Power Plant Live, a mix of restaurants and bars, is a short walk from the Inner Harbor, at Water Street and Market Place. It packs in young singles, especially on weekend nights, who come for the gigantic **Lucky's Tavern,** sports bar/rock bar; **Havana Club,** a cigar bar; and **Howl at the Moon,** a rock-'n'-roll piano bar, as well as Rams Head Live.

A number of clubs welcome smaller touring acts and local performers, from rock to jazz to folk. These are listed below.

Comedy

Baltimore Comedy Factory   See live comedy Thursday at 8pm, Friday at 8 and 10pm and midnight; and Saturday at 7, 9, and 11pm. 36 Light St. (at E. Lombard St.). ℂ **410/547-7798.** www.baltimorecomedy.com. Cover varies.

Folk & Traditional

Cat's Eye Pub   A Fell's Point bar with an Irish feel, Cat's Eye is known for its traditional Irish music, but you'll often hear blues, bluegrass, zydeco, and jazz as well. In addition to the nightly live music at 9pm, there's a back room with chessboards and game tables. Open daily from noon to 2am. 1730 Thames St. ℂ **410/276-9866.** www.catseyepub. com. Occasional $5 cover, mostly free.

Mick O'Shea's   One of Baltimore's centers for traditional Irish music, Mick O' Shea's hosts live music Thursday through Saturday nights, and food (sandwiches, soups, and Irish specialties) starting at 11:30am. 328 N. Charles St. ℂ **410/539-7504.** www.mickosheas. com. Cover about $3.

J. Patrick's   Locust Point's gathering spot for Irish music most nights of the week. Musicians welcome. 1371 Andre St. ℂ **410/244-8613.**

Jazz & Blues

An Die Musik Live!   This music shop schedules jazz and classical performances a couple times a week, held on the second floor of its Mount Vernon town house. Check the calendar online. 409 N. Charles St. ℂ **888/221-6170** or 410/385-2638. www.andiemusiklive. com. Cover varies.

Bertha's Restaurant & Bar   The Fell's Point bar/restaurant is a great venue for live jazz and blues nearly every day of the week. 734 S. Broadway. ℂ **410/327-5795.** www.berthas. com.

The **Baltimore Jazz Alliance** has set up a website listing local performances: www. baltimorejazz.com.

Bourbon Street   Three floors of live, usually rock-'n'-roll, entertainment with room for nearly 3,000 people. Thursdays are geared to the college crowd. Open Monday and Wednesday to Saturday nights. 316 Guilford Ave. ☎ 410/528-8377. www.bourbonstreet baltimore.com. Cover varies; concert tickets about $20.

The 8X10   This longtime favorite in Federal Hill has room for 400 on two floors. The focus is live music—from rock to blues to funk. Visit the website for a schedule. 8–10 E. Cross St. ☎ 410/625-2000. www.the8x10.com. Cover varies.

The Horse You Came In On   This Fell's Point bar is popular with the local college and post-collegiate crowds. The Horse features live rock or acoustic music on weekends. 1626 Thames St. ☎ 410/327-8111. Cover varies.

The Ottobar   Classic indie-rock club. 2549 N. Howard St. ☎ 410/662-0069. Cover varies.

The Recher Theatre   North of town in Towson, this former movie theater has become a magnet for local and national musicians, mostly rock but also some ska, reggae, and blues. 512 York Rd., Towson. ☎ 410/337-8316. www.rechertheatre.com. Cover varies; music lovers under 21 admitted.

Sonar   Sonar has a DJ or concerts most nights, with an emphasis on techno and house music. There are three rooms; the Main Stage room holds 1,000 people. 407 E. Saratoga St. ☎ 410/783-7888. www.sonarbaltimore.com. Cover varies.

BEER, BILLIARDS & CIGARS

Edgar's Billiards Club & Restaurant   This upscale day-and-night club near the Inner Harbor offers 17 full-size pool tables as well as smoking and nonsmoking areas and a fine selection of cigars. 1 E. Pratt St. (at Light St.). ☎ 410/752-8080.

Havana Club (Finds)   Upstairs from Ruth's Chris Steak House is this very sophisticated little spot offering appetizers, desserts, and cigars. A DJ spins tunes on Friday and Saturday. Open Wednesday through Saturday. 600 Water St. ☎ 410/468-0022. www.havanaclub baltimore.com.

Max's Taphouse   Max's is a Baltimore institution known for its tremendous beer selection: 72 rotating drafts and 300 bottles. Cigar friendly, the pub is also home to the Darthouse, with dartboards set up for both regulation play and fun. If you must stay connected, Wi-Fi is free here. 737 S. Broadway. ☎ 410/675-MAXS (6297). www.maxs.com.

THE GAY & LESBIAN SCENE

For a complete listing of nightspots, check out *Gay Life,* published by the **GLBT Community Center of Baltimore & Central Maryland** (☎ 410/837-5445; www.glccb.org), and **www.outinbaltimore.com.** Below are some longtime community favorites.

The Creative Alliance   This performance space hosts the Charm City Kitty Club, a troupe of lesbian, bi, and transgender performers. See the website for a schedule and ticket prices. 3134 Eastern Ave., Highlandtown. ☎ 410/276-3206. www.charmcitykittyclub.com.

Grand Central   This Mount Vernon pub has six bars, a video bar, and pool tables. Sapphos is a ladies' lounge. The high-tech industrial dance floor is open Wednesday through Sunday, 9pm to 2am. 1001–1003 N. Charles St. ☎ 410/752-7133. www.centralstation pub.com.

The Hippo ★ This classic has three large rooms with pool, videos, and a dance floor that attracts a primarily GLBT clientele, but all are welcome. The music is mostly house and techno. Happy hour is 4 to 8pm. Wednesday bingo is a smash hit among both gay and straight players, raising funds and fun, too. 1 W. Eager St. (at Charles St.). ☎ 410/547-0069. www.clubhippo.com. Cover varies.

FILM

The Charles Theatre The Charles, located in a historic industrial building, offers films not showing anywhere else in town—first-run independent and foreign films in particular. It has five comfortable auditoriums with stadium seating. The Charles is also a venue of the annual Maryland Film Festival, held in the spring. 1711 N. Charles St. ☎ 410/727-3456. www.thecharles.com.

IMAX Theater/Maryland Science Center Even if you have no interest in the science center, you can still see the IMAX movies. In addition to regular daytime features, there are double features each weekend on the theater's five-story-high, 75-foot-wide screen. 601 Light St. (on the harbor). ☎ 410/685-5225. www.mdsci.org.

Little Italy Open Air Film Festival On summer Fridays, you can catch a free movie. Bring a lawn chair, or use the ones already set up, to see films with an Italian accent, such as *Cinema Paradiso* and *Spartacus*. The movies are projected from the bedroom window of a nearby house. High and Stiles sts. www.littleitalymd.com.

Landmark Theatres Movies returned to downtown with the opening of this new seven-screen cinema in Harbor East. They'll even validate parking for a reasonable $3. 645 S. President St. ☎ 410/624-2622. www.landmarktheatres.com.

10 SIDE TRIPS FROM BALTIMORE

ELLICOTT CITY

Visitors have been coming to this tiny Patapsco River town, 14 miles from Baltimore, for 230 years. The town was built to support the Ellicott brothers' mill, the largest flour-milling center in Colonial America. In 1831, America's first railroad terminal was constructed here and still stands today. It was also here that the *Tom Thumb,* Peter Cooper's steam engine, raced and beat a horse-drawn vehicle. The country's first national road also ran through Ellicott City and gave farmers a route to the Atlantic.

Step back and look at the solid stone buildings still lining Main Street. The inns built in the 1800s remain—even the Colonial Inn and Opera House (now the Forget-Me-Not Factory), where John Wilkes Booth, it is said, got his start as an actor. Over the years, the town has endured fires, floods, and hurricanes. Through it all, it has survived, and its history and charm continue to draw visitors.

Essentials

GETTING THERE From Route 70, take Route 29 South to Route 40 East. Turn right on Rogers Avenue and right again on Courthouse Drive, which ends at Main Street (Rte. 144). Turn left into the historic district. From the Beltway (Rte. 695), either take Route 70 West and follow the above directions or take Route 40 West and turn left on Rogers Avenue, right on Courthouse Drive, and left on Main Street.

is open Monday through Saturday from 10am to 5pm, Sunday from noon to 5pm. Look for the side entrance on Hamilton Street. You'll find a great self-guided walking tour brochure that offers some insight into the buildings' history.

PARKING   If you look hard, you can find parking spaces in lots marked with blue "P" signs. There are metered lots off Main Street near the visitor center, down a driveway under the railroad bridge, and on Maryland Avenue near the Ellicott City B&O Railroad Museum. You can get change for the meters at the visitor center or the railroad museum. (If the parking space is lined in yellow, you have to pay; it's free if the space is white.) *Warning:* On-street parking, though not metered, has a 1- or 2-hour limit between 10am and 6pm—and cars are ticketed for staying too long.

Some lots are free: The Oella lot is across the Patapsco River Bridge near the Trolley Stop restaurant. Another free lot is down a driveway on Ellicott Mills Drive. Finally, the two lots at the courthouse, 2 blocks from the historic district, have 200 free spaces. The walk is short, though uphill on the way back to your car. A good brochure from the visitor center explains where and how to park.

Where to Dine

Ellicott City has 17 restaurants crammed along its narrow streets. For traditional French, don't miss the wonderful **Tersiguel's French Country Restaurant,** 8293 Main St. (© **410/465-4004;** www.tersiguels.com). **La Palapa Grill & Cantina,** 8307 Main St. (© **410/465-0070;** www.lapalapagrill.com), serves Mexican in a gaily decorated atmosphere. **Cacao Lane Restaurant,** 8066 Main St. (© **410/461-1378;** www.cacaolane. net), is a casual spot with a Continental menu. Light-rock musicians perform Friday and Saturday evenings. The **Ellicott Mills Brewing Company,** 8308 Main St. (© **410/313-8141;** www.ellicottmillsbrewing.com), brews its own beer to accompany the German and pub-style entrees.

What to See & Do

"Ye Haunted History of Old Ellicott City" tours are offered April through November, Friday and Saturday at 8:30pm. Reservations are essential; call © **800/288-8747.**

The **B&O Railroad Museum: Ellicott City Station,** 2711 Maryland Ave. (© **410/313-1413;** www.ecborail.org), America's oldest train station, houses artifacts and model trains. Annie Oakley and Charles Dickens once passed through here. Hours are Wednesday through Sunday from 11am to 4pm. Admission is $5 adults, $3 for children.

The **Thomas Isaac Log Cabin,** 8398 Main St. (www.thomasisaaclogcabin.net), a settler's cabin, was built about 1780—making it the town's oldest residence (Fri–Sat and Mon 1–6pm and Sun noon–5pm).

Just down Frederick Road—called Main Street in the historic district—is **Benjamin Banneker Historical Park and Museum,** 300 Oella Ave. (© **410/887-1081**). Dedicated to the first African-American "man of science," the modern museum has interactive exhibits about Banneker, who surveyed the land for construction of Washington, D.C. The park has added a log cabin, simulating Banneker's house, as well as lots of green space and nature trails. It's open Tuesday through Saturday from 10am to 4pm; a $3 donation is suggested. Take Frederick Road east across Patapsco River Bridge; turn left at Oella Avenue.

Most people come to shop at the antiques and gift stores that line Main Street and the side streets. Hours are usually 10am to 6pm; stores close on Monday or Tuesday.

For home decor, stop at **Cottage Antiques,** 8181 Main St. (© **410/465-1412**); **Joan Eve,** 8018 Main St. (© **410/750-1210**); **Taylor's Antique Mall,** 8197 Main St. (© **410/465-4444**); and **Su Casa,** 8307 Main St. (© **410/465-4100**).

Ellicott's Country Store, 8180 Main St. (© **410/465-4482**), is worth a visit for the architecture—it's considered the oldest duplex in the country. Handcrafted gifts are featured at **Discoveries,** 8055 Main St. (© **410/461-9600**).

The **Forget-Me-Not Factory,** 8044 Main St. (© **410/465-7355**), stocks magic wands and fairy wings. Musicians and coffee addicts alike will enjoy **Clef Notes Music and Cafe,** 8381 Merryman St. (© **410/461-6709**), which serves sheet music with its lattes.

HAVRE DE GRACE

Havre de Grace—tucked up near the Mason-Dixon line, 28 miles northeast of Baltimore—is primarily a sailing town now, though it was once an important Colonial crossroads. In fact, it is said that a single vote kept it from becoming the new nation's capital. Today, this picturesque town makes an excellent stop either to or from Baltimore. It's known for good restaurants, charming shops, a lighthouse, and stunning views of the spot where the Susquehanna River becomes the Chesapeake Bay.

The area was originally home to the Susquehannocks, with the first European settlers arriving in 1658. First called Harmer's Town, it soon became the location of a river ferry, which operated for 170 years. After the Revolutionary War, it adopted its current name from a suggestion by French soldiers who lovingly compared it to Le Havre back home. This was a popular destination in the early 20th century, when a famous racetrack drew the likes of the legendary Seabiscuit, Man o' War, and Citation. Today, the town is much quieter, but it remains a crossroads—for trains racing across the river, for barges carrying stone down the bay, and for people speeding along I-95.

Essentials

GETTING THERE You could sail into Havre de Grace from the lower Chesapeake Bay. Most people, however, drive here. It's only 4 minutes off I-95 at exit 89 (Rte. 155). Take Route 155 east and go under the Route 40 bridge. Turn right on Juniata Street, left on Otsego Street, and right on Water Street, and you'll be heading into town along the water's edge. Parking is available on the street, at the parks and museums, and at each end of the promenade.

VISITOR INFORMATION The **Havre de Grace Office of Tourism & Visitor Center** is at 450 Pennington Ave., between Union Avenue and Market Street (© **800/851-7756** or 410/939-2100; www.hdgtourism.com). Check the website for maps and sightseeing information. Make sure you pick up a walking-tour guide and the handy museum guide.

SPECIAL EVENTS In early May, the **reenactment of the attack on Havre de Grace in the War of 1812** (© **410/942-5780**) takes place on the Lock House grounds. Mid-August brings the **Havre de Grace Seafood Festival** (© **410/939-1525**) to Tydings Park, with auctions and a crab-calling contest. On the weekend after Labor Day, the **Duck Fair** (© **410/939-3739**) celebrates wildlife art at the Havre de Grace Decoy Museum and grounds. **First Fridays,** from April to December, feature street performances and specials at restaurants and shops.

Because Havre de Grace is down Route 40 from the Aberdeen Proving Ground, a military installation, plenty of chain hotels are nearby, such as **Best Western** (✆ 410/679-9700), **Days Inn** (✆ 410/671-9990), and **Courtyard by Marriott, Aberdeen at Ripken Stadium** (✆ 410/272-0440).

Currier House Bed & Breakfast   Location, location, location: This B&B is only a few steps from the promenade, lighthouse, and several museums. The 1790 farmhouse is filled with antiques reflecting the days when Havre de Grace attracted hunters and racing fans. It's a homey place with a wide front porch, cozy parlor, and quiet backyard. The rooms are small and simply but comfortably furnished; two have balconies with water views.

800 S. Market St., Havre de Grace, MD 21078. ✆ **800/827-2889** or 410/939-7886. www.currier-bb.com. 4 units. $95–$135 double. Rates include full breakfast. AE, DISC, MC, V. Free parking. *In room:* A/C, TV/VCR, hair dryer, no phone.

The Old Chesapeake Hotel ★★   The owners have converted several old houses near their original inn into comfortable guest suites. The main building houses a restaurant and four suites. There are also rooms in five other buildings, all on Union Avenue, except for one on Girard Street. Though there's a nod to local history, the operative word here is comfort.

400 N. Union Ave., Havre de Grace, MD 21078. ✆ **410/939-5440.** Fax 410/939-8020. www.oldchesapeake hotel.com. 30 units. $119–$149 double. Rates include continental breakfast. AE, MC, V. Free parking. No children 7 and under allowed. Children 8 and over welcome in parent's room (up to 2 kids per room allowed); children 16 and over can stay in own room. **Amenities:** Room service from adjoining restaurant. *In room:* A/C, TV, fridge, hair dryer, high-speed Internet.

The Spencer Silver Mansion Bed & Breakfast ★★★ (Value)   This grand granite lady will take you back to Havre de Grace's gay '90s. From the wraparound porch to the 12-foot ceilings, the 1896 B&B offers an elegant yet warm welcome. All that heavy furniture and Victorian-style decor could be intimidating, but the innkeeper works hard to keep it cozy. Big windows give the bedrooms an airy feel; the Iris Room even has a whirlpool tub. A carriage house just past the garden has a sitting room, kitchenette, large bedroom with two window seats, and bathroom with whirlpool; it sleeps four.

200 S. Union Ave., Havre de Grace, MD 21078. ✆ **800/780-1485** or 410/939-1485. www.spencersilver mansion.com. 5 units, 2 with shared bathroom. $85–$160 double. Rates include full breakfast. AE, DC, DISC, MC, V. Free parking. Pets accepted. **Amenities:** Parlor w/TV/VCR, stereo, and guest fridge. *In room:* A/C, TV/DVD, Wi-Fi.

Vandiver Inn   This sprawling Victorian mansion, built in 1886, is on the National Register of Historic Places. Its location on tree-lined Union Avenue is 2 blocks from the water. The bedrooms come in all sizes—some can even be connected to create a suite. A spacious honeymoon suite has a gas fireplace, four-poster bed, and whirlpool tub. Two guesthouses offer a little more privacy. New is the Monday night supper club.

301 S. Union Ave., Havre de Grace, MD 21078. ✆ **800/245-1655** or 410/939-5200. Fax 410/939-5202. www.vandiverinn.com. 17 units. $119–$159 double. Rates include full breakfast. AE, DISC, MC, V. Free parking. No children under 6. *In room:* A/C, TV, fridge, hair dryer, Wi-Fi.

Where to Dine

Laurrapin AMERICAN   Here is where the Chesapeake meets cuisine from the rest of the world. Lobster is added into the crab cake, gazpacho is seasoned with Old Bay, and salmon is served piccata, with a lemon caper sauce or Chesapeake-style with crab. Try Cioppino from the West Coast or mahimahi caught off Ocean City. Brunch only is served on Sunday.

209 N. Washington St. ℂ **410/939-4956.** www.laurrapin.com. Reservations recommended on week-ends. Main courses $7–$14 lunch, $13–$25 dinner. MC, V. Tues–Thurs 11am–3pm and 5–10pm; Fri–Sat 11am–3pm and 5–11pm; Sun 10:30am–3pm.

MacGregor's Restaurant ★★ SEAFOOD   Set high above the water, MacGregor's boasts a view from every table. Food is served on the deck and in the two-tiered dining room at lunch, dinner, Sunday brunch, and weekday happy hour. The menu is heavy on such seafood items as crab dip, crab cakes, and lobster fettuccine; the Dijon-encrusted rockfish filet has won awards. This casual spot with brick walls and duck prints is a place for fun—there's live music on Fridays and Saturdays, as well as Sundays in summer.

331 St. John St. ℂ **800/300-6319** or 410/939-3003. www.macgregorsrestaurant.com. Reservations sug-gested for dinner. Main courses $8–$14 lunch, $18–$25 dinner. AE, MC, V. Mon–Fri 11am–10pm; Sat 11am–11pm; Sun 10am–9pm.

Tidewater Grille ★★★ SEAFOOD/STEAKS   *Be forewarned:* You could get so caught up in the action on the river and beyond, you might forget to eat. Trains race past on the nearby bridge; sailboats and barges skim across the water. If you can get your mind back on the food, you're in for a treat. The same menu is available all day, everything from delicately seasoned crab cakes, burgers, soups, salads, and sandwiches to pasta, prime rib, lamb chops, and fresh fish. In pretty weather, eat on the deck—it's heaven. There are transient slips for hungry boaters, too.

300 Franklin St. ℂ **410/939-3313** or 575-7045. Reservations needed for parties of 6 or more. Main courses $8–$32. AE, DC, MC, V. Sun–Thurs 11am–10pm; Fri–Sat 11am–11pm.

What to See & Do

Lots of visitors to Havre de Grace come just for the water views—which you can see from the **promenade** ★★★, the parks, and several restaurants. The **Millard E. Tydings Memorial Park** has room for a picnic, or you can bring your fishing rod to the **Frank J. Hutchins Memorial Park.** The .5-mile promenade takes pedestrians (and bikers before 10am) along the southeast edge of town. It starts (or ends) at the Concord Point Light-house and winds through wetlands and along the shore to Tydings Park. Along the way, stop at the Havre de Grace Decoy Museum or the Havre de Grace Maritime Museum.

The town boasts six small museums and historic sites: four in town and two on the outskirts. They take only an hour or two to walk through, and admission is downright cheap. In fact, an adult can visit all six for less than $20. Hours are limited to the week-ends, except the decoy and maritime museums, which are open daily.

Concord Point Lighthouse ★★★   This stout 36-foot-tall lighthouse at the head-waters of the bay has been watching over sailors since 1827—it's one of the oldest con-tinuously operating lighthouses on the East Coast.

Concord and Lafayette sts., at north edge of promenade. ℂ **410/939-3213.** Free admission. May–Oct Sat–Sun 1–5pm. Closed major holidays.

Havre de Grace Decoy Museum ★★   Decoys are the star here, where the carved geese and ducks range from purely functional to fine art. The first-floor exhibits look at decoys as tools, while the second-floor decoys are exhibited as folk and even fine art. Don't miss the full-size figure of R. Madison Mitchell, one of the best-known carvers in this decoy-carving capital. The museum has re-created in 3-D a photo of Mitchell by the famous Baltimore photographer Aubrey Bodine.

215 Giles St. ℂ **410/939-3739.** www.decoymuseum.com. Admission $6 adults; $5 seniors, $2 children 9–18. Mon–Sat 11am–4:30pm; Sun noon–4pm. Closed Thanksgiving, Dec 25, Jan 1, and Easter.

Havre de Grace Maritime Museum Exhibits here tell the story of Havre de Grace's maritime commerce, with most of the items donated by local residents—including a replica of a shad shack and original artifacts from the last 400 years of fishing and crabbing. Expansion in 2009 has added exhibit space and provided updated ground-floor homes for the Susquehanna Flats Environmental Center's ecology programs and the Chesapeake Wooden Boat Builders School. Stop here to see boats from sailboats to canoes under construction.

100 Lafayette St. ℭ **410/939-4800.** www.hdgmaritimemuseum.org. Admission $3 adults, $2.50 seniors and students. June–Aug daily 10am–5pm; Sept–May Wed and Fri–Mon 10am–5pm.

Mount Felix Winery Wines produced at this family-owned establishment pay homage to historical figures from the area, including John Adlum, the father of American viticulture.

2000-A Level Rd. (off Rte. 155). ℭ **410/939-0913.** Free admission; tastings $5. Tasting room Tues–Sun noon–6pm.

Rock Run Historic Area at Susquehanna State Park Sure, this is a great park for hiking along the Susquehanna River, climbing the hills, and riding a bike or horse along the miles of paths through the forest—but the historic area is worth a visit, too. Start at the Jersey Toll House (now an information center for the park) for maps and to see if there are any closings. Also in this area are the Rock Run Grist Mill, built in 1794, the Rock Run Mansion which was under repairs at press time, and the Steppingstone Museum (described below).

Off Rte. 155, 3 miles northwest of Havre de Grace. ℭ **410/557-7994.** Free admission. Park daily 9am–sunset; historic buildings Memorial Day to Labor Day Sat–Sun 9am–4pm.

Steppingstone Museum ★ Steppingstone, in Susquehanna State Park, celebrates the area's agricultural history with demonstrations of the rural arts. Visitors can see the 1772 farmhouse, blacksmith forge, a 1900-era general store, veterinary office from the 1800s, and cannery. The farm is the site of a Civil War encampment in May, Scottish Festival in June, and Fall Harvest Festival in September. Of special note are the collections of quilts, toys, and hats.

461 Quaker Bottom Rd., off Rte. 155. ℭ **888/419-1762** or 410/939-2299. Admission $5 adults, free for children 13 and under. May–Sept Sat–Sun 1–4pm.

Susquehanna Museum at the Lock House ★ (Kids) This restored 1840 lock tender's home, listed on the National Register of Historic Places, sat at the end of the Susquehanna and Tidewater Canal, where the canal emptied into the river. The canal is no longer used, but the pivot bridge has been reconstructed so visitors can see how it worked. Inside the house are kitchen gadgets (which the kids can touch), a massive Steinway piano, a century-old bicycle with canvas tires, and even the last lock tender's wedding coat. You can also see changing exhibits and a video on the town's history. In early December, don't miss the candlelight boutique with gifts, wreaths, and food; it's part of the town's Christmas Candlelight Tour, held the second Sunday in December.

817 Consteto St., at northern edge of town. ℭ **410/939-5780.** www.lockhousemuseum.org. Free admission. Sat–Sun 1–5pm.

Tours & Boat Rides

The **Skipjack** *Martha Lewis* ★ (ℭ 410/939-4078; www.skipjackmarthalewis.org), docked at Tydings Park, offers cruises on most weekends from May to mid-October. Summer visitors can learn about sailing one of the last skipjacks on the bay—the 1955 boat is still a working girl, spending her winters dredging for oysters in the Chesapeake Bay. Oyster dredging trips are available in November or December. Call for reservations. The Mississippi riverboat *Lantern Queen* (© **410/939-1468;** www.lanternqueen.com) offers dinner and sunset cruises from its dock at Hutchins Park, at the foot of Congress Avenue. Call for reservations and sailing schedule.

Shopping

Havre de Grace's shops are about 7 blocks north of the promenade. Though it can be a pleasant walk along tree-lined Union Avenue or Market Street, it might be worth driving the short distance if it's a sultry day. Parking is free but limited to 2 hours.

Antiques shops dot Franklin and Washington streets. For furniture, stop at **Bayside Antiques,** 232 N. Washington St. (© **410/939-9397**). Decoy fans will want to stop at **Vincenti Decoys,** 353 Pennington Ave. (© **410/734-7709**). Chocolates are made on the premises at family-owned **Bomboy's Home Made Candy,** 329 Market St. (© **410/939-2924;** www.bomboyscandy.com) and ice cream is served in their shop across the street. **Pencilworks Gallery,** 201 St. John St. (© **410/942-0040**), offers the creations of local artisans, including jewelry, photography, and paintings.

Outdoor Activities

BIKING Two local shops rent bikes for about $15 a half-day. Take them along Havre de Grace's quiet back lanes or head over to the trails in nearby Susquehanna State Park. Both **Biller's Bikes,** 450 Franklin St. (© **443/502-2377**), and **Chesapeake Cycle and Sport,** 101 N. Washington St. (© **410/939-8735**), offer a bridge-crossing service for those who want to cross the Susquehanna to continue biking up the East Coast Greenway. Both are open Wednesday to Sunday.

BOATING Boat ramps are at Millard E. Tydings Memorial Park, Frank J. Hutchins Memorial Park, and Jean Roberts Memorial Park. The launching fee is $8. **Tidewater Marina,** at the foot of Bourbon Street (© **410/939-0950**), has transient boat slips. Experienced sailors can charter a yacht from **BaySail** (© **410/939-2869;** www.baysail. net) for a weekend or a couple hours. It also has 3- to 5-day courses for everyone from beginners to advanced sailors.

GOLFING **Bulle Rock,** 320 Blenheim Lane (© **410/939-8887;** www.bullerockgolf. com), home of several LPGA tournaments, is open to the public. Be warned; it has a reputation not only for its good looks but its challenging holes.

HIKING Trails through **Susquehanna State Park** offer pretty views of the Susquehanna River, and are open to hikers, bikers, horses, and cross-country skiers. If you go by way of the **Lower Susquehanna Heritage Greenway,** it's possible to walk to the dam—which is quite a sight. The huge concrete dam holds back the mighty river, reducing it to a shallow rocky bed.

KAYAKING **Chesapeake Cycle and Sport,** 101 N. Washington St. (© **410/939-8735**), rents kayaks for $30 for 2 hours. Beginning in spring 2010, they'll have a boat launch a block away on the Susquehanna.

PARASAILING **High Hopes** (© **410/287-5298**) offers flights from a-400 or 800-foot rope for $40 to $60 with dry takeoffs at the City Yacht Basic, 352 Commerce St. Just want to ride along? It's $10 for a half-hour.

Maryland's Two Capitals: Annapolis & St. Mary's City

Maryland's two capitals, present-day Annapolis and the state's first capital, St. Mary's City, are only 86 miles—and 3 centuries—apart. Annapolis thrives today, while St. Mary's City has disappeared. But St. Mary's is reemerging, with archaeological digs and reconstruction of the colony's first town.

Though it's a state capital, Annapolis retains much of its Colonial heritage. The State House is where George Washington resigned as commander in chief and Congress ratified the treaty to end the Revolutionary War. More than 1,500 Colonial buildings are scattered along the narrow brick streets and alleys—more than in any other town in the country.

It's also a college town, home to the United States Naval Academy and to St. John's College, known for its "Great Books" curriculum.

Lawmakers meet in the General Assembly from January to April. Midshipmen march in "The Yard" every semester. And on most weekends, Annapolis's streets bustle with packed restaurants, bars, and shops. Workboats still seek the shellfish for which the Chesapeake Bay is known. In spring, the pleasure boats arrive. Warm weather brings the festivities to the water's edge, and downtown takes on the air of a casual long-running party.

Among its long list of accolades, Annapolis has been named one of America's prettiest towns, a livable and a playful city.

1 ORIENTATION

ARRIVING

BY PLANE **Baltimore/Washington International Thurgood Marshall Airport** (ℂ **800/I-FLY-BWI** [435-9294] or 410/859-7111; www.bwiairport.com) is 24 miles north of Annapolis, off I-295 (the Baltimore–Washington Pkwy.). Domestic airlines serving BWI include **American** (ℂ 800/433-7300; www.aa.com), **Continental** (ℂ 800/525-0280; www.continental.com), **Delta** (ℂ 800/221-1212; www.delta.com), **Northwest** (ℂ 800/225-2525; www.nwa.com), **Southwest** (ℂ 800/435-9792; www.southwest.com), **United** (ℂ 800/241-6522; www.united.com), and **US Airways** (ℂ 800/428-4322; www.usairways.com).

To get to Annapolis from the airport, follow I-97 south to U.S. Route 50. Various exits will take you into town (although many chain hotels are right off Rte. 50). The Rowe Boulevard exit is the most direct one to the historic district. **SuperShuttle** (ℂ **800/258-3826;** www.supershuttle.com) charges about $30 between BWI and Annapolis. A taxi is about $45 one-way; call **BWI Airport Taxi** at ℂ **410/859-1103.**

BY TRAIN   **Amtrak** and three Annapolis-area shuttle services have teamed up to make it easier to come to Annapolis by train. For about $26, a shuttle will take Amtrak passengers from the BWI terminal directly to their hotel or other destination in the Annapolis area. Reservations are required. For details or the reservation link, go to the Northeast Corridor timetable at **www.amtrak.com**.

BY CAR   From Baltimore and points north, take I-695 (the Baltimore Beltway) to I-97 south to U.S. Route 50 east. Rowe Boulevard from U.S. Route 50 will take you into downtown. From Washington, D.C., take U.S. Route 50 east off the Washington Beltway (I-495) to Rowe Boulevard.

BY BOAT   Docking at the Annapolis City Dock or moorings in the harbor are available on a first-come, first-served basis. Moorings cost $25 for boats under 45 feet. Dock fees are $6 an hour for boats up to 50 feet, $12 for bigger vessels. Electric is extra. Pay fees at the Harbormaster's Office on the City Dock. For information, call ✆ **410/263-7973** or e-mail harbormaster@ci.annapolis.md.us.

BY BUS   **Greyhound** (✆ **800/231-2222** or 410/263-2964; www.greyhound.com) offers service to 308 Chinquapin Round Rd. **Dillon's Bus Service** (✆ **800/827-3490** or 410/647-2321; www.dillonbus.com) runs commuter buses to D.C., with stops at the Navy/Marine Corps Stadium, Harry S. Truman Park & Ride, and West Street. It costs $4.25 one-way. The **Maryland Transit Administration** (**MTA;** ✆ **800/543-9809** or 410/539-5000; www.mtamaryland.com) provides commuter bus service between Annapolis and Baltimore, as well as Washington, D.C., connecting to some of the MTA's Light Rail stops.

VISITOR INFORMATION

The **Annapolis and Anne Arundel Conference and Visitors Bureau** (✆ **410/280-0445;** www.visitannapolis.org) runs a visitor center at 26 West St., just west of Church Circle. Trolley and walking tours (p. 124) depart from here daily. The volunteers will make recommendations and reservations for tours, dinner, and accommodations. A continuously running film gives visitors a taste of Annapolis's charms (daily 9am–5pm, except Jan 1, Thanksgiving, and Dec 25). The bureau also runs an information booth at the City Dock during warm weather.

CITY LAYOUT

The streets of downtown Annapolis radiate from two circles: **State Circle** and **Church Circle.** The three main streets of the Historic District are Main, Maryland, and West. Main Street leads from Church Circle to the City Dock. Maryland Avenue stretches from State Circle to the walls of the U.S. Naval Academy. West Street runs from Church Circle to Westgate Circle and out to routes 2 and 50. The U.S. Naval Academy, surrounded by a high gray wall, is in its own enclave, east of downtown.

2 GETTING AROUND

BY SHUTTLE   The **Annapolis Department of Transportation** (**ADOT;** ✆ **410/263-7964;** www.annapolis.gov/transport) operates two free shuttles between the historic/business district and the parking area of the Navy/Marine Corps Stadium. The State Shuttle runs Monday through Friday from 6:30am to 8pm, Saturday and Sunday from 10am to 6pm; it departs every 5 minutes during rush hour, every 15 minutes the rest of the day, with stops at Church Circle, near the visitor center, and near the State House. The Navy Bus Shuttle operates May through September, leaving the Navy/Marine Corps Stadium on the hour and half-hour every day. It stops at the Naval Academy's visitors' gate, Main Street, and West Annapolis locations. *Tip:* Board any shuttle bus in the historic district—between Westgate Circle to the west and the City Dock—and ride for free.

BY BUS   Annapolis bus service can get visitors all around town, from the historic district to West Annapolis and the shopping centers near Route 50. (The Brown route shuttles between the City Dock and Annapolis Mall. Base fare is $1, except in the Free Fare Zone; exact change is required.) Buses run every half-hour, Monday through Saturday, from 6am to 7pm, Sunday from 8am to 7pm. Get a schedule at **www.annapolis. gov/transport**.

BY CAR   Car-rental firms in Annapolis include **Budget,** 2002 West St. (© **410/266-5030**); **Discount,** 1032 West St. (© **410/269-6645**); and **Enterprise,** 1023 Spa Rd. (© **410/268-7751**).

Parking is limited in the Historic District, where streets are narrow and much of the 18th-century layout is intact. Visitors are encouraged to leave their cars in a park-and-ride lot on the edge of town, off Rowe Boulevard just west of the Navy/Marine Corps Stadium for $5, and then take the free shuttle. Parking garages at about $1 an hour can be found behind the visitor center off Northwest Street; on Duke of Gloucester Street, behind City Hall; and on West Street. You can also try your luck at metered parking at the City Dock or on the street. If you park on a side street, look for parking restriction signs; without a permit, parking is limited to 2 hours. If you come on a summer weekend, look for the parking valet near the City Dock.

Cars with handicapped tags can park at meters for twice the time limit at no charge. In residential districts, they may park 4 hours.

BY TAXI   Call **Annapolis Cab** (© **410/268-0022**) or **Yellow Cab** (© **410/268-1212**) for taxi service.

BY WATER TAXI   The **Water Taxi** (© **410/263-0033**) operates from the City Dock to restaurants and other destinations along Spa and Back creeks. You can also call for a water taxi, just as you would a land taxi, and get picked up from your boat or waterfront location. If you're at a restaurant, ask the waiter to call for a ride back. It's a handy way to avoid the parking hassle as well as a pleasant sightseeing experience. Fares range from $2 to $4.50. Hours are Monday through Thursday from 9:30am to 11pm, Friday from 9:30am to 1am, Saturday from 9am to 1am, and Sunday from 9am to 11pm. Service is available in early May and in September and October.

Fast Facts   **Annapolis**

American Express   The office is near Church Circle at 9 Northwest St. (© **410/224-4200**). It's open Monday through Saturday.

Area Code   The area codes in Annapolis are **410** and **443.**

Emergencies   Dial © **911** for fire, police, or ambulance.

Hospital   Go to **Anne Arundel Medical Center,** 2001 Medical Pkwy., Jennifer Road, off Route 50 (© **443/481-1000**).

Newspapers & Magazines The local daily newspaper is the Annapolis *Capital.* The *Baltimore Sun* and the *Washington Post* are also widely available. The leading monthly magazine is *What's Up? Annapolis.*

Pharmacies Try **CVS,** 123 Main St. (© **410/295-3061**).

Post Office The main branch is at 1 Church Circle (© **410/263-1083**), open Monday through Friday from 9am to 5pm.

Taxes The local sales tax is 6%. The local hotel tax is an additional 7%.

3 WHERE TO STAY

Downtown Annapolis offers a mix of big hotels, historic inns, and bed-and-breakfasts, while Eastport is blessed with several good B&Bs. Accommodations in the historic district are convenient but pricey. *Note:* All major hotels have rooms accessible for travelers with disabilities, but most inns and bed-and-breakfasts do not. Also keep in mind that special events—the Naval Academy's Parents' Weekend in late summer, Commissioning Week in May, Army-Navy games, and the Annapolis Boat Show in October, to name a few—send hotel prices skyrocketing.

A number of more affordable chain hotels are located out on Route 50, a 15-minute ride or so to the historic district. These generally cost less and offer pools and larger rooms; some have shuttle service to downtown and Eastport. The **Country Inns and Suites by Carlson,** 2600 Housley Rd. (© **800/456-4000** or 410/571-6700; www.countryinns.com), is across the street from Westfield Annapolis and has a shuttle into downtown. The **Courtyard Annapolis,** 2559 Riva Rd. (© **800/321-2211** or 410/266-1555; www.marriott.com/bwian), has an indoor pool. **Sheraton Annapolis Hotel,** 173 Jennifer Rd. (© **800/325-3535** or 410/266-3131; www.sheraton.com/annapolis), has a downtown shuttle and indoor pool.

EXPENSIVE

The Annapolis Inn ★★★ This Georgian-themed inn was good enough for Thomas Jefferson's doctor in the 18th century, and it's perfect for a romantic getaway in the 21st century. The three bedrooms on separate levels are private, and they are shrines to comfort, with plush beds, lush seating, and bathrooms with Jacuzzis and heated marble floors. No phones, televisions if you must, and wireless Internet access only if absolutely necessary. The Murray suite is roomiest with a separate sitting room. Up under the eaves, the Rutland with its rustic fireplace is coziest. A three-course breakfast is served on china and crystal in the dining room and, in warm weather, on the intimate patio. Annapolis attractions are all close by. Want something more—perhaps a boat charter, in-room massage, string quartet, or cooking lessons? The innkeepers do what they can to make your stay just how you want it.

144 Prince George St., Annapolis, MD 21401. © **410/295-5200.** Fax 410/295-5201. www.annapolisinn. com. 3 units. $259–$479 suites. Rates include full breakfast. AE, MC, V. Street parking only. *In room:* A/C, TV upon request, free Wi-Fi.

Annapolis Marriott Waterfront ★★ The only waterfront hotel in Annapolis, and the only one with boat docks for guest use, this six-story property attracts boaters and boat lovers. It sits in the middle of all the action, beside the City Dock overlooking Ego

Alley and Spa Creek. Guest rooms, in the process of being updated in late 2007 and early 2008, are enhanced by floor-to-ceiling windows; about three-quarters of the rooms have water views or waterfront balconies, while 20 look right out over the water. Two rooms have Jacuzzis. Most rooms have pullout chair beds. "Pure" rooms have been designed for those with allergies and have special bedding and air filters, and are treated to reduce allergens. Historical photographs and ship models, including *Old Ironsides* and Hollywood's *African Queen,* adorn the public spaces.

80 Compromise St., Annapolis, MD 21401. ✆ **800/336-0072** or 410/268-7555. Fax 410/269-5864. www. annapolismarriott.com. 150 units. $269–$389 double; $349–$479 waterfront view. AE, DC, DISC, MC, V. Valet parking $19; free self-parking. **Amenities:** Indoor/outdoor restaurant and lounge; boat dock; fitness center; room service. *In room:* A/C, TV w/pay movies, fridge and microwave on request, hair dryer, Wi-Fi (fee).

The Inn at 30 Maryland ★
The symmetrical 1886 Queen Anne Victorian set in the middle of Maryland Avenue is architecturally unusual. But its owners, a former chef and his wife, have outfitted their B&B with style and comfort. Rooms are large enough to stretch out in, especially two suites. These are more like double-size rooms with sofas and refrigerators in a separate sitting area. Bathrooms were renovated in 2009. The back suite has a porch overlooking the neighboring Chase–Lloyd House's gardens. Breakfast is cooked to order and served in the dining room, "bistro" room, or outside in warm weather. Children 10 and over are welcome.

30 Maryland Ave., Annapolis, MD 21401. ✆ **410/263-9797.** www.30maryland.com. 5 suites. $175–$325. Rates include full breakfast. AE, MC, V. On-street parking. **Amenities:** Snacks and drinks in bistro; refrigerator and microwave. *In room:* A/C, TV w/satellite, fridge in 2 suites, hair dryer, free Wi-Fi.

Loews Annapolis Hotel ★★★ (Kids)
The Loews Annapolis is loaded with amenities (except for boat slips, see the Annapolis Marriott for those, and a pool, see the Westin for that) and an exceedingly friendly staff. Located near Church Circle, within walking distance of the historic district, this modern brick hotel has a tree-shaded courtyard entrance and sky-lit public areas. Guest rooms, newly redecorated but still in nautical colors, offer views of the skyline and historic area. Ask about packages for kids, grandparents traveling with children, or those who just need pampering. A shuttle is available at times when parking is tight, including the General Assembly session January into April, Commissioning Week, and other event weekends.

126 West St., Annapolis, MD 21401. ✆ **800/526-2593** or 410/263-7777. Fax 410/263-0084. www.loews hotels.com/annapolis. 216 units. $99–$329 double; $149–$379 suite. AE, DC, DISC, MC, V. Valet parking $22; free self-parking. Pets accepted for fee. **Amenities:** Restaurant; bar; coffee shop; concierge-level rooms; fitness center; spa. *In room:* A/C, TV w/pay movies, fridge and microwave upon request, hair dryer, Wi-Fi (fee).

O'Callaghan Annapolis Hotel ★★
This stylish Irish-owned hotel, sporting a contemporary Euro-style furniture in its spacious guest rooms, whispers low-key luxury—it would be vulgar to shout it. New duvets and other enhancements, including fridges in most rooms, enhanced the look in 2009. Eight units have balconies, some with table and chairs. Two suites are even roomier, situated in the back of the hotel away from West Street traffic noise. If you're here on business, note the large desks, Internet access, and extensive 24-hour business center. A shuttle bus will get you to and from the historic district. *Eco-note:* Rooms are outfitted with recycling bins.

174 West St., Annapolis, MD 21401. ✆ **410/263-7700.** Fax 410/990-1400. www.ocallaghanhotels-us. com. 120 units. $99–$209 double; $149–$299 suite. AE, DC, DISC, MC, V. Valet parking $15; free selfparking. **Amenities:** Restaurant; lounge; fitness center; room service. *In room:* A/C, TV w/pay movies and video games, fridge upon request, hair dryer, free Wi-Fi.

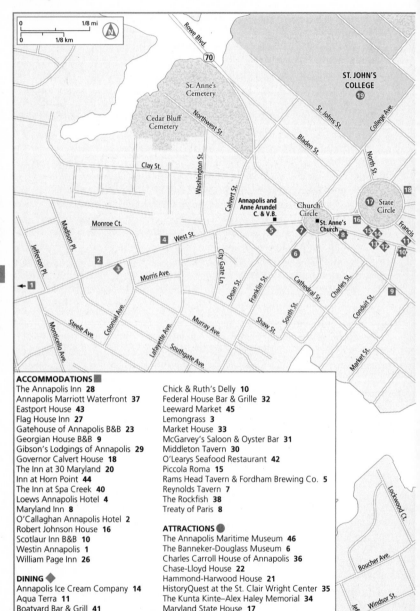

ACCOMMODATIONS ■
The Annapolis Inn **28**
Annapolis Marriott Waterfront **37**
Eastport House **43**
Flag House Inn **27**
Gatehouse of Annapolis B&B **23**
Georgian House B&B **9**
Gibson's Lodgings of Annapolis **29**
Governor Calvert House **18**
The Inn at 30 Maryland **20**
Inn at Horn Point **44**
The Inn at Spa Creek **40**
Loews Annapolis Hotel **4**
Maryland Inn **8**
O'Callaghan Annapolis Hotel **2**
Robert Johnson House **16**
Scotlaur Inn B&B **10**
Westin Annapolis **1**
William Page Inn **26**

DINING ◆
Annapolis Ice Cream Company **14**
Aqua Terra **11**
Boatyard Bar & Grill **41**
Café Normandie **12**
Carrol's Creek **39**
Castlebay Irish Pub **13**

Chick & Ruth's Delly **10**
Federal House Bar & Grille **32**
Leeward Market **45**
Lemongrass **3**
Market House **33**
McGarvey's Saloon & Oyster Bar **31**
Middleton Tavern **30**
O'Learys Seafood Restaurant **42**
Piccola Roma **15**
Rams Head Tavern & Fordham Brewing Co. **5**
Reynolds Tavern **7**
The Rockfish **38**
Treaty of Paris **8**

ATTRACTIONS ●
The Annapolis Maritime Museum **46**
The Banneker-Douglass Museum **6**
Charles Carroll House of Annapolis **36**
Chase-Lloyd House **22**
Hammond-Harwood House **21**
HistoryQuest at the St. Clair Wright Center **35**
The Kunta Kinte–Alex Haley Memorial **34**
Maryland State House **17**
St. John's College **19**
The William Paca House & Garden **25**
U.S. Naval Academy **24**

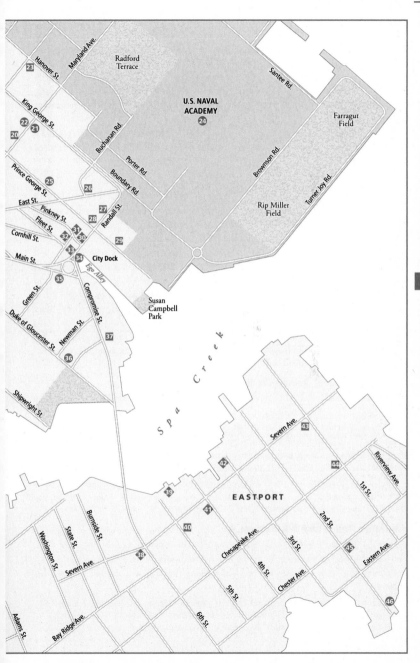

The Westin Annapolis ★★★   Annapolis's newest hotel anchors the west end of the town's redevelopment of West Street—and its sleek contemporary stylings are a breath of modern fresh air. The tea-scented lobby also houses a lounge with fireplace and a restaurant that serves breakfast, lunch, and afternoon tapas. A shuttle bus will get you to and from the historic district. The rooms feature the usual Westin luxury with big windows (great light but no great views), fluffy bedding, soothing neutral colors, and all the usual amenities. Morton's Steak House is located next door. The pool and fitness center are nicely outfitted. Packages include one with the Aveda spa nearby. Free "unwind" events are offered Monday to Friday 5 to 8pm. Shuttles travel within the historic district and to Eastport.

100 Westgate Circle (corner of Taylor Ave. and West St.), Annapolis, MD 21401. © **410/972-4300.** www. westin.com/annapolis. 225 units. $159–$409 double; $209–$509 suite. AE, DC, DISC, MC, V. Valet parking $23; self-parking $10. Small dogs accepted for fee. **Amenities:** Restaurant; lounge; room service; fitness center; indoor pool; whirlpool. *In room:* A/C, TV w/pay movies and video games, hair dryer, minibar, Wi-Fi.

MODERATE

Flag House Inn   The flags waving from the front porch offer a hint of who's staying here: The innkeepers fly the flags of their guests' home states or nations. This 1870s Victorian beauty, down the street from the Naval Academy's main gate, offers good-size rooms with either one king-size or two twin beds. Accommodations are well kept and bright, with a nice mix of modern and antique pieces. Every unit has a ceiling fan; front rooms have sound machines to soften the traffic noise outside. One room, decorated in lavender toile, is downright spacious. The innkeepers are proud parents of a 1999 USNA graduate, and the house is well located for visitors to the Naval Academy and the town itself. When you arrive, knock on the right-hand door.

26 Randall St., Annapolis, MD 21401. © **800/437-4825** or 410/280-2721. Fax 410/280-0133. www.flag houseinn.com. 5 units (shower only). $180–$300 double. Rates include full breakfast. MC, V. Free off-street parking. No children 10 and under. *In room:* A/C, ceiling fan, TV, free Wi-Fi.

The Gatehouse of Annapolis Bed & Breakfast   In the shadow of the Naval Academy, this brick town house combines Colonial style with modern convenience. Often filled with USNA relatives, it is convenient to the Naval Academy but still only a short walk from the historic district—and far enough out of the way to be quieter than places near Main Street. The best units are the two minisuites, each with a four-poster or sleigh bed, private sitting area, and bathroom. All come with fresh flowers, robes, and special soaps. The deck offers a quiet place to relax in the sun or under the stars.

249 Hanover St., Annapolis, MD 21401. © **888/254-7576** or 410/280-0024. www.gatehousebb.com. 5 units, 1 with shared bathroom. $200–$330 double. Rates include full breakfast. 2-night minimum stay and higher rates required some weekends. MC, V. Street parking only. *In room:* A/C, TV, free Wi-Fi.

Georgian House Bed & Breakfast ★   This B&B is one of the oldest structures in Annapolis. Its charm is enhanced by the modern conveniences and the location. Walk through the back gate and you're on your way down Main Street. Each unit has its own ambience: One room has a deck, one has a working fireplace, and another has a double shower.

170 Duke of Gloucester St., Annapolis, MD 21401. © **800/557-2068** or 410/263-5618. www.georgian house.com. 4 units. $189–$204 double. Rates include full breakfast. Rates higher on event weekends. AE, MC, V. Street parking only. **Amenities:** Fridge; library w/books and videos; microwave. *In room:* TV/VCR, free Wi-Fi.

The 1908 William Page Inn ★ In a town that lives and breathes Colonial style, here's a Victorian marvel, all cedar shake and wraparound porch. The first-floor bedroom has direct access to the porch; the quietest unit has a private bathroom with shower and whirlpool; and the spacious attic suite (with whirlpool, chaise, and couch) is far enough away that guests can disappear for days—and some do. Breakfast, served in the comfortable common room, is always tempting.

8 Martin St., Annapolis, MD 21401. ✆ **800/364-4160** or 410/626-1506. www.1908-williampageinn.com. 5 units, 2 with shared bathroom. $160–$245 double. Rates include full breakfast. MC, V. Free off-street parking. *In room:* TV upon request (standard in attic unit), CD player, no phone, free Wi-Fi.

INEXPENSIVE

The Barn on Howard's Cove Bed & Breakfast ★ Just a few minutes out of town, visitors can stay in a converted 1850 horse barn. But this isn't just a barn—it's a refuge. It's a little hard to find, set back on a driveway and perched on a quiet cove. A stone fireplace dominates the common room. Climb the spiral staircase to two delightful rooms—one with a queen-size bed and pullout love seat, the other with a queen-size bed, sleeping loft, and sitting room with balcony overlooking the water. In the hall is a kitchenette with fridge, microwave, coffeemaker, and video library. You can relax on the deck or in the gazebo, or launch a canoe and go exploring. If this place is booked but you want to stay on Howard's Cove, ask about **Meadow Garden,** a neighboring B&B with two rooms, or the **Farmhouse,** which has four rooms and a pool. Both are on the waterfront and have dock access. Rates are $100 a room in both B&Bs.

500 Wilson Rd., Annapolis, MD 21401. ✆ **410/266-6840.** www.barnonhowardscovebandb.com. 2 units. $150 double. Rates include full breakfast. No credit cards. Free parking. **Amenities:** Watersports equipment. *In room:* A/C, TV/VCR.

Gibson's Lodgings of Annapolis ⟨**Value**⟩ Tucked on a side street, this three-building complex is a quiet choice, yet it's only a few steps from the City Dock. Two of the buildings are historic town houses: the Patterson (a 1760s Federal Georgian with two large bedrooms) and the Berman (an 1890s house with a porch and eight bedrooms, one equipped for travelers with disabilities). Behind them is Lauer House, a 1988 addition with six suites, a full kitchen, and a sitting room that can serve as a conference room. Filled with both antiques and reproductions, the bedrooms are of varying sizes. A central garden and courtyard serve as a common area for all three buildings.

110 Prince George St., Annapolis, MD 21401. ✆ **877/330-0057** or 410/268-5555. Fax 410/268-2775. www.gibsonslodgings.com. 21 units, 4 with shared bathroom. $89–$139 double with shared bathroom; $159–$289 double with private bathroom. Rates include breakfast buffet. AE, MC, V. Free courtyard parking. Entrance is in the courtyard. *In room:* A/C, TV, hair dryer, free Wi-Fi.

Scotlaur Inn Bed & Breakfast ⟨**Value**⟩ The Scotlaur is the best value in the historic district. It's housed in the top two floors of a three-story brick building; the ground floor belongs to Chick & Ruth's Delly (see "Where to Dine," later in this chapter). Rooms are various sizes, with larger ones in front, and were updated in 2005. Room no. 301 has the disadvantage of two flights of steep stairs, but it's large, bright, and has the best view, looking out on Main Street. A parking garage behind the inn is convenient but makes the back rooms a bit noisy.

165 Main St., Annapolis, MD 21401. ✆ **410/268-5665.** www.scotlaurinn.com. 10 units. $95–$180 double. Rates for most rooms include full breakfast. MC, V. Pets accepted. *In room:* A/C, hair dryer, free Wi-Fi.

> **(Tips) Renting a Home Away from Home**
>
> During U.S. Naval Academy's Parents' Weekend or Commissioning Week, many Annapolis homeowners clear out and rent their houses to the families of mid-shipmen. **Annapolis Accommodations** (© 410/263-3262; www.stayannapolis. com) offers dozens of homes in the historic district and on the waterfront, within about 12 miles of downtown, for rental of a few days, a week, or longer. They range from one to five bedrooms. All are fully furnished, including linens and well-equipped kitchens; some have pools. Rates start at *phew!* and go to *wow!* (Luxury homes can go for as much as $1,250 a night.) House rentals are popular, with some dates such as boat-show weekends very much in demand, so if you're interested, book well in advance.

HISTORIC HOSTELRIES

Historic Inns of Annapolis   Clustered around the city's two key traffic circles, these hotels offer a taste of the historic. Some of the buildings have carved wooden banisters, wide porches, and in-room fireplaces (if you prefer a specific amenity, ask when making reservations). Because this is the 21st century, Wi-Fi is available in guest rooms at no charge. Although they're separate properties, the inns are run as one entity, with reservations handled through a central office in the Governor Calvert House.

Governor Calvert House, 58 State Circle, is both a conference center and a hotel. The property is made up of several restored Colonial and Victorian residences; it has underground parking and 55 bedrooms furnished with antiques.

The flatiron-shaped **Maryland Inn,** 16 Church Circle (at Main St.), has been operating as an inn since the 1770s. As pretty as the public rooms are, its 44 bedrooms are cramped. The location and helpful staff make it a good choice, though.

The **Robert Johnson House,** 23 State Circle (btw. School and Francis sts.), overlooks the governor's mansion and the State House. It consists of three adjoining 1773 Georgian homes. The 30 artfully restored rooms have four-poster beds and antiques; each unit also has a private bathroom.

Historic Inns of Annapolis central office, 58 State Circle, Annapolis, MD 21401. © **800/847-8882** or 410/263-2641. Fax 410/268-3613. www.historicinnsofannapolis.com. 124 units in 3 properties. $119–$399 double. Rates may be higher on holiday weekends. AE, DC, DISC, MC, V. Valet parking $24; free self-parking. Check-in at the Governor Calvert House, where free shuttle service is provided to the other inns. **Amenities:** Restaurant; coffee bar; privileges at nearby health club; local shuttle van. *In room:* A/C, TV/VCR in some rooms, hair dryer, free Wi-Fi.

ACROSS THE SPA CREEK BRIDGE

Eastport is gaining interest as a place to live and a place to play. For centuries, it was home to Annapolis's working people: watermen, boat builders, and those who worked downtown or at the Naval Academy. Sailing schools and marinas, a handful of comfortable B&Bs, and Restaurant Row—down Severn Avenue—make this an attractive part of town for tourists. It's easy and friendly and can be a lot of fun.

Eastport House ★   This is the oldest standing house in Eastport, but it's been lovingly maintained. The owner has had fun decorating the bedrooms, but she hasn't forgotten any necessities. The third-floor rooms have two double beds but sleep only two, a

guideline designed to keep everybody comfortable. Breakfast is served in the dining
room, or guests can elect to sit on the broad side porch.

101 Severn Ave., Annapolis, MD 21403. © 410/295-9710. www.eastporthouse.com. 5 units, 2 with
shared bathroom. $170–$200 double. Rates include full breakfast. MC, V. Free parking. **Amenities:** Free
bikes; fridge. *In room:* A/C, TV, Wi-Fi (fee).

Inn at Horn Point ★   A 1902 house with a wraparound porch has been turned into
a stylish B&B, filled with bright colors and bay windows. Rooms are named for Eastport's own Trumpy Yachts. While all are spacious, the king suite on the second floor has
its own private porch, two-story-high sitting area with gas fireplace, and bathroom with
claw-foot tub. The first-floor room, with roll-in shower, was specifically designed to be
wheelchair accessible.

100 Chesapeake Ave., Annapolis, MD 21403. © 410/268-1126. www.innathornpoint.com. 5 units.
$169–$219 double; $239–$269 suite. Rates include breakfast. MC, V required to guarantee room; check
or cash only for final payment. Free parking. **Amenities:** A room for those w/limited mobility. *In room:*
A/C, TV on request, high-speed Internet.

The Inn at Spa Creek   For something modern, try this tall gray-and-teal B&B, con-
veniently located across from Carrol's Creek restaurant (see below). Three bedrooms
share a two-story common area with fireplace and clerestory windows. The Garden View
room has an antique bed, French doors to the terrace, and soaking bubble tub—something like a whirlpool. The Port Hole room is down six stairs from the main floor, apart
from the rest of the house. Breakfast is served at the dining table on the top floor of the
common area, at the breakfast bar, or out on the deck under the trees.

417 Severn Ave., Annapolis, MD 21403. © 877/269-8866. www.innatspacreek.com. 3 units. $160–$250
double. Rates include breakfast. AE, DISC, MC, V. Free parking. *In room:* A/C, TV, Wi-Fi (fee).

ANNAPOLIS & ST. MARY'S CITY

6

WHERE TO DINE

4 WHERE TO DINE

You can eat in Annapolis at Colonial dining rooms, taverns, bistros, and waterside seafood houses. For families and travelers on the go, a wide selection of fast-food and family-
style eateries are clustered at the intersection of routes 50, 301, and 450, about 4 miles
from downtown, near the Annapolis Shopping Plaza.

EXPENSIVE

Carrol's Creek Waterfront Restaurant ★★★ SEAFOOD   For the best views of
the waterfront and Annapolis skyline, along with imaginative food, head for this sleek
waterfront spot in Eastport. Seating is available in a windowed dining room and on an
umbrella-shaded porch. Start with the cream of crab soup—it's one of Maryland's best.
Carrol's is definitely a seafood place. The chef is quite creative, serving herb-encrusted
rockfish, for instance, or scallops tequila. Arrive by water taxi for the full waterfront experience. Come at lunch for a sunny view and the same delicious food at a fraction of the price.

410 Severn Ave., Eastport. © 410/263-8102. www.carrolscreek.com. Reservations recommended. Main
courses $8–$18 lunch; $19–$30 dinner; $22 Sun brunch buffet. AE, DC, DISC, MC, V. Mon–Thurs 11:30am–
9pm; Fri–Sat 11:30am–10pm; Sun 10am–9pm.

Middleton Tavern ★ AMERICAN/SEAFOOD   Established in 1750 as an inn for
seafaring men, this restaurant also drew the likes of Washington, Jefferson, and Franklin.
Restored and expanded, the City Dock landmark offers many seafood entrees, as well as

steaks and chateaubriand for two. It's a nice mix of historic location and good food. At lunch, the menu includes pasta, fajitas, and sandwiches. A drink on the tavern's front porch is a favorite summer activity for both locals and visitors. There is piano music upstairs on weekends and other entertainment Tuesday to Friday.

2 Market Space (at Randall St.). ✆ **410/263-3323.** www.middletontavern.com. Call ahead for priority seating. Main courses $7–$20 lunch, $16–$32 dinner. AE, DC, DISC, MC, V. Mon–Fri 11:30am–1:30am; Sat–Sun 10:30am–1:30am.

O'Learys Seafood Restaurant ★★ SEAFOOD   Just over the Spa Creek Bridge, this Eastport spot has been a local favorite for over 20 years. Come here for the freshest seafood, prepared to order and served in a dining room awash in dark, warm tones. The menu lists other options such as duck, pork, and filet mignon. The wine list changes regularly and includes bottles from smaller vintners. Some find the main dining room noisy; if it bothers you, come on a weekday or ask to sit in the back room.

310 Third St., Eastport. ✆ **410/263-0884.** www.olearysseafood.com. Reservations recommended. Main courses $25–$33. AE, DC, MC, V. Mon–Thurs 5–10pm; Fri–Sat 5–11pm; Sun 5–9pm.

The Rockfish ★ SEAFOOD   Step out of Colonial days and into this contemporary restaurant—a "certified environmental steward"—serving fresh seafood obtained from sustainable sources, as well as a few pasta dishes, stone-hearth pizzas, and chicken and ribs. The crab soup is done right, seasoned with herbs other than the standard Old Bay Seasoning and studded with lump crab. Softshell crabs are a golden delight, and fish is accompanied by creative side dishes. Live music is scheduled most nights; there's brunch on Sunday 10am to 2pm with live jazz. From downtown, the restaurant is an easy walk across the Spa Creek Bridge. The Rockfish has its own parking lot.

400 Sixth St., Eastport. ✆ **410/267-1800.** www.rockfishmd.com. Reservations recommended. Main courses $10–$33 lunch and dinner. AE, DC, DISC, MC, V. Mon–Tues 11:30am–midnight; Wed–Sat 11:30am–1:30am; Sun 10am–midnight.

Treaty of Paris AMERICAN   Centrally located in the Maryland Inn, this cozy dining room exudes an 18th-century ambience with its brick walls, Colonial-style furnishings, candlelight, and open fireplace. The menu combines fresh seafood and meat with French-style sauces, such as salmon with Dijon cream sauce or rack of lamb with mint demiglace.

At the Maryland Inn, 16 Church Circle. ✆ **410/216-6340.** www.historicinnsofannapolis.com. Reservations recommended for dinner. Main courses $14–$21 breakfast, $18–$22 lunch, $44–$65 dinner. AE, DC, DISC, MC, V. Thurs–Fri 5:30–9:30pm; Sat 8am–2pm and 5:30–9:30pm; Sun 8am–2pm.

MODERATE

Aqua Terra ★ INTERNATIONAL   Tucked into a storefront on Main Street, this restaurant offers a sleek and modern atmosphere, with adventurous food to match. Don't look for everyday crab cakes here; expect the fresh and inventive, such as sesame-seared tuna or seafood risotto. Not so hungry? Tapas and sushi menus offer many more choices.

164 Main St. ✆ **410/263-1985.** www.aquaterraofannapolis.com. Reservations recommended. Main courses $24–$29. AE, MC, V. Mon 5:30–9pm; Tues–Thurs 11:30am–2:30pm and 5:30–10pm; Fri 11:30am–2:30pm and 5–11pm; Sat noon–3pm and 5:30–11pm; Sun noon–3:30pm and 5–9pm.

Boatyard Bar & Grill ★ AMERICAN/SEAFOOD   Big and airy by day, crowded and fun by night, locals love the Boatyard—and so do visitors. You can count on the old reliable appetizers, such as crab dip and garlic mussels, as well as burgers and a delightful crab cake served on challah. You can't miss the Caribbean/Chesapeake sailing atmosphere. The all-day menu offers everything from sandwiches to steak and crab. There's live music on Thursdays. A market on the side offers prepared foods and box lunches (for picnics or boat rides).

Severn Ave. and Fourth St., Eastport. ℂ **410/216-6206.** Reservations not accepted. Main courses $5–$9 breakfast, $9–$18 lunch and dinner. AE, DISC, MC, V. Daily 8am–midnight.

Café Normandie ★ FRENCH This rustic storefront in the heart of the historic district offers the tastes and atmosphere of a French country restaurant. From its hearty onion soup to the delicate baked Brie, every starter is a hit. Entrees include such classics as crepes, chateaubriand for two, and breast of chicken Normandie. Despite the European atmosphere, the chef uses locally produced foods and the house emphasizes sustainable practices. Breakfast is served weekends from 9am to noon.

185 Main St. ℂ **410/263-3382.** Reservations recommended. Main courses $6–$15 breakfast, $10–$18 lunch, $14–$30 dinner. AE, DC, DISC, MC, V. Mon–Fri 11am–3:30pm and 5–10pm; Sat 8am–3:30pm and 5–10:30pm; Sun 8am–4pm and 5–10pm.

Castlebay Irish Pub IRISH In a town full of Irish pubs, here's one that stands out. The specialties are shepherd's pie, fish and chips, and corned beef and cabbage; the beef and lamb stews are exceptional. The lunch menu is lighter, with burgers and corned beef. A children's menu lists smaller portions of the traditional fare. Fans of home brews should try the Three Nuns Ale. Sunday brunch includes a full Irish breakfast. Irish and pop bands play Wednesday through Saturday nights.

193A Main St. ℂ **410/626-0165.** www.castlebayirishpub.com. Reservations advised for dinner. Main courses $7–$14 lunch, $13–$27 dinner. AE, DISC, MC, V. Mon–Sat 11am–midnight; Sun 10am–midnight.

Federal House Bar & Grille AMERICAN A new restaurant has moved into this 1813 building. The space remains warm, with exposed brick, the old well-used bar, and dark-wood furnishings. The menu—available all day—mixes old (crab cakes and burgers) with new (macadamia-nut tilapia and a most welcome short-plate-platter menu for smaller appetites). Service is attentive, portions are generous, salads are crisp, and the cream of crab soup is rich with sherry. There's live music Wednesday through Friday, DJ on Saturday. Brunch is served at 10am on Sunday.

22 Market Space, City Dock. ℂ **410/268-2576.** www.federalhouserestaurant.com. Reservations recommended on Fri–Sat; none taken on holidays. Main courses $8–$25. AE, DISC, MC, V. Mon–Sat 11am–2am; Sun 10am–2am.

McGarvey's Saloon & Oyster Bar PUB FARE/SEAFOOD When you need a good sandwich, cup of chowder, or burger to go with your beer, you can't beat McGarvey's. Two narrow rooms, both dominated by bars, are set with tiny marble-topped tables. Chicken- or crab-cake–topped Caesar salads, filet béarnaise, and oyster stew are served all the time. Heartier entrees, including steaks, salmon, and crab, come out at night. The specials are usually top-notch. Brunch is served on Sunday.

8 Market Space, City Dock. ℂ **410/263-5700.** www.mcgarveys.net. Reservations accepted Mon–Thurs only. Main courses $6–$13 lunch, $19–$27 dinner. AE, MC, V. Mon–Sat 11:30am–1am; Sun 10am–1am.

Rams Head Tavern & Fordham Brewing Co. ★★ INTERNATIONAL Come for dinner in one of the cozy, brick-walled dining rooms, or a drink and appetizers on the wisteria-covered heated patio. On a summer evening, the front sidewalk is the place to be. The menu includes traditional regional favorites, from the Chesapeake's own crab to Cajun jambalaya, and steaks are available at dinner. The storefront pub serves more than 170 beers, including seasonal selections from its microbrewery, the Fordham Brewing Company. Get a sampler to try them all. It's also a venue for live entertainment (p. 129).

33 West St. © **410/268-4545.** www.ramsheadtavern.com or www.fordhambrewing.com. Reservations recommended for dinner. Main courses $7.50–$15 lunch, $12–$28 dinner. AE, DISC, MC, V. Mon–Sat 11am–2am; Sun 10am–2am. Meals served until 11pm; light fare until midnight.

Reynolds Tavern ★ TEA   After a day of visiting historic sites, why not enjoy teatime in a lovely Colonial-era tavern? It's a genteel affair, with big aromatic pots of loose tea, luscious scones piled high with jam and cream, savory tea sandwiches, and sweets. Afternoon tea is served from 11am to 5pm. Need something more filling? Hearty sandwiches, salads, and cream of crab soup are also on the lunch menu. For dinner, seafood and English favorites are served after 5pm.

7 Church Circle. © **410/295-9555.** www.reynoldstavern.org. Reservations recommended. Main courses $9–$12 lunch, $14–$30 dinner; tea $8–$23. AE, DISC, MC, V. Daily 11am–5pm; Wed–Sun 5–9:30pm.

Ristorante Piccola Roma ITALIAN   Dinnertime is romantic in this small, white table-clothed dining room, but stopping here for lunch will soothe your palate without hurting your wallet. The menu is bursting with Italian favorites—pasta, risotto, antipasti—at both lunch and dinner. A hefty wine list filled with only Italian vintages and great bread baked by the restaurant's original owner enhance the dining experience.

200 Main St. © **410/268-7898.** www.piccolaromaannapolis.com. Reservations recommended Fri–Sat nights. Main courses $9–$14 lunch, $16–$29 dinner. AE, DC, DISC, MC, V. Sun–Thurs 11:30am–2:30pm and 5:30–10pm; Fri–Sat 11:30am–2:30pm and 5–11pm.

INEXPENSIVE

Annapolis Ice Cream Company Value ICE CREAM   Super-premium ice cream stars at this little shop on Main Street. It's all made on the premises, with flavors such as Maple Walnut, Key Lime Pie, and Blackberry Cobbler. The cobblers and pies are made here and then smashed into ice cream. Sundaes and shakes are also available.

196 Main St. © **443/482-3895.** www.annapolisicecream.com. Reservations not accepted. Ice cream $3.50–$8. AE, DC, DISC, MC, V. Summer Sun–Thurs 11am–10pm, Fri–Sat 11am–11pm; shorter hours off-season.

Chick & Ruth's Delly Moments AMERICAN   An Annapolis tradition, this ma-and-pa establishment has been run by the Levitt family for 40 years. Sit wherever you like, and a waiter will take your order in the friendly deli/restaurant, famous for its sandwiches named after political figures and local attractions. Platters, pizzas, salads, sundaes, and shakes are also available. Breakfast is served all day.

165 Main St. © **410/269-6737.** www.chickandruths.com. Reservations not accepted. Main courses and lunch items $4–$10. No credit cards. Mon–Thurs 6:30am–10pm; Fri–Sat 6:30am–12:30am.

Leeward Market CAFE   Eat in at this Eastport eatery or carry out breakfast or lunch—from sandwiches to pizza—with your java. Wi-Fi is free.

601 Second St., Eastport. © **443/837-6122.** www.leewardmarket.com. Reservations not accepted. Main courses $5–$19. V. Tues–Fri 7:30am–9pm; Sat 9am–6pm; Sun 9am–4pm.

Lemongrass ★ Value THAI   Locals clamor for a seat at Lemongrass—such a tiny space but so much flavor in these spicy dishes. Arrive early or be patient for that order of hot and sweet crispy string beans, pad Thai, and tiger crying salad, and bring an

appetite—plates are piled high with spicy goodness. The menu offers lunch- and dinner-
size portions, both available all day. (Happy news: They also have takeout.)

167 West St. © **410/280-0086.** www.kapowgroup.com/lemongrass. Reservations recommended for dinner. Main courses $7–$12 lunch, $9–$15 dinner. MC, V. Mon–Thurs 11:30am–3pm and 5–10pm; Sat noon–4pm and 5–11pm; Sun 4–10pm.

Market House AMERICAN   The historic Market House, site of a market since the 1690s, offers carryout—ice cream, hot doughnuts, pizza, sandwiches, crab cakes, and baked goods. Tables are set outside the market though the City Dock is popular spot for an impromptu picnic. There's also a bank and ATM.

25 Market Place, City Dock. No phone. www.markethouseannapolis.com. Hours, credit cards, and prices vary by stall. Market open daily, hours vary by season. (It's always open for breakfast and lunch.)

5 HISTORIC ANNAPOLIS

Annapolis's National Historic District has more than 1,500 restored and preserved buildings, and its narrow streets are best seen on foot. If your visit is short, make sure to see the **United States Naval Academy,** the **Maryland State House,** the **William Paca House & Garden,** the **Hammond–Harwood House,** and the **Chase–Lloyd House.** Enjoy the stroll down pretty Prince George's Street on your way to the Paca House—it's packed with striking homes from Annapolis's 4 centuries. Tours are offered from the visitor center or HistoryQuest (see listing below).

The **City Dock,** once the destination of merchant sailing ships, now attracts pleasure boats from near and far. Sightseeing boats, both gas- and wind-powered, offer cruises from spring to fall. The area around the City Dock has plenty of good restaurants, bars, shops, and a summer theater. As if frozen in time, a **sculpture** of Alex Haley reaches out to the Chesapeake Bay to tell the story of *Roots,* his best-selling novel, to a group of children sitting on the City Dock. This display not only memorializes Haley and his African ancestor Kunta Kinte, but also recalls an actual place where enslaved Africans arrived in the New World. The sculpture is accompanied by a series of engraved plaques that complete the story and the memorial.

The Annapolis Maritime Museum (Finds   This tiny Eastport riverfront museum, headquartered in the old McNasby Oyster Company building, celebrates the waterman, the oyster, the terrapin, and other Chesapeake treasures. Even the arts are on exhibit here with a gallery of regional artwork and a Thursday concert series of traditional Chesapeake music. Activities for kids and adults are scheduled throughout the summer. Boat tours of the picturesque **Thomas Point Lighthouse,** at $70 a person, include a half-hour boat ride to the Chesapeake Bay lighthouse and a tour of the 1875 screw-pile lighthouse—the last one left in its original location and still a navigational aid. Tours are scheduled on warm Sundays. Reservations are required; see the website for details.

723 Second St. and Back Creek, Annapolis, MD 21403. © **410/295-0104.** www.amaritime.org. Free admission; donation suggested. Thurs–Sun noon–4pm.

The Banneker–Douglass Museum   This museum focuses on African Americans of the Chesapeake region from 1633 to the civil rights movement. Named after two prominent local residents, astronomer/inventor Benjamin Banneker and abolitionist Frederick Douglass, the museum has continuously changing temporary exhibits, which join its permanent exhibit on local African American history, "Deep Roots, Rising Water."

84 Franklin St. (off south side of Church Circle). 📞 **410/216-6180.** www.bdmuseum.com. Free admission. Tues–Sat 10am–4pm.

Charles Carroll House of Annapolis   This is the birthplace and home of Charles Carroll of Carrollton, the only Catholic to sign the Declaration of Independence. With sections built in 4 centuries, it sits on high ground overlooking Spa Creek, a block from City Dock. Visitors can tour the house, which is still undergoing restoration. Some features are original, including the walnut staircase, floors, and woodwork. Also take a look at the waterfront gardens and the 18th-century wine cellar. There is an elevator.

107 Duke of Gloucester St. (behind St. Mary's Church at Spa Creek). 📞 **410/269-1737.** www.charles carrollhouse.com. Free admission, except private tours. Tour fee is $5. Mar–Oct Sat–Sun noon–4pm and by appointment. Closed Nov–Feb.

Chase–Lloyd House ★★   Home of Samuel Chase, a signer of the Declaration of Independence, this historic home (built from 1769–74) is outstanding for its brilliant interior design, exquisite hanging staircase, and intricate moldings. It was designed by William Buckland, architect for the Hammond–Harwood House across the street. Only the first-floor rooms are on view, as the house continues to be a home for retired women. It's well worth the charge to see the house and formal gardens. Hours are quite limited and docents are sometimes unavailable, so call ahead.

22 Maryland Ave. (at King George St.). 📞 **410/263-2723.** Admission $4. Mon–Fri 2–4pm.

Hammond–Harwood House ★★★   If you see only one historic house in Annapolis, make it this one. A five-part classic Georgian home quite unlike the Paca mansion, with semi-octagonal wings and carved moldings, it is considered one of the 18th century's most noteworthy. The architecture, by William Buckland, is stunning. On exhibit are decorative arts from the last 3 centuries and paintings including works by the various Peales, among Maryland's finest. The collection of 18th-century items, including furniture by John Shaw, handicrafts, and textiles, is not to be missed. There are some children's things and a few "modern conveniences" of the Colonial period.

19 Maryland Ave. (northeast of State Circle, at the corner of King George St.). 📞 **410/263-4683.** www. hammondharwoodhouse.org. Admission $6 adults, $3 children 6–17. Tours Apr–Oct Tues–Sun noon–5pm on the hour (last tour 4pm). Closed Easter, Memorial Day, Labor Day, Nov–Mar except by appointment (call ext. 16), and for special events during Christmas season; see website for schedule.

HistoryQuest at the St. Clair Wright Center   The Historic Annapolis Foundation's orientation center, located at the foot of Main Street, is a restored 1790s building that once housed a bakery. Exhibits here are designed to help visitors better understand the state capital's history, architecture, and culture. It's a great place to get oriented for a tour of Annapolis, the "museum without walls." The center rents four audio tours. One offers an overview of Annapolis history and architecture. The others focus on the Revolution, the Civil War, and African-American history.

99 Main St. 📞 **410/267-6656.** Free admission. Mon–Sat 9:30am–5pm; Sun 11am–5pm.

Maryland State House ★★★   This is the oldest state house in continuous use in the nation. It opened in 1779 and served as the U.S. Capitol from 1783 to 1784. Restoration of the original Senate and House Chambers is expected to continue for 2 to 5 years, but visitors can still visit the contemporary Senate and House of Delegate chambers. George Washington came to the Old Senate Chamber here to resign as commander in chief of the Continental armies. His handwritten speech, purchased by the state in

2007, is due to go on display here when construction ends. The Treaty of Paris, ending the Revolutionary War, was ratified here. Today, Maryland's General Assembly meets here from January to mid-April. The grounds, overlooking the city and shaded by old magnolias and evergreens, are a lovely spot for a break. Enter through the Rowe Boulevard entrances up the steps or on the ground level.

State Circle. ℂ **410/974-3400.** www.msa.md.gov. Free admission. Building daily 9am–5pm; visitor center Mon–Fri 9am–5pm, Sat–Sun 10am–4pm. Tours daily 11am and 3pm. Building closed Dec 25; visitor center closed Jan 1, Easter, Thanksgiving, and Dec 25.

St. John's College   One of the oldest U.S. colleges, St. John's started in 1696 as a prep school but was chartered as a college in 1784. Self-guided tour brochures are available in Room 124, Mellon Hall. Mellon is also home to the Mitchell Art Gallery and—for a completely different style of architecture—was designed by a student of Frank Lloyd Wright. Two buildings are named for Maryland's signers of the Declaration of Independence, the Chase–Stone House and the Paca–Carroll House, both built in 1857. Don't miss the Carroll Barrister House, built about 1724 for Charles Carroll the barrister, a member of the prominent Maryland family.

60 College Ave. ℂ **410/626-2539.** www.stjohnscollege.edu. Campus open for visits during daylight hours. Brochure available in office, Mon–Fri 9am–5pm.

United States Naval Academy ★★★   Tucked behind Annapolis's historic district, standing proudly on the Severn River, the United States Naval Academy (USNA) has been educating future naval officers for more than 160 years.

For the full USNA experience, enter the Naval Academy at the pedestrian entrance near Gate 1, at Randall and King George streets, or at the other entrance closer to the City Dock at Craig Street. (The only cars allowed in the yard are those with handicapped or DOD stickers.) Start your visit at the **Armel–Leftwich Visitor Center,** just beyond the Halsey Field House, to see exhibits about midshipman life and browse the gift shop. Then, sign up for a tour to see Bancroft Hall, the world's largest dorm, and walk through the grounds.

The crisply restored **Chapel** displays Bibles belonging to Commodore John Barry and Admiral David Farragut. In the undercroft is the marble **Crypt of John Paul Jones,** along with his swords and many medals. During the American Revolution, the commodore was the first to hoist the colors of the new nation over a flagship. The chapel is open Monday through Saturday 9am to 4pm and Sunday 1 to 5pm. Worshipers are welcome to attend Sunday services.

The **Naval History Museum** in Preble Hall has finally opened after several years of renovations, with displays of naval officers, swords, medals, and other artifacts, as well as stunning ship models from the 16th to the 19th century. Famous admirals, astronauts, and one president (Jimmy Carter) have memorable exhibits. The War of 1812 flag proclaiming "Don't Give Up the Ship," which hung for decades in Bancroft Hall, is shown here. The museum is open Monday through Saturday 9am to 5pm, Sunday 11am to 5pm. *Insider's note:* Bring your government-issued ID to Gate 3 at the end of Maryland Avenue, and the Chapel and the Museum are to your right and to your left. The Severn River is straight ahead.

Monday through Friday at 12:05pm, weather permitting, you can see the midshipmen line up in **noon formation** in front of Bancroft Hall before the midday meal. **Commissioning Week,** usually held the third week in May, is a colorful time of full-dress parades, parties, and an air show by the Blue Angels.

(Fun Facts **The Colors of Annapolis**

The Historic Annapolis Foundation has spent years identifying historic buildings throughout Annapolis. When a house meets the criteria, it receives a marker decorated with the Liberty Tree, a 400-year-old tree that once graced the grounds of St. John's College. Marker colors indicate the house's style:

Green   17th-century "vernacular," built 1681 to 1708

Terra cotta   18th-century "vernacular" or Georgian, built 1715 to 1800

Bronze   Georgian of national importance, built 1730 to 1800

Blue   Federal-style, built 1784 to 1840

Verdigris   Greek Revival, built 1820 to 1860

Aubergine   Victorian, built 1869 to 1901

Gray   19th- or 20-century Annapolis vernacular, built 1837 to 1921

Ocher   Distinctive homes of all styles built in the 20th century

Armel–Leftwich Visitor Center, 52 King George St. ✆ **410/293-8687.** www.usna.edu. Free admission to grounds and visitor center (photo ID required for those 16 and over). Tours $9 adults, $8 seniors, $7 students. Visitor center Apr–June and Sept–Nov Mon–Fri 10am–3pm, Sat 9:30am–3pm, Sun 12:30–3pm; July–Aug Mon–Sat 9:30am–3pm, Sun 12:30–3pm; Dec–Mar Mon–Sat 10am–2:30pm, Sun 12:30–2:30pm. Closed Jan 1, Thanksgiving, and Dec 25. Tours offered daily, usually btw. 10am and 2:30pm; schedules vary by day and season, so call ahead or check website before coming.

The William Paca House & Garden ★★★   The home of William Paca, a signer of the Declaration of Independence and a governor of Maryland, this estate was built between 1763 and 1765 and restored by Historic Annapolis. It's one of two such houses in town (another, the Brice House, is around the corner but isn't open to the public). The five-part structure is composed of a central block, flanked symmetrically with hyphens and wings. The 45-minute house tour (every half-hour, last one at 3:30pm) offers a glimpse of life during Annapolis's "golden age." One exhibit focuses on a child's sickroom; another features Colonial leisure activities. The 2 acres of formal gardens feature a pond crossed by a Chinese Chippendale bridge and a two-story summerhouse. Climb to the top for a bird's-eye view of your surroundings. If your time is limited, at least see the gardens.

186 Prince George St. ✆ **410/267-7619.** www.annapolis.org. House and garden tours $8 adults, $7 seniors, $5 children 6–17; garden only $5. Apr–Dec Mon–Sat 10am–5pm, Sun noon–5pm. Call for hours for Jan–Mar. Closed Thanksgiving and Dec 24–25.

6 ORGANIZED TOURS & CRUISES

WALKING TOURS

To hit the high points in town, take a **Historic Annapolis Walk.** Visitors carry digital audio wands, which are customizable to enable you to go to places of the most personal interest. Tours focus on African-American Heritage, the Civil War, and the Revolution. They're available only at the Historic Annapolis Foundation's **Museum Store,** 77 Main St. (✆ **410/268-5576;** www.annapolis.org), Tuesday through Saturday from 10am to 6pm, Sunday from 11am to 6pm. The tours last about 2 hours.

Annapolis Tours (© 410/268-7601; www.annapolis-tours.com) are led by guides in Colonial costume. Tours of the historic district, which include the Naval Academy, last 2 hours and don't require reservations. From April through October, they depart daily at 10:30am from the visitor center at 26 West St. and at 1:30pm from the City Dock information booth. (If you take a morning tour, guides try to get you to the Naval Academy in time for the midshipmen's noon formation.) From November through March, there is only one tour a week, Saturday at 1:30pm, departing from the City Dock information booth. The price is $11 for adults and $6 for children 17 and under. (*Note:* Picture ID is required for those 18 and older to gain access to the Naval Academy and State House.) Other options include ghost tours on October evenings and candlelight strolls on December evenings; check the website for a schedule.

Naval Academy Walking Tours depart from the Armel–Leftwich Visitor Center of the United States Naval Academy at Gate 1 on King George and Randall streets (© 410/263-6933; www.usna.edu) daily except Thanksgiving, Christmas, and New Year's Day. In July and August, tours depart every half-hour. From September through November and April through June, tours depart every hour Monday through Friday, and every half-hour Saturday and Sunday. From December through March, tours are offered as needed. The schedule varies a lot, so call ahead or check the website before coming— or sign up when you get to the visitor center. The price is $9 for adults, $8 for seniors, and $7 for students. Bring picture ID.

Capital City Colonials (© 410/295-9715; www.capitalcitycolonials.com) offers "Annapolis in an Hour" tours for $10, as well as other historical tours. Combine food with history on the 11am tours, which include some time to rest as well as eat over a 3-hour period. They cost $42 and are scheduled Thursday through Saturday at 11am and Sunday at 1pm. Reservations are recommended.

TOURS BY BUS, TROLLEY, CARRIAGE & SEGWAY

Discover Annapolis Tours, 31 Decatur Ave. (© 410/626-6000; www.discover-annapolis. com), offers 1-hour trolley or minibus tours of the city and outlying areas. An air-conditioned 25-passenger trolley takes visitors through the historic district—by the State House, Chase–Lloyd House, Hammond–Harwood House, and St. John's College, to name a few—and areas not covered by the walking tours: Eastport, the Charles Carroll House, and the **Severn River Scenic Overlook** ★. Tours operate daily April through November, departing from the lot behind the visitor center at 26 West St. Saturday tours are available December through March. The cost is $18 for adults, $9 for children 11 to 15, and $3 for children 10 and under (free for preschoolers). A 40-minute tour is also available, leaving from HistoryQuest, 99 Main St.

Watermark Tours (© 410/268-7600) offers "Four Centuries" walking tours daily April through September and Saturdays October to March. Tickets are $16 for adults, $4 for ages 3 through 11. They include the historic district and Naval Academy. Photo ID is required; reservations are not necessary. Watermark also offers African American Heritage tours through February and Saturdays May through October, ghost tours in October, and candlelight in December. Tickets are $14 for adults, $7 for children 3 to 11.

Annapolis Carriage (© 800/639-9153; www.annapoliscarriage.com) offers 20-minute carriage rides throughout the day. The coachman points out areas of interest and gives a brief history for up to four riders (six with kids). Reserve online, by phone, or in person at HistoryQuest, 99 Main St. (© 410/267-6656; www.reservations.annapolis.org). Tours cost $35 for adults, $15 for children. Private tours are available. Hours vary by season; check the website for a schedule.

Segs in the City, 42 Randall St. (© **800/SEGS-393** [734-7393]; www.segsinthecity. net), enables visitors to explore the historic district on two-wheel Segways. Guided 1- or 2-hour tours cost $45 to $70. Trained riders can rent Segways for $50 to $150.

CRUISES & BOAT TOURS

Watermark Cruises ★, at the City Dock (© **410/268-7600;** www.watermarkcruises. com), offers excursions along Annapolis Harbor and beyond. Choices include a 40-minute kid-friendly narrated cruise aboard the *Harbor Queen* that covers the highlights of Annapolis Harbor, the U.S. Naval Academy, and the Severn River; a 40-minute tour aboard the *Miss Anne* of the Eastport waterfront along Spa Creek and the Naval Academy shore; a 90-minute Thomas Point Lighthouse Cruise on the Severn River; and a Day-on-the-Bay excursion to St. Michaels. The *Lady Sarah* offers bay lighthouse cruises. In summer, catch a ride on a pirate ship. Prices range from $12 to $40 for adults, $5 to $10 for children 3 to 11. Sailings are daily from Memorial Day to Labor Day, with abbreviated schedules in spring and fall.

Pirate tours seem to be all the rage and you can find them in Eastport. **Pirate Adventures,** 311 Third St. (© **410/263-0002**) goes out six times a day at the height of the season. Cruises aimed at 2- to 9-year-olds last 75 minutes. Kids get "tattoos," wear pirate clothes, find treasure, and engage in water-gun battles. Reservations for weekend cruises are recommended. Tickets are $18.

7 OUTDOOR ACTIVITIES

With the Chesapeake Bay and Severn River at its doorstep, Annapolis is the pleasure-boating capital of the eastern U.S. The city offers many opportunities to enjoy sailing and watersports, as well as other outdoor activities.

BIKING **Free Wheelin',** an Annapolis Transit program, loans bikes every day 9am to 5pm, June through August, to riders ages 18 and older. Bring a photo ID and plan to have the bike back by 8pm. Helmets are recommended and required on USNA grounds. Riders also get a pass to ride the transit buses, all of which have bike racks. For information, call © **410/263-7964,** ext. 101.

If the streets are too crowded for a leisurely excursion, try one of the parks and paths outside of town. The **Baltimore and Annapolis Trail** (© **410/222-6244**) is a smooth 13-mile asphalt route from Annapolis north into the suburbs. Formerly a rail corridor, it's ideal for biking or walking. The trail, which connects with the waterfront **Jonas Green Park,** under the Route 450 bridge, runs parallel to Ritchie Highway and ends on Dorsey Road at Route 648 in Glen Burnie, where it connects with the 12.5-mile BWI Trail. The trail is open daily from sunrise to sunset.

Outside the city, on the South River and Harness Creek, **Quiet Waters Park** (© **410/222-1777**) has 6 miles of biking and hiking trails with an overlook along the South River. Dogs have their own park and beach. The park is open Wednesday through Monday, 7am to dusk; you'll pay $6 per vehicle, $5 per handicapped vehicle.

SAILING SCHOOLS & SAILING TRIPS The sailing capital of the world has lots of schools that will get you at the helm for a weekend or a week. Learn to sail at the oldest sailing school in America: the **Annapolis Sailing School,** 601 Sixth St. (© **800/638-9192;** www.annapolissailing.com). With more than 50 boats and a huge support staff, this school offers programs for novices and veterans, including **KidShip** for children 5 to

15. Options range from a weekend beginner course for $475 to a 5-day vacation sailing course for $5,000 for up to six people. Grads may rent the 24-foot Rainbows. Hotel packages are also available.

Womanship, 137 Conduit St. (© **800/342-9295;** www.womanship.com), is a sailing program for women. Instruction levels range from "Chicken of the Sea" to advanced, in daytime or live-aboard settings. Learning cruises range from 2 to 7 days and from $575 to $2,750.

There are many other sailing schools in the area, so call around for one that best suits your needs. Try **JWorld Annapolis** (© **800/966-2038** or 410/280-2040; www.jworldannapolis. com) which uses the wicked fast J-boats, or **Chesapeake Sailing School** (© **800/ 966-0032** or 410/269-1594; www.sailingclasses.com), which offers courses on Back Creek.

The 74-foot schooner *Woodwind,* 80 Compromise St. (© **410/263-7837;** www. schoonerwoodwind.com), departs from the Marriott side of the City Dock for 2-hour sailing trips four times daily, April to November. Departure times vary, so call or check the website. If you like sailboat racing, you can watch the Wednesday-night races aboard the *Woodwind.* Prices are $31 to $34 for adults, $29 to $32 for seniors, and $20 for children 11 and under. Special-destination cruises, overnight trips, and bed-and-breakfast sails are also available.

LACROSSE The professional **Washington Bayhawks** (© **866/994-2957;** www.the bayhawks.com) play home games through 2011 at Navy/Marine Corps Stadium on Rowe Boulevard. The season runs May through August.

KAYAKING **Paddle or Pedal** (© **410/271-7007;** www.paddleorpedal.com) offers 3-hour sunset kayak tours in the South River on Fridays at 6pm. It also offers trips in creeks on both sides of the bay, as well as instruction and kayak rentals at Quiet Waters Park south of Annapolis. Preregistration is necessary for sunset paddles. Admission to Quiet Waters is $6 per vehicle; walk-ins and bike-ins are free.

Kayak Annapolis (© **443/949-0773;** www.kayakannapolistours.com) rents boats from its Eastport shop by Spa Creek and guides tours from nearby Truxtun Park.

SWIMMING Visitors don't have to go too far to find a Chesapeake beach. Beaches at **Sandy Point State Park,** 1100 E. College Pkwy. (© **410/974-2149**), are guarded Memorial Day to Labor Day. There are concession stands, boat rentals, picnic areas, and hiking paths, too. Admission is $6 for nonresidents. The park is open dawn to dusk. The park is located by the Bay Bridge, Route 50 off exit 32.

WATERSPORT RENTALS & CHARTERS To charter a sailboat, contact one of the sailing schools or call **South River Boat Rentals** (© **410/956-9729;** www.southriver boatrentals.com), which rents both sail- and powerboats; it's south of Annapolis by the South River Bridge on Route 2.

---

8 SHOPPING ★

Shops in Annapolis's Historic District are filled with all kinds of gifts and nautical-themed merchandise. Navy T-shirts, the classic souvenir, are everywhere. You could redecorate your house from the shops on Maryland Avenue. This town is picturesque in December—with greenery draped around every window and white lights on the trees, it's a delightful, old-fashioned place to buy those last-minute items. Finish your day with a drink at McGarvey's (p. 129) or a meal at one of the casual restaurants.

In the historic district, the main shopping streets are: **Main Street,** which runs from Church Circle to the City Dock, has many apparel and gift shops; **Maryland Avenue** has shops in the block just below the State House and State Circle, where you might find home accessories and antiques; **West Street** has added lots of new shops and restaurants; and the shops around the **City Dock** itself are mostly nautical in nature. Most stores are open Monday through Saturday from 10 or 11am to 5 or 6pm, Sunday from noon to 5pm. Many stay open until 8 or 9pm on Friday and Saturday.

At **Plat du Jour,** 220 Main St. (© **410/269-1499;** www.platdujour.net), you'll be convinced you've walked into Tuscany or Provence. It's filled with tableware, linens, toiletries, and a cookbook or two. Lovers of the Emerald Isle should head for **Avoca,** 141–143 Main St. (© **410/263-1485;** www.avoca.ie), for its Irish clothes, linens, and decorative items.

Handmade arts and crafts are available in several places. **American Craft Works,** 189B Main St. (© **410/625-1583**), features the handiwork of the League of Maryland Craftsmen. **Annapolis Pottery,** 40 State Circle (© **410/268-6153**), sells wares made on the premises; you can even watch the stock being made. **Easy Street,** 8 Francis St. (© **410/263-5556**), focuses on art glass.

For home furnishings, head for Maryland Avenue. **Peake House,** 76 Maryland Ave. (© **410/280-0410**), sells new stuff, including Mottahedeh, Quimper, and Herend. Interior designers display some of their finds at **Alex Clymer Interiors,** 86 Maryland Ave. (© **410/263-0992**), and **Be Home,** 82 Maryland Ave. (© **410/280-8616**).

For artwork to hang on the walls, check out **McBride Gallery,** 215 Main St. (© **410/267-7077;** www.mcbridegallery.com), or the juried exhibits at the Maryland Federation of Art's **Circle Gallery,** 18 State Circle (© **410/268-4566;** www.mdfedart. org). For something most definitely nautical, check out **Annapolis Marine Art Gallery,** 110 Dock St. (© **410/263-4100;** www.annapolismarineart.com). Over in Eastport, Howard L. Rogers carves teak boat signs and displays his marine paintings at his **Raven Maritime Studio,** 130 Severn Ave. (© **410/268-8639**).

For gifts and collectibles, stop by the **Annapolis Country Store,** 53 Maryland Ave. (© **410/269-6773;** www.annapoliscountrystore.com): It has Pooh, Raggedy Ann, and Curious George items. Pick up your Navy T-shirt at **Peppers,** 133 Main St. (© **800/254-6289** or 410/267-8722; www.navygear.com). For gifts for your favorite teen, see **Brown Eyed Girl,** 10 Francis St. (© **410/990-4475**). Get something stylish at **Diva,** 30 Market Space (© **410/280-9198;** www.modadiva.com). Earth-friendly and fair-trade gifts with pizazz are available at **Mixed Greens,** 48 Randall St. (© **410/216-9830.**) Next door, **Re-Sails,** 42 Randall St. (© **410/263-4982;** www.resails.net), stocks bags refashioned from old sails.

MALLS & MARKETS

Annapolis Harbour Center West of downtown, at the junction of routes 2 and 665, this shopping center is laid out like a maritime village, with more than 40 stores, services, and fast-food eateries, as well as nine movie theaters. Open Monday to Saturday from 10am to 9pm, and Sunday from noon to 5pm. 2512A Solomons Island Rd. © **410/266-5857.** www.annapolisharbourcenter.com.

Pennsylvania Dutch Farmers' Market This market is run by Amish and Mennonite families from Lancaster County, Pennsylvania. Wares range from sausages and pickles to organic produce, as well as homemade jams, fudge, and baked goods. Handmade quilts are available in a crafts section. Open Thursday from 10am to 6pm, Friday from 9am to 6pm, and Saturday from 8:30am to 3pm. 2472 Solomons Island Rd. (opposite Annapolis Harbour Center). ☎ **410/573-0770** or 573-0775.

Westfield Annapolis   Situated off Route 50, between West Street and Bestgate Road, this mall has five department stores (including Nordstrom and Lord & Taylor), more than 330 specialty shops, food court, and 11 movie theaters. Open Monday to Saturday from 10am to 9pm, and Sunday from 11am to 7pm. 2002 Annapolis Mall. ☎ **410/266-5432**. www.westfield.com/annapolis.

9 ANNAPOLIS AFTER DARK

Annapolis is a town of small venues. Most local bars feature live music on weekends—everything from pop to classic rock to blues and funk—and there are a few good local theater companies. For up-to-date listings of concerts and other events, check the Friday "Entertainment" section of the *Capital* newspaper. The visitor center gives out seasonal event calendars as well.

BARS & CLUBS

Armadillo's   This place offers a variety of live entertainment—jazz, blues, funk, classic rock, acoustic rock, and oldies—Thursday through Saturday. Music usually starts at 10pm. 132 Dock St. ☎ **410/280-0028**. Cover varies.

49 West Coffeehouse, Winebar & Gallery ★   A welcome addition to Annapolis nightlife, 49 West is located a block west of Rams Head Tavern. This coffeehouse/wine bar features live classical, jazz, and folk music every night. 49 West St. ☎ **410/626-9796**. www.49westcoffeehouse.com. Cover free–$20.

Jazz at the Powerhouse   Shows are held the fourth weekend of every month, except July and August, in a building adjacent to the Loews Annapolis Hotel. It's small, friendly, and has good music. 126 West St. ☎ **410/269-0777**. No cover.

McGarvey's Saloon & Oyster Bar   McGarvey's, O'Brien's, and the Federal House (see p. 119 for a review), all near the City Dock, make up Annapolis's most happening nightspot. McGarvey's doesn't have live music, but draws a crowd for its oysters and beer (see p. 119 for a review). It even has its own private-label Aviator Lager. The place is loud, friendly, and fun. 8 Market Space. ☎ **410/263-5700**. www.mcgarveyssaloon.com. No cover.

O'Brien's Oyster Bar & Restaurant   O'Brien's, near the City Dock, has entertainment, mostly DJs, Thursday through Sunday, starting at 10pm. 113 Main St. ☎ **410/268-6288**. www.obriensoysterbar.com. No cover.

Pusser's Caribbean Grille   The entertainment here is the boat traffic: Boaters motor up "Ego Alley" to show off their craft at the City Dock, only to turn around and head back into the harbor. Spend a summer evening on the deck with one of the specialty rum drinks. Pusser's also serves meals all day. At the Annapolis Marriott Waterfront, 80 Compromise St. ☎ **410/626-0004**. www.pussersusa.com. No cover.

Rams Head On Stage ★★★   The Rams Head has become the top nightspot in town, hosting such varied acts as Kenny "Babyface" Edmonds and the Smothers Brothers. The audience usually ranges from young adult to middle-aged; you must be 21 or over. 33 West St. ☎ **410/268-4545**. www.ramsheadtavern.com. Cover varies; advance ticket purchases recommended.

The town's largest venue, the **Maryland Hall for the Creative Arts** ★, 801 Chase St. (© **866/438-3808** or 410/263-5544; www.mdhallarts.org), presents performances by the Annapolis Symphony Orchestra, Annapolis Opera, Annapolis Chorale, and the Ballet Theater of Maryland, as well as national acts. Check out the calendar of events online. Tickets are $10 to $50.

The **Colonial Players,** 108 East St. (© **410/268-7373;** www.cplayers.com), stage five plays per year in a 180-seat theater-in-the-round. Shows are Thursday through Saturday at 8pm, Sunday at 2:30 or 7:30pm. Ticket prices are $10 to $15.

Since 1966, the **Annapolis Summer Garden Theatre** ★★, 143 Compromise St., across from the City Dock (© **410/268-9212;** www.summergarden.com), has produced three shows a summer. Reservations are encouraged; tickets cost $18.

A SIDE TRIP TO HISTORIC LONDON TOWN & GARDENS ★

There are three reasons to set aside half a day to visit the remnants of London Town, one of Maryland's oldest towns: the 1760 house set high above the South River, the lush 8 acres of gardens surrounding the property, and the ongoing archaeological research to uncover the lost buildings of this once thriving seaport. Although it was central to the state's trade, with a busy ferry in the 1600s and 1700s, by the 1800s it was just a memory. Today, only the William Brown House remains.

The three-story brick mansion, now a National Historic Landmark, is worth a look for its 18th-century furnishings and its tavern, which covers much of the first floor. Don't miss the antique clock (with only an hour hand), leather water buckets, and prints by Elizabeth Blackwell. Children will like the basement, with its toys, clothes, and hats to help them "get into" the 18th century. Knowledgeable docents lead tours on the hour of either the historic area or the Brown house, tailoring their presentations to the ages of their guests. Stop first at the new visitor center to get oriented.

In the gardens, native plants, wildflowers, camellias, and hollies cover 8 acres overlooking Almshouse Creek and the South River. The mile-long trail is delightful when the azaleas in spring or 200 camellias in fall are in bloom. The historic area re-creates activities that would have happened here including rope-making, tradesmen's houses, and a carpenter shop.

Historic London Town & Gardens (© **410/222-1919;** www.historiclondontown. org) is open year-round, except major holidays, Wednesday through Saturday 10am to 4pm and Sunday noon to 4pm. Admission is $10 for adults, $9 for seniors, and $5 for children 7 to 18. Between January and March, the Brown House is closed, but the property is open Wednesday to Friday 10am to 4pm.

To get here, take U.S. 50/Md. 301 to exit 22, Aris T. Allen Boulevard. Exit onto Route 2 south, go over the South River Bridge, and continue a half-mile. Turn left onto Mayo Road, go ¾ mile, and turn left onto Londontown Road. Go 1 mile to the end of the road and enter the site through the gates.

10 SOLOMONS ★

55 miles S of Annapolis; 80 miles S of Baltimore; 60 miles SE of Washington, D.C.; 150 miles SW of Wilmington

For more than 100 years, Calvert County—with Solomons as its centerpiece—has been a Baltimore-Washington playground. Largely agricultural, the area is becoming much more a Washington suburb, but its nearby parks, local history, outdoor activities, and marine sports continue to attract visitors.

Solomons, also known as "Solomons Island," for the island that makes up its center, is dominated by water. The island sits at the end of two peninsulas formed by the Patuxent River, Back Creek, and Mill Creek (the Patuxent's mouth into the Chesapeake is visible from the town's southern end). The island is connected to land by a bridge so short that if you blink, you'll miss it, but you'll still feel surrounded by water. A walk through town will take you past sailboats and charter fishing boats, as well as watermen's homes, the century-old Drum Point Lighthouse, and Solomons' wide public pier, the place to see beautiful sunsets over the Patuxent.

ESSENTIALS

GETTING THERE   Solomons is at the southern tip of Calvert County. Maryland routes 2 and 4 merge and run north-south across the county. To reach Solomons from Washington, D.C., and points south, take I-95 to the exit for Route 4 south; follow Route 4 all the way to Solomons. From Annapolis and points north, take the exit for Route 4 south off U.S. Route 50; follow Route 2/4 to Solomons.

VISITOR INFORMATION   Contact the **Calvert County Department of Economic Development,** in the Courthouse, Prince Frederick (© **800/331-9771** or 410/535-4583; www.ecalvert.com). In Solomons, stop by the information center at the base of the Governor Thomas Johnson Bridge, on Route 2/4 (© **410/326-6027**).

WHERE TO STAY

Back Creek Inn ★★   Housed in a blue 1880 waterman's house, this inn offers travelers a relaxing stay in a waterfront setting. The innkeepers have decorated the place with antiques, quilts, flowers, and original paintings. From the cozy sitting room, you can watch boats drift by on the Back Creek. The Lavender Room is a small cottage with a Jacuzzi, fireplace, and screened porch overlooking the creek. The Tansy, Chamomile, and Peppermint rooms also enjoy water views.

210 Alexander Lane (at Calvert St.; P.O. Box 520), Solomons, MD 20688. © **410/326-2022.** Fax 410/326-2946. www.backcreekinnbnb.com. 7 units. $105–$125 double; $155–$165 suite; $220 cottage. Additional guests $25. Rates include full breakfast. MC, V. Off-street parking. No children 12 and under. **Amenities:** Bikes; outdoor Jacuzzi. *In room:* A/C, hair dryer, free Wi-Fi.

Comfort Inn Beacon Marina   This two-story hotel is geared toward nautical enthusiasts as well as regular travelers. The complex includes a 187-slip marina with 40 covered slips. Guest rooms are clean, comfortable, and modern; 10 have Jacuzzis. Best of all, guests can open the windows to enjoy the breezes off Back Creek.

255 Lore Rd. (P.O. Box 869), Solomons, MD 20688. © **800/228-5150** or 410/326-6303. Fax 410/326-9492. www.comfortinn.com. 60 units. $109–$150 double. Rates include continental breakfast. AE, DC, DISC, MC, V. Off-street parking. **Amenities:** Waterfront restaurant and bar; hot tub; 187-slip marina; pool. *In room:* A/C, fridge, hair dryer, microwave, free Wi-Fi.

Hilton Garden Inn Solomons   The only thing this newcomer (in 2007) to Solomons doesn't have is a water view. Instead it is tucked beside a wooded lot. Ask for an even-numbered room if you prefer a view of trees to the highway. All the other amenities are covered: comfortable lobby with plenty of seating, indoor and outdoor pools, free Wi-Fi, and rooms with the level of comfort you would expect from Hilton. Most rooms feature two queen-size beds, but there are king rooms, two-room units, and six rooms with whirlpools. A free shuttle takes guests to Solomons' waterfront.

13100 Dowell Rd., Dowell, MD 20629. ☎ **410/326-0303.** www.solomons.stayhgi.com. 100 units. $149–$229. Children 17 and under stay free in parent's room. AE, MC, V. Free self-parking. **Amenities:** Restaurant; lounge; fitness center; hot tub; indoor and outdoor pools. In room: A/C, hair dryer, free Wi-Fi.

Holiday Inn Solomons Conference Center & Marina The biggest hotel in Solomons is a standard Holiday Inn, but the newly renovated rooms are comfortable and a good size. Many units have views of the marina, particularly on the second floor or above and on the southern ends of the hotel's guest wings. There are packages that include boat slips.

155 Holiday Dr. (off Rte. 4; P.O. Box 1099), Solomons, MD 20688. ☎ **410/326-6311.** Fax 410/326-1069. www.solomonsmd.hiselect.com. 326 units. $129–$159 double; $169–$239 suite. AE, DISC, MC, V. Free parking. **Amenities:** Water-view restaurant; dockside bar; executive-level rooms; fitness center; 90-slip marina; outdoor pool; sauna; tennis courts; volleyball courts. In room: A/C, hair dryer, Wi-Fi (fee).

Solomons Victorian Inn Bed & Breakfast ★ Known locally as the Davis House, this Victorian inn is decorated with antiques and reproductions. It has four public spaces, including a glassed-in porch (where breakfast is served). All but one of the bedrooms enjoy a view of Back Creek Harbor or the Patuxent River. The third-floor Solomons Sunset room features a king-size bed, microwave and galley area, whirlpool tub, and great views of the harbor on two sides. Two luxurious units in the Carriage House have private entrances, whirlpool tubs, and harbor views.

125 Charles St. (P.O. Box 759), Solomons, MD 20688. ☎ **410/326-4811.** Fax 410/326-0133. www.solomons victorianinn.com. 8 units. $100–$240 double. Rates include full breakfast. 2-night minimum stay required on holidays and event weekends. AE, MC, V. Off-street parking. No children 12 and under. In room: A/C, TV, hair dryer, free Wi-Fi.

WHERE TO DINE

The CD Cafe AMERICAN   Everybody around here recommends the CD Cafe. People crowd into the bright, cozy spot for a rich assortment of dishes such as savory cheesecake (a walnut crust filled with herbed cheeses); Cajun shepherd's pie; and breast of chicken topped with pecans, apples, and an apple-schnapps glaze. Lunchtime salads are creative and tasty—try the curried chicken. Behind the cafe is the **Next Door Lounge,** a laid-back place for light fare and drinks (Tues–Sat 4:30–11pm; Sun brunch 9:30am–2:30pm).

14350 Solomons Island Rd. ☎ **410/326-3877.** www.cdcafe.info. Reservations not accepted. Main courses $10–$15 lunch, $9–$25 dinner. MC, V. Daily 11:30am–2pm and 5:30–9:30pm (until 9pm Sun).

The Dry Dock SEAFOOD   You've got to walk through a gravelly marina parking lot and up steps to the waterfront restaurant here. Once inside, the atmosphere is about Solomons' most formal. The seasonal menu, though filled with seafood choices, includes some creative options—again, creative for Solomons. Dress up in your cleanest boating togs and get ready to dig into surf and turf, the inevitable crab cakes, or ahi tuna. With 10 tables, reservations are a must. Deck dining is available in summer.

14575 Solomons Island Rd. ☎ **410/326-4817.** www.zahnisers.com/drydock.htm. Reservations recommended. Main courses $18–$30. DISC, MC, V. Sun 10am–1pm and 5:30–9:30pm; Mon–Thurs 5:30–9:30pm; Fri–Sat 5:30–9:30pm.

Solomons Pier SEAFOOD   This casual restaurant jutting out into the water has views of the soaring bridge and Patuxent River to accompany its fresh seafood. New owners took over after Hurricane Isabel demolished the deck in 2003. The menu has a new look, too, with lots of casual fare: soups, salads, sandwiches, and plenty of appetizers, including a gooey crab pretzel. Entrees run from the expected crab cake to a wasabi-glazed tuna. If you're not hungry, get a drink to toast the sunset. Local musicians play Friday and Saturday nights from March through October.

14575 Solomons Island Rd. ✆ **410/326-2424.** Reservations accepted only for large parties. Main courses $6.25–$20. DISC, MC, V. Memorial Day to Labor Day daily 11:30am–10pm; rest of the year Sun–Thurs 11:30am–9pm; Fri–Sat 11:30am–10pm.

Stoney's Kingfishers SEAFOOD Casual, with a crab-house atmosphere, Stoney's emphasizes seafood. Its half-pound crab cake is renowned, but the "baby" version is available, too. Lunch ranges from sandwiches to soups; at dinner look for softshell crabs, steaks, and filet mignon stuffed with crab imperial. Eat in the dining rooms with picture windows overlooking the water or sit out on the deck.

14444 Solomons Island Rd. ✆ **410/394-0236.** Reservations not accepted. Main courses $9–$17 lunch, $24–$36 dinner. AE, DISC, MC, V. Memorial Day to Labor Day daily 11:30am–10pm; rest of the year Sun–Thurs 11:30am–9pm; Fri–Sat 11:30am–10pm.

ATTRACTIONS

Annmarie Garden Where else can you go for sculpture, sylvan solitude, and art-filled bathrooms? This 30-acre retreat, now affiliated with the Smithsonian Institution, features some 20 pieces of sculpture on loan from the Hirshhorn Museum. Visitors are welcomed by the *Tribute to the Oyster Tonger,* with other sculptures installed along the walking path. Rest on one of the benches designed by local children, enjoy the 113 varieties of azaleas, and don't miss those bathrooms.

13480 Dowell Rd. (off Rte. 4). ✆ **410/326-4640.** www.annmariegarden.org. Admission $3 adults, $2 seniors and children. Daily 9am–5pm.

Calvert Marine Museum and Drum Point Lighthouse ★★★ **Kids** In a state brimming with maritime museums, this is the best. It has exhibits on local industry and the environment, fossils from nearby Calvert Cliffs (see "Outdoor Activities," below), a lighthouse, and even an otter to visit. The sea-horse exhibit is intriguing—who knew they lived in the bay? The Discovery Room will have kids learning a little history while digging for fossils. Then there's the Drum Point Lighthouse, one of three remaining screw-pile lighthouses on the Chesapeake. (Thomas Point Lighthouse still operates near Annapolis, and the Hooper Strait Light is the centerpiece of the Chesapeake Bay Maritime Museum on the Eastern Shore.) You can build a little boat or take a cruise on the bugeye *Wm. B. Tennison.*

Shuttle-bus tours ($3), available daily from June to August, head to the Cove Point Lighthouse, the oldest continuously operating lighthouse in the state. Nearby is the J. C. Lore and Sons Oyster House, which has exhibits on Patuxent watermen and "deadrise" workboat building. Admission is free; it's open June through August, daily from 10am to noon and 1 to 4:30pm, plus the same hours on fall and spring weekends.

14200 Solomons Island Rd. ✆ **800/735-2258** or 410/326-2042. www.calvertmarinemuseum.com. Admission $7 adults, $6 seniors, $2 children 5–12; cruise tickets $7 adults, $6 seniors, $2 children 5–12. Daily 10am–5pm. Closed Jan 1, Thanksgiving, and Dec 25. Limited docking available for visitors.

OUTDOOR ACTIVITIES
Charter Fishing ★

Fishing is one of Calvert County's biggest draws. And for good reason: The bay waters here are filled seasonally with rockfish (striped bass), bluefish, Spanish mackerel, white perch, spot, croaker, flounder, sea trout, and black drum. Before you head out to sea, check with your charter-boat captain to find out what's in season.

Wine Tasting in Solomons

Just north of Solomons are two tiny wineries with limited bottling and even more limited hours. Those interested in the winemaking process will enjoy tasting the wares and talking to the winemakers.

Solomons Island Winery, 515 Garner Lane, Lusby (ⓒ **410/394-1933;** www.solomonsislandwinery.com), offers tastings Tuesday through Sunday noon to 5pm. From Route 4, turn left on Monticello Lane and left on Garner Lane; the winery will be on the right.

Cove Point Winery, 755 Cove Point Rd., Lusby (ⓒ **410/326-0949;** www.covepointwinery.com), has tastings every Saturday and Sunday from noon to 5:30pm, or by appointment Monday to Friday. From Route 4, turn right on Cove Point Road.

Charter fishing is available in two ways: through organized operations and through loose affiliations of captains. It's easy to charter a boat either way. In the case of an organized operation, call the office, which will supply a boat. If all its boats are full, the company will contact a local captain and have him run the charter.

It works a little differently with captains' associations. In this case, you call a contact person for the association, usually one of the captains. If that captain has an opening, he will take you out on his boat. If he doesn't, he will arrange for another captain to take you out or give you the names of captains who might be available.

Remember to ask what you'll need to bring. Most charters include fishing gear; some supply bait for free and some don't. Bring a cooler to take your catch home. The mates on charter boats work for cash tips, which should be at least 15%.

In Solomons

Bunky's Charter Boats   Bunky's operates out of a well-stocked bait-and-tackle shop across from the walking pier on Solomons Island. It has a fleet of 10 charter boats, including one 48-foot headboat, the *Marchelle*. Charter rates for up to six passengers on all boats except the *Marchelle* are $520 per half-day (6 hr.) and $620 per full day (8 hr.). Rates for six on the *Marchelle* are $600 per half-day and $700 per full day. There's a per-person charge of $70 for extra passengers. Fishing on a headboat costs $40 a person for 6 hours. Bunky's also rents 16-foot motorboats, but if you're not on a charter boat, you'll need a license to fish—which you can get here, too.

14448 Solomons Island Rd. S. ⓒ **410/326-3241.** www.bunkyscharterboats.com.

Solomons Charter Captains Association (SCCA) and Fin Finder Charters
The association runs many of its 40 boats out of the Calvert Marina Charter Dock, on Dowell Road (ⓒ **800/450-1775**). Eleven of the SCCA's boats can carry more than six people; some can carry as many as 40. Standard association rates are $525 to $675.

The *Fin Finder*, a 46-foot Chesapeake-style workboat, is Capt. Sonney Forrest's own charter boat. It carries up to 30 passengers. Rates for a full day start at $800. Cruise tours and packages are also available.

Solomons. ⓒ **800/831-2702.** www.fishsolomons.com or www.finfinder.com.

Chesapeake Beach charters are very popular, with a fleet that takes passengers to waters filled with rockfish, blues, and flounder. To get here from Annapolis, take Route 2 south to Maryland Route 260 west, which ends just north of the harbor at Maryland Route 261. From Washington, D.C., take Route 4 west to Route 260 west and follow the directions above. It's about an hour north of Solomons.

Chesapeake Beach Fishing Charters   This association of charter captains has a dozen boats. A half-day for six people costs $550; a full day goes for $700.

Chesapeake Beach. ℂ **301/855-4665.** www.chesapeakefishingcharters.com.

Rod 'N' Reel Charter Fishing   Rod 'N' Reel has a huge share of the charter-fishing operation in Maryland's portion of the Chesapeake. Charter rates for up to six people are $550 per 6-hour trip, $700 per 8-hour trip. Or get on a headboat for $55 per person; rod rentals are $5. Trips leave in the morning.

4160 Mears Ave., Chesapeake Beach. ℂ **800/233-2080** or 301/855-8450. www.cbresortspa.com.

Sportfishing

Although charter fishing is this area's forte, there are also several choice locations for sportfishing, including **Bay Front Park,** in Chesapeake Beach; and **Solomons Fishing Pier,** under the Gov. Thomas Johnson Bridge (Rte. 4) in Solomons.

Bait and tackle are available at **Bunky's Charter Boats,** in Solomons (ℂ **410/326-3241**), and **Rod 'N' Reel,** in Chesapeake Beach (ℂ **866/312-5596**).

Bike & Kayak Rentals

If you just want to meander around Solomons, **Patuxent Adventure Center,** 11380 Solomons Island Rd. (ℂ **410/394-2770;** www.paxadventure.com), rents bikes and kayaks and can arrange for tours of nearby waterways.

---

11   ST. MARY'S CITY

---

86 miles S of Annapolis; 101 miles S of Baltimore; 69 miles SE of Washington, D.C.; 173 miles SW of Wilmington

The Free State got its start here, where the Potomac River meets the Chesapeake Bay, in 1634. The settlers came here to start a colony based on freedom of conscience, and a sense of democracy that welcomed people of other faiths and other nations. It was here that the first man of color was able to participate in representative government

St. Mary's City is situated on a lovely but remote peninsula, in a county dotted with aging tobacco barns and laced with rivers and creeks. Nearby Lexington Park, the county's biggest town, is the home of the Patuxent River Naval Air Station.

St. Mary's City is a quick hop from Annapolis, Washington, or Baltimore. Or combine a visit with a stay in Solomons for a quintessential Chesapeake Bay vacation.

ESSENTIALS

GETTING THERE   St. Mary's City is located on Route 5. From Washington, take the Route 5 exit from I-495 (the Capital Beltway). Or from Annapolis, take Maryland Route 50 to Route 301 to Route 4 to Solomons and across the Gov. Thomas Johnson Bridge. Turn left a few miles past the bridge onto Route 235, right on Route 489, and left onto

Route 5 into St. Mary's City. For a more scenic drive, take Route 50 to Route 301 to Route 5 all the way to St. Mary's City—a slow and meandering route.

VISITOR INFORMATION See the **St. Mary's County Tourism Office,** 23115 Leonard Hall Dr., Leonardtown (✆ **800/327-9023** or 301/475-4200, ext. 1404).

DISCOVERING MARYLAND'S FIRST CAPITAL

Historic St. Mary's City ★★★ History happened here. Though most of the 17th-century buildings of Maryland's first capital city are gone, their foundations covered by farmland, it was here that Cecil Calvert enacted laws that permitted anyone regardless of their faith to vote and participate in government. This freedom of conscience and separation of church and state were unheard of in those days and drew a wide variety of settlers. The first Catholic chapel in English America was established here at a time when they were forbidden elsewhere. The first African American voted in the legislature here. A woman demanded the right to vote here. Nothing's perfect; her request was denied.

St. Mary's City was founded in 1634 and in its heyday was home to 20,000 people. St. Mary's City was laid out in a traditional grid pattern, with the state house at one end of the town and the church at the other end. Taverns, shops, and homes filled the spaces in between. But by the end of the 17th century, the capital had moved to Annapolis, and St. Mary's City disappeared.

Today, the site is an archaeologist's dream. Through careful archaeological digs and painstaking research, some of the buildings have been reproduced. In the summer, visitors can watch the St. Mary's College field school conduct new digs, searches in the ground for bits of old buildings, artifacts, and even the marks left in the dirt itself that recall the buildings and the people who once lived in the early Colonial town.

So what is there to see?

In the town center, you can see mostly small and simple buildings, such as an inn, an early print shop, the grander State House, and the Brick Chapel. You can even climb aboard a reproduction of a ship like the one that brought the first settlers here. Nearby are an early plantation and Indian woodland village. An archaeological museum has been built over the site of the building where the legislature sat. Allow at least 4 hours for your visit, wear comfortable shoes, and bring water, as it can get very hot and humid here. Guides will help you get a feel for 17th-century Maryland.

At the **visitor center,** get the gear for the state-of-the-art audio tour, watch the introductory video, and see an exhibit chronicling the rise and fall of St. Mary's City. It's open year-round, as is the St. John's Site Museum. Other exhibits close between Thanksgiving and Maryland Day (Mar 25).

Don't miss the **State House** or **Godiah Spray's 17th-century tobacco plantation.** While the public building is formal, the plantation shows how hard life was for the early colonists. The house is simple, the fields rough.

The reconstructed **Print Shop,** Maryland's first, was run by a woman, and was the first one south of Boston in the 17th century. It opened in 2007.

Smith's Ordinary, a reconstructed 17th-century inn, features a medieval-style fireplace and tiled inglenook. A second inn, **Farthing's Ordinary,** built in the 1600s, has a pretty good gift shop.

The newest re-creations are the **St. John's Site Museum,** which features modern galleries set atop a glass floor over the original home's foundation on display. At this site, Margaret Brent asked for a woman's right to vote and Matthias DeSousa was the first black man to participate in the legislature. The building is open year-round and there's no admission charge. The 1667 **Brick Chapel** has been built but is still empty. It is perhaps the grandest of the buildings so far reconstructed in St. Mary's. It is expected to be furnished by 2011—once the historians take their best guess about how it would have looked.

Walk down to the water to see the 76-foot *Dove,* a reproduction of a small mid-16th-century square-rigged merchant ship similar to the smaller of the two ships that brought Maryland's first settlers here in 1634. Children love to board the boat and talk with the costumed sailors.

A bonus is the waterfront setting. Walking trails through woodlands and near the water stretch 3.5 miles and recall how this area must have looked to early settlers.

Special programs are offered on **Maryland Day,** March 25; **Community and Trail Day,** in June (free admission and special events); **Tidewater Archaeology Dig day,** in late June (join the archaeologists); **Woodland Indian Discovery Day,** the weekend after Labor Day (with storytelling, Native American crafts, and exhibits); and **Grand Militia Muster Day,** in October (a gathering of 17th-c. reenactment units).

St. Mary's City. ✆ **800/762-1634.** www.stmaryscity.org. Admission $10 adults, $8 seniors, $6 students 13–18, $3.50 children 6–12; off-season (when living history exhibits are closed) $2 adults, $1 children 6–12. St. John's Museum admission free. Audio guides $3. Mid-Mar to Dec Wed–Sun 10am–5pm (all exhibits open); Jan to mid-Mar Wed–Sun 10am–5pm (only St. John's Museum, visitor center, grounds are open). Because the staff is small, it's best to call ahead to confirm hours. From Rte. 4, turn left on Rte. 235 and right on Mattapany Rd. St. Mary's City will be ahead, across Rte. 5. From Washington, take Rte. 5 to St. Mary's.

OTHER HISTORIC SITES IN ST. MARY'S COUNTY

Sotterley Plantation ★ This 1703 house is the only Tidewater-style tobacco plantation house still open to the public. The 1760 Chinese Chippendale railing is a marvel, as is the withdrawing room's intricate carving, which is estimated to have taken enslaved African Americans 20 years to complete. The original 19th-century slave quarters are open for visits. Restoration is ongoing at this National Historic Landmark, but the house is fully furnished. The grounds are open year-round for self-guided visits and walks through the formal gardens and along the trails to the Patuxent River. Check the website for special events, including wine festivals and ghost tours. *Note:* A dock is available; call ahead for a slip. It's a 20-minute walk from the dock to the house.

44300 Sotterley Lane (off Rte. 245), Hollywood. ✆ **800/681-0850** or 301/373-2280. www.sotterley.org. House tours $10 adults, $8 seniors, $5 children 6–12; grounds and self-tour admission $3. House tours May–Oct Tues–Sat 10am–4pm; Sun noon–4pm; grounds and self-tours available year-round Mon–Sat 10am–4pm, Sun noon–4pm. Site closed Jan 1, Martin Luther King Day, Presidents Day, Easter, Memorial Day, July 4, Labor Day, Thanksgiving, and Dec 25.

OUTDOOR ACTIVITIES
Point Lookout State Park ★

At the tip of St. Mary's County, at the confluence of the Potomac River and the Chesapeake Bay, **Point Lookout State Park** (✆ **301/872-5688**) offers visitors a chance to see both bodies of water at one time. The park's 1,046 acres offer a beach on the Potomac, a fishing pier on the Chesapeake, Civil War era prisoner-of-war camp Fort Lincoln, docks for boating and catching the cruise boat to Smith Island across the bay, and campsites and cabins. The lighthouse at the tip of the peninsula, built in 1830, is now dark but open to visitors 1 weekend in November. Day use at the park is $5 for state residents and $6 for nonresidents on weekends and holidays, May through September. On weekdays and out of season, the fee is $3 or $4 per vehicle. The boat-launch fee is $10, $11 for out-of-state visitors.

Day-use facilities with a guarded beach for swimming are on the Potomac side, past the fishing pier. There's a pet beach north of the causeway, too.

Visitors interested in **fishing** can cast their lines just about anywhere except the beach swimming area. Favorite areas are the pier on the bay side and the point on either the bay or riverside. The pier is closed mid-December through March. Night fishing is the only activity allowed in the park (except camping) after sunset. Campers can also fish at designated piers near campsites. A fishing license is required only for the bay shoreline. Boat and canoe rentals are available at the camp store off Route 5.

The park offers 143 **campsites** (26 with full hookups). The cost is $25 to $35 per site. Cabins sleeping four cost $50 a night. Reservations can be made up to a year in advance by calling © **888/432-2267.** The office (© **301/872-5688**) is open from 8am to 11pm in summer.

Smith Island Cruises (© **410/425-2771**; www.smithislandcruises.com) offers day trips from here to Smith Island, a 1½-hour trip across the bay, on the twin-hulled *Chelsea Lane Tyler.* From Memorial Day to Labor Day, boats depart Wednesday through Sunday at 10am and return to Point Lookout at 3:30pm. Cruises continue from September to mid-October on weekends only. Round-trip fare is $30 for adults, $15 for children 3 to 11. For details on Smith Island, see p. 178.

Fishing Charters
Chesapeake Bay Fishing Parties (© **301/872-5815**) operates the *Honey Bee* charter boat and a headboat called the *Lucky Charm* from Ridge. Charters run $550 for seven people on weekdays, $6,500 for nine on weekends and holidays ($50 for extra passengers). Headboat rates are about $60, with $5 for rod and bait.

WHERE TO STAY
St. Mary's City has only one lodging option, but nearby Lexington Park has some chain hotels, including the **Hampton Inn** (© **301/863-3200**) and the **Fairfield Inn** (© **301/863-0203**).

The Brome Howard Inn   The rich and famous drop in here—lots of Washingtonians have homes in the area—but the innkeepers will treat you with the same hospitality. The house looks out on the St. Mary's River and is decorated with antiques. The elegant bedrooms vary in decor; three have fireplaces and two combine to make a suite for families. This B&B is within walking distance of the historic site. Dinner Thursday through Sunday and Sunday brunch are by reservation only.

18281 Rosecroft Rd. (P.O. Box 476), St. Mary's City, MD 20686. © **301/866-0656.** Fax 301/866-9660. www.bromehowardinn.com. 4 units. $125–$185 double. Rates include full breakfast. AE, MC, V. Off-street parking. **Amenities:** Restaurant; bicycles; high-speed Internet access in public area. *In room:* A/C, TV/VCR, CD player, fridge, hair dryer.

WHERE TO EAT
Visitors to St. Mary's City have only a few options. Bring a picnic lunch or buy a snack in Farthing's Ordinary. You can also grab a bite at the Student Center at St. Mary's College, across Route 5 from the visitor center parking lot. There's a coffee shop on the ground floor and a dining hall serving three meals Monday through Friday and brunch and dinner on the weekends on the second floor. A couple of restaurants located near one another on Route 252 (Wynne Rd.) in Ridge are all near the water; seafood is the specialty.

Courtney's Restaurant SEAFOOD Nothing's fancy in here. It's a cinder-block building with a simple dining room and a bar with the TV going. But after a day outdoors, you'll be hungry for home cooking—and that's what Courtney's does best. You can get steamed crabs, crab cakes, or softshells. Want fresh fish? Courtney's husband comes home every morning with the day's catch. Carryout is available.

48290 Wynne Rd., Ridge. ✆ **301/872-4403.** Reservations not necessary. Main courses $6–$8 lunch, $16–$19 dinner. MC, V. Daily 7am–9pm.

Scheible's SEAFOOD Simple seafood is served in a wood-paneled dining room with vinyl table cloths. You'll have your choice of lots of fried foods, both seafood and chicken, along with club sandwiches at lunch and steaks and pasta at dinner. Portions are generous. Picture windows offer sweeping views of Smith Creek.

48342 Wynne Rd., Ridge. ✆ **301/872-0025.** Reservations recommended. Main courses $5–$12 lunch, $9–$27 dinner. AE, DISC, MC, V. Thurs–Fri 11am–9pm; Sat 6am–9pm; Sun 6am–8pm. Closed Dec–Mar.

Spinnakers Restaurant SEAFOOD Tucked in a corner of a marina, Spinnakers also features seafood. A new owner was expanding the choices at press time but count on the local fish, shellfish, and steak. Breakfast is served Sundays 8am to 1pm. Live entertainment is offered occasionally. A cabana bar and carryout are also offered.

Point Lookout Marina, 16244 Miller's Wharf Rd., Ridge. ✆ **301/872-5020.** www.pointlookoutmarina.com/spinnakers. Reservations recommended. Main courses $7–$10 lunch, $16–$21 dinner. AE, DISC, MC, V. Mon–Sat 11am–9pm; Sun 8am–9pm (longer hours in summer). Take Md. Rte. 5 or Md. Rte. 235 south to Ridge. Turn onto Wynne Rd. (Rte. 252) and go 1¹/₂ miles. Turn right on Miller's Wharf Rd. Restaurant is in the marina at end of road.

7

Around the
Capital Beltway

The suburbs of Washington, D.C., are jammed with housing developments, shopping centers, and endless miles of highway. But among the discount stores and tract housing are some delights that shouldn't be overlooked. They're easy to get to from either Baltimore or Annapolis and all are accessible from the Capital Beltway.

Among the gems are two homes connected with President Lincoln's assassination, the estate of one of Maryland's signers of the Declaration of Independence, and the home of the founder of the American Red Cross. You can visit farms and gardens, see jets and space ships, shop for antiques, and ride a roller coaster.

The following sections have been divided according to the sites' locations around the Capital Beltway. But you don't always have to use the Beltway to get where you're going; plenty of other roads will get you there, too.

A new development, National Harbor, opened in 2009. A destination on its own, it's a great jumping-off spot for Washington, D.C., visitors, too. It has its own section.

---

1 NORTHWEST

40 miles W of Annapolis; 40 miles SW of Baltimore; 8 miles NW of Washington, D.C.; 110 miles SW of Wilmington

The northwest section of the Capital Beltway is accessible by I-270, which connects to Frederick. Bethesda is home to the Discovery Channel, the National Institutes of Health, and the Bethesda Naval Hospital, and you'll find offices for a number of other federal agencies among the high-rises. It's also home to the Music Center at the Strathmore. The C&O Canal Historical Park, Clara Barton's home, and Glen Echo Park are close enough to each other to plan a day's outing with the kids. Brookside Gardens offers another respite for weary tourists. Prefer shopping? Get new stuff at White Flint Mall or old stuff on Howard Avenue (see Antique Row listing, below) in Kensington.

ATTRACTIONS

American Film Institute Silver Theatre and Cultural Center Something wonderful is always on the screen at this restored 1938 movie palace. In addition to a regular schedule of new and classic pictures, the theater hosts a series of film festivals, including the SilverDocs international documentary film series each June. Movie tickets can be reserved online. Several parking garages are within walking distance.

8633 Colesville Rd., Silver Spring. © 301/495-6720 or 495-6700 for recorded film information. www.afi.com/silver. $10 adults, $9 seniors, $6 children, $7.50 matinees. Movies daily noon–9pm. Box office opens 30 min. before screening. Parking in nearby Wayne St. Garage is free after 6pm.

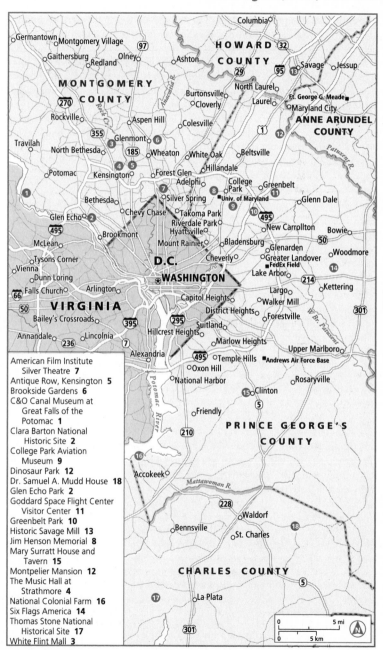

American Film Institute
Silver Theatre **7**
Antique Row, Kensington **5**
Brookside Gardens **6**
C&O Canal Museum at
Great Falls of the
Potomac **1**
Clara Barton National
Historic Site **2**
College Park Aviation
Museum **9**
Dinosaur Park **12**
Dr. Samuel A. Mudd House **18**
Glen Echo Park **2**
Goddard Space Flight Center
Visitor Center **11**
Greenbelt Park **10**
Historic Savage Mill **13**
Jim Henson Memorial **8**
Mary Surratt House and
Tavern **15**
Montpelier Mansion **12**
The Music Hall at
Strathmore **4**
National Colonial Farm **16**
Six Flags America **14**
Thomas Stone National
Historical Site **17**
White Flint Mall **3**

Antique Row   You've got two choices when you aim for the antiques shops in Kensington. Go east for knickknacks, silver, old books, and china. Or head west for the warehouses full of antique French, English, and other European furniture, chandeliers, and objets d'art. (Connecticut Ave. divides the two areas by more than traffic.) If you enjoy a day of poking around little shops, turn right off Connecticut Avenue (Rte. 185) to Kensington's historic district. You'll find 5 blocks of little shops, including **Antiques and Uniques** (℗ 301/942-3324); **Pritchard's** (℗ 301/942-1661), which also sells new decorative tiles and lighting; and the multidealer **Antique Village,** which also has a small lunch room. For serious antiques shopping, decorators (and homeowners) head to West Howard. There, among the car repair shops and other warehouses, are more than a dozen dealers who import their wares from overseas. **Sparrows** (℗ 301/530-0175) is the largest, with the most jaw-droppingly beautiful furniture. Much of it wouldn't fit in the average house. The mahogany gleams at crowded **Acanthus** (℗ 301/530-9600). **Huret Antiques** (℗ 301/530-7551) stocks 19th-century French and French-inspired designs. Most shops are open daily; free parking is plentiful.

From I-495, take exit 33 north to Rte. 185, Connecticut Ave. Turn left at Howard for the historic district. For West Howard, turn left at Knowles Ave. traffic light, right on Summit Ave., left on West Howard.

Brookside Gardens   It's just 50 acres, but it's a gem. The top draws are the conservatories with their tropical plantings and the summertime butterfly show, but don't overlook the rose and aquatic gardens or the children's Fairy Folk Garden. The serenity of the Japanese Tea House is something you'll remember. Paths are accessible for wheelchairs and strollers, and some wheelchairs are available at the visitor center. There's no picnicking, but take your lunch to neighboring **Wheaton Regional Park,** 2000 Shorefield Rd. (℗ 301/680-3803), which has lots of trees and playgrounds. There's also a miniature train and carousel to ride.

1800 Glenallan Ave., Wheaton. ℗ 301/962-1400. www.brooksidegardens.org. Free admission. Gardens daily dawn–dusk; conservatories daily 10am–5pm; visitor center daily 9am–5pm. Closed Dec 25. From I-270 and points west, take exit 4A, Montrose Rd. east, which turns into Randolph Rd. Go 7 miles and turn right onto Glenallan Ave. From I-495, the Capital Beltway, take exit 31A (north on Georgia Ave./Rte. 97) toward Wheaton. Drive 3 miles north on Georgia Ave. to Randolph Rd. and turn right. At the 2nd light, turn right onto Glenallan Ave. Park at the visitor center at 1800 Glenallan Ave. or at the conservatories at 1500 Glenallan Ave.

Chesapeake & Ohio Canal National Historical Park★   This is *the* stop on the Chesapeake & Ohio Canal. The wheelchair-accessible Olmsted Island Boardwalk runs through woods to a bridge overlooking one branch of the falls, then to the overlook where the falls crash over the rocks. The boardwalk is crowded on nice days, but when you get to the falls, you'll have plenty of space to take in the view. The strenuous Billy Goat Trail is a first-rate hike. The mule-drawn canal boat *Charles F. Mercer* takes visitors for an hour-long ride on the canal Wednesday through Sunday spring through fall. The 1831 tavern has been fully restored as a visitor center with new exhibits.

11710 MacArthur Blvd., near Falls Rd. (Md. Rte. 189), Potomac. ℗ 301/767-3714 or 299-3613. www.nps. gov/choh. Park entry fee $5 per vehicle, $3 for walk-ins. Admission valid for 3 days. Boat rides $5 a person. Daily 9am–4:45pm. Closed Jan 1, Thanksgiving, and Dec 25. Take exit 41W off I-495.

Clara Barton National Historic Site ★ Finds   The Red Cross was everything to its founder, Clara Barton. At her Glen Echo home, the closets are filled with blankets, lanterns, and other supplies for disaster relief. Her office is no-nonsense, including her chair: She cut off the back so she wouldn't rest while working. The 1891 home is a quirky thing, its design unusual inside and out, but as you wander through the rooms that sheltered Clara and her staff, you'll get to know more about the woman who made this her mission and her life. You can see the entire house in a short, fascinating visit. The guides are great with kids and never fail to keep them interested.

5801 Oxford Rd. (at MacArthur Blvd.), Glen Echo. (C) **301/320-1410.** www.nps.gov/clba. Free admission. Daily 10am–5pm; by guided tour only (given on the hour; last tour at 4pm). Closed Jan 1, Thanksgiving, and Dec 25. From I-495, take exit 40, Cabin John Pkwy., which merges with the Clara Barton Pkwy. Follow signs to Glen Echo and MacArthur Blvd. Left lane turns off with small spur to the right. Take right spur up ramp to MacArthur Blvd. Turn left to Oxford Rd.

Glen Echo Park   Combine a visit to Clara Barton's house with a trip to this cultural arts park—it's just across a parking lot. First a Chautauqua meeting ground, its emphasis on culture continues today. Call ahead or go to the website for a schedule of ballroom dancing, puppet shows, and plays. You can stop here to picnic or to ride on the 1921 hand-carved Dentzel carousel for $1.25.

7300 MacArthur Blvd., Glen Echo. (C) **301/492-6229.** www.nps.gov/glec. Free admission; tickets required for carousel; event ticket prices vary. Carousel May–June Wed–Thurs 10am–2pm, Sat–Sun noon–6pm; July–Aug Wed–Fri 10am–2pm, Sat–Sun noon–6pm; Sept Sat–Sun noon–6pm. See directions to Clara Barton site above.

The Music Center at Strathmore ★   The architecture of this music hall is striking, with an undulating roofline, picture windows letting in the light and the leafy scenery, and warm maple and birch wrapped around curved walls and floors. But it's the sound that will wow you. Every note is unmistakably clear in this cathedral to music. Nearly 2,000 seats surround the stage, which has featured everyone from the Baltimore Symphony Orchestra—this is its D.C.-area headquarters—to Queen Latifah to Patti LuPone. And it's easy to find, easy to get to, and easy to park at: Just off the Capital Beltway and I-270, the signs are well posted and there's free parking in the adjacent Metro garage and valet parking for $15. This is also home to a busy arts school that stages its performances here.

5301 Tuckerman Lane, North Bethesda. (C) **301/581-5100.** www.strathmore.org. From I-495, take exit 34 north, Wisconsin Ave. (Rte. 355) to Tuckerman Lane.

White Flint Mall   Four floors of shopping—including Bloomingdale's, Lord & Taylor, Borders, Pottery Barn, and a Dave & Buster's restaurant—offer plenty of outlets for both necessities and luxuries.

Rockville Pike at Nicholson Lane, North Bethesda. (C) **301/231-7567.** www.shopwhiteflint.com. From I-495, take exit 34 north, Wisconsin Ave. (Rte. 355), to mall. Free valet parking.

---

2 NORTHEAST

30 miles W of Annapolis; 30 miles SW of Baltimore; 9 miles NE of Washington, D.C.; 100 miles SW of Wilmington

Connected to Baltimore by routes 29, 1, and I-95, this section is dominated by the University of Maryland's main campus in College Park and Fort Meade. Laurel is home to a mill-turned-antiques center, and a resting place of George Washington. The science-minded may be interested in the Goddard Space Flight Center, while those of a fanciful bent of mind may want to pay homage to the creator of the Muppets (see Jim Henson Memorial listing, below). Prefer a picnic or roller-coaster ride? This area's got them, too.

College Park Aviation Museum (Kids) Who knew the oldest continuously operating airport in the world was right next to the University of Maryland? The museum next to the airport, a Smithsonian Institution affiliate, celebrates all the milestones of aviation, including a visit here by Wilbur Wright in 1909 and 10 aircraft from the airplane's early days. For kids, there are props to spin and even a wind tunnel. Try your hand at flying in one of the flight simulation stations.

1985 Cpl. Frank Scott Dr., College Park. ℂ **301/864-6029.** www.collegeparkaviationmuseum.com. Admission $4 adults, $3 seniors, $2 children. Daily 10am–5pm. Closed major holidays. From I-495, take exit 23 south to Paint Branch Pkwy., to Cpl. Frank Scott Dr.

Dinosaur Park Just twice a month, dinosaur fans have an opportunity to take a hike in this fossil treasure-trove with a paleontologist and see what they can find. It's just a 1-acre site but it's one of the only intact deposits of fossils from the Cretaceous Period on the East Coast. You can't take your finds (if any) with you; they go to the Smithsonian Institution. Stop when the park is closed and see the garden with plants from dinosaur times and informational signs about the fossils and local history.

13200 block Midatlantic Blvd., Laurel. ℂ **301/627-7755.** Free admission. 1st and 3rd Saturday of the month, noon–4pm; garden daily dawn–dusk.

Goddard Space Flight Center Just up the road (Rte. 295) from the aviation museum, Goddard celebrates flight into space. Exhibits focus on the beginning of space exploration (rocket pioneer Robert Goddard), the present (the latest discoveries of the Hubble Space Telescope), and the future (scientists' predictions about global warming, pollution, and other earth and space issues). Though the Hubble Space Telescope is the centerpiece of the visitor center, "Science on a Sphere" may be more fascinating to your inner geek. A ball-shaped screen shows the earth in 3-D, and you can watch weather, see the planet light up at night, or follow winds as they spread sand from China to California. Queen Elizabeth took a look during her 2007 visit here. Groups can make a reservation to tour the research facilities, including the world's largest "clean room," where scientists work on innovations for the space telescope or new satellites. The website lists science nights, model-rocket launches, and experiments.

8800 Greenbelt Rd., Greenbelt. ℂ **301/286-9041.** Fax 301/286-1781. www.nasa.gov/centers/goddard. Free admission. Sept–June Tues–Fri 10am–3pm, Sat–Sun noon–4pm; July–Aug Tues–Fri 10am–5pm, Sat noon–4pm. Closed all federal holidays. Take Rte. 295 north from Capital Beltway to E. Greenbelt Rd. (Rte. 193). Turn left onto IceSat Rd. and left to Visitor Center.

Greenbelt Park This national park is really D.C. suburbanites' backyard. With picnic tables, playground equipment, and walking trails, it's a nice getaway from all the traffic and noise. The campground is open year-round. Reservations are taken (and recommended) for summer.

6565 Greenbelt Rd., Greenbelt. ℂ **301/344-4250.** www.nps.gov/gree. Free admission; camping $16. Daily dawn–dusk. Take Rte. 295 north from Capital Beltway to W. Greenbelt Rd. (Rte. 193). Park will be on the left.

Historic Savage Mill This restored 1822 cotton mill has antiques shops, galleries, boutiques, and a couple of places to stop for refreshment. It's an interesting place that keeps its heritage alive by using the names of the buildings' original purposes in signs and maps. You have only to follow your nose to **Bonaparte Breads** (ℂ **410/880-0858**), in the Spinning Building, where you'll find coffee, French pastries, sandwiches, soup, and

Take a Walk into History

New hiking trails stretch all over Maryland, but Montgomery County offers two that allow walkers to stretch their minds along with their legs.

Underground Railroad Experience Hikes are offered Saturdays April until November at 10am on the Rural Legacy Trail. The trail begins at Woodlawn Manor, 16501 Norwood Rd., Sandy Spring. For directions and other information, call ✆ **301/370-5722.** The 2-mile hikes are free.

Rachel Carson Conservation Park Trails honor the memory of the author of *Silent Spring.* The environmental activist was also a Montgomery County resident. This 650-acre park has more than 6 miles of trails for hiking and horseback riding. (Bring your own horse.) To reach the park, go to 22201 Mt. Zion Rd., in Olney. For information, call ✆ **301/495-2595.**

other treats. In the Carding Building is the **Rams Head Tavern** (✆ **301/604-3454**), a brewpub with heartier fare. In the Carding Building and Old Weave Building, you can find antiques, handmade sweaters, and needlework supplies.

8600 Foundry St., Savage. ✆ **800/788-6455.** www.savagemill.com. Free admission. Mon–Wed 10am–6pm; Thurs–Sat 10am–9pm; Sun 11am–6pm. Closed Easter, Thanksgiving, and Dec 25. Take Rte. 32 to Rte. 1 south. Turn right at Howard St. and follow the signs.

Jim Henson Memorial Those who love Kermit and the Muppets may want to take a detour while in College Park to see the bronze-and-granite memorial to one of the University of Maryland's own, Jim Henson, who created the first Muppets while a student here in the 1950s. Jay Hall Carpenter, a nationally known sculptor, created the work, which was cast in a Baltimore foundry. Alumni raised the funds for the memorial built in 2003. You'll find Jim and Kermit sitting on a bench outside the student union.

Stamp Student Union, University of Maryland, College Park. No phone. Free admission. From I-495, take exit 27 and follow signs to exit 25, U.S. 1 S., College Park. Right on Campus Dr., go around circle, pass Hornbake Library, and Stamp Student Union will be on right. Visitors may park during the school day at the nearby Union Lane Garage or Stadium Dr. Garage. Other lots require parking permits before 4pm. They are open to the public on evenings and weekends (except during football and basketball games) and in the summer.

Montpelier Mansion (Kids) This 1780s five-part Georgian mansion, which once sat on 9,000 acres, was built by the grandson of an indentured servant and was grand enough for George and Martha Washington and Abigail Adams to spend the night. Now part of Prince George's County Parks, it has been restored to what historians think it looked like in the 1830s. The setting, now just 90 acres, is an idyllic green spot—which blazes orange and red in autumn. Christmas candlelight tours with rooms decorated by local garden clubs make the place festive. Children's hands-on programs and a boxwood maze keep kids occupied. Also on the property is the **Montpelier Arts Center** (✆ **301/377-7800**), which offers art exhibitions and performing arts events.

9650 Muirkirk Rd., Laurel. ✆ **301/377-7817.** www.pgparks.com. Admission $3 adults, $2 seniors, $1 children. Mar–Nov Mon–Thurs self-guided tours noon and 3pm, Sun guided tours on the hour noon–3pm; Dec–Feb Mon–Thurs self-guided tours noon and 3pm, Sun guided tours 1 and 2pm. Grounds daily dawn–dusk. From I-295, take exit to Rte. 197 W., left on Muirkirk Rd.

Right on Route 29 in Silver Spring is the historic **Mrs. K's Tollhouse Restaurant,** 9201 Colesville Rd. (© **301/589-3500;** www.mrsks.com). The home of the last operating tollhouse in Montgomery County, the building has been a restaurant since 1930. Surrounded by gardens and expanded over the years, it remains an elegant, old-fashioned dining establishment, serving lunch and dinner Tuesday through Saturday, brunch and dinner on Sunday. It is closed Mondays. They also have tollhouse cookies to go.

---

3 SOUTHEAST

40 miles SW of Annapolis; 50 miles SW of Baltimore; 15 miles SE of Washington, D.C.; 115 miles SW of Wilmington

These sites are accessible from exit 7A, Route 5 South. This section of the Washington suburbs is the least congested. Although more and more housing developments are popping up on farmland, you can still see vestiges of the agricultural past, perhaps even a tobacco farm or two (though few are in use around here anymore) and the fields of farmland John Wilkes Booth rode through to make his getaway. Six Flags is the exception. It is accessible from Route 214, off of I-495 or Route 301.

ATTRACTIONS

Dr. Samuel A. Mudd House   Dr. Samuel A. Mudd set John Wilkes Booth's broken leg after Booth shot Lincoln. For that action, he was incarcerated on a Caribbean island prison. The house hasn't changed much since those days. It remained the Mudd home until it was turned into a privately owned museum. In fact, Mudd family members still volunteer here. The 1830 house, surrounded by 200 acres, is filled with medical implements from Dr. Mudd's office and several items he made while in prison, including a checkerboard tabletop, a desk, and several shell-encrusted boxes. Also on the property are a farm museum and Mudd's original tombstone.

3725 Dr. Samuel Mudd Rd., Waldorf. © **301/645-6870.** www.somd.lib.md.us/museums/mudd.htm. $5 adults, $2 ages 6–16. Wed and Sat 11am–4pm; Sun noon–4pm. Last tour at 3:30pm. Closed Dec–Mar. Parking on-site.

Surratt House Museum   John Wilkes Booth slept here as he planned to kidnap and kill President Abraham Lincoln. The home's owner was hanged for her part, although how much she knew is still hotly debated. Visitors can see the tavern and family's rooms in this 1852 house, including original furnishings, such as Mary's desk. Additional Surratt family items are displayed in the visitor center next door. During the 45-minute tour, costumed volunteer guides tell how Mary got entangled in this black period of history. The house, once part of a farm, now sits on a suburban road.

9118 Brandywine Rd., Clinton. © **301/868-1121.** www.surratt.org. $3 for adults, $2 seniors, $1 ages 5–19. Thurs–Fri 11am–3pm; Sat–Sun noon–4pm. Closed mid-Dec to mid-Mar. Parking on-site.

National Colonial Farm ★ (Kids)   The sheep will greet you as you walk up the path and maybe the barn cat will insist you rub its ears at this modest two-room farmhouse surrounded by tobacco and other crops. The house's architecture is unique to this part of Prince George's County: With two fireplaces and a few luxuries (at least for colonists) this may seem a fairly well-to-do place. But this house actually recalls a middling family of the 1770s. The farm is part of the larger Piscataway Park. Its trails lead to the Potomac

River, where you can get a great view of George Washington's Mount Vernon directly across the river. Fishing is permitted here, too.

3400 Bryan Point Rd., Accokeek. (℃) **301/283-2113**, ext. 15. www.accokeek.org. Park admission free; Colonial farm admission $2 adults, 50¢ children. Park daily dawn–dusk. Colonial farm mid-Mar to Dec 23 Tues–Sun 10am–4pm; Dec 24 to mid-Mar Sat–Sun 10am–4pm. Parking on-site.

Six Flags America (**Kids**) Calling all roller-coaster fans. Six Flags has some awesome coasters: Joker's Jinx, Superman, and Batwing. Unfortunately, the lines are awesome, too. During peak times, waits can be as long as an hour. Take a break and go to Hurricane Harbor Water Park, to cool off in the wave pool, water slides, and Bahama Blast inner-tube ride. *Note:* The park requires visitors to go through metal detectors. Don't bring valuables—you'll have to put down your bags for some of the rides and to go in the water. A $15 Flash Pass allows holders to shoot to the front of the line.

13710 Central Ave., Mitchellville. (℃) **301/249-1500**. www.sixflags.com/america. Admission $50 adults, $40 children (48 in. and shorter), free for kids 3 and under. Parking $15. AE, DISC, MC, V. Apr–May and Sept Sat 10am–6pm; Memorial Day to Labor Day daily 10:30am–6pm or later; Oct Sat–Sun 1–10pm. Closed Nov–Mar. From Washington, D.C., take I-495/I-95 to exit 15A to Rte. 214 east; the park will be on the left in 5 miles. From Baltimore and points north, take I-695 to exit 7, I-97 south, then Rte. 3/301 south to Rte. 214 west to the park, 3 miles on the right. From Annapolis, go south on Rte. 3/301 to Rte. 214 west to the park.

Thomas Stone National Historical Site The youngest Marylander to sign the Declaration of Independence made his home in this unusual hyphen house. Called Haberdeventure, the home was restored by the National Park Service after the main section burned in 1977. Visitors can see exhibits in the two kitchens, the first-floor bedroom and the beautifully paneled East Room, which still holds Stone's desk. Because as many as 35 people lived here, George Washington probably didn't sleep here—but, because Stone was a friend, he probably did visit. Special programs are scheduled for the Fourth of July and there's a December candlelight tour. Stone and his wife Margaret are buried here. Walking paths take visitors around the property.

6655 Rose Hill Rd., Port Tobacco. (℃) **301/392-1776**. www.nps.gov/thst. Free admission. Summer daily 9am–5pm; Labor Day to Memorial Day Wed–Sun 9am–5pm. 30-min. tours offered 10am–4pm. Closed Jan 1, Thanksgiving, and Dec 25. Parking on-site.

WHERE TO DINE

Although you may feel you're driving near the end of the world when you're on Route 5 in Southern Maryland, you are actually very close to suburban centers. And that means you're near chain restaurants. Instead, for something locals like, stop at the **Ice Cream Factory & Café**, 13700 Old Brandywine Rd., in Brandywine ((℃) **301/782-3444;** www. icecreamfactoryandcafe.com). It's right off Route 5, between the Surratt and Mudd houses. You can get sandwiches, burgers, and subs. But the ice cream, soft-serve custard, is the real draw. They mix in one of 24 flavorings when you order. It's open April through October daily 11am to 9pm.

Another good choice is the **Casey Jones Pub, Grill & Railroom,** 417 E. Charles St., La Plata ((℃) **301/392-5116;** www.casey-jones.com), which serves some one of the best crab cakes around. The casual pub, as well the patio in warm weather, offers salads, sandwiches, and pizzas. Sushi and hearty entrees are available after 5pm. Dress up and stop next door at the **Crossing at Casey Jones (301/392-5116;** www.thecrossingatcasey jones.com), the owners' fine-dining restaurant, for filet mignon, Chilean sea bass, or pistachio chicken.

4 NATIONAL HARBOR

47 miles SW of Annapolis; 10 miles SE of Washington, D.C.; 55 miles SW of Baltimore; 115 miles SW of Wilmington

On the banks of the Potomac River, downstream from the nation's capital, a brand-new 300-acre development offers a weekend getaway on its own with restaurants, nightclubs, and waterfront activities. It can easily serve as a base for tourists visiting sights in D.C. or Mount Vernon. A short drive over the Woodrow Wilson Bridge or a water taxi ride will take you to Georgetown, George Washington's Mount Vernon, or Union Station, where you can catch a subway to anywhere in Washington.

ESSENTIALS

GETTING HERE   National Harbor is accessible with its own ramps off I-95/495 and I-295 on the Maryland side of the Potomac.

   Metrobus (✆ **202/637-7000;** www.metroopensdoors.com) service will take visitors from bus stops at the Oxon Hill Park and Ride Lot off Route 210. Buses run 20 to 30 minutes every day on the NH1 Line. Fare is $1.35 one-way.

   The **Water Taxi,** operated by Potomac Riverboat Company (✆ **703/684-0580;** www. potomacriverboat.com), takes passengers between the Gaylord complex, the main National Harbor dock, and Old Town Alexandria. Boats depart about every hour May through October with abbreviated schedules November and December. The fare is $8. Additional taxis go to Georgetown, daily May through October and weekends off-season. The fare is $16.

GETTING AROUND   National Harbor is designed for walking. Park your car in one of the huge garages or paid lots and forget about it. Garages are clearly marked with entrances on Fleet Street and Mariner Passage. Other parking is available on the fringes of the development.

WHAT TO SEE & DO

The Awakening   Don't be startled by the face and arms reaching out from the riverbank at National Harbor's waterfront. The cast-iron sculpture created by J. Seward Johnson depicts the arousing of a bearded giant.

On the waterfront.

National Children's Museum   Scheduled to open in 2012, this museum will explore environmental and sustainable practices. Even its building on St. George Boulevard will be eco-friendly. Until the new space is completed, visit the **Launch Zone,** a storefront filled with children's activities with a green theme. Visitors can also offer their own ideas for the new museum's exhibits.

112 Waterfront St. ✆ **301/686-0225.** www.ncm.museum. Free admission. Apr–May and Sept–Oct Mon–Sat 10am–5pm, Sun 11am–5pm; June to Labor Day Mon–Wed 10am–5pm, Thurs–Sat 10am–7pm, Sun 11am–7pm; Nov–Mar Mon–Fri 11am–3pm, Sat 10am–5pm, Sun 11am–5pm.

Potomac Cruises   George Washington's home in Mount Vernon is only a short boat ride away from National Harbor. The Potomac Riverboat Company gives 40-minute narrated cruises three times a day as well as daylong trips to Mount Vernon, which include a tour of Washington's home. Cruises depart from the commercial pier and the pier at the Gaylord. Call for a reservation.

At the pier. ✆ **877/511-2628** or 703/684-0580. www.potomacriverboatco.com. Day trip $40 adults, $22 children 6–11; cruise $9 adults, $5 children 6–11. Apr to early Sept Tues–Sun; mid-Sept to mid-Oct Fri–Sun, mid-Oct to Nov 1 Sat–Sun. Closed Nov–Mar.

Seadog Cruises   All this water is calling you to climb aboard a boat. Seadog's speedboats offer the fastest tours in National Harbor. In 45 minutes, you can see Old Town Alexandria, the Wilson Bridge, and Mount Vernon. Call for a reservation.

At the pier. ✆ **866/404-8439..** www.seadogcruises.com. $20 adults, $15 children 3–11. May–Oct Tues–Sun 11am–8pm.

Segway Tours   Harbor Segs offers tours throughout the day. Prices include a short riding lesson.

110 Waterfront St. ✆ **571/289-5956.** www.harborsegs.com. Tours $45–$95. Children 16 and under must be accompanied by an adult. Mon–Sat 10am–6pm; Sun noon–5pm.

WHERE TO STAY & DINE

National Harbor has 3,000 hotel rooms—and plenty are waterfront. The biggest is the **Gaylord National** (✆ 301/965-2000; www.gaylordhotels.com), a mini-version of its Opryland in Nashville, with 2,000 rooms and a convention center. The **Westin National Harbor** (✆ 301/567-3999; www.starwoodhotels.com/westin) has some of the best views, as it sits right on the waterfront. Cool, sophisticated rooms highlight **Aloft** (✆ 301/749-9000; www.aloftnationalharbor.com). There are also a **Marriott Residence Inn** (✆ 301/749-4755; www.marriott.com/residenceinn) and **Hampton Inn and Suites** (✆ 301/567-3531; www.hamptoninn.hilton.com).

National Harbor has restaurants for just about every taste. Most are chains, including the upscale **Ketchup** (✆ 301/749-7099), Ashton Kutcher's place; **McCormick and Schmick's** (✆ 301/567-6224); and the casual **Elevation Burger** (✆ 301/749-4014). **Grace's Mandarin** (✆ 301/839-3788) is the only local entry here.

SHOPPING

National chains occupy most of the glitzy shopping arcade with everything from Swarovski crystal to Godiva chocolate. **America!,** 154 National Plaza (✆ **301/686-0413**) has National Harbor and D.C.-themed souvenirs. **CakeLove,** 160 National Plaza (✆ **301/686-0340**) is owned by a local baker and Food Network host Warren Brown. National Harbor has local outlets of two D.C.-area galleries: **ArtWhino,** 173 Waterfront St. (✆ **301/567-8210**), an Alexandria gallery featuring pop-surrealism; and **Govinda,** 120 American Way (✆ **202/333-1180**), known in Georgetown for its photos of pop musicians.

The Eastern Shore

Across the Chesapeake Bay Bridge, life slows down. Turn off Route 50 or Hwy. 301 and go down a country road past cornfields. Pause by rivers and marshes where birds and rustling grass are the only sounds. Stop in small towns where mom-and-pop shops still thrive. If you love to watch trees light up with fireflies on a summer night, or cycle down a country lane, or let the breeze take your boat past farms as old as America, you'll love the Eastern Shore.

Easton is the Eastern Shore's Colonial capital—its roots are evident on every picturesque street. It is the capital of Talbot County, home to three waterfront communities within easy driving distance. Waterfront **St. Michaels** has the most shops as well as the Chesapeake Bay Maritime Museum. Boaters clog the harbor on summer weekends, but in spring and fall or midweek in summer, its charms are more accessible. **Oxford** is quieter, but it's attractive for its slower pace, waterfront park, and garden-bedecked streets. **Tilghman** (my favorite place!) hasn't bothered to beautify for the tourists—but its unique waterman's lifestyle is enough to draw them.

Cambridge, on the Choptank River, is beginning to capture the attention it deserves with the introduction of new lodging and the early stages of a downtown renaissance. Its history and outdoor activities make it worthwhile.

The southern areas of the Eastern Shore, including **Smith Island** and **Crisfield,** are the ultimate in waterman villages. Change comes slowly to these remote parts of Maryland, and residents like it that way. That very attitude draws visitors to these hard-to-reach spots.

North of the Bay Bridge, **Chestertown** is not only a Colonial town with leafy streets and elegant homes, but it's also a college town. George Washington permitted the college founders to use his name for Washington College. A dozen miles away is **Rock Hall,** a waterfront village with marinas and seafood restaurants.

Farther north is **Chesapeake City,** on the Chesapeake & Delaware Canal, which remains a crossroads for the marine traffic using the canal every day.

For the locations of these towns on the Eastern Shore, see the map inside the back cover of this book.

---

1 TALBOT COUNTY ★★★

40 miles SE of Annapolis; 60 miles SE of Baltimore; 71 miles SE of Washington, D.C.; 110 miles SW of Wilmington

Set in the middle of the Eastern Shore, Talbot (pronounced *Tall*-but) County has the most popular tourist towns north of Ocean City. Easton, the county seat, is filled with Colonial buildings. St. Michaels clings to its maritime tradition, and lots of visitors arrive by boat at one of the town's many marinas on the Miles River. Continue down Route 33 to charming and remote Tilghman, where watermen and fresh seafood reign. Oxford was once a busy seaport, home of Revolutionary War financier Robert Morris.

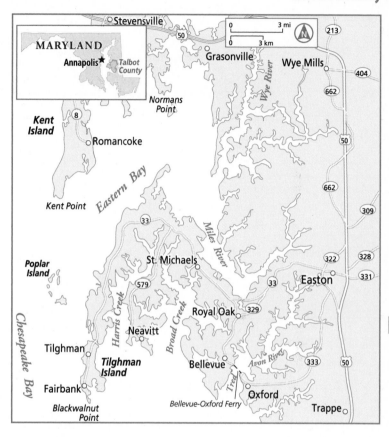

ESSENTIALS

GETTING THERE The best way to get to Easton is by car, via U.S. Route 50 from all directions. Follow the signs on Route 50 near Easton to get to St. Michaels, Tilghman, and Oxford. All are reachable by boat as well, with plenty of dock space.

Easton Airport, on U.S. Route 50 (℗ **410/770-8055**), serves local planes and runs a charter with three- and eight-passenger planes. **Greyhound** (℗ **800/231-2222** or 410/822-3333; www.greyhound.com) offers **bus** service to the Fast Stop Convenience Store, 9543 Ocean Gateway (Rte. 50), across from the airport.

VISITOR INFORMATION Contact the **Talbot County Visitors Center,** 11 S. Harrison St., Easton (℗ **410/770-8000;** www.tourtalbot.org). The *Tidewater Times,* a good pocket magazine with maps, is available in many shops.

GETTING AROUND You're going to have to drive to reach Talbot's quaint towns, though boats are a great option for St. Michaels, Oxford, and Tilghman Island. Maryland Route 33 from Easton will take you to St. Michaels and Tilghman; Maryland Route 333 goes to Oxford.

The Ultimate Crab Cake, Eastern Shore Style

Finding a good crab cake on the Eastern Shore is easy, especially in warm months when crabs are in season. Even making a list can start an argument, as everybody has his or her favorite spot. Below are two good bets—just to get the discussion started.

Ruke's Seafood Deck, Main Street, Ewell, Smith Island (© **410/425-2311**): You've got to get on a boat and go to Smith Island to get these old-fashioned, deep-fried gems. It's the local sweet crab that makes the difference.

Legal Spirits, 42 E. Dover St., Easton (© **410/820-0765**): Known for its cream of crab soup (which can be shipped), its crab cakes are tops, too.

The shortest (in miles, not time) and most scenic route from Oxford to St. Michaels is via the **Oxford-Bellevue Ferry** (© 410/745-9023; www.oxfordferry.com), across the Tred Avon River. Established in 1683, this is the country's oldest privately operated ferry. The ¾-mile trip takes 7 minutes. You can catch the nine-vehicle ferry from Bellevue, off routes 33 and 329, 7 miles from St. Michaels, or from Oxford, off Route 333. From April through October, the ferry runs every 20 minutes, Monday through Friday from 7am to sunset, Saturday and Sunday from 9am to sunset. There's no service December through February. It runs Friday to Sunday only in November. Rates for a car and driver are $10 one-way and $16 round-trip; vehicle passengers pay $1 one-way; walk-on passengers $3; bicyclists $4; and motorcycles $6. Trailers and RVs can be accommodated, but call first. This tiny ferry offers a short, fun ride to a long country road leading to either St. Michaels or Easton.

To rent a car, call **Enterprise,** Route 50 and Dover Road (© 410/822-3260). For cab service, try **Scotty's Taxi** (© 410/822-1475).

SPECIAL EVENTS   The **Waterfowl Festival** ★★★ (© 410/822-4567; www.water fowlfestival.org), held the second week in November, turns Easton into a celebration of ducks, geese, and other birds. The 3-day festival draws some 20,000 visitors. You don't have to like hunting to attend. Some 400 artists' works are displayed, and venues around town display Federal Duck Stamp paintings, duck decoys, and carvings so realistic you'll want to smooth those ruffled feathers. Admission is $10 for adults, free for children 12 and under, with free shuttle buses running from site to site. If you visit wildlife refuges around Maryland, you'll see where the proceeds of this event are used—about $5 million has been raised over the years to protect and conserve wildlife habitats.

Oxford Day (www.oxfordday.org), held the last Saturday in April, is a fun local fest, with music, entertainment, and crab races.

Tilghman Day (www.tilghmanmd.com), held the third Saturday in October, celebrates boats, crabs, and oysters and benefits the local fire department.

EASTON

Visitors to the Eastern Shore usually start at Easton. Called the "Colonial Capital of the Eastern Shore," this town values its visitors. Route 50 is filled with reasonably priced chain hotels, and the downtown district has many worthy restaurants.

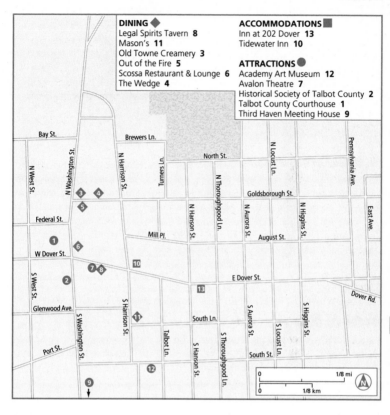

DINING ◆
Legal Spirits Tavern **8**
Mason's **11**
Old Towne Creamery **3**
Out of the Fire **5**
Scossa Restaurant & Lounge **6**
The Wedge **4**

ACCOMMODATIONS ■
Inn at 202 Dover **13**
Tidewater Inn **10**

ATTRACTIONS ●
Academy Art Museum **12**
Avalon Theatre **7**
Historical Society of Talbot County **2**
Talbot County Courthouse **1**
Third Haven Meeting House **9**

THE EASTERN SHORE

8

TALBOT COUNTY

Where to Stay

Accommodations range from your basic chain hotels on Route 50 to high style and luxury downtown. You'll pay for the luxury, especially on busy weekends during the Waterfowl Festival or hunting season. All places listed below have off-street free parking.

National chains include **Comfort Inn,** 8523 Ocean Gateway/Route 50 (② **800/228-5150** or 410/820-8333; www.comfortinn.com), and **Days Inn,** 7018 Ocean Gateway/Route 50 (② **410/822-4600;** www.daysinn.com).

Inn at 202 Dover ★★★ This stately 1874 home downtown has been restored to its preserve its elegant beginnings. Accommodations are appointed with elegant decor and bathrooms fitted with steam or rain showers and jetted tubs. The Asian Suite and the manly Safari Suite have gas fireplaces. The chintz-upholstered English Suite has the most space. **Peacock,** the inn's fine-dining restaurant, serves dinner and afternoon tea on Thursdays; reservations are required. (You don't have to be a guest to eat here.)

202 E. Dover St., Easton, MD 21601. ② **866/450-7600.** www.innat202dover.com. 5 units. $275–$475 double. Rates include full breakfast. AE, DISC, MC, V. Pets welcome. No children 15 and under. **Amenities:** Restaurant. *In room:* A/C, TV w/DVD, hair dryer, free Wi-Fi.

Getting Away From It All, Eastern Shore Style

Sometimes a room or suite isn't enough. When you want more, whether it's a waterfront view, a place that will take your dog, a pool or a dock, you might want a house. **Eastern Shore Vacation Rentals,** 28282 St. Michaels Rd., Easton (℃ **866/398-2722** or 410/770-9093) lists two- to eight- bedroom properties all over Talbot and Dorchester counties. These are modern homes, for the most part, with luxurious appointments.

The Tidewater Inn ★ New owners have taken over this gracious 200-year-old hotel. Only 2 years ago, it was remodeled, renewing it as the model of Eastern Shore hospitality it was for decades. Crisp white linens, softly colored walls, and gleaming white-tiled bathrooms are the major changes. Suites offer a smidge more room; room no. 231 has great space and a view of the renovated courtyard. A new traditional restaurant, **Hunters' Tavern,** opened in late 2009. To stay here for the Waterfowl Festival, make reservations a year ahead. Coming to hunt? Of course there's room for your dogs.

101 E. Dover St., Easton, MD 21601. ℃ **800/237-8775** or 410/822-1300. Fax 410/820-8847. www.tide waterinn.com. 75 rooms, 9 suites. $229–$259 double; $270-$410 suite. Golf and hunting packages available. AE, DC, DISC, MC, V. Valet parking $10. Pets accepted. **Amenities:** Restaurant; bar; fitness center. In room: A/C, TV w/movies, VCR (on request), fridge (on request), hair dryer (on request), free Wi-Fi.

Where to Dine

Seafood lovers, rejoice: Crabs, oysters, and fish are star attractions at restaurants all around Easton. If you're in the mood for something else, Easton is blessed with some sophisticated restaurants with creative menus.

Legal Spirits Tavern (Finds AMERICAN This casual tavern has lots of pub grub: burgers, French dip, and crab-cake sandwiches, as well as some meaty entrees that stand up to a beer. Whatever you have, start with the Shore Boys cream of crab soup. You'll want to take this soup home—and you can. It's sold by the pint, fresh or frozen.

42 E. Dover St. ℃ **410/820-0765** or 820-0747. www.shoreboys.com. Reservations recommended for dinner. Main courses $10–$18 lunch, $15–$30 dinner. AE, DISC, MC, V. Daily 11am–10pm.

Mason's AMERICAN The menu changes often at this delightful little eatery, where you can sit on the porch, on the terrace, or in the more formal dining room. Get a sandwich to go or stay for a full meal. Lunchtime choices range from sandwiches and salads to some hearty entrees from quiche to steak frites. At dinner, look for fresh seafood and roasted meats with rich sides. A coffee bar is open Monday through Saturday 9am to 5pm.

22 S. Harrison St. ℃ **410/822-3204.** Reservations recommended for dinner. Main courses $7–$15 lunch, $17–$29 dinner. AE, DC, MC, V. Mon 11:30am–2:30pm; Tues–Sat 11:30am–2:30pm and 5:30–9:30pm.

Old Towne Creamery ICE CREAM Sometimes you just need an ice-cream cone. Here's a cheery place with tiny tables, pink walls, and all kinds of cones and sundaes.

9B Goldsborough St. ℃ **410/820-5223.** Reservations not accepted. Ice-cream desserts $2–$6. No credit cards. Summer Mon–Sat 11:30am–10pm, Sun noon–1pm; hours may be shortened in cooler months.

Out of the Fire ★★ MEDITERRANEAN Trendy food flavored with seasonings from around the world has made it to Easton. This chic dining room is dominated by a wood-fired oven. Lunch means soups, pizzas, and salads. Dinner choices include pasta, meats, and poultry, all with international zing; pizza, too. The whole menu is good, but whatever you choose, at least get a sliver of their crispy-crust pizza with either traditional or exotic toppings. Pizza doesn't get any better than this.

22 Goldsborough St. ℂ **410/770-4777.** www.outofthefire.com. Reservations recommended for dinner. Main courses $9–$16 lunch, $13–$32 dinner. AE, MC, V. Mon–Fri 11:30am–2pm; Mon–Thurs 5–9pm; Fri–Sat 5–10pm.

Scossa Restaurant & Lounge ★★★ NORTHERN ITALIAN With doors that fold away to reveal the rich, sleek interior to the sidewalk, you'll be drawn by this restaurant's long banquettes and sepia-toned photos of Venice. But Scossa's real appeal is its northern Italian dishes, which feature fresh, simple ingredients. Puréed vegetables transform into velvety soups. Crusty bread is topped with olive butter. The fresh-made pastas and risottos are the star. Lunchtime salads and sandwiches have Italian style, too. And *Italian* tapas? Who knew! But it's a great way to get a taste of Scossa for $13. The wine list features Italian and California vintages with some French champagnes. Live music, mostly jazz, wafts through the dining room on weekends.

8 N. Washington St. ℂ **410/822-2202.** www.scossarestaurant.com. Reservations recommended for dinner. Main courses $7.50–$24 lunch, $17–$30 dinner. AE, DC, DISC, MC, V. Sun and Tues–Thurs 11:30am–9pm; Fri–Sat 11:30am–10pm; Mon 4–9pm.

The Wedge WINE BAR The wedge refers to cheese—and such beautiful cheese plates—but the kitchen offers lots of creative accompaniments for its wine list. Small plates here can trace their roots to cuisines all over the world. There are also salads, soups, and sandwiches. The atmosphere is relaxed. On weekends, you can enjoy performances by local musicians.

17 Goldsborough St. ℂ **410/770-3737.** Reservations recommended for dinner. Cheese and small plates $6–$12. AE, DC, DISC, MC, V. Tues–Thurs 11am–4pm and 5–9:30pm; Fri–Sat 11am–4pm and 5–10:30pm.

What to See & Do

A walk through Easton's historic district will take you past buildings that witnessed the birth of the United States and have stood through 2 centuries. The **Talbot County Courthouse,** for instance, at 11 N. Washington St., was built in 1710.

The **Historical Society of Talbot County,** 25 S. Washington St. (ℂ **410/822-0773;** www.hstc.org), offers an intimate look at life in the county and Talbot's industries, such as boat-building and duck-decoy carving. The museum is open Monday through Saturday from 10am to 4pm; admission is free. It also offers guided tours of historic Easton and of local historic houses. Don't miss the Federal-style gardens behind the museum, a quiet haven for a spot of relaxation.

The **Academy Art Museum** ★, 106 South St., at Harrison Street (ℂ **410/822-2787;** www.academyartmuseum.org), a light-filled gallery transformed from 18th-century buildings, has exhibits by regional and national artists, and a performing-arts series. Admission is free. Hours are Monday through Friday 10am to 4pm, and until 7pm Tuesday through Thursday; Saturday 10am to 3pm.

The restored Art Deco **Avalon Theatre,** 40 E. Dover St. (ℂ **410/822-7299;** www.avalontheatre.com), has been providing entertainment since 1921. Its performing-arts series draws local and national acts. For tickets, call the box office or go to **www.ticketmaster.com.**

Hunting Season

Maryland's Eastern Shore has long been considered the finest duck- and goose-hunting region on the Atlantic Flyway, with hundreds of thousands of migratory game birds passing through. More than 20 local organizations conduct guided waterfowl hunts for Canada geese (2 weeks in Nov and mid-Dec to late Jan), ducks (late Nov to mid-Jan), and sea ducks (early Oct to mid-Jan). Some quail and pheasant hunting is also available. White-tailed and sika deer may be hunted September through December.

The **Department of Natural Resources** (✆ 877/620-8DNR [8367]; www.dnr.state.md.us/huntersguide) publishes an annual guide with all hunting regulations, including bag limits, season dates, and licensing. **Albright's Gun Shop,** 36 E. Dover St., Easton (✆ 800/474-5502 or 410/820-8811; www.albrightsgunshop.com), can help plan any sort of hunting or fishing trip you have in mind, with or without guides.

Farther from downtown is **Third Haven Meeting House,** 405 S. Washington St. (✆ **410/822-0293**). Opened in 1684, this Quaker house of worship once hosted William Penn, who preached to Lord Baltimore. It is the oldest religious building in use in the U.S. Admission is free; donations are welcome. It's open daily from 9am to 5pm (meetings for worship are Sun at 10am and Wed at 5:30pm).

Shopping

Easton's main shopping is along Washington, Dover, and Harrison streets. You'll find a number of galleries, as well as antiques, clothing, and gift shops. Hours are generally daily from 9am to 5pm; some shops close midweek and have shorter hours in winter.

Albright's Gun Shop This shop stocks guns and accessories, sport clothing, watches, canvas goods, and tackle. It's an authorized Orvis dealer. Custom gunsmithing is done on the premises. 36 E. Dover St. ✆ **800/474-5502** or 410/820-8811. www.albrightsgunshop.com.

Crackerjacks Stop by this children's store for books, toys, games, dolls, stuffed animals, pinwheels, crafts, and more. 7 S. Washington St. ✆ **410/822-7716.**

Janet K. Fanto Antiques & Rare Books Look for rare books, 19th- and 20th-century furniture (mostly American), antiques, and odds and ends. The owners and watch-cat Samantha are friendly and encourage browsing. Closed some winter Wednesdays. 7 Goldsborough St. ✆ **410/763-9030.**

Tharpe Antiques and Decorative Arts Proceeds of this ritzy consignment shop benefit the Historical Society of Talbot County. It's open Tuesday to Saturday 10am to 5pm. It is located in a restored 1788 house. 30 S. Washington St. ✆ **410/822-0773.**

Troika Gallery The artist-owners present their own work, as well as pieces by local and national artists. 9 S. Harrison St. ✆ **410/770-9190.** www.troikagallery.com.

ST. MICHAELS

Since its founding in the late 1700s, St. Michaels has looked to the water for its livelihood. Shipbuilding made it famous. Log canoes were first workboats and then became better known as racing boats. Bugeyes and Baltimore clippers were built here. Watermen

(Kids) A Drive to Wye Mills

Three things in the hamlet of Wye Mills make the detour from Easton worthwhile: a flour mill, the remains of a tree, and beaten biscuits. Even if you doubt it, this could be one of those trips the kids talk about for a long time.

From Route 50, go west on Route 404 or Route 213, about 13 miles north of Easton or 14 miles southeast from Kent Island. This burg is a mile off Route 50.

Flour ground at **Old Wye Mill** ★, Old Wye Mills Road (Rte. 662), off Route 50, in Wye Mills (© **410/827-6909;** www.historicqac.org/sites/WMgristmill.htm), was sent to George Washington's troops at Valley Forge during the Revolutionary War. The mill has been in operation since 1671. Visitors can see it at work on the 1st and 3rd Saturdays of the month. Guides are good at explaining all the gear that makes the water wheel and grinding stones turn. After a visit, you can buy wheat flour or cornmeal ground here. There's no admission fee, but a $2 donation is requested. Hours are mid-April to mid-November, Friday and Saturday from 10am to 4pm and Sunday 1 to 4pm. Because volunteers staff the mill, hours may vary; it's best to call ahead.

The 450-year-old **Wye Oak** fell in a 2002 storm—but the stump of the largest white oak in the country and Maryland's official state tree remains, now surrounded by a fence. Also on the property is the tiny brick **Wye Oak House,** Talbot County's oldest school building. During daylight hours, take a peek inside.

You can't leave Wye Mills without getting a taste of an old Maryland tradition. **Orrell's Maryland Beaten Biscuits,** 14124 Old Wye Mill Rd. (Rte. 662), Wye Mills (© **410/827-6244**), in business since 1935, has limited hours, but try to schedule a stop. The dough really is beaten—usually with a hammer, though the back of an ax works too—to get the biscuits to rise. The method was used in a time when leavening was in short supply. You can try the finished product or buy some to bring home. Admission is free. They're open Wednesday (baking day) from 9am until baking is done, usually about 3pm. Call ahead (© **443/454-4361**) to visit.

If you bring your fishing rod, you can try your luck in the **Wye Mills Community Lake,** across the street from the mill. This 50-acre lake is home to bass, bluegill, and who knows what else. A non-tidal-waters fishing license is required. There are lots of grassy spots for a picnic, too.

came to sell their catch, and canneries and oyster-packing plants sprang up. Local residents are proud of the night residents here fooled the British and saved their town during the Revolutionary War.

Today, St. Michaels is a popular destination for boaters, who are crammed into the harbor on sunny weekends. It's also bed-and-breakfast heaven; many have views of the beautiful Miles River. Make time for the Chesapeake Bay Maritime Museum, where the history of the whole Chesapeake Bay is celebrated. The town's streets also offer a variety of shops and restaurants.

Aida's Victoriana Inn   Located on the harbor, this 1875 home offers comfortable rooms, many with water views. Porches and Adirondack chairs on the lawn invite guests to linger on a nice day. Rooms are of varying sizes, three of which have fireplaces. The junior suite has its own deck and fireplace. The Sharp Room has only a garden view, but its fireplace and canopy bed provide a romantic setting.

205 Cherry St., St. Michaels, MD 21663. © **410/745-3368.** www.victorianainn.com. 7 units. $169–$259 double; $249–$309 suite. Rates include breakfast. MC, V. Pets accepted for fee. Children 5 and over welcome. **Amenities:** Deck; fax; sunroom. *In room:* A/C, TV/DVD, CD player, hair dryer, MP3 dock, whirlpool tub, free Wi-Fi.

Bob Pascal's St. Michaels Harbour Inn, Marina & Spa ★   This is modern convenience in the heart of St. Michaels. The Harbour Inn has kept up with the times, replacing its kitchenettes with Jacuzzis and adding an outdoor grill to the marina deck. Every room—most are suites—has a water view, almost all have terraces, and third-floor rooms have cathedral ceilings. On-site are a waterfront restaurant and a more casual eatery.

101 N. Harbor Rd., St. Michaels, MD 21663. © **800/955-9001** or 410/745-9001. Fax 410/745-9150. www. harbourinn.com. 46 units. $189–$525 double. MC, V. **Amenities:** 2 restaurants; babysitting; bikes; health club; outdoor pool; spa; resort shuttle; watersports equipment; water taxi; Wi-Fi in public areas. *In room:* A/C, fridge, hair dryer, high-speed Internet.

Five Gables Inn & Spa (Finds)   Get pampered at this combination B&B and spa, which has expanded with new rooms and suites. Every room has a fireplace, whirlpool tub, and, because it's a spa, Aveda toiletries. Most have private porches. A small pool, sun deck, sauna, and steam room—as well as six treatment rooms for hydrotherapy, scrubs, and massages (one is for couples)—add to the pampering. A sailing or romance package can add to the spa experience.

209 N. Talbot St., St. Michaels, MD 21663. © **877/466-0100** or 410/745-0100. Fax 410/745-2903. www. fivegables.com. 20 units. $150–$425 double. Rates include continental breakfast. 2-night minimum stay required Sat–Sun. AE, MC, V. Pets accepted for fee. **Amenities:** Indoor pool; sauna; spa treatments; steam room. *In room:* A/C, TV/VCR, CD player, hair dryer, whirlpool tub, free Wi-Fi.

Hambleton Inn   Location, location, location. Set right on the harbor but steps from the shopping district, every room at this immaculate Victorian-style B&B has a water view and antique furnishings. An open second-floor porch, enclosed lower porch, and small harborside deck provide three more spots from which to view the boats docked at St. Michaels. Tell the innkeeper of special needs, especially dietary, in advance.

202 Cherry St., St. Michaels, MD 21663. © **866/745-3350** or 410/745-3350. Fax 410/745-5709. www. hambletoninn.com. 6 units. $195–$285 double. Rates include breakfast. 2-night minimum stay required on most weekends in high season. MC, V. No children 12 and under. *In room:* A/C, TV.

Harris Cove Cottages Bed 'n Boat (Kids)   Harris Cove is a throwback to a simpler, more rustic time. Though these cottages were built in the 1930s, new owners have updated them with new furniture, floors, and appliances. They remain unfussy but comfortable with full kitchens, sitting areas, and nice-size sleeping areas. Each cottage sleeps four. A one-room "stateroom" is also available. Their setting beside a quiet shallow cove—with gazebos, lounge chairs, and hammocks—makes them an old-fashioned getaway. There's also a 65-foot pier and kayaks and paddleboats to rent.

8070 Bozman–Neavitt Rd., St. Michaels, MD 21663. © **410/745-9701.** www.bednboat.com. 6 cottages, 2 units in main house. $175–$230 per cottage; $150 "stateroom" unit. No credit cards. **Amenities:** Charcoal grills; gazebos; watersports equipment. *In room:* A/C, TV/VCR/DVD, kitchen.

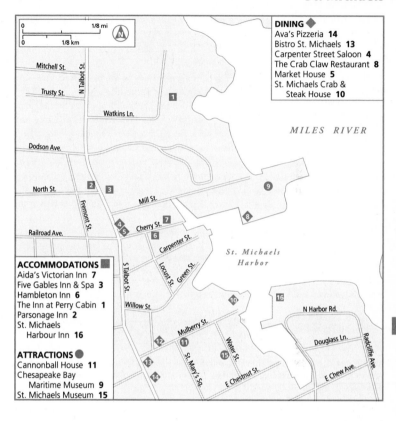

The Inn at Perry Cabin ★★ Part of the Orient Express chain, this English country–style inn on the Miles River is richly appointed and designed for stylish comfort. There are four tiers of rooms, from standard to master suite. At every level, you'll find plenty of space, river views, and luxurious linens. Some units have gas fireplaces. Amenities, such as the new Linden Spa, are fabulous and will please the most discriminating guest, although some may find service a bit cool for the Eastern Shore. It's a short walk from downtown, though right next to the maritime museum. There's access to golf, fishing, horseback riding, hunting, and a helicopter pad.

308 Watkins Lane, St. Michaels, MD 21663. ✆ **800/722-2949** or 410/745-2200. Fax 410/745-3348. www. perrycabin.com. 78 units. $390–$730 double. Ask about winter or B&B packages. AE, DC, DISC, MC, V. Pets accepted for a fee. **Amenities:** Restaurant; bar; babysitting; bikes; fitness center; outdoor pool; sauna; spa. *In room:* A/C, TV/VCR, fridge (upon request), hair dryer, high-speed Internet.

The Parsonage Inn ★ This redbrick Victorian home, built in 1883, is a beauty. It served as the parsonage to the United Methodist Church from 1924 to 1985. Today, it's a respite for travelers willing to exchange a water view for a delicious breakfast, cozy decor, and creature comforts. All rooms have brass beds, three have fireplaces, and many have ceiling fans and access to a sun deck. The first-floor room has a wood-burning fireplace. Packages combine a stay with a skipjack ride, dinner at a local restaurant, or visits to the maritime museum.

210 N. Talbot St., St. Michaels, MD 21663. ℭ **800/394-5519** or 410/745-5519. Fax 410/745-6869. www. parsonage-inn.com. 8 units. $110–$145 double. Rates include gourmet breakfast. 2-night minimum stay required most weekends. MC, V. Children welcome with prior approval. **Amenities:** Bikes; concierge service. *In room:* A/C, TV (in 6 rooms), free Wi-Fi.

Wades Point Inn on the Bay ★★

Set on a peninsula in the bay, Wades Point Inn offers an old-fashioned vacation outside St. Michaels. The sprawling house, built in 1819 by Thomas Kemp (designer of the famous Baltimore clipper ship), has been host to many a summer holiday over the past century. The main house and Kemp Guest House next door have spacious bedrooms decorated with period furniture. The Kemp rooms have porches or balconies; some have kitchenettes. A separate farmhouse has additional rooms, and can also accommodate groups of up to 13. The Victorian Summer Wing, open seasonally, has cottage-style rooms with screen doors. Breakfast includes eggs and produce from the inn's organic farm. There are kayaks, a floating dock, a swim dock, and fishing rods (the fishing's great in Eastern Bay) to help guests take full advantage of the water here.

Wades Point Rd. (P.O. Box 7), St. Michaels, MD 21663. ℭ **888/923-3466** or 410/745-2500. Fax 410/745-3444. www.wadespoint.com. 24 units. $165–$270 double. Rates include full breakfast on weekdays, continental breakfast on weekends. Children 12 and under stay free in parent's room. 2-night minimum stay required on weekends and holidays. Discounts available for seniors and for stays of 3 days or more. MC, V. Located 5 miles west of St. Michaels, off Rte. 33, at end of Wades Point Rd. **Amenities:** Bikes; executive-level rooms; walking trails; watersports equipment. *In room:* A/C, hair dryer (upon request).

Where to Dock

St. Michaels Marina Coming to St. Michaels by boat? Make a reservation for one of the marina's 54 transient slips. Rates are determined by season and boat length.

301 Mulberry St., St. Michaels, MD 21663. ℭ **800/678-8980.** 54 slips, $1.50 per ft.–$4.25 per ft. Reservations required. AE, DC, DISC, MC, V. **Amenities:** TV; fuel dock; marine store; outdoor pool; pump-out station; showers; Wi-Fi.

Where to Dine

Get your coffee and pastry (including Smith Island cake) at **Sugar Buns,** 601 S. Talbot St. (ℭ **410/745-3004**).

Ava's Pizzeria & Wine Bar PIZZA

A wood-fired oven and house-made dough and mozzarella give these pizzas their pizazz. If you opt for a sandwich, it comes with fresh-made potato chips. At dinner, entrees range from short ribs to fish and chips. And pizza, of course. Wine is offered by the glass or by the bottle, and there are 70 beers available.

409 S. Talbot St. ℭ **410/745-3081.** www.avaspizzeria.com. Reservations not accepted. Main courses $9–$15 lunch, $9–$22 dinner. AE, DC, MC, V. Daily 11:30am–9pm. Closed Tues in fall and winter.

Bistro St. Michaels ★ FRENCH

This busy restaurant in a Victorian house captures the ambience of a Paris-style bistro. The downstairs dining room can be noisy, but the dining room upstairs and the garden patio are more intimate. On a busy night, service can be leisurely. The menu is short, with choices such as broiled duck confit or chili-glazed salmon, but the wine list is extensive. A small plates menu and a seafood bar offer more choices. Locals love this place.

403 S. Talbot St. ℭ **410/745-9111.** www.bistrostmichaels.com. Reservations recommended. Main courses $27–$29. AE, DC, DISC, MC, V. Thurs–Mon 5:30–9pm.

Carpenter Street Saloon PUB FARE/SEAFOOD   A noisy, casual pub with a bar in one room and a dining room next door, this place makes a good stop for a beer and a burger—and for a family outing, too. It's got a little of everything: crab soup and crab cakes, rockfish and chips, prime rib. Locals come for their steaks. It offers a kids' menu, a few games and pool tables upstairs, a model-train track circling the ceiling, live music on Wednesday through Saturday, late-night pizza, and breakfast.

113 Talbot St., at Carpenter St. ℂ **410/745-5111.** Main courses $6–$13 lunch, $9–$24 dinner. MC, V. Daily 8am–9pm. Bar open until 2am.

The Crab Claw Restaurant ★ SEAFOOD   Many Marylanders consider this a destination restaurant. They come by the busloads for the fresh seafood, steamed crabs, and river breezes. It's casual and fun—and it's right beside the Chesapeake Bay Maritime Museum. The emphasis is crabs, served every way possible. Platters of chicken, oysters, sandwiches, and a raw bar are also available.

Navy Point, Mill St. ℂ **410/745-2900.** www.thecrabclaw.com. Reservations recommended for dinner. Main courses $18–$27. No credit cards. Mar–Nov daily 11am–10pm. Closed Dec–Feb.

Market House CAFE   Sometimes you want a good sandwich or maybe a sweet roll to go with your coffee. This chic little deli uses local ingredients for its delicious variety of soups, salads, sandwiches, subs, wraps, and burgers. Come hungry for breakfast where everything from bagels to eggs Benedict with smoked salmon or crab is offered. There's a Mouse Bites menu for the kids.

105 N. Talbot St. ℂ **410/745-4100.** Reservations not accepted. Main courses $5–$14 breakfast, $10–$17 lunch. MC, V. Daily 8:30am–5:30pm.

St. Michaels Crab and Steak House Kids SEAFOOD/STEAK   Located on the marina, this casual, family-friendly crab house offers a choice of indoor seating in a nautical setting or outdoors under an umbrella. The building is an 1830s oyster-shucking shed. The menu, which includes a children's section, features steamed crabs, crab cakes, softshells, and crab Benedict, as well other seafood, steaks, and chicken.

305 Mulberry St. ℂ **410/745-3737.** www.stmichaelscrabhouse.com. Reservations recommended for dinner. Main courses $8–$16 lunch, $13–$25 dinner. DISC, MC, V. Mid-Mar to mid-Dec Thurs–Tues 11am–10pm. Closed late Dec until last weekend in Mar.

What to See & Do

The **Chesapeake Bay Log Sailing Canoe Association** sponsors log canoe races—just about the oldest class of boat still sailing around here. Usually races are more exciting for the sailor than for the spectator. But these boats—big on sail, small on hull—have to be seen to be appreciated. Races are usually held on weekends from June to September. For information, contact the **Miles River Yacht Club** (ℂ 410/745-9511; www.milesriveryc.org).

The **Cannonball House,** on Mulberry Street at St. Mary's Square, may look like an ordinary Colonial-style house—but it was witness to the day the town outsmarted the British. When the British attempted to shell St. Michaels during the War of 1812, the townspeople blacked out the town and hung lanterns high in the trees, causing the British to overshoot the houses. Only one cannonball hit the town, striking the chimney of this house. The town was saved, and the "blackout strategy" was born. The house is privately owned and, therefore, is not open to the public.

Chesapeake Bay Maritime Museum ★★★   Celebrate the Chesapeake Bay at this unusual museum. You'll know you're in for something different when you enter the driveway—under the old Knapps Narrows Bridge. The centerpiece is the picturesque

Hooper Strait Lighthouse, and all around are fascinating exhibits about boat-building, fishing, oystering, and the people who earn their livelihood on the water. Other star attractions are the skipjack, installed in the new Oystering Building; the boatyard, where expert builders work year-round to restore historic boats; and the historic boats docked here. The grounds are open as a waterfront park after the buildings close for the day; no admission is charged then.

Navy Point, Mill St. ✆ **410/745-2916.** www.cbmm.org. Admission $13 adults, $10 seniors, $5 children 6–17. Summer daily 10am–6pm; spring and fall daily 10am–5pm; winter daily 9am–4pm. Closed Jan 1, Thanksgiving, and Dec 25. Take Rte. 33 to St. Michaels; turn right at driveway with drawbridge.

St. Michaels Museum ★   Small towns usually have small memorials to their past and that's certainly true here. Two 19th-century buildings have been joined together to create a gallery of old photos and artifacts in one while maintaining the Sewell House as it was when the Sewells and their six children lived here. Needlework samplers and a fine collection of quilts and toys are interesting. The gallery's photos, produced by a Sewell descendant, and the changing exhibits highlight the town's history as a waterman's town. Tours highlighting the waterfront and the early life of Frederick Douglass begin here. They are $10 for adults and $5 for children.

St. Mary's Square. St. Michaels. ✆ **410/745-9561.** www.stmichaelsmuseum.org. Admission $3 adults, $1 children 6–17. Fri and Sun 1–4pm; Sat 10am–4pm.

Outdoor Activities

BIKING   Rent a bike at **St. Michael's Marina,** 305 Mulberry St. (✆ **800/678-8980**).

BOAT RIDES ★   All this water, and you don't have your own boat? Not to worry: There are all kinds of ways to get on the water here. Take a ride on the *H.M. Krentz* (✆ 410/745-6080; www.oystercatcher.com), a skipjack that dredges oysters in winter and earns its keep with sailboat rides from April to October. It's docked by the maritime museum. Or perhaps you'd like a slightly more modern sailboat? The 41-foot 1926 gaff-rigged *Selina II* (✆ 410/726-9400; www.sailselina.com), captained by Iris Clarke, with room for just six passengers, offers more intimate 2-hour sails.

Go in air-conditioned comfort with **Patriot Cruises,** by the Chesapeake Bay Maritime Museum (✆ 410/745-3100; www.patriotcruises.com), which offers three 1-hour narrated cruises and one 90-minute cruise on a 65-foot tourist boat.

St. Michaels Harbor Tours & Water Taxi (✆ 410/924-2198), berthed at the foot of Mulberry Street, offers daily 25-minute tours in season, as well as water taxi service.

Shopping

Shopping is a major diversion in St. Michaels. The best shops are concentrated along Talbot Street. They're usually open from 10am to 6pm on weekends and most weekdays, with shorter hours in winter. Look for the St. Michaels/Tilghman Island visitors' guide at the visitor center, at North Talbot and Mill streets. There's a parking lot at that corner as well.

Handcrafted items are a cinch to find at **Artiste Locale,** 112 N. Talbot St. (✆ 410/745-6580); or **A Wish Called Wanda,** 110 N. Talbot St. (✆ 410/745-6763).

The town is full of fun gift shops. Stop at **Calico Gallery,** 212 Talbot St. (✆ **410/745-5370;** www.calicogallery.net), for local watercolors or toys; **Keepers,** 300 S. Talbot St. (✆ **800/549-1872** or 410/745-6388), for Orvis clothes or antique waterfowl decoys. If you prefer something nautical, stop at the **Sign of the Whale,** 208 S. Talbot St. (✆ **410/745-0680**), for something witty or elegant. Like your treasures a little older? Among the town's antiques shops, look for **Corner Antiques,** 116 N. Talbot St. (✆ **410/745-5589**), **Antiques on Talbot,** 211 N. Talbot St. (✆ **410/745-5208**); or **Oyster House Antiques,** 101 N. Talbot St. (✆ **410/745-4044**).

For the palate, get some locally produced wines at **St. Michael's Winery,** 605 S. Talbot St. (✆ **410/745-0808;** www.st-michaels-winery.com), and chocolates at the **St. Michaels Candy and Gifts,** 216 S. Talbot St. (✆ **888/570-6050** or 410/745-6060; www.candyisdandy.com).

TILGHMAN ISLAND

Keep driving southeast on Route 33, the road from Easton to St. Michaels, for about 8 miles and you'll arrive on Tilghman Island. Cross the Knapps Narrows Bridge, and you'll find yourself miles from the bustle of the city. Though some development has filled a cornfield here and there—especially at the waterline—this is the place for true Eastern Shore living: ospreys to wake you in the morning, stars to light the night, skipjacks and crabbing boats bobbing in the harbor. Come for fresh seafood, quiet roads, and water views. Tilghman is a good place to spend a day with a camera or a bike, or even a kayak. Bring your fishing pole, as there are plenty of places on the island—not to mention charter boats for hire—to cast your line. The few hotels and B&Bs are welcoming places that help you enjoy the quiet Eastern Shore way.

Where to Stay

Black Walnut Point Bed & Breakfast Inn ★ Here's a great way to escape: Drive down the main road to the very end and keep going. You'll find yourself on the southern point of Tilghman Island, with views of water on three sides, huge trees, and an 1840s white house with a wide porch to call home, at least for a while. Every room has a view of the water, but each is different: some elegant, some a bit more country style. The Tilghman Room has windows on three sides, while the Attic Hideaway is quaint but best suited for shorter people. Knotty-pine paneled cottages are compact, with living rooms, kitchens, fireplaces, and screened porches a few feet from the water.

Black Walnut Rd. (P.O. Box 308), Tilghman, MD 21671. ✆ 410/886-2452. www.blackwalnutpoint.com. 4 units in the main house, 3 cottages. $120–$225 double; $225 cottage. Rates include continental breakfast. 2- or 3-night minimum stay may be required on weekends or holidays. MC, V. No children 12 and under. **Amenities:** Hot tub; pool. In room: A/C, TVs in cottages, hair dryer, Wi-Fi (fee).

Chesapeake Wood Duck Inn ★ The thing to remember here: Make reservations for dinner when you make reservations for lodging. Dinner (cooked by the owner, who is a trained chef) is served on Saturdays—but only to 8 to 10 inn guests with reservations. The menu depends on what the watermen bring over, but your meal will include seafood paired with spices and sauces from around the world. Breakfast is hearty and memorable. The inn, which has Dogwood Harbor for a backyard, is a cozy spot with gazebo and screened porch. Each bedroom, with one exception, has a water view; and each is cheerful, with romantic or nautical decor, antiques, and original paintings.

Gibsontown Rd. at Dogwood Harbor (P.O. Box 202), Tilghman, MD 21671. ✆ 800/956-2070 or 410/886-2070. www.wooduckinn.com. 6 units in main house, 1 cottage. $129–$189 double; $199–$249 cottage. Rates include full breakfast. 2- or 3-night minimum stay may be required on weekends or holidays. Ask about winter escape packages. MC, V. In room: A/C, TV in suites, hair dryer, free Wi-Fi.

Harrison's Chesapeake House Nothing about Harrison's is fancy. Rooms are clean. Half have a water view. There's a pool, a sun porch, and a restaurant downstairs. But the real attraction is the proximity to the fishing and hunting charters run by Buddy

Harrison—ask about the many packages. An on-site gift shop, Island Treasures, sells apparel and Tilghman Island souvenirs.

21551 Chesapeake House Dr., Tilghman, MD 21671. © **410/886-2121.** www.chesapeakehouse.com. 56 units. $75–$125 double. MC, V. **Amenities:** Restaurant; lounge; pool. *In room:* A/C, TV.

Knapp's Narrows Marina and Inn (Value)

Every room here has a view of the Knapps Narrows. They're simple, fresh, and spacious—and a good value. Third-floor units have cathedral ceilings, and one suite can be turned into a meeting space if necessary. Hammocks under the trees beckon. At this full-service facility, boaters will find their vessels as welcome as they are.

Knapps Narrows (P.O. Box 277), Tilghman, MD 21671. © **410/886-2720.** www.knappsnarrowsmarina. com. 20 units. $120–$170 double; $240–$260 suite. Rates include continental breakfast. DISC, MC, V. **Amenities:** Restaurant; pool; bikes; marina. *In room:* A/C, TV, free Wi-Fi.

The Lazyjack Inn ★★

Water views, romance, and gourmet breakfasts make this a Tilghman Island delight. The Nellie Byrd Suite, with its king-size brass bed, fireplace, whirlpool tub, and harbor view, is hard to beat. But the other rooms are bright and comfortable, too. The first-floor Garden Suite has a fireplace that opens onto the bedroom and the sitting room, as well as a whirlpool. The innkeepers will accommodate any dietary needs and use organic food whenever possible.

5907 Tilghman Island Rd. (P.O. Box 248), Tilghman, MD 21671. © **800/690-5080** or 410/886-2215. www. lazyjackinn.com. 4 units. $156–$289 double. Rates include full breakfast. 2- or 3-night minimum stay may be required on weekends or holidays. MC, V. No children 12 and under. **Amenities:** Library; afternoon refreshments on Sat–Sun. *In room:* A/C, hair dryer, free Wi-Fi.

The Tilghman Island Inn ★★ (Finds)

Here's a modern inn with old-fashioned Eastern Shore hospitality. Set on Knapps Narrows across from a bird-filled marsh, the waterfront rooms take full advantage of the lovely setting, with French doors and balconies or patios. Decor varies from room to room, but all have fireplaces and most have "ultra spa baths." The inn has a cozy lounge, a restaurant named Isabel's (after the hurricane that tore through here in 2003) with a great reputation, and a waterfront bar. There's piano music in the lounge on summer weekends. The staff is ready to help you find all the treasures Tilghman has to offer.

21384 Coopertown Rd. (P.O. Box B), Tilghman, MD 21671. © **800/866-2141** or 410/886-2141. www. tilghmanislandinn.com. 20 units. $175–$300 double. Rates include continental breakfast. AE, DC, DISC, MC, V. Pets accepted. **Amenities:** Restaurant (closed Wed); lounge; outdoor pool; tennis court. *In room:* A/C, TV, VCR (on request), hair dryer, free Wi-Fi.

Where to Dine

Bay Hundred Restaurant SEAFOOD Just before you reach the Knapps Narrows Bridge, turn right to find this restaurant overlooking the marina and the bridge. It's the most casual of the area eateries, but the kitchen isn't so casual with its cooking. In fact, the chef, an acknowledged master with the mushroom, has completely revamped the menu with rich sauces, pastas, and, yes, mushrooms. You'll still find crab cakes and beef and fried rockfish sandwiches. Slips are available for boating diners.

Knapps Narrows Marina. © **410/886-2126.** www.bayhundredrestaurant.net. Reservations recommended for dinner. Main courses $6–$11 lunch, $14–$22 dinner. AE, DISC, MC, V. Sun–Thurs 11am–10pm; Fri–Sun 11am–11pm. Hours may vary in winter; it's advisable to call ahead.

Bridge Restaurant ★★ (Kids) SEAFOOD Overlooking the Knapps Narrows Bridge, this place serves traditional Eastern Shore fare along with steaks, rack of lamb, and nightly specials. Expect the freshest seafood and a professional, friendly staff. It's casual here, but good enough for a special occasion. A children's menu is available. Boat docking is available for diners at no charge.

6136 Tilghman Rd. ℂ **410/886-2330.** Reservations recommended for dinner. Main courses $5–$14 lunch, $16–$19 dinner. AE, DC, DISC, MC, V. Thurs–Sun 11:30am–8pm.

Harrison's Chesapeake House (**Kids**) SEAFOOD   This may be the best known of the Tilghman Island restaurants, and the reason has to be its hearty Eastern Shore fare: fresh seafood served by a friendly staff. The house special combines two local favorites: fried chicken and crab cakes. But you can get anything from crab to prime rib here, served family style with plates of vegetables and homemade bread and a view of the water. Look for crab feasts in summer and oyster buffets in winter.

21551 Chesapeake House Dr. ℂ **410/886-2121.** www.chesapeakehouse.com. Reservations recommended for dinner. Main courses $3.95–$16 lunch, $12–$25 dinner. AE, MC, V. Hours vary according to season, but always open Sat–Sun; call ahead to confirm.

Outdoor Activities

Rent a bike and take a long ride on flat, fairly quiet roads. Hop aboard a skipjack for a ride into history, or see what's biting from a fishing boat. Rent a kayak and poke around the many coves. Whatever you do, slow down.

BIKING   Get a bike or a motor scooter or moped (no motorcycle license required) from **Tilghman Island Marina** (ℂ 410/886-2500; www.tilghmanmarina.com). Rent for an hour or a full day. (St. Michaels is a half-hour scooter ride away.)

BOATING   **Tilghman Island Marina** (ℂ 410/886-2500; www.tilghmanmarina.com) offers kayaks, pontoon boats, skiffs with outboard motors, sailboats, and personal watercraft, as well as fishing and crabbing gear, by the hour, half-day, day, or week. Or sign up for the Poplar Island excursion: They'll tow your kayak to this small group of islands for a 4-hour expedition, box lunch included. Reservations are required for the Poplar Island excursion, and suggested for others. If you prefer others to drive, sign up for a pontoon cruise.

Look for the **Tilghman Island Water Trail** map, available at the Talbot County visitor center in Easton (ℂ 410/770-8000; www.tourtalbot.org).

CRUISING   Captain Wade Murphy will take you on a 2-hour tour on his skipjack, the *Rebecca T. Ruark* (ℂ 410/886-2176; www.skipjack.org), docked at Dogwood Harbor. As he sails the oldest working sailboat in the country, the captain talks about the history of his boat and tells tales about crabs and oysters.

Dockside Express (ℂ 888/312-7847; www.cruisinthebay.com), offers 1-hour harbor tours, crabbing cruises, and eco-tours.

The *Lady Patty* (ℂ 410/745-8077; www.sailladypatty.com), a 45-foot ketch, docked at Knapps Narrows, sails the Choptank on 2-hour, half-day, or full-day trips.

Tour the **Chesapeake Lights** aboard the MV *Sharp's Island,* a former U.S. Navy special operations vessel. Take a 3-hour cruise and see three lighthouses up close, or spend the whole day and see 10 lighthouses (ℂ 800/690-5080 or 410/886-2215; www.chesapeake lights.com).

FISHING & CRABBING   **Harrison's Sport Fishing Center** (ℂ 410/886-2121; www. chesapeakehouse.com), is the best known of the charters here. Captain Buddy Harrison has 20 charter boats and room for 1 or 100. Half-day charters are available April through December, as well as packages with breakfast and lunch or even overnight lodging. The

Miss Kim (© 410/886-2176; www.skipjack.org), a Chesapeake Bay workboat, offers half-day crabbing for six people. Other charters are available at **Knapp's Narrows Marina** (© 410/886-2720; www.knappsnarrowsmarina.com) and **Tilghman Island Marina** (© 410/886-2500; www.tilghmanmarina.com).

OXFORD

Oxford is a refined place, with a shady park and beach in the center of town. It wasn't always so quiet, though. One of the state's oldest towns, it was the Eastern Shore's first port of entry in the 1700s. It was home to many of Maryland's prominent citizens, including Robert Morris, a shipping agent, and his son Robert Morris, "financier of the Revolution," and Tench Tilghman, George Washington's aide who carried the news of Cornwallis's surrender to the Continental Congress. Tilghman is remembered with a monument in Oxford Cemetery. Although Oxford is quieter than St. Michaels, the peace is a big part of its charm. There aren't many tourists, but there is a leafy park set on a narrow beach and charming old streets that are best seen at a slow pace.

You can also ride the tiny **Oxford-Bellevue Ferry** ★, one of the oldest in the country (see p. 152 for details). Of course, you can take the ferry going the other way, making Oxford your destination.

Where to Stay

Combsberry ★★   Down a country lane, this restored 1730 manor house offers elegant and luxurious comfort. The main house, known for its fireplaces, staircase, and brickwork, has three units, while the two cottages offer room to spread out with kitchen areas and fireplaces. Every room has a water view. The carriage house features a living room with fireplace, a kitchen, and two luxuriously appointed master bedrooms. For a fireplace in the main house, ask for the Magnolia Suite (which also has a private balcony under the shade of a magnolia) or Waterford Room. Some rooms have whirlpool tubs. Gardens dotted with ancient trees surround the house, and a dock awaits boaters. Canoes are available for exploring the cove.

4837 Evergreen Rd., Oxford, MD 21654. © **410/226-5353.** www.combsberry.net. 6 units. $250–$395 double. Rates include full breakfast. AE, MC, V. Pets accepted in Oxford Cottage. No children 12 and under. **Amenities:** Boat dock. *In room:* A/C, hair dryer, no phone.

Oxford Inn (Value) (Kids)   The owners have put a lot of TLC into this well-established inn, located beside Town Creek and close to everything. It remains a good value. All rooms are decorated in French-country style, and many have window seats and views of the water. Two rooms can be combined as a family suite. Guests can relax in the cozy library with fireplace. **Pope's Tavern,** a local favorite, serves dinner Wednesday through Sunday, beginning at 5:30pm. Make reservations.

504 S. Morris St. (P.O. Box 627), Oxford, MD 21654. © **410/226-5220.** www.oxfordinn.net. 7 units. $110–$175 double. Rates include continental breakfast, plus hot dishes on Sat–Sun. AE, DISC, MC, V. **Amenities:** Restaurant; lounge. *In room:* A/C.

Robert Morris Inn   Ships' carpenters built this house in 1710 for Robert Morris, Jr., a financier of the American Revolution. It retains its Colonial character with wide floorboards, the original staircase, and traditional furnishings. Rooms differ in size and appointments: one has a four-poster bed and fireplace, and four of the original 1710 rooms face the water. Some bathrooms have claw-foot tubs and river views. Author James Michener spent time here writing *Chesapeake*.

314 N. Morris St. (P.O. Box 70), Oxford, MD 21654. © **888/823-4012** or 410/226-5111. Fax 410/226-5744. www.robertmorrisinn.com. 15 units. $130–$240 double. Rates include continental breakfast. MC, V. Closed Dec–Mar. **Amenities:** Beach at Sandaway (see below). *In room:* A/C, TV in some rooms, no phone, free Wi-Fi.

Sandaway

Sandaway The owners of the Robert Morris Inn also operate this country home built on a point jutting into the river. Among its rooms is a second-floor suite with a king-size bed that looks through French doors to the river beyond. The Sandaway Suite has a sitting room on the beach, a fireplace, TV/VCR, and lots of windows. Lots of porches at the Sandaway, trees, and chaise longues make this a comfortable retreat.

103 W. Strand (also known as Lovers Lane), Oxford, MD 21654. © **888/SANDAWAY** (726-3292) or 410/226-5111. www.sandaway.com. 18 units. $200–$370 double. Rates include continental breakfast. MC, V. Closed Dec–Mar. **Amenities:** Beach; free Wi-Fi. *In room:* A/C, no phone.

Marina

Mears Yacht Haven So you want to stay in Oxford but you're bringing your boat? Mears has 95 boat slips on an hourly, daily, weekly, or monthly basis. They can accommodate boats 20 to 130 feet. They've got the things a boater needs, including fuel pumps, showers and laundry, and things a boater wants, including cable TV, a pool, and bikes for rent.

502 E. Strand (P.O. Box 130), Oxford, MD 21654. © **410/226-5450**, or call on VHF Channel 16 as you approach Oxford. Rates vary by boat size and season. Sat–Sun rates include continental breakfast. AE, DISC, MC, V. **Amenities:** Bikes; fuel dock; marine pump-out; picnic grove; pool; showers.

Where to Dine

Latitude 38° Bistro & Spirits INTERNATIONAL/SEAFOOD   You'll forget you saw gas pumps out front once you walk into this white-tablecloth dining room—and the creative cuisine will take you away altogether. The menu—which changes every few weeks—takes advantage of the area's bounty and mixes in an international style. Lunch is served only in winter, but Sunday brunch is offered year-round. Half portions are available at dinner for smaller appetites. The bar separates the formal dining room from the more casual side. But both sides choose from the same menu, which recently featured rack of lamb, rockfish with leek sauce, and crab cakes. The bar has its own special menu each night, including $13 burgers.

26342 Oxford Rd. © **410/226-5303**. www.latitude38.org. Reservations recommended for dinner; none taken for bar area. Main courses $8–$13 lunch, $13–$29 dinner. AE, DISC, MC, V. Dinner Tues–Sun 5:30–9:30pm; brunch Sun 11am–2pm.

The Masthead at Pier Street Marina SEAFOOD   It looks a little ramshackle, but it's a truism that good seafood is often best at a place like this. (The owners also run Latitude 38°, so it has to be good.) Views of the Tred Avon River are incredible, especially from the covered deck. And so many choices: sandwiches and salads for lunch, seafood platters for dinner. Slips are available for boaters.

104 W. Pier St. © **410/226-5171**. Reservations required for dinner. Main courses $10–$28 dinner. MC, V. Daily 11:30am–9pm. Closed mid-Oct to Apr 1.

Schooner's SEAFOOD   This informal spot is on a marina with great views of the water and deck seating in season. Schooner's all-day menu offers prime rib, crab, oyster, shrimp, sandwiches, soups, and a catch of the day. It's a good place for lunch or for a boisterous evening of sailing stories, aided by several draft beer options. Bands play some summer nights. There's a kids' menu, too.

314 Tilghman St. ℰ **410/226-0160.** Reservations accepted for dining room only. Main courses $6.45–$24. AE, DC, DISC, MC, V. Daily 11am–10pm. Closed Oct–Mar.

Outdoor Activities

Surrounded by all that water, you just might want to charter a boat yourself. **Choptank Charters,** 102 S. Morris St. (ℰ **410/226-5000;** www.tays.com), offers sailing yachts for 2 days to a week and a motor yacht for 5 to 7 days. Captains are extra. Rates begin at $1,000 for 2 days on a 34-foot Sabre.

Shopping

Oxford shops are usually open Saturday and Sunday from 10am to 6pm; many close midweek when the town's pretty quiet. Hours may be cut back in winter, too.

Americana Antiques   Old treasures for sale on weekends only. 111 S. Morris St. ℰ **410/476-4348.**

Hinckley Yacht Services   The wares here range from nautical necessities and yachting apparel to gifts and games. Transient slips and boat repair are available, too. 202 Banks St. ℰ **410/226-5113.** www.hinckleyyachts.com.

Mystery Loves Company   Everybody needs a good read on vacation. Nautical books and local authors' works are for sale here, too. 202 S. Morris St. ℰ **410/226-0010.**

Oxford Market   Essentials are sold here: groceries, deli goods, ice cream, coffee, and wine. Opens at 7am daily, even in winter. 203 S. Morris St. ℰ **410/226-0015.**

The Scottish Highland Creamery   Tasty ice cream and fudge made on the premises. Truffles, though not made here, are up to the owner's high standards. 314 Tilghman St. ℰ **410/924-6298.** www.scottishhighlandcreamery.com.

Golfing the Eastern Shore

Lots of flat land, terrific water views, and beautiful weather make the Mid-Shore an up-and-coming golf destination.

The **Hog Neck Golf Course,** 10142 Old Cordova Rd., Easton (ℰ **410/822-6079;** www.hogneck.com), has been rated among the top 25 U.S. public courses by *Golf Digest.* This par-72, 18-hole course and par-32, 9-hole executive course is north of town, off Route 50. Rates are $57 Monday through Thursday, $67 Friday through Sunday, carts included.

The **Easton Club,** 28449 Clubhouse Dr., Easton (ℰ **800/277-9800;** www. eastonclub.com), has a par-72 course on Route 333 that's open to the public. Greens fees, including cart, are $64 on weekends and $54 on weekdays.

Harbourtowne Golf Resort, in St. Michaels (ℰ **800/446-9066;** www. harbourtowne.com), is a par-70 course designed by Pete Dye. Greens fees are $70 for Harbourtowne hotel guests and $85 for nonguests, including cart. Harbourtowne offers 1- and 2-night golf packages, too. Fees go down in winter.

2 CAMBRIDGE

58 miles SE of Annapolis; 85 miles SE of Baltimore; 86 miles SE of Washington, D.C.; 99 miles S of Wilmington

Since its foundation in 1684, Cambridge has drawn those who love the water. Once acting as a harbor for trading ships taking tobacco to England, and later serving as a deepwater port for 20th-century freighters, Cambridge was also a shipbuilding town. The town still draws boaters—but now they're pleasure boaters.

Cambridge lies just across the Choptank River Bridge from Talbot. Still more of a commercial center than a tourist town, it has its charms. High Street leads to the Choptank—a lovely stroll with a great view at the end. History buffs, especially those interested in the Civil War era, may be interested in the town's connections with the Underground Railroad. Nature lovers find it a nice stop on their way to Blackwater Refuge or to a hunting or fishing trip. Visitors planning a Mid-Shore visit to Easton or St. Michaels may prefer this quiet place as a base.

In its prosperity in Colonial times and again in the early 20th century, Cambridge became the home of governors, lawyers, and landowners. Their beautiful homes line High Street, Water Street, Mill Street, and Hambrooks Boulevard. Sharpshooter Annie Oakley built her house at 28 Bellevue Ave., on Hambrooks Bay. The roofline was altered so Oakley could step outside her second-story windows and shoot waterfowl coming in over the bay. The house is now privately owned, but the owners have erected a small sign in Annie's memory.

Harriet Tubman's home no longer exists, but she often walked the streets and country roads around here as she led more than 300 slaves to freedom on the Underground Railroad. She is remembered in monuments, markers, a museum in Cambridge, and a driving tour.

Anyone who has read James Michener's *Chesapeake* or John Barth's *The Sot-Weed Factor* may recognize some of the places mentioned—this is one of the towns that inspired these novels.

ESSENTIALS

GETTING THERE   Come by boat (your own; there aren't any ferries)—from the Chesapeake Bay east on the Choptank River—or come by car. Cambridge is on Route 50, about 15 miles south of Easton. Once you cross the Sen. Frederick Malkus Bridge over the Choptank, you're here. The historic district is west of the highway, which is called Ocean Gateway here.

Boat slips are available at the city marina and in front of the county offices, both on the Choptank. Boats can tie up for free for 48 hours in front of the county office building but need permission to stay longer. The city marina has slips for larger boats; reservations are required. Call 🕐 **410/228-1700** for reservations or information.

VISITOR INFORMATION   The **Dorchester Visitor Center at Sailwinds Park,** 2 Rose Hill Place, just east of the bridge in Cambridge (🕐 **410/228-1000;** www.tourdorchester. org), is full of information about Cambridge, Harriet Tubman, and the nearby Blackwater National Wildlife Refuge. The center has restrooms, a waterfront playground, and picnic tables, too. It's open daily 8:30am to 5pm.

GETTING AROUND   The quickest way to get around is by car, but because the area is so flat, many prefer bicycle. Roads are fairly quiet, making it a pleasure to drive or bike.

THE EASTERN SHORE

8

CAMBRIDGE

Be sure to stop at the visitor center for brochures and maps for walking, biking, and boating. They've got some really useful ones.

WHERE TO STAY

Cambridge House ★   This Queen Anne–style sea captain's mansion, next to Long Wharf, puts visitors in the middle of Cambridge's most beautiful street. Watch the tourists go by as you sit on the front porch, or get away from it all in the Victorian gardens. The elegant rooms, some with fireplaces, feature queen- and king-size beds. A breakfast buffet is served each morning in the dining room or on the porch. A hot tub on the back deck overlooks the garden.

112 High St., Cambridge, MD 21613. ℂ **410/221-7700.** www.cambridgehousebandb.com. 6 units. $125–$175 double. Rates include breakfast and refreshments. 2-night minimum stay required some weekends. AE, DISC, MC, V. No children 8 and under. *In room:* A/C, TV/VCR, CD player, hair dryer, free Wi-Fi.

Holiday Inn Express Cambridge   Eastern Shore hospitality and location near downtown Cambridge and Blackwater Wildlife Refuge make this a chain hotel worth mentioning. The bedding, including duvets, was updated in 2008.

2715 Ocean Gateway, Cambridge, MD 21613. ℂ **410/221-9900.** www.ichotelsgroup.com. 86 units. $84–$135 double. Rates include hot breakfast. Free baby cribs; rollaway cots available. AE, DC, DISC, MC, V. **Amenities:** Indoor pool; hot tub. *In room:* A/C, TV, hair dryer, free Wi-Fi.

Hyatt Regency Chesapeake Bay Golf Resort, Spa & Marina ★★   This resort, on 342 acres on the Choptank River, has facilities beyond any other property in the area, with enough amenities to keep families busy without ever leaving the grounds—as well as a variety of packages that take advantage of the countryside. Most rooms have balconies, though of varying size (if you want one big enough to sit on, ask for it). Corner rooms seem a little bigger. Rocking chairs and hammocks invite visitors to watch the river roll by. The spa, marina, and 18-hole par-5 golf course are open to the public. Have your heart set on a massage? Make a reservation before you arrive.

2800 Ocean Gateway, Cambridge, MD 21613. ℂ **800/233-1234** or 410/901-1234. www.chesapeakebay. hyatt.com. 344 rooms, 56 suites. $139–$240 double; $260-$400 suite. AE, DC, DISC, MC, V. Pets accepted for fee. **Amenities:** 5 restaurants; 2 bars; beach; bikes; Camp Hyatt children's program; golf course; health club; jogging trails; 150-slip marina; indoor pool; 2 outdoor pools; room service; 4 tennis courts; watersports equipment. *In room:* A/C, TV w/pay movies and games, fridge, hair dryer, Wi-Fi (fee).

Kindred Spirits Family Massage & Cottage Retreat   This one-room bed-and-breakfast offers a real sense of getting away from it all, with a massage thrown in. Run by a licensed massage therapist, the guest room is in a converted workshop behind the main house. It's a 500-square-foot room decorated with comfort in mind, with a jetted tub, a sleeper sofa, and a king-size bed. The patio has a view of the Choptank River and the massage room is adjacent to the guest room. Massage packages are offered. In keeping with the retreat idea, continental breakfast items are left in the kitchen so guests can count on total privacy. Cambridge's historic district is within walking distance via a riverside walkway.

102 Hiawatha Rd., Cambridge, MD 21613. ℂ **410/221-7575** or 725-9364. www.kindredspiritscottage retreat.com. 1 unit. $125–$150 double. Rates include continental breakfast. No credit cards; PayPal accepted. *In room:* A/C, TV w/DVD, fridge, hair dryer, free Wi-Fi.

Lodgecliffe on the Choptank ★★★ Come for the views of the Choptank River at Cambridge's only waterfront B&B. Enjoy tranquil views from every public room, the deck, the broad lawn, and the three of the guest rooms. Guest rooms are spacious; the best has its own door to the waterfront deck. But all four rooms in this 1898 home are updated in a mix of modern luxury and antique charm. Three rooms are on the first floor, one is on the second. Downtown restaurants, attractions, and shops are only a few blocks away, but sitting on the deck with a glass of wine at sunset really feels like you've gotten away from it all here.

103 Choptank Terrace, Cambridge, MD 21613. (✆ 866/273-3830. www.lodgecliffeonthechoptank bandb.com. 4 units. $180–$200 double. Rates include full breakfast. AE, DISC, MC, V. **Amenities:** Bikes. *In room:* A/C, hair dryer, free Wi-Fi.

Mill Street Inn ★★ This 1894 Victorian combines the charm of antique style with the convenience of modern technology. Breezes off the Choptank River cool the screened porch and air-conditioning cools the updated guest rooms. Visitors can choose from relaxing in a TV room with cable and a DVD player or at the chess table tucked in a turret nook. Innkeepers here aren't afraid of color, and each en-suite sleeping room is ablaze with hues as bright as cornflower blue or marigold yellow. The Cambridge Suite boasts plenty of room, a separate sitting room, and an enormous bathroom with air-jetted tub. Afternoon tea is served daily.

114 Mill St., Cambridge, MD 21613. (✆ 410/901-9144. www.millstinn.com. 3 units. $125–$200 double. Rates include gourmet breakfast and tea. AE, MC, V. *In room:* A/C, TV/DVD, hair dryer, free Wi-Fi.

WHERE TO DINE

Bistro Poplar ★★ FRENCH Classic French food in a classy bistro setting has come to Cambridge. Steak frites, croque monsieur, and onion soup share the menu with salads, including a poached lobster salad, crepes, and coq au vin. The menu, which changes seasonally, is offered from noon until the last diner heads home after 9pm. A limited menu is available after 9pm. Desserts are made in-house.

Poplar St., Cambridge. (✆ 410/228-4884. Reservations recommended during the summer and on weekends. Main courses $7–$16 lunch items, $23–$25 dinner. AE, MC, V. Thurs–Mon noon–9pm (or later.)

Kay's at the Airport (Value) AMERICAN/SEAFOOD Kay's is packing them in. The locals are filling the tables for old-fashioned favorites: Fried shrimp or chicken tender baskets, roast beef, pork chops, and crab imperial are available for lunch or dinner. Breakfast is quite a production here, too, with everything from pancakes in several flavors to breakfast wraps and full country breakfasts. Leave room for the homemade cakes and pies. A young pilot's menu is available, too. And it's really at the airport. Two-story windows overlook the private plane runways.

5263 Bucktown Rd., Cambridge. (✆ 410/901-8844. Reservations not accepted. Main courses $6–$9 breakfast, $6–$10 lunch, $11–$20 dinner. MC, V. Sun 8am–3pm; Mon–Tues and Thurs–Sat 8am–8pm.

Snappers Waterfront Cafe ★ (Kids) INTERNATIONAL/SEAFOOD Snappers is a casual place with a friendly staff. The crab dip is served in a crusty French loaf; add a couple friends, a drink, and a deck with a view of Cambridge Creek—you're going to like it here. The huge menu lists lots of seafood, Jamaican jerk chicken, pastas, and quesadillas. Kids get their own menu and a couple of video games. Sunday brunch is served from 11am to 3pm. A Tiki bar is open from Cinco de Mayo to Labor Day, Thursday through Monday from 4:30pm on, with deck parties on Sundays.

112 Commerce St., Cambridge. (✆ 410/228-0112. Reservations recommended Fri–Sat. Main courses $7–$15 lunch, $7–$29 dinner. AE, DC, DISC, MC, V. Labor Day to Memorial Day daily 11am–9pm; summer Mon–Sat 11am–10pm, Sun 11am–9pm.

Suicide Bridge Restaurant ★ SEAFOOD   This is the place to be on a Saturday night, when you'll see people waiting up to 45 minutes for their turn at seafood and crab cakes. Chicken and steak dishes are offered, but the very fresh seafood here is cooked simply and well. A lunchtime menu of panini, sandwiches, and wraps is available Tuesday through Saturday. The restaurant overlooks the Suicide Bridge—whose sad history is printed on the menu—and has a marina for boating diners. Boats must be less than 50 feet tall to fit under the Choptank River Bridge.

The restaurant operates two paddle-wheelers, the *Dorothy-Megan* and the *Choptank River Queen*. Lunch cruises are $35, dinner cruises $48, and sightseeing cruises $15. Call ✆ **410/943-4775** for a schedule.

6304 Suicide Bridge Rd., Hurlock. ✆ **410/943-4689.** www.suicidebridge.com. Reservations not accepted; call ahead for priority seating list. Main courses $9–$36; kids' menu $6–$7. MC, V. Apr–Dec Tues–Thurs 11am–9pm, Fri–Sat 11am–10pm, Sun noon–9pm; Jan 15–Mar 30 Thurs–Sat 11am–10pm, Sun noon–9pm. Closed Jan 1–15, Thanksgiving weekend, and Dec 24–26.

WHAT TO SEE & DO

Historic High Street ★, which ends at Long Wharf, is lined with 19th-century homes from a variety of periods, including French Second Empire, Queen Anne, and Federal. Take a look on your own or take the 1-hour tour offered every Saturday April through October, offered by the **West End Citizens Association** (✆ **410/901-1000**). The tours begin at 11am at Long Wharf.

Stop in the expanded **Dorchester Center for the Arts** in a new location at 321 High St. (✆ **410/228-7782;** www.dorchesterarts.org), to see the exhibits, which change every month, and browse the gift shop. Both feature local artists and artisans. It's open Monday through Thursday from 10am to 5pm, Friday and Saturday 10am to 4pm. The **Historic Ghost Walk,** which departs from here, combines a little exercise with history on Saturday nights in October. Call the center for reservations, which are a must.

The West End Citizens Association offers a 1-hour **Historic High Street Tour** Saturdays at 11am April through November. Call ✆ **410/901-1000** to reserve.

At Long Wharf, check out the *Nathan of Dorchester* (✆ **410/228-7141;** www.skipjack-nathan.org), a living museum built by local volunteers. Visitors can climb aboard the 63-foot skipjack for a 2-hour cruise on the Choptank River, offered Saturdays May through October. Stop by or call for a reservation.

Dorchester County Historical Society   The society operates several museums, including the Neild Museum (which focuses on industrial and agricultural history), the 1760s Meredith House, the 1790 Goldsborough Stables, and a Colonial-style herb garden. In 2007, the Robbins Heritage Center was added to expand the exhibits on watermen, sharpshooter Annie Oakley (who used to live in town), and the canning and seafood industries. A porch overlooks Shoal Creek and a path leads to the water.

LaGrange Plantation, 902 LaGrange Ave. ✆ **410/228-7953.** www.dorchesterhistory.org. Free admission. Tues–Sat 10am–4pm. Call ahead to schedule tours for groups.

Harriet Tubman Center   A tribute to Harriet Tubman, a former slave and conductor in the Underground Railroad, this small museum has exhibits on Tubman's life, her work as a conductor on the Underground Railroad, and her efforts during the Civil War and later. The center also offers tours of places in Dorchester County where Tubman lived, prayed, and worked. Only a few of the actual buildings still exist, but guides use the locations to tell stories about her life. Renovated in 2009–10, a new theater will show documentaries about Tubman.

Richardson Maritime Museum   Come here to find out what a bugeye is, how a log canoe sails, or what a skipjack was built to do. With builders' models, hand tools, and building plans, the museum focuses on all the boats used on the Chesapeake Bay for fishing, oystering, and trading.

401 High St. ℂ **410/221-1871.** www.richardsonmuseum.org. Free admission. Mar–Oct Wed and Sun 1–4pm, Sat 10am–4pm; Nov–Feb Sat–Sun 1–4pm. Closed Jan 1, Easter, July 4, Thanksgiving, and Dec 25.

Ruark Boatworks   Old wooden boats get a new lease on life at this wood chip–filled workshop on Cambridge Creek. Visitors are welcome to take a look, talk to the workers restoring historic vessels, or take up some tools and join in a boat-building project Monday, Wednesday, and Friday mornings.

103 Maryland Ave. at Hayward St. ℂ **410/221-1871.** www.richardsonmuseum.org. Free admission. Mon, Wed, and Fri 10am–2pm. Closed Jan 1, Easter, July 4, Thanksgiving, and Dec 25.

OUTSIDE OF TOWN

Three tributes to the Underground Railroad and its most famous conductor Harriet Tubman will be open to the public between 2011 and 2013.

A 17-acre parcel near Blackwater Wildlife Refuge is being developed as the **Harriet Tubman Underground Railroad State Park.** The park, when it opens in December 2011, will have a visitor center with artifacts about Tubman and the Underground Railroad, as well as hiking and biking paths, a picnic pavilion, and spots for paddling and viewing wildlife. This is Dorchester's first state park.

The **Harriet Tubman Underground Railroad National Historical Park** will protect 6,750 acres of farmland, forest, and wetlands over which Tubman and fleeing slaves found their way to freedom in the north. These landscapes won't really be available for the public's use but will be preserved. The state park land, which is included in this national park, of course, will be accessible.

Maps for the **Harriet Tubman Underground Railroad All American Road,** a 125-mile byway through Dorchester and Caroline counties, are available at the visitor center. New interpretive signs will be added by 2013.

For a worthwhile side trip, visit the **Spocott Windmill** ★★, 7 miles west of Cambridge on Route 343. The only existing post windmill for grinding grain left in Maryland, it's still operated at least twice a year. It's not the original—three others have been on this site since the 1700s. Also on the building are a **tenant house,** a humble 1½-story wood dwelling built around 1800; a one-room **schoolhouse,** built in 1870; and a **country museum store,** which evokes an old-time feeling with its potbellied stove and World War II–era merchandise (open only on special occasions). The sites stay open dawn to dusk every day so visitors are free to wander among the desks in the school and peek in the upstairs bedroom of the tenant house. Admission is free. Call ℂ **800/522-8687** to make arrangements for a guide.

A VISIT TO A NATURAL REFUGE

Blackwater National Wildlife Refuge ★★★, just 12 miles south of Cambridge, gives waterfowl a place to land, provides a safe haven for bald eagles and endangered Delmarva fox squirrels, and lets humans stand in awe of nature. Some 25,000 acres of marsh, freshwater ponds, river, forest, and field were set aside in 1933 for the migratory birds that use the Atlantic Flyway.

The most popular time to visit is during the fall migration, which peaks in November. Some 35,000 geese and 15,000 ducks fill the refuge. Blackwater's free open house, held the first weekend in October, is a great time to see some of the refuge residents up close.

Winter is the best time to see bald eagles. As many as 200 eagles have been seen at Blackwater, and some 18 nesting pairs have set up homes high in the trees—the greatest breeding population of bald eagles on the East Coast north of Florida.

Visitors in spring will see lots of birds headed north. Marsh and shorebirds arrive, as do the ospreys who set up house for their new families. The ospreys build huge nests on platforms in the middle of the marsh. They swoop and dive into the water for fish, and then fly back to feed their noisy offspring. The refuge hosts an Eagle Festival in March, and a youth fishing derby is held the first weekend in June.

In summer, birders can find warblers, orioles, blue herons, and even wild turkeys. *Be prepared:* Mosquitoes and flies can be fierce here in summer. Wear a hat and be on the lookout for ticks in early summer.

GETTING THERE   From Route 50, take Route 16 southwest from Cambridge; turn south on Route 335, then left on Key Wallace Drive and right to the visitor center.

VISITOR CENTER   The visitor center is on Key Wallace Drive (© **410/228-2677;** www.fws.gov/blackwater). It's open year-round, Monday through Friday from 8am to 4pm, Saturday and Sunday from 9am to 5pm. Staff members can provide maps, bird lists, and calendars of events. Exhibits explain who lives at the refuge, while an observation deck gives visitors a view of the waterfowl browsing in nearby fields. Look for the real-time cameras trained on the osprey and eagle nests. (The nest cams are on the Friends of Blackwater website, too—go to www.friendsofblackwater.org.)

FEES & REGULATIONS   The entry fee for the wildlife drive (see below) is $3 per vehicle, $1 per pedestrian or bicyclist. It's free to anyone holding a Federal Duck Stamp, Interagency Pass, Senior Pass, Access Pass, or Blackwater National Wildlife Refuge Pass. Pets are not permitted on trails but are allowed in vehicles on the drive.

WILDLIFE DRIVE   Though the refuge belongs to the wildlife, the park has set aside hiking paths and a short drive for cars and bicycles so visitors may see and hear these amazing crowds of birds. These are open from dawn to dusk.

After paying the entry fee at a self-service pay station, visitors will reach a fork in the road about ⅓-mile into the drive. Turn left for the Marsh Edge Trail and Observation Site. Then head back up the road for the rest of the drive.

The 5-mile ride meanders through woodlands and marshes that stretch to the horizon. It's quiet, except for the insects and calling birds. Bring your binoculars and camera: You might see any number of birds, deer, or the rare Delmarva fox squirrel.

Want to stretch your legs and see everything a little more closely? You can park at one of the four walking trails. The **Woods Trail** is .5 miles long and runs through a mature forest. The 2.7-mile **Key Wallace Trail** centers on forest interior birds and forest management. For a look at how Mother Nature recovers after a tornado, take a walk on the 2-mile **Tubman Road Trail.**

The .3-mile **Marsh Edge Trail** begins in the woods and ends with an 80-foot boardwalk extending into Little Blackwater River. If you visit in spring or summer, look for the osprey. In fall, you'll see waterfowl. An observation site has been set up at the end of this part of the drive, with an information kiosk. The view over the Blackwater River, with all the sights and sounds of thousands of migrating waterfowl, can be awe-inspiring.

A photo blind is at the edge of a pond and connected by a boardwalk to the drive over- looking the Little Blackwater River.

OTHER OUTDOOR ACTIVITIES

BIKING   The 5-mile wildlife drive is an easy ride on flat, mostly quiet roads. If you plan to bike from Cambridge (about 10 miles) or Vienna (about 15 miles), bring water— there aren't many places to stock up between Cambridge and Blackwater. Before you go, get the "Cycling Trails of Dorchester County" map (available at the visitor center in Cambridge or at www.tourdorchester.org). In addition, Blackwater has its own bike map with two suggested loops: a 20-mile loop from Cambridge's public high school into the refuge and a 5-mile loop crossing the refuge in two locations and winding through beau- tiful country roads. Ask about it at the visitor center.

BIRDING   Refuge volunteers offer bird walks on various weekend mornings in spring and fall. These meet at the visitor center and last about 2 hours. Call (℃ **410/228-2677** for a schedule. The visitor center also has a bird list.

BOATING & FISHING   Launching ramps for canoes and kayaks are available year- round. *Caution:* Before you start paddling in fall and winter, check the waterfowl- hunting schedule. Refuge staff advises against getting between a hunter and a goose.

To rent a kayak, motorboat, or bike, try **Blackwater Paddle and Pedal Adventures** (℃ **410/901-9255;** www.blackwaterpaddleandpedal.com), on the road to Blackwater. They also give kayak tours. Contact **'Peake Paddle Tours** (℃ **410/829-7342;** www. paddletours.com) for information on kayaking tours with knowledgeable guides.

Fishing and crabbing are permitted from April 1 to September 30 from small boats and bridges, but note that state laws apply here. A state sportfishing license is required for fishing in the Blackwater and Little Blackwater rivers. No fishing is allowed from the shores. A **Water Trails Guide** with maps is available at the visitor center.

SHOPPING

Cambridge's Downtown still needs some work but the shops they've got are worth a stop. Head to High, Poplar, and Race streets to have a look—an eclectic jumble of secondhand goods are at **Crabcatcher's Scavenger Shop,** 533 Poplar St. (℃ **410/225-5689**). At the cavernous **Sunnyside,** 500 Poplar St. (℃ **410/901-9009**), fair-trade items are available

---

(Moments   **A Bike Ride through Historic Landscapes**

The bike ride along Blackwater Wildlife Refuge's 7-mile Wildlife Drive offers effort- less pedaling along wooded paths and breathtaking water vistas. It only gets better if you start at the Bucktown Store, 4.5 miles away at 4303 Bucktown Rd. It was here, many say, that Harriet Tubman got her start assisting slaves when she defied an overseer chasing a slave. At this store he struck her and fractured her skull. The store now houses **Blackwater Paddle and Pedal** (℃ **410/901-9255**) and you can take a look around while you wait for your bike. Then on the way to Blackwater—through landscapes that were once part of the Underground Rail- road—stop at the site where Tubman was born and at the Native American long- house once used as a freed slaves' church in the 1800s. Two hours of pedaling, hundreds of years of history.

for every age, especially great greeting cards and jewelry. Even the owner's handicrafts are among the handmade items at **Joie de Vivre Gallery,** 410 Race St. ((C) **410/228-7000**). Gourmet items and wine are at **A Few of My Favorite Things,** 414 Race St. ((C) **410/221-1960**). Like duck decoys? Don't miss **Chesapeake Classics,** 317 High Street ((C) **410/228-6508**), which stocks a treasure-trove of locally-made and antique waterfowl decoys, duck calls, and fishing lures.

Out on Route 50, **Bay Country Shop** ((C) **800/467-2046** or 410/221-0700) offers mementos with Eastern Shore flair.

3 CRISFIELD & SMITH ISLAND ★★

126 miles SE of Annapolis; 153 miles SE of Baltimore; 155 miles SE of Washington, D.C.; 142 miles S of Wilmington

The remote town of Crisfield, on the extreme southern end of the Eastern Shore, offers an insider's look at the lives of the watermen and the seafood industry. Crisfield, built on acres of oyster shells, was once known as the seafood capital of the world. Even though the industry has shrunk over time, crab and oyster packing, along with services for plea- sure boaters, remain major businesses here. Indeed, the crab-packing houses now share the waterfront with marina slips for yachts and new condominiums. For visitors, Cris- field and its neighbor, Smith Island, make a great launching point for fishing and boating trips on the deep waters of the southern Chesapeake.

ESSENTIALS

GETTING THERE Crisfield is accessible by car via Maryland Route 413 from Route 50 or U.S. Route 13. You can also take your boat to Crisfield past Smith Island. (Before heading into shallow Tangier Sound, check your charts.)

VISITOR INFORMATION For helpful information about Crisfield and the surround- ing countryside, contact **Somerset County Tourism** ((C) **800/521-9189** or 410/651-2968; www.visitsomerset.com). While in town, stop at the visitor center at 1003 W. Main St. ((C) **410/968-1543;** www.crisfieldheritagefoundation.org).

SPECIAL EVENTS The **National Hard Crab Derby and Fair** ★ is a 3-day event with a crab-cooking contest, a crab-picking contest, country music, and, of course, the crab race. It's held Labor Day weekend at Somers Cove Marina; admission is about $4. Make hotel reservations well in advance. The **J. Millard Tawes Crab and Clam Bake,** held the third Wednesday in July from 1 to 5pm, is an all-you-can-eat affair; buy tickets in advance. For information on either event, call (C) **800/782-3913** or 410/968-2500.

WHERE TO STAY

Best Value Somers Cove Motel The simple old-fashioned two-story motel offers balconies or patios with views of the water. Four rooms have kitchenettes. Although ordinary, its location near the marina recommends it.

700 Norris Harbor Dr., Crisfield, MD 21817. (C) **888/315-2378** or 410/968-1900. Fax 410/968-3448. www. crisfield.com/somerscove. 40 units. $45–$150 double. DISC, MC, V. Pets accepted for a fee. **Amenities:** Outdoor pool; patio; picnic tables; grills; boat docks; boat ramps. In room: A/C, TV.

My Fair Lady ★ Pink with a wraparound porch, this 1900 B&B is within walking distance of the waterfront but set in a residential area. Rooms are filled with antiques and collectibles. A three-room suite in the attic has space for a small family. Other rooms are small but comfortable. Some have walk-in closets and all feature beautifully carved woodwork and 12-foot ceilings. All rooms have bathrooms en suite except one, and that one uses the hall bathroom with the house's original claw-foot tub.

38 W. Main St., Crisfield, MD 21817. (*©* **410/968-0352.** www.myfairladybandb.com. 6 units. $140–$380 double. MC, V. *In room:* A/C, TV, hair dryer (upon request).

WHERE TO DINE

Olde Crisfield Crab and Steak House SEAFOOD   New owners had just taken this spot over at press time, painting the exterior in bright colors and updating the steak and seafood menu. The owners have pretty good credentials—they also own the venerable Middleton Tavern in Annapolis. Outside seating is available on patios and decks by Tangier Sound. Located next door, the **Tiki Bar** serves light fare and drinks after 3pm.

204 S. 10th St., Crisfield. (*©* **410/968-2442.** Reservations not accepted, but call ahead for priority seating. Main courses $7–$22 dinner. AE, DC, DISC, MC, V. Mar–Oct daily 4–10pm. Closed Nov–Feb.

Watermen's Inn AMERICAN   Although this eatery does not boast water views, the food is the prime attraction, with an adventurous menu that ranges from softshell crabs and crab cakes to bourbon-marinated pork chops and filet with candied shallots. In summer, there's alfresco dining.

901 W. Main St., Crisfield. (*©* **410/968-2119.** www.crisfield.com/watermens. Reservations recommended for dinner. Main courses $4.95–$16 lunch, $15–$25 dinner. AE, DISC, MC, V. Summer Wed–Thurs 11am–9pm, Fri 11am–9:30pm, Sat 8am–9:30pm, Sun 8am–8pm; winter Thurs 11am–8pm, Fri 11am–8pm, Sat 8am–9pm, Sun 8am–8pm.

WHAT TO SEE & DO

The **J. Millard Tawes Historical Museum,** Somers Cove Marina, 3 Ninth St. (*©* **410/968-2501;** www.crisfieldheritagefoundation.org), was founded in 1982 to honor the Crisfield-born former governor of Maryland. Exhibits detail the town's history as well as its boat-building and seafood industries. It's open year-round, Monday through Saturday, from 9am to 5pm. Admission is $3 for adults, $1 for children 6 to 12. This is also the starting point for the **Port of Crisfield Escorted Walking Tour** ★★, offered from Memorial Day to Labor Day, Monday through Saturday at 10am. The tour winds around town and through the crab-packing plant.

While you are in the area, take a detour to **Princess Anne,** a small country town on the National Register of Historic Places about 15 miles north of Crisfield on U.S. Route 13. The town's many historic homes here are privately owned, except for the grand neoclassical **Teackle Mansion** ★, 11736 Mansion St. (*©* **410/651-2238;** www.teackle mansion.org). Built in 1801 by Littleton Dennis Teackle, a shipping magnate and an associate of Thomas Jefferson, it's open for guided tours April through mid-December, Wednesday, Saturday, and Sunday from 1 to 3pm. Inside, you'll see elaborate plaster ceilings, a 7-foot fireplace, a beehive oven, American Chippendale furniture, a Tudor-Gothic pipe organ, and an 1806 silk world map. Admission is $5 for adults, free for children 12 and under.

OUTDOOR ACTIVITIES

The 515-slip **Somers Cove Marina,** 715 Broadway (*©* **800/967-3474** or 410/968-0925), is one of the largest marinas in Maryland. It's able to accommodate both sailboats and motor yachts from 10 to 150 feet. Facilities include boat ramps, showers, a laundry room, a pool, boat storage, electricity, water, and a fuel dock.

(Moments) **Wildfowl Counterfeiters in Wood**

Walk inside the two-room shack where Lem and Steve Ward fashioned their 25,000 world-famous waterfowl decoys and you'll swear they've just stepped out for a moment. Lovingly restored by real fans, the **Ward Brothers Workshop** ★★ is outfitted with the carvers' tools and paints. Sawdust covers the floors; cigarettes sit in the ashtrays, and notes the men scribbled on the rough walls have been carefully preserved. A comprehensive story emerges of two "wildfowl counterfeiters in wood," as they called themselves, who were all in all country gentlemen and humble artists. To visit, you must make an appointment. Call the **Crisfield Visitor Center** at (©) **410/968-2501.**

Fishing trips leave from the marina and the town dock each day for flounder, trout, spot, drum, blues, and rock. To book a headboat or charter, talk with the captains along the waterfront, or call any of the following: **Capt. Keith Ward** ((©) **800/791-1470** or 410/968-0074; www.crisfield.com/prim), **Capt. Charlie Corio** ((©) **410/957-2151**), or **Capt. Larry Laird** ((©) **410/968-2545**). Charters cost $70 to $120 per person.

Janes Island State Park, 26280 Alfred Lawson Dr. ((©) **410/968-1565;** www.dnr. state.md.us), has 2,900 acres of wilderness for hiking, camping, canoeing, and boating. Located on the edge of Tangier Sound, Janes Island has beaches, 25 boat slips, and a canoe/boat trail, the only way to see the island portion of the park. In warm weather, the park rents canoes and kayaks. There are 104 campsites, 49 with electricity, and three backcountry sites; they go for $25 to $90 a night. Most are closed in winter, but four modern waterfront cabins can be rented year-round.

AN EXCURSION TO SMITH ISLAND ★

Isolated, quiet, friendly Smith Island is set apart from the rest of the Eastern Shore. No bridge connects it to the mainland; residents rely on boats to get to the doctor, the malls, even schools. But they're delighted to see visitors, offering a warm welcome in the distinct Smith Island accent. So go. Hop aboard one of the boats that leave around lunchtime from Crisfield on the Eastern Shore or Point Lookout on the Eastern Shore.

Go for the uniqueness of the place: modest streets with only a few cars, long shacks where "peelers" doff their shells to become the highly prized softshell crab, vistas of bay and wetlands.

Go for the food: crabs steamed the minute they land on the dock and multilayered Smith Island cake, the official state dessert.

Go to meet the Smith Islanders and hear the lyrical twist they put on their English. Listen to their stories about life in this out-of-the-way place.

Located 12 miles west of Crisfield, at the edge of Tangier Sound, Smith Island is a cluster of islands making up Maryland's largest inhabited offshore community. There are three towns. On one island is Ewell, where the cruise boats land, and Rhodes Point. Pretty Tylerton is on a second island; Martin National Wildlife Refuge is on the third.

A few notes: You can't bring a car. Plan on a stroll, or rent a bike or golf cart. There are no bars, as it's a "dry" island. But it's fine to bring your own bottle. Shops are few, but make sure to stop for a piece of cake or a jar of preserves made from the island's pomegranate, pear, or fig trees. Remember your bug repellent and sunscreen—black flies and mosquitoes are sure to plague you, and although the streets are shady, the sun can be fierce.

One thing's for sure: If you take the ferry for a day trip, you're going to leave wishing you had at least a few more hours here.

Essentials

GETTING THERE   The excursion boats come only in summer, but you can catch the mail boat or residents' ferry (which leave promptly at 12:30pm) if you want to visit off-season. Passenger ferryboats leave from Crisfield and from Point Lookout State Park on Maryland's Western Shore. Or you can bring your own boat.

From Somers Cove Marina in Crisfield, **Smith Island Cruises** (© **410/425-2771;** www.smithislandcruises.com) sails at 12:30pm and docks at the Bayside Inn about 40 minutes later. The boat leaves for Crisfield at 3:45pm. Service runs daily Memorial Day weekend through October 15. Round-trip fare is $25 for adults and $12 for children 3 to 11. Reservations are required.

From Point Lookout, on the Western Shore, the twin-hulled *Chelsea Lane Tyler* makes the 1½-hour trip across the Chesapeake Bay Wednesday through Sunday in summer, plus weekends in September and mid-October. See p. 138 for details.

Another option is **Capt. Otis Ray Taylor** (© **410/968-2428**) who goes to Smith Island year-round. His *Island Belle II* is the mail boat; it leaves Crisfield's City Dock at 12:30pm and departs Ewell at 4pm. Another option is **Terry Laird's** *Captain Jason* (© **410/425-5932** or 422-0620), which leaves from Crisfield for Ewell at 12:30pm and 5pm and returns to Crisfield at 7:30am and 3:30pm.

To get to Tylerton, call **Larry Laird** (© **410/425-4471** or 251-4951), whose *Captain Jason II* goes to both Tylerton and Ewell from Crisfield's City Dock. The boat departs Crisfield at 12:30 and 5pm, and leaves Smith Island at 7:30am and 4pm (3:30pm in winter).

None of these three boats requires reservations. Fare is $25 for a same-day round-trip, $40 on separate days. The *Captain Jason* I and II also take kayaks for a fee.

You can bring your own boat, but check the charts for shallow spots: Smith Island Harbor at Ewell can be 4½ feet at low tide. Water is deeper if you come from Tangier Sound via Big Thorofare. Smith Island Marina is beside the county dock and Bayside Restaurant. The gas dock in Ewell is open Monday through Saturday from 8am to 5pm. (Avoid gassing up in late afternoon, as the watermen use the pumps then.) **Smith Island Marina** (© **410/425-4220**) has transient slips, $1 a foot for overnight, $10 for daytime docking. (It is said that Ernest Hemingway once docked his boat here.)

VISITOR INFORMATION   While you are in Crisfield, stop at the visitor center at 1103 W. Main St. (© **410/968-1543**) or visit the **Tawes Museum** at Somers Cove Marina, 3 Ninth St. (© **410/968-2501**), for information.

Once in Ewell, the island's largest town (pop. 100), visit the **Smith Island Center** ★ (© **410/425-3351**), up Smith Island Road from the Bayside Inn, to get a sense of how the island is laid out, learn a little history, and see exhibits about the island. Admission is $2; from May through October, it's open daily from noon to 4pm.

GETTING AROUND   No cars are permitted on the island. Everything is within walking distance. You can bring your bike on the ferry or rent a bike or a golf cart next to the Bayside Inn.

ORIENTATION   **Ewell** is the largest town. It's where most cruise boats dock and has most of the island's seafood-packing houses. **Rhodes Point,** a mile south of Ewell and the island's center for boat repair, was once called Rogues Point because of pirates who stopped here. A marshy place, it's reachable via a wooden bridge from Smith Island or March roads. **Tylerton** may be the most remote place in Maryland, accessible by only one boat. The state's last one-room school was here until it closed in 1996.

Where to Stay & Dine

Ewell has two major restaurants. **Bayside Inn** (© 410/425-2771), with its white siding and red roof, is the first spot most visitors see. Food is hearty and served family style. For my money, the best crab cakes come from **Ruke's Seafood Deck** (© 410/425-2311), located down the road in a shabby brown building. If you don't want to eat with a crowd, bypass the restaurants and pop into **Harbor Side Groceries** (© 410/968-9090) for a snack or carryout. In Tylerton, the only place to eat is the **Drum Point Market** (© 410/425-2108). These places are all open daily in season, but may close from 3 to 6pm.

B&Bs in Ewell and Tylerton offer the only overnight accommodations.

Ewell Tide Bed & Breakfast This 100-year-old country house offers three simple but comfortable rooms. A first-floor room has an en suite bathroom. Upstairs, a room with two double beds has great water views.

20926 Tyler Rd., Ewell, MD 21824. © 888/699-2141 or 410/425-2141. www.smithisland.net. 3 units, 2 with shared bathroom. $55–$105 double. 25% discount off-season. Rates include hot breakfast. Rollaway beds available for small charge. MC, V. **Amenities:** Bikes; watersports equipment. *In room:* A/C, TV.

Inn of Silent Music Visitors can find respite in this old-fashioned farmhouse surrounded on three sides by water. All bedrooms have water views. The innkeepers pick up guests at the Tylerton dock. Dinner is available for $25 a person. The "green house," a lounge built over the marsh, offers a unique way to get away from it all.

2955 Tylerton Rd., Tylerton, MD 21866. © 410/425-3541. www.innofsilentmusic.com. 3 units. $110–$130 double. Rates include gourmet breakfast. 2-night minimum on weekends. No credit cards. Closed late Nov to mid-Mar. No children 12 and under. **Amenities:** Dinner available; bikes; watersports equipment. *In room:* A/C, fridge.

Susan's on Smith Island Both rooms offer views of the harbor. The Somerset has the better view; the Golden Pond the bigger bed. Dinner can be arranged. Susan will also arrange for excursions and other activities on the island.

20759 Caleb Jones Rd., Ewell. © 410/425-2403. www.susansonsmithisland.com. 2 units. $100–$150 double. Rates include hot breakfast. MC, V. **Amenities:** Dinner available; bikes; watersports equipment. *In room:* A/C.

4 CHESTERTOWN

48 miles NE of Annapolis; 55 miles E of Baltimore; 70 miles NE of Washington, D.C.; 50 miles SW of Wilmington

Chestertown, north of the Bay Bridge, looks terrific for a town her age. Built in 1706 on the Chester River, this was once a thriving seaport. Residents here showed their revolutionary leanings when they tossed English tea into the harbor, just as Boston's patriots did. The sea captains' homes, many built in the mid-1700s, still line Water Street—an elegant sight as you cross the Chester River Bridge. As you cross, look for the yellow reproduction of the schooner *Sultana*. Chestertown also is home to Washington College, known for the Sophie Kerr Prize, a large cash award given to a graduating writing student each year. This picturesque riverside town makes for a good day trip or a leisurely weekend visit.

ESSENTIALS

GETTING THERE   From Easton, take U.S. Route 50 north to Route 213; then follow Route 213 north into Chestertown. From I-95 and U.S. Route 40, take the Elkton exit and follow Route 213 south into Chestertown.

VISITOR INFORMATION   For a map and brochures covering Chestertown and the surrounding area, contact the **Kent County Office of Tourism,** 400 High St., Chestertown (✆ **410/778-0416;** www.kentcounty.com). While in town, stop at the visitor center at 122 N. Cross St. (✆ **410/778-9737**). It's open year-round, Monday through Friday from 9am to 5pm, Saturday and Sunday from 10am to 4pm.

GETTING AROUND   With no public transportation in Chestertown, touring by car or walking through the historic streets are the best ways to see the sights. High Street is Chestertown's main thoroughfare. Stop by the visitor center for brochures on a self-guided driving tour and a walking tour.

SPECIAL EVENTS   On Memorial Day weekend, the town reenacts the tea-tossing from the decks of brigantine *Geddes* at the **Chestertown Tea Party Festival ★★**. On May 23, 1774, after hearing of the closing of the port of Boston, local citizens boarded the British ship in the harbor and tossed its tea overboard. The festival includes boat rides, Colonial costume parades, crafts, buggy rides, and bands. For information, go to www.chestertownteaparty.com. On **First Fridays** of the month, shops and galleries are open until 8pm with special activities.

WHERE TO STAY

Brampton Bed & Breakfast Inn ★★   A curving, tree-lined driveway leads to this Greek Revival plantation house, a mile southwest of town. Built in 1860 and listed on the National Register of Historic Places, it sits on 35 acres of hills and farmland. Guests enjoy the use of two sitting rooms, a wide front porch, and extensive spruce-shaded grounds with lawn furniture. Seven rooms are furnished with authentic period antiques; nine units have fireplaces and five have whirlpool tubs. Three cottages offer space and privacy.

25227 Chestertown Rd. (off Rte. 20), Chestertown, MD 21620. ✆ **866/305-1860** or 410/778-1860. www. bramptoninn.com. 10 units. $169–$269 double; $219–$399 cottage. Rates include full breakfast and afternoon tea. 2- or 3-night minimum stay required on weekends and some holidays. AE, DISC, MC, V. Pets accepted in Russell Cottage. *In room:* A/C, TV w/VCR or DVD, hair dryer.

The Imperial Hotel ★★   With a fanciful gingerbread-trimmed triple-porch facade, this three-story brick building is a focal point along the main street of Chestertown. Inside you'll find a restaurant, parlor, and lounge/bar, with a courtyard garden in back. Guest rooms are furnished with brass beds and period antiques. The third-floor suite has a private porch overlooking High Street. The Carriage House Suite offers three bedrooms and a porch overlooking the river.

208 High St., Chestertown, MD 21620. ✆ **410/778-5000.** Fax 410/778-9662. www.imperialchestertown. com. 13 units. $75–$160 double; $150–$250 suite. Rates include continental breakfast. 2-night minimum stay required on weekends in high season. AE, MC, V. No children 12 and under. **Amenities:** Restaurant (see "Where to Dine"); bar. *In room:* A/C, TV, hair dryer (on request).

The Inn at Mitchell House If you're looking for a quiet old-world retreat surrounded by remote farmland and habitats for birds, migrating geese, white-tailed deer, and red fox, try this three-story 1743 manor house with a screened-in porch. Nestled on 10 acres overlooking Stoneybrook Pond, it sits midway between Chestertown and Rock Hall off routes 21 and 445. If you come by boat, they'll pick you up at the Tolchester Marina. Guest rooms are furnished with four-poster beds, hooked rugs, and antiques; most have a fireplace or sitting area. The "Stone's Throw Cottage" offers a bedroom, bathroom, and sitting area with fireplace and kitchen.

8796 Maryland Pkwy., Chestertown, MD 21620. © 410/778-6500. www.innatmitchellhouse.com. 6 units. $109–$149 double; $239 cottage. Rates include full country breakfast. 2-night minimum stay required on most weekends. MC, V. **Amenities:** Video library. In room: A/C, TV/VCR.

Lauretum Bed & Breakfast Inn Crowning a 6-acre spot on a shady knoll outside of town, this three-story 1870 Queen Anne Victorian (listed on the National Register of Historic Places) was named Lauretum ("laurel grove" in Latin) by its first owner, Harrison Vickers. The inn has a formal parlor with fireplace, reading room, screened porch, and sitting room. Hammocks hang under the trees. Bedrooms are bright and large; the third floor has two suites.

954 High St. (Rte. 20), Chestertown, MD 21620. © 800/742-3236. www.lauretuminn.com. 5 units. $130–$140 double; $160 suite. Rates include continental breakfast. 2-night minimum stay required on weekends in high season. AE, DISC, MC, V. **Amenities:** Video library; bikes. In room: A/C, TV/VCR, hair dryer, free Wi-Fi.

The White Swan Tavern ★★ (Finds) Washington may have only had a drink at this tavern, but now you can sleep here. This 1730 inn has six comfortable Colonial guest rooms. You can choose the former kitchen, which dates to 1706, and features brick floors and an open-beam ceiling. The Thomas Peacock Room has luxurious furnishings and a garden view. A two-room suite on the first floor is so plush you may never leave. The Bittersweet Guest Suites, two apartments next door, each sleep three. Even if you don't stay here, stop for afternoon tea, served from 3 to 5pm, for a civilized break in the day.

231 High St., Chestertown, MD 21620. © 410/778-2300. www.whiteswantavern.com. 6 units. $150–$190 double; $220–$250 suite. Rates include continental breakfast and afternoon tea. MC, V. No children 12 and under. **Amenities:** Wi-Fi. In room: A/C, fridge.

Widow's Walk Inn In the middle of all that Colonial grandeur sits this Victorian lady, an 1877 beauty with five guest rooms, all with king- or queen-size beds. A first-floor room with private bathroom is spacious, with big windows and fireplace. Another, with a private bathroom, has a claw-foot tub original to the house.

402 High St., Chestertown, MD 21620. © 888/778-6455 or 410/778-6455. www.chestertown.com/widow. 5 units, 2 with shared bathroom. $90–$160 double. Rates include continental breakfast. MC, V. **Amenities:** Fridge; TV in parlor. In room: A/C.

WHERE TO DINE

Blue Heron Cafe AMERICAN Two cheerful rooms in a low building on a side street offer diners a quiet retreat where they can find a glass of wine, a crab cake with lemon *beurre blanc*, or even veal sweetbreads. For 10 years, this quiet cafe has also been serving seafood dishes such as oyster fritters and crab frittata, and American favorites such as rack of lamb and turkey potpie. Since it's located a street off the main drag, we'll join the locals and keep this our little secret.

236 Cannon St. © 410/778-0188. Dinner reservations recommended on weekends. Main courses $12–$27 dinner. AE, DISC, MC, V. Mon–Sat 5–8:30pm.

The Front Room ★★ AMERICAN   This restaurant at the Imperial Hotel offers fine
cuisine and an elegant ambience in two intimate dining rooms and on the patio in summer. The menu changes seasonally, but house favorites include fresh fish and beef, all
accompanied by seasonal vegetables. When it's in season, the rockfish is delectable.
Brunch on Saturday and Sunday offers eggs Benedict, softshell crabs or oysters (depending on the season), and sandwiches.

208 High St. ⓒ **410/778-5000.** www.imperialchestertown.com. Reservations recommended. Main
courses $8–$17 lunch, $17–$32 dinner. AE, MC, V. Mon 11:30am–3pm and 4–8pm; Tues–Fri 11:30am–
3pm and 4–9pm; Sat 9am–3pm and 4–9pm; Sun 9am–3pm and 4–8pm.

WHAT TO SEE & DO

Take a walk down the shady streets of Chestertown. **High Street,** the main downtown
thoroughfare, takes visitors past little shops, restaurants, and inns down to the river and
the 1740s Custom House. **Water Street** is lined with the brick homes built by shipbuild-
ers, lawyers, and merchants. In midtown is the **Courthouse,** on Cross Street, the site of
a 1706 court and jail.

Behind the courthouse is the **Geddes Piper House**★, 101 Church Alley (ⓒ **410/778-
3499;** www.kentcountyhistory.org/geddes.php), home of the Kent County Historical
Society and a delightful small-town museum. The house, open Saturday and Sunday
from 1 to 4pm, is a tall 1784 three-story charmer built by James Piper. Wander through
the rooms to see fans, quilts, clothing, and toys from the 1880s.

How big are the trees in this old town? A giant American basswood, the state cham-
pion with a circumference of almost 17 feet and height of 108 feet, is on High Street,
about a block from the river. For more foliage, check out the **Virginia Gent Decker
Arboretum** at Washington College (ⓒ **800/422-1782,** ext. 7726; www.arboretum.
washcoll.edu). A wide variety of trees—from Japanese pagoda to American lindens—
grow around these historic college buildings.

About halfway between Chestertown and Rock Hall is **St. Paul's Church,** off Route
20, erected in 1713 and one of Maryland's oldest churches in continuous use. It's open
daily from 9am to 5pm; donations are welcome. The church served as a barracks for
British soldiers during the War of 1812. Actress Tallulah Bankhead is buried in the
church cemetery.

OUTDOOR ACTIVITIES

Just south of Rock Hall, **Eastern Neck National Wildlife Refuge,** 1730 Eastern Neck
Rd. (ⓒ **410/639-7056;** www.fws.gov/northeast/easternneck), is well known to nature
lovers, who flock to see migrating waterfowl all winter and the arrival of butterflies heading to South America in August and September. Like Blackwater National Wildlife
Refuge near Cambridge, this 2,286-acre wooded island, a "globally significant birding
area," is a winter haven for migratory birds, including Canada geese and tundra swan. A
water trail circles the island. Waterfowl Watch, held in mid-December, takes visitors on
guided tours of areas that are normally closed. The refuge has 6 miles of walking trails,
an accessible boardwalk, and an accessible trail with platform. There's no entry fee.

BIKING   Rent a bike for $6 an hour or $30 a day from **Bikework,** 208 S. Cross St.
(ⓒ **410/778-6940**). Discounts for multiday rentals are available. The shop also does
bike repairs and sells kayaks.

BOATING   If the *Sultana* (ⓒ **410/778-5954;** www.schoonersultana.org), a reproduction
1768 schooner, is in town, call or check the website for a schedule of cruises. Two-hour

cruises cost about $30, $15 for children 12 and under. All-day sails are $50. Reservations are recommended.

PICNICKING   Go down Water Street to find Wilmer Park, a wide-open waterfront park with gazebos, shade trees, and picnic tables.

SHOPPING

High, Cross and Cannon streets are lined with shops. Most stores are open Tuesday through Saturday from 9 or 10am to 5pm. Many have Sunday afternoon hours, too.

Village House, 103 S. Cross St. (© **410/788-5766**), stocks eye-catching wares for the home, including lamps, pillows, and knickknacks.

Twigs and Teacups, 111 S. Cross St. (© **410/778-1708**), carries a huge assortment of gifts, including stationery, soaps, toys, joke items, and teacups. Have a cup of tea and a bite to eat across the street at **Play It Again Sam,** 108 S. Cross St. (© **410/778-2688**).

Robert Ortiz Studio, 207 S. Cross St. (© **410/810-1400;** www.ortizstudios.com), sells the craftsman's high-end Shaker and Japanese-inspired furniture in a little showroom by the workshop.

The **Compleat Bookseller,** 301 High St. (© **410/778-1480**), stocks everything from classics to bestsellers, plus *Chesapeake* and other Eastern Shore favorites.

The **Artists Gallery,** 239 High St. (© **410/778-2425**), displays contemporary prints, clocks, lamps, jewelry, and accessories.

CHESTERTOWN AFTER DARK

The restored **Prince Theatre,** 210 High St. (© **410/810-2060;** www.princetheatre.org), presents classic films, community theater, and live musical performances. Shows for children are frequently on the schedule.

A SIDE TRIP TO ROCK HALL ★

This sleepy little fishing village was once a major crossroads: In Colonial times, travelers had to stop here on their way to Philadelphia. George Washington, Thomas Jefferson, and James Madison all really did sleep here. Now Rock Hall, on a peninsula between the Chesapeake and Swan Creek, is better known for its marinas, fishing charters, and some good restaurants. Water's everywhere, so pleasure boaters consider this a good destination for dinner. It's an enjoyable day trip, too.

To get here, follow Route 20 west out of Chestertown, about 15 miles away. If you come by boat and want to go into town—or if you just want to stay out of your car—get on the **Rock Hall Trolley** (© **866/RHTROLY** [748-7659]; www.rockhalltrolleys.com). It runs Friday evening and all day Saturday and Sunday between downtown and the various marinas, including Tolchester. In summer, the trolley runs every day. Call to arrange pickup. All-day fares are $3 for adults, $1 for children. The round-trip to Chestertown is $5 for adults, $3 for children.

Where to Stay

Inn at Huntingfield Creek ★★★ Lucky Rock Hall: Two of the state's finest bed-and-breakfasts are located here. This is one of them. (See the Osprey Point Inn below for the other.) The property, 70 acres of soybean, sunflower, and lavender fields, fronts the peaceful undeveloped creek. From the dock watch the sun set and the lights come on over Baltimore across the Chesapeake Bay. Bedrooms, which have private bathrooms, are spacious, with king-size beds. There's a saltwater pool just beyond the kitchen garden. Three cottages behind the main house offer more privacy with sitting rooms with pullout couches, TVs, two-sided fireplaces, and separate bedrooms with king-size beds. These are also kid- and pet-friendly. Three lovable dogs will greet you when you arrive.

4928 Eastern Neck Rd., Rock Hall, MD 21661. ℂ **410/639-7779.** www.huntingfield.com. 5 rooms, 3 cottages. $139–$249 double. Rates include gourmet breakfast. DISC, MC, V. **Amenities:** Pool; dock; gardens. *In room:* A/C, hair dryer.

Osprey Point Inn ★★★ One of the loveliest inns on the Eastern Shore, this place has the charm of a waterfront Colonial home and the space and necessities required by modern travelers. Designed to look vintage, it's less than 20 years old. There are high ceilings, fireplaces, and lots of windows. Each bedroom has its own ambience: Bolero has a fireplace and window seats overlooking the water, while the waterfront Escapade suite has a whirlpool tub in its black-marble bathroom. Five striking new units, most with water views, have been added at nearby Gratitude Marina.

20786 Rock Hall Ave., Rock Hall, MD 21661. ℂ **410/639-2194.** www.ospreypoint.com. 20 units. $125–$250 double. Rates include continental breakfast. DISC, MC, V. **Amenities:** Restaurant (see "Where to Dine," below); bar; bikes; children's play area; 160-slip marina; pool. *In room:* A/C, TV, hair dryer.

Tallullah's An old apartment building on Rock Hall's Main Street has been turned into this simple but comfortable hotel. Rooms are furnished in a retro style, each with some reference to the town's famous resident Tallulah Bankhead. All have galley kitchens, private bathrooms, and access to a shady deck. Three rooms can be combined into a suite. A two-bedroom cottage offers views of Rock Hall's tiny bayfront beach.

5750 Main St., Rock Hall, MD 21661. ℂ **410/639-2596.** 5 units and beach cottage. $125–$145 double; $250 cottage. AE, MC, V. **Amenities:** High-speed Internet. *In room:* A/C, TV, hair dryer (on request).

Where to Dine

Bay Wolf AUSTRIAN/SEAFOOD The owners here share their Austrian cuisine— Wiener schnitzel, Black Forest cake, and the like—as well as traditional Eastern Shore fare on the daily menu. Salads, soups, and the usual sandwiches (including a $10 crab cake) are featured at lunch. At dinner, you're just going to have to decide between roast pork napped in a rich brown gravy with a caraway seeded dumpling and sauerkraut, and a perfectly seasoned golden-brown crab cake. The setting is more Bavarian than Eastern Shore, with watercolors of Salzburg and the Alps and stained-glass windows. There's also a bar and sidewalk dining in summer.

Rock Hall Ave. ℂ **410/639-2000.** Reservations recommended on summer weekends. Main courses $5–$8 lunch, $17–$19 dinner. AE, DISC, MC, V. Daily noon–9pm. Closed Sun in winter.

Java Rock COFFEE This little slice of the 21st century serves coffee drinks, wireless Internet service, and a small collection of gourmet foods perfect for a picnic or stocking the boat's pantry. There's a tempting assortment of bagels, pastries, soups, and sandwiches. Eat in the airy little dining room or out on the deck, find a spot in the wireless nook, or take your goodies to go.

Sharp and Main sts. ℂ **410/639-9909.** Reservations not accepted. Coffee and pastry $1.30–$6.50. AE, DISC, MC, V. Sun–Fri 7am–5pm; Sat 7am–7pm.

Osprey Point Restaurant AMERICAN In a small but elegant Colonial-style dining room, diners have their choice of crab cakes, fresh fish, and maybe duck or lamb, all served with creative sauces and seasonal vegetables. A recent menu offered braised short ribs and pan-seared scallops. For all the formal elegance of the setting and the food, this is a place to relax and enjoy. Brunch is served on Sundays.

At the Osprey Point Inn, 20786 Rock Hall Ave. ℂ **410/639-2194.** www.ospreypoint.com. Reservations recommended. Main courses $25–$34. DISC, MC, V. Summer Wed–Thurs 5–9pm, Fri–Sat 5–9:30pm, Sun 8:30am–3pm; winter Sun 8:30am–3pm, Thurs–Sun 5–9pm. Closed Jan.

Waterman's Crab House Restaurant & Dock Bar ★ SEAFOOD   The dining room is a nice enough place for cracking steamed crabs, but the deck is made for it. Water views, bay breezes, and trays filled with the little gems make a picnic table the perfect dining spot. Waterman's has earned its reputation for good fresh seafood, seafood pasta, and prime rib. Save room for an ice-cream sundae or adult ice-cream drink. There's music on weekends in warm weather. Boat docking available.

Rock Hall Harbor, end of Sharp St. ℂ **410/639-2261.** www.watermanscrabhouse.com. Reservations recommended on weekends. Main courses $2.50–$13 lunch, $9–$25 dinner. AE, DISC, MC, V. Sun–Thurs 11am–8:30pm; Fri–Sat 11am–9:30pm.

What to See & Do

Several evenings a month, the **Mainstay** on Main Street (ℂ **410/639-9133;** www.main stayrockhall.org) presents a wide assortment of acts for $10 to $25 a ticket. It's small, with 120 seats, but it gets big acts, including the Preservation Hall Jazz Band and Bonnie Rideout, and plenty of local musicians. Buy tickets in cash at the door.

For such a small town, Rock Hall also has three museums, all with a focus on local history. **Tolchester Beach Revisited** ★, Main and Sharp streets (ℂ **410/778-5347;** www.rockhallmd.com/tolchester), is a two-room museum at the end of the Oyster Court shopping area. Anyone who has ever taken the ferry to the Eastern Shore beaches or heard stories from a grandparent will appreciate this collection of memorabilia, photos, and trinkets—all given by people who remember Tolchester Beach, the Ocean City of its day. From the 19th century until construction of the first Bay Bridge, thousands of people escaped the city heat by heading to Tolchester's beach, amusement-park rides, and hotel. The museum is free and open March through December Saturday and Sunday from 11am to 3pm, and by appointment.

The **Waterman's Museum,** Haven Harbour Marina, 20880 Rock Hall Ave. (ℂ **410/ 778-6697;** www.havenharbour.com/hhwatmus.htm), focuses on the people who harvest the bay. The reproduction shanty house has three rooms of photographs, carvings, and tools of the trade. There's free admission, and it's open daily from 10am to 5pm. Get the key from the shop at nearby Haven Harbour Marina.

The **Rock Hall Museum,** located in the Municipal Museum at 5585 Main St. (ℂ **410/639-7611;** www.rockhallmd.com/museum), features the usual small-town exhibits: boat models, old tools, a charming sleigh, and photos of all the Chesapeake Bay ferries. What makes it worthwhile is a tiny vignette in the corner, a creative display of a duck-decoy carver's studio. Admission is free, and it's open Saturday, Sunday 11am to 3pm, and by appointment.

Outdoor Activities

BIKING   This is easy biking territory, flat and quiet. Rent a bike from **Haven Harbour Marina** (ℂ **800/506-6697** or 410/778-6697; www.havenharbour.com).

BOATING   **Blue Crab Chesapeake Charters** (ℂ **410/708-1803;** www.bluecrab charters.com) has room for six on its 36-foot *Crab Imperial.* The 90-minute sail costs $50 a person; overnight charters start at $300. The 48-foot *Jennifer Ann II* (ℂ **410/705-9751** or 639-7063; www.fishfearus.com) takes six fishermen out twice a day. **Haven Harbour Marina** (ℂ **800/506-6697** or 410/778-6697; www.havenharbour.com) has slips that can accommodate visiting boats of up to 50 feet as well. Don't know the difference between tack and jibe? Learn to sail at the **Maryland School of Sailing & Seamanship** (© **410/639-7030;** www.mdschool.com). It offers 4-day live-aboard cruises for both new and experienced sailors. Rock Hall Yacht Club hosts **Friday Night Sailing Races** on the 2nd and 4th Fridays between May and August; see **www.rockhallyachtclub.org** for details.

If you like your boats smaller, see **Chester River Kayak Adventures,** 5758 Main St. (© **410/639-2001;** www.crkayakadventures.com), for kayak rentals and tours.

Shopping

Barely a block of downtown is devoted to shops. Most are open only on weekends but that is beginning to change. The shops of **Oyster Court** (© **410/708-0057**), just off Main Street, are open 9am to 5pm Wednesday through Sunday. Stop by for all kinds of gifts from gardening treasures to luscious locally made soaps. **Smilin' Jake's,** at 5745 Main St. (© **410/639-7280**), sells Hawaiian-inspired garb and is open daily. If you see something you like in **Tallullah's** window (Murano glass jewelry and gifts, mostly), call © **410/639-2596** and the innkeepers will open the shop at 5750 Main St. for you. For ice cream, stop by the 1930s-era soda counter at **Durding's Store,** at Main and Sharp streets (© **410/778-7957**). Before going home, visit **Miss Virginia's Crabcakes,** 5793 Kent St. (© **410/639-7871**), for some tasty souvenirs.

5 CHESAPEAKE CITY

75 miles NE of Annapolis; 54 miles NE of Baltimore; 40 miles SW of Wilmington; 25 miles NE of Chestertown

Chesapeake City, on the Chesapeake & Delaware Canal, remains a crossroads for the maritime traffic using the canal every day. Technically an Eastern Shore town, it is easily accessible via I-95, and thus makes an easier Eastern Shore visit than some of the other places discussed in this chapter.

The first thing you notice when driving over the 800-foot Chesapeake & Delaware (C&D) Canal Bridge is the view of the canal. Both private boats and commercial ships use this connection between the Chesapeake Bay and Delaware River. Construction of the canal brought prosperity to this town, which changed its name from the Village of Bohemia to Chesapeake City in 1839. Its inhabitants built beautiful homes, most of which still survive. Several restored Victorians now house shops and B&Bs. Boaters find it a great destination or place to stop on a cruise along the Inland Waterway.

ESSENTIALS

GETTING THERE   From Easton and other points south, take Route 301 northeast to Route 213, which leads into Chesapeake City. From Baltimore, take I-95 to the Elkton exit (Rte. 279); follow Route 213 south. Or sail into town via the canal.

VISITOR INFORMATION   For brochures, contact the **Cecil County Tourism Office,** 1 Seahawk Dr., North East (© **800/232-4595** or 410/996-6292; www.seececil.org).

GETTING AROUND   Although downtown Chesapeake City lends itself to walking, the best way to see the surrounding sights is by **car.** There is also a free seasonal passenger **ferry** service, operated by the *Miss Clare,* connecting the north and south sides of the canal. It runs Wednesday through Sunday in summer, weekends only in spring and fall. The schedule is posted on a kiosk in Pell Gardens.

ORIENTATION   The C&D Canal divides the city into north and south sides. The main commercial and historic area is on the south side of the canal. South Chesapeake City is pedestrian-friendly; its one main street, Bohemia Avenue, has stores and businesses. Look for free walking and shopping brochures in any shop. Free parking areas under the bridge and farther in town are clearly marked.

WHERE TO STAY

The Blue Max Inn ★   Built in 1844, this house was once occupied by author Jack Hunter while writing his book *The Blue Max*. The large bedrooms are decorated in period style. Thoughtful touches include chocolates, flowers, and complimentary beverages. Guests can enjoy a cozy parlor (with fireplace), dining room, gazebo, and, best of all, first- and second-floor porches overlooking the historic district.

300 Bohemia Ave., Chesapeake City, MD 21915. (C) **877/725-8362** or 410/885-2781. Fax 410/885-2809. www.bluemaxinn.com. 9 units. $105–$250 double. Rates include full breakfast and afternoon tea. 2-night minimum stay required on some weekends and holidays. AE, DISC, MC, V. No children 10 and under. **Amenities:** Bikes; fitness room; Jacuzzi. *In room:* A/C, TV/VCR, CD player, hair dryer, free Wi-Fi.

Inn at the Canal ★   The high painted ceilings in the public areas of this inn will remind visitors of the grand old post–Civil War days. Though the guest rooms are smaller, that style continues all the way up to the third-floor suite. Decorated with antiques, soft colors, and embroidered bedding, the 1868 house is welcoming and comfortable. Windows look out over the Back River Basin. The Upper Bay Suite fills the third floor with its own kitchenette, sitting area with a trundle daybed, and tiny water-view deck. The Greenbriar Point Room, though smaller, still has a good-size sitting area and windows on two sides. The innkeepers run an antiques store, **Inntiques,** in the old milking room of the house.

104 Bohemia Ave. (P.O. Box 187), Chesapeake City, MD 21915. (C) **410/885-5995.** www.innatthecanal. com. 7 units. $95–$225 double. Rates include breakfast and afternoon refreshments. 2-night minimum stay required on weekends in high season. AE, DC, DISC, MC, V. *In room:* A/C, TV (most w/VCR or DVD player), hair dryer, high-speed Internet.

WHERE TO DINE

Bayard House ★★★ AMERICAN   This 1780s house overlooking the canal has two cozy dining rooms, but who could resist the water views from the enclosed porch or brick patio? Then there's the food, artfully presented and creatively prepared. Don't miss the tournedos Baltimore: twin petite filets topped with crab cake and lobster cake, napped in Madeira cream and seafood champagne. Other options include oysters in season (prepared a number of unexpected ways), steak, and lollipop lamb chops. Lunchtime brings salads, a $10 burger, and smaller portions of the dinner entrees.

11 Bohemia Ave. (C) **887/582-4049** or 410/885-5040. www.bayardhouse.com. Reservations recommended for dinner. Main courses $10–$18 lunch, $21–$34 dinner. AE, DC, DISC, MC, V. Daily 11:30am–3pm and 4:30–9pm.

Chesapeake Inn Restaurant & Marina SEAFOOD   Walk or sail to this modern building with its own boat slips for fine or casual dining, all with waterfront views. The deck's light-fare menu (from appetizers to sandwiches to lobster pizza) and live entertainment are offered daily, with a weekend piano bar in winter. The upper-level dining room features a well-rounded wine list and a fine-dining menu of seafood, steak, veal, chicken, and pasta. From the buttery bisque to the crab cakes, crab dishes are hearty and delicious. Sunday brunch is served 10am to 2pm.

Light fare menu $9–$17; fine-dining menu $16–$28. AE, DC, DISC, MC, V. Mon–Thurs 11am–10pm; Fri–Sat 11am–11pm; Sun 10am–10pm. Deck May–Oct Mon–Thurs noon–10pm, Fri–Sat noon–1am; Nov–Apr Fri–Sun noon–1am.

WHAT TO SEE & DO

On the waterfront, the **C&D Canal Museum** ★, 815 Bethel Rd., at Second Street (© **410/885-5622**), tells the story of the giant waterway running through town. The 1829 pump house (now the museum) features the largest water wheel built in the U.S. The admission is free; it's open Monday through Friday from 9am to 4pm.

At the water's edge is **Pell Gardens,** a grassy park with a gazebo next to the town wharf. It's a good place to enjoy an ice-cream cone from the **Canal Creamery,** 9 Bohemia Ave. (© **410/885-3314**), across the street (May–Oct).

Take a cruise aboard the *Miss Clare* (© **410/885-5088**), captained by a fifth-generation resident who has plenty of stories and historical photos to share. Cruises are scheduled April through October on Saturday and Sunday.

SHOPPING

Shopping is one of the main attractions in Chesapeake City; most stores are open from 10am until 9 or 10pm on Friday and Saturday, and until 5pm on Sunday. Winter hours tend to be more limited.

Bohemia Avenue, the major thoroughfare, begins at the waterfront with a collection of galleries offering original and local art, as well as limited-edition prints. The oldest of these, **Firefly Glass Studio,** 1709 Bohemia Ave. (© **410/504-9357**), stocks stained glass in an old bank building.

Back Creek General Store, 100 Bohemia Ave. (© **410/885-5377**), is housed in an 1861 building that's packed with gifts and a large collection of Sheila and Byers Choice items, including ones of Chesapeake City. Artist and printmaker Neil Snodgrass sells his own works at **Neil's Artwork,** 226 George St. (© **410/885-5094**). His shop is open April through December.

9

Frederick & the Civil War Crossroads

Frederick has long been an important crossroads. With the building of the National Pike in the 1700s, it was linked with the port city of Baltimore and became a stop on the road west. Young Francis Scott Key grew up and practiced law in Frederick before writing the poem that would become our national anthem. When Elizabeth Ann Seton sought a place for her new community of religious women, she found a home just north of the city in Emmitsburg.

During the Civil War, thousands of wounded soldiers arrived in Frederick to recover. The first came in August 1862, following the Battle of South Mountain. More arrived the next month after the battle at Antietam, the bloodiest day of battle during the Civil War. So many wounded arrived, they outnumbered Frederick's own citizens.

In 1862, Barbara Fritchie confronted General Stonewall Jackson and was immortalized in poetry: "'Shoot if you must this old gray head; but spare your country's flag,' she said."

Two years later, Confederate general Jubal Early demanded ransom that saved the town from destruction. Battles at Harpers Ferry and Gettysburg brought more wounded before the Battle of the Monocacy was waged to the southeast.

Reminders of these sad days remain in the area's historic sites, museums, and the battlefields of **Antietam, Gettysburg, Harpers Ferry,** and **Monocacy,** maintained by the National Park Service.

Today Frederick is Maryland's third-largest city, its suburbs extending down toward Washington, D.C. Downtown is a popular spot for shopping and dining, while outside town are rolling fields and orchards, the foothills of the Catoctin Mountains, and green space for picnicking and hiking.

---

1 FREDERICK ★

---

46 miles W of Baltimore; 45 miles NW of Washington, D.C.; 33 miles S of Gettysburg

Once a largely agricultural community, Frederick is now Maryland's third-largest city (behind Baltimore and Rockville, a D.C. suburb). Though its downtown district is surrounded by housing developments that have given Frederick a population of 59,000, the 33-block historic area maintains its small-town charm. The 18th- and 19th-century buildings and cluster of church spires that make up Frederick's skyline are still a main attraction. Antiques and crafts shops dominate the shopping area, and there's a vibrant restaurant and bar scene. Like a scenic drive? Frederick lies at the junction of two national scenic byways, the Historic National Road (alternate U.S. 40) and the Catoctin Mountain Scenic Byway (Rte. 15). North and west of the city, the agricultural community still thrives, with produce stands popping up among the fields.

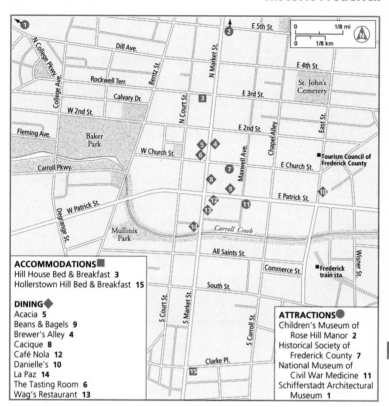

ACCOMMODATIONS ■
Hill House Bed & Breakfast **3**
Hollerstown Hill Bed & Breakfast **15**

DINING ◆
Acacia **5**
Beans & Bagels **9**
Brewer's Alley **4**
Cacique **8**
Café Nola **12**
Danielle's **10**
La Paz **14**
The Tasting Room **6**
Wag's Restaurant **13**

ATTRACTIONS ●
Children's Museum of Rose Hill Manor **2**
Historical Society of Frederick County **7**
National Museum of Civil War Medicine **11**
Schifferstadt Architectural Museum **1**

ESSENTIALS

GETTING THERE From Washington, D.C., take I-270 to Frederick, where it becomes U.S. 15 and continues north to Gettysburg. From Baltimore, take I-70 west. From points west, take I-68 east to I-70. To get to the historic district, take Route 15 to the Rosemont Avenue exit to Second Street, across the street from the exit ramp.

Greyhound (© 800/231-2222; www.greyhound.com) operates daily **bus** service to Frederick to the MARC train station, 100 S. East St. (© 301/663-3311).

The MTA's **MARC** train runs between Frederick and Washington, D.C., with service Monday through Friday. Call © 866/RIDE-MTA (743-3682) or go to **www.mta maryland.com** for schedule and fare information.

VISITOR INFORMATION The **Tourism Council of Frederick County** operates a visitor center at 151 S. East St. (opening in early 2010; © 800/999-3613 or 301/600-2888; www.fredericktourism.org). This office supplies maps, brochures, and listings of accommodations and restaurants, and conducts walking tours of the historic district. The *African American Heritage Sites* brochure outlines historic African-American sites—churches, homes, and slave quarters in Frederick and the surrounding county. Though some buildings are gone, signs mark the locations.

GETTING AROUND   The best way to get around Frederick is by **car**—that is, when you're not walking through the historic district. Parking is cheap and sometimes free: At downtown meters and garages, Monday through Friday, it's $7; Saturday $1; and Sunday it's free. Parking garages are located at 17 E. Church St., 44 E. Patrick St., and 2 S. Court St. Stop at the visitor center to have your Church Street garage ticket validated for up to 3 hours of free parking. If you park in a residential district, check for the signs that restrict nonresident parking.

Frederick County operates **TransIT** (© **301/694-2065;** www.co.frederick.md.us/transit), a **bus** service that connects outlying hotels, malls, and colleges with the historic district and Frederick-area train stations. See the website for maps and schedules.

Special Events   Fall colors are at their peak in mid- to late October—which is also the peak time for special events. Thurmont's **Catoctin Colorfest** (© **301/271-7533;** www.colorfest.org), a crafts show of enormous proportions, is held in mid-October. **First Saturday Gallery Walks** are held monthly in Frederick. Shops, galleries, and restaurants stay open until 9pm. Call © **301/698-8118** for details.

A couple of events mark the anniversaries of Civil War battles. The commemoration of the **Battle of Monocacy,** the "battle that saved Washington," is held the weekend closest to the July 9 anniversary (© **301/662-3515** for information). The **Battle of Antietam** is recalled in September (© **301/432-5124** for information).

WHERE TO STAY

There are B&Bs in the historic district, and charming inns in the countryside. A number of chain hotels are along the city's edges, many north on Route 15.

Hampton Inn Frederick   Located 2 miles south of downtown Frederick, this modern six-story hotel is standard Hampton style, newly updated in 2007. What makes it different is the bar housed in a lighthouse replica nestled beside an artificial lake and connected by footbridge to the hotel. Many guest rooms overlook the lake.

5311 Buckeystown Pike, Frederick, MD 21704 (take exit 31B off I-270 at Rte. 85). © **800/HAMPTON** (426-7866) or 301/698-2500. Fax 301/695-8735. http://hamptoninn.hilton.com. 160 units. $109–$135 double. Rates include hot breakfast. AE, DC, DISC, MC, V. Pets accepted for a fee. **Amenities:** Restaurant; fitness center; outdoor pool. *In room:* A/C, TV w/pay movies, hair dryer, Wi-Fi (fee).

Hill House Bed & Breakfast   This 1870s town house is in the historic district—just off the beaten track to be quiet, but within walking distance to everything. Accommodations are cheery and comfortable; two units have TVs. The canopy bed in the Victorian Room takes up most of the space, but luckily the bathroom is enormous. The Mexican Room has twin beds in a gaily painted setting, plus a huge plant-filled bathroom with chaise longue and access to the balcony. The Chesapeake Room also has balcony access. The Steeple Suite has a full kitchen and big windows.

12 W. Third St., Frederick, MD 21705. © **301/682-4111.** www.hillhousefrederick.com. 4 units. $105–$125 double; $175 suite. Rates include full breakfast. MC, V. *In room:* CD player, hair dryer, Wi-Fi (fee).

Holiday Inn Frederick (**Kids**)   This modern two-story hotel is a popular conference center, its public areas often bustling with activity. However, except for the handful of guest rooms overlooking the courtyard or pool, most are separated from common areas and are relatively quiet. Its indoor pool, miniature golf course, and game tables make it a great place for kids. Expect standard Holiday Inn size and decor. The hotel is adjacent to the Francis Scott Key Mall, and it's a short drive from the historic district.

5400 Holiday Dr. (I-270 at Rte. 85), Frederick, MD 21703. ⓒ **800/868-0094** or 301/694-7500. Fax 301/694-0589. www.hifrederick.com. 155 units. $139–$169 double. Children 18 and under stay free in parent's room; children 12 and under eat free. AE, DC, DISC, MC, V. Pets accepted for a fee. **Amenities:** Restaurant; lounge; fitness center; indoor pool; recreation area w/indoor miniature golf course, table tennis, and foosball; sauna; whirlpool. *In room:* A/C, TV/VCR w/pay movies, fridge and microwave in some rooms, hair dryer, free Wi-Fi.

Hollerstown Hill Bed & Breakfast

This rose-and-gray 1901 Victorian beauty is on a quiet lane at the southern end of the historic district. Guest rooms have small sitting areas and Victorian furnishings (some antiques, some reproductions—but all designed for comfort). One room has twin beds; the Dutro has a king-size bed and huge bathroom; the Cottage Garden room has a balcony nestled in the branches of an old tree. The game room has a pool table and Civil War–soldier chess set.

4 Clarke Place, Frederick, MD 21701. ⓒ **301/228-3630.** www.hollerstownhill.com. 4 units. $135–$145 double. Rates include full breakfast and afternoon tea. AE, MC, V. No children 15 and under. **Amenities:** Sitting area w/TV. *In room:* A/C, TV, free Wi-Fi.

The Inn at Buckeystown ★★

Set in a quiet country village on the Monocacy River, this 1897 mansion is rich in Italianate Victorian details, with a wraparound porch, widow's walk, and ornate trim. The interior boasts antiques, Oriental rugs, chandeliers, and five working fireplaces. Sleeping rooms have varying amenities and unique touches including fireplaces, chandeliers, or Civil War decor. The romantic Victoriana's bed is tucked into the curve of a turret. Third-floor rooms, which have shared bathrooms, can be combined with the spacious game room for a family or bridal party perhaps. Lunch, Sunday brunch, dinner, and high tea are served on Victorian china with period silver and glassware (reservations required for all meals). Check the website for murder-mystery dinners. Guests rave about the food.

3521 Buckeystown Pike (Rte. 85), Buckeystown, MD 21717. ⓒ **800/272-1190** or 301/874-5755. Fax 301/831-1355. www.innatbuckeystown.com. 9 units. $115–$175 double. Rates include breakfast. AE, DISC, MC, V. **Amenities:** Restaurant. *In room:* A/C, TV/VCR in most rooms, hair dryer, free Wi-Fi.

WHERE TO DINE

Get coffee and a bagel at the cozy **Beans & Bagels,** 49 E. Patrick St. (ⓒ **301/620-2165**). **Cafe Nola,** 4 E. Patrick St. (ⓒ **301/694-6652**), serves coffee and breakfast all day, as well as salads, sandwiches, and entrees later in the day.

Acacia Fusion Bistro NEW AMERICAN   Fill up on the $11 plate of Asian-inspired appetizers at lunch or lobster fried rice, a filet, or grilled salmon at dinner. Everything here is enticing. Most entrees have at least a smidge of Asian spiciness, but if your tastes lean more to the West, you'll find sandwiches, soups, salads, and meat or seafood entrees. The dining rooms are refined with white table cloths and warm colors.

129 N. Market St. ⓒ **301/694-3015.** www.acacia129.com. Reservations recommended on Fri–Sat. Main courses $8–$18 lunch, $8–$28 dinner. AE, DC, MC, V. Sun–Thurs 11:30am–10pm; Fri–Sat 11:30am–11:30pm.

Brewer's Alley ★ BREWPUB   Regular pub fare here is consistently good, but the specialty wood-fired pizzas are especially creative—try one topped with barbecued chicken. Beer is brewed on the premises, including the 1634 Ale designed for Maryland's 375th anniversary in 2009. It's a very popular place; on busy weekends, the wait for a table can be long. In warm weather, the sidewalk patio is delightful.

124 N. Market St. ⓒ **301/631-0089.** www.brewers-alley.com. Reservations recommended on Fri–Sat. Main courses $8–$19 lunch, $10–$21 dinner. AE, DC, MC, V. Mon–Thurs 11:30am–11:30pm; Fri–Sat 11:30am–12:30pm; Sun noon–11:30pm.

Cacique Restaurant (**Value**) SPANISH/MEXICAN Diners can sit in one of the low, cozy rooms with white tablecloths and Latino music piped in, or outside on the little sidewalk patio. The Tex-Mex and Spanish favorites include paella, fajitas, and quesadillas, with a side of undeniably fresh *pico de gallo,* sharp with lime and cilantro. The food is good, if not surprising, and the service is as friendly as you'd expect in Frederick.

26 N. Market St. ⓒ **301/695-2756.** www.caciquefrederick.com. Reservations recommended for dinner. Main courses $11–$35. AE, DISC, MC, V. Sun–Thurs 11:30am–10pm; Fri–Sat 11am–11:30pm.

Danielle's ★ AMERICAN/ITALIAN With three settings—a more formal dining room, an outdoor patio, and a casual pub—and one extensive menu filled with Italian dishes and American favorites such as crab cakes and steaks, Danielle's has something for everybody. Danielle's gained its reputation as Tauraso's and the quality has remained consistent. Half orders of pasta are a welcome idea. For lunch, you'll find sandwiches, pastas, and salads. Pizzas made in a wood-burning oven are also featured.

Everedy Sq., 6 N. East St. ⓒ **301/663-6600.** www.taurasos.com. Reservations recommended for dinner on Fri–Sat. Main courses $9–$18 lunch, $13–$26 dinner. AE, DC, DISC, MC, V. Sun 11:30am–9pm; Tues–Thurs 11:30am–10pm; Fri–Sat 11:30am–11pm.

La Paz Mexican Restaurant (**Value**) MEXICAN Two floors of dining rooms, plus a waterfront patio in warm weather, overlook Carroll Creek. The menu offers good Mexican food—fajitas, flautas, and burritos—accompanied by good margaritas. There's also a children's menu.

51 S. Market St. ⓒ **301/694-8980.** www.lapazmex.com. Reservations accepted for parties of 6 or more. Main courses $4–$17. AE, DC, DISC, MC, V. Mon–Thurs 11am–10pm; Fri 11am–11pm; Sat 11:30am–11pm; Sun 3:30–11pm.

The Tasting Room NEW AMERICAN After a day of visiting museums and quaint shops on charming little streets, this minimalist cream-and-black restaurant is a breath of fresh air. Its menu is as up to the minute as the decor, with the trendiest of ingredients, such as salmon cakes, steak salad, or pan-seared ahi tuna at lunch, or fresh fish or chowder at dinner. Choose from the 200-bottle wine list or martini specials.

101 N. Market St. ⓒ **240/379-7772.** www.tastetr.com. Reservations recommended for dinner. Main courses $6–$17 lunch, $21–$38 dinner. AE, DC, DISC, MC, V. Mon–Sat 11am–3pm and 5–10pm (until 11pm Fri–Sat).

Wag's Restaurant (**Finds**) BURGERS This basement bar is the smallest of Frederick's favorite nightspots. People come for burgers. Dripping with Wag's special sauce, they continue to be voted the best in town. There are other equally artery-clogging and wonderful sandwiches, including the Reuben and steak-and-cheese.

24 S. Market St. ⓒ **301/694-8451.** www.eatatwags.com. Reservations not accepted. Main courses $6–$9. AE, DISC, MC, V. Mon–Sat 11am–2am.

WHAT TO SEE & DO

The **Frederick Visitor Center,** located for many years at 19 E. Church St. (ⓒ **301/600-2888;** www.fredericktourism.org), plans to move to 151 S. East Street by early 2010. This is the place to stop for maps, information, and, if you parked in one of the four city garages, validation of your ticket for 3 hours of free parking. Guided walking tours of the historic district depart the visitor center at 1:30pm on Saturdays and Sundays. The cost

is $5.50 for adults, $4.50 for seniors, and $2.50 for children 12 and under. If wineries
or breweries are more your thing, or if you'd like a candlelight ghost tour, the staff can suggest plenty of options. If you love covered bridges, ask for the directions to three in Frederick County. Ghost tour fans, call ✆ **301/668-8922** for one of the Saturday evening tours offered June through November.

Frederick's 33-block historic district was honored in 2005 as a **Great American Main Street** by the National Trust for Historic Preservation. This area features shops, a handful of museums, and lots of good restaurants. Some streets are filled with tiny town houses; others are lined with one mansion after another. And you can't miss the church spires: Not only is Frederick known for them, the town's seal features them. (Look for a pair of ornate gray spires to find the visitor center and a parking garage.)

Kids can let loose at **Carroll Creek Park,** which runs east-west through the historic district between Patrick and Bentz streets. Redevelopment has added new bridges, walkways, water features, and an amphitheater. Cross Bentz Street to get to the playground and picnic tables at Baker Park. You'll find Barbara Fritchie's tiny house in the park on Patrick Street. The house, reconstructed from the original materials, recalls feisty heroine of John Greenleaf Whittier's poem, who it is said waved a flag and said, "Shoot if you must this old gray head, but spare your country's flag." Alas, the house is no longer open to the public.

Keep an eye out for the **"Angels in the Architecture"** ★★★: Local artist William Cochran painted fantastic *trompe l'oeil* angels, birds, and other objects on walls around town. "Earthbound," at the corner of West Church and North Market streets, and the Community Bridge, part of Carroll Creek Park, should not be missed.

Downtown Museums & Historic Sites

Rose Hill Manor Park & Children's Museum ★ Kids   Adults will enjoy seeing the grand architecture and decorative arts of this 1790s manor house. Kids will love looking at old-fashioned toys, trying on bonnets and hats, learning how a spinning wheel works, working a loom themselves, and touching all the labor-saving kitchen gadgets of that era. Also in the 43-acre park are an icehouse, garden, log cabin, blacksmith shop, farm museum, and carriage museum. The lawns invite picnickers to set a spell. The house tour takes about 1½ hours. Lots of events focus on kid's fun.

1611 N. Market St. ✆ **301/694-1650.** www.rosehillmuseum.com. Admission $5 adults, $4 children and seniors. House tours Apr–Oct Mon–Sat 10am–4pm, Sun 1–4pm; Nov Sat 10am–4pm, Sun 1–4pm. No tours Dec–Mar. Park is open daily 8am–4:30pm.

Historical Society of Frederick County ★   Nobody famous lived here, the guides at this 1820s Federal-style house will tell you. But, at various times, it was home to a doctor and his family; it witnessed the Civil War, with Union and Confederate troops passing through the streets just outside; and more than 100 orphaned girls called it home. Look for portraits of Roger B. Taney, chief justice of the U.S. Supreme Court and author of the *Dred Scott* decision, and Francis Scott Key, author of "The Star-Spangled Banner." There's also a library and a formal garden. The Historical Society also operates tours of the **Roger B. Taney House** at 121 S. Bentz St. It is open on Saturday 10am to 4pm and Sunday noon to 4pm. Admission is $3.

24 E. Church St. ✆ **301/663-1188.** www.hsfcinfo.org. Admission $3 adults, free for children 17 and under. Museum Mon–Sat 10am–4pm, Sun 1–4pm; library Mon–Sat 10am–4pm.

National Museum of Civil War Medicine Finds   Using display cases, wall exhibits, and particularly touching life-size dioramas with wax figures and sound effects, this museum brings to life the suffering and healing of the Civil War soldier. Exhibits focus on Civil War medicine from the initial treatment on the battlefield to the hospitals, hospital trains, operating rooms, treatments, and, finally, embalming practices used during that time. One display features Clara Barton and her efforts to bring supplies to soldiers on the battlefields. The building itself is where several thousand dead from the Battle of Antietam were housed and embalmed. The museum also operates Pry House Field Hospital Museum at Antietam Battlefield (p. 200).

48 E. Patrick St. ℂ **800/564-1864** or 301/695-1864. www.civilwarmed.org. Admission $6.50 adults, $6 seniors, $4.50 children 10–16. Mon–Sat 10am–5pm; Sun 11am–5pm. Closed Jan 1, Thanksgiving, Dec 24–25, and Dec 31.

Schifferstadt Architectural Museum Frederick's oldest standing house, one of America's finest examples of German Colonial architecture, is listed on the National Register of Historic Places. Built in 1756 by the Brunner family, who named it for their homeland in Germany, it has stone walls more than 2 feet thick, hand-hewn beams of native oak pinned together with wooden pegs, a vaulted cellar and "wishbone" chimney, and a perfectly preserved five-plate jamb stove—the only one left in the world. Guided tours are given throughout the day. Special events include Oktoberfest and Spirit tours offered Friday evenings by reservation.

1110 Rosemont Ave., on the western edge of town. ℂ **301/663-3885.** www.frederickcountylandmarks foundation.org. Suggested donation $3. Apr to mid-Dec Tues–Sun noon–4pm. Weekend visitors should call ahead to confirm hours. Closed mid-Dec to Mar.

Nearby Military Sites of the Civil War & Earlier

Fort Frederick State Park If you're driving through the area, take a look at this 1756 stone fort. Its primary role in Civil War history was as a post for Union troops, though it faced Confederate raiders once in December 1861. During the French and Indian War, it served as an important supply base for English campaigns; during the Revolutionary War, it was a refuge for settlers and a prison for Hessian and British soldiers. Daily in summer and on weekends in spring and fall, living-history reenactors show visitors about frontier life. The park also has campsites for $15 a night (ℂ **888/432-2267**), two hiking trails through woods and wetlands, and boat rentals. Nearby is the 23-mile Western Maryland Rail Trail along an old train line. The Rails to Trails Conservancy named this one of the top 12 U.S. trails for viewing fall foliage.

11100 Fort Frederick Rd. (40 miles west of Frederick, off I-70), Big Pool. ℂ **301/842-2155.** www.dnr. maryland.gov. Admission $4 adults ($1 discount for Md. residents). Fort exhibits mid-May to mid-Sept daily 9:30am–5:30pm; Apr to mid-May and mid-Sept to mid-Nov Sat–Sun 9:30am–5:30pm. Fort closed mid-Nov to Mar.

Monocacy National Battlefield This stretch of farmland was the site of a little-known but important Civil War encounter, the Battle of the Monocacy. General Jubal Early led 15,000 Confederates against a Union force of 5,800 under General Lew Wallace in July 1864. Though the Confederates won, their forces were so weakened that Union troops at Fort Stevens could push them back from Washington and save the nation's capital from capture. Today, the battlefield remains mostly unchanged. The newly built visitor center has an expanded display of uniforms (even one kids can try on), swords and medals, and an optic-fiber map that relates the battle story. An auto tour is 6 miles round-trip; five walking trails offer historic and scenic vistas. The short Gambrill Mill Trail offers a view of the railroad bridge Union troops were forced to use to retreat.

From May through August, events are scheduled the first weekend of the month; a commemoration of the battle is held on a weekend near July 9.

4801 Urbana Pike, Frederick. (☎) **301/662-3515.** www.nps.gov/mono. Free admission. Daily 8:30am–
5pm. Closed Jan 1, Thanksgiving, and Dec 25. From the north, east, or west, use I-70; take exit 54 and
proceed south on Rte. 355 to the visitor center. From the south, use I-270; take exit 26 and turn left onto
Rte. 80; then turn left onto Rte. 355 north.

SPECTATOR SPORTS & OUTDOOR ACTIVITIES

BASEBALL   The **Frederick Keys** ((☎) **877/8GO-KEYS** [846-5397]; www.frederickkeys.
com), an Orioles farm team and the 2007 Carolina League champions, play at Harry
Grove Stadium, off I-70, from May to early September. General admission is $5 to $11.

BIKING   Bikers and hikers can access the towpath of the **Chesapeake & Ohio (C&O)
Canal** at Point of Rocks, off Route 15 South; Brunswick, Route 79 off Maryland Route
340; or Sandy Hook, left off Route 340, before you cross the Potomac River. The canal
runs along the Potomac for 185 miles from Georgetown to Cumberland. Bicycle bells are
required on the towpath. The **Western Maryland Railway trail,** a 23-mile paved path,
is accessible off I-70 at exit 12, Big Pool.

Nearby, both Antietam National Battlefield and Gettysburg National Military Park are
terrific sites to tour on bike.

Rent a bike at **Wheel Base,** 229 N. Market St., Frederick ((☎) **301/663-9288**). They
sell and service bikes, too. Prices vary.

HIKING   The **Appalachian Trail** (www.appalachiantrail.org) runs along the border of
Frederick and Washington counties, through Washington Monument State Park, South
Mountain State Park, Greenbrier State Park, and Gathland State Park. You can hike the
entire Maryland portion in 3 or 4 days, but any section of it makes a great 1-day excursion.

North of Frederick, off Route 15, **Catoctin Mountain Park** ((☎) **301/663-9388**) and
Cunningham Falls State Park ((☎) **301/271-7574**) offer several miles of easy to strenuous hiking trails. (See section 5, "Serenity & Apples on Route 15," p. 207.)

SHOPPING

If you want antiques, vintage clothing, eye-popping jewelry, handcrafted gifts, or something that's just different, you're going to love Frederick's shopping. The historic district
has plenty of interesting shops, mostly on Patrick, Market, Church, and North East
streets. They're usually open from 10am to 5pm, though many close on Mondays.

ⓘTips   Following the Path of the Civil War

At the visitor center on I-70, ask for one of the **Civil War Trails** maps. With lots of
description, some photos, and a bit of a history lesson, they offer a soldier's view
of the war—only the soldiers walked, whereas visitors can drive in air-conditioned
or heated comfort. Use the maps to find Antietam or Harpers Ferry or Gettysburg, or to take the roads Union or Confederate soldiers traveled. They'll lead you
to some off-the-beaten-track sites of battles, skirmishes, hospitals, or strategic
positions for each army. The map devoted to Antietam includes Harpers Ferry.
The Gettysburg map covers much of the same territory as it describes the movement of the armies north for battle. Visit **www.civilwartrails.org** for more
information.

For **First Saturday Gallery Walks,** shops stay open until 9pm; some offer trunk shows or special merchandise and some serve refreshments.

Everedy Square/Shab Row, located around North East Street, is a cluster of specialty shops and restaurants. Everedy Square is housed in modern buildings, while Shab Row shops are located in historic town houses—even a log cabin. They stay open late every Friday night.

Antiques lovers should check out **Heritage Antiques,** 39 E. Patrick St. (✆ 301/668-0299), for china, crystal, and mahogany furniture. **Little's,** 102 E. Patrick St. (✆ 301/620-0517), also has handmade reproductions; it's closed Tuesday and Wednesday. **Emporium Antiques,** 112 E. Patrick St. (✆ 301/662-7099), has more than 130 dealers crammed into an old car dealership. You'll also find antiques dealers on East, Patrick, and Carroll streets.

Market Street offers **Molly's Meanderings,** 17 N. Market St. (✆ 301/668-8075), for vintage-look styles, and plenty of gift stores: chocolate from **Candy Kitchen,** 52 N. Market St. (✆ 301/698-0442); jewelry or animation cels from **McGuire Fine Arts,** at 110 N. Market St. (✆ 301/695-6567); or fun tableware and crafts from the **Muse,** 19 N. Market St. (✆ 301/663-3632). Teenagers love the sneakers at **Social Study** at 201 N. Market St. (✆ 301/695-5671), and clothes at **Velvet Lounge,** 203 N. Market St. (✆ 301/695-5700). **Potters' Guild of Frederick** at 227 N. Market St. (✆ 301/662-3160) markets local handicrafts.

Just off Market, **Le Savon,** 10 E. Church St. (✆ 301/694-0935), stocks homemade soap. Near Everedy Square, **Frederick Cellars,** 221 N. East St. (✆ 301/668-0311) sells local wines and chocolates by the **Perfect Truffle** (✆ 301/620-2448).

Serious antiques shoppers may want to visit nearby **New Market,** which calls itself "the antiques capital of Maryland" and is itself registered on the National Register of Historic Places. Shops line Main Street, (Rte. 144) with everything from furniture to estate jewelry. Shops are open on weekends, most 10am to 5pm. Several are open on most weekdays, as well. The **New Market Antique Dealers Association** publishes a free guide available in town or **www.newmarkettoday.com**. To reach the town, 6 miles east of Frederick, go east on I-70 and take exit 62.

FREDERICK AFTER DARK
Bars & Live Music

Most of Frederick's nightspots are on or near Market Street. **Olde Town Tavern,** 325 N. Market St. (✆ 301/695-1454), has live music and darts for its young crowd. Heading south on Market, **Bushwallers,** 209 N. Market St. (✆ 301/695-6988), hosts Irish music on Sunday and Wednesday, and live bands on Friday and Saturday. **Firestone's,** 105 N. Market St. (✆ 301/663-0330; www.firestonesrestaurant.com), has live music on Friday and Saturday. If you just need a place to hang out, go to **Brewer's Alley,** 124 N. Market St. (✆ 301/631-0089), described on p. 193 or **Wag's,** 24 S. Market St. (✆ 301/694-8451), described on p. 194. **Jackson's Restaurant & Bar,** 1A W. Second St. (✆ 301/418-6886), offers live acoustic music Wednesday through Sunday. The **Bentz Street Sports Bar,** 6 S. Bentz St. (✆ 301/620-2222; www.bentzstreetsportsbar.com), has 30 TVs tuned to sports, live entertainment on Friday, and comedy on Wednesday.

The Performing Arts

All kinds of events, including dance, music, theater, classic movies, and family entertainment, are staged year-round at the **Weinberg Center for the Arts,** 20 W. Patrick St. (✆ 301/600-2828; www.weinbergcenter.org), a 1926 movie theater.

perform at nearby Tuscarora High School. The **Maryland Shakespeare Festival Theatre** (② 301/668-4090; www.mdshakes.com) offers works by the Bard at their playhouse on West Second Street. The **Maryland Ensemble Theatre** (② 301/694-4744) performs six plays a year at 31 W. Patrick St.

2 ANTIETAM NATIONAL BATTLEFIELD ★

22 miles W of Frederick; 10 miles S of Hagerstown; 57 miles SW of Gettysburg

Antietam (or Sharpsburg to Southerners) is perhaps the saddest place you can visit in Maryland. A walk down Bloody Lane will send shivers up your spine—especially after you've seen the photographs of the corpses piled up on this road. (Photos at Antietam were the first ever taken of a battlefield before the bodies were buried.) More than 23,000 men were killed or wounded here when Union forces met and stopped the first attempted Southern invasion of the North in September 1862. It is the site of the bloodiest day of the Civil War—with more Americans killed or wounded than on any other single day of combat, including D-day. President Lincoln made a battlefield appearance shortly after the battle at Antietam to confront the Union's Gen. George McClellan over his unwillingness to pursue the retreating Confederate army. Clara Barton, who founded the American Red Cross 19 years later, nursed the wounded here.

Today, the battlefield is marked by rolling hills and farmland and attended by a visitor center, a cemetery, modest monuments, and the gentle waters of Antietam Creek. The mood is somber. Gettysburg has all the monuments and displays, but this is the place to come to consider the tragedy, rather than the triumph, of war.

FEES Admission to the battlefield is $4 for adults, $6 per family, and free for children 17 and under.

VISITOR CENTER Begin a trip to the battlefield at the **visitor center,** 1 mile north of Sharpsburg on Route 65 (② 301/432-5124; www.nps.gov/anti). It has exhibits,

---

> (Tips) **Hire a Guide**
>
> Whether you are dragging along your bored tween-agers or following the steps of your favorite Union general, an **Antietam Battlefield Guide** (② 866/461-5180 or 301/432-4329; www.antietambattlefieldguides.com) will tailor his tour to interest anyone. Since 1915, Gettysburg has had guides who show the sights and tell the stories of battle. Antietam's guides got their start in 2006 with a similar idea. They're passionate about their Civil War history—they've studied and passed tests to do this. They'll drive you around the battlefields so you don't miss a thing. And they've got stories about all the regiments, generals, and soldiers, some of whom have become well known: Clara Barton; Oliver Wendell Holmes, Jr.; Abner Doubleday. Guides charge $50 for a 2-hour tour for up to six people. Reservations are recommended, but if you come to Antietam and decide you want a guide, ask at the gift shop and someone may be available to show you around.

documentaries, a museum, a gift shop, and an observation room overlooking the battlefield. The staff provides maps, literature, and suggestions for routes to explore the battlefield and cemetery. It's open June through August daily from 8am to 7pm, September through May daily from 8:30am to 5pm; closed Thanksgiving, December 25, and January 1. *Note:* The battlefield officially closes 20 minutes after sunset.

SEEING THE HIGHLIGHTS

Antietam's quiet hills and limited number of monuments make it a stark and silent contrast to the massive memorials of Gettysburg. The park service offers an 8½-mile self-guided auto tour that can also be walked or bicycled. Maps, as well as tours on audiotape and CD, are also available at the visitor center. **Battlefield Guides** (© **866/461-5180** or 301/432-4329; www.antietambattlefieldguides.com), similar to the guides at Gettysburg, take groups or families for a 2-hour tour of the battlefield; reservations are required. Park rangers offer free battlefield walks and talks, too. You can count on a walking tour at 1:30pm, though others are offered in summer. In addition, rangers give an orientation talk at the visitor center three times a day.

Burnside Bridge crosses Antietam Creek near the southern end of the battlefield. Georgia snipers stalled 4,000 Union soldiers for over 3 hours as the Union tried to secure this stone arch bridge. Another must-see stop is the observation tower over a sunken country lane near the center of the battlefield. This road, now known as **Bloody Lane,** was the scene of a 4-hour encounter that ended with no decisive winner and 4,000 casualties. And don't miss **Dunker Church,** which figures prominently in a number of Civil War photos. These three locations are among the most memorable, graceful, and harrowing of the battlefield.

The **Pry House Field Hospital Museum** (© **301/695-1864;** www.civilwarmed.org), just a 5-minute drive off the battlefield, served as General George McClellan's headquarters during the battle. Several generals were treated here; the barn was also used as a field hospital. Admission to Pry House is $2. It's open daily 11am to 5pm Memorial Day to October 31 and in May and November, Saturday and Sunday, 11am to 5pm. It's closed December through April.

Every year on September 17, and on the weekend closest to the date, the anniversary of the battle is remembered with ranger-led hikes and special events. An Independence Day concert, featuring the Maryland Symphony Orchestra and fireworks, is held on the Saturday closest to the Fourth of July.

OUTDOOR ACTIVITIES

BIKING & HIKING The wide-open fields of Antietam Battlefield beckon both hikers and bikers with 9 miles of paved roads good for bicycling. Some 10 miles of hiking trails, including the **Final Attack Trail,** have been marked with trail maps to give visitors a chance to trek into history. For maps, stop by the visitor center.

CANOEING & KAYAKING Antietam Creek, which flows the length of the park to the Potomac, is an excellent novice-to-intermediate canoe and kayak run offering views of a small waterfall, Burnside Bridge, the ruins of Antietam Furnace, and the old C&O Canal aqueduct. **River & Trail Outfitters,** 604 Valley Rd., Knoxville (© **888/446-7529;** www. rivertrail.com), leads guided float trips down this scenic creek, and rents canoes and kayaks. **Fish N Float Adventures** (© **301/432-8469;** www.fishnfloatadventures.com) offers float trips and kayak fishing.

(Moments)   A Candlelight Remembrance

On the first Saturday of December, Antietam National Battlefield is illuminated with 23,000 candles, one for each of those killed, wounded, or missing after the battle. People come from everywhere, willing to wait an hour or more, for the chance to drive past this sad but beautiful sight. Cars start moving through the park at about 6:30pm and continue until midnight or until all the cars have passed. The only entrance is on Route 34.

WHERE TO DINE

Tiny Sharpsburg has only a few options for hungry visitors, but one place popular with locals and visitors is **Nutter's Ice Cream,** 100 E. Main St. (© **301/432-5809**).

For fine dining, go to Shepherdstown, West Virginia, across the Potomac from Sharpsburg on State Route 64. The small college town has numerous coffee shops and cafes along its main drag, East German Street. The **Yellow Brick Bank Restaurant,** 201 E. German St. (© **304/876-2208**), serves lunch, dinner, and Sunday brunch. The nearby **Bavarian Inn** ★, 164 Shepherd Grade Rd. (© **304/876-2551;** www.bavarianinnwv. com), just across the Potomac, serves hearty German fare in its Alpine-style dining room and on the terrace. Breakfast, lunch, and dinner are available.

Another option is **Old South Mountain Inn,** 6132 Old National Pike, Boonsboro (© **301/371-5400;** www.oldsouthmountaininn.com), located at the top of South Mountain ridge on Alternate Route 40 between Antietam and Frederick. It serves Saturday lunch, Sunday brunch, and dinner Tuesday through Sunday.

3 HARPERS FERRY NATIONAL HISTORICAL PARK

22 miles SW of Frederick; 54 miles W of Baltimore; 55 miles S of Gettysburg

Though you can hardly tell today, Harpers Ferry, West Virginia, was a bustling industrial center from the 1700s until the 1930s, when it was hit by the double disasters of the Depression and a flood. It's perhaps best known for abolitionist John Brown's rebellion and the town's part in the Civil War.

On October 16, 1859, Brown—already notorious from a bloody raid against slaveholders in Kansas—enlisted 19 men to raid the federal arsenal at Harpers Ferry, intent on arming the nation's slaves and starting a rebellion. Frederick Douglass warned Brown that the arsenal, in a town wedged between mountains and the Shenandoah and Potomac rivers, would be impossible to hold with so few men, and, as Douglass had foreseen, the raid failed. Brown and his men captured the arsenal but were unable to raise any significant number of slaves into rebellion. They were soon pinned in the arsenal's firehouse (later known as John Brown's Fort), and Brown was captured when U.S. Marines under Lt. Col. Robert E. Lee stormed the building. Brown was tried and convicted of "conspiring with slaves to commit treason and murder," for which he was hanged. His action polarized the nation and was one of the sparks that ignited the war. Harpers Ferry later witnessed the largest surrender of Federal troops during the Civil War; it also opened one of the earliest integrated schools in the U.S.

Today, Harpers Ferry National Historical Park is a delightful place to spend a day or weekend. Its narrow streets are lined with historic homes and restored shops that sell antiques and handicrafts. The National Park Service administers much of this tiny town. Historic exhibits focus on John Brown's raid, the town's industry, Storer College (an early African-American college), and the town's role in the Civil War, when it changed hands between the Union and the Confederacy eight times. Hills soar overhead and plunge down into the white waters of the Shenandoah and Potomac rivers. Walkers will find 4 miles of trails for a stroll or a strenuous hike. Water lovers will want to sign on for a rafting or kayaking run.

Plans have already begun for the 150th anniversary observance of the start of the Civil War. Check the park's website for events in 2011 and 2012. Events will be scheduled through 2015. Also, new trails are due to be developed on the battlefield lands coming into the park in 2010.

ACCESS POINTS   To get here, take Route 340 west from Frederick. You will cross the Potomac River Bridge (the town is off the bridge to your right) into Virginia, and then about ¾ mile later cross the Shenandoah River into West Virginia. The park's parking lot is about a mile past the Shenandoah Bridge, on the left.

FEES   Park admission is $6 per vehicle, $4 per pedestrian or cyclist. The fee includes the shuttle bus and is good for 3 days.

VISITOR CENTER   Start at the **Cavalier Heights Visitor Center,** 1 mile west of Shenandoah Bridge, off Route 340 (© **304/535-6029**). Leave your car in this parking lot (the park service has removed almost all parking from the lower town) and catch the shuttle here. The staff provides free maps and information on ranger-led tours (available in spring, summer, and fall). The visitor center is open daily from 8am to 5pm, except Thanksgiving, December 25, and January 1. Shuttles run about every 12 to 15 minutes from 8am to 5:45pm (later in summer).

SEEING THE HIGHLIGHTS

Skip the hassles of parking and take the 6-minute shuttle ride from the visitor center. Once in the lower town, stop first at the information center on Shenandoah Street (if you didn't already get brochures and trail maps at the Cavalier Heights visitor center).

The **John Brown Museum,** on Shenandoah Street, offers exhibits and displays on the abolitionist and tracks the course of his raid, capture, and conviction. Hours for the museum are the same as the park's hours, and admission is included in the park entry fee. The **Harper House** is a restored dwelling that sits at the top of the stone stairs, above High Street. The oldest remaining structure in Harpers Ferry, it was built between 1775 and 1782 and served as a tavern for such notable guests as Thomas Jefferson and George Washington.

WALKING, HIKING & WHITE-WATER RAFTING

Remember to wear sturdy shoes, so you can make the short but moderately strenuous climb farther up the stone stairs, past the lovely **St. Peter's Church,** to **Jefferson Rock** ★. At this spot, looking over the confluence of the Shenandoah and Potomac rivers, President Jefferson called the view "stupendous," and said it was worth crossing the Atlantic to see.

If you don't feel like climbing the stairs to Jefferson Rock, you might enjoy a stroll over the walking/railroad bridge across the Potomac for a view of the mighty river. On the way, you'll pass the old armory fire house, known as **John Brown's Fort,** where Brown and his men took their last stand. On the other side, you'll find the bottom of Maryland Heights (see below) and the ruins of **Lock No. 33** on the C&O Canal.

Virginius Island, a long curl of land along the Shenandoah, offers visitors an easy stroll among trees and stone ruins. This was once a booming industrial center with a rifle factory, iron foundry, cotton mill, granary, and lumberyard. It's a silent reminder of what once was. The short history trail, about a mile long, offers some explanation of what remains, and the lovely flat site is a great place to rest or let the children run.

If you're ready for a strenuous hike, head over the railroad bridge to walk up the cliffs of **Maryland Heights** to one of the most spectacular views in the state. The hike can take 3 to 5 hours, but the view of Harpers Ferry and the confluence of the two rivers makes the effort worthwhile. The park service provides trail maps for the hike to Maryland Heights as well as to nearby **Weverton Cliffs,** which also boasts a very good view. If you're planning more than a day's hike, the **Appalachian Trail** and the **C&O Canal** join briefly and pass right by Harpers Ferry, on the opposite side of the Potomac, making the town a great stop on either route.

River & Trail Outfitters, 604 Valley Rd., Knoxville, MD (© **888/446-7529;** www. rivertrail.com), offers half-day white-water rafting trips down the Shenandoah and Potomac, which pass by the town. Although this can be quite an adventure during high-water season (Feb to mid-Apr), most of the time it's a fun raft trip through beautiful scenery and a few rapids—suitable for families. Guides share local history, legends, and corny jokes. Prices depend on the season but generally run $55 to $95 per person. River & Trail also offers guided hikes up Maryland Heights, C&O bike trips, cross-country ski trips in winter, and Monocacy River paddle trips. Experienced paddlers can rent a canoe or kayak; lessons are available for every level.

Fishing is permitted in both the Potomac and Shenandoah rivers, but adults may require licenses; check with the visitor center.

WHERE TO STAY

Harpers Ferry is about 22 miles from Frederick, which has several lodging options (p. 192). Closer to the historical park, the 50-room **Comfort Inn,** at Route 340 and Union Street (© **877/424-6423** or 304/535-6391; www.comfortinn.com), is about a mile from the visitor center.

WHERE TO DINE

Good dining options are limited. You'll see numerous cafes and sandwich shops along Potomac and High streets. The food is fine, but patience is necessary on a busy day; note that a sandwich or salad can cost $7 to $10. Stop early for breakfast or wait until later in the day to eat. There are also plenty of places to stop for a drink or an ice cream—and the wait isn't as long.

---

4 GETTYSBURG NATIONAL MILITARY PARK ★★★

---

34 miles N of Frederick; 50 miles NW of Baltimore

Here on the rolling green hills just north of the Maryland-Pennsylvania line, and in the streets of a tiny town that was home to a mere 2,400 people, some 160,000 brothers met in battle. For 3 days in July 1863, the 70,000 men of the Confederate Army faced the 93,000 Union soldiers under the command of General George Meade. When the 3 days of fighting ended, the rebels had been driven back; some 51,000 were killed, wounded, or captured; and General Robert E. Lee would never mount another campaign of such magnitude again. Most important, the tide of the war had changed. The battle would become known as the "high water mark of the Confederacy."

Today, the 20,000-acre battlefield is one of the most famous in the world, drawing people to its hills and valleys, beckoning them to pause for a moment before the long rows of graves in the cemeteries and monuments in the fields. They stop, too, to recall the 272 words of Abraham Lincoln as he dedicated the cemetery on November 19, 1863.

The park surrounds the small town of Gettysburg, which still bears war wounds of its own. Plenty of small privately owned museums display collections of firearms, uniforms, and other memorabilia of those dark days.

The busiest time to visit is during the 3-day reenactment held every July 1 to July 3, when 350,000 people descend on Gettysburg. If you plan to come, make hotel reservations at least 8 months in advance—and make dinner reservations before arriving. It's a good idea to come before the reenactment to get a look around, take a tour, and gain some historical perspective. Bring a lawn chair and comfortable shoes.

Another popular event is Remembrance Day, held the Saturday closest to November 19, the anniversary of the Gettysburg Address. Weekends in spring and fall are perhaps the most pleasant times to visit. Schoolchildren flow in during the school year, and families keep the attractions filled all summer.

GETTING THERE Take U.S. Route 15 north from Frederick and I-70. After about 30 miles, you'll cross into Pennsylvania; then take the first exit and turn left on Business U.S. Route 15 north. The visitor center is 6 miles ahead on your right; the town is just past the visitor center.

Parking garages or lots are on Race Horse Alley, at Middle and Stratton streets, and on Baltimore Street between the Jennie Wade House and the Tour Center. On-street parking is available most weekends. Museums and the battlefield have their own lots.

FEES & HOURS Admission to Gettysburg National Military Park is free. The battlefield is open daily year-round: from 6am to 10pm April through October, and from 6am to 7pm November through March. The visitor center is open daily from 8am to 5pm (until 6pm in summer), except Thanksgiving, December 25, and January 1. The cemetery is open from dawn to dusk.

VISITOR CENTER Stop first at the **Gettysburg National Military Park Visitor Center** (© 717/334-1124; www.nps.gov/gett). The new 139,000-square-foot headquarters off the battlefield at 1195 Baltimore Pike (Rte. 97) has a museum focusing on Gettysburg in the Civil War, a bookstore, and Cyclorama. It is also the starting point for tours and ranger walks (see "Organized Tours," below). Rangers are glad to answer questions and provide maps of hiking trails and the 18-mile self-guided auto tour. Backpacks and large parcels are not allowed in the visitor center.

SEEING THE HIGHLIGHTS

Admission to the **Visitor Center** is free, so be sure to stop here for a map, schedule of free ranger talks and tours, and to browse the well-stocked shop and bookstore. There's also a short film and display of Civil War artifacts, as well as a large food court. The Visitor Center is open daily 8am to 5pm, and until 6pm April through October.

The major exhibits here, however, come at a price. A ticket for a movie narrated by Morgan Freeman, the extensive collections of the **Gettysburg Museum of the Civil War,** and the **Cyclorama** is $11 for adults, $9.50 for seniors, and $6.50 for children.

The film is a good introduction to the Civil War and the museum displays a good collection of weaponry and uniforms from both sides. Look for the things the soldiers carried, including musical instruments, medical supplies, and personal effects.

But it's the newly restored **Cyclorama** ★★★, a 360-degree depiction of Pickett's Charge—the climactic battle of the Gettysburg campaign—that is worth the price of admission. Brilliantly colored with gripping scenes of battle, the 1884 painting by Paul Dominique Philippoteaux is enhanced by its display, the dramatic narration, and the accompanying light-and-sound show.

The battlefield and cemetery are the main reasons for a visit here. The **Gettysburg National Cemetery** gate is on Taneytown Road. Get a map at the visitor center, walk among the gravestones, and learn about the Union and Confederate soldiers now united in this place. The graves encircle the place where Abraham Lincoln gave the Gettysburg Address and where the Soldiers' National Monument now stands.

The battlefield is so large, you must see it by car, bike, or bus. Along the ridges and valleys of the park are more than 100 monuments, dedicated by various states to their military units who fought here. The largest and most often visited is the granite-domed **Pennsylvania Memorial.** Constructed of nearly 3,000 tons of cut granite, raw stone, and cement, the monument consists of a dome supported by four arched columns, topped by a statue depicting the winged goddess of victory and peace. Other monuments recall the bravery of the troops on both sides of the battle. Of the Southern states, Virginia was the first to build a monument here. The **Virginia State Memorial,** dedicated in 1917, is topped by a brass sculpture of General Lee mounted on a horse. It's located where Pickett's Charge took place.

As you're visiting the monuments, look for the **John Burns Portrait Statue.** At over 70 years of age, this local constable and veteran of the War of 1812 asked Colonel Langhorn Wister for permission to fight with the Union troops. Although initially mocked, he earned the soldiers' respect, fighting alongside Union regiments at Gettysburg before being wounded and carried from the field.

OTHER ATTRACTIONS

The **David Wills House,** 8 Lincoln Sq. (© **866/486-5735;** www.davidwillshouse.org) located on Gettysburg's town square, is now part of the Gettysburg National Military Park but it has its own separate admission. Its exhibits focus on the man who organized the dedication of the Soldiers' National Cemetery and who invited the president to speak. Abraham Lincoln spent the night here before delivering the Gettysburg Address at the cemetery on November 19, 1863. The bed where Lincoln slept and some of his

---

Moments **Dress the Part**

A number of shops in town will help you find a stunning Civil War–style ball gown (or perhaps a more practical day or work dress). You'll need the dress, a corset, a four- or six-bone hoop, pantaloons, gloves and a bonnet. Those clothes can be suffocatingly hot, so be sure to find a lovely fan. At **A Civil Affair** on Baltimore Street (© **717/338-1565;** www.acivilaffair.com), seamstresses will alter your dress right away. Such an outfit will set you back $300 to $700 (or more). Other shops specialize in men's clothes or hats.

things are on display in the bedroom—really the best reason to pay the hefty $6.50 admission ($5.50 seniors, $4 children 6–18). The house is open May to August daily 10am to 6pm; spring and fall Wednesday to Monday 10am to 5pm, and Thursday to Monday, 10am to 5pm in winter.

Eisenhower National Historic Site ★ (www.nps.gov/eise), President Eisenhower's farm, overlooks the Gettysburg Battlefield. Eisenhower first came to Gettysburg as a West Point cadet, to study the battlefields. He and his wife Mamie bought their 189-acre farm south of town; as president, he entertained world leaders here. Today, visitors can catch a shuttle at the battlefield visitor center to tour the home and walk the grounds. Admission is $7.50 for adults, and $5 for children 6 to 12.

Gettysburg is dotted with small, privately owned museums filled with Civil War memorabilia. The best is the **Shriver House Museum,** 309 Baltimore St. (ⓒ **717/337-2800;** www.shriverhouse.org), which relates the story of a civilian family caught up in the terror of the battle. Visitors can tour the home, including the attic where sharpshooters were holed up. (If you're in town for the reenactment, stop here on Sat evening for a compelling living history tour.) Admission is $7.50 for adults, $7.25 for seniors, and $5 for children 6 to 12. It's closed January and February.

ORGANIZED TOURS

The best battlefield tours are offered by the **Association of Licensed Battlefield Guides** (ⓒ **877/594-3162** or 717/334-1124), which was set up in 1915 by Civil War veterans to ensure that visitors received accurate information about the battle. These guides can tell you about everything from troop movements to who built the Pennsylvania Memorial and how much it cost. A licensed guide will ride in your vehicle—and even drive—to give a customized tour. It's best to reserve a guide at least 3 days ahead of your visit but guides are also assigned at the visitor center on a first-come, first-served basis. A 2-hour tour costs $55 to $75 for 1 to 15 people.

Gettysburg Battlefield Bus Tours, 778 Baltimore St. (ⓒ **717/334-6296;** www. gettysburgbattlefieldtours.com), gives battlefield tours in either air-conditioned or double-decker buses. Recorded, dramatized tours cost $25 for adults and $15 for children. Licensed battlefield guides lead some tours. Buses leave from the visitor center; you can buy tickets there or at numerous locations around town.

There are plenty of free tours, too, offered by the **National Park Service.** In fact, in warm weather, up to 34 presentations are given in the cemetery and battlefield each day. These rangers' walks, talks, and tours vary—some are brief, while others include up to a 3-mile hike with lots of detail about the battles. Contact the visitor center for details.

WHERE TO STAY

With several hotels in town and more along the main routes, visitors have plenty of options—and Frederick lodgings are close enough, too. If you plan to attend the reenactment in July, reserve at least 8 months in advance.

In the heart of town, the 109-room **Quality Inn Gettysburg Motor Lodge,** 380 Steinwehr Ave. (ⓒ **800/228-5151** or 717/334-1103; www.gettysburgqualityinn.com), has outdoor and indoor pools and an exercise room.

If you'd like to sleep in a bit of history, the **Best Western Gettysburg Hotel,** 1 Lincoln Sq. (ⓒ **800/528-1234** or 717/337-2000; www.gettysburg-hotel.com), is on the town square. Down the street is the **James Gettys Hotel,** 27 Chambersburg St. (ⓒ **888/900-5275** or 717/337-1334; www.jamesgettyshotel.com), with 12 suites.

Two hotels are located at the Gettysburg Gateway complex northwest of the battlefield on Route 15. The **Wyndham Gettysburg** ★, 95 Presidential Circle (✆ 717/339-0020), has 248 rooms, indoor and outdoor pools, and a contemporary style. The **Courtyard by Marriott,** 115 Presidential Circle (✆ 717/334-5600), is slightly more casual with 152 rooms and an indoor pool. The location of these hotels is ideal for families. About 5 minutes from downtown, they offer four restaurants, a lounge, and free parking. Also here is the eight-screen **Gateway Theatres** (✆ 717/334-5575, or 334-5577 for movie schedule), which shows the 30-minute "Fields of Freedom" film about Gettysburg all day long in summer (afternoons only other times).

Outside of town, the **Quality Inn at General Lee's Headquarters,** 401 Buford Ave. (✆ 800/228-5151 or 717/334-3141; www.thegettysburgaddress.com), overlooks the battlefield of Seminary Ridge, and has an outdoor pool. The **Hilton Garden Inn Gettysburg,** 1061 York Rd. (✆ 877/782-9444 or 717/334-2040; www.gettysburg. gardeninn.com), has an indoor pool.

WHERE TO DINE

Gettysburg is dotted with little restaurants and fast-food joints. To start your day with coffee and pastry, visit **Seasons Bakery,** 100 Chambersburg St. (✆ 717/334-0377). It's open for breakfast and lunch. Closed Mondays.

Two historic taverns are experiences in themselves. The **Dobbin House,** 89 Steinwehr Ave. (✆ 717/334-2100), serves lunch and casual dinner daily in the Springhouse Tavern. Dinner is served in the Alexander Dobbin Dining Rooms. Each table in the bedroom is covered by a canopy—historic dining in bed. It's quite an experience. It's open daily at 5pm. The **Farnsworth House,** 401 Baltimore St. (✆ 717/334-8838), serves dinner in the bullet hole–covered 1863 inn. Or have a casual meal in the adjacent garden. Lunch begins at 11am. Dinner is daily at 5pm.

A SIDE TRIP TO BLACK ANKLE VINEYARDS ★

Down a country road, the corn and soybeans give way to rolling hills filled with vineyards. This may not be Napa Valley but it's the closest you can get to it in Maryland. At **Black Ankle Vineyards,** 14463 Black Ankle Rd., Mt. Airy (✆ 301/829-3338; www. blackankle.com), about 20 miles northeast of Frederick, the wines are state champions and its tasting room is a remarkable example of green construction. The walls are constructed of bales of hay (grown here), the heating system is passive solar, and the countertops in the tasting room were made from the vines and seeds left over from winemaking. The winery, which pressed its first grapes in 2006, is small, with only 2,200 cases produced annually. It's a lovely place to spend a weekend afternoon. Bring a picnic lunch, or order a cheese plate in the tasting room. Tastings are $5 and tours of the vineyards and winery are offered. Pasta dinners are served on third Sundays and musicians perform some Friday nights. The tasting room is open Wednesday to Sunday noon to 5pm.

5 SERENITY & APPLES ON ROUTE 15

20 miles N of Frederick; 60 miles W of Baltimore; 15 miles SW of Gettysburg

When planning a trip to Frederick or a drive through the Civil War sites and on to Gettysburg, reserve some time for the treasures of Route 15, the **Catoctin Mountain**

National Scenic Byway. Along the way, stop in **Thurmont,** known for its two main parks, and **Emmitsburg,** the home of St. Elizabeth Ann Seton and Mount St. Mary's University, where a replica of the Grotto of Lourdes is located. These are charming places for a weekend getaway or a day trip; both are about 90 minutes from Baltimore.

WHAT TO SEE & DO

Catoctin Mountain Park (© 301/663-9343; www.nps.gov/cato), a national park, has several good trails and is the home of presidential retreat Camp David—whose precise location is top secret. The park's entrance is on Route 77 west of Route 15. Admission is free. Tent camping here is $20 a night; cabin rentals are $55 to $140.

Cunningham Falls State Park ★★ (© 301/271-7574; www.dnr.maryland.gov) has as its centerpiece a 78-foot high waterfall, set in a canopy of 100-year-old oaks and hickories. Stay for a few minutes or the rest of the day. The park is also the site of 43-acre **Hunting Creek Lake,** which offers swimming, canoe rentals, and picnic areas. Get a guide to the many park trails at the Manor Area visitor center, off Route 15, or at Park Central, on Route 77. Four short trails will take you to the base of Cunningham Falls. Three are in the William Houck Area, off Route 77. They range from moderate to strenuous and from .5 to 2.8 miles. The fourth trail is wheelchair accessible, with a handicapped-only parking lot on Route 77 and a .3-mile boardwalk that goes all the way to the falls. Another trail ends at the **Catoctin Iron Furnace,** the remains of a Revolutionary War–era iron-making complex. The park is open daily from 8am to sunset. In peak season, fees run $3 to $4 per person; at other times they're $3 to $4 per car. Campsites are available for $25 a night, $30 with electric hookup; cabins are $50.

National Fallen Firefighters Memorial (Finds) This site, at the National Fire Academy, holds special significance since September 11, 2001: The firefighters who died at the World Trade Center have their own memorial here. The service in tribute to firefighters killed in the line of duty is held during Fire Prevention Week, in October.

16825 S. Seton Ave., Emmitsburg. © 301/447-1000. www.firehero.org. Free admission. Bring photo ID to visit, as this is a federal site. Daily dawn–dusk.

National Shrine Grotto of Our Lady of Lourdes If you know the story of St. Bernadette—the French peasant girl who saw Mary, mother of Jesus, in a grotto—but you aren't going to France anytime soon, then you might want to stop here. The site has been re-created on a mountain overlooking Mount St. Mary's University. You'll know you're here when you see the 95-foot-tall campanile topped with a golden statue of Mary. As you wander the wooded paths, you'll see other shrines and the Stations of the Cross.

Mount St. Mary's University & Seminary, 16300 Old Emmitsburg Rd., Emmitsburg. © 301/447-6122. www. msmary.edu/grotto. Free admission. Mar–Sept daily 7:30am–7:30pm; Oct–Feb daily 7:30am–5:30pm.

National Shrine of Saint Elizabeth Ann Seton ★★★ This shrine honors the first American-born saint canonized in the Roman Catholic Church. A young widow who converted to Catholicism, Mother Seton lived here with her children as she began both the Catholic parochial school system and a new order of religious women. The church, a minor basilica, is a beautiful monument, but the nearby houses—the Stone House (built about 1750) and the White House (built for her in 1810)—offer a glimpse of her life here in the mountains. The guides are quite patient with children.

333 S. Seton Ave., Emmitsburg. © 301/447-6606. www.setonshrine.org. Free admission; donations welcome. Basilica daily 10am–4:30pm; other sites Tues–Sun 10am–4:30pm. Closed Jan 1, 2nd week of Jan, Easter, July 4, Thanksgiving, Dec 24–25, and Dec 31. From Rte. 15, turn left on S. Seton Ave. The shrine is ¾ mile on the right.

Don't miss the orchard stands along your drive. There are several, all selling fruit and vegetables grown right in these foothills.

Catoctin Mountain Orchard, 15036 N. Franklinville Rd. (Rte. 15), Thurmont (© **301/271-2737;** www.catoctinmountainorchard.com), has locally baked pastries and McCutcheon's preserves, as well as fresh produce. Pick your own berries in June and July, pumpkins and apples in fall. Open May through January, daily 9am to 5pm.

Gateway Farm Market and Candyland, 14802 N. Franklinville Rd. (Rte. 15), Thurmont (© **301/271-2322**), has not only produce and fresh cider in season but also long tables filled with boxes of penny candy. Open Monday through Thursday from 8am to 9pm, Friday and Saturday from 8am to 10pm, and Sunday from 10am to 7pm.

Scenic View Orchards, 16239 Sabillasville Rd. (Rte. 550), Sabillasville (© **301/271-2149**), offers valley views along with fresh produce, preserves, and breads. It's open daily from 10am to 6pm, June through Thanksgiving.

WHERE TO STAY

The Cascade Inn ★   This white-clapboard 1890 house is worth the drive over the mountain into Cascade. Once the home of Colonel Walter Taylor, an aide-de-camp of General Robert E. Lee during the Civil War, it is now a comfortable bed-and-breakfast situated on 2 shady acres. Two units have fireplaces, the Rose Garden Suite has a sun porch with daybed, and the two-bedroom family suite has a spacious bathroom with its own whirlpool. In fact, three units have whirlpools. The first-floor Mountain Magnolia Suite is a generous size with a fireplace. The B&B is a good base for visiting Civil War sites or the Appalachian Trail, which is only 1½ miles away.

14700 Eyler Ave., Cascade, MD 21719. © **800/362-9526** or 301/241-4161. www.thecascadeinn.com. 4 units. $135–$150 double. Rates include breakfast. AE, DISC, MC, V. *In room:* A/C, TV, fridge, hair dryer, microwave (on request), free Wi-Fi.

Cozy Country Inn   The Cozy Inn has a certain charm, with premium rooms named after presidents and decorated in their style. The Reagan Cottage features a portrait of the president and horse decor, while the Roosevelt Room has a king-size bed in a style used by FDR. Every premium room has two TVs, a fireplace, and a Jacuzzi garden tub. Call ahead to reserve, especially if the president will be at Camp David—the press corps and president's staff often fill up the rooms. The shops here carry antiques, vintage clothing, and small specialties.

103 Frederick Rd. (Rte. 806), Thurmont, MD 21788. © **301/271-4301.** www.cozyvillage.com. 21 units, including 5 cottages. $62–$120 double; $117–$169 premium rooms. Rates include continental breakfast. Children 12 and under stay free in rooms with 2 beds. AE, DISC, MC, V. **Amenities:** Restaurant (see "Where to Dine," below). *In room:* A/C, fridge, hair dryer.

Sleep Inn & Suites Emmitsburg (Kids)   Emmitsburg's first and (so far) only hotel offers standard rooms but with a detail kids will like: Nintendo. One room of note is the fireplace suite, with a gas fireplace and a Jacuzzi for two. Call ahead for reservations, as the place can fill up with families and athletic teams visiting nearby Mount St. Mary's University.

501 Silo Hill Pkwy., off Rte. 15, Emmitsburg, MD 21727. © **800/SLEEP-INN** (753-3746) or 301/447-0044. Fax 301/447-3144. www.sleepinnemmitsburg.com. 79 units. $75–$159 double. Rates include continental breakfast. Children stay free in parent's room. AE, DC, DISC, MC, V. **Amenities:** Fitness room; indoor pool. *In room:* A/C, TV w/Nintendo, hair dryer, free Wi-Fi.

FREDERICK & THE CIVIL WAR CROSSROADS

Carriage House Inn ★ (Kids) AMERICAN   Plenty of people, including presidents, come to this 1857 inn for the crab cakes or hearty American fare. A stone fireplace dominates the dining room, which has wide plank floors and Early American–style furniture. It's a good place for children, whose menus are pasted inside picture books. There's a brunch buffet on Sundays.

200 S. Seton Ave., Emmitsburg. (✆) **301/447-2366.** www.carriagehouseinn.info. Reservations recommended. Main courses $8–$17 lunch, $10–$35 dinner. AE, DISC, MC, V. Sun–Thurs 11am–8pm; Fri–Sat 11am–9pm.

Cozy Restaurant (Finds) AMERICAN   Just by looking at the photos and memorabilia on the walls, you can tell the Cozy's been around a long time. It features hearty buffets as well as simple fare served in the dining rooms and on the deck in summer. Afternoon tea and special fondue suppers are other options, by reservation only. If you're a root beer fan, try the house brew.

103 Frederick Rd. (Rte. 806), Thurmont. (✆) **301/271-7373.** www.cozyvillage.com. Reservations recommended on Fri–Sat, required for candlelight fondue hideaway. Main courses $6.50–$16; buffet $8–$24. AE, MC, V. Mon–Fri 11am–8:15pm; Sat–Sun 8am–8:45pm.

Fitzgerald's Shamrock Restaurant SEAFOOD/STEAKS   This homey, friendly little restaurant proudly proclaims its Irish roots. Get a Harp or Guinness to wash down onion rings, shad in season, crab cakes, or chicken Chesapeake (a popular combination of chicken and crab). Sandwiches are available all day. No room for dessert? Take a pie with you.

7701 Fitzgerald Rd., Thurmont. (✆) **301/271-2912.** www.shamrockrestaurant.com. Reservations recommended on Fri–Sat. Main courses $7–$23. AE, MC, V. Daily 11am–10pm.

9

6 HAGERSTOWN

HAGERSTOWN

25 miles W of Frederick; 20 miles N of Antietam

Once a frontier town where Jonathan Hager built a fort to protect against Indian attack, Hagerstown is now best known for its charming city park, home to graceful swans and the remarkable Washington County Museum of Fine Arts, and perhaps for the factory outlet stores near I-70.

Hagerstown's location also makes it a convenient place to stop while visiting Civil War sites—have a picnic in City Park, visit the museum or Hager's house, or have a bite to eat in the town's arts-and-entertainment district.

WHAT TO SEE & DO

City Park   Swans on the lake, plenty of tree-shaded places for a picnic, and playground equipment to occupy the kids make this a charming spot to stop. The town began developing the 50-acre park in 1914 and Anna and William Singer chose it as the site of their art museum.

501 Virginia Ave., Hagerstown. No phone. Free admission. Daily dawn–dusk.

Discovery Station at Hagerstown   This children's museum, situated in a mid-20th-century bank, has some interesting items, but it's not a place where you can just let the kids loose. Instead, it offers adults the opportunity to wander through some dusty old memories and share them with the younger generation. These include a 15-foot model of the Titanic, a Cessna 150, and a diesel engine built in Hagerstown's Mack factory. Other exhibits focus on rocks, space, health, and agriculture. Several play areas, with blocks and toys and giant storybooks, are totally kid friendly.

101 W. Washington St., Hagerstown. © **301/790-0076** or 877/790-0076. www.discoverystation.org. $7 adults, $5 seniors, $6 children 3–17. Tues–Sat 10am–4pm; Sun 2–5pm. Closed Sun July–Sept.

The Hager House This 1740 stone house recalls the days when this was America's frontier. Jonathan Hager, a fur trader and gunsmith, designed the house to be impregnable in case of attack (which never came). Its modest collection of 17th- and 18th-century artifacts, including spinning wheels and a rare German clavichord (an early piano), makes it an interesting stop, especially for those already visiting the park or art museum.

110 Key St., City Park, Hagerstown. © **301/739-8393.** www.hagerhouse.org. $3 adults, $2 seniors, $1 children 6–12. Tues–Sat 10am–4pm; Sun 2–5pm. Closed mid-Nov to 1st Tues of Dec and Jan–Mar.

Hagerstown Roundhouse Museum There's nothing fancy about the design here, and the exhibitions are amateurish. But what makes this museum worth a look are the model train layouts. If you love O-gauge trains and marveling at cute little houses, you're going to enjoy yourself. Certainly the Trains of Christmas layout, open November through March, is the big draw but during the rest of the year, two other train layouts feature local sites and topography. Artifacts from Hagerstown's history as a "hub city" and a Brio train layout for kids to play with round out the visit. Outside, the CSX trains rumble by local tracks holding decommissioned trains owned by the museum. The cabooses are open for visits in spring and fall.

300 S. Burhans Blvd., Hagerstown. © **301/739-4665.** www.roundhouse.org. $3.50 adults, 50¢ children. Fri–Sun 1–5pm.

Washington County Museum of Fine Arts (Finds) Rodin's sculptures are here, as are paintings by Whistler, Courbet, seven members of Charles Wilson Peale's family, and Joshua Johnson. The museum, overlooking the City Park lake, was built in 1931 thanks to the generosity of local girl Anna Brugh and William Henry Singer, a steel heir and painter. The eclectic 7,000-piece collection has pieces from Europe, America, and Asia, most from the 18th to the 20th centuries. One gallery focuses on the Singers with their portraits, landscapes painted by Singer, and other works from their friends. With only 13% of the collection on the walls at a time, exhibits change regularly.

91 Key St., City Park, Hagerstown. © **301/739-5727.** www.wcmfa.org. Free admission. Tues–Fri 9am–5pm; Sat 9am–4pm; Sun 1–5pm.

WHERE TO STAY & DINE

Hagerstown's Potomac Street has a couple of good restaurants. Local favorites are the **Rhubarb House,** 12 Public Sq. (© **301/733-4399;** www.rhubarbhouse.com), with sandwiches and burgers, and the charming **Schmankerl Stube Bavarian Restaurants,** 58 S. Potomac St. (© **301/797-3354;** www.schmankerlstube.com), serving Bavarian favorites such as sauerbraten and Wiener schnitzel.

Chain hotels line Route 40, including a **Clarion Hotel,** 901 Dual Hwy. (© **301/733-5100**), **Comfort Suites,** 1801 Dual Hwy. (© **301/791-8200**), and **Hampton Inn,** 1716 Dual Hwy. (© **301/739-6100**).

You'll have to leave town for more interesting options. Here are a couple good choices, both only a short drive to the Antietam battlefield as well as Hagerstown.

Inn BoonsBoro ★   Novelist Nora Roberts mixes old-fashioned romance with up-to-the-minute luxury in the B&B she opened in 2008 in a 1798 stone structure in tiny Boonsboro, 10 miles from Antietam. Each room has its own ambience and is even named for a different romantic couple. The "Jane and Rochester" room boasts an enormous canopy bed while "Nick and Nora" is Art Deco chic. All the rooms are spacious with flatscreen TVs and DVD players, and have access to a small porch; some rooms have private entrances and two have gas fireplaces. The penthouse also has a whirlpool tub (guests enter by the back door).

1 N. Main St., Boonsboro, MD 21713. ℂ **301/432-1188.** www.innboonsboro.com. 8 units. $220–$300 double. Rates include full breakfast. AE, DISC, MC, V. No children 12 and under. **Amenities:** Library w/high-speed Internet access. *In room:* A/C, TV/VCR, hair dryer.

Jacob Rohrbach Inn ★   Inhabitants of this three-story stone house, built at the turn of the 19th century, once heard the gunfire of the battle of Antietam. Confederate soldiers woke the house's namesake and shot him dead. Today, the home is now an elegant inn. The four largest rooms have private entrances. One is located in a spacious separate cottage with sitting room and private porch.

7138 W. Main St., Sharpsburg, MD 21782. ℂ **877/839-4242** or 301/432-5079. www.jacob-rohrbach-inn. com. 5 units. $111–$192 double. Rates include full breakfast. 2-night minimum stay required on weekends and holidays. AE, DISC, MC, V. No children 10 and under. **Amenities:** Bikes. *In room:* A/C, TV w/VCR or DVD, hair dryer, free Wi-Fi.

Western Maryland

Western Maryland is a haven for lovers of the outdoors. Garrett and Allegany counties offer a wide variety of outside activities in any season. More than 100,000 acres of parkland stretch over mountains and into valleys. Gently rolling mountains draw visitors to their hiking and biking paths and ski slopes. Rivers and streams, particularly the Youghiogheny and the Savage, attract fly fishermen and white-water rafters. The centerpiece is Deep Creek Lake.

Western Maryland, which begins at the state's skinniest section at Hancock and ends at the West Virginia border, is easy to reach by way of interstate highways. From Baltimore, take I-70. Washingtonians can connect with I-70 from I-270. When I-70 turns north into Pennsylvania near Hancock, it connects to I-68, which heads west into West Virginia. I-81 joins I-70 near Hagerstown to bring visitors from Pennsylvania and Virginia. U.S. Route 219 intersects I-68 and heads south to Deep Creek Lake.

For a more scenic route, the old U.S. Route 40, the nation's first national pike, connects Frederick to Cumberland and other points west and east. It's slower going but much more interesting.

1 THE GREAT OUTDOORS IN WESTERN MARYLAND

Western Maryland's gently rolling mountains are part of the Appalachians, with Backbone Mountain (elevation 3,360 ft.) marking the eastern Continental Divide. Outdoors enthusiasts can find forests, mountain lakes, and miles of streams and rivers. White-water rafters come to meet the challenges of the Youghiogheny (pronounced Yok-a-*gain*-ee; those in the know just call it the "Yough"). Boaters flock to Garrett's seven lakes. Skiers head for the hills of Wisp Resort, and cross-country skiers glide along the state parks' trails. There are also plenty of opportunities for windsurfing, snowmobiling, fly-fishing, mountain biking, golfing, hunting, hiking, and camping.

Of the 100,000 acres of protected wilderness in Western Maryland, 40,000 are part of Green Ridge State Forest, east of Cumberland, while 53,000 are in the Savage River State Forest, near Deep Creek Lake. The area is great for wildlife-watching and fishing: Some species, notably hawks and black bears, began to disappear from the landscape, but they are returning in force to the region's parks and forests. And although mining runoff once threatened Garrett County's water, the Casselman, North Branch Potomac, and Youghiogheny rivers now boast some of the best fly-fishing around.

In other chapters of this book, the sections on outdoor pursuits are organized by activities such as biking and camping. But in Western Maryland, you can do just about anything, anywhere. This chapter instead has a rundown of each of the parks—except Deep Creek Lake State Park, which is described in the section about the lake itself—and some of their unique qualities to help you decide exactly where you want to go and what you want to do. For more information, call the individual state parks for brochures and maps (see numbers below), or go to **www.dnr.maryland.gov**. To reserve a campsite anywhere in Maryland, call ℂ **888/432-2267** or reserve online at **http://reservations. dnr.state.md.us**. *Note:* As of 2009, it is illegal to consume or possess liquor in a state park, except in motor homes and full-service cabins.

ALLEGANY COUNTY

Allegany has two outstanding state parks, plus the terminus of the C&O Canal, which is popular with bikers, hikers, and history buffs.

The **Chesapeake & Ohio Canal National Historical Park** (ℂ **301/722-8226;** www. nps.gov/choh) is an ideal place for a trek on the flat, wide canal towpath. Both cyclists and hikers enjoy all or part of the 184-mile route along the Potomac River, all the way from Cumberland to Georgetown, in D.C. Any portion can make a great 1-day biking trip. The canal passes by numerous sites, including Paw Paw Tunnel, Fort Frederick, Harpers Ferry, and **Great Falls** ★. The trip from Cumberland is almost all gently downhill. Because flooding can make some of the towpath impassable, check with the park service to see if the route you intend to bike is clear.

Green Ridge State Forest, exit 64 off I-68 (ℂ **301/478-3124**), is home to 46,000 acres of abundant wildlife and scenic vistas over the Potomac River. Adirondack-style shelters are placed along the 24-mile backpacking trail. Mountain bikers have access to the park's roads, most of the 43 miles of hiking trails, and a separate bike trail and racecourse. At the oak-hickory forest's southern end, you'll find the Paw Paw Tunnel on the C&O Canal (p. 223). Primitive camping is available at 100 sites ($10 per night). The park's activities include off-road driving, hunting, canoeing, kayaking, and fishing. The shooting range is open Wednesday through Saturday and Monday from 10am to sunset, Sunday from noon to sunset.

Rocky Gap State Park ★, exit 50 off I-68 (ℂ **301/722-1480**), has great trails with views of 243-acre Lake Habeeb, mountain overlooks, and a stout 5-mile trail up Evitts Mountain to the remains of a 1784 homestead. Walk along Rocky Gap Run to see the mile-long gorge and hemlock forest. The lake has three swimming beaches, two boat ramps, and boat, canoe, kayak, and paddleboat rentals. Boats are permitted on the lake 24 hours a day. Fishing licenses are required. The park has 278 campsites, including 14 minicabins ($50–$65 per night). Reservations here are recommended.

Suppliers & Guides in Allegany County

C&O Bicycle, 9 S. Pennsylvania Ave., Hancock (ℂ **301/678-6665;** www.candobicycle. com), rents and sells bikes in its shop, located between the C&O Canal towpath and the 20-mile Western Maryland Rail Trail. C&O also repairs bikes and operates a general store with lodging in the bunkhouse (reservations are a good idea). Shuttle service available. Closed Tuesday through Thursday in cold weather.

Adventure Sports, 113 E. Main St., Frostburg (ℂ **301/689-0345**), rents, sells, and services bikes, skis, and canoes.

The staff at **Cumberland Trail Connection,** Canal Place, Cumberland (ℂ **301/777-8724;** www.ctcbikes.com), right on the C&O tow path, know both the towpath and the Allegheny Highlands Trail. They rent and sell bikes, cycling equipment, and camping gear.

Allegany Expeditions (ℂ **800/819-5170** or 301/722-5170) rents canoes, kayaks, cross-country skis, and camping equipment. It offers guided trips for hiking, rock climbing and rappelling, cave exploration, and canoeing. Call to inquire about cross-country ski packages in New Germany State Park as well as fly-fishing and bass-fishing expeditions.

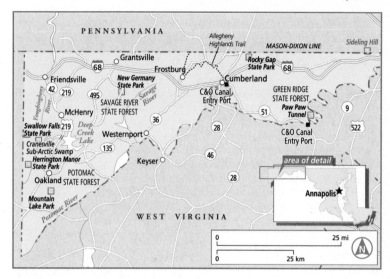

GARRETT COUNTY

Garrett County is covered by state forests and parks. It's the home of swimming holes, the state's highest waterfall, and an intriguing preserve owned by the Nature Conservancy. To find a park that best suits you, visit **www.dnr.maryland.gov**.

Swallow Falls State Park ★★★ (© 301/387-6938) has 10 miles of hiking trails. Follow the Youghiogheny River for views of Swallow Falls and the even more spectacular Muddy Falls, which drops 63 feet. The walk through one of Maryland's last virgin forests of giant pines and hemlocks shouldn't be missed—you won't forget its quiet beauty. The park has the area's largest camping facility, with 65 improved sites and modern bathhouses with showers and laundry tubs. Camping costs $25 to $50 per night; reservations can be made up to a year in advance. Pets are permitted on leashes in designated camping areas and in day-use areas in the off-season. A 5.5-mile trail good for hiking or cross-country skiing connects the park with Herrington Manor.

Herrington Manor State Park (© 301/334-9180) draws cross-country skiers to its 10 miles of groomed trails. It offers ski and snowshoe rentals ($15 a day), sled rentals ($6 a day), 20 furnished cabins, and stone warming rooms. Trails and rental facilities are open from 8:30am to 4pm during good skiing conditions. In summer, the park's trails draw hikers and bikers. The 53-acre Herrington Lake has guarded beaches and canoes, rowboats, and paddleboats to rent from May through September. Bring your tennis racquet or volleyball: Courts are waiting. Campers can reserve 1 of 20 furnished log cabins year-round; book as much as a year ahead. Rentals range from $20 to $100 for a full-service cabin. Pets are allowed only in day-use areas.

Savage River State Forest (© 301/895-5759), which surrounds New Germany and Big Run, is the largest of Maryland's state forests, at more than 54,000 acres. It features miles of rugged hiking trails. It's also home to many bears, so plan accordingly. The longest trail, Big Savage, follows a 17-mile path along the ridge of Big Savage Mountain

Tips Great Allegheny Passage

With the completion of the **Great Allegheny Passage,** it is now possible to walk or cycle 335 miles from Pittsburgh to Washington, D.C. The Passage and the C&O Canal towpath come together in Cumberland, and Maryland's section of the trail, the **Allegheny Highlands Trail** (www.ahtmtrail.org), stretches from Cumberland to Frostburg. Enthusiasts see this as a trail to conquer, but it's actually the fulfillment of George Washington's dream to connect the Chesapeake Bay to the Ohio River.

This path to gorgeous mountain vistas is an opportunity to test your endurance up hills and over miles. The climb from Cumberland to the Eastern Continental Divide marker is 1,700 feet. Riders go through three tunnels in Maryland, including the 3,294-foot-long Big Savage Tunnel (closed late Nov to early Apr). Along the trail you'll find lodging, camping areas, restrooms, and restaurants. There's also the possibility of meeting up with bears, turkeys, and copperhead snakes. And at one point, the trail parallels the Western Maryland Scenic Railway tracks.

Local bicycle shops provide rentals, equipment, and repairs, and some will shuttle cyclists to various trail heads. (See suppliers and guides listings for both Allegany and Garrett counties, below.) For a map, go to **www.ahtmtrail.org**. For information, call ℂ **888/282-2453.**

at an average elevation of 2,500 feet. Also popular is Monroe Run, which traverses the forest between New Germany and Big Run. Mountain bikers may use all trails except Big Savage and Monroe Run. Snowmobiles and off-road vehicles have their own trails; permits are required and available at park headquarters. Stop by for trail maps, including one delineating 10 miles of cross-country-ski trails. Savage River Lake was the site of the 1989 world white-water championships; only nonpowered watercraft are allowed on the water. Fifty-two primitive campsites are spread throughout the forest—you may not see another camper while you're here. Backwoods camping is also permitted, but fires are not allowed at some sites. Camping is available year-round at $10 per night, with sites offered on a first-come, first-served basis with self-registration. Pets are permitted on leashes. If you don't have the time or the inclination to stay for a while, at least drive through the park, as many motorcyclists do on weekends. The roads are public, and the feeling of escape that comes from all those acres of trees is worth the ride.

New Germany State Park ★★ (ℂ **301/895-5453**) has 12 miles of trails, well marked for cross-country skiing. It also offers equipment rentals, cabins, and large stone warming rooms where skiers can stop and get a snack. Trails and rental facilities are open from 8am to 4pm during good skiing conditions. The park has 39 improved campsites with clean bathhouses and hot showers. All sites are large, private, and located in a wooded glen; the cost is $20 per night. These can be rented up to a year in advance for visits between April and Labor Day; September through October, the sites are offered on a first-come, first-served basis. Available year-round are 11 furnished cabins—with electricity, fireplaces, and room for two to eight persons—for $90 to $120 a night, with a 2-night minimum required. You can reserve cabins up to a year in advance. The park also has a 13-acre lake popular for swimming and boating, with boat rentals available. The day-use fee for Marylanders is $2 on weekends and holidays, $3 during ski season. Non-residents pay $1 more. Pets are not permitted.

Big Run State Park (© 301/895-5453), just down the road, offers fishing and hiking along Monroe Run and Big Run. You can launch your boat at Savage River Reservoir. The 300-acre park has 30 rustic campsites with chemical toilets and running water. Some are in wooded areas along Monroe Run and Big Run, others on the shore of the Savage River Reservoir. Sites at Big Run are open year-round and cost $15 per night (available on a first-come, first-served basis). Pets are permitted on leashes.

Potomac–Garrett State Forest (© 301/334-2038) is spread over 19,000 acres in two separate tracts in the lower westernmost corner of the county. With plenty of streams, beaver ponds, and cranberry bogs, it offers beautiful scenery, including the highest point in any Maryland state forest: Backbone Mountain, in Garrett State Forest near Route 135 and Walnut Bottom Road. There are 8 miles of mountain-biking trails, as well as trails for snowmobiles, dirt bikes, and ATVs. Off-road-vehicle permits are required and can be obtained at each park's headquarters. Hikers can choose from 30 miles of trails, many easy enough for day hikes and many with mountain views that can only be seen off the road. Geocaching is also big here. The fishing here is some of the best in Western Maryland, with 21 miles of first-class trout streams, including 9 miles of the North Branch of the Potomac River. Here's the place to catch the Maryland Grand Slam: brook, brown, 'bo, and cutthroat trout. Potomac–Garrett also offers five primitive camping areas, open year-round. Getting to them may take some effort, however: The sites are beautiful and generously spaced, and a few have three-sided wooden shelters, but the roads to the sites are not well maintained. The cost is $10 for regular sites, $15 for a site with a shelter. Pets are permitted off-leash if they're under control.

Jennings Randolph Lake (© 301/359-3861) covers 952 acres and has 13 miles of shoreline. It straddles the Maryland–West Virginia line. On the Maryland side, there's a boat ramp at Mt. Zion Road via Route 135 and a scenic overlook at Walnut Bottom Road. The lake is open for boating, fishing, and water-skiing. Hiking trails on the Maryland side start at one of the overlooks. White-water rafting is available in spring. For the dam release schedule, see **www.nab.usace.army.mil/recreation/jenran.htm**. Call © 304/355-2890 for lake conditions. Pets on leashes are permitted in some areas.

Broadford Lake, near Oakland (© 301/334-9222), is open from March 31 to early November during daylight hours. The 140-acre park has a guarded beach as well as a boat launch and rentals. Electric boat motors only are permitted. There are picnic pavilions, playgrounds, and ball fields. Pets on leashes are permitted in some areas. Admission is $2 per car on weekdays and $3 per car on weekends.

Cranesville Swamp Preserve ★ (© 301/897-8570; www.nature.org) is a vestige of the last ice age. Operated by the Nature Conservancy, it's a 1,600-acre peat bog home to sedges, cranberry, sphagnum moss, and tamarack trees—a species usually not found south of Alaska. Quiet and wild, the four trails lead through a cathedral of pine forests and cross a 1,500-foot boardwalk to see the unusual plants, some carnivorous. To get to the entrance (which is in West Virginia), go south on U.S. Route 219; turn right on Mayhew Inn Road, left on Bray School Road, right on Oakland Sang Run Road, left on Swallow Falls Road, and right on Cranesville Road at the fork. Turn left on Lake Ford Road, right at the next fork. It's about a fifth of a mile on the right. The preserve is open dawn to dusk year-round. Admission is free. Pets are not allowed. Wear boots and bring water and bug repellent. There are no restrooms.

The Wild Rivers of Garrett County

The "three sisters"—the Youghiogheny, Casselman, and North Branch Potomac rivers—have become so popular that the area is often featured on national fly-fishing shows. The

Casselman is a fertile catch-and-release river; anglers here have been known to catch 40 fish a day. The Youghiogheny supports a strong population of brown and rainbow trout, but be aware that dam releases cause substantial increases in the water level below the Deep Creek Lake power plant. Call ℂ **315/413-2823** or visit **www.deepcreekhydro. com** for a dam-release schedule.

Garrett County offers myriad opportunities for white-water rafting, kayaking, and canoeing. The Youghiogheny, the North Branch Potomac, and the Savage are the area's best-known runs. Although they can be challenging all year, they're at their fiercest in the spring after snowmelt. In 1976, the Youghiogheny River between Millers Run and Friendsville became Maryland's first officially designated Wild and Scenic River. This portion, known as the Upper Yough, contains approximately 20 class IV and V rapids. Fortunately for the inexperienced paddler, outfitters have sprung up all over the area to take people down this exciting river. If you'd prefer a little less excitement, the Middle Yough offers class I and II rapids, and the Lower Yough is a class III run. There are also several rivers just across the border in West Virginia—the Cheat, Gauley, Big Sandy, and Russell Fork—that are rated class IV or higher.

Kayakers hoping to avoid raft traffic would do well to visit the North Branch Potomac and Savage rivers (both class III/IV); however, they can only be run after heavy rains or snowmelt. For open canoeing, the Casselman River (class II) to the west is good in winter and spring.

Most outfitters run raft trips on several or all of these rivers; see below for options.

Suppliers & Guides in Garrett County

Guided rafting trips cost $100 to $140 per person for an (expert) Upper Yough trip. Middle Yough (novice) trips cost about $50; Lower Yough (intermediate) trips are $75 to $135 depending on the level of service. Family float trips cost around $30. *Note:* Remember to tip your guide—$3 to $5 per person is appropriate.

Friendsville has become a white-water center, as it's located on the Upper Youghiogheny. Friendsville is at the intersection of I-68, Maryland Route 42, and the Yough; from Deep Creek Lake, take U.S. Route 219 north to Maryland Route 42 into town.

Precision Rafting, in Friendsville (ℂ **800/477-3723;** www.precisionrafting.com), and **Cheat River Outfitters** (ℂ **888/99-RIVER** [997-4837]; www.cheatriveroutfitters. com) offer trips in the Upper Yough's Class V waters (depending on the dam release schedule). Precision also offers raft trips down all of the rivers and paddling lessons. Cheat River offers trips on the Class II, III, and IV Cheat River in West Virginia, about 45 minutes from Deep Creek.

Several outfitters based in nearby Ohiopyle, Pa., offer similar trips. Try **Mountain Streams & Trails** (ℂ **800/RAFT-NOW** [723-8669]; www.mtstreams.com), which also does kid-oriented trips, or **Laurel Highlands River Tours** (ℂ **800/4-RAFTIN** [472-3846]; www.laurelhighlands.com). To get to Ohiopyle from Deep Creek Lake, take U.S. Route 219 north to U.S. Route 40 west (just past the intersection with I-68). Go into Pennsylvania and turn north onto State Route 381 to Ohiopyle. It's about an hour from Deep Creek Lake.

Allegany Expeditions (ℂ **800/819-5170**) offers equipment rentals and various guided excursions. See "Suppliers & Guides in Allegany County," above, for details.

Perhaps unique to Garrett County is its **Adventuresports Institute** ★, Garrett College, 687 Mosser Rd., McHenry (ℂ **301/387-3330;** www.adventuresportsi.org). This division of Garrett College offers an associate's degree in adventure sports, but its classes are open to nonmatriculated students. If you want to learn how to paddle white water rather than just ride along in a raft, enroll in a 4-day kayaking class. The institute rents equipment and teaches classes in mountaineering, rock climbing, and ice climbing. For a list of course offerings and prices, call or visit the website.

For tackle and bait, stop by **Bill's Outdoor Center,** 20768 Garrett Hwy. (U.S. Rte. 219), McHenry (© **301/387-FISH** [3474]).

High Mountain Sports, 21327 Garrett Hwy., Oakland (© **301/387-4199**), sells, rents, and services bicycles. It also offers water-ski and kayak lessons and tours, and mountain-bike tours, from this location. At its location next to Wisp Resort, 8527 Sang Run Rd., McHenry (© **301/387-2113**), it rents skis, snowshoes, and snowboards.

Rent kayaks from **Deep Creek Marina,** 1899 Deep Creek Dr. (© **301/387-6977**).

Snowshoes can be rented at **Herrington Manor State Park** (© **301/334-9180**) and **Deep Creek State Park** (© **301/387-5563**) for $15 for a full day.

2 CUMBERLAND & ALLEGANY COUNTY

140 miles W of Baltimore; 140 miles NW of Washington, D.C.; 113 miles SE of Pittsburgh

The city of Cumberland sits on a tight bend of the Potomac River in the heart of the Allegheny Mountains, with a portion of the C&O Canal as its centerpiece. Once a large industrial city, it is now quieter, though tourism is a growing industry. Visitors come to see the canal, George Washington's headquarters, and the surrounding mountains.

At the turn of the 20th century, Cumberland was Maryland's "Queen City," second in size only to Baltimore. Many reminders of those days remain: a long street of Victorian mansions, the ornate storefronts of the rejuvenated shopping district, the black smoke of the *Mountain Thunder* coal-powered train.

Since the construction of I-68 cut right through—you might say right on top of—Cumberland, the city has become more accessible to the rest of the state. People come to see not only Cumberland, but also Rocky Gap State Park (known for Lake Habeeb) with its resort, golf course, and area parks.

The Allegheny Mountains are particularly beautiful in autumn, and the area is becoming popular with bikers and hikers who find Cumberland and nearby Frostburg cheaper and closer to home than Deep Creek Lake to the west.

ESSENTIALS

GETTING THERE I-68, which runs right through the center of Cumberland, is the fastest route by car from either the east or west. From the east and north, I-70 will take you to I-68. For a more scenic drive, you can get off I-70 or I-68 onto the Old National Pike (U.S. Rte. 40).

Amtrak (© **800/872-7245;** www.amtrak.com) serves Cumberland on its Capitol Limited train route, which travels from Washington, D.C., to Chicago. It stops at the station on East Harrison Street.

The **Greater Cumberland Regional Airport** (© **304/738-0002;** www.cumberland airport.com) is actually in Wiley Ford, West Virginia, 2½ miles off Route 68 at exit 43B. It serves only private planes.

VISITOR INFORMATION Walking-tour brochures, maps, and information about the Cumberland are available at the visitor center operated by **Allegany County Tourism** (www.mdmountainside.com) at the **Western Maryland Railway Station,** 13 Canal St., Cumberland (© **800/425-2067**), open daily from 9am to 5pm.

SPECIAL EVENTS The **Heritage Days Festival** (① **301/722-0037**), held in mid-June in Cumberland, fills the streets with arts and crafts, entertainment, and train rides. **C&O Canal and Rail Fest** (① **301/722-8226**), in mid-July at Canal Place, celebrates Cumberland's transportation heritage with living-history demonstrations, crafts, entertainment (often by nationally known performers), and food.

WHERE TO STAY

The Cumberland-Frostburg area offers an inviting blend of historic inns, modern hotels and motels, and homey B&B lodgings. Most are moderately priced and offer very good value. All have free parking.

Failinger's Hotel Gunter ★ This 1897 landmark hotel boasts guest rooms and public areas, particularly the centerpiece oak staircase, that are a work of Victorian charm. Modern conveniences are plentiful, but original oak doors, brass fixtures, claw-foot tubs, and delicate sconces remain. Rooms are individually furnished, with canopy or four-poster beds, armoires, and pastel fabrics; several of them were redecorated in 2009. Room no. 307, the Roy Clark Room, named after the country singer who stayed here in 1990, is the most masculine of the rooms with black-and-white Victorian trimmings.

11 W. Main St., Frostburg, MD 21532. ① **301/689-6511**. Fax 301/689-6034. www.failingershotelgunter. com. 14 units. $95 double; $110 suite. Rates include continental breakfast. AE, DC, DISC, MC, V. **Amenities:** Free Wi-Fi. *In room:* A/C, TV, fridge and microwave available.

Holiday Inn Cumberland This modern six-story hotel sits at the east end of Cumberland's shopping promenade, providing easy walking access to the downtown area. King and double rooms are clean and comfortable, as you would expect from a Holiday Inn. Railroad enthusiasts might like a room overlooking the nearby tracks (the trains aren't too loud); everyone else will prefer the town side, where there's less noise.

100 S. George St., Cumberland, MD 21502. ① **877/426-4672** or 301/724-8800. Fax 301/724-4001. www. hicumberland.com. 130 units. $129–$209 double. Children 19 and under stay free in parent's room; children 12 and under eat free with parent. AE, DC, DISC, MC, V. Pets accepted for a fee. **Amenities:** Restaurant; lounge; billiards; fitness center; outdoor pool. *In room:* A/C, fridge, microwave, Wi-Fi (fee).

Inn at Walnut Bottom ★★ (Kids) The owners have combined the warmth and charm of a B&B with standard hotel amenities and a few niceties of their own, including delicious breakfasts featuring crème brûlée French toast or some other hot delight. You might need to borrow one their bikes to burn off those calories afterward. Then, consider Afspaending—a relaxation therapy that combines localized massage techniques with gentle stretches and exercises. It's offered by the inn's co-owner, who is trained in the technique, and is a relief for sore cycling muscles. The inn is composed of two 19th-century homes just a block from historic Washington Street: the Cowden House (1820) and the Dent House (1890). Guest rooms are spacious, with high ceilings, large windows, antiques and period reproductions, and down comforters. Children are welcome.

120 Greene St., Cumberland, MD 21502. ① **800/286-9718** or 301/777-0003. www.iwbinfo.com. 12 units, 4 with shared bathroom. $120–$170 double. Rates include full breakfast. AE, DISC, MC, V. **Amenities:** Bikes; relaxation therapy. *In room:* A/C, TV w/cable, hair dryer, free Wi-Fi.

Rocky Gap Lodge & Golf Resort Situated beside Lake Habeeb and the rolling hills of Rocky Gap State Park, Rocky Gap Lodge mixes luxury accommodations with a challenging 18-hole Jack Nicklaus golf course—populated by wild critters unafraid of flying golf balls—and the beauty of the Appalachian mountains. Golf-package guests should check with the manager to extend their checkout time (tee times and golf clinics can run much later than the usual checkout time). Rocky Gap also offers a year-round program of outdoor activities, including rappelling, rock climbing, caving, kayaking, horseback riding, fly-fishing, biking, horse-drawn carriage or sleigh tours, cross-country skiing, and boating. Or you can just pull up a lounge chair beside the lake or choose from the many treatments offered at the Garden Spa.

16701 Lakeview Rd. NE, Flintstone, MD 21530. ✆ **800/724-0828** or 301/784-8400. Fax 301/784-8408. www.rockygapresort.com. 216 units. $119–$239 double; $199–$619 suite. Children 18 and under stay free in parent's room. AE, DC, MC, V. **Amenities:** 2 restaurants; lounge; golf; health club; indoor pool; spa; tennis courts. *In room:* A/C, TV w/pay movies and Nintendo, hair dryer, Wi-Fi (fee).

Savage River Lodge ★★★   Tucked in the woods of the Savage River State Forest down a winding 1½-mile road, this lodge will take you away from the world. Cellphone reception may be spotty but the scenery is a sure bet. Eighteen individual log cabins with front porches, spacious but simple, combined with an elegant restaurant (see "Where to Dine," below) and plenty of outdoor activities make this a spot you won't want to leave. Pets are welcome in most of the cabins; several are pet-free to accommodate those with allergies.

1600 Mt. Aetna Rd., Frostburg, MD 21532 (about 5 miles off I-68). ✆ **301/689-3200.** www.savageriver lodge.com. 18 cabins (sleep 4). $185–$240; higher in Oct and Dec. Rates include continental breakfast. AE, DISC, MC, V. **Amenities:** Restaurant; lounge; outdoor activities; TV in lodge; 10 miles of hiking trails; Wi-Fi in lodge. *In room:* A/C, gas fireplace, fridge, hair dryer, high-speed Internet.

WHERE TO DINE
Cumberland

Oxford House Restaurant ★   AMERICAN/INTERNATIONAL   This restaurant is a standout in the region. The atmosphere is intimate, the food and service excellent. The chef mixes European flavors with American ones—and that makes for a menu with a lot of spice. Fish is featured; salmon dishes, such as the almond-crusted preparation, are winners, but there are also meat and vegetarian choices. Be sure to check the wine list.

129 Baltimore St. ✆ **301/777-7101.** www.oxfordhouserestaurant.com. Reservations recommended. Main courses $19–$30, lunch $9–$15. AE, DISC, MC, V. Mon–Sat noon–9pm; brunch on the last Sun of each month, Easter, and Mother's Day 10am–3pm.

Queen City Creamery Coffee Bar & Deli COFFEE/ICE CREAM   Mix nostalgia with your ice cream at this soda fountain, which has a counter, booths, and a 1952 jukebox. Coffee drinks, soups, and sandwiches are available. A shop at Canal Place is open weekends.

108 Harrison St. ✆ **301/777-0011.** www.queencitycreamery.com. Reservations not accepted. Sandwiches $2–$7. MC, V. Mon–Thurs 7am–9pm; Fri 7am–10pm; Sat 8am–10pm; Sun 8am–9pm.

Ristorante Ottaviani (Kids) ITALIAN   Sit up front for a quieter, more intimate dinner. If you sit in back, you just might feel you've become part of a big Italian family (one in which children 8 and under get a complimentary beverage and bowl of pasta). Everybody greets everybody else, music blares from the sound system, and the mood is jovial as waitresses pass by with plates of great pasta.

25 N. Centre St. ✆ **301/722-0052.** www.ristoranteottaviani.com. Reservations recommended on Fri-Sat. Main courses $13–$27. MC, V. Tues–Sat 5–10pm.

Frostburg

Start your day with a cup of joe in Frostburg at **Mountain City Coffeehouse and Creamery,** 60 E. Main St. (✆ **301/687-0808**). They've got Deep Creek Lake's famous Lakeside Creamery ice cream, too. They are open every morning but Monday.

Au Petit Paris Restaurant Français ★ (Finds) FRENCH   Au Petit Paris is a find in this small town—a fine, intimate French restaurant, worth the drive from Cumberland or Deep Creek Lake. Even other area restaurateurs recommend it. The interior has a Parisian feel, with French posters and bistro-style furnishings. The restaurant, celebrating its 50th anniversary in 2010, is a favorite for classic French fare, such as chateaubriand (order 24 hr. in advance) and coq au vin. If you're planning to eat here, make a reservation.

86 E. Main St. ℭ **301/689-8946.** www.aupetitparis.com. Reservations recommended. Main courses $20–$32. AE, DISC, MC, V. Tues–Sat 5:30–9:30pm.

Giuseppe's Italian Restaurant (Value) ITALIAN   In the heart of town and a block from the Frostburg State University campus, this spot is popular with the college community and locals. And it deserves the attention with first-rate food and cozy atmosphere. The pizzas are first-rate and you can't beat all the usual Italian favorites, such as pasta, shrimp scampi, veal parmigiana, and a wonderful array of antipasti, as well as a few unusual dishes such as crab carbonara.

11 Bowery St. ℭ **301/689-2220.** www.giuseppes.net. Reservations recommended on Fri–Sat. Main courses $8.50–$27. AE, DISC, MC, V. Sun 3–9pm; Mon–Sat 4:30–11pm.

The Savage River Lodge ★★★ AMERICAN   Even if you don't stay here, it's worth the drive down the long road to sit in the rustic dining room or out on the porch. You'll eat well, whether it's the weekend breakfast with omelets, crab Benedict, and rich French toast or a simple lunch of soup, salad, or a sandwich. For dinner, choose from steak, seafood, or maybe a portobello mushroom with lemon couscous.

1600 Mt. Aetna Rd. (about 5 miles off I-68). ℭ **301/689-3200.** www.savageriverlodge.com. Reservations required. Main courses $8–$12 breakfast, $9–$13 lunch, $18–$35 dinner. AE, DISC, MC, V. Mon–Fri 11:30am–1:30pm and 5–8:30pm; Sat–Sun 10am–2pm and 5–8:30pm.

WHAT TO SEE & DO

One of the highlights of a visit to Cumberland is a stroll through the **Victorian Historic District** ★★★ along Washington Street on the western side of town. This area includes the site of the original Fort Cumberland (now the Emmanuel Episcopal Church) and more than 50 residential and public buildings built in the 1800s, when Cumberland was at its peak. Listed on the National Register of Historic Places, Washington showcases homes with stained-glass windows, cupolas, and mansard roofs. You'll see architectural styles ranging from Federal, Queen Anne, Empire, Colonial Revival, Italianate, and English Country Gothic to Georgian Revival, Gothic Revival, and Greek Revival. A self-guided walking tour available from the visitor center offers a glimpse into their history. Two homes are open for tours (see below).

Brooke Whiting House of Art   Whiting, a curator of rare books for UCLA, bequeathed his 1911 bungalow and collection to the Allegany County Historical Society, which has opened the house for tours. Memorabilia from his world travels, including paintings, Asian ceramics, and Murano and Tiffany glass, are on display.

632 Washington St. ℭ **301/777-7782.** www.thewhitinghouse.org. Admission $5. Hours by appointment only. Regular hours will begin spring 2010.

Canal Place (Chesapeake & Ohio Canal National Historical Park/Cumberland Visitor Center)   The C&O Canal opened here in 1850. For more than 75 years, it was an important transport line and had a major impact on the development of the town. Visit the Western Maryland Station Center at track level, check out the exhibits on the history of the canal (including a model of the Paw Paw Tunnel), and pick up

a brochure. Then explore the towpath, a nearly level trail for walkers, hikers, and bikers.
There are remnants of locks, dams, lock houses, and other features along the way.

13 Canal St. ✆ **301/722-8226.** www.nps.gov/choh. Free admission. Daily 9am–5pm.

C&O Canal Paw Paw Tunnel ★

Construction on the Paw Paw Tunnel, part of the C&O Canal National Historical Park, started in 1836 when engineers decided to build the Canal right through, rather than around, an intervening mountain. The result was an engineering marvel lined with more than six million bricks passing ¾ mile through the hill. Today, the tunnel is open to walkers, who can make the one-way trip in 20 minutes. This is not for the claustrophobic or those afraid of the dark (you must walk down a narrow towpath bounded by a guardrail, with the canal on one side and a sloping brick wall on the other). If you're up for it, pass through the massive brick arch into the darkness, then head for the light at the end of the tunnel. A flashlight is a must.

Rte. 51 and the Potomac River, south of Cumberland. ✆ **301/722-8226.** www.nps.gov/choh. Free admission. Daily dawn–dusk.

Emmanuel Episcopal Church

This church, located in Cumberland's historic district, is built on the 1755 foundations of Fort Cumberland, where George Washington began his military career. Although the Emmanuel parish dates from 1803, the cornerstone of the current building was laid in 1849. The church contains original Tiffany stained-glass windows and a scale model of Fort Cumberland. The grounds are part of the Fort Cumberland Walking Trail.

16 Washington St. ✆ **301/777-3364.** emmanuelparish.ang-md.org. Free admission. Mon–Fri 9am–5pm, except during services. Services Wed 5:30pm; Thurs 10:30am; Sun 8 and 10am, 6pm.

George Washington's Headquarters

This log cabin, believed to be the only remaining structure from the original Fort Cumberland, was used by then-colonel George Washington as his official quarters during the French and Indian War. The one-room cabin is not open to the public but has a window with an audio description.

In Riverside Park, Greene St. (at the junction of Wills Creek and the Potomac River). ✆ **301/777-5132.** Free admission. Daily 24 hr.; exterior viewing only.

Gordon-Roberts House

Built as a private residence in 1867 for the president of the C&O Canal, this fascinating 18-room Second Empire home is now in the hands of the Allegany County Historical Society. It's filled with antiques, such as a Victorian courting couch and an 1840 square grand piano. Other features include a research room, a walled garden, and a basement kitchen with antique utensils and fireplace.

218 Washington St. ✆ **301/777-8678.** www.gordon-robertshouse.com. Admission $7. Wed–Sat 10am–5pm. Last tour at 4pm.

Queen City Transportation Museum ★ (Kids)

The Cumberland branch of the Thrasher Carriage Museum (see below), this museum celebrates the National Road, the U.S. government's first public-works project, which began in Cumberland. The exhibits, with 32 vehicles from Conestoga wagons to carriages to the automobile, are in chronological order. Children's activities are squeezed between the buggies.

210 S. Centre St. ✆ **301/777-1776.** www.queencitytransportationmuseum.com. Admission $5 adults, $3 children 6–12. May–Oct Tues–Sat 10am–5pm; Nov–Apr Tues–Sat 10am–4pm. Last tour an hour before closing.

Thrasher Carriage Museum ★

Housed in a renovated train warehouse opposite the Western Maryland Railroad depot in Frostburg, this museum houses an extensive collection of late-19th- and early-20th-century horse-drawn carriages, featuring more than 50 vehicles from the collection of the late James R. Thrasher. Highlights include the inaugural coach used by Teddy Roosevelt, several Vanderbilt sleighs, elaborate funeral wagons, formal closed vehicles, surreys, and open sleighs.

Depot Center, 19 Depot St., Frostburg. © **301/689-3380.** www.thethrashercarriagemuseum.com. Admission $4 adults, $2 children 6 and over. May–Oct Thurs–Sun 10am–2pm; Nov to mid-Dec Sat–Sun 10am–2pm; late Dec to Apr by appointment.

The Western Maryland Scenic Railroad ★★ (Kids) The 32-mile round-trip excursion between Cumberland and Frostburg—enhanced by live commentary—follows a mountain valley route through the Cumberland Narrows, with many panoramic vistas and a 1,300-foot elevation change between the two destinations. All trains depart from and return to Cumberland. The trip takes 3½ hours, including a 1½-hour layover in Frostburg, where you can visit the nearby Thrasher Carriage Museum or get a snack. The railroad also offers weekend murder-mystery dining excursions. The website lists dates and times. Diesel trains are used May through August and in October to help meet the demand for tickets. Santa Express trips, offered Thanksgiving weekend through December, are aboard the steam train.

Western Maryland Station Center, 13 Canal St. © **800/872-4650** or 301/759-4400. www.wmsr.com. Tickets $30 adults, $28 seniors, $16 children 12 and under; first-class tickets that include lunch $55 adults, $53 seniors, $35 children 12 and under. Reservations required. Excursions generally leave at 11:30am; special excursions leave at 6pm; 4:30pm departures added in Oct. From I-68, take downtown Cumberland exit 43C (westbound) or Johnson St. exit 43A (eastbound) and follow signs.

SHOPPING

Cumberland's pedestrian mall along Baltimore Street is worth a stroll. Most shops are open every day. **Monkey Business,** 62 Baltimore St. (© **301/724-2050**), features upscale women's fashions. The **Saville Gallery,** 9 N. Centre St. (© **301/777-2787;** www.alleganyartscouncil.org), is operated by the Allegany Arts Council and features the work of Western Marylanders. Just off the pedestrian mall is the **Book Center,** 15 N. Centre St. (© **301/722-2284**), where you'll find a large selection of books on Maryland, local history, railroading, and canals.

Canal Place, adjacent to the Western Maryland Railway Station (© 800/989-9394; www.canalplace.org), is home to **Arts at Canal Place** (© 301/777-8199), **Cumberland Trail Connection Bicycle Shop** (© 301/777-8724), and **Tree House Toys** (© 301/759-4869). For a bite to eat, options include the **Crabby Pig** (© 301/724-7472), **Queen City Creamery** (© 301/777-2552), and **Wild Mountain Cafe** (© 301/759-9453).

CUMBERLAND AFTER DARK

Something is always going on in one of the three area theaters or at nearby Frostburg State University's **Performing Arts Center** (© **301/687-7462;** www.frostburg.edu). Check with the **Allegany Arts Council,** 9 N. Centre St. (© **301/777-ARTS** [2787]; www.alleganyartscouncil.org), for a schedule of concerts and cultural events.

The **Cumberland Theatre,** 101 N Johnson St. (© **301/759-4990;** www.cumberland theatre.com), in a renovated church, presents a professional program of musicals and comedies as well as mysteries and dramas June through November.

The **New Embassy Theatre,** 49 Baltimore St. (© **301/722-4692**), a 1931 Art Deco movie theater, hosts classic films, live music, theater, and dance. Its restoration was featured on Bob Villa's *Restore America.* Call for a schedule and tickets.

Windsor Hall, 37 Baltimore St. (© **301/724-6800**), means live music with blues, jazz, rock and occasionally, stand-up comics.

3 DEEP CREEK LAKE ★★★ & GARRETT COUNTY ★

50 miles SW of Cumberland; 190 miles W of Baltimore; 120 miles SE of Pittsburgh

Garrett County's mountain scenery has beckoned visitors for centuries. Native American hunters combed these hills a thousand years ago looking for game. In Colonial days, this was the American frontier, populated mostly by Indians and trappers. Few settled here until the coming of the Baltimore & Ohio Railroad in the 1850s. Farmers, coal miners, and loggers were the first to arrive. During the Civil War, the railroad provided a needed supply link, and Garrett towns became the targets of Confederate attack. Once peace returned to the country, Garrett became a vacation destination. Three presidents—Grant, Cleveland, and Harrison—vacationed here.

Once Deep Creek Lake was created in the 1920s and the Wisp Resort built in 1944, leisure travelers had even more reasons to make the trip to Garrett County. Deep Creek Lake is now the state's largest freshwater lake, nearly 12 miles in length, with 65 miles of shoreline occupied by private vacation homes and chalets. The northern end is where the action is—the commercial centers, the Wisp Resort, and the waterfront hotels and inns are all located here. Summer temperatures, averaging a comfortable 66°F (19°C), draw visitors escaping the heat and humidity of the big cities. In winter, Deep Creek Lake is Maryland's premier ski resort, with an average temperature of 28°F (2°C) and a yearly snowfall of more than 100 inches.

In recent years, Garrett County has become a four-season destination as well as *the* place for mid-Atlantic residents to buy a second home. It's centrally located between Pittsburgh, Baltimore and Washington, and eastern Ohio cities, a 3- to 4-hour drive from each. Visitors can hike or bike the scenic trails; go skiing, snow-tubing, or snowshoeing; take to the waters and try boating, fly-fishing, kayaking, or white-water rafting; and visit antiques and crafts stores. Or they can do nothing but sit back and enjoy the old-time charm that this region has long been known for.

ESSENTIALS

GETTING THERE   From the east or west, take I-68 to exit 14 and drive south on U.S. Route 219.

VISITOR INFORMATION   The visitor center is on U.S. Route 219, near the bottom of the Wisp Resort's ski runs. It's open daily from 9am to 5pm. Ask for a vacation guide, which contains a calendar of events and information on local history, restaurants, hotels, and shopping. For information, call ☎ **301/387-4386** or go to **www.garrettchamber. com**.

> **Fun Facts**   **Venice in the Mountains**
>
> Skip the car and head to lakeside establishments by boat in summer. Businesses have added piers so visitors can get to the store, the movies, and even church by boat. The visitor center has a "Travel by Boat" map listing all the places with docks. Call ☎ **301/387-4386** for information.

For ski conditions, call ☏ **301/387-4911** or visit **www.visitdeepcreek.com/ski report.php**.

GETTING AROUND Businesses in Deep Creek Lake sometimes have mailing addresses in McHenry or Oakland. Deep Creek Lake and McHenry are, for all intents and purposes, the same place, and you can count on those addresses to be on the lake or close by. Oakland, the county seat of Garrett County, is several miles south of Deep Creek Lake. Some businesses maintain mailing addresses there; others are actually just off the lake, outside the Deep Creek Lake/McHenry postal zone. Proximity to the lake resort areas is indicated in the listings in this section.

U.S. Route 219 runs beside the northern half of Deep Creek Lake and swings south toward Oakland. The Glendale Road Bridge crosses the middle of the lake and leads to Deep Creek Lake State Park (where you'll find the best public beach and a nature center). North of this bridge is where all the action is. South of this bridge, it's quieter and more remote. Most sailors sail their boats here; look for the weekend regattas.

SPECIAL EVENTS Garrett County celebrates autumn with a 5-day **Autumn Glory Festival** (☏ **301/387-4386**), usually held the second weekend in October. In early June, Scottish pride shows during the **McHenry Highland Festival** (☏ **301/387-3093**)—come for the sounds of bagpipe, harp, and fiddle, plus dance and athletic competitions, bluegrass music, crafts, and food. The **Garrett Lakes Arts Festival** (☏ **301/387-3082; www.artsandentertainment.org**), a series of performances held March through September, includes a sampling of music and drama.

WHERE TO STAY
Vacation Rentals

The Deep Creek Lake area offers plenty of vacation properties—cabins, town homes, and mountain chalets—for rent by the week or in 2- and 3-day intervals. They come in all sizes, from a two-bedroom lakeside cottage or slopeside town house to eight-bedroom behemoths with extra everything (fireplaces, hot tubs, decks, boat slips, and even ski-in/ski-outs are available). Many allow pets. They generally come with all the linens, appliances, and tools you'll need. Most homes are individually owned and rented through agencies. Reputable ones are **Railey Mountain Lake Vacations** (☏ **866/544-3223; www.deepcreek.com**), **Long & Foster Resort Vacation Rentals** (☏ **800/336-7303; www.deepcreekresort.com**), and **Coldwell Banker Deep Creek Realty** (☏ **410/387-6187; www.deepcreekrealty.com**).

Hotels, Motels & B&Bs

Carmel Cove Inn ★★ You'll notice this little B&B, with its steeples and clock tower, looks a bit like a monastery—and it was once a Carmelite priory. Tucked in a wooded area off Glendale Road, you'll feel the serenity of the place as you stroll its 2 acres, down to the cove and dock. Inside, these are no monks' cells. The comfortable guest rooms offer a variety of amenities. Some units have hot tubs; others have private decks or fireplaces. Breakfast is delivered to premier and terrace rooms; appetizers are offered in the evening. The parlor has a striking stone fireplace and a billiards table.

105 Monastery Way, Swanton, MD 21561. ☏ **301/387-0067.** www.carmelcoveinn.com. 11 units. $175–$195 double. Rates include full breakfast and snacks. DISC, MC, V. No children 12 and under. **Amenities:** Complimentary beverage bar; billiards table; DVD library; snow- and watersports equipment; tennis court; Wi-Fi w/laptop available for guests' use. *In room:* A/C, TV/DVD, hair dryer.

Haley Farm Bed & Breakfast ★★ If you dream of a real country vacation, surrounded by orchards, wildflowers, and horses, this could be your spot. Set on 65 acres, Haley Farm offers country living in luxurious accommodations. Rooms range from spacious to cavernous; most are suites with fireplaces, Jacuzzis, and traditional furnishings. Three units have kitchenettes. More private (and downright huge) accommodations are available in the carriage house and barn. Need more room and privacy? The lakeside cottage offers the amenities of an entire house with boat dock and hot tub. The inn offers spa treatments, such as massages and facials (reservations required). Ask about packages and group retreat programs.

16766 Garrett Hwy., Oakland, MD 21550. ⓒ 888/231-FARM (3276) or 301/387-9050. Fax 301/387-9050. www.haleyfarm.com. 10 units. $155–$235 double; $400 cottage. Rates include full breakfast. 2-night minimum stay required on weekends. DISC, MC, V. No children 12 and under. **Amenities:** Sauna; snow- and watersports equipment. In room: A/C, TV/VCR, free Wi-Fi.

Lake Pointe Inn ★★ Built in the 1800s, this inn has a variety of accommodations. Room sizes vary, from small to spacious enough for three. Expect dreamy beds, warm earth tones, and arts-and-crafts-style furnishings. Most units have gas fireplaces and Jacuzzis, some have steam showers, and you can count on a view of the lake. A couple units, including the spacious McCann, have balconies. South-facing rooms offer the best views, but all have comfortable amenities. The blazing fire in the living room may keep you from heading outdoors—but the lake and the ski slopes, both within walking distance, are bound to beckon. If you're allergic to down pillows and comforters, alternatives are available. Reserve ahead for spa treatments.

174 Lake Pointe Dr., McHenry, MD 21541. ⓒ 800/523-LAKE (5253) or 301/387-0111. www.deep creekinns.com. 10 units. $250–$292 double. $15 off-season discount. Rates include full breakfast. 2-night minimum stay required on weekends. DISC, MC, V. No children 16 and under. **Amenities:** Bikes; massage room; sauna; steam room; tennis court; video library; watersports equipment. In room: A/C, TV/VCR, hair dryer, MP3 dock, free Wi-Fi.

Riverside Hotel (Value Set on the a quiet section of the Youghiogheny River, this small 1889 inn offers simple eco-friendly lodgings and a hearty vegetarian dinner that are popular with the kayakers. Though newly refurbished, the hotel contains some of the original hotel's beds. Room no. 5, really a suite with separate sitting room, has river views. Room no. 2, the only room that's air-conditioned, also has a fireplace. Dinner, served 4 to 8pm Friday to Monday, is open to the public. Other days, dinner is available by reservation for groups of six or more. Though breakfast isn't served here, the accurately named **Friendly Cup,** 641 Water St. (ⓒ **410/859-3608**), next door, opens at 7am Friday through Monday with organic coffee, sweet treats, and free Wi-Fi.

609 Water St., Friendsville. ⓒ **301/746-5253.** www.riversidehotel.us. 3 units. $65–$105 double. DC, DISC, MC, V. Closed Nov–Mar. **Amenities:** Free Wi-Fi. In room: Fridge, microwave.

Suites at Silver Tree Privately owned condominium units overlooking the lake are rented out in this hotel-like enterprise. Each unit is furnished according to the owners' tastes, with a variety of one-bedroom, one-bedroom-with-loft, and studio apartments. All have kitchenettes, gas fireplaces, and TVs. The majority of units have lake-view balconies and most will accommodate four people. Silver Tree takes advantage of its picturesque cove location with a gigantic deck and plenty of Adirondack chairs. Two massive stone fireplaces dominate the lobby overlooking the lake.

565 Glendale Rd., Oakland, MD 21550. ⓒ **800/711-1719.** www.suitesatsilvertree.com. 33 units. $145–$314 in season; $103–$261 off-season. AE, DISC, MC, V. **Amenities:** Restaurant; lounge w/weekend entertainment; fitness center; marina; sauna. In room: A/C, TV, kitchenette, hair dryer, free Wi-Fi.

Will O'the Wisp (Kids) Variety makes this a place to consider. Room layouts vary from a one-room efficiency to a two-story, three-bedroom apartment. For example, unit no. 308 adjoins unit no. 408 for a two-story unit. All have decks or balconies with direct views of the swimming beach and lake. Units are individually owned with varying levels of furnishings, though everything is clean and well-kept. When you call to book, ask how long ago the units were updated. Also, if you want a clearer view of the lake in summer, ask for a unit ending in 01 to 05. In every case, there's maid service every day. An indoor pool, huge game room, and great restaurant—the Four Seasons—make this a great spot.

20160 Garrett Hwy., Oakland, MD 21550. ℂ **888/590-7283** or 301/387-5506. www.willothewisp.com. units. $145–$400 in season; $105–$235 off-season. AE, DC, DISC, MC, V. **Amenities:** Restaurant; lounge; beach; dock; fitness center; indoor pool; sauna. *In room:* A/C, TV, hair dryer, free Wi-Fi.

Wisp Resort ★★ (Kids) With accommodations overlooking the slopes and ski lockers just inside the door, Wisp makes it easy on skiers. Recently refurbished, Wisp offers two-room suites in the tower or standard rooms or efficiencies with kitchenettes in the Lodge; all have queen-size beds and sofa beds. Two rooms have fireplaces, and the tower suites have Murphy beds in the sitting room. A center for kids 3 to 14, with half- and full-day skiing and snowboarding classes, makes things easy on parents. The resort offers a huge variety of outdoor activities throughout the year, including mountain biking, boat tours, and off-road vehicles.

290 Marsh Hill Rd. (off U.S. Rte. 219, on north side of Deep Creek Lake), McHenry, MD 21541. ℂ **800/462-9477** or 301/387-5581. Fax 301/387-4127. www.wispresort.com. 169 units. $79–$229 double. AE, DC, DISC, MC, V. Pets accepted for a fee. **Amenities:** Restaurant; coffee shop/pizzeria; 2 lounges; warm-weather mountain biking; scenic chairlift rides; children's center; concierge; fitness center; 18-hole golf course; hot tub; paintball; indoor pool; spa; skate park; ski shop; ski/snowboard program for children 3–14; tennis court. *In room:* A/C, fridge, hair dryer, Wi-Fi (fee).

WHERE TO DINE

Note: Garrett County liquor regulations prohibit alcohol sales on Sunday, except when served with a meal. No alcohol can be served before 1pm.

Canoe on the Run DELI This unpretentious sandwich shop serves gourmet sandwiches, coffee, and pastries; there are even a few vegetarian options, a rarity in these parts. The dining area is spare but quiet and cozy, with a gas fireplace. In warm weather, the outdoor deck is available. Beer and wine are sold here.

2622 Deep Creek Dr., McHenry. ℂ **301/387-5933.** Reservations not accepted. Sandwiches and salads $5–$8. AE, DISC, MC, V. Mon–Fri 8am–2:30pm; Sat–Sun 8am–3:30pm.

The Deer Park Inn ★ FRENCH For fine dining in a turn-of-the-20th-century atmosphere, it's hard to beat this lovely 1889 inn, built deep in the country as a summer home for Baltimore architect Josiah Pennington. The restored 17-room "cottage" is listed on the National Register of Historic Places. Furnished with Victorian antiques, it is a romantic setting for candlelit French cuisine with an American flair. The menu recently included confit of duck with braised red cabbage and garlic mashed potatoes, salmon en croûte, and filet with cabernet sauvignon sauce. The inn also offers three bedrooms upstairs ($145–$165 double).

65 Hotel Rd., Deer Park. ℂ **301/334-2308.** www.deerparkinn.com. Reservations recommended. Main courses $20–$29. DISC, MC, V. Summer Mon–Sat 5:30–9:30pm; winter Thurs–Sat 5:30–9:30pm. Located 9 miles southeast of the Deep Creek Lake Bridge, off Sand Flat Rd. and Rte. 135; look for signs.

Four Seasons ★ AMERICAN Four Seasons is more formal than many of the other eateries in Deep Creek, with lots of polished wood, stone trim, and gigantic picture windows overlooking the lake. Come for the food, too. An ambitious menu offered for breakfast, lunch, and dinner makes this a good choice all day long. Try the rich omelets or banana nut French toast for breakfast, the burgers for lunch, or the meat and fish dishes at dinner served with a variety of savory sauces.

At Will O' the Wisp, 20160 Garrett Hwy. (U.S. Rte. 219), Oakland. ⓒ **301/387-5503**, ext. 2201. Reservations recommended for dinner. Main courses $4–$10 breakfast, $5–$8 lunch, $14–$30 dinner. AE, DISC, MC, V. Daily 7am–2pm and 5–9:30pm. Located just south of the Deep Creek Lake Bridge.

Lakeside Creamery ICE CREAM If you see a crowd outside the Lakeside Creamery in the morning, you know it must be close to opening time. The homemade ice cream draws people by car, on foot, and even by boat. It offers 22 flavors. Try the handmade waffle cones, too.

20282 Garrett Hwy. (U.S. Rte. 219), Oakland. ⓒ **301/387-2580.** www.lakesidecreamery.com. Reservations not accepted. Most items $2–$6. MC, V. Summer daily 11am–11pm; off-season Mon–Fri 11am–9pm, Sat–Sun 11am–10pm. Closed mid-Oct to May.

Mountain State Brewing Company ★ BREWPUB Two standouts here are beer and flatbread pizza. Brewed in Thomas, West Virginia, the beers range from the lightest Cold Trail Ale to the deepest oatmeal stout. Flatbread pizza is baked in a wood-fired oven. They want you to set a spell here in this casual spot. Play a game or sit on the deck and watch the sun set over the mountains. Listen to the live music on summer weekends. Takeout pizza and beer (no beer sales on Sun, though) are available.

6690 Sand Run Rd., McHenry. ⓒ **301/387-3360.** www.mountainstatebrewing.com. Reservations recommended. Main courses $6–$21. DISC, MC, V. Mon–Wed 11am–10pm; Thurs–Sat 11am–11pm; Sun noon–10pm.

Uno Chicago Grill ⟨Kids⟩ PIZZA Everybody comes here. It's a family place, with a playground and wide lawn by the lake so the kids can wear themselves out while waiting for a table. (And there *can* be a wait, especially on weekends.) A central fireplace dominates the dining room, covered outside seating overlooks the lake, and a deck at the Honi-Honi Bar has entertainment on warm weekends. The food is the usual for Uno's: pizza, pastas, sandwiches, soups, salads, and a children's menu.

19746 Garrett Hwy., Oakland. ⓒ **301/387-4866.** Reservations not accepted. Main courses $7.95–$27. AE, DC, DISC, MC, V. Mon–Sat 11am–midnight (until 11pm in winter); Sun 11am–11pm.

Wendy's Towne Restaurant ⟨Value⟩ CAFE Wendy opened this Oakland restaurant in the midst of a recession after waitressing for 27 years. She collected recipes from friends and family and turned a run-down space into a charming cafe. Wendy serves good home-cooking for breakfast, lunch, and dinner in a congenial atmosphere. Try Logan's chocolate chip pancakes, or maybe Collin's fried pickles. Sandwiches at lunch, including old-time favorites such as liver and onions and honey-dipped chicken, keep people coming back. Breakfast is served all day.

230 Alder St., Oakland. ⓒ **410/334-3300.** Reservations not accepted. Main courses $3–$15. DISC, MC, V. Mon–Sat 6am–8pm (until 11pm in winter); Sun 7am–7pm.

OUTDOOR ACTIVITIES

BOATING Summer activities focus on watersports. You can rent just about any kind of powerboat, from a ski boat for one to a pontoon boat for 12. Paddleboats, canoes, and fishing boats are also available at many marinas around the lake. A water-ski boat costs about $90 for 2 hours, runabouts are $25 to $50, and a pontoon boat runs around $65 an hour. Some of the leading firms along U.S. Route 219 at Deep Creek Lake are

Aquatic Center (✆ 301/387-8233), **Bill's Marine North** (✆ 800/607-BOAT [2628] or 301/387-5677), **Bill's Marine Service** (✆ 301/387-5536), **Crystal Waters** (✆ 301/387-5515), and **Deep Creek Marina** (✆ 301/387-6977).

If you don't want to rent a boat, **Wisp Resort** (✆ **301/387-4911**) offers pontoon and kayak tours of the lake and Savage River Reservoir kayak tours.

If you want to sail, you'll have to bring your own boat, as none are available for rent. Or you can learn to sail at **Deep Creek Sailing School** (✆ **301/387-4497;** www.deep creeksailingschool.com). Courses run 5 days and cost $235 to $250. Private lessons may also be arranged.

CAMPING **Deep Creek Lake State Park** (✆ **301/387-5563**) offers 112 improved campsites (26 with electric hookups) plus a yurt, Adirondack-style cabin, and two mini-camper cabins. Facilities include bathhouses with showers. Rentals are $25 to $65 a night. Reservations are recommended; call ✆ **800/432-2267.** Pets are permitted in designated loops. See the Garrett County section of "The Great Outdoors in Western Maryland," earlier in this chapter, for other camping options.

CROSS-COUNTRY SKIING Cross-country skiing is available at **Herrington Manor State Park** (✆ 301/334-9180) and **New Germany State Park** (✆ 301/895-5453), both described in "The Great Outdoors in Western Maryland," earlier in this chapter. **Deep Creek Outfitters** (✆ 301/387-2200), **Allegany Expeditions** (✆ 800/819-5170), and **High Mountain Sports** (✆ 301/387-4199; www.highmountainsports.com) rent cross-country skis.

DOG-SLEDDING A local outfitter offers dog-sledding in area parks. The weather must be cool enough for the dogs (50°F/10°C or lower). If there's no snow, sleds on wheels are available. Reservations are required. They even have kennel visits ($15 a person) available if all you want to do is get to know one of these Siberian or Alaskan beauties. **Husky Power Dogsledding** (✆ **301/746-7200;** www.huskypowerdogsledding. com) offers dog-sled rides and learn-to-mush tours around local forests for $150 to $195.

DOWNHILL SKIING & SNOWBOARDING Deep Creek Lake is the home of Maryland's only ski area. With an elevation of 3,115 feet and a vertical drop of 700 feet, the **Wisp Resort** ★★, 296 Marsh Hill Rd., McHenry (✆ 301/387-4911; www.skiwisp. com), offers 32 ski runs and trails. Beginners can ski or ride on several of the long, scenic trails, while black-diamond skiers can head for the face, which is straight down the front of the mountain with lots of moguls. Trails through the forest can be fast enough for both intermediates and experts. Lift tickets range from $39 on weekdays to $57 on weekends, with reduced rates for night skiing, 2-day tickets, early- or late-season skiing, and children. Kids 6 and under ski free. The ski season runs from early December (sometimes Thanksgiving weekend) to March. Wisp also operates a ski school for kids 3 to 14, child-care facility, rental service, and ski shop.

ECO-TOURS Deep Creek Lake State Park's **Discovery Center** (✆ **301/387-7067**) houses an exhibit on local geology, fauna, and flora. It's also the starting point for fun (and, dare I say, educational) outdoor adventures. Interpretive programs, campfires, hikes, and star-gazing are among the possibilities throughout the year. Activity schedules are available here and at the visitor center on U.S. Route 219. It's open daily in summer 10am to 5pm, and other times 10am to 4pm Friday to Sunday.

All Earth Eco Tours (✆ 800/446-7554 or 301/746-4083; www.allearthecotours.com) offers adventure tours, from Savage Reservoir kayaking and photography workshops to cross-country skiing and hikes. Toddler Tuesdays at the Discovery Center are a big draw.

Tips **White-Water Rafting Without Fear**

A white-water course at the top of Marsh Hill enables rafting wannabes the chance to get their feet wet before venturing over to the Yough. **Adventure Sports Center International** (✆ 877/300-2724; www.adventuresportscenter. com) offers 2-hour sessions for beginners. Or bring your own raft or kayak. The course can be changed to accommodate the rafters' abilities, from easy for first-timers to Class IV for a white-knuckle thrill.

FISHING   Deep Creek Lake is home to about 22 species of fish, including yellow perch, bass, bluegill, catfish, crappie, chain pickerel, northern pike, walleye, and trout. Four world-class rivers in the area make this fly-fishing heaven. Come for the cutthroat, rainbow, brown, and brook (wild) trout. Fishing is best April through June, but ice fishing in January and February is becoming popular. The state of Maryland requires a fishing license, which can be bought at most tackle shops.

The Casselman, North Branch of the Potomac, and Yough rivers are good trout areas, too, of course. The Casselman is home to brook and brown, the North Branch has rainbow, and the Yough has rainbow and brown. A trout stamp is required if you intend to remove trout from nontidal waters.

Try **Bill's Outdoor Center** (✆ 301/387-3474), **Deep Creek Outfitters** (✆ 301/387-2200) or **Deep Creek Marina** (✆ 301/387-0732) for tours, equipment, and boat rentals. The **Orvis** fly-fishing shop at Wisp (✆ 301/387-4911) offers tours, too.

GOLF   The **Golf Club at Wisp,** Wisp Resort Golf Course, 296 Marsh Hill Rd., McHenry (✆ 301/387-4911; www.wispresort.com), has reconfigured its 18-hole, par-72 championship facility built beside (and on) the ski slopes. It's open daily from April to mid-October. Fees for 18 holes are $40 to $65. A pro shop and driving range are on the grounds. The **Oakland Golf Club,** Sang Run Road, Oakland (✆ 301/334-3883; www.golfatoakland.com), has an 18-hole, par-71 championship course and driving range, open April through October. Fees range from $25 to $58.

HIKING   Five trails ranging from easy to challenging are in **Deep Creek Lake State Park,** south of McHenry on State Park Road (✆ 301/387-5563). The most scenic is Indian Turnip Trail, which is approximately 2.5 miles and winds along Meadow Mountain and across the ridge top. Entry fee is $2 per vehicle; the park is open daily from 8am until sunset in summer, until 4pm in winter. **Wisp Resort** (✆ 301/387-4911) offers scenic chairlift rides after the snow melts for a mountaintop view and a downhill hike. See the Garrett County section of "The Great Outdoors in Western Maryland," earlier in this chapter, for other hiking options.

MOUNTAIN COASTER   Downhill thrills without snow! **Wisp Resort** (✆ 301/387-4911) has erected this roller-coaster-style ride on its slopes. Riders fly down the 5,000 foot track at a speed they are comfortable with—these coasters for one or two people have brakes. Take it slow and the ride lasts about 5 minutes. Forgo the brakes and you'll be down in a minute and a half. It's $10 a ride.

SLEIGH RIDES   **Pleasant Valley Dream Rides** (✆ 301/334-1688; www.pleasant valleydreamrides.com) offers horse-drawn sleigh and carriage rides on the hour, from 10am to 10pm; $14 for adults and $10 children 3 to 10.

WESTERN MARYLAND

10

DEEP CREEK LAKE & GARRETT COUNTY

SNOW TUBING   **Wisp Resort** offers the Bear Claw Snow Tubing Park (© **301/387-4911**), a fast dash down a groomed run on a big inflatable tube and a tow back to the top. Two-hour sessions cost $15 to $20. Reservations are a must.

SWIMMING   **Deep Creek Lake State Park** (© **301/387-5563**) features an 800-foot guarded sandy beach with bathhouses and lockers nearby. It's one of the only public places for swimming. Entry fees to the park are $3 to $4 a person in season. Off-season fees are $3 to $4 per vehicle, with free admission for seniors and children in restraint seats. The park is open from 8am until sunset. Lifeguards are on duty from Memorial Day to Labor Day, Thursday through Sunday from 10am to 6pm.

OTHER ATTRACTIONS IN GARRETT COUNTY

Church of the Presidents   Presidents Grant, Harrison, and Cleveland attended services here, as did Chester Arthur (before he took office). Built in 1868 as a Presbyterian church, it's made of the same sandstone used for B&O railroad bridges.

St. Matthew's Episcopal Church, 126 E. Liberty St., Oakland. © **301/334-2510.** Sun services at 8 and 10:45am.

Deep Creek Cellars   Paul Roberts and Nadine Grabania built this little winery in their home in the northwest corner of Maryland. It produces 14,000 bottles of some of Maryland's best wine every year, and the owners take great pride in their work. (You can find their wines throughout Maryland and Washington, D.C.) Wander through the vineyard. At harvest time, you can see the juice as it's pressed from the fruit. Best of all, try the final product in the tasting room. Even the trip up Route 42 is scenic.

177 Frazee Ridge Rd., Friendsville. © **301/746-4349.** www.deepcreekcellars.com. Tasting room Apr 20–Nov 20 Wed–Sat 11am–6pm; call ahead for winter and holiday hours.

Garrett County Historical Society Museum   This quaint museum staffed by friendly volunteers has a pioneer cabin and rooms focusing on local history (the B&O Railroad, military life, and so on). There's an amazing array of local artifacts, including those of the famous hunter Meshach Browning, plus an elegant 1908 surrey.

107 S. Second St., Oakland. © **301/334-3226.** Free admission; donations accepted. May–Dec Mon–Sat 11am–4pm; Jan–Apr Thurs–Sat 11am–4pm.

Oakland Train Station (**Finds**)   The restored Queen Anne–style station is striking, with its bell-shaped turret and stained glass. Built in 1884 for the growing resort clientele, it now houses a visitor center and a handicrafts shop.

117 E. Liberty St., Oakland. © **301/334-1243.** Free admission. Daily 9am–5pm.

Simon Pearce ★   Cross the catwalk over the furnaces and workbenches of glass artisans as they create the crystal-clear pieces for which Simon Pearce is famous. Most artisans work until 3pm, but there's usually at least one team working until 5pm and on weekends. The showroom is filled with the elegant, modern wares created here and at the other Simon Pearce factories around the country.

265 Glass Dr., Mountain Lake Park. © **800/774-5277.** www.simonpearce.com. Daily 9am–5pm. Located south of Deep Creek Lake and Oakland: Take Rte. 219 south to Rte. 135; turn left and then turn right on Glass Dr.; the factory is on the left.

SHOPPING

Around the lake you'll find a few shops for clothing and souvenirs. New on the scene is **Deep Creek Sweets,** 1550 Deep Creek Dr., at the Fort in McHenry (© **301/387-7979**), stocked with locally made chocolates and fudge.

Kids **Working Farms**

If you want your kids to see a real farm, stop by the Deep Creek visitor center for the brochure called *Visit Our Working Farms, Share Our Heritage,* which lists farms that welcome visitors.

At **Cove-Run Farms,** 596 Griffith Rd., Accident ((C) **301/746-6111**), there's a corn maze built into 10 acres—Maryland's largest such autumn attraction. The corn is tall and the paths are tricky, but it's fun to hear the kids squeal as they make their way through. It's open mid-August through October, Friday from noon to 10pm, Saturday from noon to 9pm, and Sunday from 2 to 6pm.

A few places in outlying areas of Deep Creek Lake are worth a stop. **Schoolhouse Earth,** 1224 Friendsville Rd., north of the lake off Route 42 ((C) **301/746-8603;** www. schoolhouseearth.com), specializes in country accessories, gourmet food, jewelry, and home and garden decor. It's open daily from 10am to 6pm.

In Oakland, the **Book Mark'et & Antique Mezzanine,** 111 S. Second St. ((C) **301/334-8778**), has children's books, fiction, history, and biography, as well as antiques and collectibles. It is open Monday through Saturday from 9:30am to 5:30 or 6pm, Sunday from 11am to 4pm.

Located 8 miles south of Oakland on U.S. Route 219, just past the intersection of U.S. Route 50, is the 1,200-square-foot **Red House School Antiques** ((C) **301/334-2800**). It carries antiques and crafts. It's open Monday through Saturday from 10am to 5pm, Sunday from 11am to 5pm.

AN EXCURSION TO GRANTSVILLE ★

The historic National Road, which once connected the East Coast to the Ohio Valley, still comes through here: You can see the tall mile markers along the road. Plan to stop in pretty little Grantsville for some shopping and a home-cooked meal.

To get here from Route 68, take exit 19 north (Rte. 495) to U.S. 40 east. The first stop is the **Casselman River Bridge.** This was the largest single-span stone bridge ever built when it was constructed in 1813. It was closed to traffic in 1953, but you can walk across it to a small riverside park.

At one end of the bridge is the **Spruce Forest Artisan Village ★★,** 177 Casselman Rd. ((C) **301/895-3332;** www.spruceforest.org). Old homes, schoolhouses, and shops were relocated here from other parts of Western Maryland; some date from Revolutionary War days. Twelve structures house studios where you can watch artisans carve wooden birds, beat iron into jewelry, and weave shreds of wood into baskets. Studio hours vary, but something is always open Monday through Saturday from 10am to 5pm between Memorial Day and the last Saturday in October, plus one December weekend. Off-season you take your chances, but the artisans do work here when the weather's agreeable. Music is offered Saturdays in summer. The restored 1797 **Stanton's Mill** offers tours by appointment. (See www.spruceforest.org.)

The **Old Red Barn,** 146 Casselman Rd. ((C) **301/895-5347**), has two floors of goods a home cook will love, as well as Frostburg-made McFarland Candies.

WESTERN MARYLAND

10

DEEP CREEK LAKE & GARRETT COUNTY

The Casselman Inn (Value) AMISH/PENNSYLVANIA DUTCH   You'll notice the wonderful aromas from the bakery as soon as you enter this 1824 inn, and the hearty food here is a bargain. You'll find homemade bread, honey-dipped chicken, and grilled ham. A children's menu is available. The dining room is usually filled with families and seniors on day trips.

113 E. Main St. (Alt. Rte. 40, off I-68, exit 19), Grantsville, MD 21536. (C) **301/895-5055** for lodging, 301/895-5266 for restaurant. www.thecasselman.com. Reservations not accepted. Main courses $4–$6 breakfast, $4–$16 lunch and dinner. DISC, MC, V. Mon–Thurs 7am–8pm; Fri–Sat 7am–9pm.

Penn Alps Restaurant & Craft Shop ★ (Value) REGIONAL   Remember those old-fashioned restaurants with simple, homemade fare served by the kindest of waitresses? Come here for the hearty breakfasts or substantial lunch and dinner fare. There are buffets every Friday and Saturday night, as well as a Saturday breakfast buffet and Saturday and Sunday brunch. Dishes include roast pork and sauerkraut, fried chicken, steaks, and seafood. Lighter items include sandwiches, soups, salads, and burgers, plus children's and seniors' menus. You can buy fresh-baked breads or pies here, or handmade goodies from the crafts shop. The restaurant is across the parking lot from the Spruce Forest Artisan Village and an easy walk to the Casselman River Bridge. An 1818 stagecoach inn makes up part of the building. Look for the double fireplace, which has warmed visitors for nearly 2 centuries.

125 Casselman Rd., Grantsville. (C) **301/895-5985.** www.pennalps.com. Reservations not accepted, except for large groups. Main courses $2–$7 breakfast, $4–$10 lunch, $11–$19 dinner. AE, DISC, MC, V. Nov to day before Memorial Day Mon–Thurs 9am–7pm, Fri–Sat 9am–8pm, Sun 9am–8pm; Memorial Day to Oct Mon–Sat 9am–8pm, Sun 9am–3pm. Closed several days at Christmas.

The Stonebow Inn ★★   Set away from Deep Creek Lake—but close enough to get there or to Cumberland in 20 minutes—this 1870 inn on 6½ acres may offer the perfect getaway. In addition to its classic Victorian style, its location puts visitors right in the middle of the goings-on in Grantsville. You can visit Spruce Forest Artisan Village, dine at Penn Alps, and take a walk or fish along the Casselman River. Guest rooms differ in size and amenities; some have a fireplace, microwave, or CD player. A first-floor room is spacious and convenient for those who don't like steps. Two separate and spacious cottages make the escape complete. Two rooms are pet-friendly.

146 Casselman Rd., Grantsville, MD 21536. (C) **800/272-4090** or 301/895-4250. www.stonebowinn.com. 9 units. $140–$160 double; $180–$200 cottage. Rates include full breakfast. AE, DISC, MC, V. Pets accepted with prior arrangements. Children 12 and under accepted in cottages. **Amenities:** Sauna. *In room:* A/C, TV/VCR, hair dryer, free Wi-Fi.

Maryland & Delaware's Atlantic Beaches

A trip to the beach, or "downy ocean" in local parlance, is the only true vacation for many Marylanders and Delawareans. And any beach is fair game: Bethany's vacationers can't keep away from Rehoboth's shops and restaurants or Ocean City's amusements. Anglers head to Ocean City and Lewes for the charter boats. The beaches of Delaware Seashore State Park are the quietest. If you want to party, head for the nightspots of Delaware's Dewey

Beach or the boardwalk of Ocean City, Maryland.

Delaware beaches are quite different from Maryland beaches. For one thing, all Maryland beaches are public, whereas Delaware has private beaches. In this chapter, we'll give you a snapshot of each, starting at the north end of Delaware and heading south to Maryland, focusing on the individual delights and differences of each.

1 THE BEACHES IN BRIEF

DELAWARE BEACHES

Stretched along 25 miles of ocean and bay shoreline, Delaware's five beach towns—Lewes, Rehoboth Beach, Dewey Beach, Bethany Beach, and Fenwick Island—have their own personalities and ambience.

For information on dinner specials, coupons, and local news, grab one of the free publications piled up in restaurants and hotels. Look for *The Wave, Sunny Day,* and *Southern Delaware Explorer.*

LEWES With such a quaint little town to keep your attention, you just might forget there's a beach in Lewes, just on the other side of the canal. Metered parking at the beach is available. There are also bathhouses and lifeguards in season. The water is calm and the sand white. The best beach is at **Cape Henlopen State Park** (© 302/645-8983; www.destateparks.com/park/cape-henlopen), 1 mile east of Lewes. Admission is $8 per out-of-state car—and it's worth it. The beaches are never wall-to-wall with bodies as they can be in Ocean City. Even the water at the confluence of Delaware Bay and the ocean seems calmer. You can take a walk or ride a bike on a nature trail here and look for shorebirds.

REHOBOTH & DEWEY Swimming at Rehoboth's and Dewey's wide sandy beaches is one of the area's top activities. All the beaches have public access and are guarded, but there are no bathhouses.

At Rehoboth, look for the NO SWIMMING signs between Brooklyn Avenue and Laurel Street that warn against swimming near two sunken ships. Though the ships have been cut down to the waterline, it's best to avoid this dangerous spot. *Tip:* Rehoboth offers complimentary "Beach Wheels," wheelchairs designed for beach use, at the boardwalk and Maryland Avenue or Laurel Street. They're available on a first-come, first-served basis. Call © 302/227-2400 for details.

Just south of Dewey is perhaps Delaware's finest, quietest beach. A narrow strip of land between the ocean and Rehoboth and Indian River bays, **Delaware Seashore State Park** ★ (© **302/227-2800;** www.destateparks.com/park/delaware%2Dseashore) offers ocean waves and quiet bay waters. Besides 6 miles of beach—two of them guarded from 9am to 5pm in summer—there's a 310-slip full-service marina and boat ramp, plus 500 sites for RVs and campers. Part of the beach is set aside for surfing. Unguarded beach is available for surf fishing. With a yearly license, you can drive onto the beach. With a day pass, you can walk on. Concessions are available at the guarded beaches. Admission is $4 for Delaware cars, $8 for out-of-state vehicles. *Note:* The Indian River Inlet Bridge is being replaced; construction is expected to last until 2011. Besides creating noise, dust, and traffic snarls, this will result in the closure of some camping facilities and limit some fishing. See **www.destateparks.com** for updates.

BETHANY & FENWICK Bethany's public beach is small and can be very crowded. Visitors staying in oceanside houses and condos have their own private beaches, in most cases, and don't have to worry about crowds as much. You'll hear about dolphin sightings all around the Delaware beaches, but they're quite common here. The beach in front of the boardwalk is free and open to the public. It is guarded from Memorial Day weekend to Labor Day, Monday through Friday from 10am to 5pm, weekends and holidays from 9:30am to 5:30pm. There are large, clean bathhouses behind the bandstand. **Bethany Resort Rental** (© **800/321-1592** or 302/539-6244) operates a rental concession on the beach, with 8-foot umbrellas, surf mats, boogie boards, chairs, and more.

Fenwick, on the border with Maryland, has more public beaches than Bethany. It's slightly more relaxed than Ocean City, but not as quiet as Bethany. Its claim to fame is the very narrow but long **Fenwick Island State Park** (© **302/227-2800;** www.destate parks.com/park/fenwick-island), where you can watch the sun rise over the ocean and later watch the sun set over Assawoman Bay. The 3-mile beach offers public space for swimming, sunbathing, surf fishing, and surfing. Facilities include showers, changing rooms, a first-aid room, lifeguards, a gift shop, picnic tables, nonmotorized boat rentals, and refreshments. Admission is $4 for Delaware cars, $8 for out-of-state cars. Entry is free weekdays in spring and fall and all week in winter. Hours are 8am to sunset year-round.

MARYLAND BEACHES

Ocean City has the most public beaches—and some of the most crowded. If you want to make friends, come here. The beach near the southern tip of O.C. is the widest and usually least crowded; a huge parking lot makes this a convenient place for day-trippers. The beach along the boardwalk actually gets quite narrow in a few places. Still, for those who love the boardwalk and all its shops and restaurants, this is the best beach. In northern Ocean City, land of high-rise condos, the beach widens. Crowds depend on the size of the building, but it's easy to find a place for your blanket here.

The inlet at Ocean City's southern end divides touristy O.C. from the wild and pristine beaches of **Assateague Island,** which doesn't have a single restaurant, gas station, or hotel. Although you can see it across the inlet from Ocean City, it's about an 11-mile drive to the visitor center and parking lots. Most of the 30-mile strip of barrier island is not open to vehicles. It's home to an enormous number of shorebirds, sika deer, and the wild ponies made famous by Marguerite Henry's *Misty of Chincoteague* books. The visitor center and campgrounds are the only buildings here.

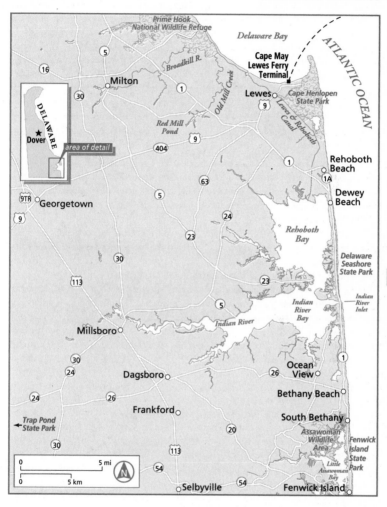

The entire 10-mile stretch of Ocean City beach is open to the public free of charge. Lifeguards are on duty from 10am to 5:30pm all summer. Beach chairs, umbrellas, rafts, and boogie boards can be rented by the day or week. Attendants will position your umbrella and, if you rent for the week, have your umbrella and chairs ready when you arrive each day. They usually accept cash only.

Wicomico Street Bathhouse is at Wicomico and Philadelphia streets, near the southern end of O.C. It's privately operated and charges a fee. Public restrooms are along the boardwalk at Worcester, Caroline, 9th, and 27th streets.

The beach at the inlet at the southern end of the island is set aside for surfers on weekdays in summer. On weekends, check with local radio stations to find out which areas are designated "surf beaches." Signs are also posted, and of course you can also check at local surf shops, including **Quiet Storm,** 74th Street (© **410/723-1316**), or **Endless Summer Surf Shop,** 38th Street (© **410/289-3272**).

Surf fishing is not permitted within 50 yards of swimmers between 9am and 6pm, so the big poles usually come out in the evening or early morning. When the swimmers go home in the fall, the surf fishermen take over.

---

2   LEWES

86 miles SE of Wilmington; 34 miles N of Ocean City; 107 miles SE of Baltimore; 121 miles E of Washington, D.C.

Delaware's northernmost and oldest beach resort, Lewes (pronounced *Loo*-is) is also its oldest town, founded in 1681 as a Dutch whaling station named Zwaanendael. The community maintains strong ties both to its Dutch heritage, which you can learn about at the Zwaanendael Museum, and to the sea—as a beach resort, a boating marina, and a port for dozens of fishing fleets.

Though Lewes is where the Delaware Bay meets the Atlantic Ocean, the town has grown up west of the Lewes–Rehoboth Canal, turning away from the water. Here you'll find the historic sites, small shops, restaurants, and inns. The result is a quaint, friendly little town that also happens to have a beach.

Beach fans must take an easy walk across the Savannah Road Bridge to the water. Parking is available in a paid lot. And lots of Lewes vacationers head to nearby Cape Henlopen State Park for the wide, sandy beaches there.

Lewes seems more like a Cape Cod resort than a Delmarva beach resort. With its small-town atmosphere and proximity to beaches, it's a good choice for anybody tired of the bustle of the other resorts.

ESSENTIALS

GETTING HERE   **By Car**   From points north, take routes 113 and 13 to Route 1 and then to Route 9 (Savannah Rd.) into town. From the south, take Route 113 to Georgetown, and then take Route 9 east to Lewes. From Ocean City or Rehoboth, take Route 1 to Route 9. From the west, take Route 50 across the Bay Bridge ★★ to Route 404 east, and then to Route 9.

By Ferry   Many visitors from the north come to Lewes via the **Cape May-Lewes Ferry,** an 80-minute Delaware Bay minicruise that connects southern New Jersey to mid-Delaware and saves considerable driving for north- or southbound passengers along the Atlantic coast. In operation since 1964, this ferry service maintains a fleet of five vessels, each holding up to 800 passengers and 100 cars. Departures are daily year-round, with almost hourly service in the summer months from 8:15 to 9pm. Rates for passengers (and passengers with bikes) are $7.50 one-way off-season, $10 in high season; the charge for vehicles ranges from $25 to $43, with reduced prices for motorcycles. Reservations are required for vehicles. In New Jersey, the **Cape May Terminal** is at the end of the Garden State Parkway. The **Lewes Terminal** is by the Cape Henlopen State Park entrance, about a mile from the center of town. For reservations and information, call © **800/64-FERRY** (643-3779) or visit **www.cmlf.com**. Shuttle service is available to both Cape May and Lewes every day in summer and on weekends in spring and fall for an extra $3; children 6 and under ride free.

By Plane   Visitors arriving by plane should fly into the **Salisbury–Ocean City–Wicomico Regional Airport.** See p. 266 for details.

See p. 266 for details.

VISITOR INFORMATION   Contact the **Lewes Chamber of Commerce and Visitors Bureau** (✆ 877/465-3937 or 302/645-8073; www.leweschamber.com). The chamber's office is in the Fisher-Martin House at 120 Kings Highway, next to the Zwaanendael Museum. It's open year-round, Monday through Friday from 10am to 4pm. In summer, it's also open Saturday from 9am to 3pm and Sunday from 10am to 2pm. Restrooms are located in the park behind the house. You can also get a visitors' guide from the **Southern Delaware Tourism Office** (✆ 800/357-1818; www.visitsoutherndelaware.com).

GETTING AROUND   The **Seaport Taxi of Lewes,** 306 Savannah Rd. (✆ 302/645-6800), operates a taxi service from the terminal to downtown, as well as local service. Ferry passengers can call from the information station at the ferry terminal.

SPECIAL EVENTS   The first weekend in October brings the Boast the Coast/Coast Day weekend. **Boast the Coast,** sponsored by the Lewes Chamber of Commerce, celebrates the town's nautical history. The highlight is the lighted boat parade in the canal. **Coast Day** (✆ 302/831-8083; www.decoastday.org) is sponsored by and held at the University of Delaware College of Marine Studies in Lewes. The fair includes lectures, ship tours, aquariums, and a crab-cake cook-off. The events are free except for parking.

The **Great Delaware Kite Festival** (✆ 302/645-8073) is held at Cape Henlopen State Park on Good Friday.

The **World Championship Punkin Chunkin** (✆ 302/684-8196; www.punkinchunkin.com), held the first weekend in November, is held in a field near Bridgeville, off Route 404. Contestants enter their own mechanical contraptions (no explosives allowed) to see which can hurl a pumpkin the farthest—and that can be 4,000 feet or more. In addition, there are food and crafts vendors, live bands, and entertainment for kids. It's silly, rowdy, and a lot of fun—and up to 35,000 people attend. Admission is $9; parking is $2.

WHERE TO STAY

Lodging options in Lewes include handsome inns as well as traditional motels. Prices range from moderate to expensive in summer—and can be a bargain in the off-season. Some places require minimum stays. Reservations are mandatory in summer months and recommended at other times. Parking is at a premium; metered parking on the street may be necessary at some local inns.

For vacation rentals, call a real-estate agent. One reputable company is **Jack Lingo,** 1240 Kings Hwy. (✆ 800/331-4241 or 302/645-2207; www.jacklingo.com). Most rentals are houses or town houses in Lewes, some with views of or frontage on Delaware Bay.

Moderate

The Blue Water House ★★   Hole up at this brightly colored inn and you might feel you've been transported far beyond Delaware's shore. In fact, the inn is tucked between town and beach, closer to the beach, though a bit off the beaten track. Its charm lies in its feeling of seclusion and its beautiful rooms. Accommodations are spacious, decorated with a sense of island fun, and look out on a big balcony hung with hammocks. The sitting room has a flatscreen TV and game tables, while a lookout provides panoramic views and a good place to relax.

407 E. Market St. (across the canal on the bay side of town), Lewes, DE 19958. (C) **800/493-2080** for reservations, or 302/645-7832 for information. www.lewes-beach.com. 9 units. $140–$180 double. Rates include hot buffet breakfast. 2- or 3-night minimum stay required in high season, on spring and fall weekends, and on holidays. AE, MC, V. Free parking. No children. **Amenities:** Bikes; beach equipment; movie library; massage; watersports equipment. *In room:* A/C, TV/VCR, fridge, hair dryer, free Wi-Fi.

Hotel Blue ★★   The glass bathroom basins glow with a blue light. Every room has a fireplace and private balcony. There are pillows that look like beach balls, a rooftop pool with a fireplace and seating area off to the side, and tower suite rooms with the queen-size bed tucked into a curved wall of windows. And the style is colorful and contemporary— about as far as you can get from the fishermen's hotel, the Angler, that used to sit on this site. This is all just about fun for adults. The hotel is just a short walk to the beach or the historic district, and the rooms look over the canal's marinas or the wetlands behind it. If you get a ground level room, your balcony will look over a koi pond rather than the parking lot.

110 Anglers Rd., Lewes, DE 19958. (C) **800/935-1145** or 302/645-4880. www.hotelblue.info. 16 units. $150–$320 double. Minimum stays on weekends required. AE, MC, V. Free parking. Children 18 and under not allowed. **Amenities:** Fitness room; pool; rooftop deck w/fireplace. *In room:* A/C, flatscreen TV, coffeemaker, fridge, hair dryer, microwave, robes, free Wi-Fi.

Hotel Rodney ★   Modern styling covers the elegant old bones of this 1926 hotel in the heart of the historic district. Formerly the Zwaanendael Inn, the inn has been converted into a boutique-style hotel. Antique furnishings have been restored and recovered; modern headboards, custom fabrics, and flatscreen TVs have been added. The sleek contemporary lobby is comfortable and hints at the decor throughout. Corner rooms with bright windows are a delight. Master suites have extra room and a pullout couch. Computers for guests' use have been added; bikes can be rented. A new gym is on the lower level next to a cozy lounge with a new bistro off the lobby.

142 Second St. (at Market St.), Lewes, DE 19958. (C) **800/824-8754** or 302/645-6466. www.hotelrodney delaware.com. 23 units. $90–$250 double; $130–$300 suite. Weekly rates available. 2-night minimum stay required on weekends in high season. AE, DISC, MC, V. Free parking. **Amenities:** Cafe; bikes; fitness room; free Wi-Fi in lobby. *In room:* A/C, TV, fridge (in suites), hair dryer, iPod docking stations.

The Inn at Canal Square ★   This four-story property overlooking the canal has a casual country-inn atmosphere with the amenities of a full-service hotel. Its spacious, traditionally styled rooms come in every size, from a standard unit with two queen-size beds to a full apartment. Most have views of the canal, though two parlor suites overlook Lewes. Fourth-floor rooms have extra comforts, like honor bars, CD players, robes, and oversize balconies. The Commodore Suite and Admiral's Quarters come with kitchen, fireplace, and sun deck. A massage studio was added in 2007; make an appointment at the front desk.

122 Market St., Lewes, DE 19958. (C) **888/644-1911** or 302/644-3377. www.theinnatcanalsquare.com. 24 units. $125–$310 double; $525–$625 cottage suite. Rates include European-style breakfast. Children 5 and under stay free in parent's room. Seasonal getaway packages. AE, MC, V. Free parking. Pets welcome in courtyard room for a fee. **Amenities:** Fitness center. *In room:* A/C, TV, hair dryer, free Wi-Fi.

An Inn by the Bay   Set between beach and downtown Lewes, this beach house-style bed-and-breakfast offers casual style and something spooky: tales of a friendly ghost. The master suite has windows on three sides with great views of town and the water. It has a private feel, since it's separated from the other rooms. A two-bedroom suite in the back has smallish bedrooms but a comfortable living room and small porch with a water view.

7 units. $100–$250 double. 2-night stay required on weekends in high season. AE, MC, V. Off-street parking. Small pets accepted off-season. *In room:* A/C, TV, hair dryer, free Wi-Fi.

The John Penrose Virden House ★ This 1888 ship's pilot's house has the best location of the B&Bs in Lewes, right in the heart of the business district. With a mix of antique and modern furnishings, it's both gracious and comfortable. Breakfast is served in the dining room, where an old ship's bar serves as a buffet, and on the patio in summer. In winter, dining by the fireplace of the sitting room is cozy, too. Two well-appointed guest rooms offer views of the town or the canal. A separate cottage off the garden offers extra privacy.

217 Second St., Lewes, DE 19958. ℭ **302/644-0217** or 644-4401. www.virdenhouse.com. 3 units. $150–$240 double. Rates include full breakfast and afternoon refreshments. No credit cards. Free parking. Children not accepted. **Amenities:** Bikes; beach equipment; garden. *In room:* A/C, TV, fridge, free Wi-Fi.

Inexpensive

The Beacon Motel This motel near Fisherman's Wharf, opened in 1989, occupies the top two floors of a three-story property, with the ground level devoted to shops and a reception area. Guests can spread out in the large rooms, which feature bamboo furnishings in beach colors; suites have trundle twin beds.

514 E. Savannah Rd. (P.O. Box 609), Lewes, DE 19958. ℭ **800/735-4888** or 302/645-4888. www.beaconmotel.com. 66 units. $95–$210 double. Rates include morning coffee and tea. Children 12 and under stay free in parent's room. AE, DISC, MC, V. Free parking. Closed Nov–May. **Amenities:** Outdoor pool; sun deck. *In room:* A/C, TV w/free movies, fridge, hair dryer, free Wi-Fi.

WHERE TO DINE
Expensive

The Buttery ★★★ NOUVEAU FRENCH This is as close as you'll get to a Paris bistro on the Delaware shore: a restored Victorian mansion with candlelit dining rooms, a bar, and an extensive wine list. It may well be the most romantic restaurant at the beach. In warm weather, the veranda is a lovely spot. The menu takes advantage of local seafood (crab cakes, pan-seared yellowfin tuna, bouillabaisse), with a few beef and poultry options as well. Sunday champagne brunch is delightful. The best deal is the elegant $28 prix-fixe dinner served nightly from 5 to 6:30pm. Casual diners may prefer the light fare menu offered in the bar and on the veranda 2:30 to 5pm everyday.

102 Second St. ℭ **302/645-7755.** www.butteryrestaurant.com. Reservations recommended. Main courses $12–$18 lunch, $22–$38 dinner. MC, V. Sun–Thurs 11am–8pm; Fri–Sat 11am–9pm.

Gilligan's Restaurant and Bar SEAFOOD Gilligan's menu always includes a variety of straightforward seafood dishes, with a zing here or there. The heft of the 8-ounce crab cakes, which have earned honors as the "best in Delaware," make them a great option. Seafood is always a good choice here, such as the salmon in miso ginger broth or macadamia-encrusted grouper. The look here has a slightly upscale but casual, tropical vibe. An outdoor bar overlooks the canal.

134 Market St. (at Front St.). ℭ **302/644-7230.** www.gilliganswaterfront.com. Reservations accepted only for parties of 5 or more. Main courses $8–$17 lunch, $23–$31 dinner. AE, DISC, MC, V. Late May to Sept daily 11am–3pm and 5–9pm; Apr to mid-May and Oct–1st week of Dec Tues–Sun 11am–3pm and 5–9pm; dinner until 10pm Fri–Sat Apr–Dec. Closed Dec–Mar.

Half Full PIZZA How can you go wrong with creative personal pizzas paired with a glass of wine or beer? The food is great in this tiny restaurant so let's complain about the seating. Bar stools with no backs make it impossible to really relax. So go ahead, lean on your elbows and enjoy the Margherita, black and white (with truffles), or spinach salad pizzas. Pizzas are big enough for most people to share. The owners also run Striper Bites Bistro (see below) so we're sure they know what they're doing.

113 Market St. ⓒ 302/645-8877. www.halffulllewes.com. Reservations not accepted. Main courses $8–$13. AE, DISC, MC, V. Tues–Thurs 4–10pm; Fri–Sat 4pm–midnight.

Jerry's Seafood SEAFOOD   Washingtonians may feel at home at this beach outlet of a D.C. institution. It's the home of the "crab bomb" (a 10-oz. crab cake), as well as a raw bar, a few salads and sandwiches at lunch, and filet mignon and chicken dishes at dinner. The reputation for crab cakes—they're jumbo lump meat bound with a whisper of filler—is well earned.

108 Second St. ⓒ 302/645-6611. www.jerrys-seafood.com. Reservations recommended for dinner. Main courses $8–$32 lunch, $13–$32 dinner. AE, MC, V. Daily 11am–4pm and 4:30–10pm (Sun until 8pm).

Moderate

Lewes Bakery and Notting Hill Coffee Roastery, 124 Second St. (ⓒ 302/645-0733), roasts its fair-trade coffee and bakes its pastries right there.

Café Azafrán MEDITERRANEAN   This is just a little cafe where you order at the counter for lunch, though waiters come to your table at dinner. Sandwiches, soups, and salads at lunch taste of olives and Manchego and Serrano ham. At dinner, choose from traditional tapas or a small variety of "large plates" such as tuna with Moroccan marinade, veal tenderloin, or a vegetarian platter. Desserts have a Mediterranean accent, too. There's a "tapas happy hour" on Wednesdays, and Thursday night is paella night; reservations are mandatory. The cafe opens for coffee and pastries daily at 7am. Takeout is available.

109 Market St. ⓒ 302/644-4446. www.cafeazafran.com. Reservations recommended for dinner. Main courses $7–$13 lunch, $19–$29 dinner. AE (at dinner only), MC, V. Nov–Apr daily 7am–3:30pm; May–Oct daily 7am–3:30pm and 6–10pm.

Striper Bites Bistro ★ SEAFOOD   Bright and airy, this casual spot celebrates seafood. Sure, you can find steak or chicken on the intriguing menu here, but seafood reigns. You can't go wrong with the rich crab bisque or the melt-in-your-mouth pan-seared tuna. Grilled salmon, blackened-tuna pasta, and lump crab cake are all fresh and served by a friendly waitstaff. Fifteen wines are available by the glass.

107 Savannah Rd. ⓒ 302/645-4657. www.striperbites.com. Reservations not accepted. Main courses $9–$14 lunch, $12–$31 dinner. AE, DISC, MC, V. Mon–Sat 11:30am–3:30pm and 5–9pm.

WHAT TO SEE & DO

Pretty Lewes is more than a beach and shopping town. Its historic roots shine through—in the eye-catching Zwaanendael Museum and in a complex of buildings that are part of the Lewes Historical Society. A little fun, a little history—what could be better?

Fort Miles   Bit by bit, this World War II army outpost on Cape Henlopen is being restored to its appearance in 1942. Tour guides dressed in war-era uniforms take visitors around the low, beige buildings and talk about how this base was built early in the 20th century to defend the Delaware Bay (and thus the cities of Wilmington and Philadelphia) from naval attack. It remained on active duty until 1958. Tours are offered three times a week. There are also lantern tours at dusk and a firepower tour, which focuses on the artillery here. Restoration is ongoing in the 420-foot bunker, which houses the massive 12-inch gun trained on the bay. One of the concrete towers that line Delaware's

beaches is open to visitors here. Climb the 100-plus steps of the spiral staircase for birds'- **243**
eye views of Lewes and the beach. A visit to the tower is worth the price of admission.

Cape Henlopen State Park, 15099 Cape Henlopen Dr., Lewes (*C* 302/644-5007. www.destateparks.com/
park/cape-henlopen or www.fortmiles.org. Admission Mar–Nov $8 out-of-state vehicle per day ($2 discount for in-state plates); Dec–Feb free. Daily 8am–sunset.

The Lewes Historical Society ★★ This collection of 12 historic buildings includes the **Ryves–Holt House,** the Lewes Life-Saving Station, and the Dr. Hiram Burton House, built about 1665 and the oldest house in Delaware. Tours are offered throughout the summer on the hour. Get tickets either at the Ryves-Holt House at 218 Second St. or the Hiram Burton House at 110 Shipcarpenter St.

110 Shipcarpenter St. (*C* 302/645-7670. www.historiclewes.org. Admission $5. Mid-June to mid-Sept Mon–Sat 11am–4pm.

Zwaanendael Museum This towering red Dutch-style building is unlike anything else in Lewes. Built for the town's 300th anniversary in 1931, it resembles the city hall of Hoorn, in the Netherlands. Exhibits celebrate Delaware's "First Town in the First State"; maritime archaeology, including artifacts from the sunken ship the HMS *DeBraak* (even a ketchup bottle); and local, maritime, and military history.

102 Kings Hwy. at Savannah Rd. (*C* 302/645-1148. Free admission. Tues–Sat 10am–4:30pm; Sun 1:30–4:30pm.

OUTDOOR ACTIVITIES

Cape Henlopen State Park ★ ((*C* 302/645-8983; www.destateparks.com/park/cape-henlopen), with its 3,143 acres bordered on one side by the Atlantic and on another by Delaware Bay, offers beach swimming, tennis, picnicking, nature trails, crabbing, and pier fishing, accessible from all the Delaware beach resorts. It's also the home of the 80-foot **Great Dune,** the highest sand dune between Cape Hatteras and Cape Cod. For those who enjoy a good climb, a refurbished World War II observation tower (115 steps) offers some of the best coastal views for miles. Walking with kids? Ask for the *Seaside Interpretive Trail Guide;* it tells about things you'd probably just walk by without noticing. The park is open year-round from 8am to sunset. Entry fee to the park is $8 for out-of-state visitors and $6 for Delaware residents from May through October; it's free the rest of the year.

BIKING Even if you're not a serious cyclist, it's good to bring a bike to Lewes: The historic streets and shoreline paths are ideal for cycling, and it's a great way to avoid the parking problem in the shopping district. All of Southern Delaware is easy to bike with flat terrain and pleasant views of farmland, villages, and wetlands; and most roads are wide, with good shoulders. The **Delaware Bicycle Council** ((*C* 302/760-2453; www.deldot.gov) produces *Delaware Maps for Bicycle Users.* All roads are marked and color-coded according to their suitability for cyclists, so there's no guesswork involved in planning your route. Maps can be obtained online.

Bicycling on your own near the beaches is a breeze thanks to the level terrain and the wide back roads. Even a trip up Route 1 from Bethany to the Indian River Inlet is easy. For family excursions, biking is a great way to see **Cape Henlopen State Park** ((*C* 302/645-8983; www.destateparks.com/park/cape-henlopen). Paved bike routes run through the park and take you places that cars can't go. The terrain is mostly flat, with just a few hills on routes to overlooks. Or head to **Trap Pond State Park** (see below) which opened new hiking and biking trails in 2008 or to the 6-mile **Junction and Breakwater Trail** that connects Lewes and Rehoboth Beach via a crushed stone trail suitable for walkers, joggers, bikers, and wheelchairs; motorized vehicles are prohibited. To access the wooded trail, find the trail head off Wolf Neck Road off Route 1, where there's a parking lot and visitors' services. A map is available at **www.destateparks.com/downloads/trails/j-and-b-trail.pdf**.

Delaware state law requires that children 16 and under wear bicycle helmets while riding. You can also rent bikes from **Lewes Cycle Sports,** in the Beacon Motel, Savannah Road (📞 888/800-BIKE [2453] or 302/645-4544).

BIRD & WILDLIFE-WATCHING Lewes, located between Cape Henlopen and Prime Hook, is the best base for birders on the Delaware coast. **Cape Henlopen State Park** (📞 302/645-8983; www.destateparks.com/park/cape-henlopen) is prime breeding ground for the endangered piping plover. (Access is restricted certain times of the year to protect the nesting grounds.) Whales and dolphins appear regularly off the coast of Cape Henlopen, though usually a little farther south. About 10 miles north of Lewes, **Prime Hook National Wildlife Refuge,** off Route 16 (📞 302/684-8419; www.fws.gov/northeast/primehook), is the best place around for birding and wildlife photography. The refuge has two hiking trails and a 7-mile self-guided canoe trail (bring your own canoe); they're great places to view migrating waterfowl in spring and fall, plus shorebirds, warblers, amphibians, and reptiles in spring. Admission is free; the refuge is open daily from 30 minutes before sunrise to 30 minutes after sunset. The visitor center is open Monday through Friday from 7:30am to 4pm, plus Saturdays and Sundays between April and November from 9am to 4pm. *Note:* Bring bug repellent, especially in late summer.

CAMPING Campgrounds at **Cape Henlopen State Park** are open March 1 to November 30. Reservations must be made at least 24 hours in advance. Call 📞 877/987-2757. Two sites are accessible for those with disabilities, and 12 are set aside for tent camping only. It's an inexpensive option in a resort area. The 159 sites sit on pine-covered dunes, with water hookup and access to clean bathhouses with showers. The sites are all fairly spacious, but the ones in the center loops are not terribly private. The largest and most private are located in the back loop, but they aren't well suited for trailers or motor homes. Rates are $25 to $31 per night. As with all camping on the Atlantic coast, mosquitoes can be a problem, so bring bug repellent.

Another option is **Trap Pond State Park'**s 142 campsites, including eight rustic cabins overlooking the pond. Call 📞 877/987-2757 for reservations. Rates for out-of-state campers are $19 for tent sites, $28 for electric and water sites, $49 for one of the two yurts, and $59 for a cabin. The park also has boat rentals and pontoon boat tours in the summer.

CANOEING The creeks and ponds of Sussex County make for lovely canoe excursions. A 5-mile canoe trail along the Hitch Pond and James branches of the Nanticoke River will take you past the two largest trees in Delaware, one of which is estimated to be 750 years old. The wide, glassy pond is surrounded by the northernmost stand of naturally-planted bald cypress tress, one some 300 years old. The trail begins at **Trap Pond State Park,** 33587 Baldcypress Lane, Laurel (📞 302/875-5153; www.destateparks.com/park/trap-pond), where you can rent canoes or kayaks for $8 to $11 an hour.

Nearby in Laurel is the smaller, wilder **Trussum Pond,** which looks and feels more like the Florida Everglades or a bayou than southern Delaware. From Route 24, take Route 449, which goes by the entrance to Trap Pond State Park, to Road 72 (Trussum Pond Rd.). A small park and parking area are located next to the pond, where you can paddle among abundant lily pads and the last graceful trees from a prehistoric bald cypress stand. You'll have to do the navigating yourself; there aren't any trail markers.

Prime Hook National Wildlife Refuge, 11978 Turkle Rd., Milton (© 302/684-8419; www.fws.gov/northeast/primehook), offers 15 miles of streams and ditches, including a 7-mile self-guided canoe trail. Electric-powered boats can also use the waterways. There's a boat launch behind the visitor center, but bring your own boat—there are no rentals at the 10,000-acre refuge. Admission is free.

DISC GOLF Did you know there were disc-golf stars? They get together at **Trap Pond State Park,** 33587 Baldcypress Lane, Laurel (© 302/875-5153; www.destateparks.com/tpsp/tpsp.htm), for a series of tournaments through the wooded areas of the park. The course is available for amateurs, too.

FISHING With easy access to both Delaware Bay and the Atlantic, Lewes offers a wide variety of sportfishing opportunities. The fishing season starts when the ocean fills with huge schools of mackerel in late March through April. Large sea trout (weakfish) arrive in early May and June; flounder arrive in May and remain throughout the summer, as do bluefish and shark. As the ocean warms up in June, offshore species such as tuna and marlin begin roaming the waters. Bottom fishing in the bay for trout, flounder, sea bass, and blues continues all summer, with late August through September often providing the largest catches. October and November bring porgies, shad, and blackfish. Delaware now requires licenses for all fishermen ages 16 to 64.

Arrange headboat ocean and bay fishing excursions and cruises at **Fisherman's Wharf,** Anglers Road (© 302/645-8862), or at **Angler's Fishing Center,** Anglers Road (© 302/644-4533; www.anglersfishingcenter.com). Call for full-day, half-day, or nighttime excursions. There are even family shark-fishing excursions.

Cape Henlopen is great for shore and surf fishing. In Lewes, try the **Lewes Harbor Fishing and Boating Outfitters,** 217 Anglers Rd. (© 302/645-6227), for supplies.

HORSEBACK RIDING **Winswept Stables** (© 302/645-1651; www.winsweptstables.net) offers horseback excursions along trails or on the beach.

KAYAKING **Quest Fitness and Kayak** (© 302/644-7020; www.questfitnesskayak.com) offers tours to watch the sunset, look for dolphins, or pass by lighthouses. The Pints and Paddles tour is designed for the beer enthusiast. Rentals are also available.

SHOPPING

Lewes is the best shopping destination on the shore for arts, crafts, and antiques. All of the places listed below are in Lewes. Most shops are open daily from 10 or 11am to 5 or 6pm, with extended hours in summer.

Auntie M's Emporium Head here for lots of old stuff: kitchenware, books, furniture, and garden sculptures. 116 W. Third St. © 302/644-1804.

Cape Artists Gallery Local artists bring their original works to display here. 110 Third St. © 302/644-7733.

Kids' Ketch Get your beach toys here—or perhaps something to while away those rainy days. 132 Second St. © 302/645-8448. www.kidsketch.com.

Lewes Gourmet This gourmet shop has international goodies, as well as Food Network cooks' wares. 110 Front St. © 302/645-1661.

Peninsula Gallery Across the canal below the Beacon Hotel, this gallery displays mainly works by regional artists. Closed Mondays January through March. 520 E. Savannah Rd. © 302/645-0551. www.peninsula-gallery.com.

A Delaware Brewery & Winery

Nassau Valley Vineyards, 32165 Winery Way (just off Rte. 1, on Rte. 14B), Lewes (*C* 302/645-9463; www.nassauvalley.com), offers self-guided tours and tastings Monday through Saturday from 11am to 5pm, Sunday from noon to 5pm. You can see where the wine ferments; look at displays on viniculture, viticulture, coopering, and bottling; and taste the locally produced chardonnay, cabernet, and rosé. It won't take long, but it's a nice break from the beach.

If a brewery tour is more your style, try the **Dogfish Head Craft Brewery,** 3 miles west of Lewes, off Route 16 in Milton (*C* 302/684-1000; www.dogfish. com). Locals are big fans of Dogfish Head's quirky brews, which also sell in 27 states and four countries. You can see this locally made ale go from grain to bottle in fragrant and free tours offered Tuesday through Saturday afternoons year-round. Reservations are required.

Puzzles Exercise your brain with the games and puzzles here, including jigsaws, crosswords, and brainteasers. 108 Front St. *C* 302/645-8013.

Stepping Stone Look for American crafts here, with something new every visit. Front and Market sts. *C* 302/645-1254.

Thistles This shop carries fine, unusual decorative items, including stained glass, pottery, glassware, and silver. 203 Second St. *C* 302/644-2323.

Two Friends Pretty gifts for your best bud or her home, with wares from Mariposa and Vera Bradley. 205 Second St. *C* 302/644-0477.

ORGANIZED CRUISES

A good way to see the Delaware Bay and the Lewes Canal harbor is by sea. You can pick up a self-guided tour brochure from the visitor center in the Fisher–Martin House, on Kings Highway. It covers more than 40 sites with brief descriptions of each one. For sightseeing cruises from Lewes, call **Fisherman's Wharf Fishing & Cruising,** 217 Anglers Rd. (*C* 302/645-8862; www.fishlewes.com), which operates narrated excursions around the harbor of Lewes and the Delaware breakwater areas. Trips include a 2-hour dolphin-watching cruise, a 3-hour whale- and dolphin-watching cruise, and a 2-hour sunset cruise. Prices are $15 to $35. Most tours are offered June through September; call for details and departure times.

3 REHOBOTH & DEWEY BEACHES ★

88 miles SE of Wilmington; 27 miles N of Ocean City; 110 miles SE of Baltimore; 124 miles SE of Washington, D.C.

Rehoboth is the most popular of the Delaware beaches. It's small-town friendly and beach-resort casual, yet has a touch of style, too. Visitors can choose from beachfront condominiums, boardwalk hotels, and old-fashioned cottages. On the south side of

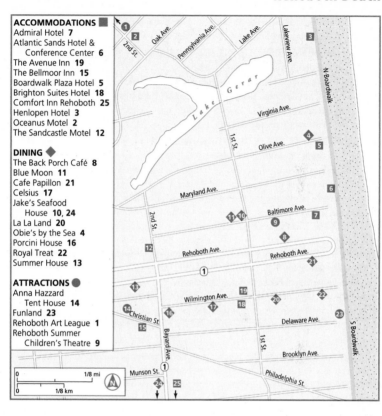

ACCOMMODATIONS ■
Admiral Hotel **7**
Atlantic Sands Hotel &
Conference Center **6**
The Avenue Inn **19**
The Bellmoor Inn **15**
Boardwalk Plaza Hotel **5**
Brighton Suites Hotel **18**
Comfort Inn Rehoboth **25**
Henlopen Hotel **3**
Oceanus Motel **2**
The Sandcastle Motel **12**

DINING ◆
The Back Porch Café **8**
Blue Moon **11**
Cafe Papillon **21**
Celsius **17**
Jake's Seafood
House **10, 24**
La La Land **20**
Obie's by the Sea **4**
Porcini House **16**
Royal Treat **22**
Summer House **13**

ATTRACTIONS ●
Anna Hazzard
Tent House **14**
Funland **23**
Rehoboth Art League **1**
Rehoboth Summer
Children's Theatre **9**

town, grand homes overlook Silver Lake. The town's shops offer a lovely diversion, with everything from home fashions to hippie accessories. Just outside town on Route 1, Rehoboth has become synonymous with outlet shopping—and Delaware has no sales tax. Frequent visitors can rejoice that major construction of the town's entrance has been completed after 4 years of dust and disruption. The results look good, too.

Rehoboth Beach is also a popular destination for gay and lesbian travelers, a mid-Atlantic alternative to Provincetown or Fire Island, with a number of gay-owned and predominantly gay venues.

Head south from Rehoboth and you hit Dewey Beach. It's a more casual suburb of Rehoboth, with a trolley connecting the towns in summer. Dewey is noted for its night-spots. Ruddertowne, in particular, draws young crowds for its party atmosphere. The beach is good, and the Rehoboth Bay is only a couple of blocks from the ocean.

ESSENTIALS

GETTING THERE **By Car** From the north, take routes 113 and 13 to Route 1, and then Route 1A into Rehoboth. From the south, take Route 113 north to Route 26 east to Bethany Beach, and take Route 1 north to Rehoboth. From the west, take Route 50 across the Bay Bridge to Route 404 east; then take Route 9 east to Route 1 south. From Ocean City, continue up Coastal Highway as it turns into Route 1 to Dewey.

By Plane　For visitors arriving by plane, the nearest airport is **Salisbury–Ocean City– Wicomico Regional Airport.** See p. 266 for details.

VISITOR INFORMATION　The **Rehoboth Beach-Dewey Beach Chamber of Commerce,** 501 Rehoboth Ave. (© **800/441-1329,** ext. 12 or 302/227-2233; www.beach-fun. com), is open year-round Monday through Friday from 9am to 5pm and Saturday from 9am to 1pm. The **Welcome Grove** offers visitors a little history museum, playground, and farmer's market in summer, as well as the visitor center. Gay and lesbian travelers should visit **www.camprehoboth.com**.

GETTING AROUND　**By Public Transportation**　From mid-May to mid-September, **DART First State** (© **800/355-8080** or 302/739-3278; www.dartfirststate.com) operates a daily shuttle service down Route 9 from Georgetown to Lewes, and down Route 1 to Rehoboth and on to the border with Ocean City. Buses go down Savannah Road in Lewes and travel along Rehoboth Avenue to the Rehoboth boardwalk, the park-and-ride lot, and the shopping outlets. They stop at Ocean City, where passengers can catch the Ocean City bus. A daily pass is $2.10 per person—or $7 per carload when parking at the park-and-ride lot on Shuttle Road off Delaware Route 1. Your pass is also good for one ride on Ocean City's bus; likewise, an Ocean City pass is good for one ride in Delaware.

　The **Jolly Trolley of Rehoboth Beach** (© **302/227-1197;** www.jollytrolley.com) operates a shuttle between Rehoboth Beach and south Dewey Beach. Buses runs Memorial Day through Labor Day, daily every half-hour from 8am to 2am; limited service is available in May and September. The fare is $2 for adults ($3 after midnight), $1 for children 6 and under. Bus stops are posted. Call for guided tours of Dewey and Rehoboth.

By Car　Parking in Rehoboth Beach can be difficult. Metered parking at $1.50 an hour is in effect from Memorial Day weekend to mid-September, daily from 10am to midnight. The meters take only quarters but electronic meters along Rehoboth Avenue also take credit and debit cards—and more of these machines are coming. Change machines are located in the first and second blocks of Rehoboth Avenue.

　To park in a nonmetered area Memorial Day to Labor Day, get a **parking permit.** Permits for daily, weekly, or seasonal parking are available from the Parking Meter Division, 30½ Lake Dr. (behind City Hall), from the Visitor Center at 501 Rehoboth Ave., or from real-estate offices. They cost $45 for a week, $30 for a 3-day weekend, $13 for a weekend day, and $8 for a weekday. The police will explain the rules and help you get change. Call © **302/227-6181** for information. Once you've parked, leave your car and walk. Almost everything is within a few blocks of the boardwalk and the main street, Rehoboth Avenue.

SPECIAL EVENTS　Greyhound lovers converge on Dewey and Rehoboth beaches on Columbus Day weekend for the **Greyhounds Reach the Beach Weekend** ★ (www. adopt-a-greyhound.org/dewey). This social gathering was started in 1995 by greyhound lovers who met informally over the Internet. About 3,500 ex-racers and their humans usually take part. It's a lot of fun to see and meet these graceful animals and their gracious owners.

　The 3-day **Sea Witch Halloween and Fiddler's Festival** at the end of October features a costume parade, trick-or-treating, a 5K race, and a fiddling contest. For information, contact the Rehoboth Beach–Dewey Beach Chamber of Commerce (© **800/ 441-1329** or 302/227-2233).

The **Rehoboth Beach Independent Film Festival** (📞 **302/645-9095** or www.rehoboth
film.com) takes place the first weekend in November.

WHERE TO STAY

Most accommodations in Rehoboth and Dewey are moderately priced. In July and August, however, you may encounter difficulty finding any room (single or double occupancy) near the beach for under $200 a night. Even though Rehoboth and Dewey are seasonal destinations, don't expect dramatic off-season discounts like those you'll find in Ocean City. The outlets are a huge attraction for holiday shoppers, so the shoulder season extends through December (but ask your hotel about weekday packages). There are sometimes significant discounts in January, February, and March. In any case, reservations are always necessary in summer and strongly recommended through the holiday shopping season.

House rentals are popular, so they can be tough to get. But for families, they can be a good idea: lots of space, kitchens, and maybe two bathrooms for about $1,000 per week and up—way up. Larger houses go for up to $5,000 a week, but a condo is considerably more reasonable. **Crowley Associates Realty** (📞 **800/242-4213** or 302/227-6131; www.crowleyrealestate.com) is a popular rental agent in the Rehoboth/Dewey area. Reservations should be made as early as possible—there's so much return business here, families often put in their request when they return the keys at the end of their vacation. If you'd like to rent a house or condo, be sure to call soon after Labor Day. Then again, something, probably older or farther from the beach, could be available in spring. As with other beach resorts, most condos come well equipped, except for linens, towels, and paper products; plan to bring those.

You could "rough it" and rent a cottage at the **Indian River Inlet Marina,** at the Delaware State Seashore Park. There are only 12 available—and with the amenities they offer, they're popular. Each has two bedrooms and a loft (sleeping a total of six people comfortably), full kitchen, fireplace, satellite TV, washer/dryer, and screened porch. Who called this camping? In summer, they can be rented for $325 a night. Off-season rates run about $250. Two- and 3-night minimums are required on weekends and peak times. Reserve online at **www.delaware.reserveworld.com** or call 📞 **877/98-PARKS** (987-2757).

Rehoboth Beach
Very Expensive

Atlantic Sands Hotel & Conference Center ★ The Atlantic Sands, right on the boardwalk, is Rehoboth's largest hotel. Sun worshipers love it for its spacious deck and large pool right on the oceanfront. Guest rooms, all with new bedding, feature dark-wood furniture and balconies with a water view. Some units have a whirlpool, wet bar, or microwave.

101 N. Boardwalk (btw. Baltimore and Maryland aves.), Rehoboth Beach, DE 19971. 📞 **800/422-0600** or 302/227-2511. www.atlanticsandshotel.com. 182 units. $185–$445 double. AE, DC, DISC, MC, V. Free parking. **Amenities:** Restaurant; poolside bar; health club; outdoor pool; spa; rooftop sun deck; free Wi-Fi in lobby. *In room:* A/C, fridge, hair dryer.

The Bellmoor Inn ★★★ This family-run establishment doesn't skimp anywhere. The lobby and library—with English-country decor, fireplace, and sumptuous furnishings—offer the first clue. Accommodations, though standard in layout, are richly furnished with thoughtful touches. Some units are part of a 1960s-era motel, but they are cleverly disguised and set in a soothing garden. Rooms in the newer section are equally well appointed and somewhat larger. Choose from standard rooms, junior suites, king rooms (with fireplace and whirlpool tub), or full apartments. One pool is for adults only; a second one is for families. A full-service spa completes the luxury.

6 Christian St., Rehoboth Beach, DE 19971. © 302/227-5800. Fax 302/227-0323. www.thebellmoor.com. 78 units. $99–$499 double; $269–$589 suite. Rates include full breakfast and afternoon tea. 2- or 3-night minimum stay required on weekends and holidays. AE, DISC, MC, V. Free parking. **Amenities:** Concierge-level suites; 2 outdoor pools and sun deck; health club; indoor hot tub (adults only); spa; Wi-Fi in garden and first floor. *In room:* A/C, fridge, hair dryer, high-speed Internet.

Boardwalk Plaza Hotel ★★   Step into the dark, ornate Victorian parlor of a lobby—complete with two tropical birds—and enjoy the old-fashioned hospitality of this friendly staff, who go out of their way to serve you in style. The fourth-floor concierge level is decorated with Victorian antiques, while the lower floors have pretty good reproductions. Most rooms are oceanfront or oceanview suites; a few have whirlpools. There are also a few standard rooms in the back of the hotel plus a spacious corner apartment. The pool is quite small but has an abundance of whirlpool jets.

Olive Ave. and the boardwalk, Rehoboth Beach, DE 19971. © 800/33-BEACH (332-3224) or 302/227-7169. Fax 302/227-0561. www.boardwalkplaza.com. 84 units. $269–$569 double. Children 6 and under stay free in parent's room. AE, DC, DISC, MC, V. Free parking. **Amenities:** Restaurant; bar; concierge-level rooms; health club; Jacuzzi; indoor/outdoor pool and sun deck. *In room:* A/C, TV/DVD, hair dryer, high-speed Internet.

Expensive

Avenue Inn & Spa   You might have trouble finding this place if you're on Rehoboth Avenue—step back and then you'll see it. Shops on the ground floor obscure it (though the entrance is really on Wilmington). Once inside, you'll find a comfortable, country-inn kind of place. Some rooms have TV/VCRs, fireplaces (electric, with heat optional), and Jacuzzis. The inn is filled with dark English-country furniture and burgundy fabrics, which might make you forget the hundreds of tourists outside, browsing in all those shops.

33 Wilmington Ave., Rehoboth Beach, DE 19971. © 800/433-5870 or 302/226-2900. Fax 302/226-7549. www.avenueinn.com. 48 units. $165–$330 double. Rates include continental breakfast, afternoon wine and cheese, and cookies served by the lobby fireplace. 2-night minimum stay required on some weekends. AE, DISC, MC, V. Free parking. **Amenities:** Fitness center; outdoor hot tub; indoor pool and deck; spa. *In room:* A/C, fridge, hair dryer, microwave, free Wi-Fi.

Brighton Suites Hotel ★   For families, this all-suite hotel a short walk from the beach is a good choice. The sandy-pink, four-story property's bedrooms have one king-size or two double beds, a large bathroom, and a separate living room with pullout sofa. The hotel's DVD library, with about 250 choices, is popular on rainy days.

34 Wilmington Ave., Rehoboth Beach, DE 19971. © 800/227-5788 or 302/227-5780. Fax 302/227-6815. www.brightonsuites.com. 66 units. $269–$649 suite. Ask about packages, especially for stays of 3 or more nights. 2- or 3-night minimum stay required on summer weekends and holidays. AE, DISC, MC, V. Free parking. **Amenities:** Beach equipment; fitness center; DVD library; indoor pool; rooftop sun deck. *In room:* A/C, TV/DVD, fridge, hair dryer, microwave, wet bar, free Wi-Fi.

Henlopen Hotel ★   On the north end of the boardwalk, this beachfront lodging is a tradition dating from 1879, when the first Henlopen Hotel was built here. Recently modernized, the rooms are simple. All 12 oceanfront rooms and 80 oceanview rooms have their own balconies. Families will like the suites.

511 N. Boardwalk, Rehoboth Beach, DE 19971. © 800/441-8450 or 302/227-2551. Fax 302/227-8147. www.henlopenhotel.com. 92 units. $169–$399 double. 2- or 3-night minimum stay required on

Hotel Rehoboth ★   This stylish newcomer (in 2008) offers a few welcome amenities. Besides the well-appointed rooms, there are the rooftop pool (big enough for a dip but forget the laps), continental breakfast, evening reception, and the jaunty shuttle to the ocean 3 blocks away. The best rooms are perhaps the second floor rooms with balconies overlooking the action on Rehoboth Avenue.

247 Rehoboth Ave., Rehoboth Beach, DE 19971. © **877/247-7346** or 302/227-4300. Fax 302/227-1200. www.hotelrehoboth.com. 65 units. $199–$399 double. AE, DISC, MC, V. Free parking. *In room:* A/C, TV/ DVD, fridge, hair dryer, MP3 dock, free Wi-Fi.

Moderate

Admiral Hotel (Kids)   In the heart of the beach district, this modern five-story motel is a favorite with families. It has a terrific indoor pool inside a glass pavilion, plus a lovely deck with whirlpool. All units have a partial ocean view. Families can opt for six-person suites with a kitchen.

2 Baltimore Ave., Rehoboth Beach, DE 19971. © **888/882-4188** or 302/227-2103. www.admiralrehoboth. com. 73 units. $168–$239 double. Supplementary charges apply on some peak or holiday weekends. Children 12 and under stay free in parent's room. 2- or 3-night minimum stay required in summer. AE, DISC, MC, V. Free parking. **Amenities:** Microwave in lobby; indoor pool; sun deck; whirlpool. *In room:* A/C, TV, fridge, hair dryer, free Wi-Fi.

Comfort Inn Rehoboth ★   Within sight of the Rehoboth outlets, this hotel is perfectly located for serious shoppers, and it's just 2 miles to the beach. Opened in 1996, its guest rooms are clean, comfortable, and spacious. Some have a microwave or whirlpool tub. The DART bus to the beach stops right outside.

4439 Hwy. 1, Rehoboth Beach, DE 19971. © **800/590-5451** or 302/226-1515. Fax 302/226-1550. www. comfortinnrehoboth.com. 96 units. $130–$220 double. Rates include deluxe continental breakfast. 2-night minimum stay required on summer weekends. AE, DC, DISC, MC, V. Free parking. **Amenities:** Health club; outdoor pool. *In room:* A/C, TV w/pay movies, fridge, hair dryer, free Wi-Fi.

Heritage Inn & Golf Club   This hotel has its own 9-hole golf course, open to non-guests. It's located just between Lewes and Rehoboth's beach—each is 3 miles away. Rooms have red, white, and blue Early American decor; three units have whirlpools; and six are family suites.

Rte. 1 and Postal Lane (P.O. Box 699), Rehoboth Beach, DE 19971. © **800/669-9399** or 302/644-0600. www.rehobothheritage.com. 86 units. $169–$229 double. Rates include continental breakfast. AE, DISC, MC, V. **Amenities:** 9-hole golf course (greens fees $15–$35); health club; outdoor pool. *In room:* A/C, TV w/free movies, coffeemaker, fridge, hair dryer, microwave, free Wi-Fi.

Oceanus Motel (Value)   This L-shaped, three-story motel—a classic mid-1960s design— lies 2 blocks from the beach and just off Rehoboth Avenue in a quiet neighborhood. Each room shares a porch overlooking the good-size pool.

6 Second St. (P.O. Box 324), Rehoboth Beach, DE 19971. © **800/852-5011** or 302/227-8200. www.ocean usmotel.com. 38 units. $169–$199 double. Supplementary charges of $10–$20 apply on certain weekends. Children 12 and under stay free in parent's room. Rates include continental breakfast. DISC, MC, V. Free parking. Closed Nov to late Mar. **Amenities:** Outdoor pool. *In room:* A/C, TV, fridge, hair dryer, microwave, free Wi-Fi.

The Sandcastle Motel ★   You can't miss this motel, built in the shape of a sugary-white sand castle right off the main thoroughfare. Its location, though about 5 blocks from the beach, is ideal for shopping and walking to restaurants. Each large, well-laid-out room has a private balcony. The pool has a lifeguard on duty.

123 Second St. (off Rehoboth Ave.), Rehoboth Beach, DE 19971. © **800/372-2112** or 302/227-0400. www. thesandcastlemotel.com. 60 units. $159–$249 double. 2- or 3-night minimum stay required on some weekends and holidays. AE, DISC, MC, V. Free parking in enclosed garage. Closed Nov–Mar. **Amenities:** Indoor pool; sauna; sun deck. *In room:* A/C, TV w/free movies, fridge, hair dryer.

Dewey Beach

Atlantic Oceanside Motel
This modern three-story structure is on the main beach highway, equidistant from the bay and the ocean (both about a block away). The rooms are of the standard motel variety, but the motel's convenience to the beach and Dewey nightlife recommend it. Families may prefer the Oceanside Suites—efficiencies and one-bedroom suites in a quieter area 2 blocks from Dewey.

1700 Hwy. 1, Dewey Beach, DE 19971. © **800/422-0481** or 302/227-8811. www.atlanticoceanside.com. 61 units. $35–$249 double; $45–$299 suites. 3-night minimum stay required on summer weekends. AE, DC, DISC, MC, V. Free parking. Closed mid-Nov to mid-Mar. Pets accepted in off-season for fee. **Amenities:** Outdoor pool; sun deck. *In room:* A/C, TV w/free movies, fridge, microwave, Wi-Fi (fee).

The Bay Resort Motel (Kids)
It's a little out of the way in Dewey (read: quieter), but this three-story complex, set on a strip of land between the bay and the ocean, is the ideal place to watch the sun set on Rehoboth Bay. From the 250-foot pier on the bay, you can drop a fishing line or watch the sailboats drift by. Each unit has a balcony facing either the pool or the bay.

126 Bellevue St. (P.O. Box 461), Dewey Beach, DE 19971. © **800/922-9240** or 302/227-6400. www.bay resort.com. 68 units. $159–$229 double. Rates include continental breakfast. Children 15 and under stay free in parent's room. 2- or 3-night minimum stay required on summer weekends and holidays. DISC, MC, V. Free parking. Closed Nov–May. **Amenities:** Outdoor pool. *In room:* A/C, TV w/free movies, hair dryer, kitchenette, free Wi-Fi.

Best Western Gold Leaf
A block from both the beach and the bay, this modern four-story motel is across the street from the Ruddertowne complex and convenient to all of Dewey's attractions. Each bright, comfortable room has a balcony and a view of the bay, ocean, or both. Four king rooms feature whirlpool tubs. Renovations to all the rooms were due to be completed in time for the summer 2010 season.

1400 Hwy. 1 (at Dickinson St.), Dewey Beach, DE 19971. © **800/422-8566** or 302/226-1100. Fax 302/226-9785. www.bestwesterngoldleaf.com. 75 units. $89–$229 double. Ask about reduced-rate packages Nov–Mar. 2- or 3-night minimum stay required in summer and on holiday weekends. Children 17 and under stay free in parent's room. Rates include continental breakfast. AE, DC, DISC, MC, V. Free garage parking. Pets accepted in off-season for a fee. **Amenities:** Rooftop pool; sun deck. *In room:* A/C, TV, fridge, hair dryer, high-speed Internet.

WHERE TO DINE

Rehoboth Beach

Expensive

The Back Porch Café ★ INTERNATIONAL   For more than 20 years, diners have sat back and enjoyed the Key West atmosphere along with the fresh, creative fare. Flavors are global though the food is local and seasonal: scallops with red Thai curry, chicken salad flecked with lemon and basil. The sweetbreads are popular, and prosciutto-crusted loin of rabbit is always on the menu. The bartenders offer potent creations, including the house coffee flamed table-side. Besides the cozy dining room, there are three outdoor decks. Live, mellow music brings in crowds Thursday and Friday nights. New is the "apres-surf" menu, perfect with a cocktail before dinner.

59 Rehoboth Ave. © **302/227-3674.** www.backporchcafe.com. Reservations recommended on Fri–Sat. Main courses $11–$15 lunch, $29–$32 dinner. DISC, MC, V. June–Sept daily 11am–10pm; early Oct Fri–Sun 11am–10pm. Closed late Oct to May.

Blue Moon (Finds) AMERICAN/INTERNATIONAL   Located off the main drag, this restaurant is housed in a bright blue-and-mango cottage. The interior features curved banquettes and exotic flowers. The menu changes three times a year. You can count on rack of lamb, salmon, and duck—and small plates are another option—but the presentations are unexpected. So is the entertainment, from singing impersonators to a jazz brunch.

35 Baltimore Ave. © **302/227-6515.** www.bluemoonrehoboth.com. Reservations recommended. Main courses $23–$32. AE, DC, DISC, MC, V. Mon–Sat 6–10pm; Sun 10:30am–2pm and 6–10pm. Closed Jan.

La La Land INTERNATIONAL   This acclaimed restaurant, on a side street off the boardwalk, offers a variety of seafood and meat dishes served up with creative touches: veal chop with mascarpone polenta or lobster tail with crabmeat gratin. Sit inside in the art-filled pink, purple, and periwinkle dining room and get a table on the patio set in a bamboo garden.

22 Wilmington Ave. © **302/227-3887.** www.lalalandrestaurant.com. Reservations recommended (and it's okay to ring the doorbell to reserve a table). Main courses $20–$44. AE, DC, DISC, MC, V. Mid-Apr to mid-Nov daily 6–10pm; may close Mon–Tues in shoulder seasons. Closed Dec–Mar.

Nage ★★ NEW AMERICAN   A tiny delight tucked into the corner of the Shore Plaza shopping center on Route 1, Nage is newly expanded to make room for 100 clamoring for their menu filled with creative gems. *Nage,* French for "swims," specializes in seafood but has become known for—of all things—burgers. Sandwiches include the divine lobster knuckle sandwich. At dinner, choose from scallops or their signature seafood stew in a lobster and saffron broth. Or pair wines and starters for a small-plate feast. If meat's your thing, go for the organic chicken or their prime rib burger. Whatever you choose, you'll swim away satisfied.

19730 Coastal Hwy. © **302/226-2037.** www.nage.bz. Reservations required for dinner. Main courses $9–$16 lunch, $15–$34 dinner. AE, MC, V. Lunch Tues–Sat 11:30am–2:30pm; dinner daily 5–9pm.

Moderate

Celsius ★ (Value) CONTINENTAL   Cross over the threshold and leave the beach for an evening on the Mediterranean. Three small dining rooms are decorated with yellow walls, sun-splashed murals of faraway places, and red-and-yellow table cloths. But the tastes aren't confined to the Riviera. Entrees have sauces inspired by a variety of ethnic traditions, both European and Asian. So you can choose from ahi tuna, paella, or a crab cake. A crab lovers' menu, a wide choice of tapas/appetizers and a children's menu should please everybody. On a budget? Try the three-course $29 prix-fixe menu.

50 Wilmington Ave. (at First St.). © **302/227-5767.** Reservations recommended on Fri–Sat. Main courses $15–$26. MC, V. Mon–Sat 5–10pm; Sun 10am–2pm and 5–10pm.

Jake's Seafood House ★ SEAFOOD   Both locations are spacious, with plenty of dining rooms, though still noisy. But who cares? The seafood is fresh, prepared well, and can be paired with some affordable wines. Started by a Baltimore family, Jake's specializes in seafood the way locals like it. Grilled fish (including a delectable tuna), crab cakes (done Baltimore style—very traditional and very good), sandwiches, and a few beef dishes are straightforward. Petite portions are a welcome addition.

Two locations: 29 Baltimore Ave. (at First St.; ℂ **302/227-6237**), and 4443 Hwy. 1 (ℂ **302/644-7711**). www.jakesseafood.com. Reservations not accepted. Main courses $8–$14 lunch, $14–$45 dinner. AE, DC, DISC, MC, V. Daily 11:30am–10pm. Downtown location closed Oct–Mar.

Obie's by the Sea AMERICAN   You can't dine any closer to the ocean than here beside the boardwalk. Obie's offers both indoor and open-air dining. A casual atmosphere prevails, with an all-day menu of sandwiches, burgers, ribs, salads, and "clam bakes" (clams, shrimp, chicken, corn, and biscuits). There's DJ music and dancing on weekends.

On the boardwalk (btw. Virginia and Olive aves.). ℂ **302/227-6261.** Reservations not accepted. Main courses $4.95–$19. AE, MC, V. Mid-May to mid-Sept daily 11am–1am; Apr to mid-May and mid-Sept to early Nov Fri–Mon 11am–1am. Closed mid-Nov to Mar.

Porcini House NORTHERN ITALIAN   Gone are the formal French atmosphere along with the Chez La Mer label. The vibe is more casual and the menu is completely new with a gourmet take on everything from pizza to hot dogs. The dog, for example, is Kobe beef. French fries have their own menu—including one with black truffles. Six kinds of risotto, flat bread pizzas, and pastas round out the menu. As expected, you can find mushrooms on everything (if you want.)

210 Second St. ℂ **302/227-6494.** Reservations recommended. Main courses $12–$30 dinner, $7–$12 lunch. AE, DC, DISC, MC, V. Daily 11am–10pm.

Inexpensive

Cafe Papillon (Finds) FRENCH   This tiny little walk-up on "Penny Lane" has plenty of inviting treats for breakfast or lunch: filled croissants, sweet or savory crepes, sandwiches, and cappuccino. The counter and tables are all outside, so this is definitely a seasonal delight.

Penny Lane, 42 Rehoboth Ave. ℂ **302/227-7568.** Reservations not accepted. Crepes $4–$8; sandwiches $5–$8. No credit cards. June–Aug daily 8am–11pm; May and Sept–Oct Sat–Sun 8am–11pm.

Royal Treat ★ BREAKFAST/ICE CREAM   The family-owned Royal Treat continues to fry up a hearty breakfast for the hungry sun-worshipers who crowd into the three cheery dining rooms or the screened porch. Then they come back later for ice cream. This old-fashioned Rehoboth landmark near the boardwalk must be doing something right—it's been serving breakfast for 3 decades.

4 Wilmington Ave. ℂ **302/227-6277.** Reservations not accepted. All items $2–$10. No credit cards. May–Sept daily 8–11:30am and 1–11:30pm.

Summer House (Kids) SEAFOOD   The party just keeps going on in this Rehoboth landmark, which serves such casual fares as sandwiches, burgers, and salads. The dinner menu offers plenty of seafood and meat choices, as well as daily specials.

228 Rehoboth Ave. ℂ **302/227-3895.** http://summerhousesaloon.com. Reservations not accepted. Main courses $11–$22. AE, DC, DISC, MC, V. Daily 11:30am–1am.

Dewey Beach

Rusty Rudder ★★ AMERICAN/SEAFOOD   This California-style restaurant right on the bay has been a favorite of young beachgoers since 1979. It offers great views from its dining rooms, decks, and terraces. Dinner entrees include crab cakes, prime rib, and enormous seafood platters. A land-and-sea buffet is offered nightly in summer, Friday

and Saturday in the off-season. The star of dinner, however, is the overflowing salad bar.
Lunch favorites include sandwiches, salads, and seafood specialties. There's nightly entertainment, with better-known acts on weekends.

113 Dickinson St. (on the bay). (℃) **302/227-3888.** www.deweybeachlife.com. Main courses $5.95–$15
lunch, $12–$49 dinner. AE, DC, DISC, MC, V. Summer daily 11:30am–10pm (Sun brunch 10am–2pm);
Oct–Apr Thurs–Sun 11:30am–9pm.

WHAT TO SEE & DO

Rehoboth and Dewey offer a quieter, more relaxed alternative to Ocean City, Maryland,
but both towns have nightlife and shops that stay open past 5pm, which you won't find
at Bethany, Lewes, or Fenwick Island. If the sandy beaches, good restaurants, and intriguing little shops don't interest you, maybe the outlets will.

Indoor Attractions

The **Rehoboth Art League,** 12 Dodds Lane (℃ **302/227-8408**), is nestled in the Henlopen Acres section of town amid 3 acres of gardens, walking paths, and an outdoor
sculpture area. The facility includes three galleries, a teaching studio, and a restored cottage. It offers exhibits by local and national artists. Admission is free, except for some
special events. Galleries open year-round, Monday through Saturday from 10am to 4pm
and Sunday from 1 to 4pm. It's closed January 1, Columbus Day, Veterans Day, Thanksgiving, the Friday after Thanksgiving, and December 25.

The **Anna Hazzard Tent House,** 17 Christian St., off Rehoboth Avenue (℃ **302/226-
1119**), is one of the original tiny tent buildings erected in the 19th century when
Rehoboth was a summer retreat for Methodists. Admission is free, and it's open May
through October, Wednesday and Saturday from 10am to 2pm.

Especially for Kids

Funland, on the boardwalk between Delaware and Brooklyn avenues (℃ **302/227-
1921;** www.funlandrehoboth.com), has rides and games. The rides for the preschool set
are varied enough to keep the youngsters busy for hours; rides for kids 8 and over or so
are more limited. It's open from Mother's Day weekend to Labor Day, the arcade from
10am, the rides from 1pm. It closes when everybody's ready to go home.

About 1½ miles north of town is **Jungle Jim's Adventure Land,** Route 1 and Country
Club Road (℃ **302/227-8444**), which offers go-carts, miniature golf, bumper boats, a
rock-climbing wall, outdoor rides, and a water park with slides and rides. It's open weekends in May and September and daily from Memorial Day to Labor Day from 10am to
11pm.

Pirate Adventures (℃ **302/539-5155**) take off from the pier at Harpoon Hanna's,
142nd Street and the bay, seven times a day. There's treasure, sea chanteys, storytelling
and other pirate stuff. Tickets are $18 for those 3 and over and $8 for baby pirates.

Rehoboth Summer Children's Theatre (℃ **302/227-6766;** www.rehobothchildrens
theatre.org) puts on shows for the kids at venues around the Rehoboth area, including
the All Saints Episcopal Church, the Bay Center in Ruddertowne, and the Holiday Inn
Express, in Bethany. Favorites such as *Cinderella* and *Jack and the Beanstalk* are performed
selected weeknights in summer. Curtain time is usually 7pm. The theater also offers
morning acting workshops and an apprentice program. Call for reservations.

Shopping the Outlets & the Boardwalk

The **Tanger Outlets** ★, stretching for 2 miles down Route 1 (℃ **866/665-8682** or
302/226-9223; www.tangeroutlet.com), have become a destination in their own right.

(Moments) The Life-Saving Stations

Just south of Dewey and beside the Ocean City Inlet are two buildings that memorialize the men of the U.S. Life-Saving Service.

The pumpkin-and-brown **Indian River Life-Saving Station,** on Route 1, south of Dewey (℃ **302/227-6991;** www.destateparks.com/attractions/life-saving-station/index.asp), has been restored to its 1905 appearance. Built in 1876 as an Atlantic-coast outpost to look out for ships in distress, it was transferred to the U.S. Coast Guard in 1915, decommissioned in 1962, and restored in 1998. Listed on the National Register of Historic Places, its spare interior recalls the heroic rescuers who saved sailors from sinking ships. Admission is $4 for adults, $3 for seniors, and $2 for children 6 to 12. Guided tours are available until a half-hour before closing. Or use your cellphone for an audio tour. From April through October, it's open daily from 8am to 4:30pm. Off-season, it's open select weekends 8:30am to 4pm. Call ahead.

In Ocean City, the white-and-red **Ocean City Life-Saving Station Museum,** at the Inlet end of the Boardwalk (℃ **410/289-4991;** www.ocmuseum.org), recalls the men who saved 4,500 sailors off these shores. Artifacts include a restored surf rescue boat and a pictorial history of storms that have raged here. Other exhibits focus on O.C. history, including bathing suits and lifeguards. Admission is $3 for adults, $1 for children 6 to 12. Hours are June through September daily from 10am to 10pm, and May and October daily from 10am to 4pm. In April, it's open weekends 10am to 4pm. Call ahead for winter hours.

Clothing stores include Brooks Brothers, Liz Claiborne, L.L.Bean, OshKosh B'Gosh, and Polo Ralph Lauren. Some 150 outlet stores offer accessories, housewares, china and crystal, sneakers, and handbags. Two centers are on the western side of Route 1; the third stretches between them on the east. You can't walk from center to center—and you have to be dedicated if you want to hit all the shops in a single day. Get a map so you can plan the most efficient route. Parking can be a challenge on weekends or rainy days, and Route 1 traffic can slow to a crawl. This place is so popular, New Jersey residents hop on the Cape May-Lewes Ferry to spend a day shopping in sales-tax-free Delaware. Hours are Monday through Saturday from 9am to 9pm and Sunday from 11am to 7pm. In summer, Sunday hours begin at 9am.

In downtown Rehoboth, there are a few shops on the mile-long boardwalk but most are along Rehoboth Avenue, which intersects the boardwalk at its midpoint. Most stores open from 10am to 6pm, with extended evening hours in summer.

Azura The owners design the stylish clothes sold here. Look for jewelry, furnishings, and accessories as well. 139 Rehoboth Ave. ℃ **302/226-9650.**

Carlton's When you discover you haven't packed your party dress, country club clothes, or sport coat, stop here for something classic but stylish. 31 Rehoboth Ave. ℃ **302/227-3590.**

Christmas Spirit You can always find Santas, angels, and ornaments in this festive shop. 161 Rehoboth Ave. ℃ **302/227-6872.**

Ibach's   Head here for chocolates: nonpareils, cashew turtles, cherry cordials. There's saltwater taffy, too. 9 Rehoboth Ave. (℘ **877/270-9674** or 302/227-2870. www.dolles-ibachs. com.

Scandinavian Occasion   Sweet lace curtains, colored glass and semiprecious stone jewelry are just the beginning of the treasures you'll find here. 125 Rehoboth Ave. (℘ **302/227-3945.**

Sea Shell Shop   This is a treasure-trove of seashell art, lamps, and jewelry, as well as loose shells, sponges, and hermit crabs. Little hands, the owners say, are always welcome. 119 Rehoboth Ave. (℘ **302/227-6666.** www.seashellshop.com.

Tickled Pink   Stop in for Lilly Pulitzer's pink-and-green country-club style. 235 Rehoboth Ave. (℘ **866/536-7456** or 302/227-7575. www.tickledpinkapparel.com.

Spas

Sometimes you just need a little pampering. Rehoboth has become something of a spa resort, with plenty of places to choose from. **Avenue Apothecary & Spa,** 110A Rehoboth Ave. (℘ **302/227-5649;** www.avenueinn.com), offers European facials, waxing, makeup, and hair and nail care. It has a spa shop as well. The **Spa at the Bellmoor,** 6 Christian St. (℘ **800/425-2355** or 302/227-5800; www.thebellmoor.com), offers massage, facials, body treatments, waxing, and nail care. The **Spa by the Sea,** 19266 Coastal Hwy. (℘ **302/227-8640;** www.thespabythesea.com), offers traditional massage, facials, manicures, and other treatments.

OUTDOOR ACTIVITIES

BIKING   With its flat terrain and shady streets, Rehoboth is ideal for bicycling. Bikes are allowed on the boardwalk between 5 and 10am from May 15 to September 15, and anytime off-season.

A scenic 6-mile **Junction and Breakwater Trail** connects Rehoboth and Lewes via a crushed stone trail suitable for walkers, joggers, bikers, and wheelchairs; motorized vehicles are prohibited. The 15 mile round-trip takes 2 hours or more, depending on where and how long you stop. Find the trail head behind the Tanger Outlets shopping area on the east side of Route 1. A map is available at **www.destateparks.com/ downloads/trails/j-and-b-trail.pdf**.

Insider's note: If you stop by one of the bike shops, they can give you directions from downtown Rehoboth to the trail. It's an easy ride. Stop at **Atlantic Cycle,** 18 Wilmington Ave. (℘ **302/226-2543**), **Bob's Bikes,** 1st and Maryland Ave. (℘ **302/227-7966**), or **Bike to Go,** 174 Rehoboth Ave. (℘ **302/227-7600**), and rent a bike for about $6 an hour or $12 to $16 a day.

GOLF   The public 9-hole course at **Heritage Inn & Golf Club** is on Route 1 in Rehoboth (℘ **800/669-9399** or 302/644-0600; www.rehobothheritage.com).

The number of public golf courses between Fenwick and Rehoboth has grown in recent years to include the **Rookery,** 27052 Broadkill Rd., Milton, DE (℘ **302/313-4653;** www.rookerygolf.com), an 18-hole course off the Broadkill River; **Baywood Greens,** 32267 Clubhouse Way, Long Neck, DE (℘ **302/947-9800;** www.baywood-greens.com), 18 holes set among flowers, ponds, two tunnels, and eight bridges; **Bear Trap Dunes,** 11 Willow Oak Ave., Ocean View, DE (℘ **302/537-5600;** www.beartrap dunes.com), 27 holes set among wetlands and sand dunes; and **Bayside,** 31806 Lakeview Dr., Selbyville, DE (℘ **302/436-3400;** www.livebayside.com/golf), a Jack Nicklaus course with views of Assawoman Bay.

TENNIS   There are public courts at **Rehoboth City Courts,** on Surf Avenue between Rehoboth Beach and North Shores; at Rehoboth Junior High School, on State Street; and in Dewey Beach on the bay at McKinley Street.

WATERSPORTS   **Bay Sports,** 111 Dickinson St., Dewey Beach (✆ **302/227-7590**), rents kayaks, pedal boats, sailboats, Hobie catamarans, and jet skis by the half-hour, hour, or day. A kayak or pedal boat goes for $15 to $25 an hour. Hobie cats are $50 to $65, depending on size. Stop by **DB Parasailing,** Route 1 at Dickinson Street (✆ **302/227-9507**), to go parasailing. Reservations are recommended; rides cost $60 to $70.

REHOBOTH & DEWEY BEACHES AFTER DARK

Sandwiched between the quiet family resorts of Bethany Beach and Fenwick Island to the south and Lewes to the north, Rehoboth and Dewey beaches offer the only consistent nightlife on the Delaware coast.

Clubs & Bars

REHOBOTH BEACH   Live acts are scheduled on weekends at **Dogfish Head Brews and Eats,** 320 Rehoboth Ave. (✆ **302/226-2739**). In summer, **Irish Eyes,** 52 Rehoboth Ave. (✆ **302/227-5758**), schedules DJs on Saturday nights. There's also a pool table and 16 TVs to catch all the football action in fall and winter. Feeling mellow? Try **Victoria's,** located at Olive and the Boardwalk (✆ **302/227-0615**), for piano Friday and Saturday 6 to 10pm.

DEWEY BEACH   Dewey Beach's rocking nightlife revolves around two mainstays: the **Rusty Rudder,** 113 Dickinson St., on the bay (✆ **302/227-3888**), and the **Bottle & Cork,** Hwy. 1 and Dagsworthy Street (✆ **302/227-7272**). The crowd tends to be 20- to 35-year-olds looking to party. The Rudder holds deck parties and has occasional bands or other activities; the cover varies. The Bottle & Cork, open only in spring and summer, is a surprisingly large rock club that hosts both local and nationally known bands; the cover varies. When Better Than Ezra or Sugar Ray is in the house, expect a big crowd.

The **Starboard,** 2009 Hwy. 1 (✆ **302/227-4600;** www.thestarboard.com), is usually crowded with young people. It serves breakfast, lunch, and dinner only in summer—the Bloody Marys are famous. Go to the website for special events.

Gay & Lesbian Rehoboth

A number of Rehoboth nightspots cater to a GLBT clientele. **Aqua Grill,** 57 Baltimore Ave. (✆ **302/226-9001;** aquagrillrehoboth.com), draws a young crowd of mostly men for the drinks and live entertainment. The **Blue Moon,** 35 Baltimore Ave. (✆ **302/227-6515**), has a happy hour popular with the men. DJs and the mellow lounge in back at **Cloud 9,** 234 Rehoboth Ave. (✆ **302/226-1999**), draw a mixed clientele. **Dogfish Head Brews & Eats,** 320 Rehoboth Ave. (✆ **302/226-2739**), is primarily straight but draws a mixed crowd for its craft beer and live entertainment. A lesbian crowd goes to the **Frogg Pond,** 3 S. First St. (✆ **302/227-2234;** www.thefroggpond.com). Dancing's the thing at **Purple Parrot,** 134 Rehoboth Ave. (✆ **302/226-1139**).

The Performing Arts

The newly rebuilt open-air **Rehoboth Beach Memorial Bandstand,** at Rehoboth Avenue and the boardwalk (✆ **302/227-2233**), hosts more than 40 free concerts and other events on summer weekends, starting at 8pm. Check with the visitor center for an up-to-date schedule.

For something lighthearted, go to the **Theatre of the Arts,** 20 Baltimore Ave.
(© **302/227-9310;** www.rehobothbeachtheatre.com), where you might find a Jimmy
Buffett or Bee Gees tribute band or stand up comedian.

4 BETHANY BEACH & FENWICK ISLAND ★

100 miles SE of Wilmington; 120 miles SE of Baltimore; 130 miles SE of Washington, D.C.

Nicknamed the "Quiet Resorts," Bethany Beach and Fenwick Island have the most laid-
back atmosphere of the Maryland and Delaware beach resorts and are a calm alternative
to the bustle of Ocean City to the south and the sophistication and shopping of
Rehoboth to the north. This pleasant stretch of condominium communities, state parks,
and public and private beaches may be quiet at night, but it offers visitors—especially
families—so much during the day: It's a great place to just sit back and enjoy the beach,
swim in the surf, bicycle along quiet roads, bird-watch in the dunes or coastal waterways,
and stroll on the tiny Bethany Beach boardwalk.

ESSENTIALS

GETTING THERE **By Car** Whether you're approaching from points north or south,
it is best to take Route 113 and to avoid the frequently crowded Route 1—particularly
in July and August. To reach Bethany Beach, take Route 26 east at Dagsboro; to reach
Fenwick Island from the north, take Route 20 south (just outside of Dagsboro); and to
get to Fenwick from the south, turn west on Route 54 at Selbyville. From the west, take
Route 50 across the Bay Bridge to Route 404 east, then turn south on Route 113 and
follow the directions above.

By Bus Bus service is no longer available here. **Greyhound** (© **800/229-9424;** www.
greyhound.com) does provide bus service to Ocean City; see p. 268 for details.

By Plane Visitors arriving by plane can fly into the **Salisbury–Ocean City–Wicomico
Regional Airport;** see p. 266 for details.

VISITOR INFORMATION The **Bethany-Fenwick Area Chamber of Commerce**
(© **800/962-SURF** [7873] or 302/539-2100; www.bethany-fenwick.org) is on Route 1,
adjacent to the Fenwick Island State Park. It publishes a helpful booklet called *The Quiet
Resorts* and stocks plenty of brochures. It's open year-round, Monday through Friday
from 9am to 5pm, Saturday and Sunday from 10am to 4pm. Bethany's **Town Hall,** 214
Garfield Pkwy. (© **302/539-8011**), also has brochures and a small museum telling the
story of Bethany's origins.

GETTING AROUND Since Bethany Beach and Fenwick Island are within 5 miles of
each other, most people take a car, but bikes and inline skates are also useful. All motels
provide free guest parking; most restaurants also have access to parking for customers.
Many Bethany and Fenwick streets are subject to metered or permit parking, and rules
are strictly enforced. Bethany's meters are enforced May 15 to September 15 from 10am
to 11pm. *Tip:* Skip the meters—just stop at the kiosk for a parking permit. These run
$13 a day or $84 a week and eliminate the need to keep the meters fed all day. The kiosk
and change machines around town will also make change.

Once you park, get around Bethany Beach (but not to Sea Colony or South Bethany)
via the **Beach Trolley.** It costs a quarter (exact change) to ride and runs from 9:30am to
7:30pm.

ORIENTATION If it weren't for the little signs in the median on Route 1, you'd never know there were three communities here. But officially, there are Bethany Beach, South Bethany, and Fenwick Island. North of the town of Fenwick is the Fenwick Island State Park, all beach and parking lot with no restaurants, shops, or hotels. Fenwick Island is like a hyphen, connecting Ocean City to Delaware. Traveling north from O.C., you'll hardly know you've left the state.

Head north to Bethany Beach and its quieter, all-residential neighbor, South Bethany. Bethany Beach is home to a small shopping area and boardwalk. Between the two is the huge condo resort called Sea Colony. Bethany and South Bethany have public beaches; Sea Colony's are private.

SPECIAL EVENTS The **Bethany Beach Boardwalk Arts Festival** (© 302/539-2100), a juried festival of fine arts and crafts, is held the Saturday after Labor Day from 10am to 5pm. In late September, join in the **Make-a-Wish Triathlon at Sea Colony** (www.midatlanticcommunity.org/tri) or just cheer on the athletes. The **Fall Surf-Fishing Tournament** is held in October; the **Spring Surf-Fishing Tournament** takes place on a weekend in early May. For information, call © 302/539-2100.

WHERE TO STAY

Bethany Beach and Fenwick Island are packed in summer, with more and more people booking a week in a condominium unit or beach house. New developments are springing up on Route 24, a short drive from the beach, now that almost every oceanfront parcel has been developed.

Bethany has a variety of accommodations, from oceanfront mansions to houses in town, from duplexes and town houses to condos tucked under trees. The condo resort **Sea Colony** ★★★ is an attractive option, with many rental units in nine oceanfront high-rises and a variety of condos on the west side of Route 1. With 12 pools, one is close to every unit. Tennis villas are surrounded by 34 courts, four indoor. There are also walking and biking paths, a fitness center, and a children's center. Shuttles take Sea Colony West guests to the beach. Guests need a recreation pass for the beach, pools, tennis courts, fitness centers, and shuttles; these cost $35 per person per week in season.

Look for your vacation rental early: Bookings are accepted up to a year in advance though you might still find a nice place a few weeks before you arrive. Rentals range from $500 per week for a small unit up to the thousands for oceanfront homes with room for extended family. Some good rental companies to call include **Century 21 Wilgus** (© 800/441-8118), **Coldwell Banker** (© 302/539-1777), **Seacoast Realty** (© 800/928-8800 or 302/539-8600), **Tansey-Warner, Inc.** (© 800/221-0070 or 302/539-3001), and **Tidewater Realty, Ltd.** (© 800/888-7501 or 302/539-7500). **Resort Quest** (© 888/500-4254 or 302/537-8888; www.resortquestdelaware.com) specializes in Sea Colony units. All of them will send brochures describing their rental properties.

Hotel rooms for July and August are booked months in advance, have higher rates, and often require weekend surcharges and 2- or 3-night minimum stays. Get your beach fix at a budget rate by visiting in spring or especially the fall when the weather can be beautiful and the water is warm. Beaches are fairly quiet in early June and after mid-August when schools reopen.

Bethany Beach

The Addy Sea Bed & Breakfast ★ You'll find this romantic Victorian jewel far from the Bethany-size crowds but right by the ocean. A century-old cedar-shake cottage with wraparound porch, the Addy Sea offers quiet comfort along with a grand view from most rooms. Corner rooms (nos. 6 and 7) are brighter and have the best vistas. Room no. 12 has a king-size bed, Jacuzzi, and TV, while room no. 10 has a niche with windows offering a 180-degree view.

99 Ocean View Pkwy. (at N. Atlantic Ave.), Bethany Beach, DE 19930. ✆ **800/418-6764** or 302/539-3707. Fax 302/539-7263. www.addysea.com. 13 units. $100–$400 double. Rates include full breakfast, afternoon tea, and lunch in summer. 2- or 3-night minimum required on weekends and holidays. AE, DISC, MC, V. Free parking. **Amenities:** Communal TV; beach equipment. *In room:* A/C, hair dryer, free Wi-Fi.

Bethany Arms Motel & Apartments (Kids) Ideal for families who want to be close to the ocean, this complex offers basic motel units with fridges and microwaves, as well as apartments with full kitchens and ocean views. Two buildings are on the boardwalk, with three more in back between the boardwalk and Atlantic Avenue.

Atlantic Ave. and Hollywood St. (P.O. Box 1600), Bethany Beach, DE 19930. ✆ **302/539-9603.** www. beach-net.com/bethanyarms.html. 50 units. $75–$250 double. Surcharges may apply. 2- or 3-night minimum stay required on summer weekends and holidays. MC, V. Free parking. Closed late Oct to early Mar. *In room:* A/C, TV, fridge, microwave.

Fenwick Island

Fenwick Islander Motel (Value) On the bay side of the highway, just north of the Maryland–Delaware state line, this bright three-story motel offers simple, clean accommodations. All units have kitchenettes; second- and third-floor rooms have balconies. Rooms in back are off the highway and quieter, with a view of the canal.

Rte. 1 and S. Carolina Ave. (btw. S. Carolina and W. Virginia aves.), Fenwick Island, DE 19944. ✆ **800/346-4520** or 302/539-2333. Fax 302/537-1134. www.fenwickislander.com. 63 units. $49–$199 double. Children 9 and under stay free in parent's room; children 10–16 stay for $5 each per night. Surcharges and minimum-stay requirements may apply on weekends and holidays. Weekly rates available. AE, DISC, MC, V. Free parking. Closed Nov–Mar. **Amenities:** Outdoor pool. *In room:* A/C, hair dryer (upon request), kitchenette.

Ric-Mar Apartments (Kids) The homey Sea Charm Motel that stood here is gone, but the adjacent apartments remain. The family-owned Ric-Mar offers Fenwick's closest accommodations to the beach, just 100 feet away. Guests can choose from snug studio efficiencies or one- and two-bedroom apartments. Three units that sleep six rent only by the week in summer. The units are old, but clean and "beachy."

Delaware and Bunting aves., Fenwick Island, DE 19944. ✆ **302/539-9613.** 14 units. $110–$155 efficiency; $120–$250 apt. 3-night minimum stay required in high season. DISC, MC, V. Free parking. Closed mid-Sept to mid-May. **Amenities:** Patio and deck w/grills; outdoor pool. *In room:* A/C, TV, kitchenette.

Seaside Inn At this highway-side motel located a half-block from the beach, rooms are simply furnished. Larger king and two-queen units have sleeper sofas and a smidge more room. A tiny pool is tucked behind the office. The only bad news: no water views.

1401 Coastal Hwy., Fenwick Island, DE 19944. ✆ **800/417-1104** or 302/251-5000. www.seasideinn fenwick.com. 61 units. $39–$185 double. Surcharges and minimum-stay requirements on some weekends and holidays. AE, DISC, MC, V. Free parking. Closed mid-Oct to mid-May. **Amenities:** Outdoor pool. *In room:* A/C, TV, fridge, hair dryer (upon request), microwave.

WHERE TO DINE

The restaurants of the Bethany Beach and Fenwick Island area provide a pleasant blend of waterside and inland dining, mostly at moderate prices. Family-oriented, lower priced restaurants mix easily with fine-dining establishments that offer quality, ambience, and creative food. Unless otherwise noted, most restaurants serve alcohol. (Note that in Bethany, alcoholic beverages are available only in restaurants—there are no bars.)

11

Note: Hours in the "Quiet Resorts" can change as crowds diminish off-season. Always call ahead if you're visiting in the off-season—that is, before Memorial Day and after Labor Day. Fenwick stays a bit livelier until the greyhounds have left after Columbus Day weekend.

Since motels in Bethany and Fenwick do not serve breakfast, you may want to check out some of the following places, particularly Frog House and Warren's Station.

Bethany Beach

Baja Beach House Grill MEXICAN   Fresh Mexican is on the menu at this *muy* casual eatery owned by a Bethany native. Burritos, tacos, and fajitas, as well as burgers and sandwiches, are cooked as soon as you order them at the counter. You can get carryout or stay to eat inside this sleek, California-style shop. Breakfast is served daily.

109 Garfield Pkwy., Bethany Beach. © **302/537-9993.** www.bajabeachhouse.com. Reservations not accepted. You can call ahead to place carryout orders. Main courses $3.25–$12. AE, MC, V. Hours vary depending on season, but always open for breakfast, lunch, and dinner in summer, plus long weekends in the spring and fall off-season; call ahead.

The Cottage Cafe Restaurant AMERICAN   This homey place has updated its country-cottage look but kept the comfort foods that make it so popular. The menu offers everything from old-fashioned pot roast and meatloaf to sandwiches, soup-and-salad combos, and pastas. In summer, a breakfast buffet is served on Saturday and Sunday from 8am to noon. Early-bird specials are offered before 6pm.

Rte. 1 at Hickman Plaza, Bethany Beach. © **302/539-8710.** www.cottagecafe.com. Reservations not accepted. All items $7–$28. AE, DC, MC, V. Mon–Fri 11am–1am; Sat–Sun 8am–1am.

Frog House (Kids) AMERICAN   You can sleep in and still get breakfast at the Frog House, where it's served until 2pm. The 12 kinds of pancakes range from apple to chocolate chip. Lunchtime favorites include sandwiches, burgers, and salads; dinner brings fried chicken, steamed shrimp, and crab cakes. This is a great place to take the whole family—it's casual, friendly, and reasonably priced.

116 Garfield Pkwy., Bethany Beach. © **302/539-4500.** Reservations not accepted. Main courses $2.50–$8.75 breakfast, $4.75–$6.25 lunch, $7.65–$17 dinner. DISC, MC, V. Mar–May Fri–Sat only; Memorial Day to Labor Day daily 7am–9pm; Sept–Nov 8am–2pm. Closed Dec–Feb.

Grotto Pizza PIZZA   The crowds keep coming to Grotto Pizza. There are outlets throughout Delaware, and Bethany is lucky enough to have two—which are both packed at dinnertime. It's no wonder, with the crispy crust, savory sauce, and cheese—and the perfect white pizza, which combines spices, onions, and cheese. The menu also has salads, subs, and pastas. Grotto has branches in Dewey and Rehoboth; delivery is available, too.

793 Garfield Pkwy., Bethany Beach (© **302/537-3278**), and 8–10 York Beach Mall, South Bethany (© **302/537-6600**). www.grottopizza.com. Reservations not accepted. Pizza $9.75–$20. AE, DISC, MC, V. Summer Sun–Thurs 11am–11pm, Fri–Sat 11am–midnight; hours vary in off-season, so call ahead. The York Beach Mall location closes in off-season.

Kingston Grille FRENCH   This noisy, 12-table bistro continues making waves among those who love traditional French cooking. Foie gras may be teamed with a baked Brie or crab may top the filet mignon. When local seafood is available, you can be sure it will turn up on the menu tucked into the soups or starring on its own.

14 Pennsylvania Ave. (at Campbell Place), Bethany Beach. © **302/539-1588.** Reservations required. Main dishes $24–$40. MC, V. Wed–Sun 5–10pm. Closed Jan–Feb.

Mango Mike's SEAFOOD The beach vibe makes this casual place a lot of fun. Friendly waitstaff make it pleasant. And a seat on the deck overlooking the ocean makes it a place to linger (if there isn't a long line of hungry people waiting). Inside, the decor is beach-shack modern. The menu features fresh seafood and slightly Caribbean dishes, such as coco-loco shrimp salad and jerk-chicken salad.

Garfield Parkway and the Boardwalk, Bethany Beach. ℂ 302/537-6621. www.mangomikes.com. Reservations accepted only for 5–6pm. Main dishes $15–$30. AE, MC, V. June–Sept daily 11:30am–11:30pm; Apr–May and Oct–Thanksgiving weekend Fri–Sat 11am–9pm, Sun 11am–3pm. Closed Dec–Mar.

McCabe's Gourmet Market DELI This deli and market is a local favorite for sandwiches, salads (such as a chicken-walnut option), and fresh-baked breads and pastries. *Tip:* Visitors in South Bethany walk from the beach to pick up sandwiches for their beachside picnic—it's that close. Call ahead and your order will be waiting.

Rte. 1, in the York Beach Mall (just north of Fenwick Island State Park), South Bethany. ℂ 302/539-8550. www.mccabesgourmet.com. Reservations not accepted. Sandwiches $4.25–$7.95. AE, DISC, MC, V. Summer daily 7am–5pm (or later); fall and spring Tues–Sat 7am–5pm, Sun 7am–4pm. Closed Jan to mid-March.

Sedona ★ AMERICAN Offering some welcome sophistication in Bethany Beach, Sedona is a great place to sneak away from the kids and have an adult meal (although well-behaved children are welcome). The sleek interior has room for 70 diners; in summer, make a reservation or be prepared to wait. Traditional recipes get a contemporary accent here. Choices range from rack of lamb to seared tuna, and sometimes there's antelope.

26 Pennsylvania Ave., Bethany Beach. ℂ 302/539-1200. www.sedona-bethany.com. Reservations recommended. Main courses $24–$36. AE, DISC, MC, V. Daily 5–10pm in summer; winter Fri–Sat 5–10pm.

Fenwick Island

David Twining's Nantuckets ★ SEAFOOD This is a place for grown-ups, with bright dining rooms, white tablecloths, and an innovative menu offering rich beef, garlicky mashed potatoes, famous quahog *chowdah*, and a lobster shepherd's pie that doesn't need a crust. If you like a more casual dining experience (although shorts are welcome in the dining rooms), try the adjacent bar, a cheerful place to grab a cold drink, appetizer, or whole meal. Service is top-notch. Early-bird specials are available before 5:45pm; there's happy hour in the taproom from 4 to 7pm.

Rte. 1 and Atlantic Ave. ℂ 800/362-3463 or 302/539-2607. www.nantucketsrestaurant.com. Reservations recommended. Main courses $9–$30. AE, DC, DISC, MC, V. Daily 4–10pm in taproom; 5pm–midnight in dining rooms (until 9pm in off-season).

Harpoon Hanna's ★ (Kids) SEAFOOD This huge, wood-paneled bayside restaurant occasionally has its ups and downs, but you can always count on fresh fish, along with a crisp tropical salad with mandarin orange and tiny shrimp. What *really* draws the crowds are the warm breads—raisin, rye, and coconut muffins—and the fresh fish prepared three ways. The waitstaff is young but works hard to please. In summer, arrive early—about 4:30pm or so—or plan on a long wait. The Tiki Bar has nightly parties, sometimes with live entertainment. Children are welcome; docks available for diners arriving by boat.

142nd St. (at Rte. 54). ℂ 800/227-0525 or 302/539-3095. www.harpoonhannasrestaurant.com. Reservations not accepted. Main courses $8–$11 lunch, $8–$25 dinner. AE, DISC, MC, V. Daily 11am–9pm (Sun brunch 10am–3pm), with extended hours in summer.

Warren's Station (Value) AMERICAN Families have been coming here since the 1960s. The big, white restaurant, which resembles a lifesaving station, serves good-size portions of traditional foods, including a turkey dinner; beef, chicken, and seafood entrees; and a heavenly "crab cutlet," a big fluffy crab cake from an old Deal Island Church recipe. Not that hungry? Try a burger, sandwich, or salad. Leave room for homemade pie. No alcohol is served.

Ocean Hwy. (Rte. 1, btw. Indian and Houston sts.). ℂ 302/539-7156. www.warrensstation.com. Reservations not accepted. Main courses $2–$9 breakfast, $3–$9 lunch, $9–$18 dinner. DISC, MC, V. Mid-May to Labor Day daily 8am–9pm; Sept 4:30–8:30pm. Closed Oct to mid-May.

WHAT TO SEE & DO

The 1-mile-long **Bethany Beach Boardwalk** has only a few businesses on it. It's more of a promenade, perfect for a leisurely walk near the beach. Most of the shops and fast-food eateries are on **Garfield Parkway,** which intersects the boardwalk midway. **Fenwick Island** has no boardwalk between its hotels and its wide-open beach with gentle dunes. Shops and businesses are concentrated along Route 1.

To see real sunken treasure, head to the **DiscoverSea Shipwreck Museum** ★, Route 1 and Bayard Street, Fenwick Island (ℂ **302/539-9366;** www.discoversea.com), a small private museum above the Sea Shell City shop. The collection includes jewelry, coins, china, and a seashell display. Admission is free. Hours are Memorial Day through Labor Day daily from 11am to 8pm, September through May Saturday and Sunday from 11am to 4pm.

Built in 1859, the **Fenwick Island Lighthouse,** on the Transpeninsular Line, Route 54, about a quarter-mile west of Route 1, is one of Delaware's oldest. The lighthouse is still in operation; its beams can be seen for 15 miles. Its grounds and ground floor are open to the public July and August, Thursday through Tuesday 10am to 2pm, and September through October 12, Friday to Monday 10am to 2pm. Find the gate on 146th Street in Ocean City. Admission is free.

Across from the lighthouse is the **Viking Golf Theme Park,** routes 1 and 54, Fenwick Island (ℂ **302/539-1644**), an inland amusement park with miniature golf, a water park, and go-carts. Hours vary according to weather. The water park is open from Memorial Day weekend to Labor Day, daily from 10am to 8pm. Miniature golf is open from Easter weekend to October, on warm weekends from 10am to 11pm, and in summer daily from 10am to midnight.

OUTDOOR ACTIVITIES

BIKING   The flatland along Route 1 in Bethany Beach and Fenwick Island is ideal for bicycling; however, caution is advised during peak traffic season in July and August. Bethany also has bike lanes through town.

Prefer a quiet ride under a canopy of loblolly pines? **Assawoman Wildlife Area** offers several bike-accessible roads that wind through tidal marshland and forests. To get here, take Route 26 west and turn left on Double Bridges Road, left to Camp Barnes Road, and follow signs to Assawoman. The park, which charges no admission, is open 7am to sunset.

Bethany Cycle and Fitness Shop, 7792B Garfield Pkwy. (ℂ **302/537-9982**), rents beach bicycles for $5 to $12 an hour or $20 per day.

FISHING   Fishing, both in the bay and in the surf, is a major draw in this area, but licenses are now required for those 16 and over. They are available online at **http://egov. dnrec.delaware.gov** or at the park office. Off-road vehicles must have a surf fishing tag to be permitted on the beaches. Surf fishing is permitted when lifeguards are off-duty. The Bethany–Fenwick Area Chamber of Commerce sponsors two surf-fishing tournaments a year, in early May and October; for information, call ℂ **302/539-2100.**

Fenwick Island State Park has 3 miles of seacoast beach, most of which is open to surf fishing, and considerable tracts of open bay, ideal for both fishing and crabbing. There are also dune crossings for off-road vehicles; a surf-fishing vehicle permit is required. Call ✆ **302/539-9060** for vehicle permits and maps of fishing areas. Similar facilities are available at **Delaware Seashore State Park** (✆ **302/227-2800**).

HIKING & BIRDING   During the off-season, **Fenwick Island** and **Delaware Seashore** state parks, both on Route 1, are great places for a walk along deserted beaches. In high season, however, when these beaches are covered with sunbathers, it's best to head out at sunrise or venture a little inland. *Tip:* Bring bug repellent.

Assawoman Wildlife Area (see "Biking," above) welcomes hikers on its few miles of dirt roads through tidal marsh and forests. An observation tower on the way to Mulberry Landing makes it easy to view a variety of shorebirds.

KAYAKING & SAILING   To tour the quieter waters of Assawoman Bay, a salt marsh, Assateague Island, or a nearby cypress stand, stop by **Coastal Kayak** (✆ **877/445-2925** or 302/539-7999; www.coastalkayak.com). It has a stand on the bay across from Fenwick Island State Park. Tours cost $40 to $50 for adults and $10 less for children; they last 90 minutes to 2 hours. It also rents kayaks, sailing catamarans, and windsurfers—and it delivers. (Get a coupon from the website.)

TENNIS   Although there's not much tennis for the general public, **Sea Colony** (p. 260) is the largest tennis resort on the East Coast, sporting 26 courts, including four outdoor lighted courts, four clay courts, and four indoor courts. If tennis is your game, contact a real-estate agent about renting a condo in Sea Colony's tennis villas.

SHOPPING

BETHANY BEACH   Most of the shopping in Bethany Beach is along or near Garfield Parkway, with a few shops on the boardwalk. They're generally open daily from 10am to 5pm, with extended hours in summer.

Bethany Beach Books, 99 Garfield Pkwy. (✆ **302/539-2522**), is the perfect place to pick up some beach reading. For your sweet tooth, head to the **Fudge Factory,** 3 Town Center (✆ **302/539-7502**), or follow your nose to the delectable aromas at **Fisher's Popcorn,** 108 Garfield Pkwy. (✆ **888/436-6388** or 302/539-8833).

Stop in **Alice H. Klein,** on Garfield Parkway (✆ **302/539-6992;** www.tkodirect. com), for delicate, handcrafted jewelry. Bethany's premier boutique is the eclectic **Japanesque,** 16 Pennsylvania Ave. (✆ **302/539-2311**), which carries a wide selection of Japanese jewelry, home furnishings, and books.

FENWICK ISLAND   Shopping in Fenwick is limited, but if you like country items, visit the **Seaside Country Store** (✆ **302/539-6110**). This big, red store on Route 1, surrounded by strip malls, has room after room of merchandise with a country feel—from gifts and clothing to home decor to candy. It's closed December through February. **Pottery Place** (✆ **302/539-3603**) has lots of beachy nature, but those in the know show up at 7am for their first cup of joe. The coffee bar in the back of the shop has famous coffee, including those fattening wonderful coffee drinks. It's open at 7am for your caffeine fix year-round.

NIGHTLIFE IN BETHANY

Hanging out on the boardwalk is all the rage—but there really isn't much to do at night. Still, it is the place for teens to meet their friends and everyone else to take a stroll and enjoy the ocean breezes.

Bethany Beach's **bandstand** features shows beginning at 7:30pm. The performances are all family oriented, with orchestras, bluegrass bands, and puppet shows. Sometimes there are dance lessons or talent shows. The town posts a schedule on the boardwalk and at the town hall on Garfield Parkway.

5 OCEAN CITY, MARYLAND ★★★

116 miles S of Wilmington; 144 miles SE of Baltimore; 130 miles SE of Washington, D.C.

For many Marylanders, heading "downy ocean" or "to the shore" means only one thing: a summer vacation in Ocean City, a 10-mile stretch of skinny barrier island. It's often quite crowded on the beach, in the restaurants, and on Coastal Highway, but it's still Marylanders' favorite place to enjoy the sun and the water. So many visitors arrive that for 3 months of the year, Ocean City is the second-largest city in the state. (Only Baltimore has more people.) Ocean City's entire beach is open to the public.

The 3-mile-long boardwalk, which stretches to 27th Street in the oldest part of Ocean City, is crowded with hotels, some of them dating back to the 1920s. Restaurants, ice-cream stands, and shops fill in the gaps. The boardwalk ends near the fishing pier, which has amusement rides and a huge Ferris wheel.

Out on Coastal Highway, shopping centers, restaurants, hotels, and condos demand your attention and your money. Miniature-golf courses are exceedingly popular: They're all crowded after dark, and there are some dandies (p. 281). The quieter waters surrounding Ocean City—the bays of Assawoman, Sinepuxent, and Montego—attract fishermen, sailors, parasailers, and kayakers.

ESSENTIALS

GETTING THERE **By Car** Route 50 goes right to Ocean City. To reach the southern end of town, continue on Route 50 to the bridge that enters O.C. at Caroline Street. For those staying at 60th Street or above, take Route 90 and cross the bridge at 62nd Street. An alternative route (but only one lane each way) is to turn on Route 404 East past Queenstown; follow it into Delaware. Turn south onto Route 113 south. Route 26 east connects with Bethany. Turn south on Route 1 to Ocean City. Or take Route 54 to Fenwick to Route 1. However you get there, avoid Route 1 in Rehoboth—especially on weekends, when traffic slows to a frustrating crawl most of the day. *Tip:* Call ✆ 877/229-7726 on your way to the Bay Bridge for up-to-date traffic reports.

By Plane The **Salisbury–Ocean City–Wicomico Regional Airport,** 30 minutes west of Ocean City, near Salisbury (✆ 410/548-4827), handles nonstop commuter flights to and from Baltimore, Washington, D.C., Philadelphia, and points south via **US Airways** (✆ 800/428-4322; www.usairways.com). Private planes also fly into that airport, as well as **Ocean City Municipal Airport,** 3 miles west of town off Route 611 (✆ 410/520-5412).

If you arrive via Baltimore Washington International Airport, then you can arrange to have the **BayRunner Shuttle** (✆ 410/912-6000; www.bayrunners.com) pick you up; it makes five trips daily.

Car rentals are available from **Avis** (✆ 410/742-8566; www.avis.com) and **Hertz** (✆ 410/749-2235; www.hertz.com), both at the Wicomico Regional Airport. At the Ocean City airport, **Express** (✆ 410/213-7336) rents cars.

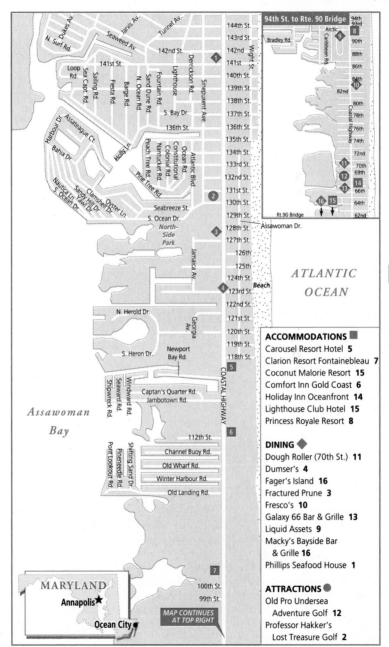

94th St. to Rte. 90 Bridge

ACCOMMODATIONS ■
Carousel Resort Hotel **5**
Clarion Resort Fontainebleau **7**
Coconut Malorie Resort **15**
Comfort Inn Gold Coast **6**
Holiday Inn Oceanfront **14**
Lighthouse Club Hotel **15**
Princess Royale Resort **8**

DINING ◆
Dough Roller (70th St.) **11**
Dumser's **4**
Fager's Island **16**
Fractured Prune **3**
Fresco's **10**
Galaxy 66 Bar & Grille **13**
Liquid Assets **9**
Macky's Bayside Bar & Grille **16**
Phillips Seafood House **1**

ATTRACTIONS ●
Old Pro Undersea Adventure Golf **12**
Professor Hakker's Lost Treasure Golf **2**

ATLANTIC OCEAN

Assawoman Bay

MARYLAND
Annapolis ★
Ocean City

By Bus Greyhound (© 800/231-2222; www.greyhound.com) has daily service into Ocean City from points north and south, with nonstop buses from Baltimore, Washington, D.C., and Salisbury. Buses stop at the **West Ocean City Park & Ride,** 12848 Ocean Gateway (© 410/289-9307).

VISITOR INFORMATION The **Ocean City Convention and Visitors' Bureau** operates a visitor center in the Roland E. Powell Convention Center, 4001 Coastal Hwy., at 40th Street, bay side (© 800/626-6232 or 410/289-8181; http://ococean.com). It's open daily from 8:30am to 5pm.

If you're heading into town from Route 50, stop at the information center run by the **Greater Ocean City Chamber of Commerce,** routes 707 and 50, 1½ miles from Ocean City (© 410/213-0552; www.oceancity.org). It's a great place to pick up brochures and coupons. Open daily from 8:30am to 4:30pm.

Tip: If you have only 1 night to stay at the beach, check with the staff at either center. Although most hotels advertise 2- or 3-night minimum stays on weekends, they can probably find you accommodations.

Look for coupons and event schedules in *Ocean City Visitors' Guide, Sunny Day, Beachcomber,* and *Beach Guide,* available in restaurants, stores, and hotels.

GETTING AROUND **By Bus** In peak season, when parking is scarce, the bus is the most convenient way to get around. Buses run 24 hours a day. They follow one route, from the Delaware border south along Coastal Highway to the inlet, returning north along Baltimore Street and Coastal Highway. In summer, buses run every 10 minutes; from October 20 to Memorial Day, they run every half-hour. The fare is $2 for a 24-hour period; exact change is required. For information, contact the **Ocean City Transportation Department,** 66th Street, bay side (© 410/723-1606).

A **park-and-ride lot,** on Route 50 in West Ocean City (on the western side of the bridge), has free parking. Visitors can board a shuttle to South Division Street near the inlet to either spend the day there or catch a bus to other O.C. destinations. It costs $1 for the entire day.

By Boardwalk Tram ★ The tram travels 2½ miles between the inlet and 27th Street, stopping to pick up passengers who signal the driver. In summer, it runs every 10 minutes from 7am to midnight daily. On weekends from Easter to May, and in September and October, it runs every 15 minutes. To get off, raise your hand and the tram will stop. The fare is $3 one-way, or get a frequent rider card at the tram station for $20 for eight rides. It's great for parents with tired children—and a good way for first-time visitors to become familiar with the boardwalk.

By Taxi Taxi service has expanded in recent years—serving those who've had too much to drink as well as nondrivers. Among the growing number of services are **Sunset Taxi** (© 410/250-8294) and **Eastern Shore Taxi** (© 410/524-6647).

PARKING Parking is difficult at the height of the season. A majority of public facilities, such as shopping centers and restaurants, offer free parking. Eight public lots, mostly around the southern end of Ocean City, and most downtown streets have meters which must be fed $1.25 an hour 24 hours a day April 15 through October 15. Parking is free off-season. You can find change machines at several lots: Worcester Street; Somerset Street and Baltimore Avenue; Dorchester Street and Baltimore Avenue; North Division Street and Baltimore Avenue; and Fourth Street and Baltimore Avenue. The largest public lot is the Hugh T. Cropper parking lot at the inlet, with 1,200 paid spaces. The first 30 minutes here are free; then the rate is $1 an hour, $1.50 on weekends. If you plan to

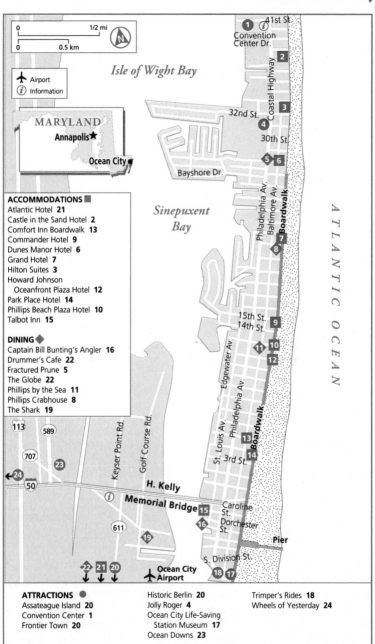

Isle of Wight Bay

✈ Airport
ⓘ Information

MARYLAND
Annapolis★
Ocean City●

ACCOMMODATIONS ■
Atlantic Hotel **21**
Castle in the Sand Hotel **2**
Comfort Inn Boardwalk **13**
Commander Hotel **9**
Dunes Manor Hotel **6**
Grand Hotel **7**
Hilton Suites **3**
Howard Johnson
  Oceanfront Plaza Hotel **12**
Park Place Hotel **14**
Phillips Beach Plaza Hotel **10**
Talbot Inn **15**

DINING ◆
Captain Bill Bunting's Angler **16**
Drummer's Cafe **22**
Fractured Prune **5**
The Globe **22**
Phillips by the Sea **11**
Phillips Crabhouse **8**
The Shark **19**

Sinepuxent
Bay

Bayshore Dr.

41st St
Convention
Center Dr.

Coastal Highway

32nd St.
30th St.

Philadelphia Av.
Baltimore Av.
Boardwalk

ATLANTIC OCEAN

15th St.
14th St.

Edgewater Av.
Philadelphia Av.

St. Louis Av.
Philadelphia Av.
3rd St.

Boardwalk

H. Kelly
Memorial Bridge

Keyser Point Rd.
Golf Course Rd.

Caroline
St.
Dorchester
St.

Pier

S. Division St.

Ocean City
Airport

ATTRACTIONS ●
Assateague Island **20**
Convention Center **1**
Frontier Town **20**

Historic Berlin **20**
Jolly Roger **4**
Ocean City Life-Saving
  Station Museum **17**
Ocean Downs **23**

Trimper's Rides **18**
Wheels of Yesterday **24**

park here for nighttime activities, be aware that hundreds of other people will have the same idea—and the wait to get in the lot, and later to get out, can be long.

ORIENTATION Ocean City stretches for 10 miles, with one main north-south thoroughfare, Coastal Highway. It becomes two one-way streets on the southern end at around 32nd Street: Philadelphia goes south; Baltimore heads north. Cross streets are designated by numbers (from First to 145th), with numbers decreasing to the south. It's vital to know the cross street when looking for a shop or restaurant (though if you have a street address, the first two numbers usually tell you the cross street). Attractions and businesses on the cross streets are designated as either ocean side (east of Coastal Hwy.) or bay side (west of Coastal Hwy.). If you see an address that says Atlantic Avenue, it's oceanfront.

SPECIAL EVENTS Ocean City's party atmosphere is enhanced by festivals throughout the year; below is just a selection of the largest and most popular.

Everybody in O.C. is Irish on the Sunday closest to St. Patrick's Day for the **St. Patrick's Day Parade and Festival.** Every year, more and more people decide this is the place for the "wearin' of the green." The 4-day **Springfest,** held the first week of May, brings crafts, music, and food to the inlet parking lot. Lots of businesses open now, as O.C. prepares for summer.

On the **Fourth of July,** some 300,000 people crowd into Ocean City. Fireworks over Assawoman Bay top off the family-style picnic held at Northside Park beginning at 1pm. A second fireworks display takes place at North Division Street, at the south end of the boardwalk. Festivities begin with a concert at 8pm; fireworks begin at both locations at 9:30pm.

The **White Marlin Open** ★ (www.whitemarlinopen.com) is held the first full week in August. Some 400 boats register for this annual fishing expedition. In 2009, prize money for the biggest white marlin, blue marlin, shark, and tuna totaled more than $2 million. Stop by the Harbor Island Marina on the bay side for the weigh-ins every night from 4 to 9pm. They reel in some whoppers. A 1,062-pound blue marlin broke a state record in 2009.

The 4-day **Sunfest** festival, held the third week of September, officially ends the summer season with crafts, music, and food at the inlet. From mid-November to New Year's, holiday displays make up the **Winterfest of Lights** ★★. The first takes place at the inlet, where you can drive past the lit displays. The second takes place in Northside Park. For $3 for those 12 and older, you can ride the tram through the light displays and then stop to see Santa, have hot chocolate, and browse the gift shop.

Family activities are scheduled nearly every summer evening on the beach or at North Side Park: Sundae Sundays, movies, concerts, and bonfires. Check with the visitor center.

(*Fast Facts* **Ocean City**

Area Code Ocean City's area codes are **410** and **443.**

Beach Wheelchairs Free beach-accessible chairs are available on a first-come, first-served basis from the Ocean City beach patrol. Or reserve your chair at the convention center or police department by calling ✆ **410/723-6610.**

Dentists Emergency work is provided at **Atlantic Dental Associates,** 12308 Ocean Gateway, at Route 50 (✆ **410/213-7575**).

Emergencies Dial 📞 **911** for fire, police, or ambulance.

Eyeglass Repair The local choice is **Accurate Optical,** 118th Street, near the Food Lion supermarket (📞 **410/524-0220**).

Hospitals Go to the **75th Street Medical Center,** 7408 Coastal Hwy. (📞 **410/524-0075**); the **Atlantic General Hospital,** 9733 Healthway Dr., Berlin (📞 **410/641-1100**); or the **Peninsula Regional Medical Center,** 100 E. Carroll St., Salisbury (📞 **410/546-6400**).

Library The North Ocean City Library is at 100th Street and Coastal Highway (📞 **410/524-1818**).

Newspapers Ocean City's weekly newspaper is *Ocean City Today.* Dailies from Baltimore, Washington, and Philadelphia are also available.

Pharmacies Go to **Bailey's,** Eighth Street and Philadelphia Avenue (📞 **410/289-8191**), or **CVS,** Coastal Highway and 120th Street (📞 **410/524-7233**).

Police If it's not an emergency, dial 📞 **410/723-6610** for Ocean City police, 📞 **410/641-3101** for state police, or 📞 **410/289-7556** for beach patrol.

Post Office The main post office is located at 71st Street and Coastal Highway, bay side (📞 **410/524-7611**). Also at the visitor center on Route 50 west of the bridge into Ocean City.

Taxes The state sales tax is 6%.

Transit Information Dial 📞 **410/723-2173.**

Visitor Information Dial 📞 **800/OC-OCEAN** (626-2326) or 410/289-2931.

Weather Dial 📞 **800/OC-OCEAN** (626-2326) or 410/548-9262.

WHERE TO STAY

More than in any other part of Maryland, lodgings here rely on a high season. Summer—especially July and early August—commands the highest rates, often with weekend supplements. In many cases, minimum stays of 2 or 3 nights are required, so check in advance. Reservations are essential for weekends. Most hotels have pools (ask if it's important to you), but those with indoor pools can fill up in the off-season, especially on holiday weekends. Every hotel has rooms that are accessible for those with disabilities; nearly all have free parking.

Rates are a little lower on rooms without an ocean view or with a partial view. January rates are bargain basement (for good reason), but tariffs in spring and fall are also economical, and many hotels offer packages. Spring can be rainy, but September is terrific: The beach is nearly empty (except on weekends), lots of restaurants are still open, and the water is warm. I hate to give this secret away, but early June can also be a good time—as long as you're willing to put up with "June Bugs" (new high-school graduates celebrating their freedom). Since the grads are occupied elsewhere, you'll find lots of room in restaurants, shops, and nightspots; drive carefully. Valentine's Day and Christmas also draw a crowd; look for hotel packages and special menus for each holiday, as well as light displays and New Year's Eve parties.

For many families, renting a condo or town house is the only way to go. With several bedrooms and bathrooms, full kitchens, and living rooms, these offer a convenient way to take everybody to the beach. Most rent from Saturday to Saturday. Several real-estate companies offer hundreds of units on both the ocean and the bay; try **Coldwell Banker** (© 800/633-1000; www.cbvacations.com) or **Long and Foster** (© 800/843-2322) for rentals in Ocean City, as well as in the "suburbs" of west Ocean City. Rates start at $1,000 a week and take off from there. Every unit is different, so read the thick brochures and check the firms' websites. Generally, units are well kept, with fairly new furniture, appliances, and often a stash of paperbacks and board games for rainy days. Bring your own paper products and linens. Just about everything else is usually provided. (Check the listings to be sure.) The best units—that is, the newest and closest to the beach—are snapped up by January or February, but if you decide in May to go to the beach, you'll still have plenty of choices.

Expensive

Carousel Resort Hotel ★★

The Carousel is an attractive choice for families and couples. One of the oldest of north Ocean City's high-rises, it offers plenty of amenities, including pools indoor and out, restaurants, a beach bar and grill, a playground, and even pizza delivery. Rooms are well-equipped, if small, and even have kitchenettes. If those 237 rooms aren't enough, 102 two- and three-bedroom oceanfront condo units are available in the 22-story tower. Some are decorated by the hotel; others are privately owned with varying decor. Carousel is a conference center and can be fully booked. Off-season, the hotel offers some great values.

11700 Coastal Hwy., Ocean City, MD 21842. © 800/641-0011 or 410/524-1000. Fax 410/524-7766. www. carouselhotel.com. 339 units. $59–$349 double; $179–$499 condo. Weekly rates available. AE, DC, DISC, MC, V. Free parking. **Amenities:** 2 restaurants; deli/coffee bar; 2 bars; fitness room; Jacuzzi; indoor ice rink (open to the public); indoor and outdoor pool; sauna; tennis court. *In room:* A/C, TV, DVD or VCR (in condos), fridge, hair dryer, high-speed Internet, microwave.

Clarion Resort Fontainebleau ★★

On the ocean, far from the boardwalk and in the midst of Condo Row in northern Ocean City, this hotel offers oversize rooms and suites, all with tiny, standing-room-only balconies and views of the ocean and the bay. The seven two-story cabana suites, with sitting rooms and huge bedrooms, are spacious and fun. The Clarion also rents 73 one-, two-, and three-bedroom units at the adjacent Marigot Beach Condominiums.

10100 Coastal Hwy. (at 101st St.), Ocean City, MD 21842. © 800/638-2100 or 410/524-3535. Fax 410/524-3834. www.clarionoc.com. 250 units. $99–$389 double; $119–$479 condos. AE, DC, DISC, MC, V. Free valet and self-parking. Pets okay in hotel for fee. **Amenities:** Restaurant; beach bar and grill; 2 lounges; beach equipment; fitness center; playground; indoor pool; spa; terrace. *In room:* A/C, TV, fridge, hair dryer, microwave, free Wi-Fi.

Coconut Malorie ★★

Stylish with a tropical flair, this Fairfield resort offers suites overlooking Isle of Wight Bay. The lobby—with a waterfall, marble floors, and palm trees—is inviting. Suites are decorated in the same Caribbean style: big British colonial beds, Haitian art, luxurious bathrooms with whirlpool tubs, and plenty of space. Wi-Fi is available in the lobby and by the pool. The resort offers a variety of activities, a concierge service, and good recreation facilities. A footbridge connects the hotel to **Fager's Island** (see "Where to Dine," below).

200 59th St., Ocean City, MD 21842. © 800/767-6060. Fax 410/524-9327. www.coconutmalorie.com. 85 units. $89–$275 double. AE, DC, DISC, MC, V. Free parking. **Amenities:** Poolside bar; fitness room; outdoor pool. *In room:* A/C, hair dryer, high-speed Internet, kitchenette.

Dunes Manor Hotel ★

If you like your hotels old-fashioned, the Dunes Manor is for you. On 28th Street, just beyond the boardwalk, this 11-story hotel tries its best to capture days gone by. The Victorian-style facade, cupolas, and wide porch with rocking chairs are just the beginning. Tea and crumpets are offered every summer afternoon. Each unit is up-to-date in every way, with an oceanfront view, a balcony, one king-size or two double beds, and a decor of light woods and floral fabrics. Rooms on upper floors have the best views; nine units have kitchenettes.

2800 Baltimore Ave., Ocean City, MD 21842. (C) **800/523-2888** or 410/289-1100. Fax 410/289-4905. www.dunesmanor.com. 170 units. $45–$304 double; $109–$359 efficiency. Weekly rates available. AE, DC, DISC, MC, V. Free parking. **Amenities:** Restaurant; lounge; fitness center; indoor/outdoor pool; sun deck; whirlpool. *In room:* A/C, TV, fridge, hair dryer, microwave, free Wi-Fi.

Hilton Suites Ocean City Oceanfront ★★★
New on the oceanfront, you can't miss the blue-and-white, 12-story tower dominating the skyline in O.C.'s midsection. And the Hilton has it all, including spacious rooms and amenities such as a swim-up pool bar, a huge children's pool, an outdoor hot tub, and changing rooms for guests staying after checkout. The 225 suites feature sitting rooms with flatscreen TVs and pullout sofas, well-stocked kitchens, spacious bathrooms with jetted tubs, and bedrooms with two queen- or one king-size bed. Specialty corner, terrace, and penthouse suites are available.

3200 Baltimore Ave., Ocean City, MD 21842. (C) **866/729-3200** or 410/289-6444. www.oceancityhilton. com. 225 suites. $199–$499 suite. 3-night minimum in peak season. Weekly rates available. AE, DISC, MC, V. Free self- and valet parking. **Amenities:** Restaurant; lounge; swim-up pool bar; fitness room; oceanfront grill; outdoor hot tub; 2 outdoor pools (1 children's, 1 adult's); indoor pool. *In room:* A/C, 2 TVs w/ movies and video games, hair dryer, kitchen, MP3 dock, free Wi-Fi.

Lighthouse Club Hotel ★★★
Empty your wallet and pamper yourself in this unique boutique hotel, perched on Isle of Wight Bay. You can't miss the inn, which resembles a gabled, red-roofed screw-pile lighthouse from the Route 90 bridge. Inside, the lobby soars to a skylight three stories up. A circular staircase takes guests to their rooms, decorated in tropical white and rattan. Balconies overlook the bay. Eight units have fireplaces and Jacuzzis. Light-keeper suites offer more spacious surroundings.

The adjacent **Edge** (where rates begin at $209 a night) may be even more luxurious, with two-story guest rooms, private Jacuzzis, wide-open sitting areas, gas fireplaces, and DVD players. Each unit has a balcony overlooking the pool. The Left Bank suite has a Jacuzzi placed by picture windows overlooking the bay. Two penthouse suites top the hotel.

201 60th St. (on the bay), Ocean City, MD 21842. (C) **800/371-5400** or 410/524-5400. Fax 410/524-3928. www.fagers.com/hotel. 23 units in the Lighthouse; 12 units in the Edge. $79–$180 double; $209–$339 suite. Off-season packages are a good deal in winter. Rates include continental breakfast. AE, DC, DISC, MC, V. Free parking. **Amenities:** Restaurant (see Fager's Island, under "Where to Dine," below); Jacuzzi; pool. *In room:* TV/DVD, fridge w/soda, hair dryer, free Wi-Fi.

Princess Royale ★ (Kids)
All of the suites were updated in 2008, but what makes this the place to stay is the Olympic-size indoor pool. Even if it rains, the pool is big enough for everybody—and not many hotels can say that. It's part of a recreation center, glassed in with a sauna, Jacuzzis, and a poolside cafe that will keep your kids happy. Rooms are rented in the lower five floors; the upper floors are condo units. One-bedroom suites sleep two to six people, two-bedrooms sleep six to eight, and three-bedrooms sleep up to 10.

9100 Coastal Hwy., Ocean City, MD 21842. (C) **800/4-ROYALE** (476-9253) or 410/524-7777. Fax 410/524-1623. www.princessroyale.com. 310 units, 25 condos. $79–$349 double; $169–$565 condo. Children 12 and under stay free in parent's room. AE, DISC, MC, V. Free parking. **Amenities:** 2 restaurants; bar; comedy club; fitness center; Jacuzzi; minigolf; indoor pool; sauna; tennis courts; beach volleyball court. *In room:* A/C, TV, hair dryer, kitchenette (full kitchen in condos), free Wi-Fi.

Castle in the Sand Hotel (Value)   A good choice for families who don't want to break the bank, this modern hotel with a castlelike exterior is set on the beach at 37th Street, about 10 blocks from the boardwalk. Standard rooms have the usual amenities; for something bigger, check into a condo or one of the quaint apartments in 36 beach cottages. Two-bed, two-bathroom condos go for about $1,200 a week; apartments run a little less. Outside are a pool and a beachside restaurant with live music daily mid-May to mid-September.

3701 Atlantic Ave., Ocean City, MD 21842. ✆ **800/552-SAND** (7263) or 410/289-6846. Fax 410/289-9446. www.castleinthesand.com. 180 units. $99–$249 double (standard, suites, and efficiencies). Weekly rates available. AE, DC, DISC, MC, V. Free parking. Closed mid-Nov to mid-Feb. **Amenities:** Restaurant; bar and grill; children's summer activities; outdoor pool. *In room:* A/C, TV/DVD w/movies, kitchen (in some), fridge, hair dryer, microwave (in some); free Wi-Fi.

Commander Hotel   Set right in the center of the boardwalk, this successor to one of O.C.'s oldest hotels offers lots of conveniences and comforts. A variety of accommodations—from efficiencies to suites—fits a variety of guests. The Promenade Suites lead right out onto the second-story deck and pool, while the corner Captain's Suites offer a bit more room, with lots of windows overlooking the boardwalk and beach. Cabana Suites, though a good size, overlook Baltimore Avenue.

1401 Atlantic Ave., Ocean City, MD 21842. ✆ **888/289-6166** or 410/289-6166. www.commanderhotel. com. 110 units. $75–$309 double. Weekly rates available. Children 5 and under stay free with 2 parents. MC, V. Free parking. Closed Nov to mid-Mar. **Amenities:** Restaurant; lounge; outdoor and indoor pools; oceanfront sun deck. *In room:* A/C, TV, fridge, hair dryer, microwave (in most rooms).

Grand Hotel   First, it's really not "grand"—more like big and comfortable. Overlooking a wide swath of beach, the Grand is a good family choice. It's right on the boardwalk, but at the quiet north end. It's got standard rooms, plus a variety of eateries and shops at the boardwalk level. If you're coming without the kids, you might prefer the 12th-floor whirlpool rooms or the bay-view suites.

2100 Baltimore Ave., Ocean City, MD 21842. ✆ **800/447-6779** or 410/289-6191. Fax 410/289-7591. www.grandhoteloceancity.com. 251 units. $115–$600 double. AE, DC, DISC, MC, V. Free parking. **Amenities:** Restaurant; lounge; pool bar; indoor and outdoor pools w/sun deck; sauna. *In room:* A/C, TV, fridge, hair dryer, microwave, free Wi-Fi.

Holiday Inn Oceanfront ★★   Right in the center of O.C., directly on the beach, this eight-story hotel is convenient to everything. Its resort amenities make it a good choice for a weekend or a week. There are hammocks by the pool, a newly resurfaced tennis court, and a 10-person Jacuzzi. Each long, narrow room has a balcony and sitting area on one side, sleeping area in the middle, and kitchenette by the door. Units on the top three floors have fireplaces (electric—romantic, but not hot, in summertime). Room no. 813 has views of both ocean and bay.

6600 Coastal Hwy. (oceanfront at 67th St.), Ocean City, MD 21842. ✆ **800/837-3588** or 410/524-1600. Fax 410/524-1135. www.holidayinnoceanfront.com. 216 units. $54–$334 double. Weekly rates available. AE, DC, DISC, MC, V. Free parking. **Amenities:** Restaurant; poolside bar and grill; children's summer programs; fitness center; outdoor and indoor pools; sauna; tennis; whirlpool; free Wi-Fi in lobby. *In room:* A/C, TV/VCR w/movies, fridge, hair dryer, kitchenette.

Howard Johnson Oceanfront Plaza Hotel ★   Newly renovated in 2009, this moderately priced choice on the boardwalk offers guest rooms decorated in rich colors and textures. Each room has a balcony with full or partial ocean views. Deluxe oceanfront units have sleeper sofas.

1109 Atlantic Ave., Ocean City, MD 21842. ℂ **800/926-1122** or 410/289-7251. Fax 410/289-4901. www. hjoceanfrontplaza.com. 90 units. $49–$299 double. Children 18 and under stay free in parent's room. AE, DC, DISC, MC, V. Free parking. **Amenities:** Restaurant; bar; Jacuzzi.; indoor and outdoor pools. *In room:* A/C, fridge, hair dryer, safe, microwave, free Wi-Fi.

Inexpensive

Comfort Inn Gold Coast (Value)   For value and great location, this bayside hotel is a good choice. Set back from the highway, its bayside rooms boast a lovely view—and the higher rates to prove it. Not every room has a view, but all are comfortable. The hotel's location, next door to the Gold Coast Mall, with restaurants and movie theaters, is a shopper's dream.

11201 Coastal Hwy. (at 112th St.), Ocean City, MD 21842. ℂ **800/228-5150** or 410/524-3000. Fax 410/ 524-8255. www.comfortgoldcoast.com. 202 units. $39–$295 double. Children 17 and under stay free in parent's room. AE, DISC, MC, V. Free parking. **Amenities:** Children's play area; health club; Jacuzzi; indoor pool. *In room:* A/C, TV, fridge, hair dryer, microwave, free Wi-Fi.

Park Place Hotel   Owned by a longtime O.C. hotelier family, the Park Place is designed to meet vacationing families' every need. Built in 2000, the hotel has standard rooms with space enough for all that beach paraphernalia. All have kitchenettes and pullout sofas; oceanfront rooms have balconies; and bay-view rooms are a bit bigger. Bay-view king rooms have Jacuzzis as well.

Second and Third sts., Ocean City, MD 21842. ℂ **888/212-7275** or 410/289-6440. Fax 410/289-3389. www.ocparkplacehotel.com. 89 units. $50–$259 double. Weekly rates available. Children 12 and under stay free in parent's room. AE, DC, DISC, MC, V. Free parking. Closed Dec–Jan but open New Year's Eve. **Amenities:** Outdoor bar and grill; DVD/VCR rental; pool w/sun deck. *In room:* A/C, TV, fridge, hair dryer, microwave, free Wi-Fi.

Phillips Beach Plaza Hotel   Victorian chandeliers, wrought-iron fixtures, and a fireplace give this old-time hotel's lobby more elegance than you'd expect to find in O.C. But upstairs, the guest rooms are pretty standard. Still, a number of features make this place worth a second look: a variety of single rooms, 27 one- to three-bedroom apartments (some with full kitchens), a big porch with rocking chairs overlooking the boardwalk and ocean, and the Phillips by the Sea restaurant (see "Where to Dine," below). If you want to stay at the beach for a week but avoid weekend traffic, you can book a week here from weekday to weekday.

1301 Atlantic Ave. (btw. 13th and 14th sts.), Ocean City, MD 21842. ℂ **800/492-5834** or 410/289-9121. Fax 410/289-3041. 96 units. $70–$230 double; $90–$300 apt. Weekly rates available. 2-night minimum stay required on weekends. AE, DC, DISC, MC, V. Free parking. Closed Jan–Mar. **Amenities:** Restaurant. *In room:* A/C, hair dryer (on request).

Talbot Inn (Value)   The Talbot Inn is a great spot for fishermen and those who love the boardwalk. It's an easy walk to the Talbot Street Pier (where you can find a fishing boat or take a ride on the *O.C. Rocket*), to the inlet and its rides and shops, and to the widest part of the beach. The inn has two three-story buildings, one bayfront and the other without a view. Units range from efficiencies to two-bedroom apartments. Rooms without a view are a few feet wider and can sleep up to six. Apartments have enclosed balconies. Though this is an older property, it's well maintained and has that fantastic location. **M.R. Ducks,** the bar and clothing shop, is next door.

Talbot St., on the bay (P.O. Box 548), Ocean City, MD 21842. ℂ **800/659-7703** or 410/289-9125. Fax 410/ 289-6792. www.talbotstreetpier.com. 36 units. $39–$159 double. Weekly rates available. 3- or 4-night minimum stay required on summer weekends and holidays. DISC, MC, V. Free parking. **Amenities:** Restaurant; bar; marina. *In room:* A/C, TV, kitchenette.

As you might expect, seafood is a favorite here. For the most part, a casual atmosphere prevails—although for the better restaurants, it's always wise to make reservations and check on the dress code. Casual places don't take reservations and the wait can last an hour. In summer, restaurants are rarely closed: Some open as early as 5am and continue serving until 10 or 11pm. Most places have full bar facilities. The season winds down from Columbus Day to Valentine's Day but nowadays there's always some place to go.

Expensive

Fager's Island ★ AMERICAN/PACIFIC RIM   Fager's Island plays up its bayfront location, with lots of decks, a gazebo, a pavilion, and a pier. The "1812 Overture" celebrates every sunset—it's a tradition here. The menu has a few Asian-inspired dishes, such as the Chilean sea bass with plum glaze, but you can also get a strip steak, crab cakes, a burger, quesadillas, or a sandwich. The pricey kids' menu lists beef tenderloin and crab cakes along with chicken tenders. The bar is shorts-and-T-shirt casual; you can stay late and enjoy live entertainment there. Head upstairs for more formal dining. Sunday jazz brunch is offered 11am to 3pm.

201 60th St. (on the bay). ✆ **888/371-5400** or 410/524-5500. www.fagers.com/restaurant. Reservations recommended for dinner. Main courses $3–$10 brunch, $7–$17 lunch, $22–$36 dinner. AE, DC, DISC, MC, V. Daily 11am–10pm.

Fresco's ITALIAN ★   Overlooking a serene scene of bayside grasses dancing amid the gentle waves, the dining room is designed for a romantic dinner. A pianist in the bar adds to the ambience, and though the bar dominates one side of the restaurant, it remains subdued. And the food? Fresh and beautifully prepared. You can't go wrong with their salty, sweet cream of crab soup, fresh tomatoes with mozzarella, or pasta bathed in a simple sauce and studded with lump crabmeat. The wine list features 40 choices, half by the glass. A light fare menu offers less expensive options such as a lobster club, pizza, or a burger. (You can bring the kids; there's a children's menu.)

8203 Coastal Hwy. (on the bay). ✆ **410/524-8202.** www.ocfrescos.com. Reservations recommended for dinner. Main courses $22–$36. AE, DC, DISC, MC, V. Sun–Thurs 4:30–10pm; Fri–Sat 4:30–10:30pm.

Galaxy 66 Bar & Grille INTERNATIONAL   Although it can't claim ocean or bay views, this purple-and-gold restaurant offers a sleek interior and an innovative menu that mixes familiar and exotic flavors. The menu, which changes regularly, recently included filet mignon with truffle demiglace and fish with lemonade sauce. Lunchtime features sandwiches, soups, and salads. Views are available in the Skye Bar, a rooftop deck open for night owls.

6601 Coastal Hwy. ✆ **410/723-6762.** www.galaxy66barandgrille.com. Reservations recommended for dinner. Main courses $9–$14 lunch, $18–$36 dinner. AE, DC, DISC, MC, V. Daily 11:30am–4pm and 5–10pm (light fare until midnight); Oct–Apr Tues–Sun 11:30am–4pm and 5–9pm.

The Hobbit Restaurant ★★★ SEAFOOD   The quaint Hobbit filled with Lord of the Rings decor was torn down but a new Hobbit arrived in 2008. Quaint gave way to sleek but the menu is back and we are glad. Seasonal favorites are featured alongside fish and beef dishes and the always in demand veal pistachio. The wine list is extensive, and early birds can get a good deal. The new room is noisy when there's a crowd but the big picture windows look out on tranquil waters.

81st St. (on the bay). ✆ **410/524-8100.** www.thehobbitrestaurant.com. Reservations necessary. Main courses $21–$27. AE, DISC, MC, V. Daily 5–10pm. Closed Jan–Mar.

Jules ★ AMERICAN   An unassuming dining room in a nondescript shopping center, Jules offers creative takes on local food. Even better, they have a great Early Bird deal, three courses with a glass of wine for about $30. Dishes celebrate local seafood, beef, and even tomatoes and corn with classic sauces and seasonings inspired by the world's cuisine. It's casual but feels swank enough for a low-key celebration

11805 Coastal Hwy. ℰ **410/524-3396.** www.julesoc.com. Reservations recommended on Fri–Sat. Main courses $24–$32. AE, DISC, MC, V. Daily 5–10pm (closed Mon Dec–Feb).

Liquid Assets Martini & Wine Bar ★★ TAPAS/WINE BAR   Tucked behind a wine shop, this casual dining room offers wines and martinis, and plenty of small plates to pair with them. Choose from seafood appetizers, cheese plates, salads, or wings. If you prefer heartier fare, there are burgers, sandwiches, steaks, and seafood. The restaurant also offers lunch and carryout.

9301 Coastal Hwy. ℰ **410/524-7037.** www.ocliquidassets.com. Reservations not accepted. Entrees $9–$15 lunch, $10–$24 dinner. AE, DC, DISC, MC, V. Sun–Thurs 11:30am–11pm; Fri–Sat 11:30am–midnight.

Moderate

Captain Bill Bunting's Angler AMERICAN   This spacious restaurant, at the marina of Ocean City, has been a favorite since 1938. It features an air-conditioned dining room with nautical decor, plus a deck overlooking the bay—an ideal spot to see the fishermen bringing back their bounty. The extensive menu revolves around daily fresh-fish specials, plus steaks and seafood platters. Early-bird diners are entitled to an after-dinner cruise. Lunch focuses on raw-bar selections, fish sandwiches, salads, and burgers. *Note:* For early risers, doors open at 6am for breakfast.

Talbot St. (on the bay). ℰ **410/289-7424.** Reservations recommended for dinner. Main courses $6–$13 lunch, $14–$29 dinner. AE, DISC, MC, V. May–Oct daily 6am–11pm. Bar until 2am Sat–Sun. Closed Nov–Apr.

Macky's Bayside Bar & Grill AMERICAN/REGIONAL   Watch the sun set (as Kate Smith sings "God Bless America") while you sit outside with a crab cake or steak. Designed like an old beach shack, the tables on the "beach" fill up first. The food's okay; the atmosphere is the real draw. The lunch menu includes sandwiches and salads. A kids' menu is available. Or come late and stay for the party.

54th St. (on the bay). ℰ **410/723-5565.** www.mackys.com. Reservations not accepted. Main courses $7–$13 lunch, $14–$28 dinner. AE, DC, DISC, MC, V. Daily 11am–2am (dinner served until 10pm; light fare until 1am). Closed mid-Oct to Mar.

Phillips Seafood Restaurants SEAFOOD   The Phillips family dynasty began with a small crab house at 21st Street and Philadelphia Avenue. This used to be Ocean City's finest restaurant. Four decades later, all three outlets are hugely popular, even if the food is only okay.

Phillips Crabhouse, at 21st Street, is casual, with white paper on the tables and a huge menu that emphasizes crab. A seafood buffet is also popular. It's open for lunch.

Phillips by the Sea, at the Beach Plaza Hotel, drips with Victorian ambience. It offers the same Phillips' menu. The dining room can be noisy; in good weather, the front porch is better. Breakfast is offered every morning. They take reservations here.

Phillips Seafood House, at 141st and Coastal Highway, is situated along O.C.'s condo strip. It's designed to resemble the original and offers the same dinner menu. The lines look like the original's, too.

Phillips Crabhouse: 2004 Philadelphia Ave. (at 21st St.). © **410/289-6821.** Reservations not accepted. Main courses $8–$14 lunch, $11–$35 dinner. AE, DISC, MC, V. Apr–Oct daily noon–10pm. Closed Nov–Palm Sunday. **Phillips by the Sea:** 1301 Atlantic Ave., on the boardwalk. © **800/492-5834** or 410/289-9121. Reservations recommended for dinner. Main courses $11–$35 dinner. AE, DISC, MC, V. Daily 8am–1pm and 5–10pm. Closed Jan–Feb. **Phillips Seafood House:** 14101 Coastal Hwy. © **800/799-2722** or 410/250-1200. Reservations not accepted. Main courses $11–$35 dinner. AE, DISC, MC, V. Mon–Fri 5–9:30 or 10pm; Sat–Sun 4–9:30 or 10pm (closing time depends on season). Call for off-season hours. Closed Dec–Jan.

The Shark SEAFOOD   Local seafood rules here in this restaurant that rises above the commercial fishing docks in West Ocean City. Small plates and entrees featuring seafood caught from the boat, along with local organic produce and dairy, rise above the usual, too. Steamed shellfish options are succulent, and mako shark (of course) is a specialty. Another fun option is a wine flight with a few of the small plates. Lunch features $5 specials.

12924 Sunset Ave., West Ocean City © **410/723-5565.** www.ocshark.com. Reservations recommended. Main courses $7–$14 lunch, $17–$32 dinner. AE, DISC, MC, V. Daily 11:30am–10pm.

Inexpensive

Dough Roller PIZZA   Ocean City has some good pizza joints, but this one is also pretty with each of the five locations decorated with carousel horses and gingerbread woodwork. Also on the menu are burgers, sandwiches, subs, New England grinders, and pasta. Pancakes are served all day. There are several locations around town.

2 boardwalk locations: S. Division St. (© **410/289-3501**) and Third St. (© **410/289-2599**). Reservations not accepted. Main courses $9–$24. AE, MC, V. Summer daily 7am–midnight; call for winter hours, which are much more limited (1 location is always open).

Dumser's (Kids) AMERICAN/ICE CREAM   An O.C. favorite since 1939, this eatery began as an ice-cream parlor but is now a popular restaurant. The atmosphere is homey, with comfort foods such as fried chicken, roast turkey, and crab cakes. Lunch choices include sandwiches, salads, subs, and soups. There's a kids' menu; no liquor is served. Save room for dessert: Dumser's is still an ice-cream parlor at heart, with more than 20 sundaes. A second location with a more limited menu, **Dumser's Drive-In,** 49th Street and Coastal Highway (© **410/524-1588**), is also open year-round. Both are good options for families. Three boardwalk locations serve ice cream only.

12305 Coastal Hwy. © **410/250-5543.** Reservations not accepted. Main courses $3–$11 breakfast, $4–$9 lunch, $7–$17 dinner. MC, V. Mid-June to Labor Day daily 7am–11pm; Sept to early June daily 7am–9pm.

Fractured Prune ★ (Finds) CAFE   If you like doughnuts, don't come to O.C. without stopping at one of the three Prunes. Outrageous doughnuts are made to order, dipped in one of a variety of glazes, toppings, and sugars and served hot. You can mix the cherry glaze with the chocolate chips, or top chocolate glaze with peanuts or coconut. There are also locations at 127th St., Coastal Hwy. (© **410/250-4400**), and 9636 Stephen Decatur Hwy., West Ocean City (© **410/213-9899**).

28th St. and Coastal Hwy. (© **410/289-4131**). www.fracturedprune.com. Reservations not accepted. Doughnuts $9.95 a dozen. No credit cards. Daily 6am–1pm.

WHAT TO SEE & DO

A fascinating self-guided **Walking Tour of Historic Downtown Ocean City** is available at the visitor center on 40th Street.

Wheels of Yesterday   Car enthusiasts will enjoy strolling through the rows and rows of classic cars, plus a few kiddie cars and even a replica of a 1950s service station. Curator Jack Jarvis will lead you through the exhibits, most of which are part of the private collection of Granville D. Trimper, owner of many of the rides and amusements on the boardwalk. Favorites include a 1928 seven-passenger Lincoln, Jack Benny's Overland, cars used in the movies *Hoosiers* and *Tuck Everlasting,* and a shiny gold 1960 Studebaker Hawk.

12708 Ocean Gateway (Rte. 50). ℰ 410/213-7329. Admission $5 adults, $3 children 12 and under. June–Sept Mon–Sat 9am–9pm, Sun 9am–5pm; Oct–May daily 9am–5pm. Take the Rte. 50 bridge out of Ocean City. The museum is on the left, across from the shopping outlets.

Especially for Kids

Ocean City, which claims to be the number-one family resort on the East Coast, is home to several amusement parks and child-oriented activities. Before you head for the attractions, look for coupons for everything from miniature golf to go-carts, at either the visitor center or in one of the local newspapers, such as *Sunny Day* or *Beachcomber.*

Frontier Town ★ (Kids   Frontier Town has been stuck in time for almost 50 years—it was a winner in 1959 and still is today. The cowboys and outlaws try hard to make you think you're in the Old West, with train rides, pony rides, cancan shows, bank holdups, and gunfights. In a separate park (with separate admission), there's a water park and miniature golf. Campsites on Sinepuxent Bay are also available from April to October.

Rte. 611, 4 miles south of Rte. 50. Old West ℰ 410/289-7877. Water park ℰ 410/641-0693. www.frontiertown.com. Combination admission for both parks $24 taller than 42 inches; $20 shorter than 42 inches. For Old West park, $14 ages 11 and over and $12 ages 10 and under. Water park and miniature golf $14 taller than 42 inches; $12 shorter. Golf day or night, $4 taller than 42 inches; $2 shorter. Mid-June to Labor Day daily 10am–6pm (miniature golf until 10pm). Free parking. Take Rte. 50 west and turn left on Rte. 611 toward Assateague.

Jolly Roger   Newly revamped in 2009, this park is home to Speedworld (the largest go-cart racing complex of its kind in the U.S.), two minigolf courses, a water park, and more than 30 other attractions. Go-cart tracks have minimum-height requirements.

30th St. and Coastal Hwy. ℰ 410/289-3477. www.jollyrogerpark.com. Water park $35. Passport entrance fees $25–$100. Daily Memorial Day to Labor Day: rides noon–midnight; Speedworld 2pm–midnight; golf 9am–5pm; water park 10am–8pm. Speedworld and golf also open Apr to Memorial Day, Sept, and weekends in Oct. Closed Nov–Mar. Free parking.

Ocean Bowl Skate Park   Skateboards are forbidden from most of Ocean City, so skaters head over to the 17,000-square-foot concrete bowl on Third Street and St. Louis Avenue. The park, the country's oldest municipal skate park, has areas suitable for beginner to advanced. Pads and helmets, which are required, can be rented here.

Third Street and St. Louis Ave. 410/289-BOWL (2695). www.oceanbowl.com. Mon–Fri $12, Sat–Sun days $15, weekly pass $40. Daily in summer 9:30am to dark; off-season weekends and holidays 11:30am to dark.

Pier Rides   Rides here appeal mostly to older kids and teens who like centrifugal force, but the Ferris wheel is a highlight for all ages. Rising high above everything else in old Ocean City, it offers spectacular views of the ocean, the beach, and the boardwalk. It's a wonderful place to be at sunset. The rest of the rides seem to change every season, although the Venetian double-decker carousel is always in its place.

On the inlet in downtown Ocean City. ℰ 410/289-3477. Rides about $5 or so each. Easter to late Sept Sat–Sun 11am–midnight; summer daily noon–midnight.

Trimper's Rides & Amusements   Established in 1887, this is the granddaddy of O.C. amusement areas. It has over 100 indoor and outdoor rides, including a water flume and a fanciful 1902 merry-go-round with hand-carved animals. The indoor rides are open year-round, but only on weekends in cooler months.

Boardwalk near the inlet (btw. S. Division and S. First sts.). ℂ **410/289-8617.** www.trimpersrides.com. Most rides $2–$8. A $22 wristband allows unlimited rides Sat–Sun noon–6pm and Mon–Fri 1–6pm. May–Sept daily noon or 1pm–midnight; Mar–Apr and Oct–Nov Sat–Sun noon–closing; hours vary Dec–Feb.

GOLF

Ocean City promotes itself as a major golfing destination; many courses offer vacation packages with O.C. hotels. The courses listed below welcome visitors and can be contacted directly or through the **Ocean City Golf Getaway Association,** 9935 Stephen Decatur Hwy. (ℂ **800/462-4653;** www.oceancitygolf.com).

All courses are open year-round from dawn to dusk. Most courses in the area use a multitiered system for greens fees, which means they vary from morning to afternoon to evening. However, fees generally range from $40 to $96, with cheaper rates in the off-season and on summer afternoons. Fall rates are usually the highest; if you're a January golfer, you'll find bargains then. *Tip:* Consider starting a round at about 4pm; the rates often drop in the early evenings, and the temperatures go down, too.

The Bay Club   Eight miles from the boardwalk, the Bay Club offers two 18-hole par-72 courses. Features include a driving range, practice green, club rentals, and lessons.

9122 Libertytown Rd., Berlin. ℂ **410/641-4081.** www.thebayclub.com.

The Beach Club Golf Links   A reserved tee time is recommended at this semiprivate club, which has two 18-hole par-72 courses. It has a pro shop, club rentals, driving range, and putting green.

9715 Deer Park Dr., Berlin. ℂ **800/435-9223** or 410/641-GOLF (4653). www.beachclubgolflinks.com.

Eagle's Landing Golf Course   The scenery here may distract you from your game. This public 18-hole course also offers club rentals, lessons, a pro shop, practice facilities, and a clubhouse restaurant. Reservations are recommended.

12367 Eagle's Nest Rd., Berlin. ℂ **800/283-3846.** www.eagleslandinggolf.com.

GlenRiddle Golf Club   Ocean City's newest course occupies the farmland where famous racehorses Man O'War and War Admiral were raised. The two courses are named for the horses. Man O'War resembles British links and the historic training track is a cross hazard on 3 holes. War Admiral is a private club. A Ruth's Chris Steakhouse is on the premises.

11501 Maid at Arms Lane, Berlin. ℂ **888/632-4747** or 410/213-2325. www.glenriddlegolf.com.

Ocean City Golf Club   Founded in 1959, this club has two USGA-rated 18-hole championship courses, a seaside par-72, and a bayside par-73. Facilities include a clubhouse with a restaurant, bar, and pro shop.

11401 Country Club Dr., Berlin. ℂ **800/442-3570** or 410/641-1779. www.oceancitygolfclub.com.

Pine Shore Golf   Features a 27-hole midlength course and driving range.

8219 Stephen Decatur Hwy., Berlin. ℂ **877/446-5398** or 410/641-5100. www.pineshoregolf.com.

(Kids) Minigolf Mania

Ocean City may have the highest concentration of minigolf courses of any barrier island on earth. Here's a rundown of the best on the island.

Jungle Golf, Jolly Roger Park, 30th Street and Coastal Highway (✆ **410/289-3477**): Plastic lions and a rhino look on as you negotiate 18 holes that climb the sides of a series of man-made waterfalls. Although this course has 1 lame hole early on—a flat, straight 10-foot putt—most are fun. Challenging holes on the back 9 ensure that you'll end your round with a thrill. Open Memorial Day to Labor Day.

Lost Galaxy Golf, 33rd Street and Coastal Highway (✆ **410/524-4FUN** [4386]): Here you can play golf in outer space. Sure, the special effects are cheesy and the water is the oddest blue, but you've got to love the spaceships, aliens, and fun maze of holes. This is one of the few courses open year-round.

Old Pro Golf, 68th Street and Coastal Highway (✆ **888/OLDPRO1** [653-7761]; www.oldprogolf.com): All seven Old Pro courses at four locations are good, but this is the best. Enclosed in a hangarlike barn, it's one of the most fun O.C. places to be when it's raining. Props include a submarine and a plaster killer whale. If you *really* like minigolf, get the Old Pro Pass for $15, which lets you play every Old Pro course as much as you'd like until 5pm. Takes about 7 hours. Open year-round.

Professor Hakker's Lost Treasure Golf, 139th Street and Coastal Highway (✆ **410/250-5678**): You can't miss this place—it's got an airplane in the roof. There are two courses: Gold and Diamond. The decor is reminiscent of the *Indiana Jones* movies, with water traps, caves, and even a bridge. Closed December through March.

River Run Golf Club A Gary Player 18-hole signature course, the par-71 River Run is a favorite in West O.C. Facilities include a pro shop, locker room, PGA golf pros, carts, a driving range, and putting greens. Reserving a tee time is recommended.

11605 Masters Lane, Berlin. ✆ **800/733-7786** or 410/641-7200. www.riverrungolf.com.

Rum Pointe Seaside Golf Links This 18-hole par-72 championship course, designed by the father-son team of P. B. and Pete Dye, has 17 holes overlooking Sinepuxent Bay and nearby Assateague Island. Facilities include a pro shop, driving range, and clubhouse with restaurant. Reserving a tee time is recommended.

7000 Rum Pointe Lane, Berlin. ✆ **888/809-4653** or 410/629/1414. www.rumpointe.com.

OTHER OUTDOOR ACTIVITIES

BIKING An early-morning ride down the boardwalk is traditional for lots of families. Boardwalk biking is allowed between 2 and 10am in summer, and anytime in the off-season. Cyclists on Coastal Highway share a lane with the buses. A headlight and rear reflector are required on all bikes on the road after dark. Rental rates vary, but expect to pay $6 an hour for a two-wheeler, $12 an hour for a tandem, and $8 for "funcycles" (recumbent tricycles). Two good sources are **Continental Cycle,** 73rd Street and Coastal Highway (© 410/524-1313), and **Mike's Bikes,** 10 N. Division St. (© 410/289-5404).

COAST CRUISES   For sightseeing at top speed and a splash, *Sea Rocket,* Dorchester Street at the bay (© 410/289-5887), and the *O.C. Rocket,* Talbot Street Pier (© 410/289-3500), offer a great diversion from the beach. Both are 70-foot, 150-passenger open-top speedboats that zoom along the waters of Ocean City and beside Assateague Island. The trips last about 50 minutes; they cost about $16 for adults, $8 for children 7 to 10. Departures run every hour or two from late May to September. *Tip:* People in the very back tend to get very wet (people in the front get less wet, and those in the middle get the least wet). Save this ride for a warm day, when a little sea spray is a welcome thing.

Assateague Adventure (© 410/289-3500; www.assateagueadventure.com) offers nature cruises to Assateague Island three or four times a day. These 90-minute tours, which leave from Talbot Street Pier, include 30 minutes on the island, an opportunity to dredge for clams or put your hand in the touch tank. The cost is $8 to $16; everybody pays an additional $1 landing fee. Reservations are suggested.

Duckaneer (© 410/289-3500) departs the Talbot Street Pier on a pirate adventure several times a day. Daytime cruises are geared to the kiddies; adults might find the evening cruises more fun. Cruises cost $9 for ages 1 to 4 and $19 for everybody else. Reservations are not necessary (but a good idea).

11

FISHING   Because Ocean City is surrounded by the Atlantic and four bays, fishing boats abound. Departures usually run from April to October. Rates range from $325 for makeup charters up to $2,400 for tuna, shark, or white marlin. Get a spot on the rail of a headboat for about $28. Trips leave as early as 5am. Rod rentals are available.

Most boats set sail from one of O.C.'s three main fishing marinas: the **Ocean City Fishing Center,** in West Ocean City (© 800/322-3065; www.ocfishing.com); the **Bahia Marina,** on the bay at 22nd Street (© 410/289-7438; www.bahiamarina.com); and the **Sunset Marina,** 12911 Sunset Ave. (© 877/514-3474; www.ocsunsetmarina.com). Call them for information on the kinds of boats available, as well as their rates and departure times. The *Angler* (© 410/289-7424), a reliable headboat, also takes morning trips from the Talbot Street Pier on the bay.

HORSE RACING (**Kids**   Four miles west of Ocean City, **Ocean Downs,** 10218 Racetrack Rd. (Rte. 589), just off Route 50, in Berlin (© 410/641-0600; www.oceandowns. com), features up to 10 harness races Wednesday through Sunday nights June through August. Live racing runs from 7:25 to about 11pm. Simulcast TV racing from other tracks begins daily at noon year-round. Grandstand admission and parking are free. Clubhouse admission is extra. The racetrack is very kid friendly: Winning trotters are led to the winner's circle, where children gather around for a close look. A parade of horses starts each evening's races, with the lead horse getting close enough for the kids to pet. Many horses and their drivers are local, too. There's also a restaurant and lounge, as well as the slots parlor opening in 2010 (see below).

KAYAKING   **Assateague Explorer** runs kayaking tours off Assateague between Memorial Day and Columbus Day six times a day for $40 for adults, $36 for children. Call © 757/336-5956 or www.assateagueisland.com/kayaktours.htm.

SLOTS   **Ocean Downs,** 10218 Racetrack Rd., Berlin (© 410/641-0600; www.ocean downs.com), won approval for the state's first slots parlor in September 2009. By Memorial

SURF FISHING   Surf fishing is permitted on all public beaches. However, between 9am and 6pm you cannot fish within 150 feet of swimmers or of anyone on the beach, which, in peak season, can be impossible. **Public fishing piers** are at Inlet Park (this one charges a tiny fee), as well as on the bay side at the Third Street Pier, Ninth Street Pier (which is lighted), and Northside Park (at 125th St.). For fishing supplies, visit **Bahia Marina,** on the bay at 22nd Street (© 410/289-7438).

SURFING   The beach between the fishing pier and the inlet has been set aside for surfers on all summer weekdays. On weekends, different beaches rotate as designated surf beaches. Go to www.ococean.com/ocbp for each day's location. **K-Coast Surfshop,** on 35th Street (© 410/524-8500), or on 78th Street (© 410/723-3330), keeps an up-to-date schedule and also offers lessons and rentals. The 24-hour surfing info line is © 410/524-7685.

WATERSPORTS   From April through October, O.C. is a hotbed of sailing, parasailing, windsurfing, jet-skiing, powerboating, water-skiing, and more. For information on jet skis, contact **Bay Sports,** on the bay between 21st and 22nd streets (© 410/289-2144). For skiff and pontoon-boat rentals, try **Bahia Marina,** on the bay at 22nd Street (© 410/289-7438), or **O.C. Parasail,** Talbot Street Pier, near the inlet and at 54th Street and the bay (© 410/723-1464). For pontoon-boats, jetboats, or tubing, call **Bayside Rentals** (© 410/524-1948) for a wide variety of watersport rentals. Check the visitor center for brochures with up-to-date information.

SHOPPING

The shopping in Ocean City may not be high class, but there's a lot of it. The boardwalk, the outlet center, dozens of strip malls along Coastal Highway, and small-town antiques shops in nearby Berlin are all happy to take visitors' money.

If you enter town from the Route 50 bridge, you can't miss the **Ocean City Factory Outlets** (www.ocfactoryoutlets.com), a half-mile from the bridge, on the mainland at the intersection of Golf Course Road. The 20-plus brand-name outlets include Harry and David's, Gap, and Jos. A. Bank. Parking is free and plentiful; a daily shuttle also stops at a variety of O.C. hotels from late July to mid-September (check the website for a schedule). The complex is open Sunday through Thursday from 10am to 6pm (until at least 8pm June–Aug), and Friday and Saturday from 10am to 9pm.

The **Tanger Outlets,** in Rehoboth, have a much bigger selection—and Delaware charges no sales tax. Serious shoppers may want to head north. See p. 255.

Perhaps the most popular and populated shopping destination in O.C. is the boardwalk—27 blocks of souvenirs, candy, restaurants, snack shacks, and, of course, T-shirts. You'll find much of the same merchandise in all the souvenir shops, but there are a couple places worth visiting. **Ocean Gallery World Center,** at Second Street (© 410/289-5300; www.oceangallery.com), is a trashy standout, with its mosaiclike facade of art from around the world—and that's on the outside. Its three stories are full of art posters, prints, and original sofa-size oil paintings. The **Kite Loft,** at Fifth Street (© 410/289-6852), has a large selection of kites (from simple to really cool), flags, windsocks, and toys. You may even see a pig fly. There's another location on 131st Street.

For something sweet, **Candy Kitchen** specializes in fudge and saltwater taffy and has numerous locations. If you're down near the inlet, stop in **Wockenfuss Candy,** First Street and the Boardwalk (© 410/289-7013), for fine chocolates.

Moments **The Fish That Didn't Get Away**

For 1 week in August, Ocean City is the center of the angling universe. Even if you didn't bring your 50-foot yacht and your thousand-dollar entry fee, you can join in the excitement of the **White Marlin Tournament,** where the winning fish can garner a prize worth $1.5 million or more. Head to the docks for the nightly weigh-in. The boats come in between 4 and 9pm—with most arriving around 7pm. See the fish that didn't get away: blue and white marlins, wahoo, and dolphinfish (mahimahi), all of impressive size. Entrepreneurs set up booths for food, drink, and mementos. The city provides a shuttle from the convention center, relieving visitors of the worries of where to park and where the heck this dock is.

OCEAN CITY AFTER DARK

From people-watching on the boardwalk to a game of miniature golf to cocktails at the hundreds of beach and bayside bars, high-season Ocean City has almost as much nightlife as it has sand. There's something for everybody—certainly lots of places for singles to meet, as well as a few spots just to relax with a beer. Many are open on weekends year-round—and you can count on a party for New Year's Eve and St. Patrick's Day. Below are a few fun places to try.

B.J.'s on the Water   B.J.'s has live entertainment on Wednesdays and weekends at 9pm in high season, plus a sports bar, raw bar, and full menu. 75th St., on the bay. ☏ 410/524-7575. www.bjsonthewater.com.

Fager's Island   Fager's Island's bar is a popular watering hole for the well-heeled over-30 set, with deck parties in the summer and live music most nights spring through fall. 60th St., on the bay. ☏ 410/524-5500. www.fagers.com/restaurant.

The Greene Turtle Sports Bar & Grille   DJs spin the tunes on weekends, and a game's always on TV. There's a second location on Route 611 in west Ocean City (☏ 410/213-1500). 116th St. and Coastal Hwy. ☏ 410/723-2120. www.greeneturtle.com.

Party Block   Three clubs in 1 block—the Paddock, Big Kahuna's, and Rush—make this one of *the* places for the college-age crowd to meet and dance. Paddock features live music and bikini contests; Kahuna's the place for '80s, '90s and dance music; and Rush plays techno and hip-hop. Cover usually charged after 10pm. 17th St. and Coastal Hwy. ☏ 410/289-6331. www.partyblock.com.

Seacrets, Jamaica   Seacrets is a Caribbean-themed mega beach bar and grill, decorated with palm trees, dangling lights, and sand (leave the high heels in your room). At the large, covered dance area, crowds of young and old are treated to live reggae or party music. Seacrets also serves light fare, but it's best to come very early if you want to eat. Even kids are welcome early; they'll enjoy the theme-park decor. *Tip:* Much of Seacrets is outside, so it might not be the best choice if rain is in the forecast. 49th St., on the bay. ☏ 410/524-4900. www.seacrets.com. Cover varies; usually $3 or more.

JUST DOWN THE ROAD IN SALISBURY

Just a few minutes away is the small shore town of Salisbury, which hosts a museum and baseball team and is just a short drive or bus ride from O.C.

Delmarva Shorebirds   The Class A South Atlantic League affiliate of the Baltimore Orioles were league champs in 1997 and 2000.

Arthur W. Perdue Stadium, Hobbs Rd., Salisbury. © 410/219-3112 for tickets. www.theshorebirds.com. From O.C., take Rte. 50 west to Salisbury. Turn left on Hobbs Rd. after the Rte. 13 bypass.

The Ward Museum of Wildfowl Art ★★   Named for Lem and Steve Ward, brothers from Crisfield who turned decoy carving into an art, this museum houses the world's largest collection of contemporary and classic wildfowl art, with works by the Ward brothers and galleries tracing the history of decoy making, from Native American reed figures to the most recent winners of the Ward World Championship Carving Competition, held each spring in Ocean City. The museum has programs for children, workshops on carving for adults, and an exceptional gift shop.

909 Schumaker Dr., Salisbury. © 410/742-4988. www.wardmuseum.org. Admission $7 adults, $5 seniors, $3 students; $17 per family. Mon–Sat 10am–5pm; Sun noon–5pm. Closed Jan 1, Thanksgiving, and Dec 25. From Rte. 50, turn onto Rte. 13 south; turn left onto College Ave., which will veer left and become Beaglin Park Dr.; the museum is on the right.

Restaurant 213 ★★★ (Finds) FRENCH   Those who love good food may want to venture out to this tiny restaurant along an unassuming stretch of Business Route 13 in Fruitland, south of Salisbury. The chef-owner—who has cooked at the White House—has crammed 13 tables into a low space and topped them with white cloths and stylish white dishes. Those plates are filled with silky sauces, which pair with fish and meat in a most heavenly way. The wine list runs 50 pages and includes descriptions, pictures of the labels, and a chart listing which wines pair with the regular menu items. Dinner includes an *amuse bouche* and, at the end, a package with something for breakfast—a nice touch. Sunday's prix-fixe menu offers five courses for $35.

213 N. Fruitland Blvd. (Rte. 13 Business N.), Fruitland. © 410/677-4880. www.restaurant213.com. Reservations recommended on Fri–Sat. Main dishes $29–$36. AE, MC, V. Tues–Sat 5–9pm.

6 ASSATEAGUE ISLAND NATIONAL SEASHORE ★★

161 miles S of Wilmington; 57 miles S of Ocean City; 174 miles SE of Baltimore; 177 miles SE of Washington, D.C.

Imagine yourself here on a sunny afternoon—enjoying the surf, ocean breezes, and warm sand with your family, your friends, and a fat white-and-brown pony. The famous wild horses of Assateague are not shy. The band of bachelor ponies isn't, anyway. The majority of the horses try to stay away from people, but the rest hang around the parking lot, poke their noses in open car windows, pose for pictures along the highway, or stand completely still on the beach while the wind tosses their manes.

More than 2.5 million people come to Assateague Island each year to enjoy this pristine barrier island and those ponies. On the Maryland half of this 37-mile-long island, you can see some of the 150 ponies up close. They are harder to see on the Virginia side, where they tend to stay farther from the walking trails.

Heed the warnings and don't touch or feed the ponies. They are wild and can be unpredictable. They're pretty, but they do bite and kick.

Most visitors are drawn to the guarded beaches in front of the state park's store, refreshment stands, and restrooms, or the nearby campgrounds. But you don't have to

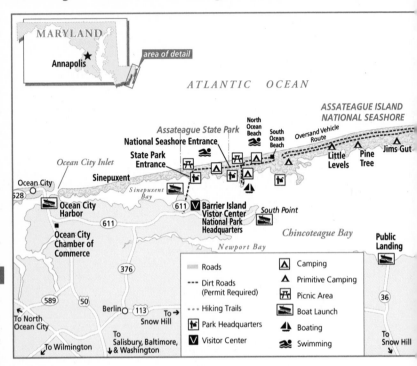

walk too far to find deserted beaches, inhabited only by the aforementioned horses and a few sika deer and shorebirds, including the endangered piping plover.

Wherever you go, be aware of Assateague's second-most-famous inhabitants—mosquitoes. They really are as bad as the brochures, guidebooks, and park rangers tell you, so come prepared with bug spray, citronella candles, and long sleeves. Compared to nearby Ocean City, Assateague is still wild and primitive—no hotels, restaurants, convenience stores, or gas stations. Just people. And ponies. And mosquitoes.

Assateague is part state park and part national seashore. The descriptions of rules, regulations, and activities that follow indicate which authority has jurisdiction over which parts. For specifics on the Virginia side of the island, see *Frommer's Virginia.*

ACCESS In Maryland, take Route 611 south from Route 50 west from Ocean City. In Virginia, take Virginia Route 175 west across Chincoteague Island. The roads do not connect in the middle.

VISITOR CENTERS The National Park Service operates the **Barrier Island Visitor Center,** on Route 611 before you cross the bridge onto Assateague (② **410/641-1441**), and the **Campground Office,** inside the park (② **410/641-3030**). It's open daily from 9am to 5pm. It's closed Easter and December 25. An expanded, waterfront visitor center is due to open in mid-2010 with expanded exhibits, aquariums, videos, as well as the usual brochures and gift shop. Maryland also operates **Assateague State Park**

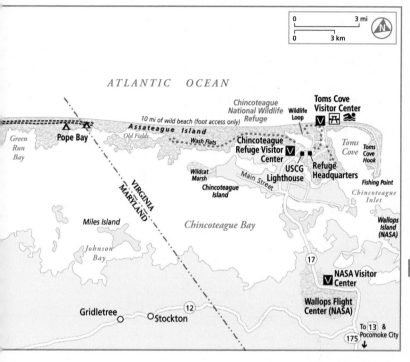

(© **410/641-2918**), at the northern end of the island. It connects to the national park but has its own amenities, regulations, and fees.

FEES & REGULATIONS **Assateague State Park** (© **410/641-2918**) charges an entry fee daily from Memorial Day to Labor Day: $3 per state resident, $4 per out-of-state resident. Admission is free in the off-season.

Entry to the **Assateague Island National Seashore** is $15 per car year-round, good for a week. Walk-in and biking visitors enter free. Most national-park regulations apply. Permits are required for backcountry camping and off-road vehicle use. Pets are allowed only in the Maryland side of the park and must be leashed. Alcohol use is prohibited in the state park. And ***don't feed the ponies.***

SEASONS Maryland's state park is open for day use from April 1 to December 1. Assateague Island National Seashore and Chincoteague National Wildlife Refuge are open year-round. There is no daily closing time on the Maryland side of the island, but only surf fishermen and campers staying in designated spots may stay overnight.

AVOIDING THE CROWDS & THE BUGS Weekends in summer are crowded. If you plan to camp, make reservations. The human population is not the biggest nuisance: Mosquitoes, biting flies, and ticks are abundant from April through September, and mosquitoes are especially a problem beginning at the end of July and following a heavy or steady rain. They're also much worse on the bay side of the island, so try to get an oceanside site if you're camping in the national park. Your best bet for avoiding the bugs is to wait until it gets cold enough to kill them all off. The good news is that sea breezes from the Atlantic keep the mosquitoes pretty much off the beach itself—so once you make it near the surf, you're safe.

RANGER PROGRAMS   The National Park Service offers a wide variety of ranger-led programs on a weekly basis throughout the summer, including nature hikes, surf-rescue demonstrations, canoe trips, campfire programs, and surf fishing and shellfishing demonstrations. For a complete rundown of these activities, pick up a copy of *Assateague Island Times,* a visitors' guide to activities and events; it's available at the visitor centers or through Assateague Island National Seashore, 7206 National Seashore Lane, Berlin (© 410/641-1441).

SEEING THE PONIES

It may come as quite a surprise to learn that finding and viewing the famed wild horses takes almost no effort, especially on the Maryland side of the island, where the ponies have free reign. In fact, you'll probably have to stop for a few begging ponies along the side of the road as you enter. (For your own safety, that of the ponies, and that of your car, roll up your windows and do not feed them.) When you're camping, you may hear a pack of horses stroll by your tent in the middle of the night or see the telltale signs in the morning. For a more picturesque setting, stop by the beach in the evening after the crowds have left when the ponies roam the beach. *Tip:* Visitors have a free chance to take a drive and pull over to watch the ponies or deer along 2 miles of Bayberry Drive between the state and national park entrances. Bikers are welcome, too.

In Virginia, the ponies are less accessible; you can generally see them—often in the distance—along the paved road called the Wildlife Tour, in the fenced marshes south of Beach Road, and from the observation platform on the Woodland Trail.

The annual **Pony Penning and Auction** ★, a unique exercise in population control, is held on Chincoteague Island, a barrier island adjoining Assateague, on the last Wednesday and Thursday of July. The Chincoteague "cowboys" round up the Virginia herd on Wednesday, and thousands of spectators watch as the horses swim from Assateague to Chincoteague, where the foals are auctioned off the next day. Campsites and hotel rooms (only available on Chincoteague and the mainland) fill up fast, so reserve well in advance. If you're staying in Ocean City, get up before dawn and drive the 60 miles to Chincoteague. You'll make it in time for the pony swim and be back in O.C. for dinner.

Although it's exciting to see the ponies swim across the channel, be aware that tens of thousands of people come to witness the annual event. You may only see the ponies as tiny dots as you wait along the shore shoulder-to-shoulder with hundreds of new friends. Traffic on the small island is almost too much to handle.

OUTDOOR ACTIVITIES

Unlike any other ocean beaches in the area, **campfires** are allowed in the national park. They must be built below the high-tide mark. It's easiest to bring your own wood—sometimes you can find places to buy it right along Route 611. Fires must be extinguished until cold with water, not sand; never leave a fire unattended.

CANOEING, KAYAKING & BOATING   The only launch facility on the island is for canoes. It's at the end of Ferry Landing Road on the Maryland side. Larger boats can be

> **Tips** **Don't Horse Around with the Ponies**
>
> When you see the horses, remember: They are wild. Do not be fooled by their gentle appearance and willingness to approach you and your car looking for handouts. The ponies are prone to unpredictable behavior—and they will bite and kick—so do not attempt to feed or pet them. Also, please drive carefully; at least one pony a year is hit and killed by a car.

launched for the day from the state park's marina just west of the bridge (across from the Barrier Island Visitor Center). The fee is $10.

Waters at the Maryland end of Chincoteague Bay are usually ideal for canoeing, though the tidal currents around Chincoteague Island are strong. The bay is generally shallow, so operators of larger boats should watch for sandbars. In summer, you can rent canoes from the concession at the end of Bayside Drive. Four backcountry canoe-in campsites are located in the national park. Permits are required and can be obtained at the ranger station in Maryland or at the Toms Cove Visitor Center in Virginia.

Coastal Kayak (© 877/445-2925 or 302/539-7999; www.coastalkayak.com) offers eco-tours of the Assateague back bay. Tours cost about $40 for adults and $30 for children. (Get a coupon from their website.) **Assateague Explorer** (© 757/336-5956; www.assateagueisland.com/kayaktours.htm) runs kayaking tours off Assateague between Memorial Day and Columbus Day six times a day for $40 for adults, $36 for children.

The park's own **Coastal Bays Program** (© 410/726-3217) offers canoe rentals for $40 a day, kayak rentals for $45, bicycles for $20, and clam rakes for $10. Hourly rentals as well as overnight and weekend are also available.

CRABBING, CLAMMING & FISHING   Pick up the *Shellfishing in Maryland* brochure at the visitor center for a map showing the best places to catch crabs, clams, and mussels. The best time to crab is late summer to early fall, in the morning or early evening. The most common approach is the string, bait, and net method: Attach a piece of bony chicken or a fish head to a string (chicken necks are the preferred bait) and cast out in shallow water. When you feel a tug, gently tow the line in. If there's a crab on the end, net it before you take it out of the water, then transfer it to a basket or other container and continue crabbing.

A single collapsible crab pot or trap may also be used, if it is attended at all times. You can purchase a crab pot at bait-and-tackle shops; they look like large chicken-wire boxes. Place bait in the center of the trap; drop it in clear, shallow water; and pull it up as soon as a crab walks in. All crabs must measure 5 inches point to point, and all egg-bearing females must be released. Limits are 1 bushel per person per day, or 2 bushels per boat per day. Crabbing is prohibited January through March.

Signing and raking are accepted methods for clamming. The mudflats at Virginia's Toms Cove are more suitable for signing. To sign for clams, walk along the mudflats at low tide and look for small keyhole openings, or "signs," indicating the presence of a clam. Then dig it out with a hand trowel or small digging tool. Raking can be done at any tide level, but you need a clamming rake, which has a basket to catch the clams. Drag the rake through the mud until the tines scrape a shell; then dig up the mud, shake it loose, and catch the clam in the basket. Clams must be 1 inch wide; the limit is 1 bushel per person per day.

Mussels and oysters are rare in the waters surrounding the island. Oysters are rarely found off the private leased beds (and trespassing is prohibited). The park service asks that you take only what you will consume in mussels and oysters.

No saltwater license is required for surf fishing on the coast, though an after-hours permit is required on the Virginia end of the island. Fishing is prohibited on the guarded beaches and in the designated surf zones.

HIKING & BIKING   Conditions and trails for hiking and biking are better at the Virginia end of the island, but there are three .5-mile self-guided hiking trails on the Maryland end of the national park: Life of the Marsh, Life of the Forest, and Life of the Dunes. All are short, and all require bug repellent. Cyclists can use the 3-mile paved bike path along Bayberry Drive and the Oceanside campground.

In Virginia, about 5 of the 15 miles of trails are paved for cycling. The Wildlife Tour is closed to car traffic until 3pm each day, so hikers and bikers can have it all to themselves. The Woodland Trail, which leads to a pony observation platform, is also paved. These wooded paths are serene but exciting if you find the sought-after ponies.

OFF-ROAD VEHICLES   The vast majority of Assateague is not accessible by car; however, off-road (or over-sand) vehicle routes stretch for 12 miles. Permits are required and are issued for a $70 to $150 annual fee. Call ✆ **410/641-3030** or see **www.nps.gov/asis** for information and ORV regulations.

SWIMMING   The state park has guarded beaches Memorial Day weekend through Labor Day weekend daily 10am to 5pm.

CAMPING

Accommodations on the island are limited to a state-run campground and two campgrounds and several backcountry campsites run by the National Park Service.

The campground run by **Assateague State Park** (✆ **410/641-2120,** ext. 22; 888/432-2267 for state camping reservations) is open April 1 through October 31. It has 311 sites on the ocean side of the island, with bathhouses (with flush toilets and hot showers), a camp store, and a snack bar. Reservations are accepted up to a year in advance. Sites are on the ocean side of the island and cost $30 to $40 per night.

The **National Park Service** (✆ **410/641-3030** for information, or 877/444-6777 for reservations) operates oceanside and bayside campgrounds that are slightly more primitive than the state-park facility. Both NPS campgrounds have chemical toilets, drinking water, and cold showers. There are also flush toilets and cold showers at the beach bathhouse. Reservations are recommended from April 15 to October 15—and are essential in warm weather. The rest of the year, campsites are available on a first-come, first-served basis. If possible, reserve a site at the oceanside campground for fewer pesky bugs. The cost is $20 per night from April 15 to October 15, $16 per night the rest of the year. There is no camping on the Virginia side.

In addition, the park has several backcountry or hike-in/paddle-in campsites along the Maryland end of the island. Each site has a chemical toilet and picnic table, but no drinking water. To use these sites, you must pick up a $5 backcountry permit from the ranger station during regular business hours.

Another camping and kayaking alternative is the picturesque **Pocomoke River State Park** (✆ **410/632-2566**), which is about a 45-minute drive from the Virginia or Maryland end of Assateague and is less crowded and more comfortable. It offers 230 improved campsites and 12 mini one-room cabins (some air-conditioned) in two wooded sites along both sides of the unspoiled Pocomoke River. **Shad Landing** offers a few extras:

marina, canoe, kayak, and boat rentals; a nature center; a swimming pool; and hiking and ORV trails. Its 201 campsites are available year-round: $30 for electric, $25 for nonelectric, and $50 for the eight cabins. Across the river, **Milburn Landing** is smaller, quieter, and open only from April to mid-December. Its 38 campsites cost $25 for electric, $20 for nonelectric; four cabins are $50. To make reservations for May through September, call © **888/432-2267**, ext. 762, or visit **www.dnr.maryland.gov**. To get here, take Route 113 south. The park is 20 miles south of Berlin.

Paddling fans, once you see the shady Pocomoke, you're going to want to get out on it. Bring your own boat, rent one for a couple of hours at the park, or sign up for a tour with the **Pocomoke River Canoe Company** (© **410/632-3971**; www.atbeach.com/amuse/md/canoe). They're located on the river in nearby Snow Hill.

WHERE TO STAY NEARBY

Prefer a real bed? **Ocean City** is close, or you can try accommodations in nearby **Berlin,** about a 15-minute drive from Assateague (see below).

A SIDE TRIP TO BERLIN, MARYLAND

Barely 20 minutes away from the Ocean City boardwalk is the historic town of Berlin. Its quaint stores and antiques shops have long been a favorite side trip for vacationers in Ocean City. It also has two charming places to stay, a good restaurant, and a little theater featuring live entertainment. These amenities and a location roughly equidistant from Assateague and Ocean City make Berlin a good diversion.

To get to Berlin from Ocean City, take the Route 50 bridge out of O.C. and follow Route 50; take a left on Route 113; from there, you'll hit Berlin in less than a mile.

Where to Stay

Atlantic Hotel ★   Richard Gere and Julia Roberts came here to film *Runaway Bride*. This three-story 1895 Victorian beauty was refurnished with "new" antiques in 2009 along with fresh new feather beds and comforters and flatscreen TV/DVD units. The Anna Suite includes sitting room and kitchen. Larger units are quite comfy while the smaller units can be a bit tight but are comfortable enough for the price. No. 20 is the Richard Gere Room (his room in the movie) but the corner No. 10 is larger and airier. For a bit of extra privacy, opt for the Gardner's Cottage behind the hotel with its sitting room and tiny front porch.

2 N. Main St., Berlin, MD 21811. © **800/814-7672** or 410/641-3589. Fax 410/641-4928. www.atlantic hotel.com. 17 units. July–Aug $115–$315 double; Apr–May and Sept–Oct $125–$240 double; Nov–Mar $125–$240 double. AE, DC, DISC, MC, V. Free parking. No children. **Amenities:** Restaurant; bar. *In room:* A/C, TV/DVD, hair dryer.

Merry Sherwood Plantation ★   Drive through the gates and enter a hideaway filled with fragrant flowers, butterflies, and, at the end of the drive, an 1859 plantation house. Inside, the rooms are filled with antiques, sunshine streams through the porch windows, and breezes cool the high-ceilinged rooms. Front bedrooms are sunnier, but those in back are quieter. All but two units have private bathrooms; the two that share a bathroom are spacious and well-appointed, and the claw-foot tub is equally charming. The honeymoon suite has a whirlpool tub, while the Stokes has a fireplace. And don't miss the cupola; it's a good place to catch a breeze—or ponder the universe.

8909 Worcester Hwy. (2½ miles south of Berlin on Rte. 113), Berlin, MD 21811. © **800/660-0358** or 410/641-2112. www.merrysherwood.com. 8 units, 2 with shared bathroom. $100–$175 double off-season, $125–$200 double in season. Rates include full breakfast. MC, V. Free parking. *In room:* A/C, free Wi-Fi.

Drummer's Café ★★ TRADITIONAL New owners closed the bigger Solstice Restaurant to make room for banquets and reopened the Victorian-style Drummer's Cafe—and it's welcome news. A traditional lunch menu of soups, salads, sandwiches, and quiche of the day stay on the menu for dinner, too. Heartier entrees, crab cakes, fish, and beef are available after 5pm. Diners prefer the screened porch in the summer but the paneled dining room is cozy. The bar fills with music Monday, Thursday, and Sunday.

At the Atlantic Hotel, 2 N. Main St. ✆ **410/641-3589.** www.atlantichotel.com/drummers-cafe. Reservations required for dinner. Main courses dinner $24–$35, lunch $9–$14. AE, DC, DISC, MC, V. Daily 11am–10pm; Sun brunch 11am–3pm. From Ocean City, take Rte. 50 west 7 miles to Rte. 818 (Main St.).

The Globe AMERICAN/REGIONAL A former movie theater, the Globe still uses its little stage for weekend jazz performances. Sit by the stage to listen to the music with a drink and appetizer or take a table farther back to focus on the Asia-inspired dishes. There are all kinds of choices of soup, sandwiches, salads, noodle dishes, and, after 5pm, entrees such as pasta, tuna, crab cakes, and steak. The **Balcony Art Gallery** upstairs features local artwork.

12 Broad St. ✆ **410/641-0784.** www.globetheater.com. Reservations recommended for dinner. Main courses $16–$28 dinner, $8–$16 lunch. AE, DISC, MC, V. Sun 10am–11pm; Mon–Thurs 11am–11pm; Fri–Sat 11am–midnight.

What to See & Do

Many shop owners have a story to tell about the time Julia Roberts stopped by or the day the cameras moved in for a close-up of their store window. Those stories and the shopping make a visit here amusing. For more lore, stop by the town's own museum.

Calvin B. Taylor House Museum Lovingly preserved by local residents, this Federal-style home features some fine antiques and dazzling faux-finish woodwork, as well as exhibits recalling the life of the banker-owner and the town itself. Seabiscuit fans will want to see the portrait of War Admiral—he was raised on a farm nearby.

208 N. Main St. ✆ **410/641-1019.** www.taylorhousemuseum.org. Free admission, but donations appreciated. June–Oct Mon, Wed, and Fri–Sat 1–4pm. Closed Nov–May.

Shopping

Most shops are open daily from 10am to 5pm, though on Sundays hours are limited mostly to 11am to 3pm with a few open until 4 or 5pm.

Local artists show their work at the **Worcester County Arts Council Gallery and Shop,** 6 Jefferson St. (✆ **410/641-0809**), and at **Water's Edge Gallery,** 2 S. Main St. (✆ **410/629-1784**). **Jeffrey Auxer Designs** displays traditional Venetian glass in Auxer's studio, 19 Jefferson St. (✆ **443/513-4210;** www.jeffreyauxer.com). You'll find fun clothes and accessories at **Bruder Hill,** 25 Commerce St. (✆ **410/629-1260**). For locally-made jewelry and an eclectic collection of gifts go to **Beach House Boutique,** 14 Broad St. (✆ **410/629-1010**). **TaDa,** 18 William St. (✆ **410/641-4430**), features striking home furnishings painted by the owner. **Town Center Antiques** (✆ **410/629-1895**) has its wares at 1 N. Main St. and also at 113 N. Main St.

Wilmington

At first glance, Wilmington is all business, as it has been since the first Swedish settlers arrived in 1638. An important industrial center since the American Revolution, it is now home to a number of large corporations, including banking, insurance, and pharmaceutical companies, as well as DuPont.

On weekends, the city puts away the briefcase and puts on its running shoes.

The parks and Riverfront trail are filled with joggers and picnickers. It seems everyone gathers around a restaurant table with friends. The museums, theaters, and nearby Brandywine Valley beckon, too. And visitors are most welcome: Hotels deals are plentiful and there's more than enough room in the restaurants, along the trails, and at any of the city's attractions.

1 ORIENTATION

ARRIVING

BY PLANE **Philadelphia International Airport** (② 800/745-4283; www.phl.org) is about a half-hour from downtown Wilmington. Car-rental agencies at the airport include **Avis** (② 800/331-1212) and **Hertz** (② 800/654-3131).

Delaware Express (② 800/648-5466 or 302/454-7800; www.delexpress.com) offers van service from the Philadelphia airport to Wilmington for about $34. For the most prompt service reserve by phone or online at least 24 hours in advance. Otherwise, look for the phone near the customer service center at baggage claim.

BY TRAIN **Amtrak** (② 800/USA-RAIL [872-7245]; www.amtrak.com) serves Wilmington on its Northeast Corridor line, with Acela, Metroliner, and regional trains stopping here several times daily. The Wilmington Amtrak station is at 100 S. French St. (at Martin Luther King, Jr. Blvd.), on the Riverfront. There's a taxi stand outside.

BY CAR I-95 cuts across the city's center. The Delaware Memorial Bridge (part of I-295) connects Wilmington to the New Jersey Turnpike and points north. From southern Delaware and the Eastern Shore, Route 13 will bring you into the city.

BY BUS **Greyhound** (② 800/231-2222; www.greyhound.com) and **Peter Pan** (② 800/343-9999; www.peterpanbus.com) provide daily bus service into the **Wilmington Transportation Center,** 101 N. French St. (② 302/655-6111).

VISITOR INFORMATION

Information on Wilmington, the Brandywine Valley, and New Castle is available from the **Greater Wilmington Convention and Visitors Bureau,** 100 W. 10th St., Ste. 20 (② 800/652-4088 or 302/295-2210; www.visitwilmingtonde.com). It's open Monday through Friday from 9am to 5pm. For motorists, the visitor center at the **I-95 Delaware Travel Plaza,** south of town between exits 1 and 3 (② 302/737-4059) was torn down in late 2009 with a new center due to be open by summer 2010; it's open daily, except December 25, from 8am to 8pm.

For 10 days in June, music lovers turn out for free jazz at the **DuPont Clifford Brown Jazz Festival.** Visit **www.cliffordbrownjazzfest.com** for a schedule. The **Delaware Antiques Show** is held the first weekend in November. It is sponsored by Winterthur; go to www.winterthur.org for details.

CITY LAYOUT

Three rivers surround Wilmington: the Brandywine, the Christina, and the Delaware. The **downtown** business area, wedged between the Brandywine and Christina, is laid out in a grid system, less than 20 blocks wide and long. *Note:* Though the downtown area is relatively small, the attractions, restaurants, and hotels are spread out, with most either south of downtown or in the northern suburbs. Aside from a few museums and shops along Market Street, you can't or wouldn't want to walk between major attractions.

Two areas of Wilmington also worth a visit are the **Riverfront** and the suburban north side. The Riverfront is about a 5-minute drive south of downtown between I-95 and the Christina River. To reach this home of arts venues, restaurants, offices, and condos, take Martin Luther King, Jr., Blvd. to Madison St. and follow the signs. Or head back to I-95 and take exit 6. Riverfront has lots of free parking.

The **north side** of Wilmington (north of Rte. 52 and northwest of I-95) features modest-to-lavish brick houses, parks, the trendy **Trolley Square** neighborhood, and nearby **Little Italy,** with plenty of restaurants. The main thoroughfares are Delaware Avenue to Route 52 (also known as Pennsylvania Ave. and Kennett Pike); as you drive out Route 52, the city soon gives way to rolling hills of the Brandywine Valley.

MAIN ARTERIES & STREETS   Market Street runs north-south in downtown Wilmington. The east-west cross streets are numbered from First to 16th, with the lowest number on the southern end. The north-south streets bear the names of presidents and local heroes west of Market, and trees east of Market. Most streets are one-way, except for Fourth Street. I-95 enters Wilmington via two main avenues: Delaware (Rte. 52) at the north, and Martin Luther King, Jr., Boulevard at the south.

From I-95 and downtown, approach Wilmington's north side by using Route 52, which splits into Pennsylvania Avenue (Rte. 52) and Delaware Avenue about 2 blocks north of I-95. Both routes 52 and 202 take you out to Brandywine Valley sites.

MAPS   *Greater Wilmington and Brandywine Valley: America's Cultural Gem,* a booklet produced by the Greater Wilmington Convention and Visitors Bureau, has detailed maps of downtown and the Wilmington region with major attractions marked.

2 GETTING AROUND

BY BUS   Wilmington is served by the **DART First State** (© **800/355-6066;** www. dartfirststate.com) bus system. Blue-and-white signs indicating stops are located throughout the city, and regular routes can take you to some hotels, museums, theaters, and parks, as well as to the malls and historic New Castle. Fares are based on a zone system; the minimum fare for one zone is $1.15. Exact change is required. For information on schedules and fares, call or visit the website.

BY SHUTTLE   DART also operates the **Trolley,** a 25¢ bus (exact change required) that takes visitors from Rodney Square to the Amtrak station to the Riverfront. The route

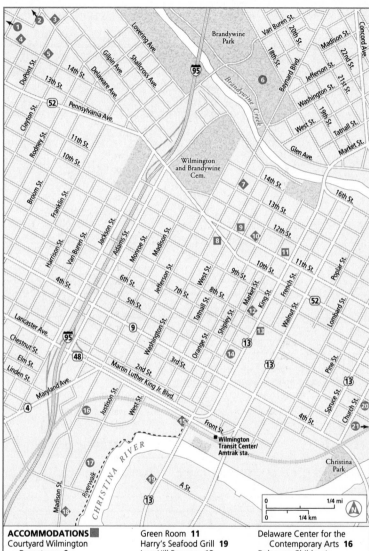

WILMINGTON

12

GETTING AROUND

ACCOMMODATIONS ■
Courtyard Wilmington
    Downtown **9**
Doubletree Downtown **13**
Hotel du Pont **11**
Sheraton Suites Wilmington **8**

DINING ◆
Deep Blue Bar & Grill **10**
Domaine Hudson **7**
Govatos **12**

Green Room **11**
Harry's Seafood Grill **19**
Iron Hill Brewery **18**
Kelly's Logan House **3**
Kid Shelleen's **4**
Riverfront Market **15**
Toscana Kitchen + Bar **5**

ATTRACTIONS ●
Brandywine Zoo **6**
Delaware Art Museum **2**

Delaware Center for the
    Contemporary Arts **16**
Delaware Children's
    Museum **17**
Delaware History Museum **14**
Kalmar Nyckel Foundation **21**
Marian Coffin Gardens
    at Gibralter **1**
Old Swedes Church **20**

goes up Walnut Street north via Rodney Square and West Street to 13th Street and down Market Street and King Street. Service is provided every 30 minutes. The whole ride takes about 15 minutes. Shuttles run Monday through Saturday from 7:30am to 7:30pm. Get a schedule from the visitor center or DART.

BY CAR Because Wilmington's attractions are scattered around town—and because so many pair a visit to the city with Brandywine Valley attractions—a car is necessary. If you aren't driving, rent a car from either **Enterprise,** 422 Delaware Ave. (© **302/425-4404**), or **Budget,** 100 N. Walnut St. (© **302/652-0629**).

BY TAXI There's a taxi stand at the Amtrak station, across the street from the bus station. To order a taxi, call **Yellow Cab** (© **302/658-4340**).

(*Fast Facts* **Wilmington**

Area Code Wilmington's area code is **302.**

Camera Repair For camera repair, supplies, or processing, try **Cameras Etc.,** 4101 N. Market St. (© **302/764-9400**).

Emergencies Dial **Wilmington Optical,** 616 Market St. (© **302/654-0530**).

Hospitals Downtown options include **St. Francis Hospital,** Seventh and Clayton streets (© **302/421-4100**), and **Wilmington Hospital,** 14th and Washington streets (© **302/428-4280**).

Libraries The library is at 10th and Market streets (© **302/571-7400**).

Newspapers & Magazines The city's daily newspaper is the *News Journal.* The best monthly magazine is *Delaware Today.*

Pharmacies A local chain, **Happy Harry's Discount Drugs,** has locations at 839 N. Market St., at Ninth Street (© **302/654-1834**), and at Trolley Square, Delaware Avenue and DuPont Street (© **302/655-6397**).

Police For nonemergencies, call © **302/343-3600.** For emergencies, dial © **911.**

Post Office The main downtown post office is at 500 Delaware Ave., Ste. 1 (© **302/656-0228**).

Taxes There is no sales tax in Delaware, but an 8% to 10% lodging tax applies to stays at city hotels.

Transit Information Call **DART First State** (© **302/652-3278**).

3 WHERE TO STAY

Because Wilmington is a major destination for business travelers, numerous hotels cater to them downtown. That said, no matter where you go in Delaware, when you hear people refer to "The Hotel," they mean the Hotel du Pont in Wilmington. For more than 80 years, this hotel has dominated the Delaware lodging scene.

Most local hotels charge top prices Sunday through Thursday—spiking in late spring and early fall—but on weekends, rates drop. Summer, by the way, is low season around here and prices plummet, even at the Hotel du Pont. Look also for packages combining accommodations with tickets to area attractions.

DOWNTOWN
Expensive

Hotel du Pont ★★★   Opened in 1913 and owned by E. I. du Pont de Nemours and Company, this has the grandest accommodations in town. The 12-story Italian Renaissance structure in the heart of the city is a showcase of marble, coffered ceilings, carved walnut, and genteel service. Each unit was updated in 2007 with new fabrics (DuPont's latest fibers, of course) and fixtures. They're spacious and luxurious, with comfortable sitting areas. Corner suites are even grander, with living and dining rooms. Two floors are decorated in a more contemporary style to appeal to a hipper crowd. Weekend guests are offered a variety of packages, and some really good deals.

11th and Market sts., Wilmington, DE 19801. 🕻 **800/441-9019** or 302/594-3100. Fax 302/549/3108. www.hoteldupont.com. 217 units. $159–$429 double; $699–$899 suite. Weekend packages available. AE, DC, DISC, MC, V. Valet parking $22; self-parking $16. Pets under 20 lb. accepted with deposit. **Amenities:** 2 restaurants; lobby lounge for cocktails and afternoon tea; coffee shop; airport limousine service; concierge; fitness center; golf course nearby; room service; tennis nearby. *In room:* A/C, flatscreen TV w/pay movies, hair dryer, minibar, MP3 alarm clock, Wi-Fi (fee).

Sheraton Suites Wilmington ★★   In Wilmington's financial section but convenient to Route 52, this contemporary 16-story hotel offers comfortable, spacious suites with two queens or one king-size bed. Each has a full bedroom with dressing area and a separate living room with large-screen TV, wet bar, and desk (furniture and white bedding was new as of 2007). **Basil's** serves breakfast, lunch, and dinner.

422 Delaware Ave., Wilmington, DE 19801. 🕻 **800/325-3535** or 302/654-8300. Fax 302/654-6036. www. starwoodhotels.com/sheraton/suiteswilmington. 223 units. $125–$300 double. Weekend rates available. AE, DC, DISC, MC, V. Parking Sun–Thurs $16, Fri–Sat $12. **Amenities:** Restaurant; lounge; concierge-level rooms; fitness room; indoor pool; room service; sauna. *In room:* A/C, 2 TVs, hair dryer, kitchenette, Wi-Fi (fee).

Moderate

Courtyard Wilmington Downtown   Converted from a 10-story office building, this hotel does not fit the mold of the Marriott chain—but it does offer good value for downtown. Three room styles are available, with 80 king-bed rooms, 25 two-queen, and 18 spa rooms with a king-size bed and whirlpool tubs. Room size and configuration sizes vary but all have contemporary furniture and most have sleeper sofas. The equipment in the fitness center was upgraded in 2009.

1102 West St., Wilmington, DE 19801. 🕻 800/321-2211 or 302/429-7600. Fax 302/429-9167. www. marriott.com. 123 units. $99–$199 double. Children stay free in room. AE, DC, DISC, MC, V. Self-parking $9.50, free parking Fri–Sat nights. **Amenities:** Restaurant; lounge; fitness center; room service. *In room:* A/C, TV, fridge, hair dryer, microwave, free Wi-Fi.

SUBURBS
Expensive

Hilton Wilmington/Christiana ★   This hotel, nestled amid grassy grounds off exit 4B of I-95, is a good choice in the 'burbs—it's located near the University of Delaware and surrounded by shopping malls. The modern four-story brick building surrounds a courtyard with gazebo and pool. In front is a pond that's home to a family of swans (public feedings scheduled daily). The hotel was completely redecorated in 2008. Rooms are typical size and style for Hilton with contemporary furnishings and Brandywine artwork. An executive level includes continental breakfast, evening reception, and rooms a smidge bigger (for $25 extra.)

100 Continental Dr., Newark, DE 19713. ℂ **800/348-3133** or 302/454-1500. Fax 302/454-0233. www. hiltonchristiana.com. 266 units. $139–$284 double. Lower weekend rates available. AE, DC, DISC, MC, V. Free parking. Pets welcome for a fee. **Amenities:** Restaurant; lounge; concierge; fitness center; outdoor pool; room service; free shuttle to downtown and UDel. *In room:* A/C, TV w/movies, fridge, hair dryer, Wi-Fi (fee).

The Inn at Montchanin Village ★★★   Why sleep in a hotel room when you can wake up in a historic village surrounded by autumn's glory or fragrant gardens? Just a few miles from downtown Wilmington and set among the Brandywine treasures, Montchanin Village is part of du Pont family history: It was once home to workers in the black powder mills and factories along the Brandywine. The whole village is listed on the National Register of Historic Places.

Eleven buildings, completed between 1870 and 1910, became the Inn at Montchanin Village in 1996. Nine of these buildings, once the workers' residences, have been converted into 28 guest rooms, including one- and two-level suites. Six superior suites have king-size beds, marble bathrooms with oversize tubs, and gas fireplaces. All rooms open onto an outdoor sitting area, and first-level rooms and suites have private gardens. The blacksmith shop houses the inn's restaurant, **Krazy Kat's** (see "Where to Dine," below), while the health club and spa can be found in the Dilwyn Barn.

Rte. 100 and Kirk Rd. (P.O. Box 130), Montchanin, DE 19710. ℂ **800/269-2473** or 302/888-2133. Fax 302/888-0389. www.montchanin.com. 28 units (11 with shower only). $192–$244 double; $290–$399 suite. AE, DC, DISC, MC, V. Free parking. **Amenities:** Restaurant; lounge; health club; room service; spa. *In room:* A/C, TV/VCR or DVD, hair dryer, high-speed Internet, kitchenette.

Moderate

Best Western Brandywine Valley Inn ★ (Finds)   Though very much a motor lodge, its innkeepers have gone to great lengths to make guests forget that once they step inside. Court units serve business travelers with queen-size or two double beds, high-speed Internet, mostly Wi-Fi, desks with printers and cordless phones, and limousine service. The charming Country French Boudoirs, in contrast, are cozy, smaller rooms with romantic wallcoverings and linens for a real bed-and-breakfast feel. (Blue rooms are a bit roomier than the red rooms.) For pure luxury, ask for one of the three Winterthur rooms, outfitted with rich fabrics and fabulous Winterthur reproduction furniture—over-the-top in both decor and comfort. The location is perfect for Brandywine tourists and business travelers alike, right on Route 202 near Nemours.

1807 Concord Pike (Rte. 202), Wilmington, DE 19803. ℂ **800/537-7772** or 302/656-9436. Fax 302/656-8564. www.brandywineinn.com. 96 units. $97–$130 double; $325–$425 Winterthur chambers and suite. Packages available. Rates include bagel breakfast in lobby. Children 18 and under stay free in parent's room. AE, DC, DISC, MC, V. Free parking. **Amenities:** Fitness center; hot tub; outdoor pool. *In room:* A/C, TV/DVD, fridge, hair dryer, free Wi-Fi.

Doubletree Hotel Wilmington   Popular with business travelers and weekend tourists, this modern seven-story hotel on the busy Route 202 corridor, is about halfway between downtown Wilmington and the major Brandywine museums and gardens. The guest rooms were redecorated in late 2008 with white duvets, marble-top chests, and flatscreen TVs. Corner rooms have bigger bathrooms and a bit more space. "Green" features are designed to save energy, too. Fitness fans may use the jogging tracks at Widener University next door. For shoppers, Concord Mall is on the other side of the hotel. Fans of Doubletree visiting Wilmington on business may prefer the **Doubletree Downtown,**

700 N. King St. (© **302/655-0400**). It has 218 rooms on nine floors, an indoor pool, restaurant, lounge, and free Wi-Fi. It's 9 blocks to the train station.

4727 Concord Pike (U.S. Rte. 202), Wilmington, DE 19803. © **800/222-TREE** (8733) or 302/478-6000. Fax 302/477-1492. www.doubletreehotels.com. 244 units (45 with shower only). $109–$259 double. Weekend packages available. AE, DC, DISC, MC, V. Free parking. **Amenities:** Restaurant; lounge; fitness center; hot tub; indoor pool; courtesy shuttle service within 5-mile radius, including downtown Wilmington. *In room:* A/C, TV or TV/VCR, hair dryer, MP3 dock, Wi-Fi (fee).

Inexpensive

Fairfield Inn Wilmington Newark/Christiana Mall (Value) This three-story property off of I-95 is an inexpensive option for both business travelers and guests. Most rooms are furnished in simple modern style with two doubles or a king-size bed, desk, and dresser. Despite the hotel's proximity to the highway, rooms are well-insulated against noise. To ensure a quieter night, ask for accommodations with a lower room number. Rooms ending in 47 to 50 face the highway.

65 Geoffrey Dr., Newark, DE 19713. © **800/228-2800** or 302/292-1500. Fax 302/292-8655. www.marriott. com. 133 units. $97–$130 double. Rates include continental breakfast. AE, DISC, MC, V. Free parking. **Amenities:** Fitness center; outdoor pool. *In room:* A/C, TV w/pay movies, fridge, hair dryer, free Wi-Fi.

---

4 WHERE TO DINE

DOWNTOWN

Expensive

Deep Blue Bar and Grill ★ SEAFOOD How do you like your seafood: sashimi, raw bar, traditional, or Pacific Rim style? Deep Blue's got it all. Set in a parking garage, of all things, this restaurant draws a crowd of 30-somethings to its popular bar. (In this sleek modern setting, nothing can muffle the noise—so ask for a table away from the bar.) The menu is filled with interesting options, from the five-spice ahi tuna to crab-and-spinach-mousse-stuffed perch. The wine list offers more than 170 choices. A $35 pre-theater dinner menu is available before 6pm, and servers will make sure you arrive before curtain time.

111 W. 11th St. © **302/777-2040.** www.deepbluebarandgrill.com. Reservations recommended for dinner. Main courses $11–$17 lunch, $24–$33 dinner. AE, DC, DISC, MC, V. Mon–Fri 11:30am–2pm; Mon–Sat 5:30–10pm.

Green Room ★★ CONTINENTAL/FRENCH When you want to treat yourself to a night on the town, make reservations at the Green Room. From the moment you enter the sumptuous surroundings of carved ceilings, paneled walls, soaring windows, and grand chandeliers, you'll know you've stepped into luxury. You'll be reminded when you see the menu, too—prices soar as high as the ceilings, but the food is exquisite. Some may find the atmosphere a little stiff; others may call it refined. The tuxedoed waiters try hard to please, though service can be uneven. The meals are perfect though, with rich sauces and artful desserts. Brunch is served on Sunday. A new tasting menu at lunch is a great way to enjoy the Green Room's best.

At the Hotel du Pont, 11th and Market sts. © **302/594-3154.** www.hoteldupont.com. Reservations required. Jackets required for men Fri–Sat. Main courses $11–$22 lunch, $27–$37 dinner. AE, DC, MC, V. Mon–Sat 7–11am; 11:30am–2pm, and 6–10pm; Sun 10am–2pm and 5–9pm.

Harry's Seafood Grill SEAFOOD   The soaring dark-blue dining room of this Riverfront restaurant is dominated by a glittery sea star on the ceiling; the windows overlook the Christina River. The menu changes daily to reflect the fresh seafood available—there's everything from lobster in the rough to fish and chips, sushi to raw oysters. Rather than focus on Chesapeake-style seafood, the chef here has gone global, with recipes representing the Far East, Portugal, and regional American cuisine. The impressive wine list is designed for those who want to try something new—tasting flights are available.

101 S. Market St. 🕐 **302/777-1500.** www.harrysseafoodgrill.com. Reservations recommended, even for lunch. Main courses $8.95–$20 lunch, $16–$53 dinner. AE, DC, DISC, MC, V. Mon–Thurs 11am–10pm; Fri–Sat 11am–11pm; Sun 4–9pm.

Moderate

Domaine Wilmington ★★ WINE BAR   Come here for the wine: The list, though not as extensive as at bigger restaurants, is filled with selections you won't find anywhere else in Delaware. But stay for the food, too: The chef has created dishes to pair with your wines, which come in tastes (1½ oz.) and 3- or 5-ounce servings. Cheese plates feature artisanal choices from around the world. Then there's a choice of soups, salads, and entrees, with the menu and wine list changing seasonally. Half portions give you the opportunity to pair a few outstanding dishes with different wines. The servers can be helpful without being overbearing. Don't miss the baked Brie salad, the lamb, or the duck if they're listed. This wine bar is cozy and maybe a little noisy, but it's always fresh and fun.

1314 N. Washington St. 🕐 **302/655-WINE** (9463). www.domainehudson.com. Reservations recommended. Small plates $8–$15; main courses $15–$27. AE, DISC, MC, V. Tues–Sun 4:30–10:30pm.

Kelly's Logan House AMERICAN   Built in 1864, this old tavern by the railroad tracks once saw the likes of Al Capone and Wild Bill Hickok. Kelly's may still draw a few characters, but now they're coming for dinner washed down by a cold brew. Located right on Delaware Avenue, it's a good stop on your way to Brandywine Valley attractions. The menu is varied—hearty sandwiches, wraps, pasta, salmon, and burgers, plus brunch on Sunday. Thai and Cajun seasonings add interest to the usual fare. Live music draws lots of young people Tuesday through Saturday nights (p. 308).

1701 Delaware Ave. 🕐 **302/655-6426.** www.loganhouse.com. Main courses $12–$15. AE, DISC, MC, V. Tues–Sat 11am–1am; Sun noon–8pm; Mon 11am–11pm.

Kid Shelleen's AMERICAN   Tucked in a residential area on the city's north side, just north of Trolley Square, this lively indoor/outdoor restaurant, known for its open charcoal grill, is always hopping. Inside, you'll find a pub atmosphere: exposed brick, dark wood, and some game on the TV. But the food is better and the offerings more extensive than your average pub fare. Entrees include grilled salmon, barbecued ribs, "black and bleu" steak salad, and pastas. A big, friendly open bar area in the middle of the restaurant is dominated by a large-screen TV.

1801 W. 14th St. (at Scott St.). 🕐 **302/658-4600.** www.kidshelleens.com. Reservations recommended. Main courses $9–$20. AE, DC, DISC, MC, V. Mon–Sat 11am–1am; Sun 10am–2pm and 3pm–1am. Live music Wed and DJ on Thurs, both at 10pm.

Toscana Kitchen + Bar ★ ITALIAN/TUSCAN   As soon as you step into Toscana's dimly lit dining room (even at lunchtime), you'll be enveloped by the subdued din of conversation, the bustle of the waitstaff, and the piquant aromas flowing from the open kitchen and the wood-burning oven. From the warm breadsticks to the hefty panini, generous pasta servings and deftly sauced entrees, you'll know you'll be satisfied here.

Pizzelles, either a traditional Margherita or topped with something exotic, are another **301** good option. Half portions and small plates are the answer to a weight-watcher's prayer. Wines by the bottle or by the glass are mostly Italian.

1412 N. DuPont St. ⓒ **302/654-8001.** www.toscanakitchen.com. Reservations accepted only for parties of 6 or more. Main courses $8–$12 lunch, $9–$26 dinner. AE, DC, DISC, MC, V. Mon–Fri 11:30am–2pm; Mon–Thurs 5–10pm; Fri–Sat 5–11pm; Sun 5–9pm.

Inexpensive

Govatos AMERICAN   Established in 1894, this Wilmington tradition makes an ideal midcity choice for breakfast or lunch. The menu offers sandwiches, burgers, salads, and home-style favorites. The main attractions, however, are the desserts, because this place produces Delaware's largest selection of homemade chocolates and candies.

800 Market St. ⓒ **302/652-4082.** www.govatoschocolates.com. Breakfast items $4–$8; lunch items $6–$12. MC, V. Mon–Fri 8am–3pm.

SUBURBS
Expensive

Celebrity Kitchens ★ CONTEMPORARY/REGIONAL   This is dining as entertainment—and a Food TV fan's dream come true. Guest chefs prepare the night's feast, demonstrating as they go, answering questions, and debating the merits of food fads or TV chefs. For 2½ hours, fresh ingredients get sliced, sautéed, beaten, and baked into a four-course meal served with wine. As entertainment, it's amusing. As for the food, expect fine ingredients expertly prepared, with a mix of flavors to savor. The nightly menus are online; you'll see a featured ingredient or cuisine.

1601 Concord Pike, Independence Mall. ⓒ **302/427-2665.** www.celebritykitchens.com. Reservations required. 4-course dinners $50–$65. AE, DC, DISC, MC, V. Mon–Sat 6–8:30pm.

Krazy Kat's ★★★ NEW AMERICAN   The warm, candlelit dining room set in the old blacksmith shop at the Inn at Montchanin Village has a funny name, and even funnier animal "portraits" adorning its walls. But the real reason to come here is the serious food. The seasonal menu is filled with creative combinations: silky crab bisque with Meyer-lemon crème fraîche, or salmon with nutty Brussels sprouts. The wine list is extensive, too. And the service is polished and relaxed in the warm, candlelit dining room set in the old blacksmith shop—this is destination dining, after all. The dessert menu is as interesting as the dinner menu. Prix-fixe menus at lunch and dinner offer creative combinations that are easy on the wallet.

At Montchanin Village, Rte. 100 and Kirk Rd. ⓒ **302/888-4200.** www.montchanin.com/dining.html. Reservations recommended. Jackets suggested for men at dinner. Main courses $8–$18 lunch, $16–$30 dinner. AE, DC, DISC, MC, V. Mon–Fri 7–10am, 11:30am–2pm, and 5:30–9:30pm; Sat–Sun 8–11am and 5:30–9:30pm; Sun brunch 11am–2pm.

Moderate

Feby's Fishery ★ SEAFOOD   Feby's is known for good food in a family-style atmosphere. The nautically themed restaurant—on the city's southwest side, west of the junction of Route 100 South—also has a seafood market, a sure sign of fresh fish on the premises. The menu lists as many as 18 different species of fish, plus daily specials and creative combinations. For landlubbers, there's always a good piece of beef.

3701 Lancaster Pike (Rte. 48). ⓒ **302/998-9501.** www.febysfishery.com. Reservations recommended for dinner. Main courses $8–$15 lunch, $18–$40 dinner. AE, MC, V. Mon–Thurs 11am–9:30pm; Fri 11am–10pm; Sat–Sun 4–9:30pm.

5 ATTRACTIONS

Though many visitors to Wilmington head out to the Brandywine Valley attractions, the city itself has several museums and sites of interest.

Blue Ball Barn (Kids) This newly restored and enlarged 1914 barn houses the only state-run folk-art museum in the country. In just two barn-size rooms, you'll find 120 works by 50 artists, including flowers made from horseshoes, quilts reflecting African-American history, salvage and "Outsider" art, as well as paintings and collages, decoys, and sculpture. Amish, Native American, and early European cultures are also represented. The park also has a "Can-Do" playground, designed to be usable by children of all abilities.

Alapocas Run State Park, 1914 W. Park Dr., off Rte. 202, Wilmington. ℂ 302/577-1164. www.destate parks.com/blueball. Admission to park May–Oct $6 per vehicle ($3 discount for Md. residents); Nov–Apr free. Daily 9am–4pm. Closed Thanksgiving and Dec 25.

Brandywine Zoo (Kids) This is just a 12-acre place with 150 animals, but the petting zoo, the Siberian tiger, and the cute-as-a-button binturongs make it a good diversion for children. Especially interesting are the cages filled with curious little monkeys, most of them tamarins that are as interested in the humans as the humans are in the monkeys. Set in Brandywine Park, a 180-acre urban oasis just off Van Buren Street, it's a good way to get away from the noise and heat of the city, too.

1001 N. Park Dr. ℂ 302/571-7788. www.brandywinezoo.org. Admission $5 adults, $4 seniors, $3 ages 3–11. Daily 10am–4pm. Free parking.

Delaware Art Museum ★★ The Delaware Art Museum, home of 12,000 works of art, is best known for its dazzling collection of pre-Raphaelite art. The entrance, overlooking the sculpture garden, is crowned with a colorful Dale Chihuly glass sculpture. First-floor galleries are devoted to the pre-Raphael works, local artist Howard Pyle and his fellow illustrators of the Brandywine school, and John Sloan and early-American modernism. A second-floor bridge lets visitors get a closer look at the Chihuly glass as they head to galleries filled with more contemporary art, including works by Jacob Lawrence, Edward Hopper, and Jamie Wyeth. There is a 9-acre sculpture garden, a children's area, a cafe, and museum store.

2301 Kentmere Pkwy. ℂ 302/571-9590. www.delart.org. Admission Wed–Sat $12 adults, $10 seniors, $6 college students, $6 children 7–18; Sun free. Wed–Sat 10am–4pm; Sun noon–4pm.

Delaware Center for the Contemporary Arts Housed in an impressive building on Wilmington's Riverfront, this seven-gallery space focuses on contemporary visual arts by local and nationally known artists. As a noncollecting museum, exhibits are always changing, with about 30 each year. Also featured are the works of the 26 artists who keep their studios here. There's a small gift shop with handcrafted items.

200 S. Madison St. ℂ 302/656-6466. www.thedcca.org. Free admission. Tues and Thurs–Sat 10am–5pm; Wed and Sun noon–5pm.

Delaware Children's Museum (Kids) With exhibits that focus on the environment, transportation and—well, this town is a major financial center—banking, as well as a climbing structure, the DCM was due to open on the Riverfront in April 2010.

550 Justison St. ℂ 302/654-2340. www.delawarechildrensmuseum.org. At press time, admission is expected to be about $12 for adults and children. Hours are expected to be daily 9am–4:30pm.

Delaware History Museum ★ (Kids) In big, bright displays with lots of artifacts right at toddler level, the "Distinctly Delaware" exhibit tells all about the 200-plus years of Delaware history. DuPont is heavily featured, of course, but visitors will also learn about agriculture, the state's role in the Underground Railroad, and the famous Delawareans portrayed in wax, including civil-rights attorney Louis Redding and Emily Bissell, who created Christmas Seals. Grandma's Attic is a delightful place for kids to play and try on clothes. Children's programs are offered, too.

504 Market St. (near south end of Market St. Mall). ① 302/655-7161. www.hsd.org. Admission $4 adults, $3 students and seniors, $2 children 3–18. Wed–Fri 11am–4pm; Sat 10am–4pm.

Kalmar Nyckel A grand ship brought the first 24 Swedish settlers to the Delaware Valley in 1638. Now, on the shores of the Christina River near Old Swedes Church and Fort Christina Park, the *Kalmar Nyckel* Foundation has re-created the three-masted ship with its fine carvings and richly appointed captain's cabin. When it's not sailing, visitors can tour the 139-foot-long electric-blue ship and take a look at its seven guns, 7,500 square feet of sail, and 10-story-high main mast. The best time to find the *Kalmar Nyckel* at home is November through April. It sails along Delaware's coast—with 1 month each summer in Lewes—May through October. It also sometimes docks at the Riverfront Park downtown. Ninety-minute sailing excursions are offered during its Wilmington stay. Three-hour sails are offered from Lewes. See the website for schedule and fees.

The Sail Loft Museum at the shipyard has a few displays about shipbuilding and sailing the *Kalmar Nyckel*. Off-season, visitors may also see the crew hard at work repairing sails and lines for the coming year's sailing season.

1124 E. Seventh St. ① 302/429-7447. www.kalmarnyckel.org. Free admission to museum. Cruises $35–$60. Sat–Sun 10am–4pm. To get to shipyard, take Fourth St. east to Church St. Turn left on Church St.; turn right on Seventh St.

Marian Coffin Gardens (Finds) This newly preserved du Pont green spot is just off busy Route 52 near downtown Wilmington. A project of Preservation Delaware, the gardens feature a fragrant formal garden, reflecting pool, wooded paths, and a charming teahouse with seating (but no tea). Walk up to the stone terrace for a bird's-eye view of the layout. Bridal photographers use the garden as a backdrop for lots of portraits. The 1840s Gibraltar mansion is not open to the public.

1405 Greenhill Ave. (off Rte. 52). ① 302/651-9617. www.preservationde.org/gibraltar. Free admission. Daily dawn–dusk. Limited parking available on-site. DART bus stops nearby.

Old Swedes Church ★ Formally known as Holy Trinity Episcopal Church, this stone-and-brick building overlooking the Christina River is the oldest church in continuous use in the U.S. It was built in 1699 as part of the Swedish Lutheran Church. Today, artifacts tell of the parish's vibrant history. Parishioners donated the black-walnut pulpit; the king of Sweden presented the altar candles in 1988; Tiffany created one of the luminous stained-glass windows; and the church chest dates from 1713. Hendrickson House, moved here and restored in 1958, contains artifacts of rural Delaware from 1690 to 1800. A labyrinth is located here, as well.

606 Church St. (at Seventh St.). ① 302/652-5629. www.oldswedes.org. $2 tour. Guided tours Wed–Sat 10am–4pm. Take Fourth St.; turn left on Church St.

Riverfront Wilmington ★★★ On a bend in the Christina River, Wilmington has built brick-and-board walkways with views both urban and wild. Beginning at the train station and ending at the Russell W. Peterson Urban Wildlife Refuge, this 1⅓-mile path takes visitors past shops, museums, and a series of signs illustrating Wilmington's history. Watch a rowing team glide by, discover a Canada goose on the shore, or catch a ride on the River Taxi.

Start at the **Tubman–Garrett Riverfront Park,** at Water and South French streets. Twenty-one placards spaced along the walkway tell the history of the Christina River and the city, beginning with the development of industry, shipbuilding, and other transportation here. The Underground Railroad, which ran through Wilmington, is remembered as well, as are efforts to restore wetlands and excavate archaeological sites. Sometimes you can also see the *Kalmar Nyckel,* a reproduction of the ship that brought Wilmington's first settlers. **Dravo Plaza,** lined with huge cranes, recalls the city's shipbuilding history and its contributions to World War II.

Hungry yet? The number of restaurants just keeps going up. Among them are **Harry's Seafood Grill,** 101 S. Market St. (© **302/777-1500**), reviewed on p. 300, and **Iron Hill Brewery,** 710 S. Madison St. (© **302/658-8200**). If you just want a sandwich or snack, stop at the **Riverfront Market,** 1 S. Market St. (© **302/425-4454**), where you can also pick up meats, fish, and produce to take home. It's open Tuesday through Friday from 9am to 7pm, Saturday from 9am to 6pm.

The **Delaware Theatre Company** and **Delaware Center for the Contemporary Arts** are resident arts organizations here. The Riverfront also hosts festivals and concerts at Dravo Plaza and along the walkway. Sports fans can see the Blue Rocks play minor-league baseball at **Frawley Stadium,** a short walk off the Riverfront.

If you get tired of walking, the **River Taxi** (© **302/530-5069**) will take you to your next stop for $3. From April to November, the 40-passenger pontoon boat shuttles passengers along a 30-minute loop. Call in cooler weather if you don't see the taxi.

Visitors who make it to the end of the Riverfront will reach the **Russell W. Peterson Urban Wildlife Refuge.** The 225 acres of marshland have become home to many birds and other creatures. Newly opened in late 2009 is the **DuPont Environmental Education Center,** with touch-screen exhibits, free weekend nature activities, a boardwalk across the freshwater tidal pond, and a colorful garden path. The center is open Tuesday through Friday 11am to 3pm, Saturday 10am to 3pm, and Sunday noon to 4pm. Admission is free.

Madison St. (on the west) and Water St. (on the north) are the closest to the park. © **302/425-4890.** www.riverfrontwilm.com. Plentiful parking at free lots near the Shipyard Shops, 900 S. Madison St., the Chase Center on the Riverfront, 800 S. Madison St., and near the Riverfront Market, 1 S. Market St. Some paid parking available near the Amtrak station, 100 S. French St. (at Martin Luther King, Jr., Blvd.).

Rockwood Museum ★★ This rural Gothic mansion, furnished in 17th-, 18th-, and 19th-century decorative arts, is a treasure. Built in 1850 by Joseph Shipley and set on 72 acres, it was expanded by the home's only other occupants, the Bringhursts, who lived here from 1891 to 1965. Rockwood boasts a pink parlor with gilded fireplace and moldings, a lush conservatory, and spacious bedrooms, decorated as they might have been in the Bringhursts' time. A new highlight is the changing displays of beaded, brocade, and velvet Victorian clothing. Decorative painting in many of the rooms adds a touch of whimsy, especially in the newly reinterpreted kitchen. Rockwood is the centerpiece of a New Castle County–owned park with hiking trails, many of them paved and lighted. Get a trail map at the museum. The Butler's Pantry, a self-serve cafe, gives visitors an opportunity to rest in one of the many colorful parlors. Thousands of tiny lights illuminate trees around the house in December.

610 Shipley Rd. (℃ **302/761-4340.** www.rockwood.org. Free admission to park; tours $5 ages 13 and
older, $2 ages 2–12. Gardens and park daily dawn–dusk; house tours on the hour Wed–Sun 10am–3pm;
Butler's Pantry Wed–Sun 8am–3pm. From I-95 north, take exit 9 (Marsh Rd.); follow the signs.

6 SPECTATOR SPORTS & OUTDOOR ACTIVITIES

BASEBALL The **Wilmington Blue Rocks** (℃ **302/888-BLUE** [2583]; www.blue
rocks.com), a Class A Kansas City farm team who finished in first place in their division
in 2009, play at the 5,900-seat Daniel S. Frawley Stadium, off I-95 near the Riverfront.
Box seats are $10; reserved seats are $9; general admission is $6; and children, seniors,
and military pay $4. Parking is free. Frawley Stadium is also home of the **Delaware
Sports Museum and Hall of Fame** (℃ **302/425-3263;** www.desports.org), open April
through October, Tuesday through Saturday from noon to 5pm. Admission is $4 for
adults, $3 for seniors, and $2 for youths 12 to 19.

GOLF The rolling hills around Wilmington make for challenging golf. The following
courses welcome visitors.

The **Delcastle Golf Course & Restaurant,** 801 McKennan's Church Rd. (℃ **302/998-
9505;** www.delcastlegc.com), located near Delaware Park racetrack, offers a par-72
18-hole championship course, pro shop, and full restaurant open from 7am to dark.
Nearby are a driving range and miniature golf. Greens fees range from $30 to $35.

The **Ed Oliver Golf Club,** 800 N. DuPont Rd. (℃ **302/571-9041;** www.edoliver
golfclub.com), in a residential area off Route 52 (Pennsylvania Ave.), has a par-69
18-hole championship course, driving range, pro shop, and restaurant; it also offers lessons and group clinics. Greens fees range from $28 to $48.

The **Three Little Bakers Golf Course & Country Club,** 3540 Three Little Bakers
Blvd. (℃ **302/737-1877**), nestled in the Pike Creek Valley southwest of Wilmington,
has a par-71 18-hole course open daily to the public, except after 3pm on Thursday and
Friday. Facilities include a pro shop, club rental, golf lessons, and bag storage. Greens fees
range from $29 to $59.

HORSE RACING & SLOTS For half a century, racing fans have placed their bets at
Delaware Park, 4½ miles south of Wilmington, off I-95 exit 4B, Stanton (℃ **800/417-
5687** or 302/994-2521; www.delawarepark.com). Thoroughbred racing is offered April
through October Saturday and Monday to Wednesday; post time is 1:15pm. Simulcast
racing is offered year-round. Slot machines are available 24 hours a day. There are restaurants and weekend entertainment.

PUBLIC PARKS Wilmington's playground is **Bellevue State Park,** 800 Carr Rd.
(℃ **302/761-6963;** www.destateparks.com), on the northeast perimeter of the city. This
328-acre park was once the estate of the William du Pont family. Facilities include picnic
areas, garden paths for walking, fitness trails for jogging, clay tennis courts, and an eques-
trian facility, plus ice-skating in winter.

Southwest of Wilmington is **Lums Pond State Park,** 1068 Howell School Rd., off
Route 71, Bear (℃ **302/368-6989;** www.destateparks.com). Stretching along the
Chesapeake & Delaware Canal, this 1,790-acre park contains the state's largest freshwa-
ter pond and is home to beaver colonies and waterfowl. The pond offers sunbathing (no

swimming), fishing, and boating. Bring your own boat or rent a rowboat, canoe, paddle-boat, or sailboat during the summer and on weekends in May and September; rates range from $7 to $14 per hour. The surrounding parklands include hiking and walking trails; a nature center; picnic areas; football, soccer, and baseball fields; basketball and tennis courts; and campsites.

Entry fees to Delaware state parks are seasonal, with no admission charged from November through April. Otherwise, the fee is $6 per out-of-state vehicle and $3 per Delaware-registered car. Both parks are open from 8am to sunset year-round.

A SIDE TRIP TO FORT DELAWARE STATE PARK ★

Fort Delaware State Park, located on Pea Patch Island, in Delaware City (© **302/834-7941;** www.destateparks.com), is about 16 miles south of Wilmington, in the Delaware River. Take Route 13 or I-95 south from Wilmington to Route 9 (turn left), which will take you to Delaware City. A 5-minute ferry ride will take you to the park, which surrounds a five-sided granite fortress where prisoners of war were held during the Civil War. Serious business went on here but it doesn't stop a costumed reenactor from using a little humor as he greets visitors just before they enter through the sally port and explains the fort's role in 1864. Presentations throughout the day include guided tours and musketry and blacksmithing demonstrations. Not to be missed are the armory, the re-created laundry, kitchen, and offices, and the view of the Delaware River from the battlements. Nature lovers should save time to walk the trails beyond the fort and visit the observation tower to see the nesting birds and other wildlife. The ferry departs from Battery Park in Delaware City about every hour. Once on the island, a trolley will take you from the dock to the fort.

The ferry fare, which includes admission to the park, is $11 for adults, $10 for those 62 and over and $6 for children 12 and under. The site is open on weekends April through October, plus Wednesday through Friday from mid-June to Labor Day; call for exact hours, the ferry schedule, and the schedule of events. Reenactments and living-history demonstrations are held throughout the summer. The witty guided tours by Confederate and Union reenactors and the very loud musket, artillery, and cannon demonstrations are great for both children and adults. Ghost tours and paranormal investigations have added a spooky dimension for autumn visiting.

7 SHOPPING

Two of the Wilmington area's biggest shopping malls are **Concord Mall,** 4737 Concord Pike (© **302/478-9271**), and **Christiana Mall,** 435 Christiana Mall Rd., I-95 exit 4A (© **302/731-9815**). The downtown area offers some shopping, mostly on Ninth Street and along Market Street. **Govatos,** 800 Market St. (© **302/652-5252;** www.govatos chocolates.com), has made its own chocolates and candies since 1894. The shop is open Monday through Friday from 8am to 5pm; October through April, it also opens Saturday from 8am to 3pm. There's a second shop in the Talleyville Shopping Center, 4105 Concord Pike (© **302/478-5324**). On the Riverfront, the **Riverfront Market,** 3 S. Orange St. (© **302/422-9500;** www.riverfrontwilm.com), is a great place to stop for a sandwich or cup of soup. Fresh seafood, meat, and produce are also available. It's open Monday through Friday from 9am to 6pm, Saturday from 9am to 4pm. Some places open early for breakfast.

For the latest information on area entertainment, consult the *News Journal*'s entertainment guide called *Spark*. It's available free around town or online at **www.sparkweekly. com**. *Out & About* magazine also lists entertainment events.

THE PERFORMING ARTS
Classical Music & Opera

For such a small city, Wilmington has a lively performing-arts scene, and the **Grand Opera House** ★, 818 N. Market St. (© **302/658-7897** for information, 800/374-7263 or 302/652-5577 for tickets; www.grandopera.org), is the center of it, right in the heart of downtown. Built in 1871 as part of a Masonic temple, this restored Victorian showplace is one of the finest examples of cast-iron architecture in America. The auditorium seats 1,100 and is home to the Delaware Symphony Orchestra and Opera Delaware. It also offers ballet, jazz, chamber music, pop music, and theater.

The **Delaware Symphony Orchestra** (© **302/656-7442** for information, 800/374-7263 or 302/652-5577 for tickets; www.desymphony.org) is led by David Amado. The DSO's 90-plus performances a year range from classical to pops. Performances are usually held in the Grand Opera House in Wilmington, but chamber-music concerts are given in the Hotel du Pont or Winterthur. Tickets run $27 to $57.

How do you like your opera—grand Italian, light operetta, or maybe something for the kids? **Opera Delaware** (© **302/658-8063** for information, 800/374-7263 for tickets; www.operade.org) offers three operas a year, ranging from $25 to $68. Supertitles are provided; those who don't like them can sit in sections where the projections can't be seen.

Theater & Dance

The **DuPont Theatre,** at 10th and Market streets (© **800/338-0881** or 302/656-4401; www.duponttheatre.com), has brought touring shows to downtown Wilmington for more than 80 years. Set in the Hotel du Pont, it has a 1,239-seat capacity amid vintage Victorian decor. In addition, local companies often stage performances here—including the Wilmington Ballet's "Nutcracker."

City Theater Company Off-Broadway productions are staged in the black-box theater of Opera Delaware Studios. Some plays are edgy; others appeal to kids. So look for anything from *Humpty Dumpty* to *Sweeney Todd* to world premieres. Buy tickets online or with cash only at the door. 4 S. Poplar St. © **302/220-8285.** www.city-theater.org.

Delaware Theatre Company (**Finds**) At the foot of Orange Street on the Riverfront, this 389-seat facility has no seat more than 12 rows from the stage. The theater is home to Delaware's only resident professional company, which presents classic and contemporary plays, as well as children's theater. 200 Water St. © **302/594-1100** for box office. www.delawaretheatre.org.

The New Candlelight Theatre A big red barn in the northern suburb of Ardentown has been home to this dinner theater for more than 25 years. Admission includes a buffet dinner. On Thursday, Friday, and Saturday, the show is at 8pm; the Sunday show is at 3pm; Wednesday's matinee begins at 1pm. The house opens 2 hours earlier for the buffet. 2208 Millers Rd. (signposted off Harvey Rd.), Ardentown. © **302/475-2313.** www.newcandlelighttheatre.com. Tickets $55 adults, $32 children, no children's prices on Sat.

Dravo Plaza, on Wilmington's Riverfront, is the place to hear music: outdoor jazz, reggae, classical, and blues concerts are offered on Thursdays in summer. The nightlife elsewhere is pretty mellow, dominated by folk music, blues, and hotel piano bars.

Catherine Rooney's   Set in Trolley Square, just down the street from Kelly's Logan House, CR has a double personality on Saturday nights with a DJ in one room and a live rock party going on in another. DJs are featured on Fridays, too, with acoustic music on Thursdays. Trolley Sq., 1616 Delaware Ave. ℂ 302/654-9700. www.catherinerooneys.com. Cover varies.

Kelly's Logan House   This old tavern rocks with local music on Tuesday through Saturday. Musicians play on the second floor, making a nice background for diners on the first floor and terrace (see p. 300 for restaurant review). 1701 Delaware Ave. ℂ 302/655-6426. www.loganhouse.com. Cover varies.

Mojo 13   This indie-rock club shakes things up in Delaware with different acts every night, from rock to ska, and they're usually local. 1706 Philadelphia Pike. ℂ 302/798-5798.

FILM

Theatre N at Nemours   This 221-seat theater shows independent and foreign films usually Friday and Saturday at 8pm, plus Friday, Saturday, and Sunday matinees at 2pm. Tickets are available an hour before showtime, online or by calling ℂ **302/571-4699.** Nemours Building, 1007 Orange St. ℂ 302/658-6070. www.theatren.org.

ESPECIALLY FOR KIDS

The **Delaware Children's Theatre,** 1014 Delaware Ave. (ℂ **302/655-1014;** www.dechildrenstheatre.org), presents plays based on fairy tales and other children's stories. Tickets are $10, with performances on select Saturdays and Sundays at 2pm. *Note:* Adult visitors will enjoy visiting this ornate three-story building for its historic and architectural value. Listed on the National Register of Historic Places, it was designed in 1892 by a woman as a women's club—which continues to own and operate the building. Parking for performances is free.

The Brandywine Valley & Historic New Castle

The Brandywine Valley combines natural beauty with the best in art and craftsmanship. The valley's hills, rivers, and forests are dotted with mansions, gardens, and museums.

Here, between Wilmington and across the Pennsylvania line, you'll find the famous homes and gardens of the du Pont family—which give the Brandywine the nickname "Château Valley"—as well as the rolling hills and woodlands where three generations of the Wyeth family have lived and found inspiration for their art.

South of Wilmington, New Castle, Delaware's original capital, recalls the First State's early days. The town has preserved its 18th-century past with cobblestone streets, brick sidewalks, and 200-year-old homes. New Castle also offers some good antiques shops and restaurants.

1 THE BRANDYWINE VALLEY

10 miles N of Wilmington; 35 miles W of Philadelphia; 73 miles N of Baltimore

Meandering north from Wilmington, the Brandywine River has a long, storied history. The river and its valley provided for early settlers, powered the first du Pont industry, and inspired a school of art. To the Native Americans, the river was the *Wawset* or *Suspecoughwit*, cherished as a bountiful shad-fishing source. The Swedes and Danes later called it the Fishkill. Quakers and other English settlers renamed it the Brandywine and made it an important mill center in the 18th and 19th centuries. At its peak, more than 100 water-powered mills along the river produced everything from flour, paper, and textiles to snuff and black powder, on which the American du Ponts first made their fortune. In more recent times, the valley has been home to a school of artists and illustrators, beginning with Howard Pyle and Frank Schoonover and including the Wyeth family—N. C.; Andrew, who still lives and paints here; and Jamie.

The Brandywine Valley begins near Wilmington and stretches into Pennsylvania. Those who wish to see Winterthur and Longwood Gardens can do both in a day, since they're only a 20-minute drive apart. Some Pennsylvania sights are included because they're part of the area; the Pennsylvania side is also explored in *Frommer's Philadelphia & the Amish Country*. Two main arteries, routes 52 and 100, comprise the Brandywine Valley Scenic Byway—see **www.byways.org** for a map that works well with this chapter.

ESSENTIALS

GETTING THERE The valley's attractions in Delaware are spread out north of Wilmington, but most are along Route 52. By car, take I-95 into Wilmington to Delaware Route 52 North. The main attractions in Pennsylvania are along U.S. Route 1. From Wilmington, routes 52 and 100 both lead to U.S. Route 1. Alternate routes from I-95 are U.S. Route 202, which goes all the way to U.S. Route 1, and Route 141 to Route 52.

Bus service from Wilmington is available through **DART** (© 302/652-3278; www. dartfirststate.com). See p. 294 for information on rail and air transportation.

VISITOR INFORMATION   Contact the **Greater Wilmington Convention and Visitors Bureau,** 100 W. 10th St., Ste. 20, Wilmington (© 800/652-4088; www.visit wilmingtonde.com), open Monday through Friday from 9am to 5pm; or stop by the branch at the **I-95 Delaware Travel Plaza,** between exits 1 and 3 near Newark, Delaware, open daily from 8am to 8pm. (The old center was demolished in 2009 with a new one to open in summer 2010.) Or stop at the **Chester County Visitor Center,** on U.S. Route 1 at the entrance to Longwood Gardens, Kennett Square, Pennsylvania (© 800/228-9933 or 610/388-2900; www.brandywinevalley.com), open Monday to Saturday from 11am to 5pm and Sunday noon to 5pm.

AREA CODE   Brandywine Valley attractions located in the Wilmington suburbs use the 302 area code. Pennsylvania sights, inns, and restaurants use the 610 area code.

SPECIAL EVENTS   **Longwood Gardens** (© 610/388-1000) has seasonal displays including the **Christmas Display** ★★★, featuring hundreds of poinsettias and a lighted outdoor display. **Yuletide at Winterthur** (© 800/448-3883) is always a sensation, with rooms decorated according to customs from throughout history. The **Battle of Brandywine Reenactment** (© 610/459-3342), held in September, recalls local American Revolution history. In May, the **Winterthur Point to Point Races** (© 800/448-3883) is a good place to see horses and to *be* seen.

WHERE TO STAY

Wilmington area hotels are convenient bases from which to tour the Brandywine Valley, so check p. 296 for more places to stay. For a full DuPont experience, you may want to consider the Inn at Montchanin Village, originally part of the DuPont powder mills; see p. 298. Below are several inns and hotels in nearby Pennsylvania. Ask about packages that include entrance to area attractions when you make reservations.

Brandywine River Hotel ★ (**Value**)   This hotel, on a hillside in the heart of the valley, is one of the area's best values—lots of amenities, good location, and stylish rooms for the price of an average chain hotel. Designed to meld with the scenic region, with a facade of brick and cedar shingle, it is set among shops, restaurants, and galleries. Decorated with traditional furnishings, accommodations include standard doubles and executive units with sofa beds. The best rooms are the premium suites with fireplaces; they are roomy and cozy for a weekend getaway.

Routes 1 and 100 (P.O. Box 1058), Chadds Ford, PA 19317. © **800/274-9644** or 610/388-1200. www. brandywineriverhotel.com. 40 units. $129–$199 double; $159–$199 suite. Rates include continental breakfast and afternoon tea. AE, DC, DISC, MC, V. Free parking. Pets under 20 lb. accepted for $20 per day; must be crated when unattended. **Amenities:** Lobby bar; fitness center; room service. *In room:* A/C, TV/ VCR, hair dryer, free Wi-Fi.

Fairville Inn Bed & Breakfast   This gracious 1857 inn, listed on the National Register of Historic Places, is set on 5 leafy acres near Winterthur. Its Colonial-style decor is warm and cozy. The main house has five bedrooms; if you'd like more space or a private porch (or even a fireplace), ask for a room in the Springhouse or the Carriage House. These outbuildings offer extra privacy as well.

506 Kennett Pike (Rte. 52), Chadds Ford, PA 19317. © **877/285-7772** or 610/388-5900. www.fairvilleinn. com. 15 units. $165–$285 double. Rates include full breakfast and afternoon tea. 2-night minimum Apr– Dec weekends. AE, DISC, MC, V. Free parking. *In room:* A/C, TV, hair dryer, free Wi-Fi.

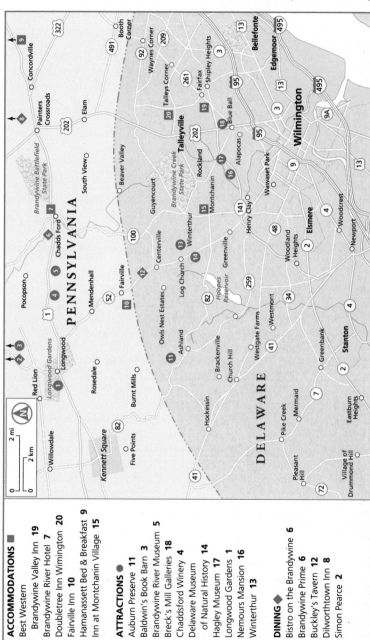

THE BRANDYWINE VALLEY & HISTORIC NEW CASTLE

13

THE BRANDYWINE VALLEY

ACCOMMODATIONS ■

Best Western
Brandywine Valley Inn **19**
Brandywine River Hotel **7**
Doubletree Inn Wimington **20**
Fairville Inn **10**
Hamanassett Bed & Breakfast **9**
Inn at Montchanin Village **15**

ATTRACTIONS ●

Auburn Preserve **11**
Baldwin's Book Barn **3**
Brandywine River Museum **5**
Breck's Mill Galleries **18**
Chaddsford Winery **4**
Delaware Museum
  of Natural History **14**
Hagley Museum **17**
Longwood Gardens **1**
Nemours Mansion **16**
Winterthur **13**

DINING ◆

Bistro on the Brandywine **6**
Brandywine Prime **6**
Buckley's Tavern **12**
Dilworthtown Inn **8**
Simon Pearce **2**

Hamanassett Bed & Breakfast ★★   This romantic 1856 country house with Palladian windows and a wide porch has long been a B&B. Owners Ashley and Glenn Mon, up from New Orleans, have worked to make it as luxurious as possible. You'll feel far from the crowds—though Brandywine attractions are only about 20 minutes away. Trees and flowers line the walking trails; nearby horses beg for a treat; a waterfall spills into the koi pond. The inn itself offers a casual solarium, a library, and spacious bedrooms decorated with antiques and luxurious beds. A charming cottage with two bedrooms is available for families or pet owners. And always, always expect Southern hospitality from these gracious hosts.

P.O. Box 336, Chester Heights, PA 19017. ℂ **877/836-8212** for reservations or 610/459-3000. www.hamanassett.com. 7 units. $160–$225 double; $190–$235 suite; $350–$550 cottage. Rates include full breakfast. AE, DISC, MC, V. Free parking. Pets accepted for a fee. Children 12 and under accepted in cottage. **Amenities:** Day pass to nearby YMCA; fridge stocked w/complimentary beverages; game room w/ billiards; video library. *In room:* A/C, TV/VCR or DVD, MP3 dock, free Wi-Fi.

WHERE TO DINE

Bistro on the Brandywine ★★ FRENCH/AMERICAN   This popular casual bistro has diners waiting in line on weekends. They come for the French onion soup, the inventive salads, the panini, and such main courses such as cassoulet. Locally-grown mushrooms are often featured in the dishes here. Sharing plates for both lunch and dinner are a great way to try a few new dishes. Make sure to leave room for homemade ice cream, crème brûlée, or crepes.

1623 Baltimore Pike (routes 1 and 100), Chadds Ford, PA. ℂ **610/388-8090.** www.bistroonthebrandywine.com. Reservations recommended. Main courses $9–$16 lunch, $12–$21 dinner. AE, MC, V. Mon–Sat 11:30am–9pm; Sun 4–9pm.

Brandywine Prime Seafood & Chops at Chadds Ford Inn AMERICAN   Old restored farmhouse meets contemporary style and cuisine at this stylish chophouse. The focus here is dry-aged beef, seafood, and a raw bar. The wine list includes local vintages, but if you have a favorite, feel free to bring it along. Sunday brunch is offered and the bar has its own selection of sandwiches and small plates to go with a cocktail.

Corner of routes 1 and Old 100, Chadds Ford, PA. ℂ **610/388-8088.** www.brandywineprime.com. Reservations recommended. Main courses $10–$39. AE, MC, V. Mon–Thurs 5am–10pm; Fri–Sat 5–11pm; Sun 10am–2pm and 4–9pm.

Buckley's Tavern AMERICAN   This casual roadside restaurant in the quaint borough of Centreville has been feeding people since the 1800s. But the menu is up to date, with trendy small plates, hearty sandwiches, salads, and intriguing entrees. Lunchtime favorites include a flavorful mustard-crusted chicken sandwich, while at dinner, crab cakes are paired with roasted corn béarnaise. It's a busy place, from the porch on a sunny day to the very casual bar to the more formal Colonial dining room. Brunch is served on Sundays. The location is perfect for a Sunday drive—pair brunch with a visit to one of the local museums or some of the antiques shops that pop up along Route 52.

5812 Kennett Pike (Rte. 52), Centreville, DE. ℂ **302/656-9776.** www.buckleystavern.org. Reservations recommended for dinner; not accepted for weekend lunch or brunch. Main courses $9–$13 lunch, $10–$22 dinner. AE, DC, MC, V. Mon–Thurs 11:30am–9:30pm; Fri–Sat 11:30am–11pm; Sun 10am–2:30pm and 4–9pm.

Dilworthtown Inn ★ CONTINENTAL   Located on the road that was once the principal connection between Wilmington and West Chester, this establishment was built in 1758 and restored in 1972. The 15 dining rooms include the house's original kitchen and an outside stable area for warm-weather dining. Colonial furniture, dark-wood beams, 11 fireplaces, gas lamps and candlelight, and Andrew Wyeth paintings set the mood. The menu changes weekly and includes an array of fine-dining options. Start with Dilworthtown mushroom soup or escargot; move on to rack of lamb or sea scallops. Pair these with an offering from the 800-bottle wine cellar.

1390 Old Wilmington Pike and Brinton Bridge Rd. (off Rte. 202), West Chester, PA. ✆ **610/399-1390.** www.dilworthtown.com. Reservations required; jackets for men recommended. Main courses $22–$32. AE, DC, DISC, MC, V. Mon–Fri 5:30–9:30pm; Sat 5–9:30pm; Sun 3–8:30pm. Closed Wed before Labor Day to the following Tues.

Simon Pearce AMERICAN The name usually associated with fine modern crystal also has a restaurant in the Brandywine Valley. Naturally, Simon Pearce tableware graces the tables, with creative modern cuisine served at lunch and dinner. Try the calamari salad or shepherd's pie at lunch, or perhaps the duck or Pennsylvania lake trout for dinner. Brunch is served on Sunday. The restaurant is on the second floor of the glass-blowing factory, with floor-to-ceiling windows overlooking Brandywine Creek. Make sure to stop to see the glass blowers at work.

1333 Lenape Rd., West Chester, PA. ✆ **610/793-0949.** www.simonpearce.com. Reservations not necessary. Main courses $11–$14 lunch, $29–$31 dinner. AE, DISC, MC, V. Daily 11:30am–3pm and 5:30–9pm.

THE DU PONT HOMES & GARDENS

If you've seen only one du Pont home, you're just getting started. Each reflects the personality of its owners and their lifestyles. For sheer splendor, visit the newly reopened **Nemours Mansion.** If your tastes are more of a garden variety, **Longwood Gardens** has the most varied grounds. Even if you skip the house (though it's a nice one), don't miss the conservatories. The charms of world-famous **Winterthur** are more academic; remember, this is more a museum than a house. The room with the Chinese wallpaper has earned its world-class reputation; this house tells more about the decorative arts than about the personality who gathered them here. (Marylanders should check out the Chestertown room and the Baltimore alcove.) Leave time for the gardens, especially the children's Enchanted Woods (but if you have time for only one garden in the Brandywine Valley, go to Longwood). The **Hagley Museum** is worth visiting to see how regular Americans lived and worked when the country was new. Its grounds beside the river offer a spectacular display of autumn foliage.

Hagley Museum and Library ★★★ **Kids** The du Pont fortune got started along this wooded riverbank. French émigré Eleuthère Irénée du Pont de Nemours built the first of his gunpowder mills here in 1802, and the first du Pont home in 1803. The mills grew in number and size, later to include workers' homes and a school. A visit to the 235-acre site can take a couple of hours or an entire day. Just the walk along the river, past the ruins of the old roll mills, will keep kids busy.

The **visitor center** features an exhibit demonstrating how mills work, as well as the DuPont Science and Discovery display (including a NASCAR car and a spacesuit). Kids will love the adjacent **Hydroelectric Plant,** where they can learn about simple machinery at the "Easy Does It!" exhibit.

Walk along the river and millrace to see the roll mills, the narrow-gauge railroad, and the dangerous steps it took to make gunpowder in the 1800s. Visit what remains of one of the workers' communities, the Gibbons House, the Sunday school, and the **Belin House Restaurant** (Mar–Dec daily 11:30am–4pm; closed Jan–Feb). The **Millwright Shop** dioramas and live demonstration explain how gunpowder was made. The exhibit

13

on a deadly 1920 explosion, right along the path of the powder yards, serves as a bit of archaeological dig while highlighting the importance of safety.

Visitors to the family house, **Eleutherian Mills,** can catch a bus that offers a narrated tour through the powder yards to the Georgian-style residence where five generations of du Ponts lived. Rooms reflect the periods of the house's history from the 1800s to the 1920s. The French gardens, barn, and First Office are also worth a look.

Hagley's Family Fun Events include dollar days, the Invention Convention in January, and bike and hike days; check the website for details.

Rte. 141, Wilmington, DE. ℂ **302/658-2400.** www.hagley.org. Admission $11 adults, $9 students and seniors, $4 children 6–14. Visitor center daily 9:30am–4:30pm. Tours Mar 15–Dec daily 9:30am–4:30pm; Jan–Mar 14 Mon–Fri at 10:30am and 1:30pm and Sat–Sun 9:30am–4:30pm. Closed Thanksgiving, Dec 25, and Dec 31. From Wilmington, take I-95 to Rte. 52 N. Turn right on Rte. 141; museum entrance is on the left.

Longwood Gardens ★★★ Kids One of the world's most celebrated horticultural displays, Longwood Gardens showcases more than 11,000 different types of plants and flowers amid 1,050 acres of outdoor gardens and woodlands. For sheer size, Longwood is spectacular. But the ever-blooming displays throughout the grounds and conservatory are both creative and delightful, thanks to Pierre S. du Pont, who purchased the existing farm and arboretum in 1906, and from 1907 to 1954 designed most of what is enjoyed today.

Everybody has a favorite spot: the tropical paradise of the **Conservatory;** the eye-popping seasonal displays; the flower-garden walk that explodes in seasonal color; the understated **Chimes Tower** (with carillon); the **Idea Garden** to inspire home gardeners; the **Flower Garden Fountains,** the **Italian Water Garden,** or the **Main Fountain Garden,** whose 380 fountains and spouts rise over 130 feet high during one of the 5-minute displays throughout the day. There are also illuminated displays in the fountain garden on Tuesday, Thursday, and Saturday evenings June through September, plus fireworks displays on several evenings in summer (check the website for a schedule). The recently restored **East Conservatory** is filled with water features among the plantings (serious gardeners will enjoy the audio-wand tours). Behind the ballroom is an organ museum with interactive displays for children. The **Indoor Children's Garden** was reopened in 2007, delighting children and adults with its whimsical fountains and garden paths. Three fanciful **Treehouses** scattered among the gardens outside offer a bird's eye view of the gardens for kids and adults alike.

Longwood's attractions also include seasonal plant displays (Christmas and Easter gardens are noteworthy) and hundreds of performances—even ice-skating in December; check the website for a schedule. Facilities include the **Peirce–du Pont House;** a large museum shop; and the **Terrace Restaurant,** which has both a cafe and full-service dining room. Reservations are recommended for the dining room. Electric scooters, wheelchairs, and strollers are available for rental.

Rte. 1 (just north of Rte. 52), Kennett Square, PA. ℂ **610/388-1000.** www.longwoodgardens.org. Admission $16 adults, $14 seniors, $6 ages 16–22, $2 ages 6–15. AE, DC, DISC, MC, V. Mid-Jan to Mar daily 9am–5pm; Apr–May daily 9am–6pm; Memorial Day to Labor Day Mon–Wed and Sun 9am–6pm, Thurs–Sat 9am–10pm; Sept–Oct daily 9am–6pm; early Nov to Thanksgiving daily 9am–5pm; Thanksgiving to early Jan daily 9am–9pm.

Nemours Mansion & Gardens ★★★ It took 4 years and $39 million—and finally the restoration of this 1909 47,000-square-foot château was completed in mid-2009. The home of Alfred I. du Pont and his family, and named after the du Pont ancestral home in France, the 102-room Louis XVI–style château is a model of extravagance. It boasts acres of marble, dozens of glittering chandeliers, paintings from 4 centuries, a clock that once belonged to Marie Antoinette, and gates from palaces of Henry VIII and Catherine the Great. Just as dazzling as the house are the 100 acres of European-style gardens: a maze, sunken gardens, a reflecting pool, a colonnade, and wonderful sculptures. It takes about 3 hours to wander the gardens after the house tour. Tour reservations are a must. Tours begin at the visitor center; arrive 15 minutes before tour time.

Rte. 141 (Powder Mill Dr.) and Alapocas Rd., Wilmington, DE 19803. ℭ **800/651-6912** or 302/651-6912. www.nemoursmansion.org. Admission $15. Tours every 2 hr. on the hour Tues–Sat 9am–3pm; Sun 11am–3pm. Closed Dec 31–May 1.

Winterthur Museum & Country Estate ★★★ **Kids** Named after a town in Switzerland and pronounced "win-ter-tour," this eight-story mansion and country estate features one of the world's premier collections of American antiques and decorative arts. The estate was the country home of Henry Francis du Pont, a collector of furniture, who in 1951 turned the place into a museum for American decorative arts. The 85,000 objects made or used in America, including Chippendale furniture, silver tankards by Paul Revere, and a dinner service made for George Washington, are displayed in the 175 period rooms. The galleries include exhibits of furniture styles, life at Winterthur, Early American craftsmen, and the Campbell collection of soup tureens.

It takes more than one visit to see all of Winterthur. A variety of 1-hour **Discovery Tours** focus on everything from entertaining to du Pont collections to seasonal topics. The introductory Elegant Entertaining tour, for instance, covers only one floor, high-lighting the dining room, sitting rooms, and other period public rooms. The Winterthur Experience pass, good for 2 consecutive days, includes one Discovery Tour, admission to the galleries, and a tram tour of the 966-acre grounds. Additional hour-long tours can be added for $5 for adults. Reservations are recommended. The popular **Yuletide Tour** ($22 for adults; $12 for children) is offered from mid-November to December 31. Download **iPod tours** about the collection from the website.

Children 8 and under are permitted on three of the tours, as well as the Yuletide Tour. Kids (and adults, too) will love the **Enchanted Woods,** a 3-acre fairy-tale garden filled with places to play, including a Faerie Cottage and Troll Bridge. Other facilities include two restaurants, an expansive museum store, and a bookshop.

5105 Kennett Pike (Rte. 52), Winterthur, DE. ℭ **800/448-3883** or 302/888-4600. www.winterthur.org. Galleries and garden admission $15 adults, $13 seniors and students, $5 children 5–11. Guided Discovery Tours of house and garden $20 adults, $18 seniors and students. Special interest tours $10 additional. AE, DISC, MC, V. Tues–Sun 10am–5pm (last tour at 4pm). Closed Thanksgiving and Dec 25. Call for other winter closings. Located on Rte. 52, 6 miles northwest of Wilmington and 5 miles south of Rte. 1.

OTHER ATTRACTIONS

Auburn Heights Preserve **Kids** Wilmington fans of trains and antique cars have visited this home of an impressive collection of Stanley Steamer cars and a miniature train for special events for years. A state park historic site since 2008, it opens to tourists 8 Sundays a year and the Friday and Saturday after Thanksgiving. Additional openings should be added by 2010. Visitors can look over the collection of pristine Stanley Steamer automobiles lovingly collected by the Marshall family, ride the one-eighth scale steam engine train around the property, enjoy performances, bring a picnic, and tour the 1897 granite Victorian home. The 200 wooded acres are lovely and peaceful.

3000 Creek Rd., Yorklyn, DE 19736. ℭ **800/349-2134.** www.auburnheights.org or www.destateparks. com/attractions. Admission $10 adults, $7 ages 2–12; house tour $8 additional. See website for opening times. Also open by appointment. From Rte. 52 North, take Campbell Rd. to New London Rd. to Pyles Ford Rd. to Creek Rd.

Baldwin's Book Barn (Finds)

Okay, technically this is a store—but for true bibliophiles, it's a can't-miss experience. With five floors of 300,000 rare and used books, maps, and prints in an 1822 stone barn, it's easy to while away hours getting lost among the stacks or perusing a book in the cozy reading room. There's no admission, but just try to get out of here without spending any money.

865 Lenape Rd. (routes 100 and 52), West Chester, PA. (C) 610/696-0816. www.bookbarn.com. Mon–Fri 10am–8pm; Sat–Sun 10am–6pm. From Rte. 1, take Rte. 52 north. The barn is 6 miles past Rte. 1 on the left.

Brandywine Battlefield Historic Site

On these rolling hills, George Washington's troops fought with the British for control of strategic territory near Philadelphia. The September 11, 1777, defeat had its victories, too: The Marquis de Lafayette saw his first military action here, witnessed the courage and determination of the Americans, and helped convince the French to form an alliance with the colonists. House tours of two Quaker farmhouses, which served as George Washington's headquarters and the quarters of Lafayette, are offered on the hour March to November. On-site are picnic areas and a visitor center with exhibits, dioramas, and a museum shop. Check the website for three driving tours.

1491 Baltimore Pike (Rte. 1), Chadds Ford, PA. (C) 610/459-3342. www.ushistory.org/brandywine. Admission $6 adults, $5 seniors, $4 children 6–17. Wed–Sat 9am–4pm; Sun noon–4pm.

Brandywine River Museum ★★★

This Civil War–era gristmill in a pristine wooded setting—near the home and studio of three generations of Wyeth artists—has been converted into a museum that embraces not only the art of the Brandywine School but also the setting that inspired it. Huge, sweeping windows overlook the valley and river below. Inside are the paintings of Howard Pyle and the artists he taught, including N. C. Wyeth, Frank Schoonover, and Maxfield Parrish. Works by N. C.'s children Andrew, Henriette, and Caroline hang here, too, as well as paintings by Jamie Wyeth, of the third generation of the family. Andrew Wyeth has a gallery all his own, with his comments accompanying most of his pieces. Tours of N. C. Wyeth's house and studio are offered Tuesday through Sunday from April to November. The studio is worth seeing: Wyeth's paint-splattered smock still hangs near his palette and the painting he was working on at the time of his death. The big museum shop and restaurant have great views, too.

Rte. 1 and Pa. Rte. 100, Chadds Ford, PA. (C) 610/388-2700. www.brandywinemuseum.org. Admission $20 adults, $6 seniors and students; studio tour $5; audio tour $3. Daily 9:30am–4:30pm. Closed Dec 25. Just south of Rte. 100 on the Brandywine River.

Breck's Mill galleries

Two fascinating galleries are housed in this 1814 stone mill building downstream from the Hagley Museum. The **Somerville Manning Gallery** is devoted to 20th- and 21st-century art, including the works of the Wyeth family and other artists trained in the Brandywine School tradition. The **André Harvey Studio** on the second floor displays Harvey's realistic bronze sculptures of people and animals, as well as sculptural gold jewelry. There's a U.S. Post Office on-site, too.

Andre Harvey Studio: 101 Stone Block Row, Greenville, DE. (C) 302/656-7955. www.andreharvey.com. Free admission. Mon–Sat 10am–4:30pm and by appointment. Somerville-Manning Gallery: 101 Stone Block Row, Greenville, DE. (C) 302/652-0271. www.somervillemanning.com. Free admission. Mon–Sat 10am–5pm.

Chaddsford Winery Walk in the door of this restored barn, and you'll be greeted with a sample of wine made in Pennsylvania's largest winery. Then take a self-guided or guided half-hour tour. In-depth winemaking tours are also offered Fridays at 3pm and Saturdays at 1pm. For $8, buy a glass and try a wide variety of regional wines. Check the website for classes and festivals. This is also a good place to start on the Brandywine Valley Wine Trail, a collection of area wineries and vineyards. Get a map at Chaddsford or go to www.bvwinetrail.com. (Bring your GPS; the map's just a guide.)

632 Baltimore Pike (U.S. 1), Chadds Ford, PA. ℂ **610/388-6221.** www.chaddsford.com. Free admission; full tasting session $8. Tours daily noon–6pm. Located 5 miles south of Rte. 202, just past the Brandywine River Museum. Closed Thanksgiving, Dec 25, and Jan 1.

Delaware Museum of Natural History ⟨**Kids**⟩ Visitors are greeted by a giant squid "swimming" overhead in the glass entrance—perfect for a museum known for its mollusk and bird collections. (Did you know a squid is a mollusk?) Following a loop, visitors can look up at an Allosaurus, one of Delaware's only dinosaurs, or tiptoe over the Great Barrier Reef exhibit located under the Plexiglas floor. The shell, gemstone, and mineral cases glitter with color and light. In warm weather, take a break on the patio by the butterfly garden. The museum is bound to intrigue the kids.

4840 Kennett Pike (Rte. 52), Wilmington, DE. ℂ **302/658-9111.** www.delmnh.org. Admission $7 adults, $5 seniors, $6 children 3–17. Mon–Sat 9:30am–4:30pm; Sun noon–4:30pm. Located 5 miles northwest of Wilmington on Rte. 52. Closed Jan 1, Easter, July 4th, Thanksgiving, and Dec 25.

2 HISTORIC NEW CASTLE

7 miles S of Wilmington; 40 miles SW of Philadelphia; 70 miles NE of Baltimore

New Castle, Delaware's original capital, was a major Colonial seaport. Peter Stuyvesant, who established a Dutch settlement named Fort Casimir, purchased the area from Native Americans in 1651. (It's said that Stuyvesant designed the town's central green by "pegging it off" with his wooden leg.) Later captured by the Swedes and then the English, who renamed it New Castle, this stretch of land along the west bank of the Delaware River remains much the way it was in the 17th and 18th centuries. Original houses and public buildings have been restored and preserved, along with brick sidewalks and cobblestone streets.

Park your car (no meters here) and stroll past old homes and churches, a few tiny shops, and restaurants. Everything is close by—even the expansive Battery Park by the river. Cool breezes, green places, and playground equipment make it a nice break for both children and adults.

ESSENTIALS

GETTING THERE From Wilmington, either take U.S. Route 13 south to Delaware Route 273 east to New Castle, or follow Delaware Route 9 south directly to New Castle. From the south, take Route 301 to Route 13 North. (It's a good day trip from Baltimore or Annapolis, too.)

VISITOR INFORMATION For information, contact the **New Castle Historical Society** (ℂ **302/322-2794;** www.newcastlehistory.org) or stop by the Court House for a map and brochure about the town.

SPECIAL EVENTS **A Day in Old New Castle** (ℂ **877/496-9498;** www.dayinold newcastle.org), held the third Saturday in May, gives visitors a chance to tour the town's

(Kids) Wilmington & the Brandywine Valley for Kids

Wilmington and its suburbs are home to palatial residences, elegant hotels, and immense gardens, not places you'd think of as kid-friendly. Fortunately, several sites welcome kids. All of the following are described in detail earlier in this chapter, except the Delaware History Museum, Delaware Children's Museum, and Fort Delaware State Park, listed in chapter 12, "Wilmington."

Brandywine Zoo (p. 302)   A tiny zoo set in the green Brandywine Park has just 150 animals, but pint-size goats willing to be petted and curious little monkeys make this a child's delight.

Delaware Children's Museum (p. 302)   Although we didn't get to preview it by press time, the Children's Museum looks like it will offer fun ways for kids to look at themselves, their world, and the adult world of banking.

Delaware History Museum (p. 303)   This museum of First State history, housed in an old Woolworth's store in Wilmington, is bright and colorful, and has fun exhibits. Its hands-on Discovery Room lets kids touch artifacts and hear stories.

Delaware Museum of Natural History (p. 317)   Children can run wild here (carefully, of course) while looking at dinosaur skeletons, lots of shells, special exhibits, and their own Discovery Room.

Fort Delaware State Park (p. 306)   Kids will love this Civil War fort on an island in the Delaware Bay. Not only is there a boat ride to the island and a trolley ride to the fort, but reenactors lead guided tours laced with humor and give LOUD artillery demonstrations in summer.

Hagley Museum (p. 313)   The family-friendly museum, set on the shady banks of the Brandywine River, tells the story of the du Pont family's early gunpowder mill. Kids love the gunpowder testing demonstration.

Longwood Gardens (p. 314)   This is a sprawling landscape with fountains, animal-shaped hedges, and conservatories. Little ones shouldn't miss the children's indoor garden or the whimsical treehouses.

Winterthur's Enchanted Woods (p. 315)   These 3 acres will delight the young ones with a labyrinth, fountains, and a kid-size cottage. Pick up the amusing brochure that tells the tale of the Enchanted Woods.

private homes and gardens, as well as public buildings, gardens, and museums. The **Historic New Castle Antiques Show** is held in Battery Park the last Sunday in August. **A New Castle Spirit o Christmas** features house tours, carolers, and carriage rides in mid-December; contact the **New Castle Historical Society** (© **302/322-2794;** www. newcastlehistory.org) for details.

WHERE TO STAY

New Castle is an easy drive from Wilmington, 7 miles away, especially because the town has few accommodations.

The Terry House Bed and Breakfast (Value) This 1860 brick town house is the rare B&B in historic New Castle. Its 6 guest rooms have queen-size or double beds and en suite bathrooms. Porches along the back of the house overlook Battery Park and the Delaware River. Rooms are spacious with antiques and chandeliers, though bathrooms are merely serviceable. Suite no. 7, on the third floor, has enough room for a family of four, and a spacious attic room looks over the trees to the park and river below. Lined with books, it's a bit like living in a library. The house is filled with collections from china to kitchen tools and the walls are covered with portraits, photos, and prints. Once you meet the scholarly, charming innkeeper, you'll feel you've arrived for a visit at your grand-mother's house.

130 Delaware St., New Castle, DE 19720. © **302/322-2505.** www.terryhouse.com. 4 units. $90–$110 double. Rates include full or continental breakfast. No credit cards. On-street parking. **Amenities:** Porch and garden w/access to Battery Park. In room: A/C, TV, free Wi-Fi.

WHERE TO DINE

The Arsenal at Old New Castle AMERICAN The same folks who operate Jessop's Tavern (see below) offer more refined dining down the street in this big brick building, which originally served as an ammunition storage house for the War of 1812. You have your choice of a casual tavern or more elegant dining room, both with Colonial-style ambience. Menu choices are classic preparations of fish and beef plus a few hearty sand-wiches. Entertainment is on the schedule every night: karaoke, live jazz or blues, piano bar.

30 Market St. © **302/323-1812.** www.arsenal1812.com. Reservations recommended for dinner. Main courses $18–$25 dinner. AE, DC, DISC, MC, V. Wed–Sat 5pm–1am. Kitchen closes at 10pm.

Jessop's Tavern ★ AMERICAN Don't miss this tiny tavern tucked into a 1724 building. The atmosphere and menu are designed to reflect the area's history, with Colo-nial potpie (a delight), pot roast, fresh seafood, and English pub fare like fish and chips and shepherd's pie. At lunchtime, the salads, soups, and sandwiches on hearth-baked breads will keep you happy for the rest of the afternoon. Sweet-potato fries are a specialty. It's a casual place, a reminder of the town's seafaring days. Just need a quick bite? Stop next door at the **Shoppe of the Three Crowns** (© **302/221-0773**) for a sandwich or ice cream or even Afternoon Tea. (The Motor Oil ice cream is to die for.)

114 Delaware St. © **302/322-6111.** Reservations not accepted, except for large parties. Main courses $7–$15 lunch, $10–$24 dinner. AE, DC, DISC, MC, V. Mon–Thurs 11am–10pm; Fri–Sat 11:30am–11pm; Sun noon–8pm.

Prince on Delaware ★ MODERN AMERICAN Tucked inside a Colonial brick-front is this ode to modern American cuisine. You'll know it's different the second you step inside. The dark-wood tables are left bare so their chrome bases gleam on the old hardwood floors. The white leather chairs are a nice contrast to the rusty red and choco-late brown walls. And the food is fresh and organic. The recipes recall American favor-ites—crab cakes, pork chops, and fish, for example—but the sauces are spiked with new flavors. And this chef is not afraid of herbs and spices. Brunch, with a complimentary mimosa or Bellini, is served on Sunday.

124 Delaware St. © **302/326-1130.** www.princeondelaware.com. Reservations recommended on Fri-Sat. Main courses $8–$14 lunch, $14–$27 dinner. AE, DC, DISC, MC, V. Mon–Thurs 11am–9pm; Fri–Sat 11am–10pm; Sun 11am–3pm.

Many historic buildings in New Castle are privately owned and thus not open to the public. Stop by the Court House to pick up a map and guide to the town's historic buildings, which points out the ones open to the public. *Note:* Almost everything (except a few restaurants and shops) is closed on Mondays and weekdays in winter.

A notable building is the 1820 **Immanuel Episcopal Church on the Green,** at Second and Harmony sts., which was the first parish of the Church of England in Delaware. Extensively damaged by fire in 1980, it has been carefully restored. The adjoining cemetery is the resting place of many prominent Delawareans, including George Read I, signer of the Declaration of Independence. Another is the **New Castle-Frenchtown Railroad Ticket Office,** a tiny white building and a stretch of track in Battery Park that recalls the 1820s horse-drawn railway, once part of an important commercial route.

The historic district has only a few shops. For country items, stop by **Almost History,** 302 Delaware St. (© 302/322-6434). Crafters will find **Two Morrow's Stitches That Count,** 306 Delaware St. (© 302/328-7888), useful.

Amstel House   Dating from the 1730s, this house is a fine example of Georgian architecture. It was likely the most elegant home in town when constructed. Today, it's furnished with antiques and decorative arts of the period.

2 E. Fourth St. © 302/322-2794. www.newcastlehistory.org. Admission $3 adults, $1.50 children; combination ticket with the Dutch House $6 adults, $2.50 children. May–Dec Wed–Sat 11am–4pm; Sun 1–4pm. Closed holidays.

Dutch House   One of the oldest brick houses in Delaware, this building has remained almost unchanged since its construction around 1700. The early Dutch furnishings include a courting bench; also on display is a 16th-century Dutch Bible. During seasonal celebrations, the dining table is set with authentic foods and decorations.

32 E. Third St., on the green. © 302/322-2794. www.newcastlehistory.org. Admission $3 adults, $1.50 children; combination ticket with the Amstel House $6 adults, $2.50 children. May–Dec Tues–Sat 11am–4pm; Sun 1–4pm.

Old New Castle Court House ★   This building was Delaware's Colonial capital and the meeting place of the state assembly until 1777. Built in 1732 on the fire-charred remains of an earlier courthouse, it's been restored and modified over the years, though always maintaining its role as the focal point of town. You'll find portraits of men important to Delaware's early history, the original speaker's chair, and excavated artifacts. An exhibit on the Underground Railroad tells the thrilling story of a runaway slave and her family who were jailed here. Free guided tours are available.

211 Delaware St., on the green. © 302/323-4453. www.history.delaware.gov. Free admission. Wed–Sat 10am–3:30pm; Sun 1:30–4:30pm.

Old Library Museum   This fanciful hexagonal building, erected in 1892 by the New Castle Library Society, holds exhibits by the New Castle Historical Society. Its Victorian styling is attributed to the architectural firm of Frank Furness of Philadelphia.

40 E. Third St. © 302/322-2794. www.newcastlehistory.org. Free admission. May–Dec Sat–Sun 1–4pm. Closed Jan to mid-May.

Read House & Gardens ★   A walk through this 22-room Federal-style house overlooking the river is a walk through New Castle history. Originally the home of George Read II, son of a signer of the Declaration of Independence, it had only two other owners. Rooms from each "period" pay homage to them all. The soaring Palladian windows

Finds **Attention Hog Fans**

Is it a restaurant, a museum, or a motorcycle dealership? Actually, **Mike's Famous Harley-Davidson,** 2160 New Castle Ave., New Castle (📞 **800/FAMOUS-HD** [326-6874]; www.mikesfamous.com), is all three. Just off the Delaware Memorial Bridge at I-295 South and Route 9 in New Castle, motorcycle enthusiasts can eat at **Mike's Warehouse Grill;** visit the **Museum of the American Road;** and shop for a new or used Harley parts, clothes, or baby gear. The grill describes its cuisine as "regional American roadside," serving what *Delaware Today* has called the best chili in the area. The museum (admission $4 adults; $3 children 4–10, seniors, students, and military) features the Harley ridden around the world. Store, restaurant, and museum hours vary seasonally, but all are open daily. Mike's also hosts bike runs, parties, and other events, and offers motorcycle rentals as well. Check the website for hours and special events.

and intricate composition-work moldings were part of the original design. Don't miss Mr. Read's law office or the second-floor bathing room, to which servants carried hot water. The second owner added the formal gardens in the mid-1800s, now the oldest surviving gardens in Delaware. The third owner's contributions included the European-style rathskeller built in the basement during Prohibition; it's a hoot.

42 The Strand. 📞 **302/322-8411.** www.hsd.org/read.htm. Admission $5 adults, $4 seniors and students, $2 children. Mar–Dec Wed–Fri 11am–4pm, Sat 10am–4pm, Sun 11am–4pm; Jan–Feb Sat 10am–4pm, Sun 11am–4pm. Last tour is at 3:30pm.

Dover &
Central Delaware

To race-car fans, Dover means NASCAR twice a year. To gamblers, it's a place to play the slots. To history buffs, this town is where the U.S. Constitution got its first "yea" vote.

Set in the middle of this tiny state, Delaware's capital has its share of museums and attractions. Problem is, too many people fail to slow down on their way to the beach! What a shame.

At least the wildlife is smart enough to stop: Bombay Hook National Wildlife Refuge offers migrating visitors 16,000 acres of marsh and wetlands.

1 DOVER

45 miles S of Wilmington; 84 miles E of Baltimore; 43 miles N of Rehoboth

Plotted in 1717 according to a charter by William Penn, Dover was originally designed as the Kent County seat. By 1777, this rich grain-farming community's importance had increased, and the state legislature, seeking a safe inland location as an alternative to the old capital of New Castle, relocated to the more central Dover. Delaware became the "first state" on December 7, 1787, when its delegates assembled at Dover's Golden Fleece Tavern to ratify the Constitution of the United States, the first state to do so.

Today, Dover continues to be a hub of state government and business. Its history is showcased at a sprawling agricultural museum, a museum of American art stocked with lavish works donated by Delaware art collectors, and the Old State House. On the city's southern edge, Dover Air Force Base, the largest airport on the East Coast, is home to its own museum of aircraft.

ESSENTIALS

GETTING THERE   From the north, take I-95 to Wilmington and head south on Route 1 or Route 13 (also known as the DuPont Hwy.) to Dover. Route 13, which runs the length of Delaware, is also the best way to approach Dover from the south. From Washington, D.C., and west, take Route 50 across the Bay Bridge to Route 301 North. Follow 301 to 302 east, then take Route 454. From 454, take Route 8 into Dover.

Bus service to Dover is available through **Greyhound** (© **800/231-2222;** www.greyhound.com), which stops at 716 S. Governors Ave. (© **302/736-5183**).

VISITOR INFORMATION   Head first to the **Delaware Visitor Center,** 406 Federal St., at Duke of York Street, Dover (© **302/739-4266**). It offers information, exhibits, restrooms, and a gift shop, and is open Monday through Saturday from 9am to 4:30pm, Sunday from 1:30 to 4:30pm. Reservations are a must for its 30-minute tours around the Green—a good introduction to Dover history—offered Tuesday through Saturday. You can also stop by the **Kent County Convention and Visitors Bureau,** 435 N. DuPont

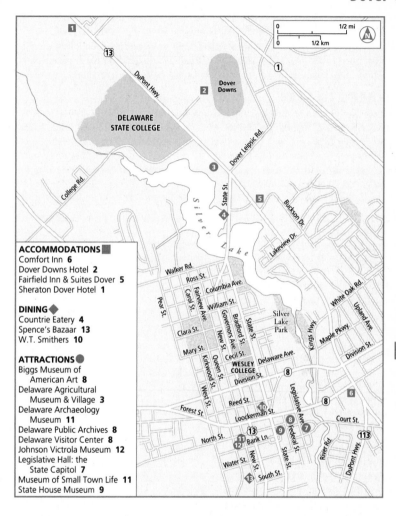

ACCOMMODATIONS ■
Comfort Inn **6**
Dover Downs Hotel **2**
Fairfield Inn & Suites Dover **5**
Sheraton Dover Hotel **1**

DINING ◆
Countrie Eatery **4**
Spence's Bazaar **13**
W.T. Smithers **10**

ATTRACTIONS ●
Biggs Museum of
   American Art **8**
Delaware Agricultural
   Museum & Village **3**
Delaware Archaeology
   Museum **11**
Delaware Public Archives **8**
Delaware Visitor Center **8**
Johnson Victrola Museum **12**
Legislative Hall: the
   State Capitol **7**
Museum of Small Town Life **11**
State House Museum **9**

Hwy. (© **800/233-5368** or 302/734-4888; www.visitdover.com), or the **Smyrna Visitor Center,** 5500 DuPont Hwy., 11 miles north of Dover (© **302/653-8910**).

GETTING AROUND You'll need a car. To rent one, contact **Avis** (© **302/734-5550**) or **Hertz** (© **302/678-0700**). For reliable 24-hour taxi service, call **City Cab of Dover** (© **302/734-5968**). *Note:* Amish buggies are common on the area's highways and byways, usually on the shoulders. Please drive with care and pass them slowly.

SPECIAL EVENTS The two **"Monster Mile"** NASCAR weekends, in June and September at Dover International Speedway (© **800/711-5882;** www.doverspeedway.com), are the biggest events in Dover. Make your hotel reservations up to a year in advance. In late April or early May, several privately owned historic homes and gardens open to the public for **Old Dover Days** (🕿 **800/233-5368;** www.visitdover.com). Costumed guides, maypole dancing, and crafts demonstrations take place on the Green. Cyclists come for the **Amish Country Bike Tour** (🕿 **800/233-5368;** www.visitdover.com), held the Saturday after Labor Day. **Christmas in Odessa** (🕿 **302/378-4900;** www.christmas inodessa.com) is held the first Saturday in December, with house tours, music, and crafts.

WHERE TO STAY

Generally, Dover accommodations are moderately priced—but don't go looking for hotel rooms for NASCAR weekends. Believe it or not, most rooms are booked before racing fans even get a chance to call. Look for lodging about an hour away: at the beach resorts, Wilmington, or on Maryland's Eastern Shore. Local hotels also tend to book up on summer weekends. Most of Dover's hotels are on Route 13 (DuPont Hwy.); these are largely modern chains with ample free parking.

Comfort Inn   Businessmen and families head for this Comfort Inn, just off Route 13 at Loockerman Street. The closest motel to the historic district, this brick-fronted inn has two adjoining wings. The decor and furnishings are typical of the chain.

222 S. DuPont Hwy. (Rte. 13), Dover, DE 19901. 🕿 **800/228-5150** or 302/674-3300. www.comfortinn. com/hotel-dover-delaware-DE400. 94 units. $110–$300 double. Rates include continental breakfast. AE, DC, DISC, MC, V. Pets accepted. **Amenities:** Fitness center; outdoor pool. *In room:* A/C, fridge, hair dryer (upon request), microwave, free Wi-Fi.

Dover Downs Hotel ★   This luxury hotel adjacent to the slots and racetracks offers track-view rooms and plenty of pampering—whether you won or not. After its 2008 expansion, the hotel is now Delaware's largest with 500 rooms. Most units are spacious, with standard furnishings. Spa suites with Jacuzzi tubs, wet bars, and separate sitting rooms are available. Other suites feature billiard tables or fireplaces.

1131 N. DuPont Hwy., Dover, DE 19901. 🕿 **866/4-RESERV** (473-7378) or 302/674-4600. www.dover downshotel.com. 500 units. $129–$350 double; $165–$805 suite. Children 18 and under stay free in parent's room. AE, DISC, MC, V. **Amenities:** 8 restaurants; 2 lounges; concierge; concierge-level rooms; fitness center; indoor pool; room service; spa; shuttle service to downtown Dover. *In room:* A/C, TV w/pay movies, fridge, hair dryer, Wi-Fi (fee).

Fairfield Inn & Suites Dover ★   This Marriott franchise has room for families and amenities for business travelers. Decorated in bright colors—no solemn tans and mauves here—the suites have a pullout sofa, second TV, CD player, fridge, and microwave. Standard rooms are almost as spacious, but the fitness center is small.

655 N. DuPont Hwy., Dover, DE 19901. 🕿 **302/677-0900.** www.marriott.com. 77 units. $95–$159 double; $119–$189 suite. Rates include hot breakfast. AE, DC, DISC, MC, V. **Amenities:** Fitness center; indoor pool; spa. *In room:* A/C, TV, CD player (in suites) hair dryer, free Wi-Fi.

Sheraton Dover Hotel ★   A favorite spot for business executives and conference attendees, this seven-story hotel is the most complete facility along the north-south corridor. Guest rooms are traditionally furnished, with mahogany reproduction furniture and rich earth tones.

1570 N. DuPont Hwy. (Rte. 13), Dover, DE 19901. 🕿 **302/678-8500.** Fax 302/678-9073. www.sheraton dover.com. 156 units. $99–$199 double; $119–$535 suite. AE, DC, DISC, MC, V. **Amenities:** Restaurant; lounge; club-level rooms; fitness center; indoor pool. *In room:* A/C, TV w/movies, hair dryer, free Wi-Fi.

Chain restaurants line DuPont Highway. For something local, a few options are:

Countrie Eatery AMERICAN   One thing draws the locals here: breakfast. They come for the omelets, the pancakes, and the bottomless cup of joe. Lunch and dinner are served, too, with home-style meatloaf, hot turkey sandwiches, and country dinners.

950 N. State St. (©) **302/674-8310.** Reservations not accepted. Main courses $4–$9 breakfast, $4–$10 lunch, $7–$16 dinner. No credit cards. Mon–Thurs 6:30am–8pm; Fri–Sat 6:30am–9pm; Sun 6:30am–4pm.

Sambo's Tavern ★ SEAFOOD   About 7 miles northeast of Dover Downs, this family-owned tavern has seafood delivered fresh from the Delaware Bay and produce from local farms every day. The rooms are rustic with wood-paneled walls, big picture windows overlooking the Leipsic River, and local newspapers on the tables. Try the crab cakes, fried golden brown, or dig into a mound of steamed hard-shell clams. Sandwiches, salads, soups, and seafood platters round out the all-day menu. Boat docking is available.

283 Front St., Leipsic, DE 19901. (©) **302/674-9724.** Reservations recommended. Main courses $5–$31. DISC, MC, V. Mon–Sat 11am–10pm. Bar Mon–Sat 9am–11pm. Closed Nov–Mar.

Spence's Bazaar MARKET   This old-time market has plenty of options for carryout: tasty pies and breads, sandwiches, hot pretzels, and candies, all made by members of Mennonite and Amish communities. Hours vary, so it's best to call ahead if you have your heart set on shoofly pie. Don't get lost among the huge number of stalls that make up the flea market and auction business surrounding the market.

550 S. New St. (©) **302/734-3441.** Tues and Fri 7:30am–5pm.

W. T. Smithers AMERICAN   This Victorian-style eatery is dainty enough for a girls' night out, but the bar is big enough for all your friends. Stop for lunch and enjoy over-stuffed sandwiches (skip the crab cake though), a luscious cream of crab soup, or a salad. The dinner menu runs the gamut from fish and steak to a wide array of shrimp, scallops, fish, and crab dishes. Or come for the party: a DJ on Wednesdays and Saturdays and karaoke most Fridays.

140 S. State St. (©) **302/674-8875.** www.wtsmithers.us. Reservations recommended. Main courses $7–$10 lunch, $7–$22 dinner. AE, DC, DISC, MC, V. Daily 11am–1am.

WHAT TO SEE & DO

The major museums of Dover, as well as Legislative Hall and the state archives, have been designated the **First State Heritage Park at Dover.** A "park without boundaries," the various sites, nevertheless, have hours. Start your visit at the **Green,** where Delaware became the first state to ratify the U.S. Constitution in 1787. Most of Dover's historic sites, government buildings, and museums are located around or within walking distance of here. From Route 13, follow signs for the historic district and take State Street, which goes right through the center of the Green. Other attractions, along with Dover's hotels and motels, are concentrated east of the historic district, along Route 13, also known as DuPont Highway. You'll need a car to get around this strip, which is home to Dover Downs, the Delaware Agricultural Museum and Village, and the Dover Air Force Base.

Museums & Historic Sites

Biggs Museum of American Art ★   In galleries spread over the second and third floors of the Delaware State Visitor Center, you'll see rooms filled with antique furniture; gorgeous silver tea services produced locally; and the works of the Hudson River School, the Peales, and local painters and sculptors. The collection of Sewell C. Biggs, a local art patron, spans 2 centuries and includes 20th-century Impressionism.

406 Federal St. (C) **302/674-2111.** www.biggsmuseum.org. Free admission. Wed–Fri 9am–4:30pm; Sat 9am–5pm; Sun 1:30–4:30pm.

Delaware Agricultural Museum & Village   A huge barn right on DuPont Highway houses an enormous collection of tractors and other farm equipment—including a 1930s farm kitchen, log cabin, and crop-dusting plane. Outside, you'll find an 1890s village, complete with barn, farmhouses, train station, windmill, and church.

866 N. DuPont Hwy. (C) **302/734-1618.** www.agriculturalmuseum.org. Admission $5 adults, $3 seniors and children 6–17. Jan–Mar Mon–Fri 10am–4pm; Apr–Dec Tues–Sat 10am–4pm, Sun 1–4pm. Across from Dover Downs on Rte. 13.

Delaware Public Archives   For part of every year, Delaware's copy of the Bill of Rights goes on display here. The document is only one of seven extant from the first official imprint. The exhibit is open December 7 (Delaware Day) to July 4; the rest of the year it returns to the National Archives. In an agreement with the National Archives, the Bill of Rights will return to Delaware for half of each year for the next 20 years.

121 Duke of York St. (C) **302/744-5000.** http://archives.delaware.gov. Free admission. Mon–Sat 9am–4:30pm; Sun 1:30–4:30pm.

Delaware State Museums ★★ (Value)   Five of the state's museums are in Dover (the others are the Zwaanendael in Lewes and the New Castle Court House). The museums in Dover highlight the accomplishments of Delawareans since prehistoric times. Admission to all of these is free. *Note:* It is difficult to see all of these museums in 1 day at a relaxing pace. Go first to the museum you want to see the most.

Start at the **Delaware State Visitor Center,** 406 Federal St. ((C) **302/739-4266;** http://history.delaware.gov), to get a map and see its own exhibits. (The Biggs Museum of American Art is here, too; see above for details.) Nearby, the **Green,** the English-style town square at Bank Lane and State Street, was designed by William Penn more than 300 years ago, and soldiers gathered here to join the Revolutionary War troops of General Washington. Look for the sign remembering the Golden Fleece Tavern, where Delaware's legislators voted to ratify the U.S. Constitution.

At the **Delaware Archaeology Museum,** 316 S. Governors Ave. ((C) **302/739-4266**), learn about the methodology of archaeology, look over artifacts from a Native American burial ground, and peruse pottery from digs—all on view in a 1790 Presbyterian church that shares a free parking lot with the Johnson Victrola Museum. Open Tuesday through Friday from 10am to 3:30pm, Saturday 9am to 5pm.

Next door, the **Museum of Small Town Life** ★, 316 S. Governors Ave. ((C) **302/739-4266**), housed in an 1880s Sunday school, offers visitors a chance to walk down Main Street as it was a century ago. Stop by the printing office, the drugstore, the woodworking shop, and the all-important general store. Open Tuesday through Friday from 10am to 3:30pm, Saturday 9am to 5pm.

The **Johnson Victrola Museum** ★, at New Street and Bank Lane ((C) **302/739-4266**), is packed with old records and antique phonographs that pay tribute to the man who made the Victrola a must-have in the early 1900s. Eldridge R. Johnson, a Delaware boy who founded the Victor Talking Machine Company, invented a way to make the original phonograph (with the big horn) more compact and control its volume. His invention made the machine popular—and made him a millionaire. Open Tuesday through Friday from 10am to 3:30pm, Saturday 9am to 5pm.

The **State House Museum,** on the Green (📞 302/739-4266), dates to 1792. To
mark the U.S. bicentennial in 1976, the Georgian-style Court House, with its 18th-century courtroom, legislative chambers, and deeds office where freed slaves filed their manumission papers, was restored to its original appearance. Although the state's General Assembly moved to the nearby Legislative Hall in 1933, the State House continues to be used for ceremonial events. Restoration had closed the museum at press time; call for hours (usually the same as the other museums.)

Legislative Hall: The State Capitol   This Georgian-style building, which has housed the state's General Assembly since 1933, is open to visitors (bring photo ID). Tours are available 9am to 5pm on the first Saturday each month.

152 Legislative Ave. 📞 **302/739-9194.** www.delaware.gov. Free admission. Mon–Fri 9am–3pm when General Assembly is not in session; Mon–Fri 9am–noon on General Assembly session days.

Nearby Attractions

Air Mobility Command Museum (Dover Air Force Base) ★★ (**Kids**)   The name of this museum, located in a restored World War II hangar listed on the National Register of Historic Places, doesn't do it justice. The collection of vintage aircraft and artifacts here reflect the history of Dover Air Force Base since the early days of World War II and through the Berlin airlift and remind us of the brave men who flew and serviced these craft. Not only will you see the museum's first plane, a C-47A used in the 1944 D-day paratroop drop over Normandy, you may have a chance to walk inside it. Several of the historic planes are open every day. Cargo planes, air refueling planes, and jets that broke the sound barrier are here, along with a flight simulator, open whenever a volunteer is available, which gives visitors 10 and over a chance to "fly."

1301 Heritage Rd. (off Rte. 113). 📞 **302/677-5938.** www.amcmuseum.org. Free admission. Tues–Sat 9am–4pm. Closed federal holidays. Take Rte. 9 (left from Dover) and look for the signs.

Dover Downs Casino   Dover Downs' slots casino draws busloads hoping to make a million. The 80,000-square-foot facility, adjacent to the racetrack, has 3,100 slot machines and electronic games. You can play until 4am. You must be 21 to play.

1131 N. DuPont Hwy. 📞 **800/711-5882** or 302/674-4600. www.doverdowns.com. Daily 24 hr. Closed Easter and Dec 25.

John Dickinson Plantation   The home of John Dickinson, one of Delaware's fore-most statesmen of the Revolutionary and Federal periods, was originally built in 1740. Destroyed by fire in 1804, the brick house was rebuilt in 1896. Guides dressed in period clothing give visitors a glimpse of the daily life of the Dickinson family, tenants, and slaves. It's located near the Air Mobility Command Museum.

340 Kitts Hummock Rd. 📞 **302/739-3277.** http://history.delaware.gov. Free admission. Wed–Sat 10am–3:30pm. Arrive at least 30 min. before closing time. Take Rte. 113 south from Dover to Kitts Hummock Rd., past the Dover Air Force Base.

SPECTATOR SPORTS & OUTDOOR ACTIVITIES

HARNESS HORSE RACING   **Dover Downs** (📞 800/711-5882; www.doverdowns. com) offers harness racing November through April. Races run Monday through Thursday at 4:30pm, Saturday and Sunday at 5:30pm. Simulcast racing is offered year-round, daily from noon to midnight. **Harrington Raceway,** Route 13, Harrington (📞 302/398-7223; www.harringtonraceway.com), has 90 race days from April through June and August through October, Sunday through Thursday with post time at 5:15pm. Simulcast is available daily from noon to midnight. Like Dover Downs, Harrington has a 24-hour

(Moments) **Historic Houses of Odessa**

The quiet town of Odessa comes to life on the first Saturday of December, when 30 historic houses spanning 3 centuries open for **Christmas in Odessa** (℗ 302/378-4900; www.christmasinodessa.com). Public buildings and private homes are open for daytime and candlelight tours. Music, carriage rides, food, and a crafts shop are also available. Tickets are sold that day at the Old Academy, at Fourth and Main streets, for $20.

But you don't have to wait for December to visit. The town, which dates back to the 17th century when it was called Cantwell's Bridge, was once a thriving crossroads. When trains and highways bypassed the town, Odessa became a sleepy place. The charming Georgian homes built just before the American Revolution by William Corbit and David Wilson are the centerpieces of the **Historic Houses of Odessa** (℗ 302/378-4119; www.historicodessa.org). These two houses—along with a wood-sided working family's home and a 19th-century bank and hotel—are open to the public March through December. Original furnishings, a great Underground Railroad story, and the opportunity to walk through the old town, itself a historic district, make this a worthwhile stop. Tours are offered Thursday through Saturday 10am to 4:30pm, Sunday 1 to 4:30pm. Tickets are $10 adults, $8 seniors and students.

Odessa is 23 miles north of Dover and 22 miles south of Wilmington. To get here, take Route 13 and follow the signs to the historic district.

slots parlor (closed Easter and Dec 25). The track is located on the state fair grounds, about 15 miles south of Dover.

STOCK-CAR RACING   Twice a year, NASCAR fans flock to **Dover International Speedway,** 1131 N. DuPont Hwy. (Rte. 13), Dover (℗ 800/411-3219; www.dover speedway.com). These two major race weekends draw some of the world's top drivers to Dover's 140,000-seat track. Tickets for adults start at $27 for general admission. Reserved seating for Sunday's race runs about $100; order online or call ℗ **800/441-7223.** Tickets go on sale 10 months prior to each race.

DART First State (℗ **302/652-DART** [3278]; www.dartfirststate.com) offers express shuttle buses from the State Danner Campus, 800 Bay Rd., in Dover and Christiana Mall in Wilmington. Tickets are $20 per carload from Danner and $10 per person round-trip from the mall. Call or check the website for a schedule; bring exact change.

SILVER LAKE & KILLENS POND STATE PARK

Dover's beautiful **Silver Lake** is the core of a 182-acre recreation area in the heart of the city. Biking, swimming, and picnicking draw most people, but the park also has a boat ramp, exercise circuit, volleyball court, and walking/jogging trail. The park has entrances on Washington Street and Kings Highway; it's open year-round from sunrise to sunset. Contact the **Dover Parks and Recreation Department** (℗ **302/736-7050**) for additional information.

Some 13 miles south of Dover, about a half-mile east of Route 13, is **Killens Pond State Park** ★, 5025 Killens Pond Rd., Felton (℗ **302/284-4526;** www.destateparks.

Tips **Put Yourself in the Driver's Seat**

Want to ride in a Winston Cup car? Maybe even drive it yourself? **Monster Racing Driving School** (🕿 **800/468-6946;** www.monsterracing.com) will let you get behind the wheel to "tame the monster" at Dover Speedway. For $99, you can ride the course for four laps with an instructor. Packages range from $389 to $899 to drive a race car for 30 laps, with shorter and less expensive alternatives in between.

com/park/killens-pond). Covering 1,444 acres, with a 66-acre millpond, Killens Pond is a natural inland haven with picnic areas, shuffleboard courts, horseshoe pits, biking and hiking trails, volleyball courts, boat rentals, pond fishing, and camping. The **Killens Pond Water Park** has lap lanes, a mushroom fountain, and a lily-pad fun walk. Park entry fees daily May through October are $3 for Delaware-registered cars and $6 for out-of-state vehicles. Water-park admission is an additional $2 for adults and $1 for children 15 and under. The park is open year-round; the water park is open Memorial Day through Labor Day.

Also at the park are 77 campsites, with 10 cabins, 17 tent-only sites, and 1 pond-view cottage, open year-round. Reservations are taken up to 7 months in advance; call 🕿 **877/987-2757.** Fees are $19 to $29 for tent sites and $28 to $32 for sites with water and electric hookup. *Note:* NASCAR fans fill the campsites quickly on race weekends in April and September. Be sure to reserve 7 months in advance.

THE PERFORMING ARTS

Schwartz Center for the Arts   This performing-arts venue brings back to life the beloved 1904 Dover Opera House. It is home to the Dover Symphony Orchestra and plays host to a wide variety of performers, from the Second City comedy troupe to the Preservation Hall Jazz Band. Film, plays, and ballet are also on the schedule, which can be found on the website. Children's programming is quite extensive.

226 S. State St. 🕿 **302/678-3583.** www.schwartzcenter.com.

2 BOMBAY HOOK NATIONAL WILDLIFE REFUGE ★

45 miles S of Wilmington; 107 miles E of Baltimore; 53 miles N of Rehoboth

Thanks to its abundance of wildlife refuges, the Delmarva Peninsula is a haven for migrating birds and those who watch them. Bombay Hook, established in 1937 as part of a chain of refuges extending from Canada to the Gulf of Mexico, is the largest of Delaware's refuges. Though its primary (and loudest) inhabitants and visitors are wintering ducks and geese, Bombay Hook also hosts herons, egrets, sandpipers, willets, and the occasional bald eagle, as well as a more permanent mammal, amphibian, and reptile population. If you've visited Maryland's Blackwater National Wildlife Refuge, Bombay Hook will be quite a contrast. The facilities are considerably more primitive—roads aren't paved, the trails are well marked but not well worn, and there are fewer ranger programs and visitor services. This means there are also fewer human visitors, so you may have the place all to yourself, especially in the off-season.

GETTING THERE   Take Route 13 north of Dover to Route 42; travel east (left) on Route 42 to Route 9 and then north on Route 9 for 1½ miles; turn right onto Whitehall Neck Road, which leads to the visitor center.

VISITOR CENTER   The visitor center/ranger station (✆ **302/653-6872;** http://bombayhook.fws.gov) is open year-round, Monday through Friday from 8am to 4pm, plus spring and fall weekends from 9am to 5pm. The park is open daily from sunrise to sunset.

FEES & REGULATIONS   Entrance fees are $4 per car or $2 per person 16 and older on bike or on foot. Admission is free on hunting days—but access is limited, too. Deer, snow goose, and Canada goose hunting are permitted under special regulations in designated portions of the refuge during the regular Delaware hunting season.

SEEING THE HIGHLIGHTS

Like most wildlife refuges, much of Bombay Hook is not accessible to the public. However, the 12-mile round-trip auto route, several nature trails, and three observation towers offer opportunities to see birds and other wildlife. The driving tour, which can be biked, begins and ends at the visitor center and takes you by the three major wetland pools: Raymond Pool, Shearness Pool, and Bear Swamp Pool. The roads are well marked and offer plenty of spots to park. Cyclists should note that the roads throughout the refuge are dirt and gravel—though they are flat. The visitor center has audiocassettes and binoculars for visitors' use. To see the most birds, come in May or June, when the shorebird population hits its peak. Or visit in October or November, when the most ducks and geese are here—they can number 150,000.

BIRD-WATCHING   Birds can be seen all along the auto tour, but for the best vantage point, hike to one of the three 30-foot observation towers, one overlooking each of the pools. Part of the trail to Bear Swamp Observation Tower is accessible; an observation platform at ground level below the tower provides a good view, and a viewing scope at wheelchair level has been installed on the dock.

The best times to see migratory birds are October through November and mid-February through March. Some 256 species have been counted. **Canada, tundra,** and **snow geese** begin arriving in early October, while **ducks**—pintail, mallard, American widgeon, and others—increase through November. **Shorebird** migration begins in April; their populations in the refuge peak in May and June.

The refuge is the year-round home to **bald eagles,** though they can be difficult to spot. Eggs begin hatching in April; the baby eagles begin to leave their nests in June. Shearness Pool serves as their roosting and nesting area. Parson Point Trail will take you to the back of the pool for a closer look. During mating and nesting season (Nov–June), however, this trail may be closed. Bring binoculars or stop at the observation tower along the auto route to get a glimpse of the eagles.

HIKING   Hiking in the refuge is primarily a means of observing and photographing wildlife, so the nature trails aren't terribly strenuous or long. All of the trails are flat and range from .25 mile to 1 mile long. Bring insect repellent and wear long sleeves from July through September. The Bear Swamp Trail is partially wheelchair accessible; the Parson Point Trail is the longest option. The Boardwalk Trail offers visitors a look at four different refuge habitats—woodland, freshwater pond, brackish pond, and salt marsh. Another trail leads to the Raymond Tower, set in a meadow.

15

Fast Facts

1 FAST FACTS: MARYLAND & DELAWARE

AREA CODES The area code for all of Delaware is 302. Some Brandywine Valley attractions are in Pennsylvania; their area code is 610. Maryland has four area codes: 301 and 240 in the western half of the state, 410 and 443 in the eastern half, including Baltimore and Annapolis. In Maryland, you must always dial the area code first.

AUTOMOBILE ORGANIZATIONS Motor clubs will supply maps, suggested routes, guidebooks, accident and bail-bond insurance, and emergency road service. The **American Automobile Association (AAA)** is the major auto club in the United States. If you belong to a motor club in your home country, inquire about AAA reciprocity before you leave. You may be able to join AAA even if you're not a member of a reciprocal club. For membership information or for emergency road service, call AAA (© **800/222-4357**; www.aaa.com).

BUSINESS HOURS Most businesses are open every day. Store operating hours are usually 10am to 5pm or later. Mall stores close at 9pm or later. Many tourist attractions, however, have had to cut back their hours and quite a few have eliminated opening hours on Monday, Tuesday, and sometimes Wednesday. Winter hours at the beach may be even more limited, Saturday and Sunday, if they open at all.

DRINKING LAWS The legal age for purchase and consumption of alcoholic beverages is 21; proof of age is required and often requested at bars, nightclubs, and restaurants, so it's always a good idea to bring ID when you go out.

Do not carry open containers of alcohol in your car or any public area that isn't zoned for alcohol consumption. The police can fine you on the spot. Don't even think about driving while intoxicated.

Beer, wine and liquor are available only in licensed liquor stores. In Ocean City, beer and wine are sold more widely than hard liquor, which is available only from a county-run outlet. In most areas, alcohol sales are permitted on Sunday though in Bethany Beach, Del., Cambridge, Md., and Garrett County, Md., Sunday sales are restricted to those drinking alcohol with a meal. There are no package sales on Sunday in Cambridge and Garrett County. Bars may not sell alcohol in Maryland and Delaware after 2am.

DRIVING RULES See "Getting There & Getting Around," p. 30.

ELECTRICITY Like Canada, the United States uses 110–120 volts AC (60 cycles), compared to 220–240 volts AC (50 cycles) in most of Europe, Australia, and New Zealand. Downward converters that change 220–240 volts to 110–120 volts are difficult to find in the United States, so bring one with you.

EMBASSIES & CONSULATES All embassies are located in the nation's capital, Washington, D.C. Some consulates are located in major U.S. cities, and most nations have a mission to the United Nations in New York City. If your country isn't listed below, call for directory information in Washington, D.C. (© 202/555-1212) or check **www.embassy.org/embassies**.

The embassy of **Australia** is at 1601 Massachusetts Ave. NW, Washington, DC 20036 (© **202/797-3000;** usa.embassy.gov/au).

The embassy of **Canada** is at 501 Pennsylvania Ave. NW, Washington, DC 20001 (© **202/682-1740;** www.canadianembassy.org). Other Canadian consulates are in Buffalo (New York), Detroit, Los Angeles, New York, and Seattle.

The embassy of **Ireland** is at 2234 Massachusetts Ave. NW, Washington, DC 20008 (© **202/462-3939;** www.irelandemb.org). Irish consulates are in Boston, Chicago, New York, San Francisco, and other cities. See website for complete listing.

The embassy of **New Zealand** is at 37 Observatory Circle NW, Washington, DC 20008 (© **202/328-4800;** www.nzembassy.com). New Zealand consulates are in Los Angeles, Salt Lake City, San Francisco, and Seattle.

The embassy of the **United Kingdom** is at 3100 Massachusetts Ave. NW, Washington, DC 20008 (© **202/588-7800;** http://ukinusa.fco.gov.uk/en). Other British consulates are in Atlanta, Boston, Chicago, Cleveland, Houston, Los Angeles, New York, San Francisco, and Seattle.

EMERGENCIES Dial © **911** for any emergency requiring police, firefighters, or ambulance.

GASOLINE (PETROL) Maryland and Delaware gas prices tend to be at or below the national average. Taxes are already included in the printed price. One U.S. gallon equals 3.8 liters or .85 imperial gallons.

HOLIDAYS Banks, government offices, post offices, and many stores, restaurants, and museums are closed on the following legal national holidays: January 1 (New Year's Day), the third Monday in January (Martin Luther King, Jr., Day), the third Monday in February (Presidents' Day), the last Monday in May (Memorial Day), July 4 (Independence Day), the first Monday in September (Labor Day), the second Monday in October (Columbus Day), November 11 (Veterans Day/Armistice Day), the fourth Thursday in November (Thanksgiving Day), and December 25 (Christmas). The Tuesday after the first Monday in November is Election Day, a federal government holiday in presidential-election years (held every 4 years, and next in 2012).

For more information on holidays see "Calendar of Events," in chapter 3

INSURANCE For information on traveler's insurance, trip cancellation insurance, and medical insurance while traveling please visit www.frommers.com/planning.

INTERNET ACCESS Internet access is available in most hotels, as well as at a number of coffee shops, including Panera Bread and Starbucks. Local libraries offer computer access and Wi-Fi free of charge. FedEx Office also offers computer and Internet access. Cybercafes are difficult to find; try www.cybercafe.com.

LEGAL AID If you are "pulled over" for a minor infraction (such as speeding), never attempt to pay the fine directly to a police officer; this could be construed as attempted bribery, a much more serious crime. Pay fines by mail, or directly into the hands of the clerk of the court. If accused of a more serious offense, say and do nothing before consulting a lawyer. Here the burden is on the state to prove a person's guilt beyond a reasonable doubt, and everyone has the right to remain silent, whether he or she is suspected of a crime or actually arrested. Once arrested, a person can make one telephone call to a party of his or her choice. International visitors should call your embassy or consulate.

MAIL   At press time, domestic postage rates were 28¢ for a postcard and 44¢ for a letter. For international mail, a first-class letter of up to 1 ounce costs 98¢ (75¢ to Canada and 79¢ to Mexico); a first-class postcard costs the same as a letter. For more information go to **www.usps.com.**

If you aren't sure what your address will be in the United States, mail can be sent to you, in your name, c/o General Delivery at the main post office of the city or region where you expect to be. (Call ✆ **800/275-8777** for information on the nearest post office.) The addressee must pick up mail in person and must produce proof of identity (driver's license, passport, and so on). Most post offices will hold your mail for up to 1 month, and are open Monday to Friday from 8am to 6pm, and Saturday from 9am to 3pm.

Always include zip codes when mailing items in the U.S. If you don't know your zip code, visit www.usps.com/zip4.

NEWSPAPERS & MAGAZINES   The Sun and the Washington Post are Maryland's major newspapers. In Annapolis, look for the Capital, and in the Mid-Shore, the Star Democrat. You'll find the Wilmington News-Journal and the Philadelphia Inquirer in Delaware. They are easy to find in drug stores, supermarkets, and convenience stores.

POLICE   Dial ✆ **911** in an emergency anywhere in either Maryland or Delaware.

SMOKING   Smoking in restaurants, bars, and other public places is illegal in Maryland and Delaware. A few Delaware hotels offer rooms for smokers—but the majority of bed-and-breakfasts do not.

TAXES   The United States has no value-added tax (VAT) or other indirect tax at the national level. Delaware has no sales tax but does have an 8% to 10% lodging tax. Maryland's sales tax is 6% on everything except groceries, and lodging taxes range from 4.5% to 7.5%. These taxes will not appear on price tags or quoted prices.

TELEPHONES   Public phones are getting harder to find in Maryland and Delaware, with very few available on the street.

Many convenience groceries and packaging services sell **prepaid calling cards** in denominations up to $50; for international visitors these can be the least expensive way to call home. Many public pay phones at airports now accept American Express, MasterCard, and Visa credit cards. **Local calls** made from pay phones in most locales cost either 25¢ or 35¢. Most long-distance and international calls can be dialed directly from any phone. **For calls within the United States and to Canada,** dial 1 followed by the area code and the seven-digit number. **For other international calls,** dial 011 followed by the country code, city code, and the number you are calling.

Calls to area codes **800, 888, 877,** and **866** are toll-free. However, calls to area codes **700** and **900** (chat lines, bulletin boards, "dating" services, and so on) can be very expensive—usually a charge of 95¢ to $3 or more per minute, and they sometimes have minimum charges that can run as high as $15 or more.

For **reversed-charge or collect calls,** and for person-to-person calls, dial the number 0 then the area code and number; an operator will come on the line, and you should specify whether you are calling collect, person-to-person, or both. If your operator-assisted call is international, ask for the overseas operator.

For **local directory assistance** ("information"), dial 411; for long-distance information, dial 1, then the appropriate area code and 555-1212.

TIME   Maryland and Delaware are situated in the Eastern Standard Time zone. The continental United States is divided into **four time zones:** Eastern Standard Time (EST), Central Standard Time (CST), Mountain Standard Time (MST), and Pacific Standard Time (PST). Alaska and Hawaii have their own zones. For example, when it's 9am in Los Angeles (PST), it's 7am in Honolulu (HST),10am in Denver (MST), 11am in Chicago (CST), noon in New York City (EST), 5pm in London (GMT), and 2am the next day in Sydney.

Daylight saving time is in effect from 1am on the second Sunday in March to 1am on the first Sunday in November, except in Arizona, Hawaii, the U.S. Virgin Islands, and Puerto Rico. Daylight saving time moves the clock 1 hour ahead of standard time.

TIPPING   In hotels, tip **bellhops** at least $1 per bag ($2–$3 if you have a lot of luggage) and tip the **chamber staff** $1 to $2 per day (more if you've left a disaster area for him or her to clean up). Tip the **doorman** or **concierge** only if he or she has provided you with some specific service (for example, calling a cab for you or obtaining difficult-to-get theater tickets). Tip the **valet-parking attendant** $1 every time you get your car.

In restaurants, bars, and nightclubs, tip **service staff** and **bartenders** 15% to 20% of the check, tip **checkroom attendants** $1 per garment, and tip **valet-parking attendants** $1 per vehicle.

As for other service personnel, tip **cabdrivers** 15% of the fare; tip **skycaps** at airports at least $1 per bag ($2–$3 if you have a lot of luggage); and tip **hairdressers** and **barbers** 15% to 20%.

TOILETS   You won't find public toilets or "restrooms" on the streets in most U.S. cities but they can be found in hotel lobbies, bars, restaurants, museums, department stores, railway and bus stations, and service stations. Large hotels and fast-food restaurants are often the best bet for clean facilities. Restaurants and bars in resorts or heavily visited areas may reserve their restrooms for patrons.

VISITOR INFORMATION   In Maryland, contact the **Maryland Office of Tourism Development** (© **866/639-3526** or 410/767-3400; www.visitmaryland.org). Its website has links to county websites as well. For information on Baltimore and the vicinity, contact **Visit Baltimore** (© **877/ BALTIMORE** [225-8466] or 410/659-7300; www.baltimore.org). Annapolis visitors should contact the **Annapolis and Anne Arundel County Conference and Visitors Bureau** (© **888/302-2852** or 410/280-0445; www.annapolis.org).

For information on parks, forests, and wildlife refuges, contact the **Maryland Department of Natural Resources** (© **877/620-8DNR** [8367] or 410/260-8DNR [8367]; www.dnr.maryland.gov).

In Delaware, contact **Delaware Tourism Office** (© **866/2VISITDE** [284-7483] or 302/672-6834; www.visitdelaware.com). For beach and Dover information, contact **Southern Delaware Tourism** (© **800/357-1818** or 302/856-1818; www.visitsouthern delaware.com). For information on Wilmington and the Brandywine Valley, contact the **Greater Wilmington Convention and Visitors Bureau** (© **800/422-1181** or 302/652-4088; www.visitwilmingtonde.com).

WEATHER   For Baltimore and Annapolis, check on the day's weather forecast by calling © **410/936-1212**. In Wilmington, dial © **302/429-9000** for weather, time, and a few ads.

INDEX